BRAVE NEW
WORLD

ALSO BY
FRED FORDHAM
To Kill A Mockingbird: A Graphic Novel
The Adventures of John Blake

BRAVE NEW WORLD

A GRAPHIC NOVEL

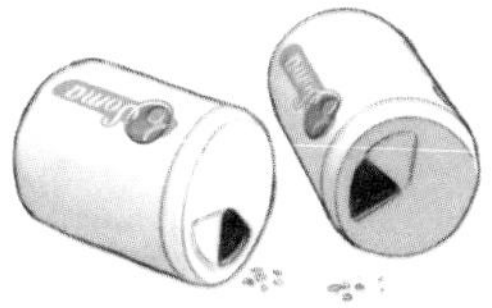
Soma
Soma

ADAPTED AND ILLUSTRATED BY

FRED FORDHAM

BRAVE NEW WORLD. Original text copyright © 1932, 1946 by Aldous Huxley. Illustrations and adaptation of text copyright © 2022 by Fred Fordham. All rights reserved. Printed in Canada. No part of this book may be used or reproduced in any manner whatsoever without written permission except in the case of brief quotations embodied in critical articles and reviews. For information, address HarperCollins Publishers, 195 Broadway, New York, NY 10007.

HarperCollins books may be purchased for educational, business, or sales promotional use. For information, please email the Special Markets Department at SPsales@harpercollins.com.

FIRST EDITION

Designed by Kyle O'Brien

Library of Congress Cataloging-in-Publication Data has been applied for.

ISBN 978-0-06-305525-4

22 23 24 25 26   TC   10 9 8 7 6 5 4 3 2 1

ACKNOWLEDGMENTS

Special thanks to Mary Gaule and Jennifer Civiletto for overseeing this project and keeping all the plates spinning; to Camille Johnston and Ros Asquith for their essential editorial feedback; to my agent, Jenny Savill, for her constant support; and to the Huxley Estate for involving me in bringing this strange and insightful piece of philosophy/fiction to a new medium.

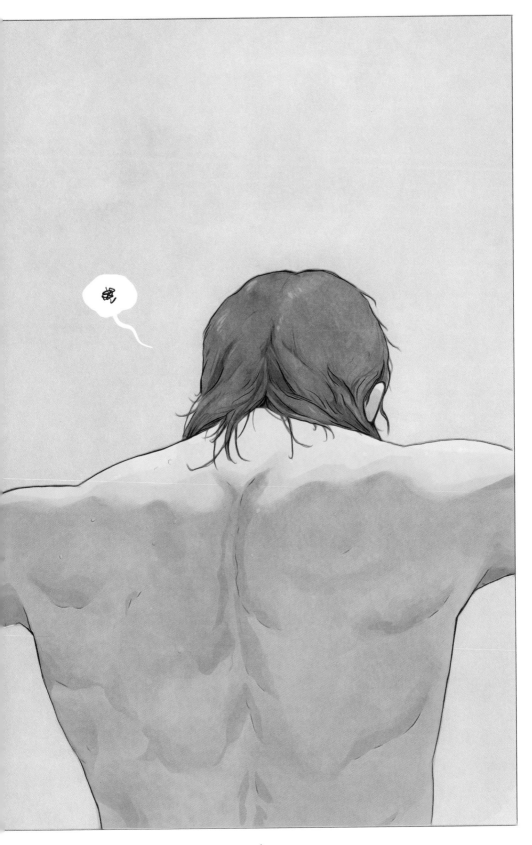

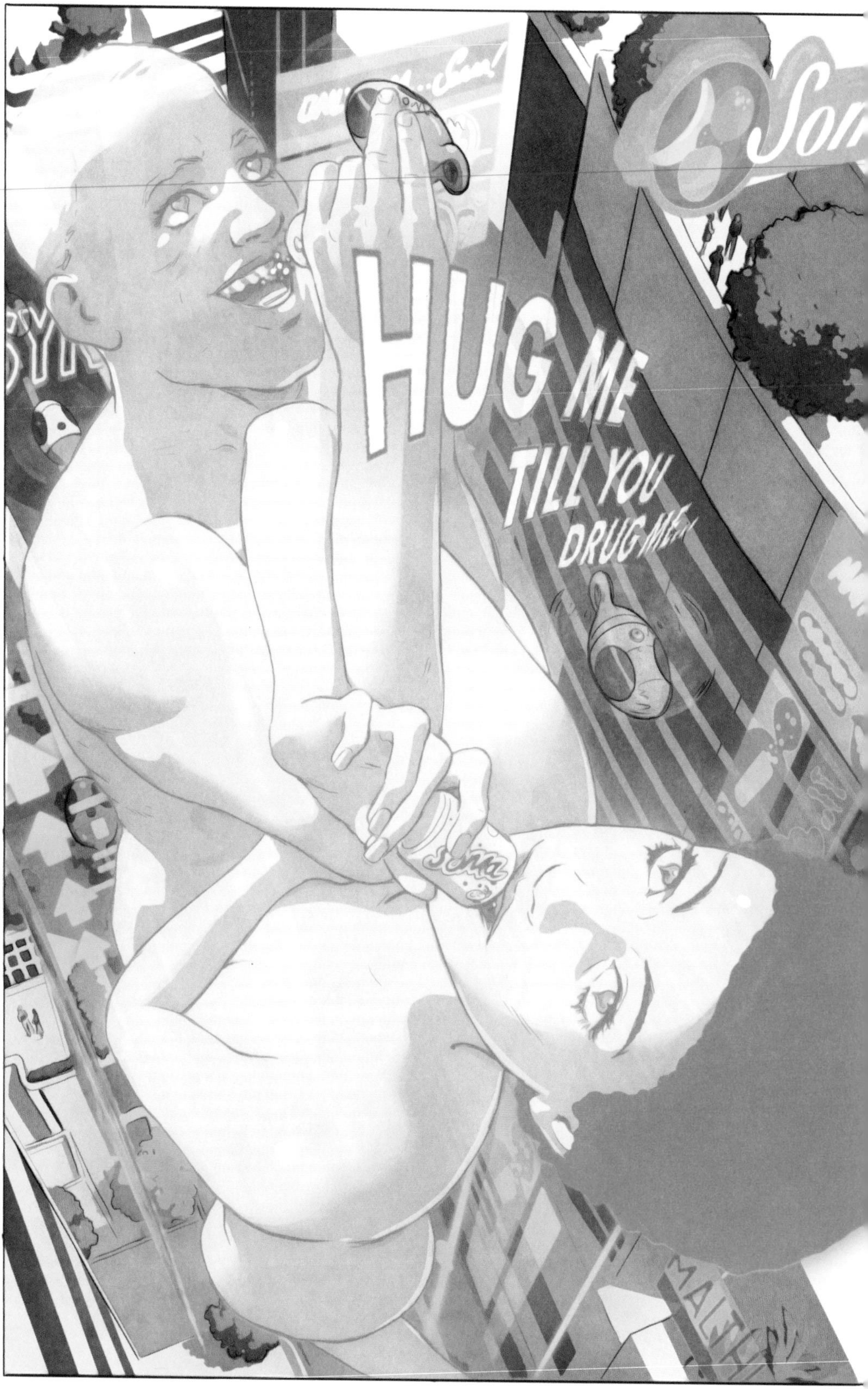
HUG ME
TILL YOU
DRUG ME...
Soma

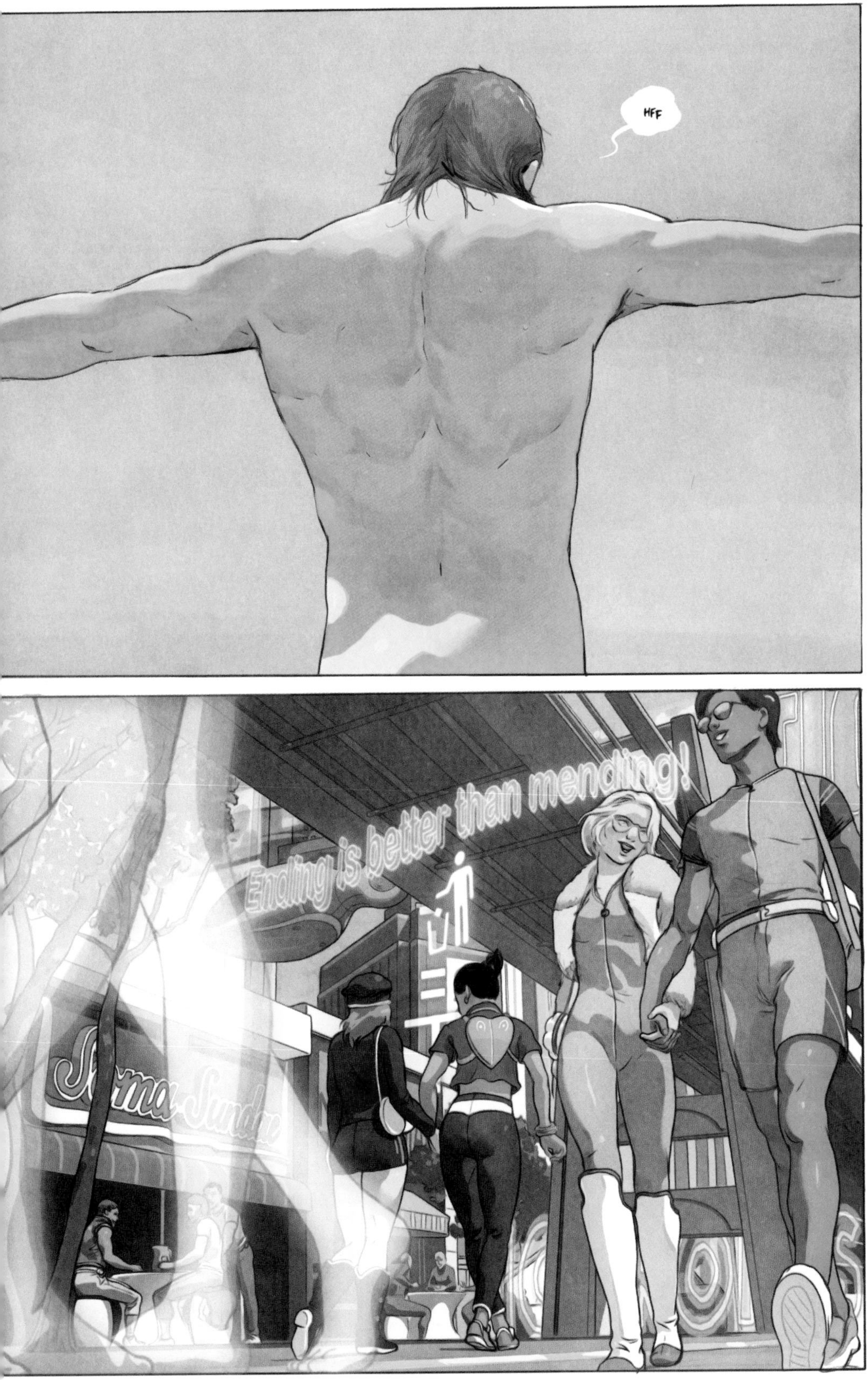
HFF
Ending is better than mending!

HWUH
OBSTACLE GOLF

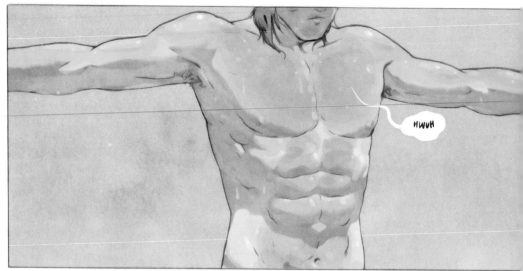

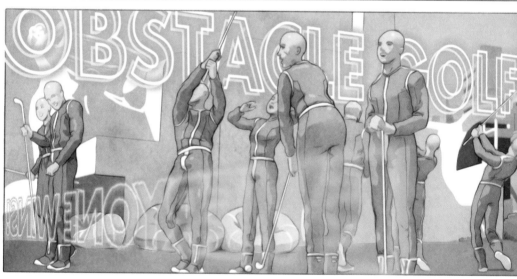

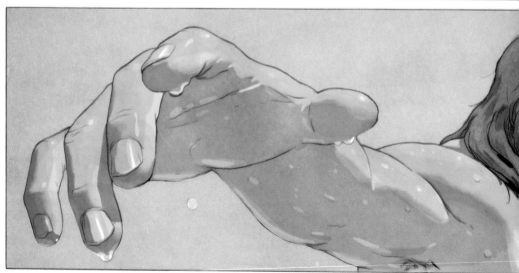

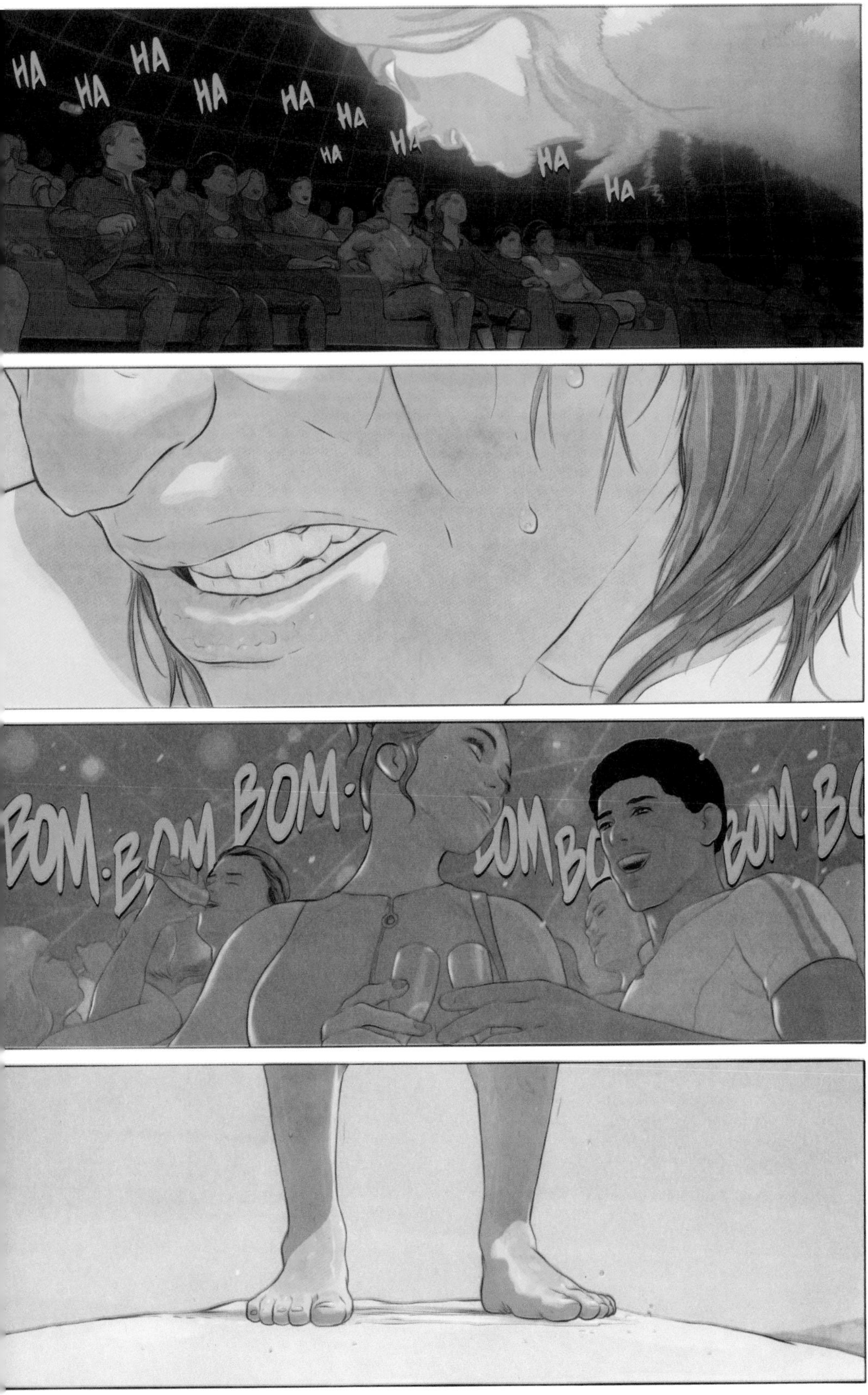
HA HA HA HA HA HA HA HA HA HA HA
BOM·BOM BOM·
BOM·

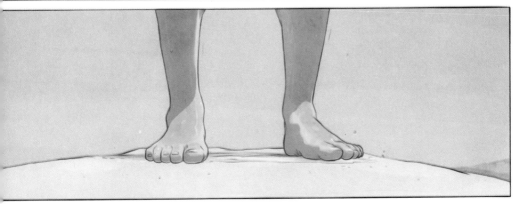

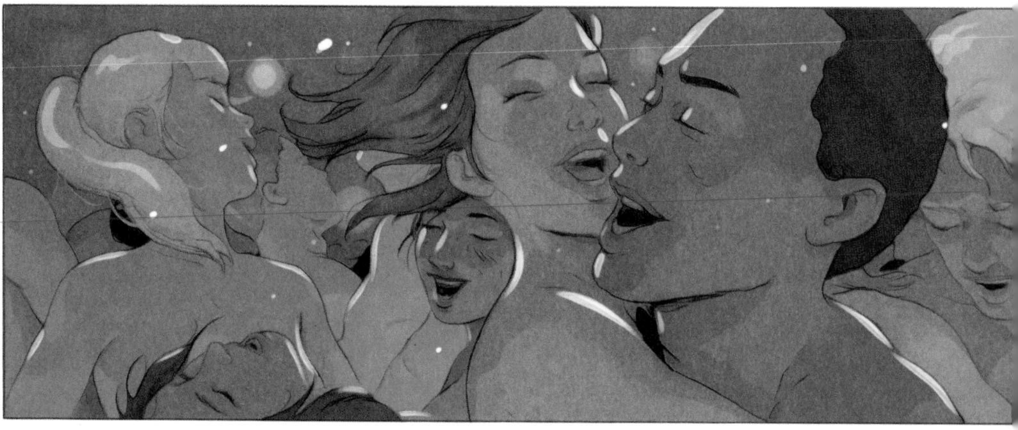

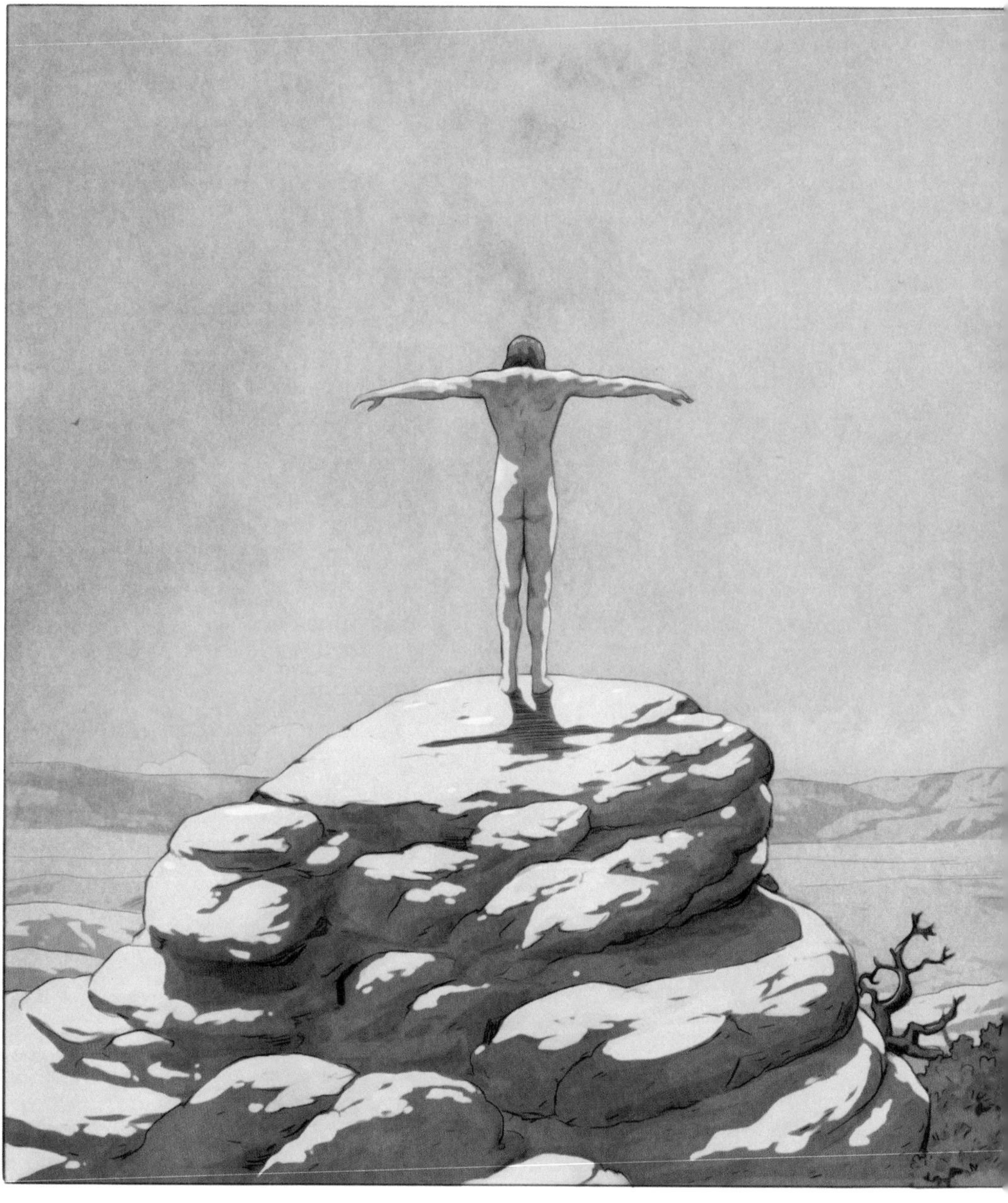

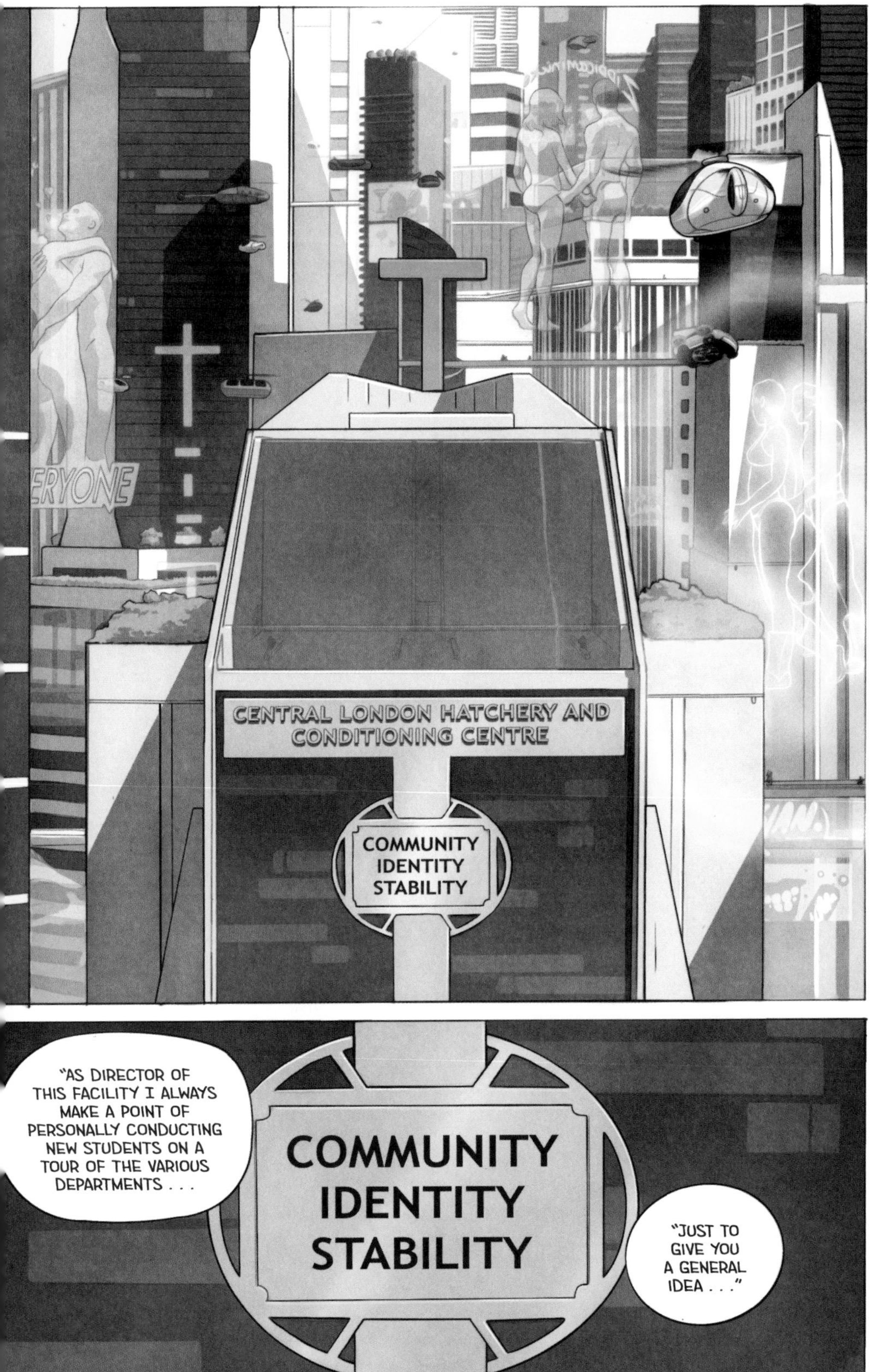
CENTRAL LONDON HATCHERY AND CONDITIONING CENTRE
COMMUNITY IDENTITY STABILITY
"AS DIRECTOR OF THIS FACILITY I ALWAYS MAKE A POINT OF PERSONALLY CONDUCTING NEW STUDENTS ON A TOUR OF THE VARIOUS DEPARTMENTS . . .
COMMUNITY IDENTITY STABILITY
"JUST TO GIVE YOU A GENERAL IDEA . . ."

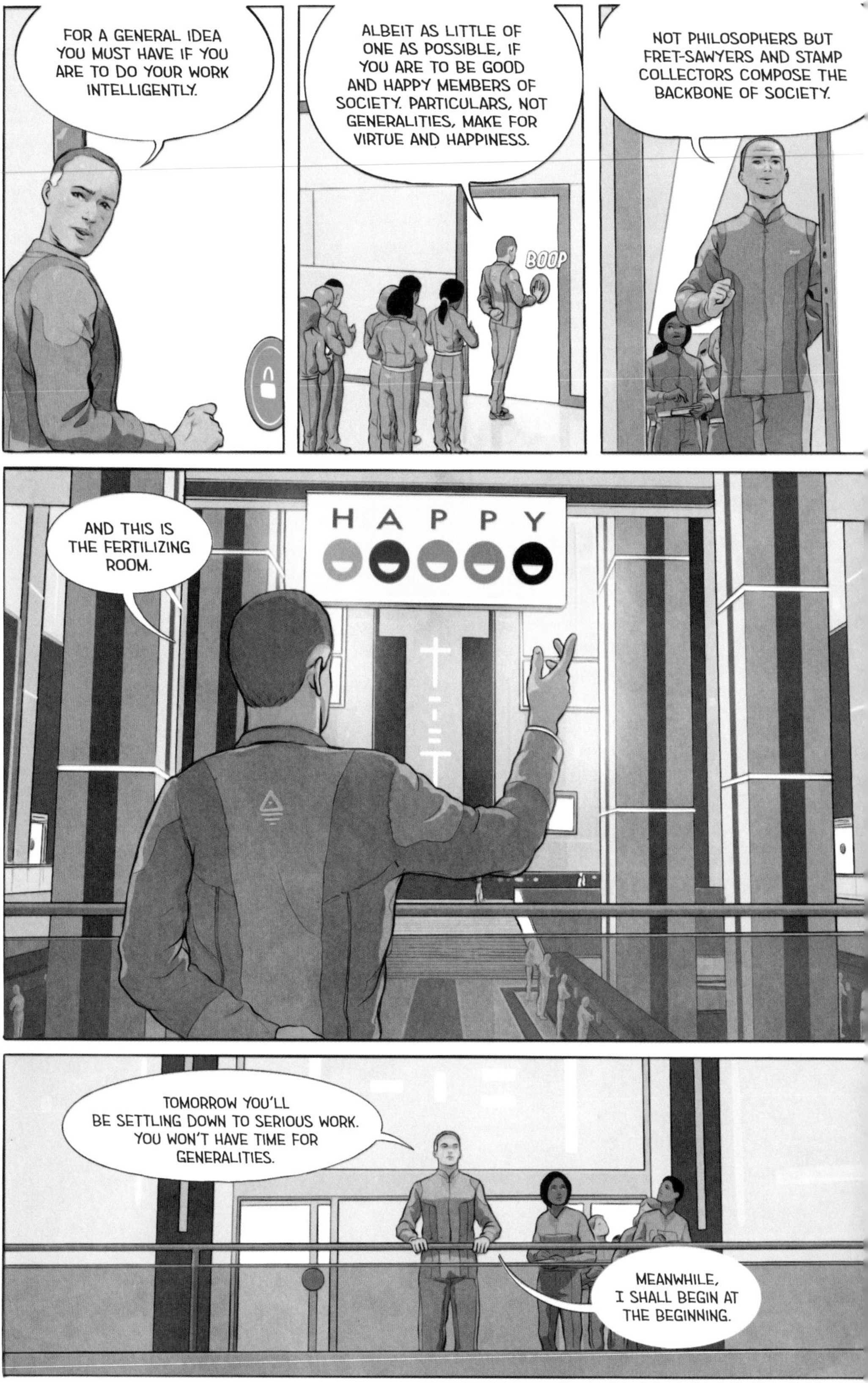
FOR A GENERAL IDEA YOU MUST HAVE IF YOU ARE TO DO YOUR WORK INTELLIGENTLY.
ALBEIT AS LITTLE OF ONE AS POSSIBLE, IF YOU ARE TO BE GOOD AND HAPPY MEMBERS OF SOCIETY. PARTICULARS, NOT GENERALITIES, MAKE FOR VIRTUE AND HAPPINESS.
BOOP
NOT PHILOSOPHERS BUT FRET-SAWYERS AND STAMP COLLECTORS COMPOSE THE BACKBONE OF SOCIETY.
HAPPY
AND THIS IS THE FERTILIZING ROOM.
TOMORROW YOU'LL BE SETTLING DOWN TO SERIOUS WORK. YOU WON'T HAVE TIME FOR GENERALITIES.
MEANWHILE, I SHALL BEGIN AT THE BEGINNING.

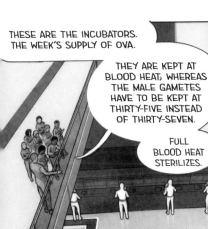

THESE ARE THE INCUBATORS. THE WEEK'S SUPPLY OF OVA.

THEY ARE KEPT AT BLOOD HEAT, WHEREAS THE MALE GAMETES HAVE TO BE KEPT AT THIRTY-FIVE INSTEAD OF THIRTY-SEVEN.

FULL BLOOD HEAT STERILIZES.

RAMS WRAPPED IN THERMOGENE BEGET NO LAMBS.

GAMETES
- Males at blood heat —
- Rams wrapped i
  beget no lar

THE MODERN FERTILIZING PROCESS BEGINS, OF COURSE, WITH A SURGICAL PROCEDURE. THIS IS UNDERGONE VOLUNTARILY FOR THE GOOD OF SOCIETY, NOT TO MENTION THE FACT THAT IT CARRIES A BONUS AMOUNTING TO SIX MONTHS' SALARY.

ONCE COUNTED AND INSPECTED FOR ABNORMALITIES, THE OVA ARE THEN IMMERSED IN A WARM BOUILLON CONTAINING FREE-SWIMMING SPERMATOZOA.

THE FERTILIZED OVA ARE THEN RETURNED TO THE INCUBATORS.

ALPHAS AND BETAS REMAIN UNTIL DEFINITELY BOTTLED, WHILE GAMMAS, DELTAS, AND EPSILONS ARE REMOVED AGAIN AFTER THIRTY-SIX HOURS TO UNDERGO BOKANOVSKY'S PROCESS.

THIS BEING THE MASS PRODUCTION OF IDENTICAL TWINS, AND ONE OF THE MAJOR INSTRUMENTS OF SOCIAL STABILITY.

- Fertilized ova → incubators.
- Gammas, deltas and epsilons → Bok process.
Bok process
- Major instrume

STANDARDIZED MEN AND WOMEN IN UNIFORM BATCHES. AN ENTIRE FACTORY STAFFED WITH THE PRODUCTS OF A SINGLE BOKANOVSKIFIED EGG.

THE PRINCIPLE OF THE ASSEMBLY LINE AT LAST APPLIED TO BIOLOGY.

PROGRESS.

MR. FOSTER, CAN YOU TELL US THE RECORD NUMBER OF INDIVIDUALS FOR A SINGLE OVARY?

SIXTEEN THOUSAND AND TWELVE IN THIS CENTER.

IN ONE HUNDRED AND EIGHTY-NINE BATCHES OF IDENTICALS.

THEY'VE DONE MUCH BETTER IN SOME OVERSEAS CENTERS. STILL, WE MEAN TO BEAT THEM IF WE CAN.

THAT'S THE SPIRIT I LIKE!

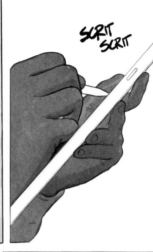

SCRIT SCRIT

COME ALONG WITH US, MR. FOSTER, AND GIVE THESE STUDENTS THE BENEFIT OF YOUR EXPERT KNOWLEDGE.

WITH PLEASURE.

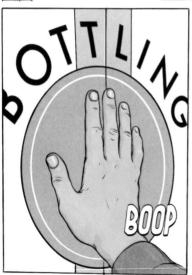

BOTTLING

BOOP

THE SOCIAL PREDESTINATORS SEND THEIR FIGURES TO THE FERTILIZERS.

WHO GIVE THEM THE EMBRYOS THEY ASK FOR.

AND THE BOTTLES COME IN HERE TO BE PREDESTINED IN DETAIL.

AFTER WHICH THEY ARE SENT DOWN TO THE EMBRYO STORE.

WHERE WE NOW PROCEED OURSELVES.

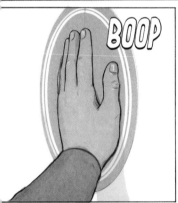

BOOP

EMBRYOS ARE LIKE PHOTOGRAPH FILM. THEY CAN ONLY STAND RED LIGHT.

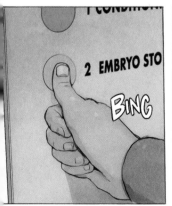

1 CONDITION
2 EMBRYO STO
BING

SCRIT SCRIT

11

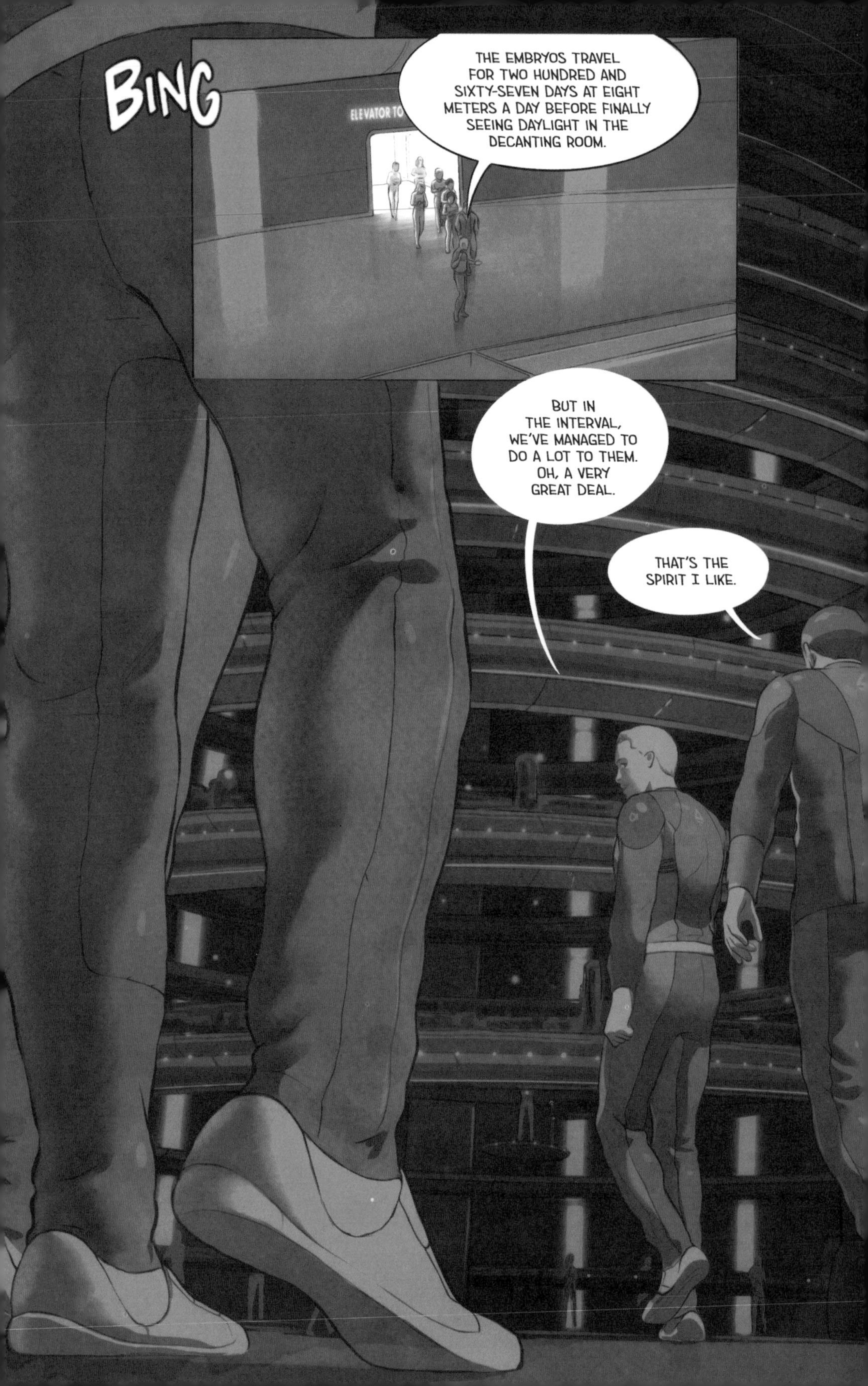
BING
ELEVATOR TO
THE EMBRYOS TRAVEL FOR TWO HUNDRED AND SIXTY-SEVEN DAYS AT EIGHT METERS A DAY BEFORE FINALLY SEEING DAYLIGHT IN THE DECANTING ROOM.
BUT IN THE INTERVAL, WE'VE MANAGED TO DO A LOT TO THEM. OH, A VERY GREAT DEAL.
THAT'S THE SPIRIT I LIKE.

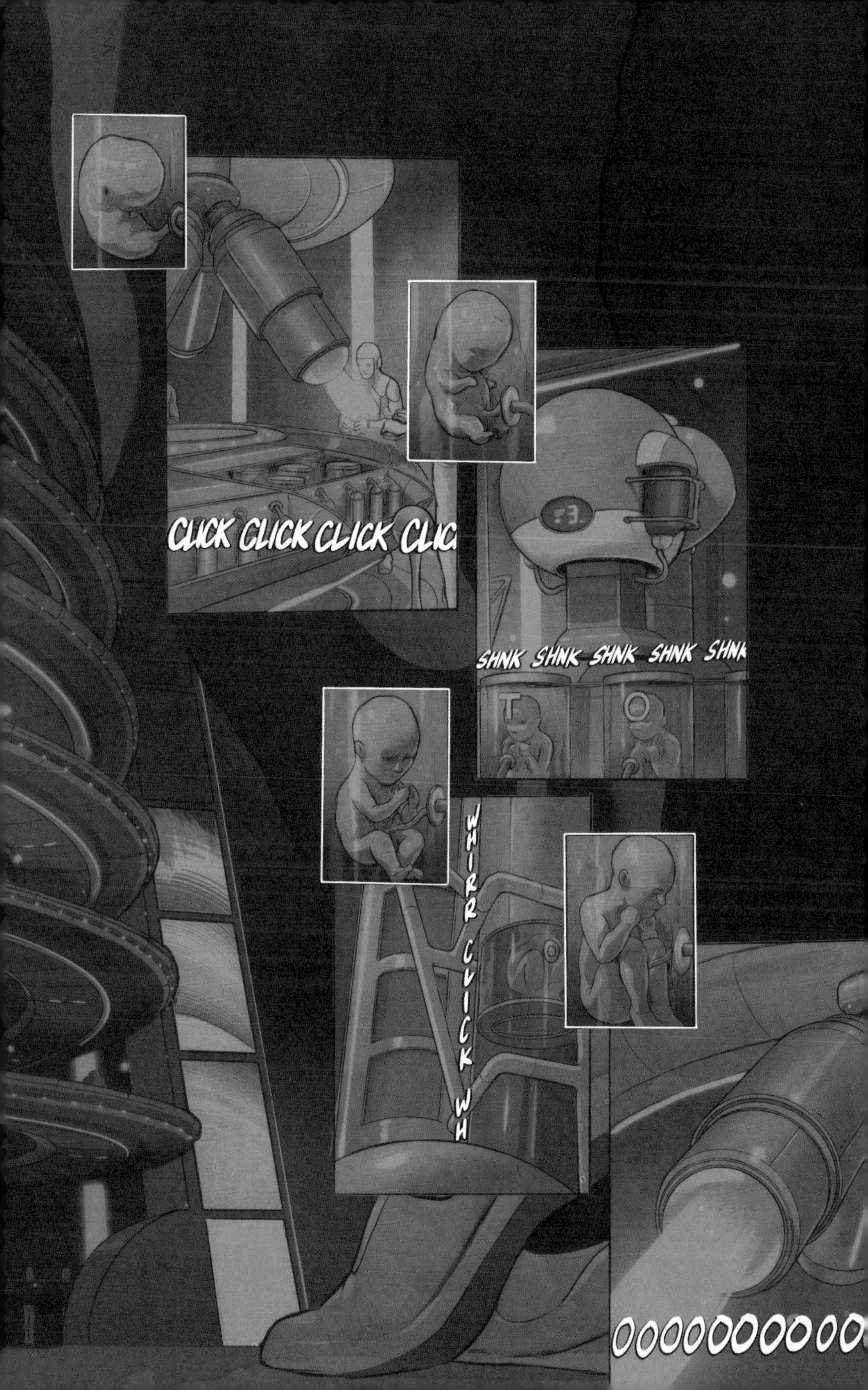
CLICK CLICK CLICK CLIC
F3.
SHNK SHNK SHNK SHNK SHNK
T O
WHIRR CLICK WH
OOOOOOOOOO

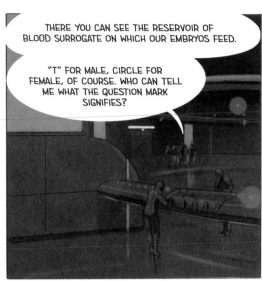

THERE YOU CAN SEE THE RESERVOIR OF BLOOD SURROGATE ON WHICH OUR EMBRYOS FEED.

"T" FOR MALE, CIRCLE FOR FEMALE, OF COURSE. WHO CAN TELL ME WHAT THE QUESTION MARK SIGNIFIES?

FREEMARTINS, SIR.

QUITE SO. FOR OF COURSE IN THE VAST MAJORITY OF CASES, FERTILITY IS MERELY A NUISANCE. THOSE DECANTED AS FREEMARTINS ARE STRUCTURALLY QUITE NORMAL, BUT STERILE.

AND WE DO NOT CONTENT OURSELVES WITH MERELY HATCHING OUT EMBRYOS. ANY COW CAN DO THAT. WE ALSO PREDESTINE AND CONDITION. WE DECANT OUR BABIES AS SOCIALIZED HUMAN BEINGS, AS ALPHAS OR EPSILONS, AS FUTURE SEWAGE WORKERS OR FUTURE DIRECTORS OF HATCHERIES.

DOWN HERE WE CONDITION THEM TO THRIVE ON THAT FOR WHICH THEY ARE PREDESTINED.

AND OUR COLLEAGUES UPSTAIRS TEACH THEM TO LOVE IT.

AND THAT IS THE SECRET OF HAPPINESS AND VIRTUE--LIKING WHAT YOU'VE *GOT* TO DO.

TEN TO THREE.

WE MUST GO UP TO THE HYPNOPAEDIA NURSERIES BEFORE THE CHILDREN HAVE FINISHED THEIR AFTERNOON SLEEP . . .

THANK YOU FOR YOUR TIME, MR. FOSTER.

INFANT NURSERIES
CONDITIONING

DECANTING, EMBRYO STORE,
BOTTLING, FERTILIZING

NEO-PAVLOVIAN

BOOP

WATCH
CAREFULLY.

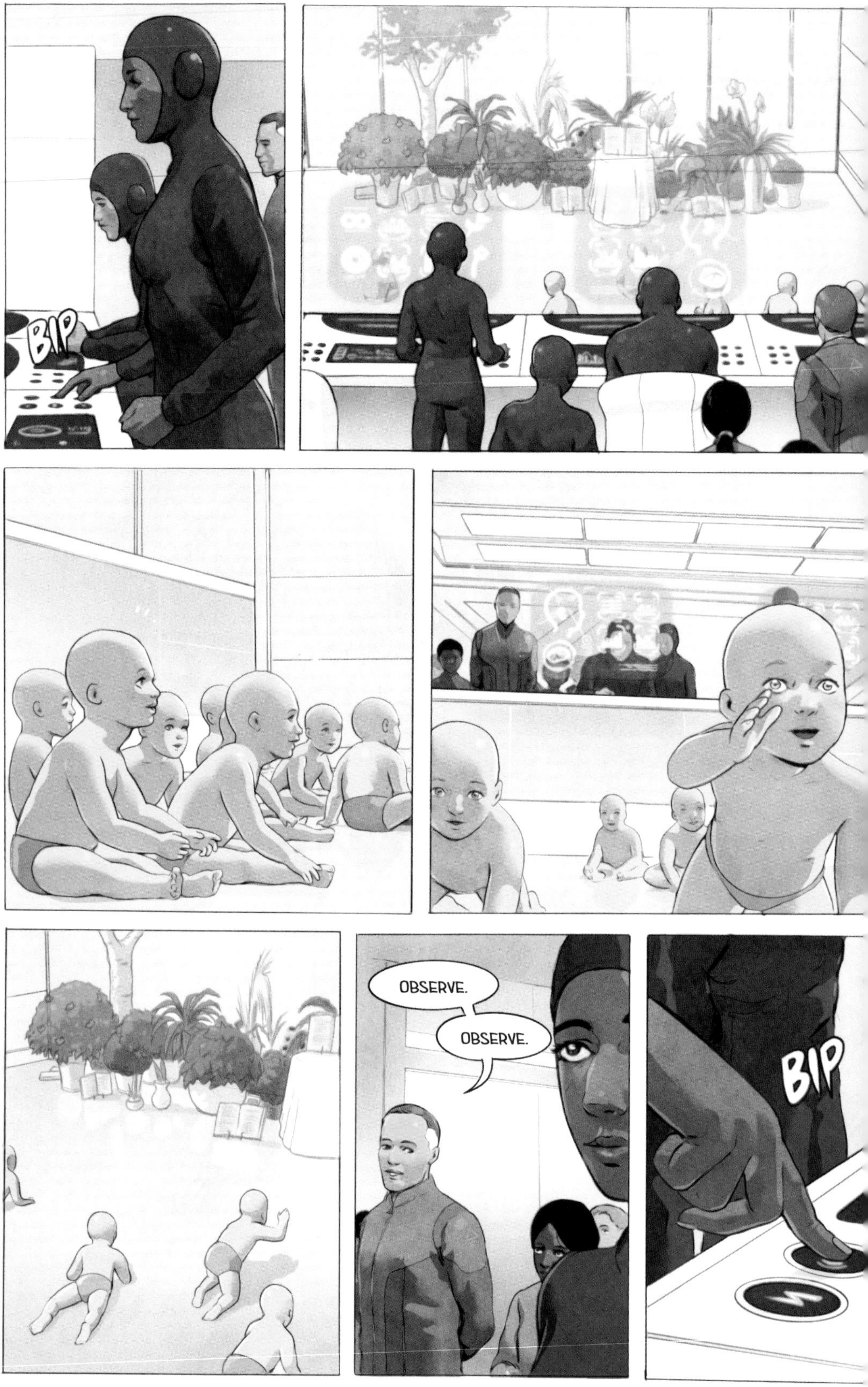
BIP
OBSERVE.
OBSERVE.
BIP

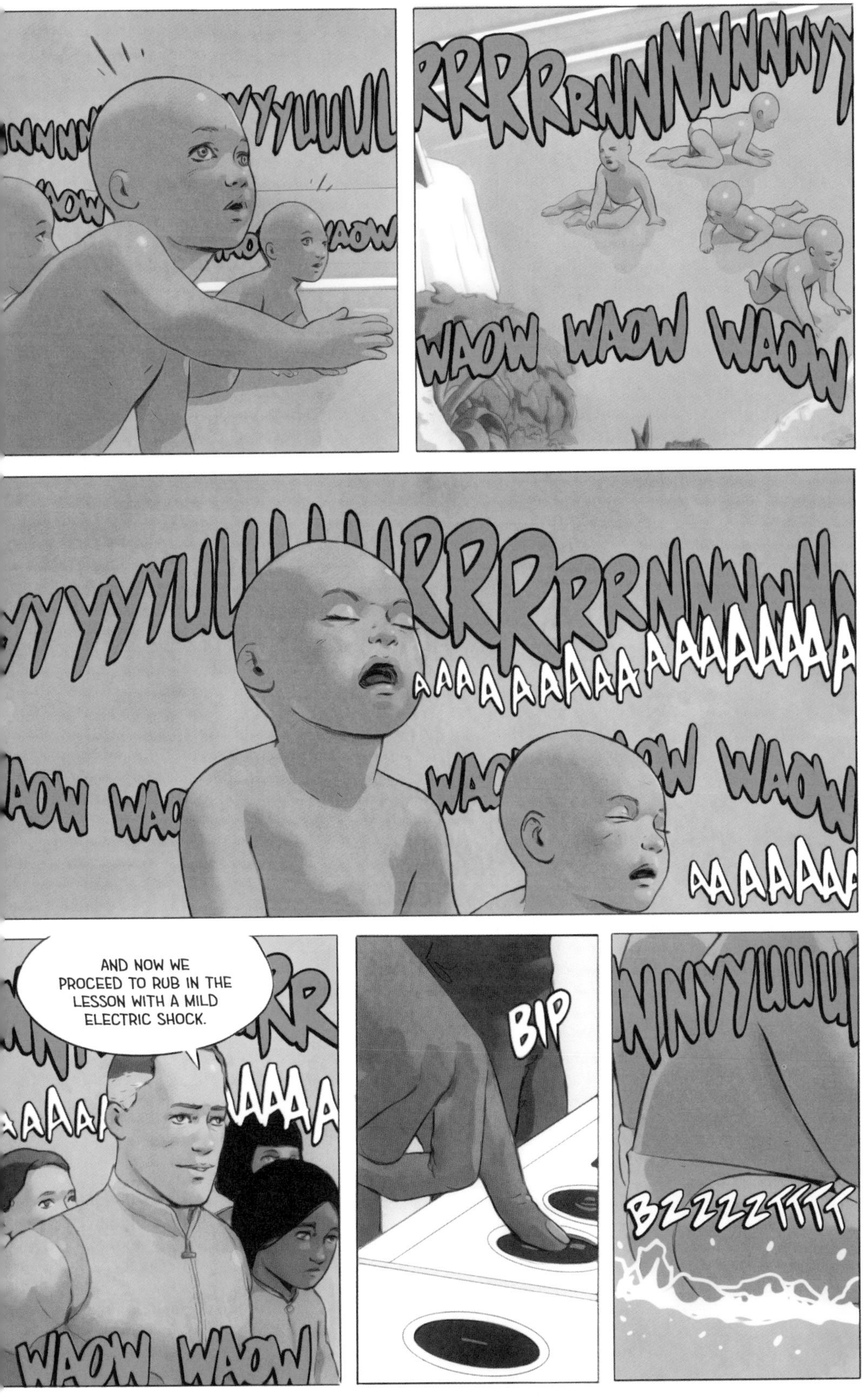
NNNN
YYUUUL
WAOW
WAOW
RRRRNNNNNNNYY
WAOW WAOW WAOW
YYYYUU
RRRRNN
AAAAAAAAAAAAAAAAA
AOW WAO
WAO
W WAOW
AAAAAA
AND NOW WE PROCEED TO RUB IN THE LESSON WITH A MILD ELECTRIC SHOCK.
AAAA
AAAA
WAOW WAOW
BIP
NNYYUUUL
BZZZZTTTT

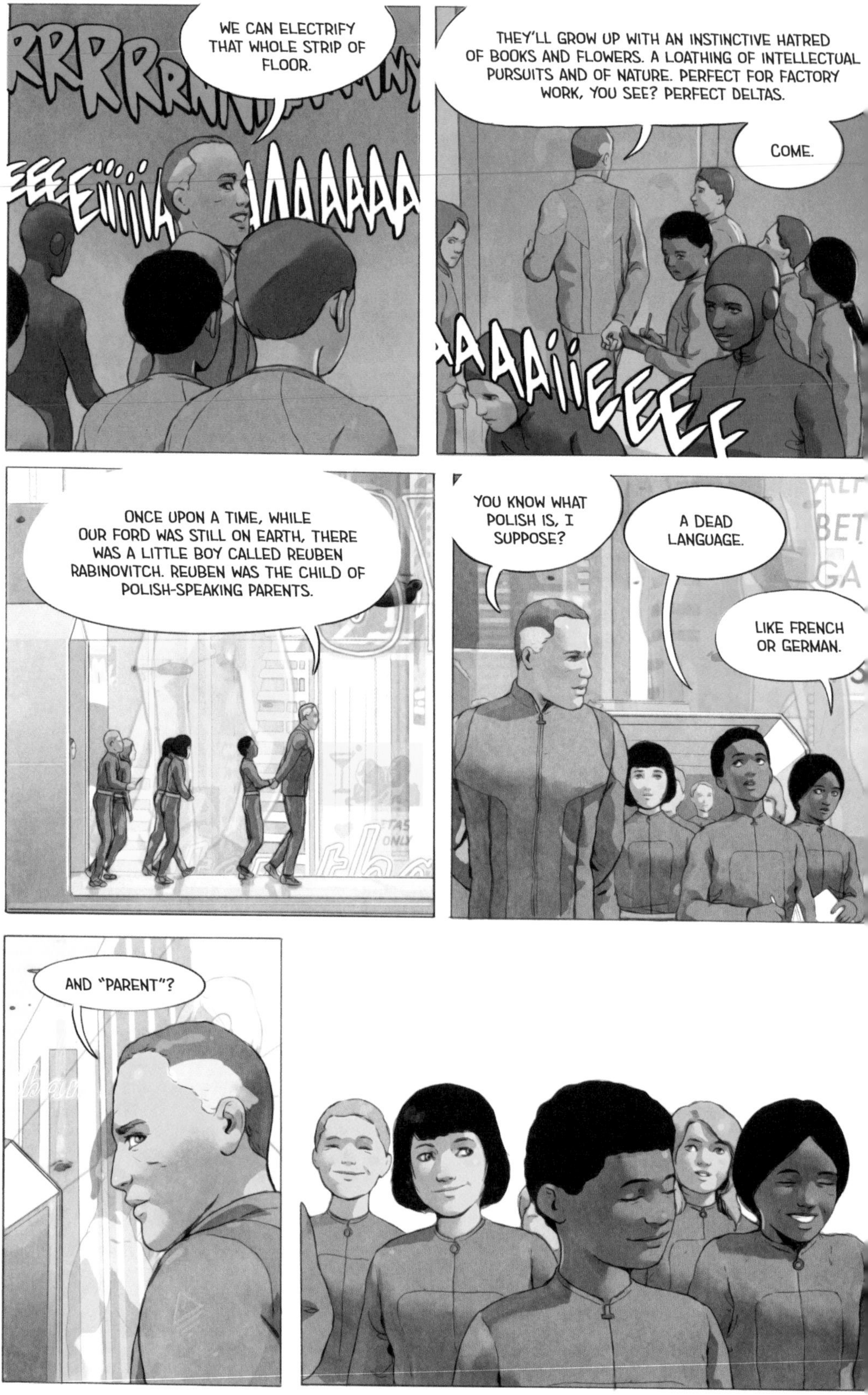
WE CAN ELECTRIFY THAT WHOLE STRIP OF FLOOR.
RRRRRNNNNNMMMMMNY
EEEEEIIIIIAAAAAAAAAAAA
THEY'LL GROW UP WITH AN INSTINCTIVE HATRED OF BOOKS AND FLOWERS. A LOATHING OF INTELLECTUAL PURSUITS AND OF NATURE. PERFECT FOR FACTORY WORK, YOU SEE? PERFECT DELTAS.
COME.
AAAAIIEEEF
ONCE UPON A TIME, WHILE OUR FORD WAS STILL ON EARTH, THERE WAS A LITTLE BOY CALLED REUBEN RABINOVITCH. REUBEN WAS THE CHILD OF POLISH-SPEAKING PARENTS.
YOU KNOW WHAT POLISH IS, I SUPPOSE?
A DEAD LANGUAGE.
LIKE FRENCH OR GERMAN.
AND "PARENT"?

WELL? IT IS SCIENCE, AFTER ALL, NOT SMUT.

H-HUMAN BEINGS USED TO BE...

WELL, THEY USED TO BE VIVIPAROUS.

QUITE RIGHT.

AND WHEN THEY WERE DECANTED...

"BORN."

WELL, THEN THEY WERE THE PARENTS-- I MEAN, NOT THE BABIES, OF COURSE; THE OTHER ONES...

IN SHORT, THE PARENTS WERE THE FATHER AND THE MOTHER.

MOTHER.

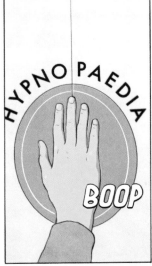

HYPNO PAEDIA

BOOP

THESE ARE UNPLEASANT FACTS, I KNOW. BUT THEN, MOST HISTORICAL FACTS ARE UNPLEASANT.

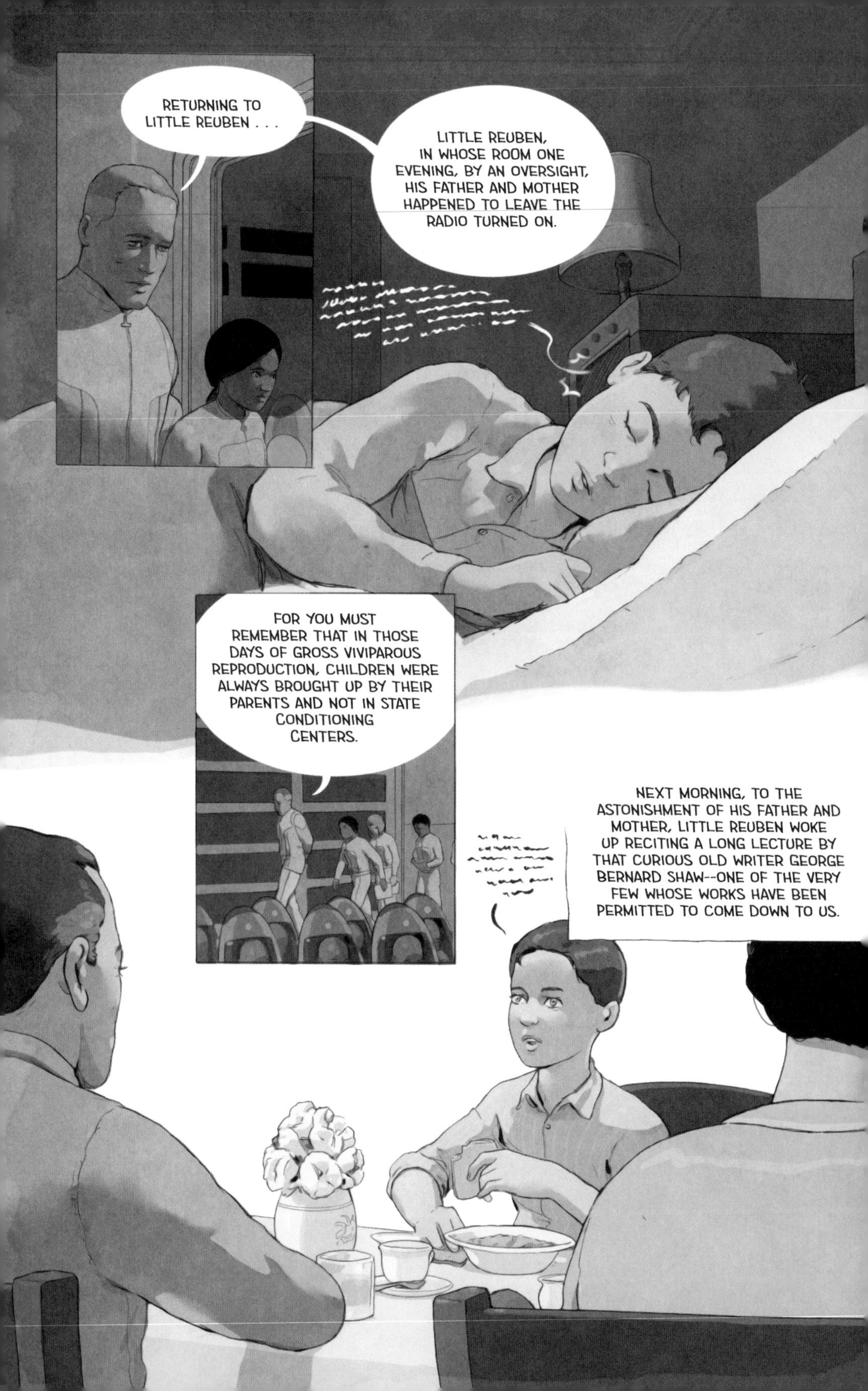
RETURNING TO LITTLE REUBEN . . .
LITTLE REUBEN, IN WHOSE ROOM ONE EVENING, BY AN OVERSIGHT, HIS FATHER AND MOTHER HAPPENED TO LEAVE THE RADIO TURNED ON.
FOR YOU MUST REMEMBER THAT IN THOSE DAYS OF GROSS VIVIPAROUS REPRODUCTION, CHILDREN WERE ALWAYS BROUGHT UP BY THEIR PARENTS AND NOT IN STATE CONDITIONING CENTERS.
NEXT MORNING, TO THE ASTONISHMENT OF HIS FATHER AND MOTHER, LITTLE REUBEN WOKE UP RECITING A LONG LECTURE BY THAT CURIOUS OLD WRITER GEORGE BERNARD SHAW--ONE OF THE VERY FEW WHOSE WORKS HAVE BEEN PERMITTED TO COME DOWN TO US.

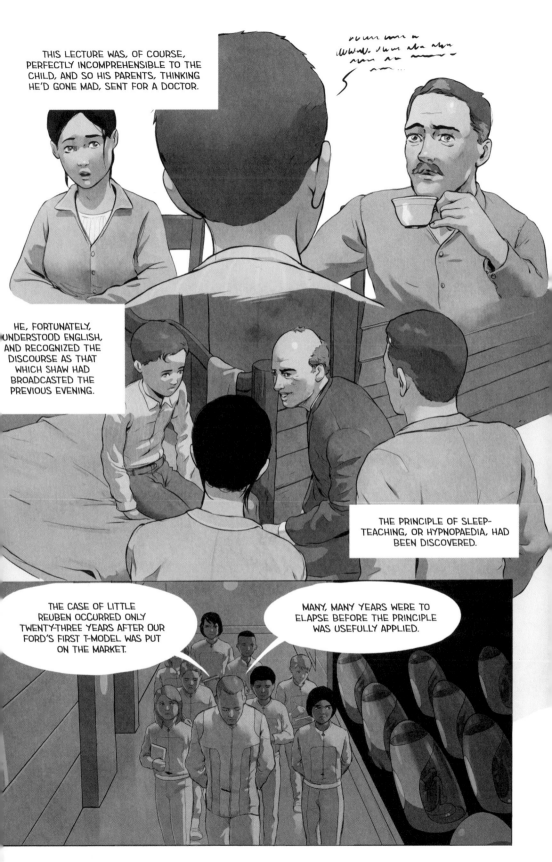

THIS LECTURE WAS, OF COURSE, PERFECTLY INCOMPREHENSIBLE TO THE CHILD, AND SO HIS PARENTS, THINKING HE'D GONE MAD, SENT FOR A DOCTOR.

HE, FORTUNATELY, UNDERSTOOD ENGLISH, AND RECOGNIZED THE DISCOURSE AS THAT WHICH SHAW HAD BROADCASTED THE PREVIOUS EVENING.

THE PRINCIPLE OF SLEEP-TEACHING, OR HYPNOPAEDIA, HAD BEEN DISCOVERED.

THE CASE OF LITTLE REUBEN OCCURRED ONLY TWENTY-THREE YEARS AFTER OUR FORD'S FIRST T-MODEL WAS PUT ON THE MARKET.

MANY, MANY YEARS WERE TO ELAPSE BEFORE THE PRINCIPLE WAS USEFULLY APPLIED.

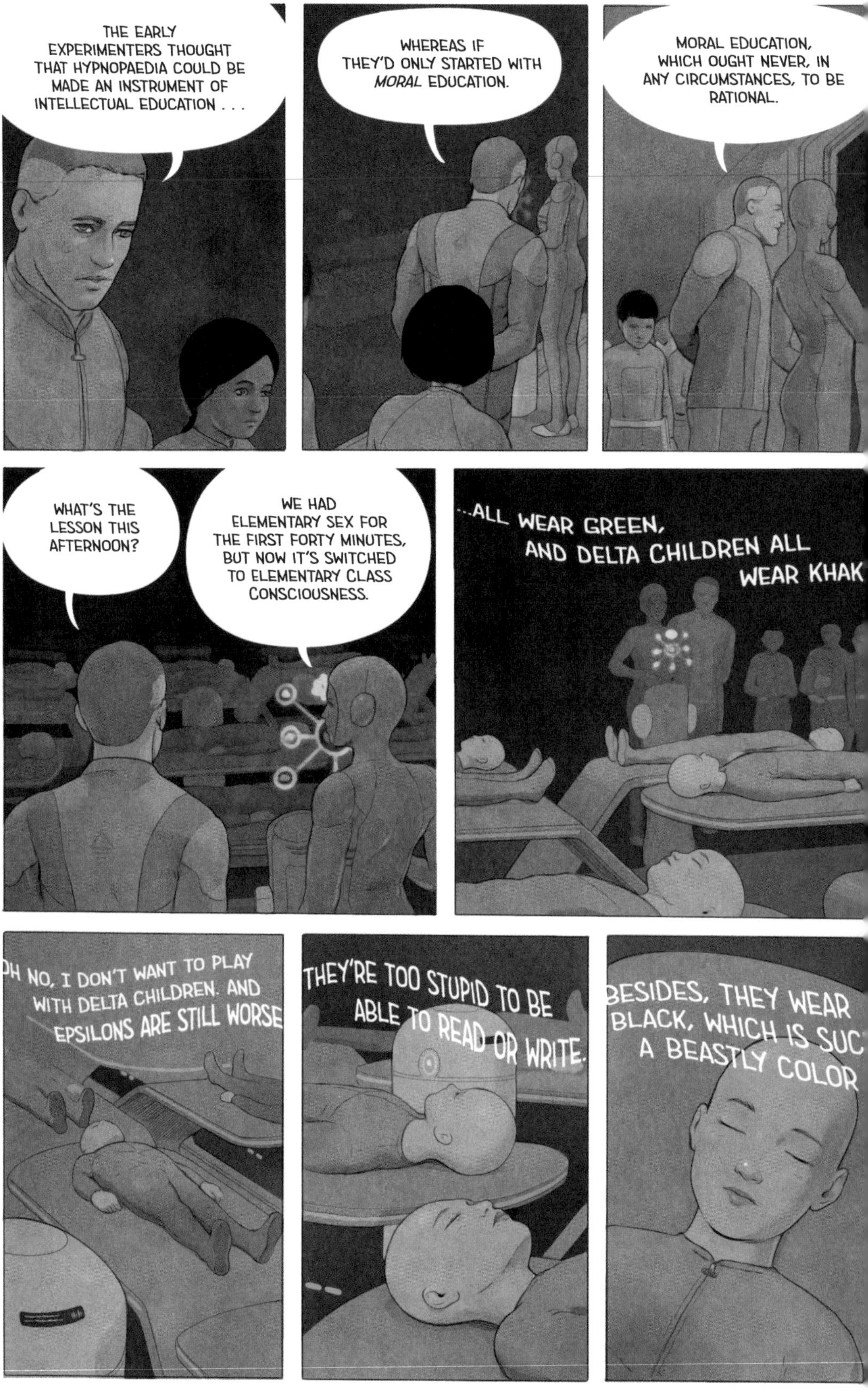
THE EARLY EXPERIMENTERS THOUGHT THAT HYPNOPAEDIA COULD BE MADE AN INSTRUMENT OF INTELLECTUAL EDUCATION . . .
WHEREAS IF THEY'D ONLY STARTED WITH *MORAL* EDUCATION.
MORAL EDUCATION, WHICH OUGHT NEVER, IN ANY CIRCUMSTANCES, TO BE RATIONAL.
WHAT'S THE LESSON THIS AFTERNOON?
WE HAD ELEMENTARY SEX FOR THE FIRST FORTY MINUTES, BUT NOW IT'S SWITCHED TO ELEMENTARY CLASS CONSCIOUSNESS.
...ALL WEAR GREEN, AND DELTA CHILDREN ALL WEAR KHAK
H NO, I DON'T WANT TO PLAY WITH DELTA CHILDREN. AND EPSILONS ARE STILL WORSE
THEY'RE TOO STUPID TO BE ABLE TO READ OR WRITE.
BESIDES, THEY WEAR BLACK, WHICH IS SUC A BEASTLY COLOR

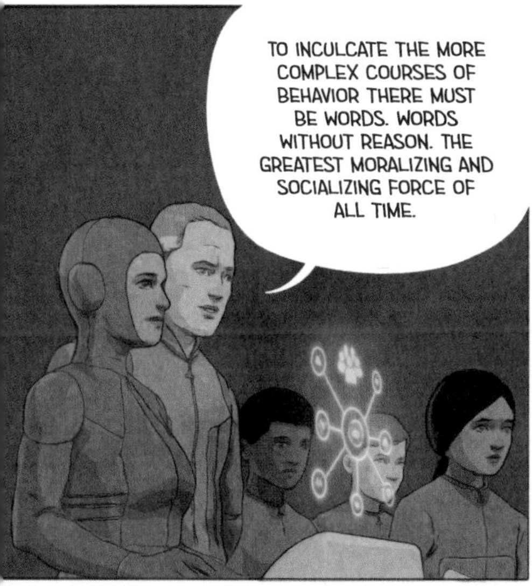
TO INCULCATE THE MORE COMPLEX COURSES OF BEHAVIOR THERE MUST BE WORDS. WORDS WITHOUT REASON. THE GREATEST MORALIZING AND SOCIALIZING FORCE OF ALL TIME.

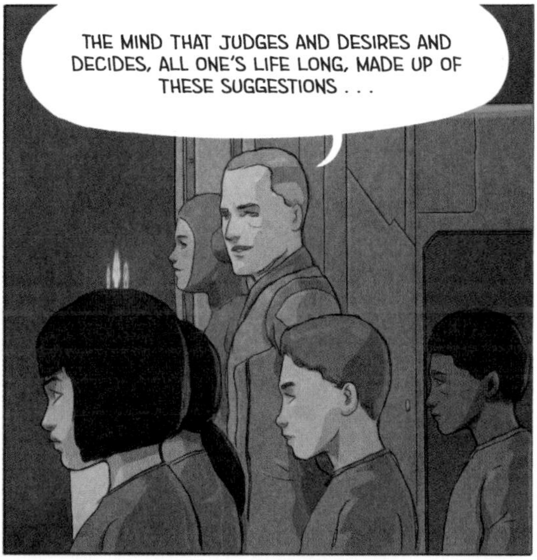
THE MIND THAT JUDGES AND DESIRES AND DECIDES, ALL ONE'S LIFE LONG, MADE UP OF THESE SUGGESTIONS . . .

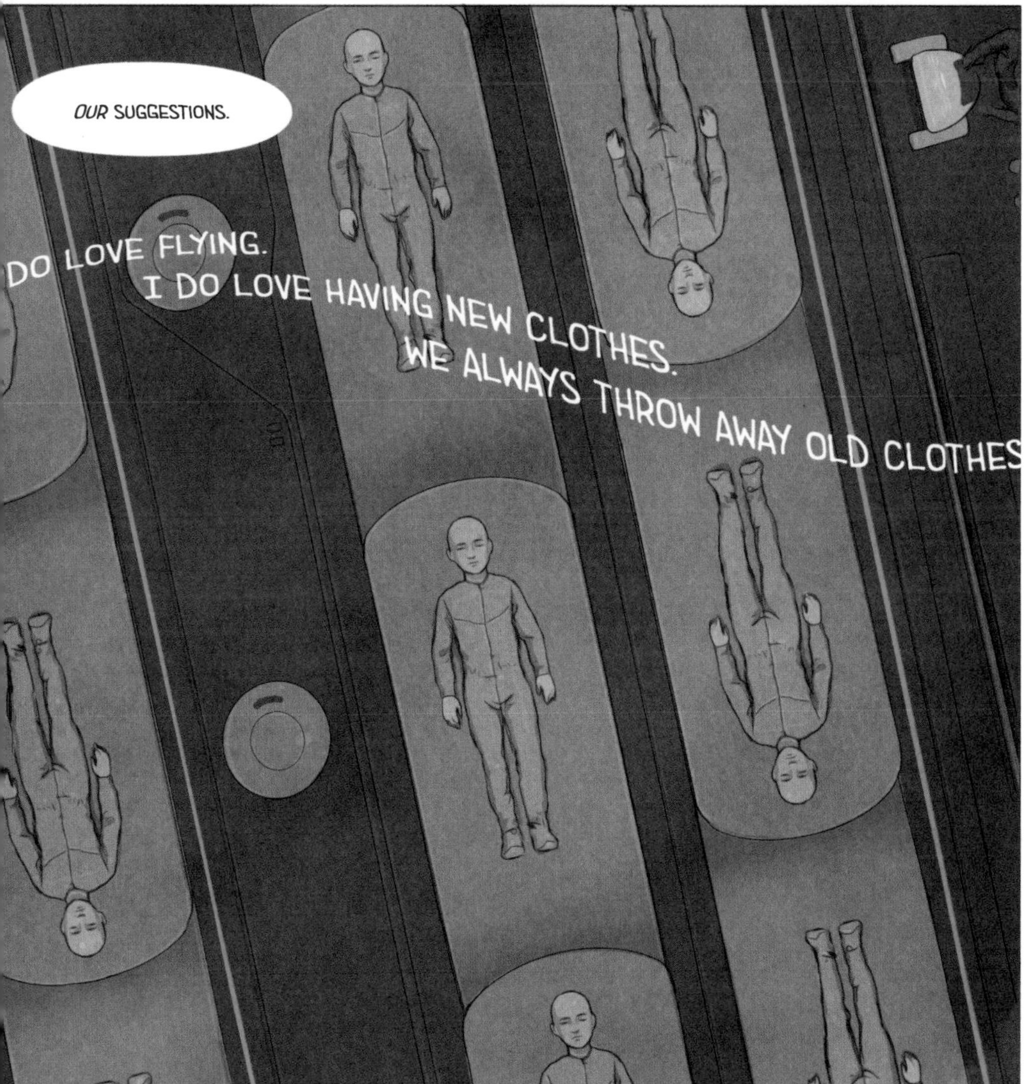
OUR SUGGESTIONS.
DO LOVE FLYING.
I DO LOVE HAVING NEW CLOTHES.
WE ALWAYS THROW AWAY OLD CLOTHES

MAIN DAY-SHIFT OFF DUTY. SECOND DAY-SHIFT TAKE OVER. MAIN DAY-SHIFT OFF . . .

. . . DUTY. SECOND DAY-SHIFT TAKE OVER. MAIN DAY-SHIFT OFF DUTY. SECOND DAY-SHIFT TAKE OVER . . .

BETA CHANGING ROOMS

BERNARD MARX

Have a gre
Evening, Bern

BERNARD MARX

MEN'S CHANGING ROOMS

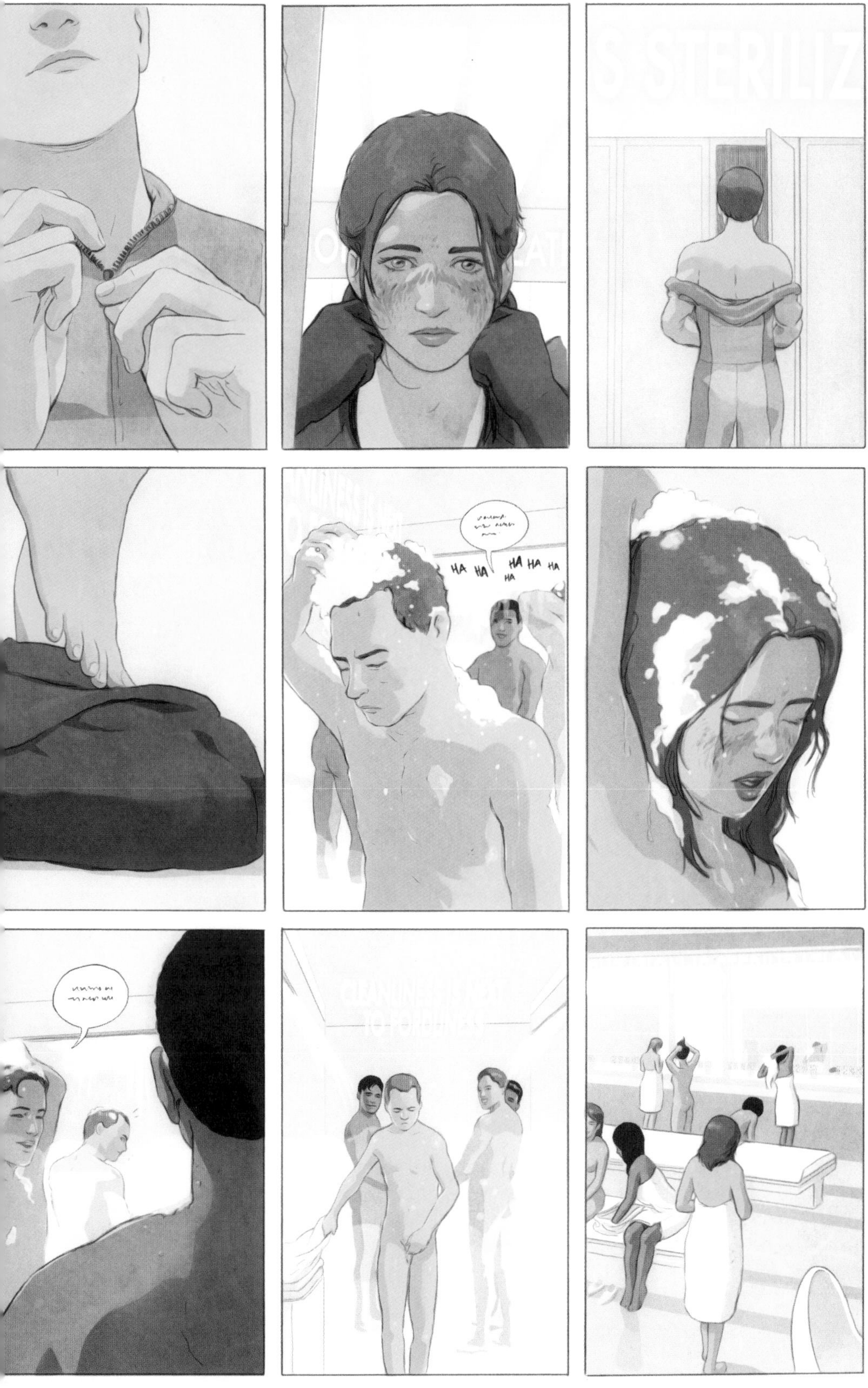
S STERILIZ
HA HA HA HA HA HA

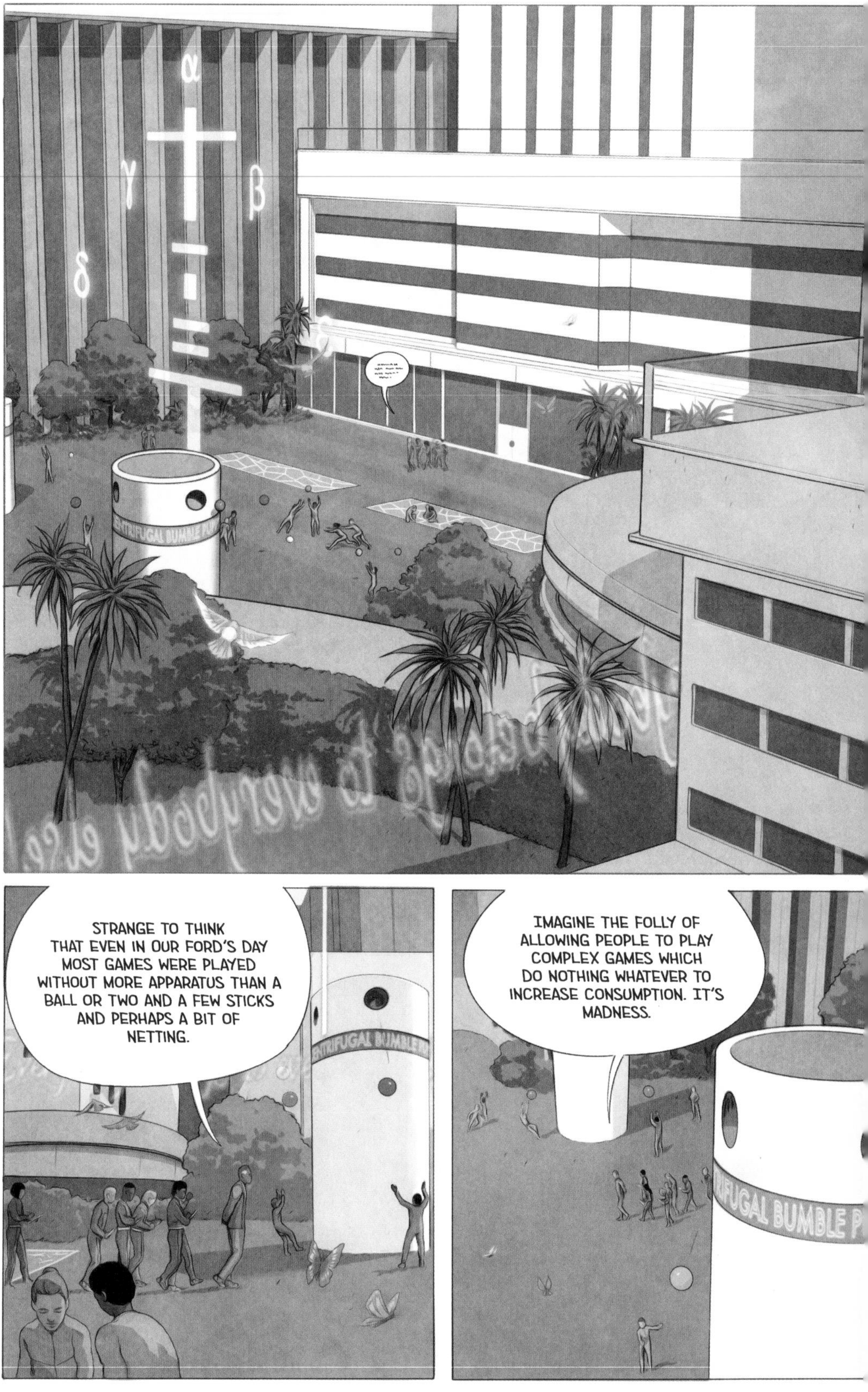
STRANGE TO THINK THAT EVEN IN OUR FORD'S DAY MOST GAMES WERE PLAYED WITHOUT MORE APPARATUS THAN A BALL OR TWO AND A FEW STICKS AND PERHAPS A BIT OF NETTING.
IMAGINE THE FOLLY OF ALLOWING PEOPLE TO PLAY COMPLEX GAMES WHICH DO NOTHING WHATEVER TO INCREASE CONSUMPTION. IT'S MADNESS.

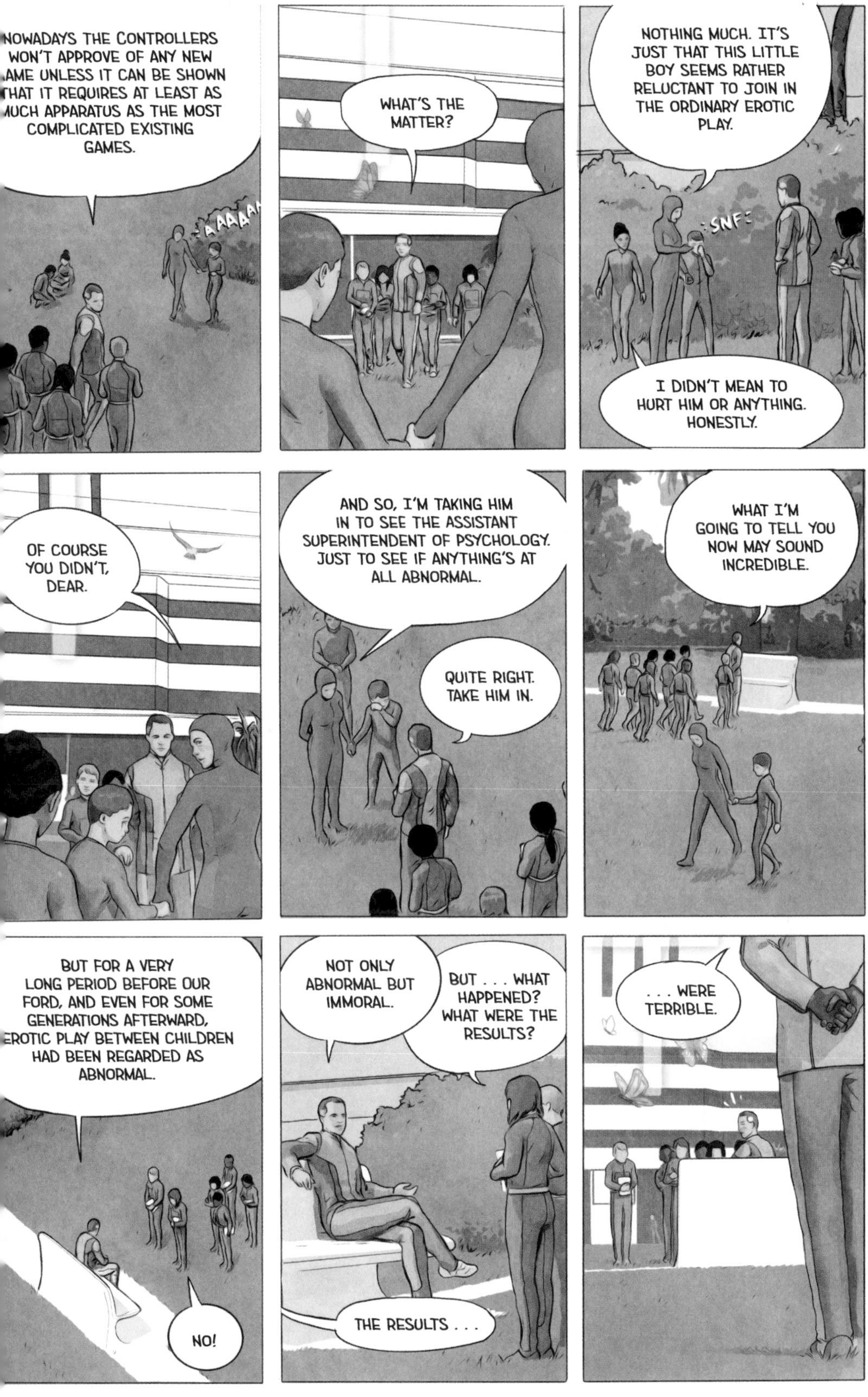
NOWADAYS THE CONTROLLERS WON'T APPROVE OF ANY NEW AME UNLESS IT CAN BE SHOWN THAT IT REQUIRES AT LEAST AS UCH APPARATUS AS THE MOST COMPLICATED EXISTING GAMES.
AAAAA
WHAT'S THE MATTER?
NOTHING MUCH. IT'S JUST THAT THIS LITTLE BOY SEEMS RATHER RELUCTANT TO JOIN IN THE ORDINARY EROTIC PLAY.
SNF
I DIDN'T MEAN TO HURT HIM OR ANYTHING. HONESTLY.
OF COURSE YOU DIDN'T, DEAR.
AND SO, I'M TAKING HIM IN TO SEE THE ASSISTANT SUPERINTENDENT OF PSYCHOLOGY. JUST TO SEE IF ANYTHING'S AT ALL ABNORMAL.
QUITE RIGHT. TAKE HIM IN.
WHAT I'M GOING TO TELL YOU NOW MAY SOUND INCREDIBLE.
BUT FOR A VERY LONG PERIOD BEFORE OUR FORD, AND EVEN FOR SOME GENERATIONS AFTERWARD, ROTIC PLAY BETWEEN CHILDREN HAD BEEN REGARDED AS ABNORMAL.
NO!
NOT ONLY ABNORMAL BUT IMMORAL.
BUT . . . WHAT HAPPENED? WHAT WERE THE RESULTS?
THE RESULTS . . .
. . . WERE TERRIBLE.

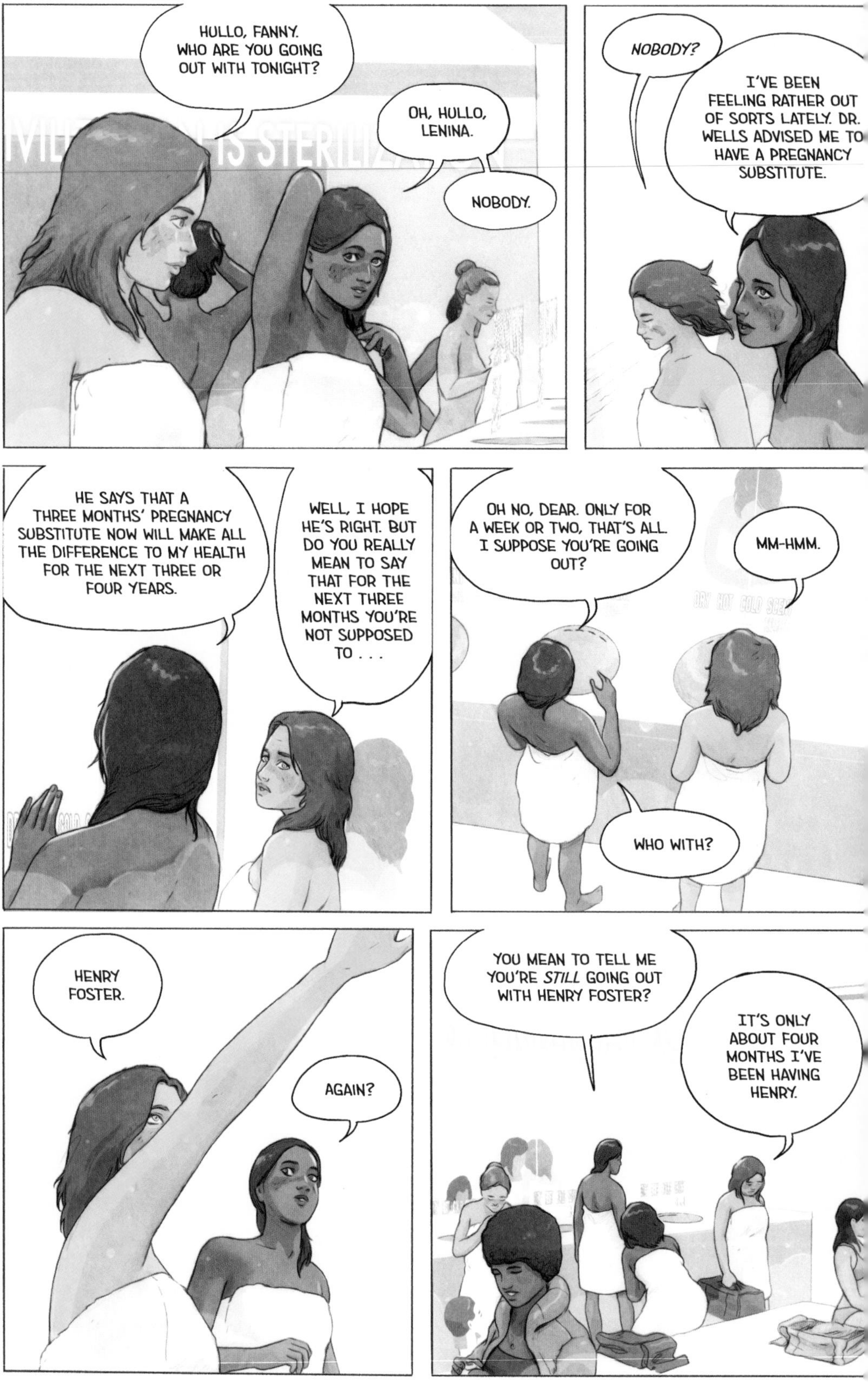
HULLO, FANNY. WHO ARE YOU GOING OUT WITH TONIGHT?
OH, HULLO, LENINA.
NOBODY.
NOBODY?
I'VE BEEN FEELING RATHER OUT OF SORTS LATELY. DR. WELLS ADVISED ME TO HAVE A PREGNANCY SUBSTITUTE.
HE SAYS THAT A THREE MONTHS' PREGNANCY SUBSTITUTE NOW WILL MAKE ALL THE DIFFERENCE TO MY HEALTH FOR THE NEXT THREE OR FOUR YEARS.
WELL, I HOPE HE'S RIGHT. BUT DO YOU REALLY MEAN TO SAY THAT FOR THE NEXT THREE MONTHS YOU'RE NOT SUPPOSED TO . . .
OH NO, DEAR. ONLY FOR A WEEK OR TWO, THAT'S ALL. I SUPPOSE YOU'RE GOING OUT?
MM-HMM.
WHO WITH?
HENRY FOSTER.
AGAIN?
YOU MEAN TO TELL ME YOU'RE *STILL* GOING OUT WITH HENRY FOSTER?
IT'S ONLY ABOUT FOUR MONTHS I'VE BEEN HAVING HENRY.

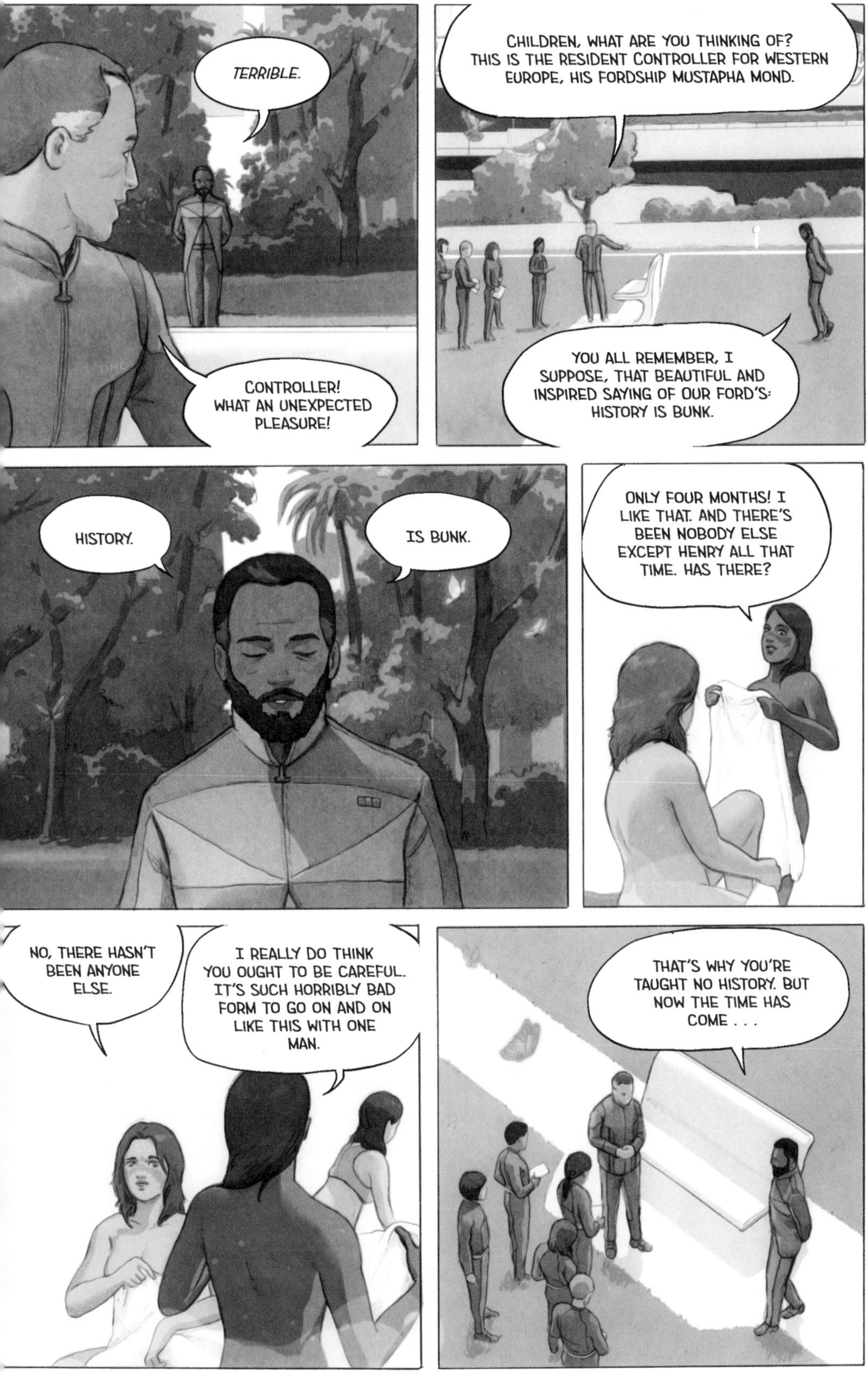
TERRIBLE.
CONTROLLER! WHAT AN UNEXPECTED PLEASURE!
CHILDREN, WHAT ARE YOU THINKING OF? THIS IS THE RESIDENT CONTROLLER FOR WESTERN EUROPE, HIS FORDSHIP MUSTAPHA MOND.
YOU ALL REMEMBER, I SUPPOSE, THAT BEAUTIFUL AND INSPIRED SAYING OF OUR FORD'S: HISTORY IS BUNK.
HISTORY.
IS BUNK.
ONLY FOUR MONTHS! I LIKE THAT. AND THERE'S BEEN NOBODY ELSE EXCEPT HENRY ALL THAT TIME. HAS THERE?
NO, THERE HASN'T BEEN ANYONE ELSE.
I REALLY DO THINK YOU OUGHT TO BE CAREFUL. IT'S SUCH HORRIBLY BAD FORM TO GO ON AND ON LIKE THIS WITH ONE MAN.
THAT'S WHY YOU'RE TAUGHT NO HISTORY. BUT NOW THE TIME HAS COME . . .

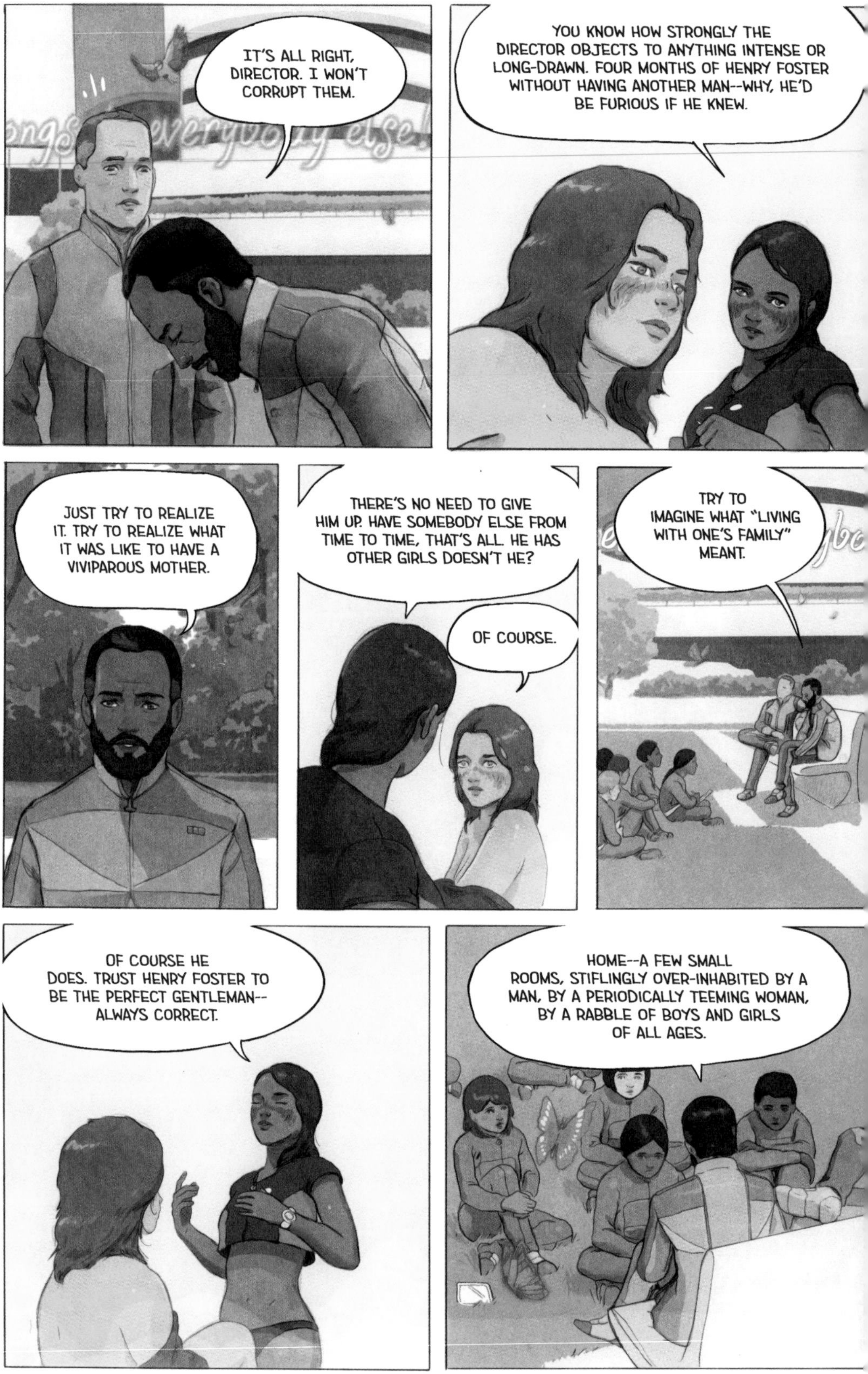
IT'S ALL RIGHT, DIRECTOR. I WON'T CORRUPT THEM.
YOU KNOW HOW STRONGLY THE DIRECTOR OBJECTS TO ANYTHING INTENSE OR LONG-DRAWN. FOUR MONTHS OF HENRY FOSTER WITHOUT HAVING ANOTHER MAN--WHY, HE'D BE FURIOUS IF HE KNEW.
JUST TRY TO REALIZE IT. TRY TO REALIZE WHAT IT WAS LIKE TO HAVE A VIVIPAROUS MOTHER.
THERE'S NO NEED TO GIVE HIM UP. HAVE SOMEBODY ELSE FROM TIME TO TIME, THAT'S ALL. HE HAS OTHER GIRLS DOESN'T HE?
OF COURSE.
TRY TO IMAGINE WHAT "LIVING WITH ONE'S FAMILY" MEANT.
OF COURSE HE DOES. TRUST HENRY FOSTER TO BE THE PERFECT GENTLEMAN--ALWAYS CORRECT.
HOME--A FEW SMALL ROOMS, STIFLINGLY OVER-INHABITED BY A MAN, BY A PERIODICALLY TEEMING WOMAN, BY A RABBLE OF BOYS AND GIRLS OF ALL AGES.

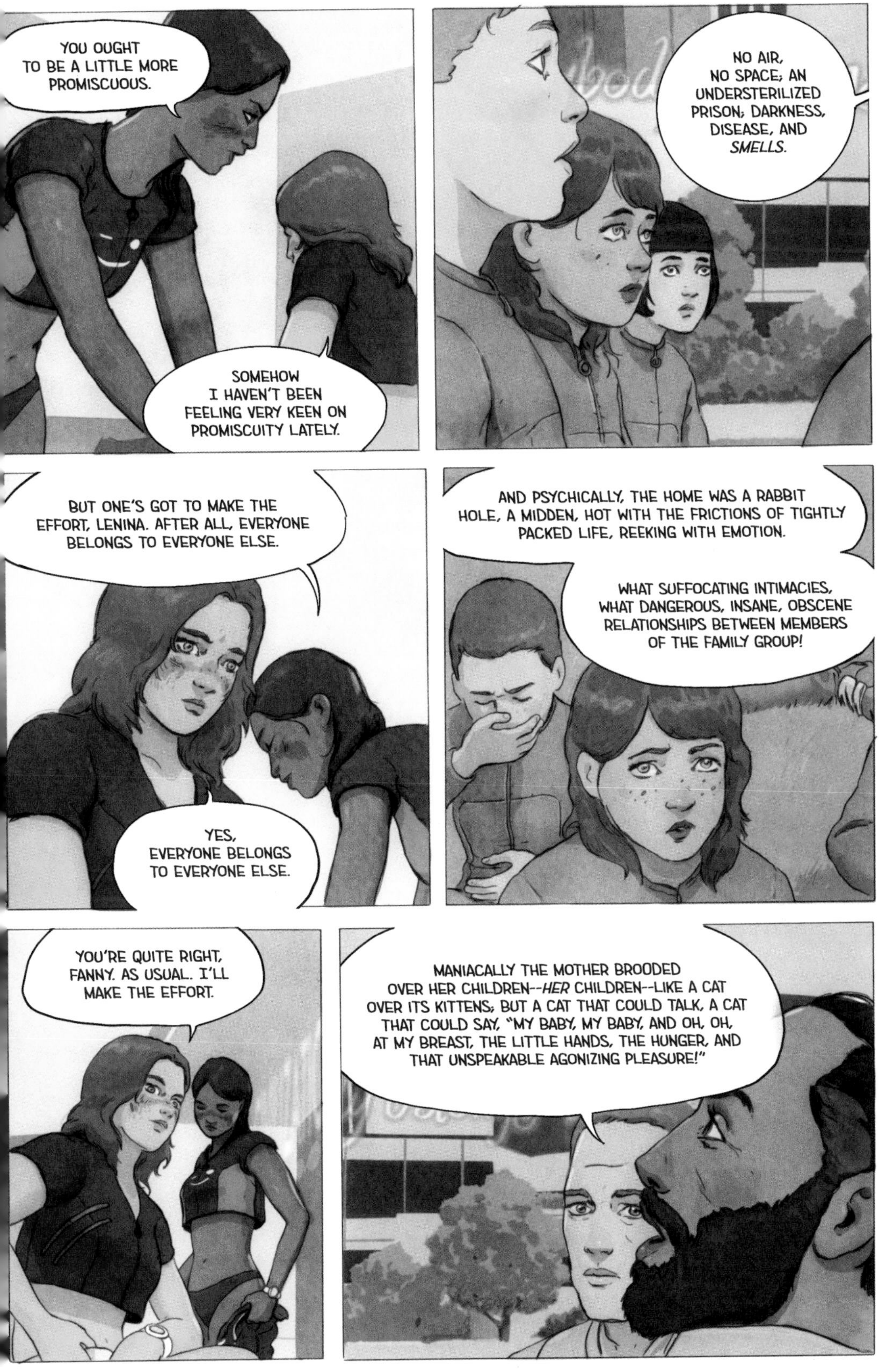
YOU OUGHT TO BE A LITTLE MORE PROMISCUOUS.
SOMEHOW I HAVEN'T BEEN FEELING VERY KEEN ON PROMISCUITY LATELY.
NO AIR, NO SPACE; AN UNDERSTERILIZED PRISON; DARKNESS, DISEASE, AND *SMELLS*.
BUT ONE'S GOT TO MAKE THE EFFORT, LENINA. AFTER ALL, EVERYONE BELONGS TO EVERYONE ELSE.
YES, EVERYONE BELONGS TO EVERYONE ELSE.
AND PSYCHICALLY, THE HOME WAS A RABBIT HOLE, A MIDDEN, HOT WITH THE FRICTIONS OF TIGHTLY PACKED LIFE, REEKING WITH EMOTION.
WHAT SUFFOCATING INTIMACIES, WHAT DANGEROUS, INSANE, OBSCENE RELATIONSHIPS BETWEEN MEMBERS OF THE FAMILY GROUP!
YOU'RE QUITE RIGHT, FANNY. AS USUAL. I'LL MAKE THE EFFORT.
MANIACALLY THE MOTHER BROODED OVER HER CHILDREN--*HER* CHILDREN--LIKE A CAT OVER ITS KITTENS; BUT A CAT THAT COULD TALK, A CAT THAT COULD SAY, "MY BABY, MY BABY, AND OH, OH, AT MY BREAST, THE LITTLE HANDS, THE HUNGER, AND THAT UNSPEAKABLE AGONIZING PLEASURE!"

YES, YOU MAY WELL SHUDDER.

TO TELL THE TRUTH, I'M BEGINNING TO GET JUST A TINY BIT BORED WITH NOTHING BUT HENRY EVERY DAY.

DO YOU KNOW BERNARD MARX?

GOING TO THE FEELIES TONIGHT, HENRY?

I HEAR THE NEW ONE AT THE ALHAMBRA IS FIRST-RATE.

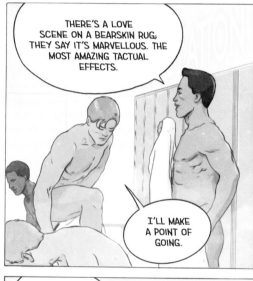

THERE'S A LOVE SCENE ON A BEARSKIN RUG; THEY SAY IT'S MARVELLOUS. THE MOST AMAZING TACTUAL EFFECTS.

I'LL MAKE A POINT OF GOING.

OUR FORD--OR OUR FREUD, AS, FOR SOME INSCRUTABLE REASON, HE CHOSE TO CALL HIMSELF WHENEVER HE SPOKE OF PSYCHOLOGICAL MATTERS--HAD BEEN THE FIRST TO REVEAL THE APPALLING DANGERS OF FAMILY LIFE.

LENINA, YOU DON'T MEAN TO SAY . . .?

WHY NOT? BERNARD'S AN ALPHA-PLUS.

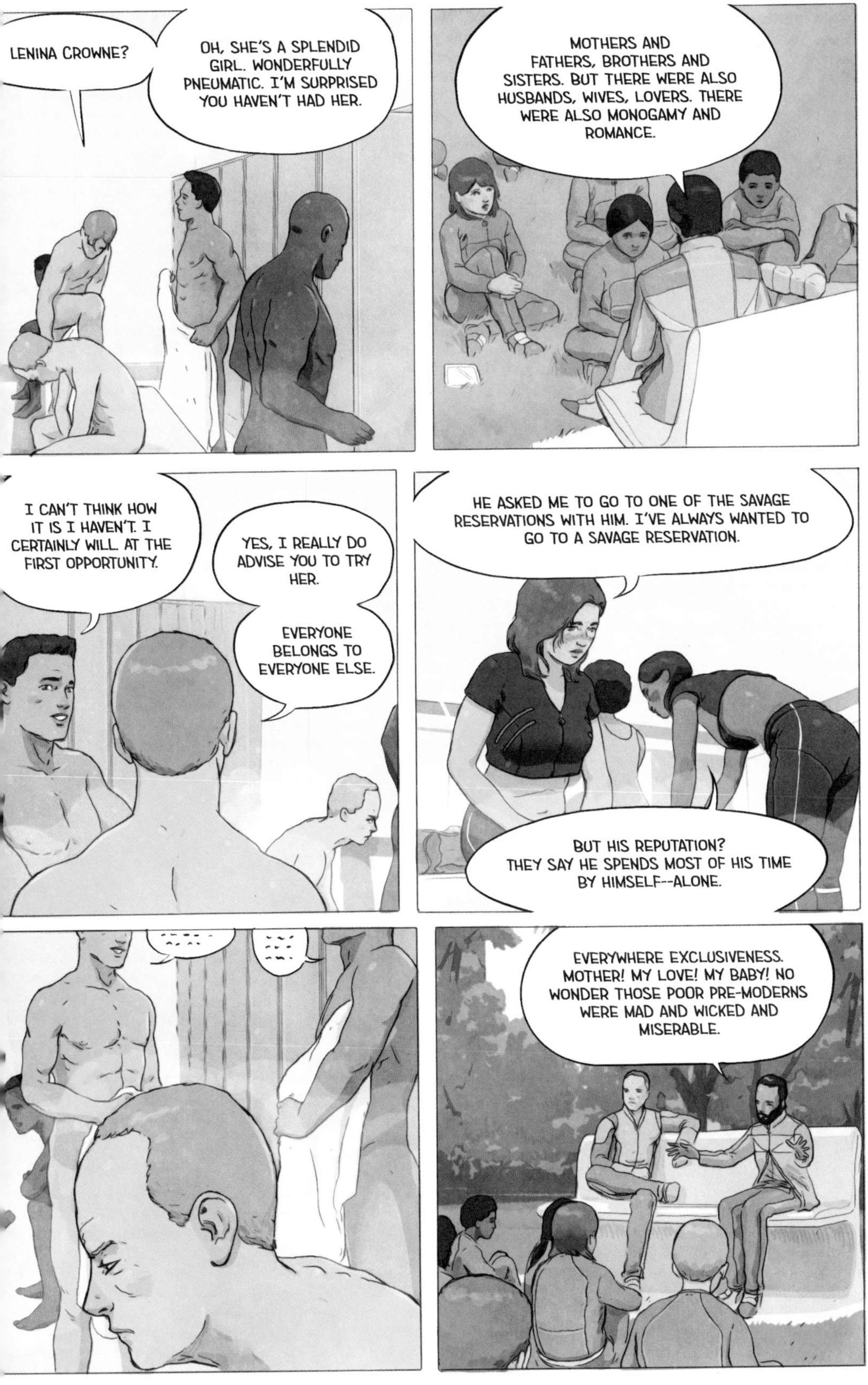
LENINA CROWNE?
OH, SHE'S A SPLENDID GIRL. WONDERFULLY PNEUMATIC. I'M SURPRISED YOU HAVEN'T HAD HER.
MOTHERS AND FATHERS, BROTHERS AND SISTERS. BUT THERE WERE ALSO HUSBANDS, WIVES, LOVERS. THERE WERE ALSO MONOGAMY AND ROMANCE.
I CAN'T THINK HOW IT IS I HAVEN'T. I CERTAINLY WILL. AT THE FIRST OPPORTUNITY.
YES, I REALLY DO ADVISE YOU TO TRY HER.
EVERYONE BELONGS TO EVERYONE ELSE.
HE ASKED ME TO GO TO ONE OF THE SAVAGE RESERVATIONS WITH HIM. I'VE ALWAYS WANTED TO GO TO A SAVAGE RESERVATION.
BUT HIS REPUTATION? THEY SAY HE SPENDS MOST OF HIS TIME BY HIMSELF--ALONE.
EVERYWHERE EXCLUSIVENESS. MOTHER! MY LOVE! MY BABY! NO WONDER THOSE POOR PRE-MODERNS WERE MAD AND WICKED AND MISERABLE.

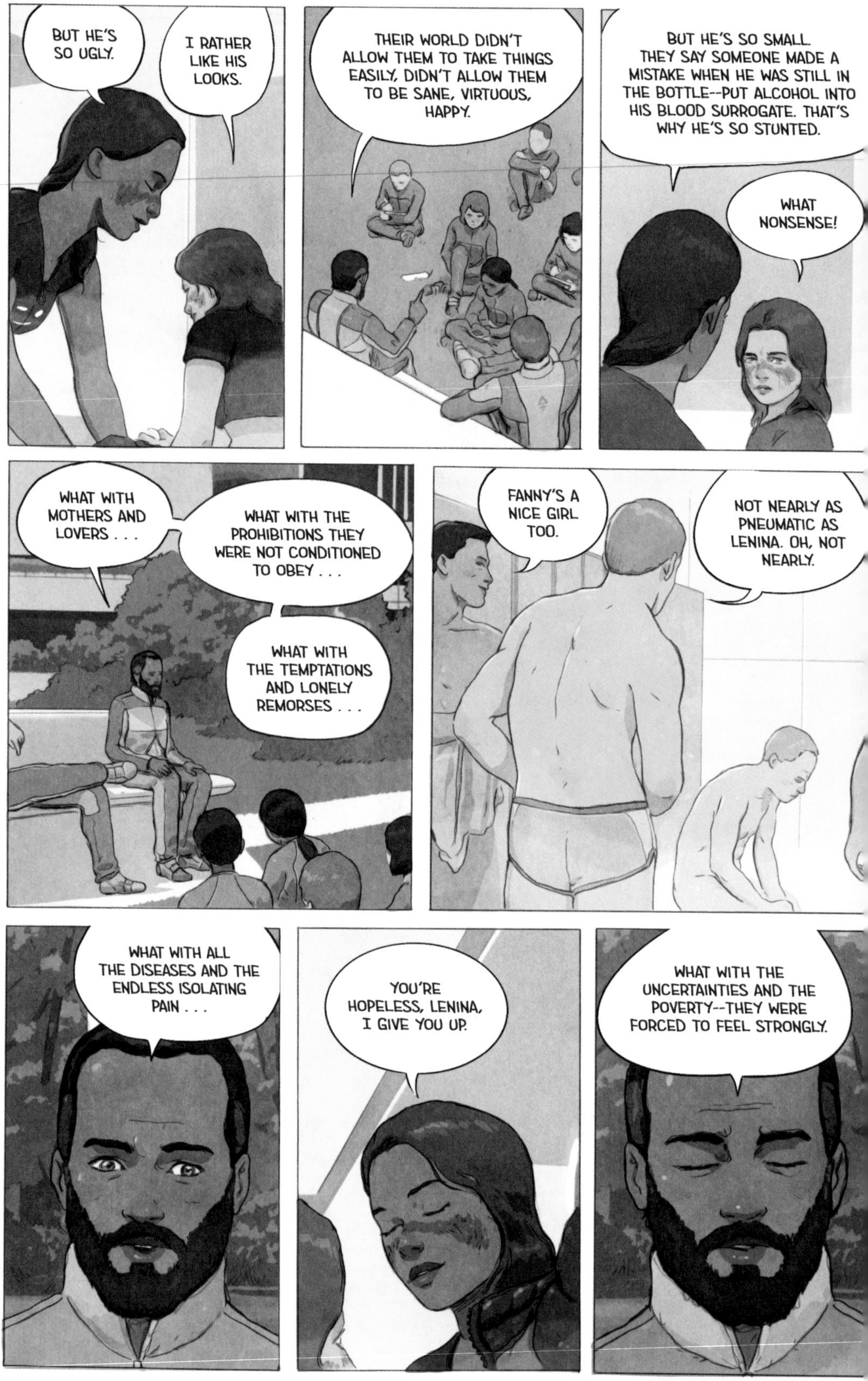
BUT HE'S SO UGLY.
I RATHER LIKE HIS LOOKS.
THEIR WORLD DIDN'T ALLOW THEM TO TAKE THINGS EASILY, DIDN'T ALLOW THEM TO BE SANE, VIRTUOUS, HAPPY.
BUT HE'S SO SMALL. THEY SAY SOMEONE MADE A MISTAKE WHEN HE WAS STILL IN THE BOTTLE--PUT ALCOHOL INTO HIS BLOOD SURROGATE. THAT'S WHY HE'S SO STUNTED.
WHAT NONSENSE!
WHAT WITH MOTHERS AND LOVERS . . .
WHAT WITH THE PROHIBITIONS THEY WERE NOT CONDITIONED TO OBEY . . .
WHAT WITH THE TEMPTATIONS AND LONELY REMORSES . . .
FANNY'S A NICE GIRL TOO.
NOT NEARLY AS PNEUMATIC AS LENINA. OH, NOT NEARLY.
WHAT WITH ALL THE DISEASES AND THE ENDLESS ISOLATING PAIN . . .
YOU'RE HOPELESS, LENINA, I GIVE YOU UP.
WHAT WITH THE UNCERTAINTIES AND THE POVERTY--THEY WERE FORCED TO FEEL STRONGLY.

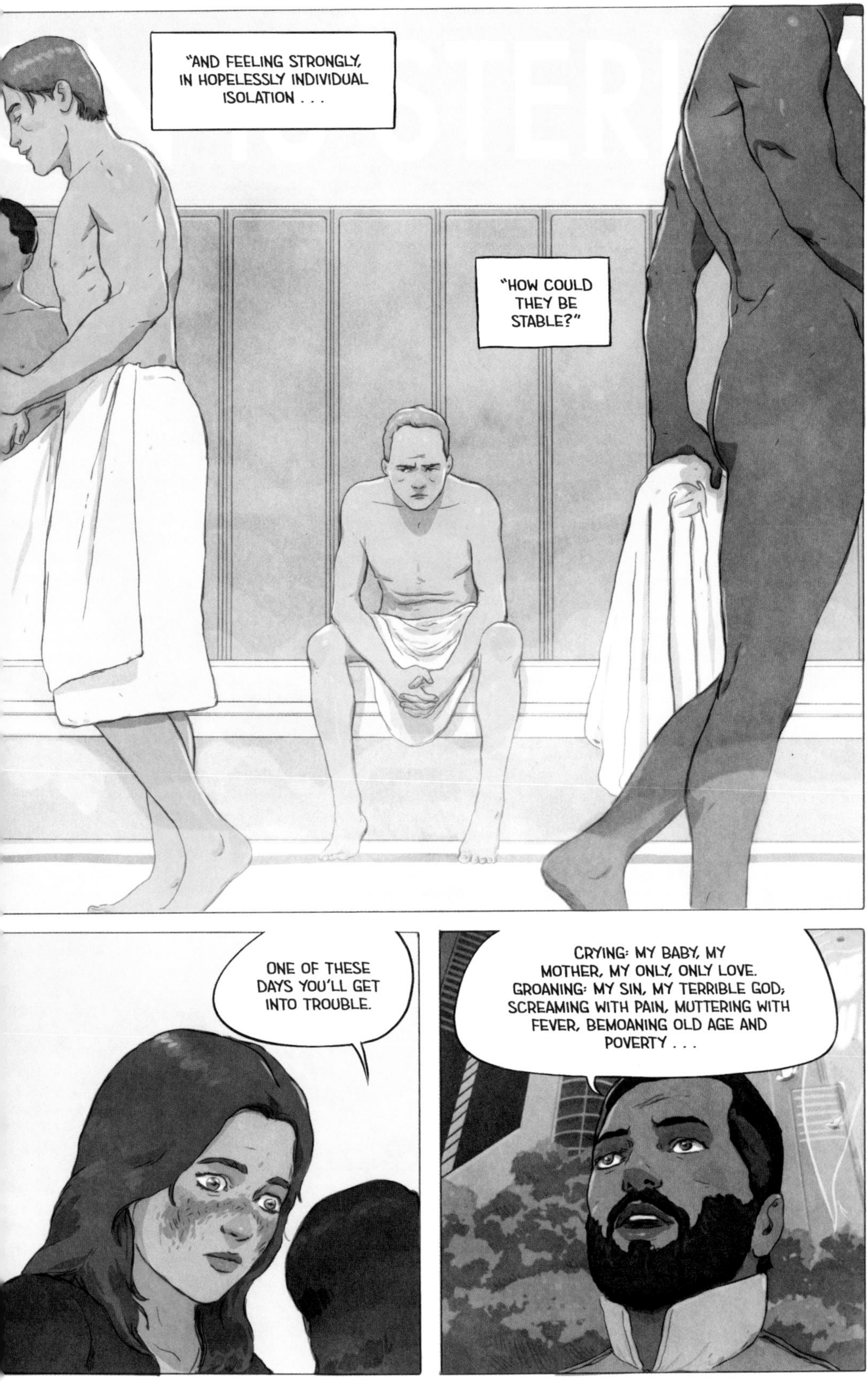
"AND FEELING STRONGLY, IN HOPELESSLY INDIVIDUAL ISOLATION . . .
"HOW COULD THEY BE STABLE?"
ONE OF THESE DAYS YOU'LL GET INTO TROUBLE.
CRYING: MY BABY, MY MOTHER, MY ONLY, ONLY LOVE. GROANING: MY SIN, MY TERRIBLE GOD; SCREAMING WITH PAIN, MUTTERING WITH FEVER, BEMOANING OLD AGE AND POVERTY . . .

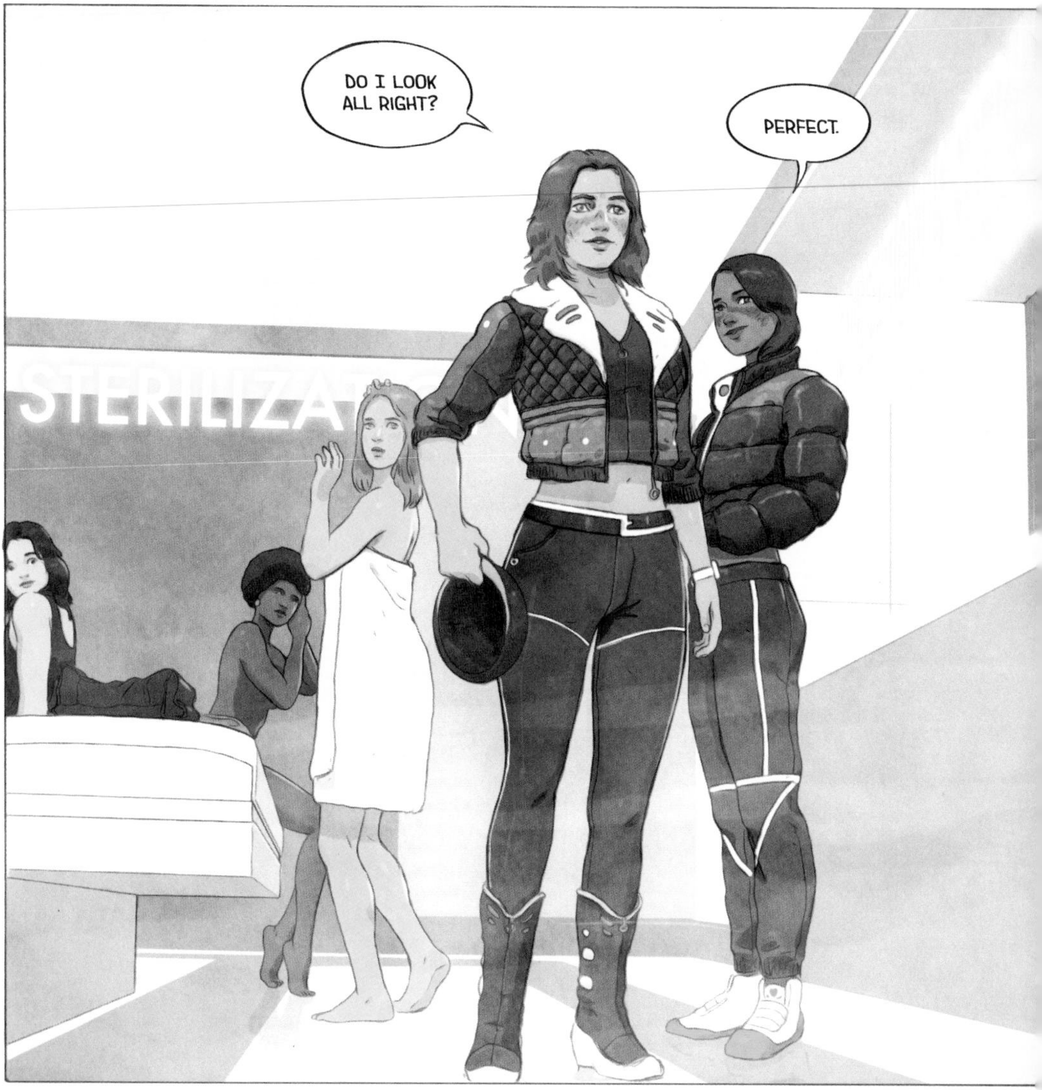
DO I LOOK ALL RIGHT?
PERFECT.
STERILIZA

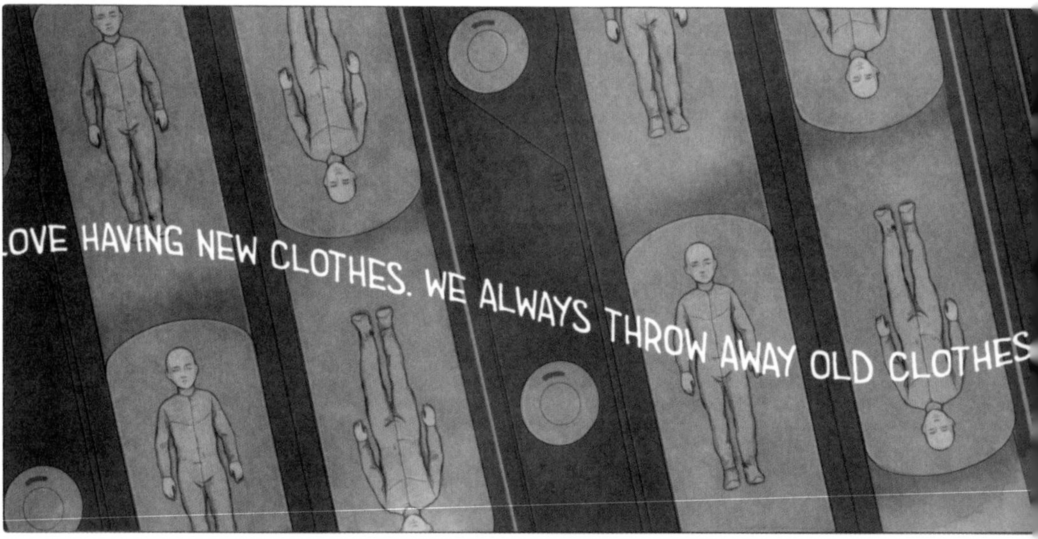
LOVE HAVING NEW CLOTHES. WE ALWAYS THROW AWAY OLD CLOTHES

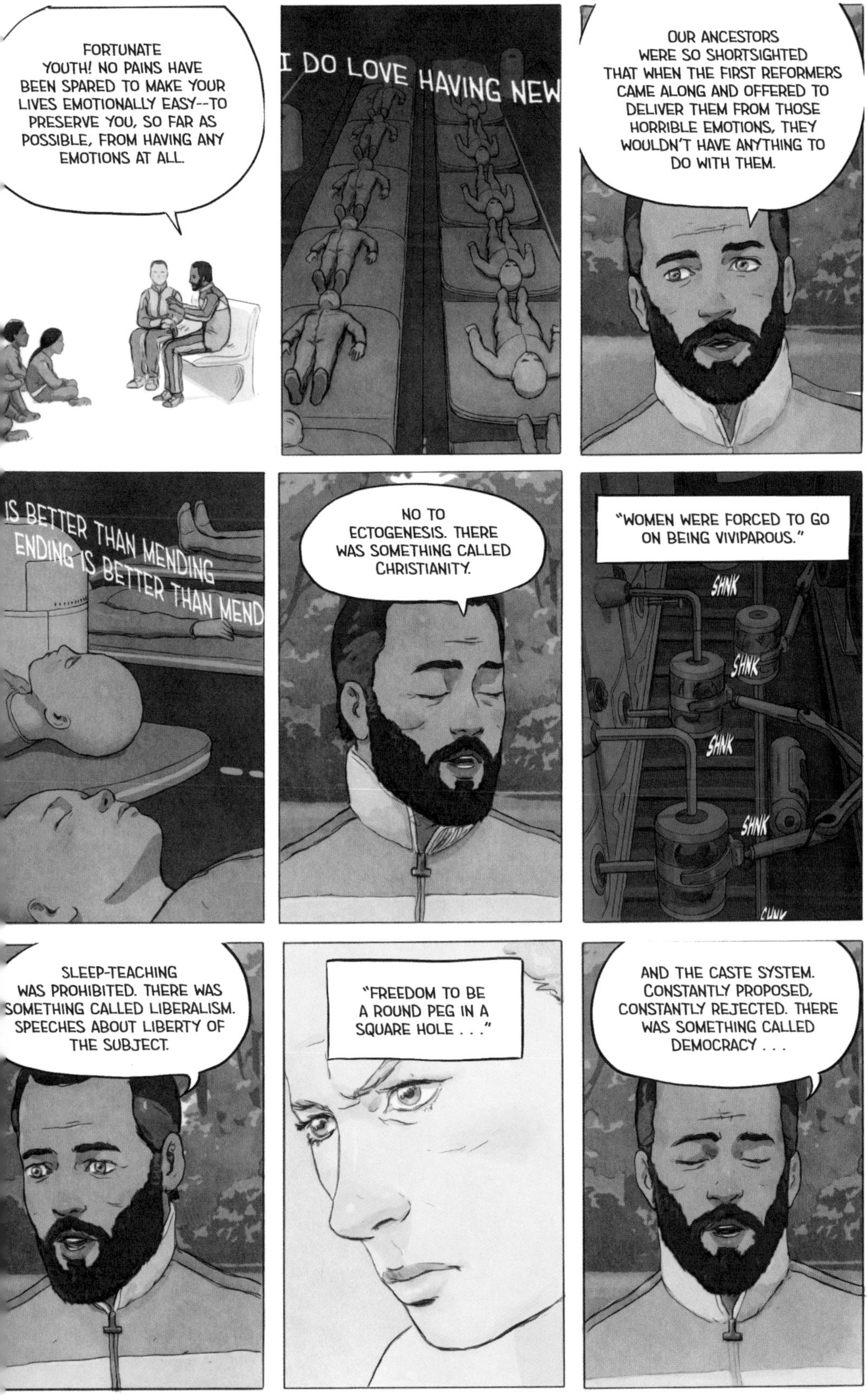
FORTUNATE YOUTH! NO PAINS HAVE BEEN SPARED TO MAKE YOUR LIVES EMOTIONALLY EASY--TO PRESERVE YOU, SO FAR AS POSSIBLE, FROM HAVING ANY EMOTIONS AT ALL.
I DO LOVE HAVING NEW
OUR ANCESTORS WERE SO SHORTSIGHTED THAT WHEN THE FIRST REFORMERS CAME ALONG AND OFFERED TO DELIVER THEM FROM THOSE HORRIBLE EMOTIONS, THEY WOULDN'T HAVE ANYTHING TO DO WITH THEM.
IS BETTER THAN MENDING
ENDING IS BETTER THAN MEND
NO TO ECTOGENESIS. THERE WAS SOMETHING CALLED CHRISTIANITY.
"WOMEN WERE FORCED TO GO ON BEING VIVIPAROUS."
SHNK
SHNK
SHNK
SHNK
SLEEP-TEACHING WAS PROHIBITED. THERE WAS SOMETHING CALLED LIBERALISM. SPEECHES ABOUT LIBERTY OF THE SUBJECT.
"FREEDOM TO BE A ROUND PEG IN A SQUARE HOLE . . ."
AND THE CASTE SYSTEM. CONSTANTLY PROPOSED, CONSTANTLY REJECTED. THERE WAS SOMETHING CALLED DEMOCRACY . . .

"AS THOUGH HUMAN BEINGS WERE MORE THAN PHYSICO-CHEMICALLY EQUAL."

HE DOES LOOK GLUM.

LET'S BAIT HIM.

THEN THE NINE YEARS' WAR BEGAN IN A.F. 141. PHOSGENE, CHLOROPICRIN, ETHYL IODOACETATE, DIPHENYLCYANARSINE, TRICHLORMETHYL . . .

GLUM, MARX, GLUM.

WHAT YOU NEED IS A GRAM OF SOMA.

. . . CHLOROFORMATE, DICHLORETHYL SULPHIDE, HYDROCYANIC ACID . . .

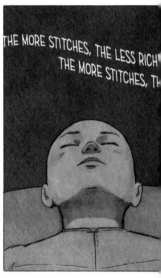

THE MORE STITCHES, THE LESS RICH THE MORE STITCHES, TH

. . . THE GREAT ECONOMIC COLLAPSE . . .

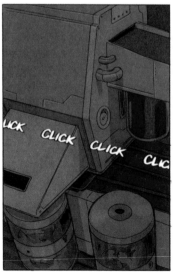

CLICK CLICK CLICK CLIC

. . . CHOICE BETWEEN WORLD CONTROL AND DESTRUCTION.

ENDING IS BETTER THAN MENDING
ENDING IS BETTER THAN MEND'

LIBERALISM WAS DEAD OF ANTHRAX . . .

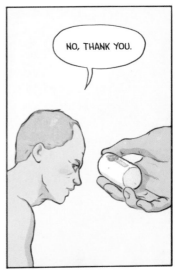

NO, THANK YOU.

FST FST FST FST

THERE WAS CONSCRIPTION OF CONSUMPTION. EVERY MAN, WOMAN, AND CHILD COMPELLED TO CONSUME . . .

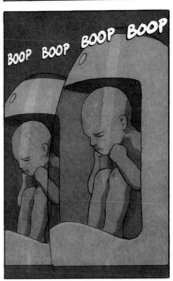

BOOP BOOP BOOP BOOP

TAKE IT. TAKE IT.

CONSCIENTIOUS OBJECTION ON AN ENORMOUS SCALE. ANYTHING NOT TO CONSUME.

BIP

39

BACK TO CULTURE. YOU CAN'T CONSUME MUCH IF YOU SIT STILL AND READ.

AAAAAAAAAA
AA
AAAA
AAAA

... EIGHT HUNDRED SIMPLE LIFERS MOWED DOWN BY MACHINE GUNS AT GOLDERS GREEN ...

SHNK SHNK SHNK SHNK SHNK

... THE FAMOUS BRITISH MUSEUM MASSACRE. TWO THOUSAND CULTURE FANS GASSED WITH DICHLORETHYL SULPHIDE ...

I LOVE NEW CLOTHES,
I LOVE NEW CLOTHES,
I LOVE NEW CLOTH

... ACCOMPANIED BY A CAMPAIGN AGAINST THE PAST; BY THE CLOSING OF MUSEUMS, THE BLOWING UP OF HISTORICAL MONUMENTS ...

"... SUPPRESSION OF ALL BOOKS PUBLISHED BEFORE A.F. 150."

BIP

NO. THANK YOU.

THERE WERE SOME THINGS CALLED PYRAMIDS . . .

BIP

. . . A MAN CALLED SHAKESPEARE . . .

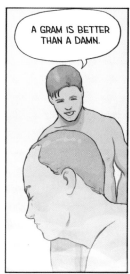
A GRAM IS BETTER THAN A DAMN.

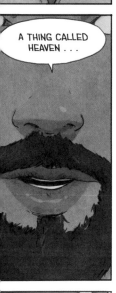
A THING CALLED HEAVEN . . .

AAAA

AAA

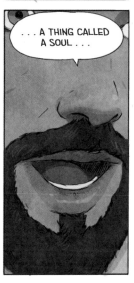
. . . A THING CALLED A SOUL . . .

OOOOOOOOO

. . . A THING CALLED IMMORTALITY . . .

BIP

. . . ENORMOUS QUANTITIES OF ALCOHOL, MORPHIA, AND COCAINE . . .

DAMN YOU.

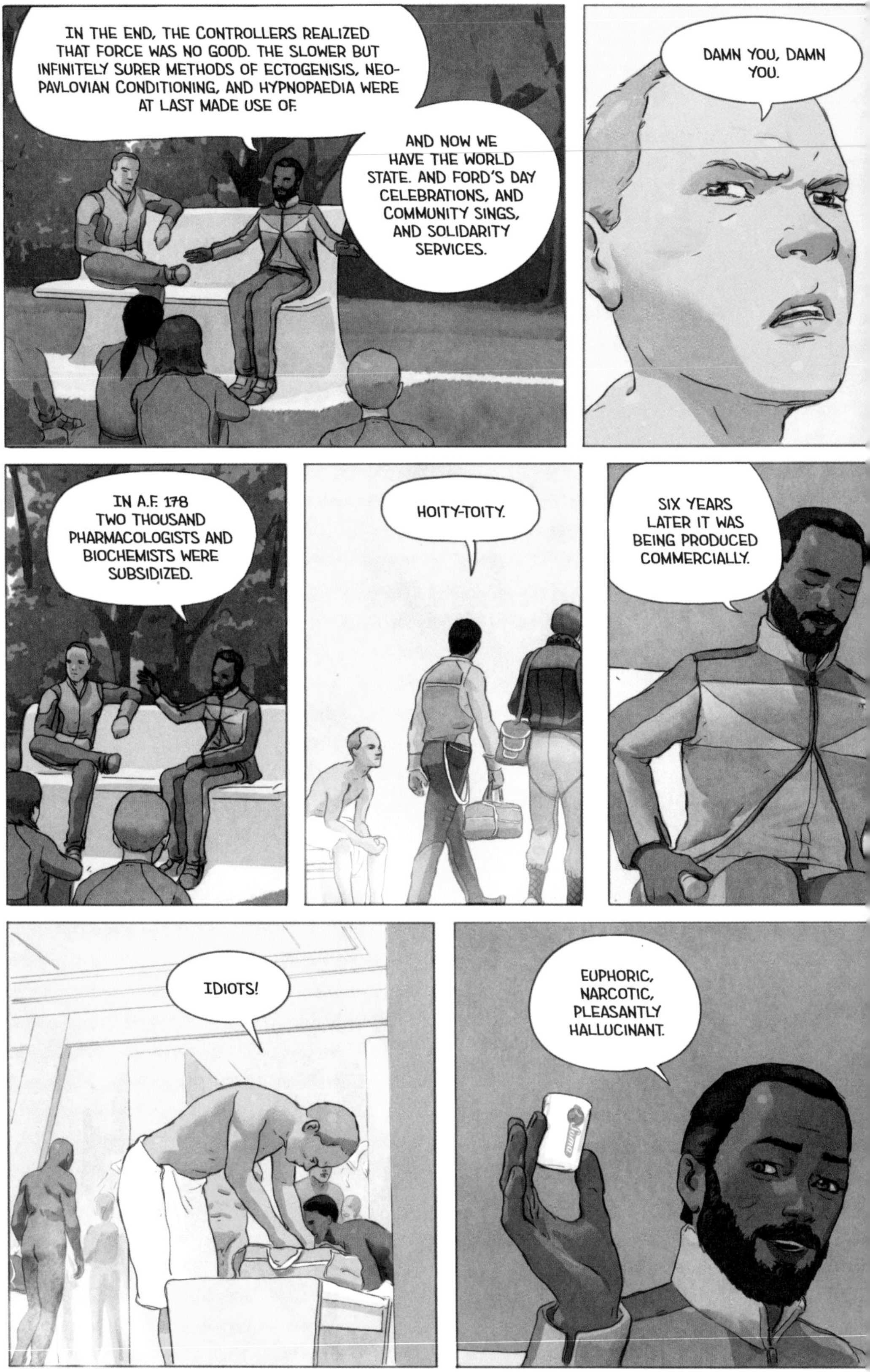
IN THE END, THE CONTROLLERS REALIZED THAT FORCE WAS NO GOOD. THE SLOWER BUT INFINITELY SURER METHODS OF ECTOGENISIS, NEO-PAVLOVIAN CONDITIONING, AND HYPNOPAEDIA WERE AT LAST MADE USE OF.
AND NOW WE HAVE THE WORLD STATE. AND FORD'S DAY CELEBRATIONS, AND COMMUNITY SINGS, AND SOLIDARITY SERVICES.
DAMN YOU, DAMN YOU.
IN A.F. 178 TWO THOUSAND PHARMACOLOGISTS AND BIOCHEMISTS WERE SUBSIDIZED.
HOITY-TOITY.
SIX YEARS LATER IT WAS BEING PRODUCED COMMERCIALLY.
IDIOTS!
EUPHORIC, NARCOTIC, PLEASANTLY HALLUCINANT.

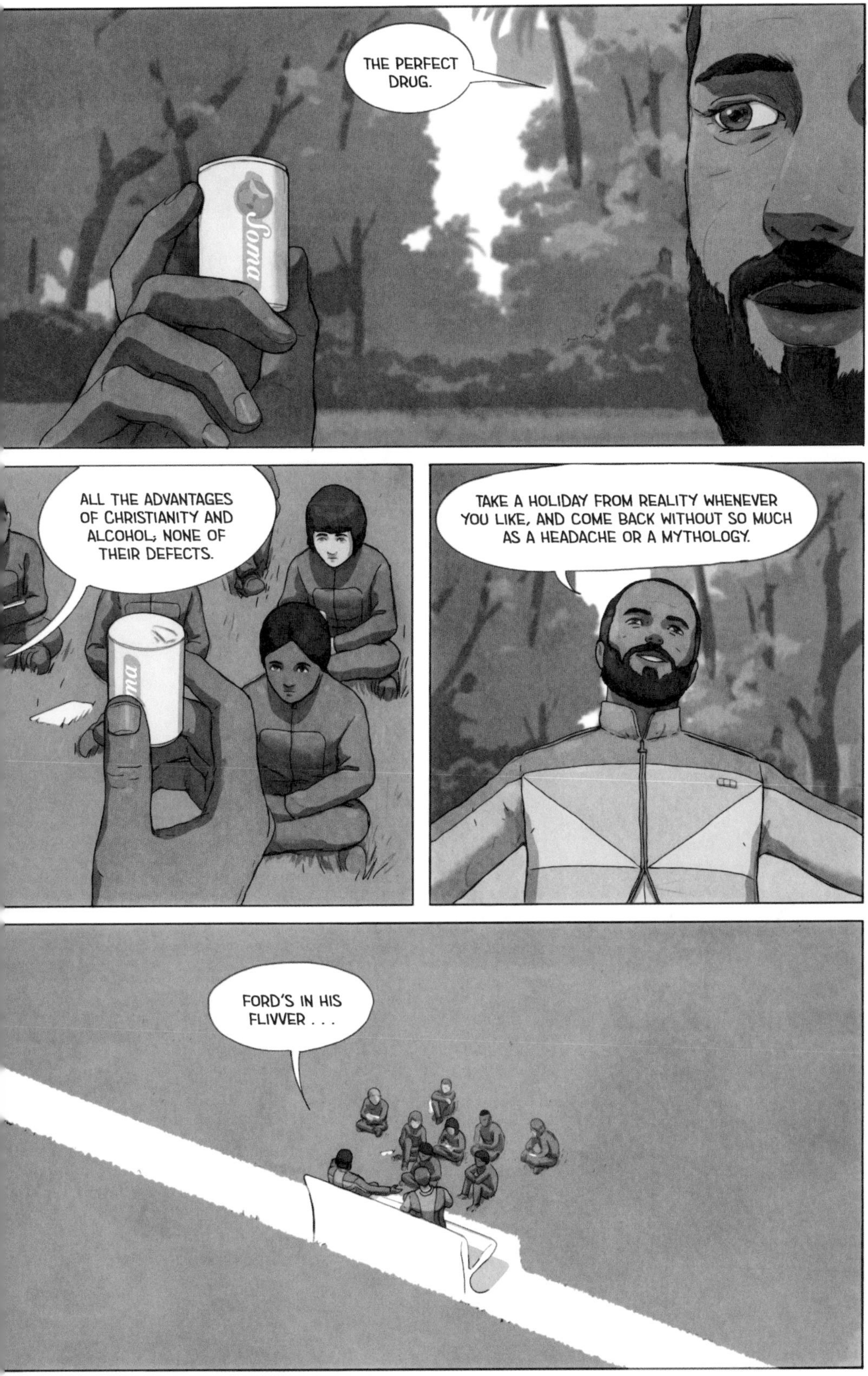
THE PERFECT DRUG.
Soma
ALL THE ADVANTAGES OF CHRISTIANITY AND ALCOHOL; NONE OF THEIR DEFECTS.
TAKE A HOLIDAY FROM REALITY WHENEVER YOU LIKE, AND COME BACK WITHOUT SO MUCH AS A HEADACHE OR A MYTHOLOGY.
FORD'S IN HIS FLIVVER . . .

". . . ALL'S WELL WITH THE WORLD."

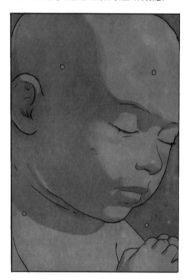

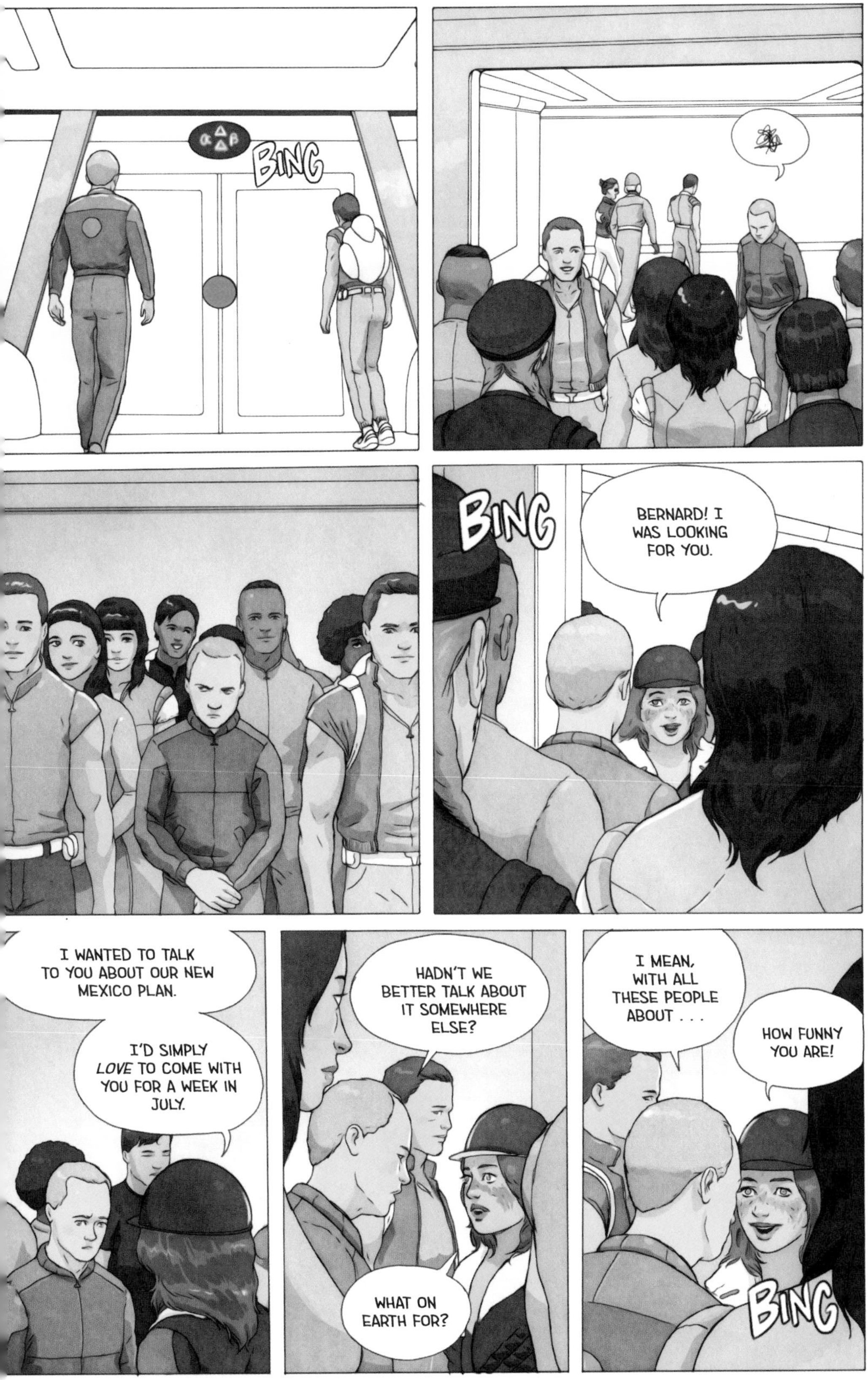
BING
BING
BERNARD! I WAS LOOKING FOR YOU.
I WANTED TO TALK TO YOU ABOUT OUR NEW MEXICO PLAN.
I'D SIMPLY *LOVE* TO COME WITH YOU FOR A WEEK IN JULY.
HADN'T WE BETTER TALK ABOUT IT SOMEWHERE ELSE?
WHAT ON EARTH FOR?
I MEAN, WITH ALL THESE PEOPLE ABOUT . . .
HOW FUNNY YOU ARE!
BING

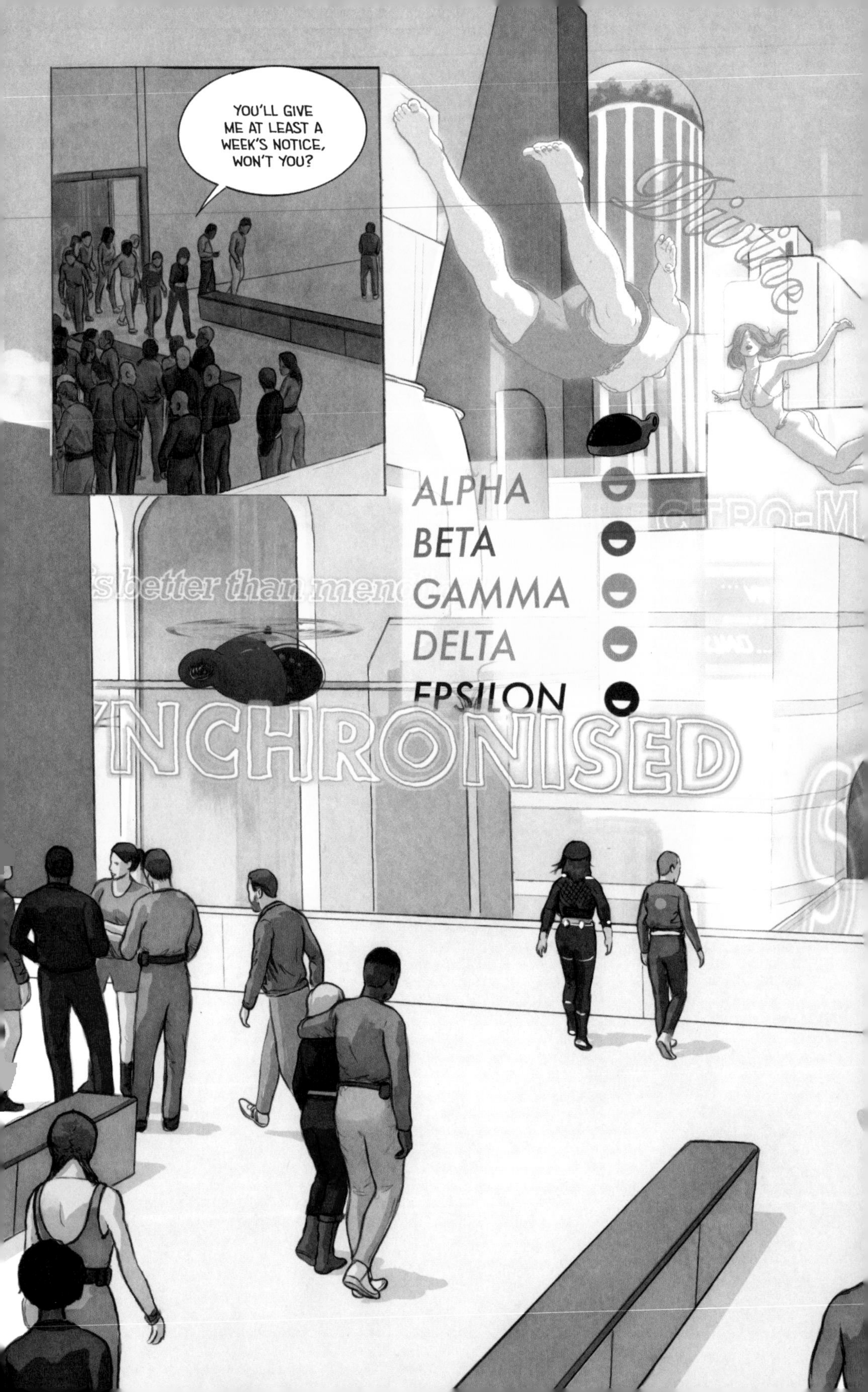
YOU'LL GIVE ME AT LEAST A WEEK'S NOTICE, WON'T YOU?
ALPHA
BETA
GAMMA
DELTA
EPSILON
NCHRONISED

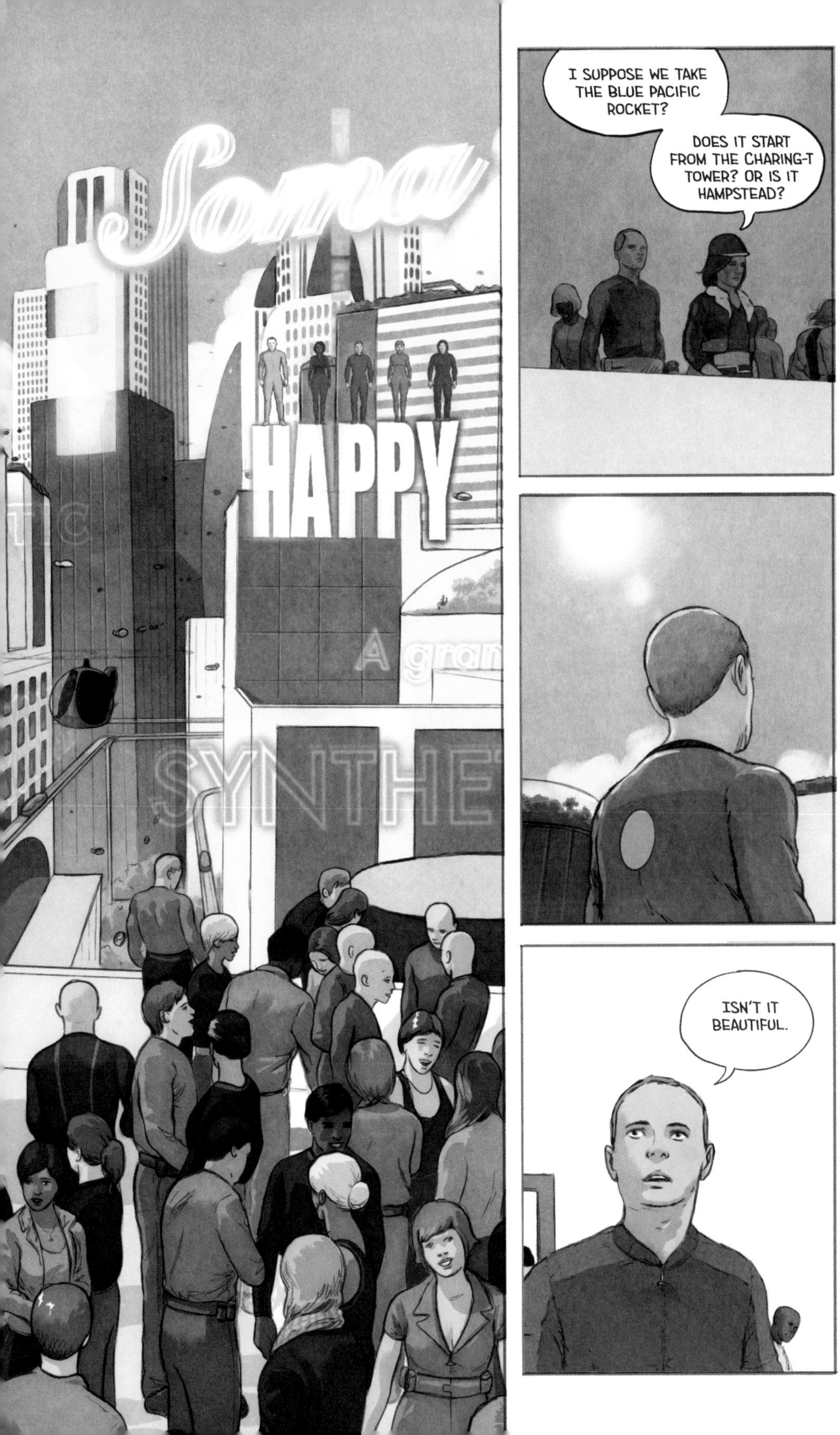
Soma
HAPPY
A gram
SYNTHE
I SUPPOSE WE TAKE THE BLUE PACIFIC ROCKET?
DOES IT START FROM THE CHARING-T TOWER? OR IS IT HAMPSTEAD?
ISN'T IT BEAUTIFUL.

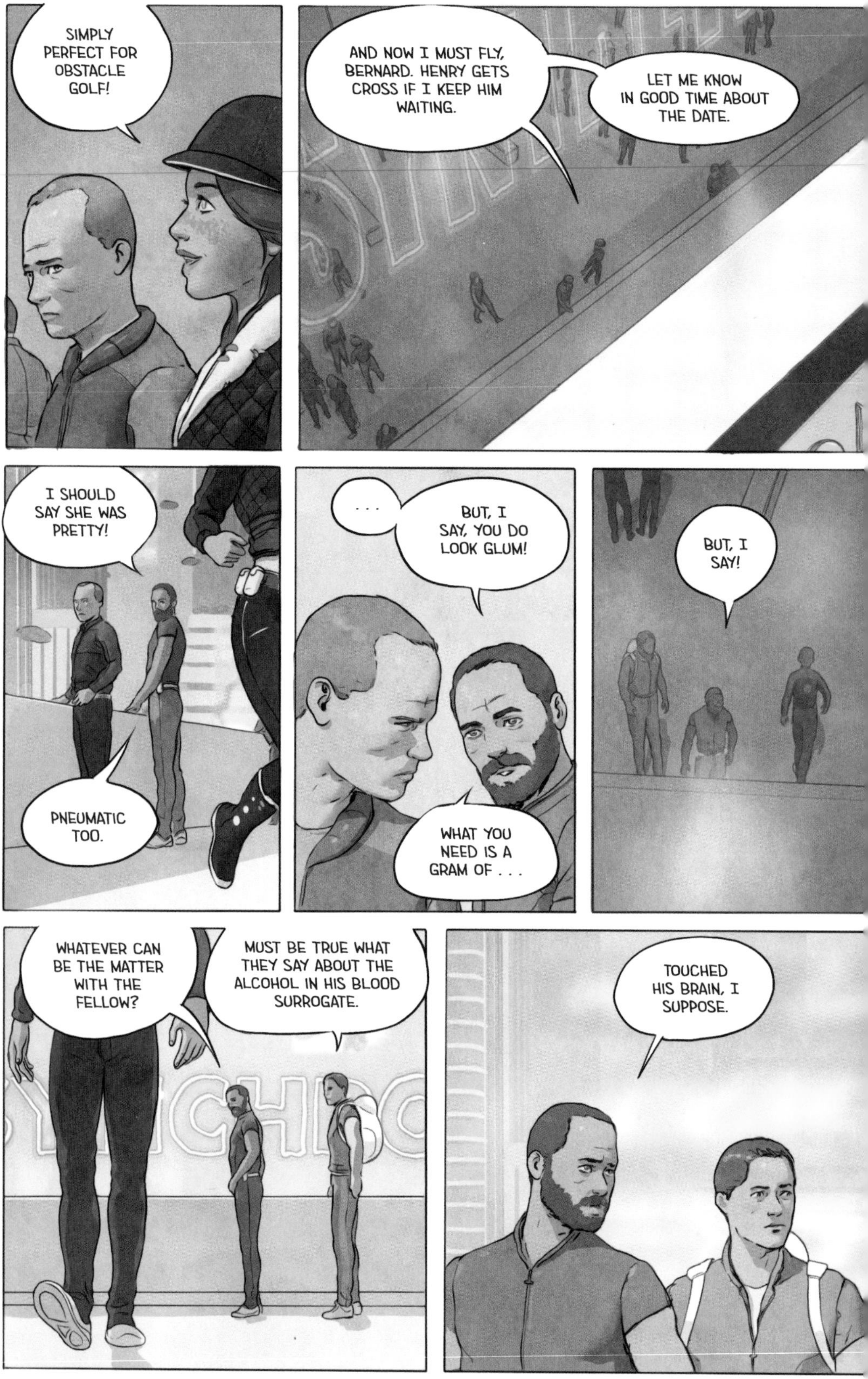
SIMPLY PERFECT FOR OBSTACLE GOLF!
AND NOW I MUST FLY, BERNARD. HENRY GETS CROSS IF I KEEP HIM WAITING.
LET ME KNOW IN GOOD TIME ABOUT THE DATE.
I SHOULD SAY SHE WAS PRETTY!
PNEUMATIC TOO.
. . .
BUT, I SAY, YOU DO LOOK GLUM!
WHAT YOU NEED IS A GRAM OF . . .
BUT, I SAY!
WHATEVER CAN BE THE MATTER WITH THE FELLOW?
MUST BE TRUE WHAT THEY SAY ABOUT THE ALCOHOL IN HIS BLOOD SURROGATE.
TOUCHED HIS BRAIN, I SUPPOSE.

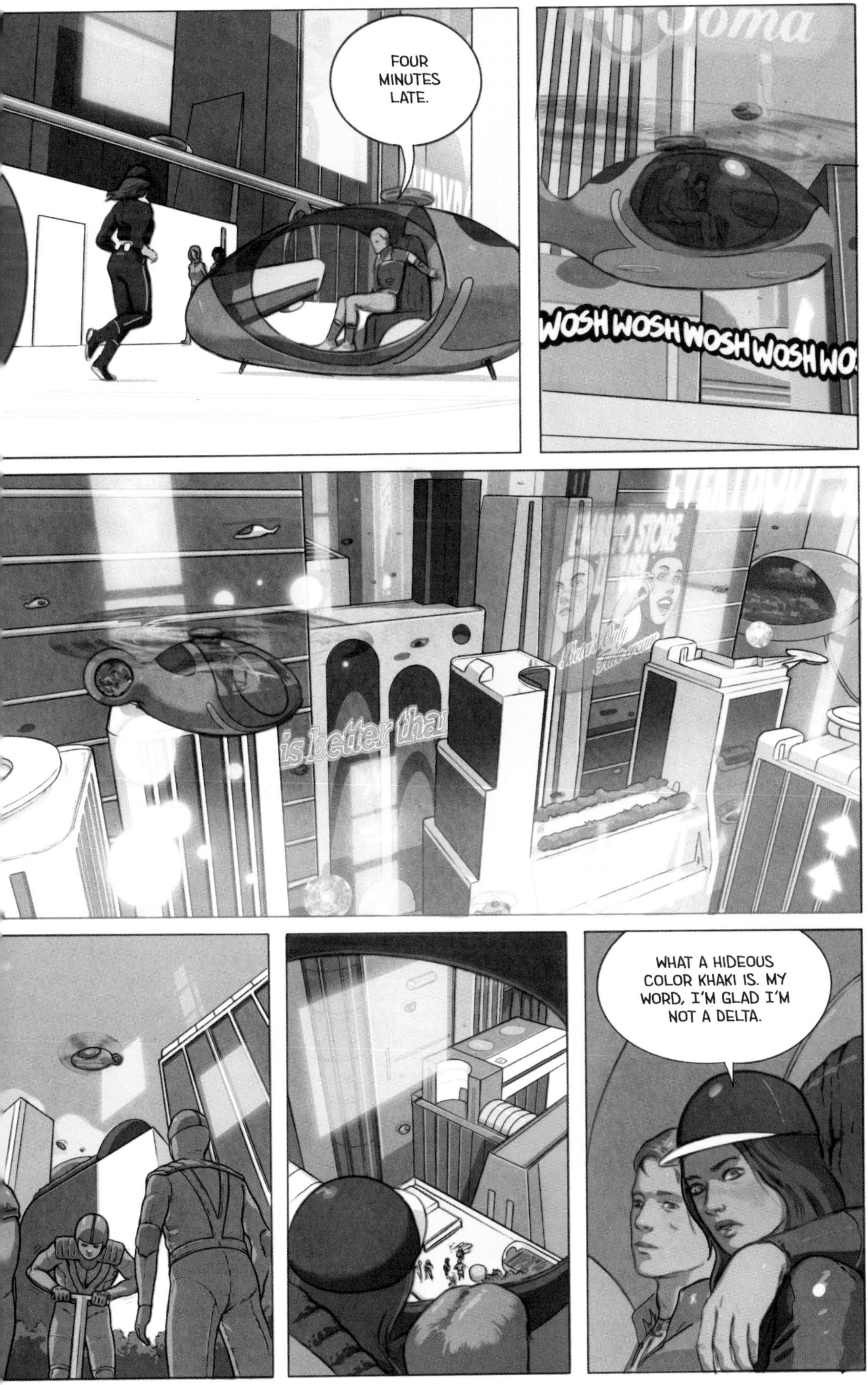
FOUR MINUTES LATE.
WOSH WOSH WOSH WOSH
WHAT A HIDEOUS COLOR KHAKI IS. MY WORD, I'M GLAD I'M NOT A DELTA.

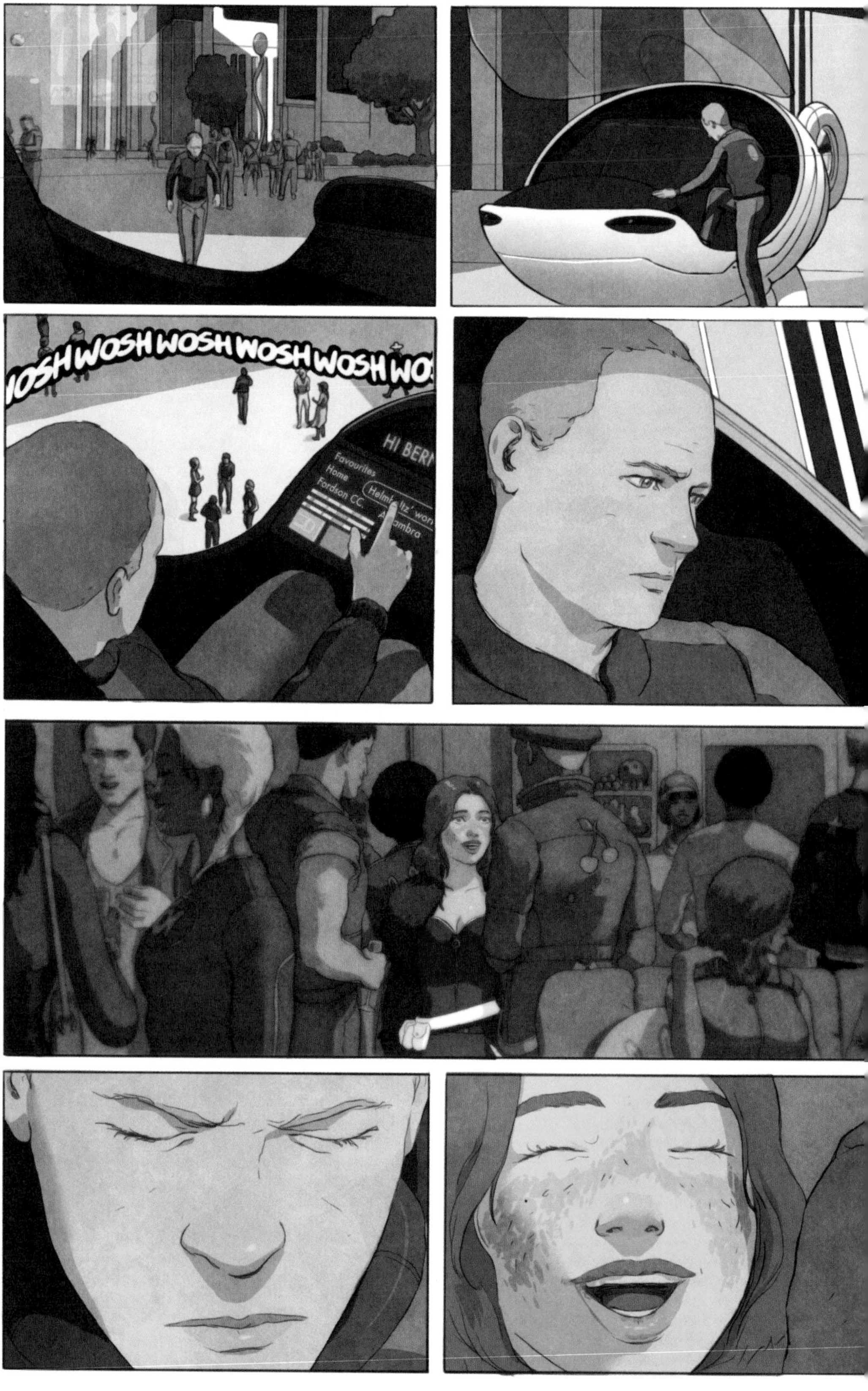
WOSH WOSH WOSH WOSH
HI BERN
Favourites
Home
Fordson CC.

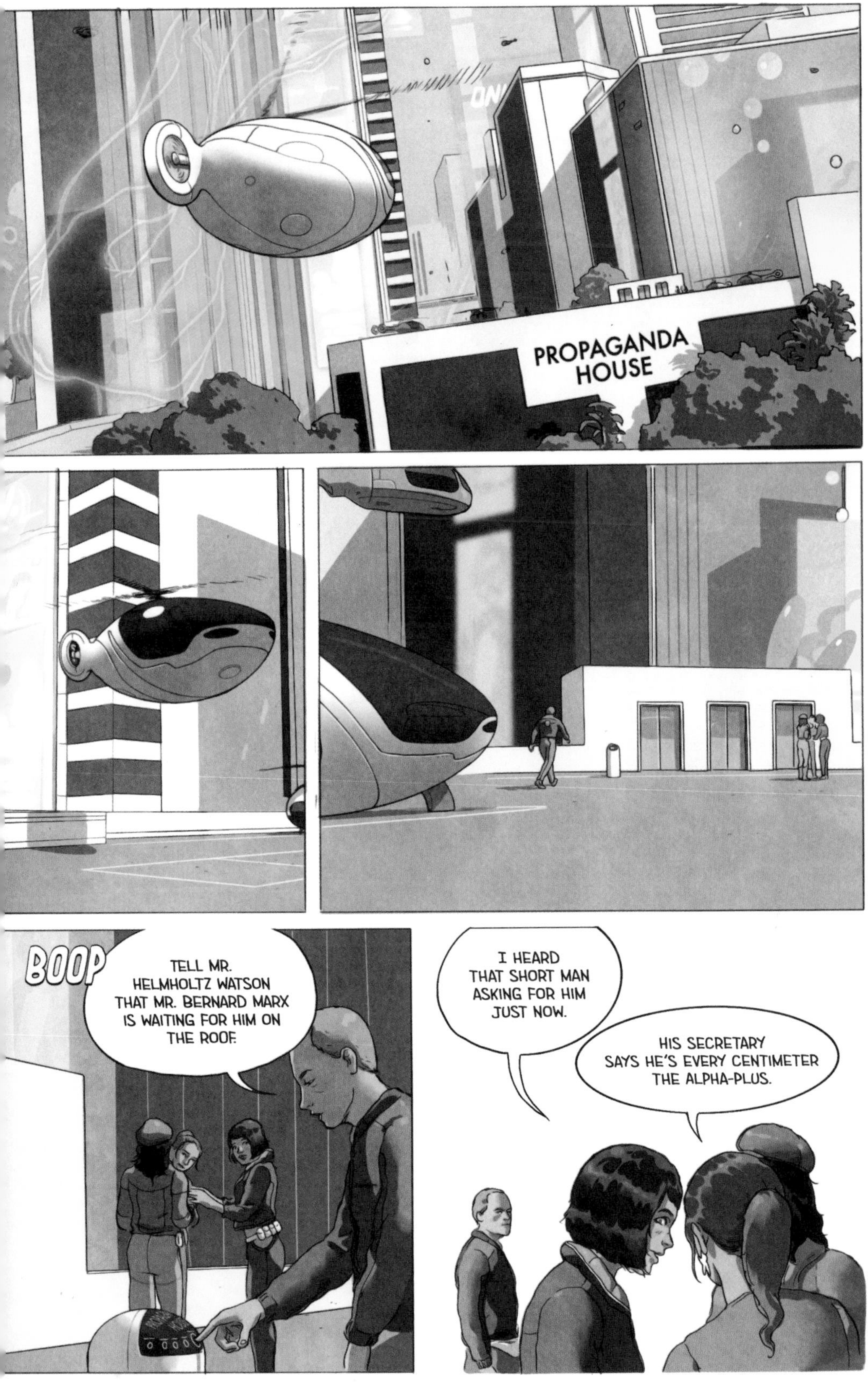
PROPAGANDA HOUSE
BOOP
TELL MR. HELMHOLTZ WATSON THAT MR. BERNARD MARX IS WAITING FOR HIM ON THE ROOF.
I HEARD THAT SHORT MAN ASKING FOR HIM JUST NOW.
HIS SECRETARY SAYS HE'S EVERY CENTIMETER THE ALPHA-PLUS.

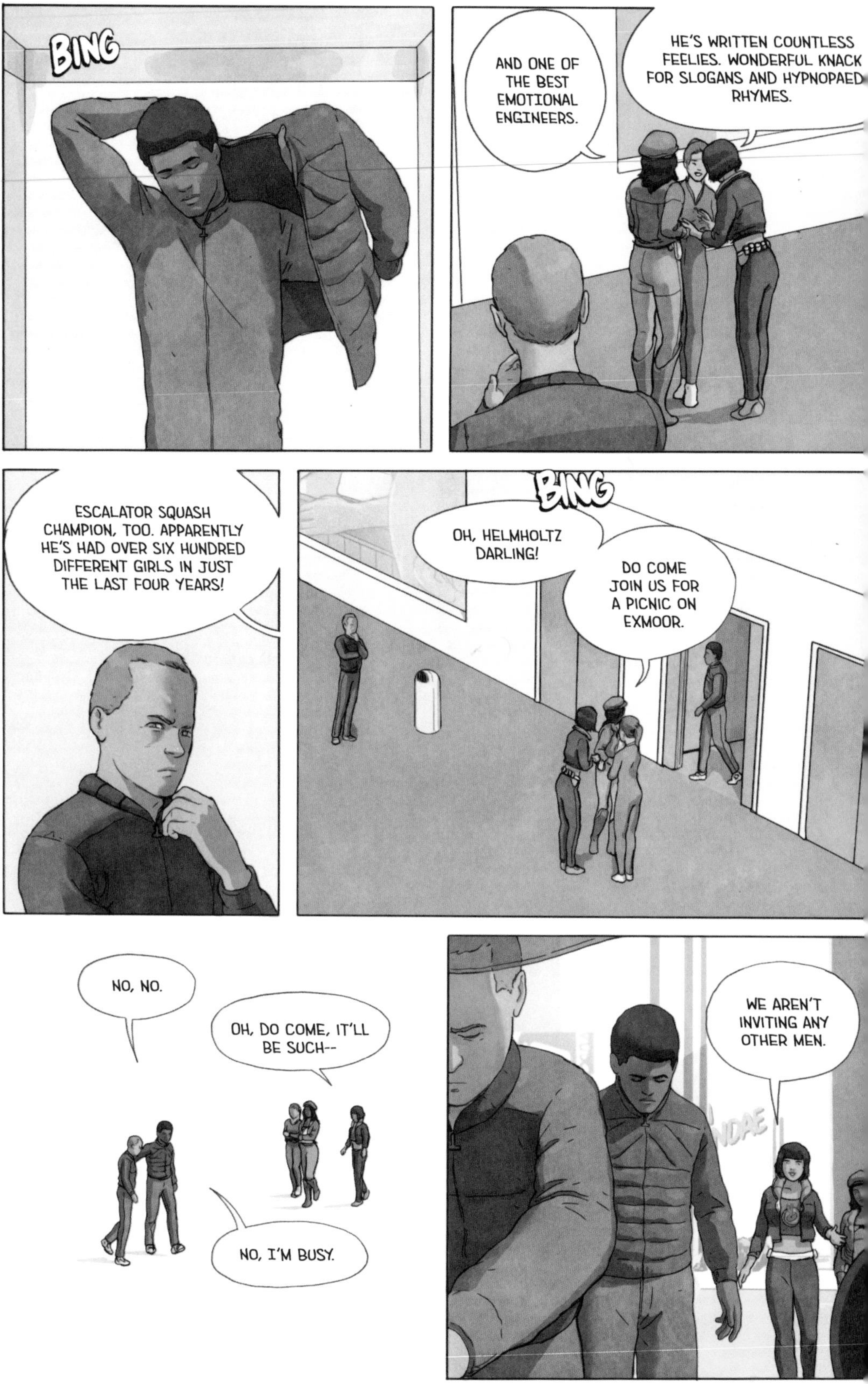
BING
AND ONE OF THE BEST EMOTIONAL ENGINEERS.
HE'S WRITTEN COUNTLESS FEELIES. WONDERFUL KNACK FOR SLOGANS AND HYPNOPAED RHYMES.
ESCALATOR SQUASH CHAMPION, TOO. APPARENTLY HE'S HAD OVER SIX HUNDRED DIFFERENT GIRLS IN JUST THE LAST FOUR YEARS!
BING
OH, HELMHOLTZ DARLING!
DO COME JOIN US FOR A PICNIC ON EXMOOR.
NO, NO.
OH, DO COME, IT'LL BE SUCH--
NO, I'M BUSY.
WE AREN'T INVITING ANY OTHER MEN.

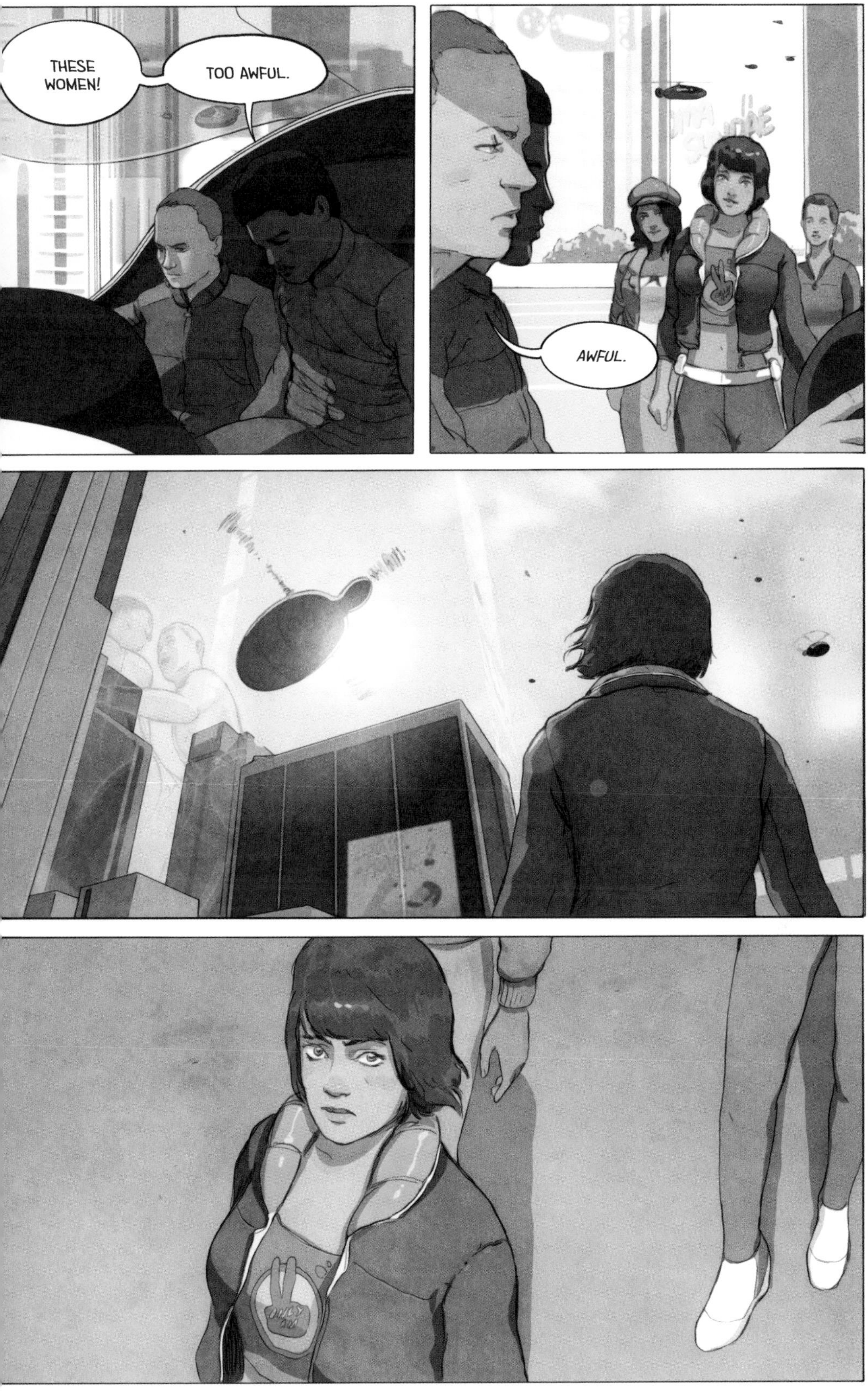
THESE WOMEN!
TOO AWFUL.
AWFUL.

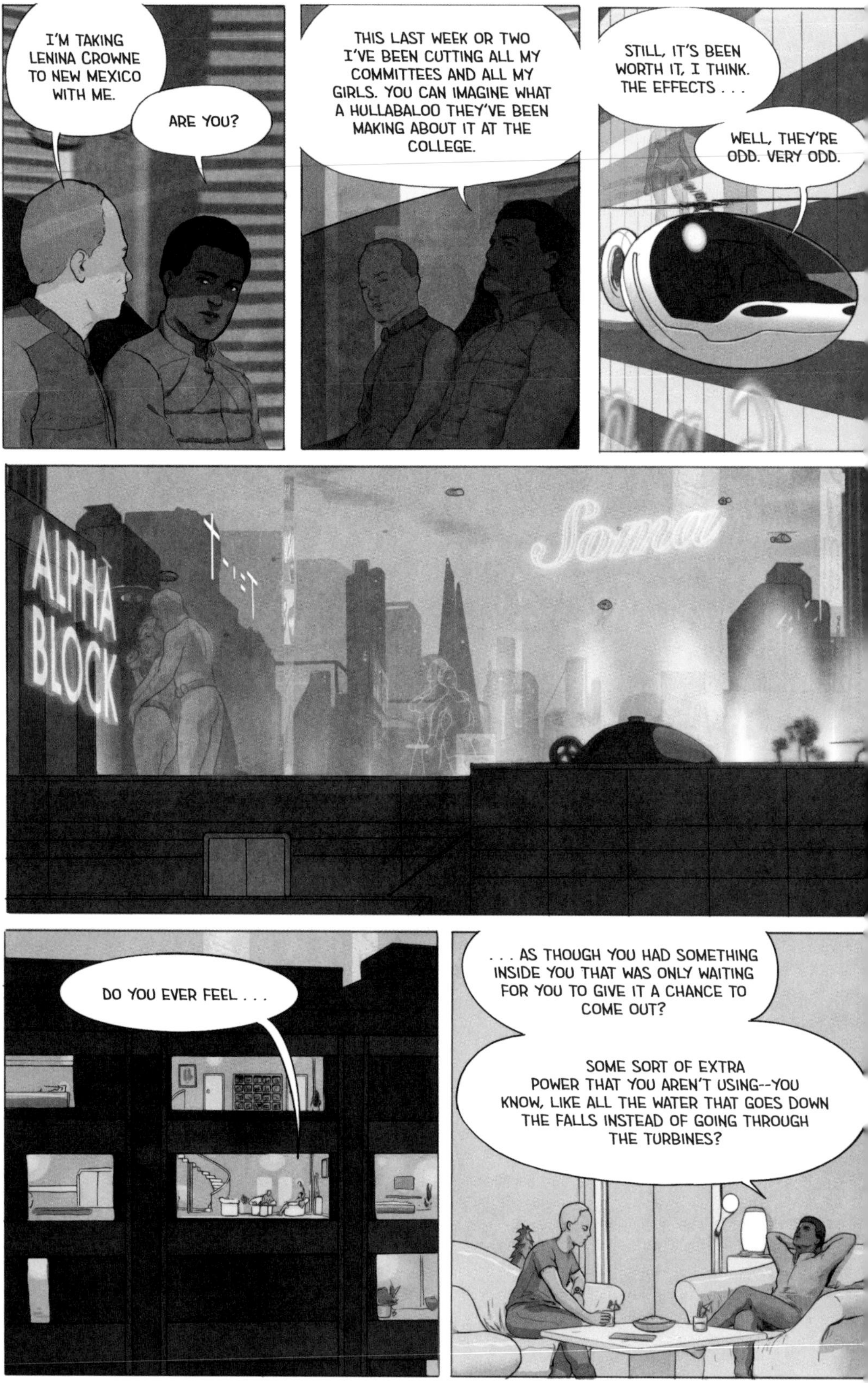
I'M TAKING LENINA CROWNE TO NEW MEXICO WITH ME.
ARE YOU?
THIS LAST WEEK OR TWO I'VE BEEN CUTTING ALL MY COMMITTEES AND ALL MY GIRLS. YOU CAN IMAGINE WHAT A HULLABALOO THEY'VE BEEN MAKING ABOUT IT AT THE COLLEGE.
STILL, IT'S BEEN WORTH IT, I THINK. THE EFFECTS . . .
WELL, THEY'RE ODD. VERY ODD.
ALPHA BLOCK
Soma
DO YOU EVER FEEL . . .
. . . AS THOUGH YOU HAD SOMETHING INSIDE YOU THAT WAS ONLY WAITING FOR YOU TO GIVE IT A CHANCE TO COME OUT?
SOME SORT OF EXTRA POWER THAT YOU AREN'T USING--YOU KNOW, LIKE ALL THE WATER THAT GOES DOWN THE FALLS INSTEAD OF GOING THROUGH THE TURBINES?

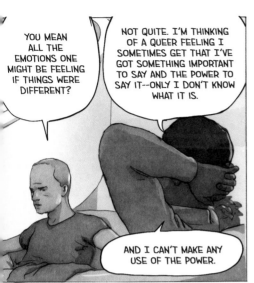

YOU MEAN ALL THE EMOTIONS ONE MIGHT BE FEELING IF THINGS WERE DIFFERENT?
NOT QUITE. I'M THINKING OF A QUEER FEELING I SOMETIMES GET THAT I'VE GOT SOMETHING IMPORTANT TO SAY AND THE POWER TO SAY IT--ONLY I DON'T KNOW WHAT IT IS.
AND I CAN'T MAKE ANY USE OF THE POWER.
IF THERE WAS SOME DIFFERENT WAY OF WRITING . . .
OR ELSE SOMETHING ELSE TO WRITE ABOUT.
A gram in time saves nine!
SYNCHRO
YOU SEE, I'M PRETTY GOOD AT INVENTING PHRASES--THE SORT OF WORDS THAT SUDDENLY MAKE YOU JUMP, THAT SEEM SO NEW AND EXCITING EVEN THOUGH THEY'RE ABOUT SOMETHING HYPNOPAEDICALLY OBVIOUS.
BUT THAT DOESN'T SEEM ENOUGH.
I FEEL I COULD DO SOMETHING MUCH MORE IMPORTANT. YES, AND MORE INTENSE, MORE VIOLENT.
BUT WHAT?
AND HOW CAN ONE BE VIOLENT ABOUT THE SORT OF THINGS ONE'S EXPECTED TO WRITE ABOUT? CAN YOU MAKE WORDS REALLY PIERCING WHEN YOU'RE WRITING ABOUT A COMMUNITY SING, OR THE LATEST IMPROVEMENT IN SCENT ORGANS?
CAN YOU SAY SOMETHING ABOUT NOTHING? THAT'S WHAT IT FINALLY BOILS DOWN TO. I TRY AND I TRY . . .

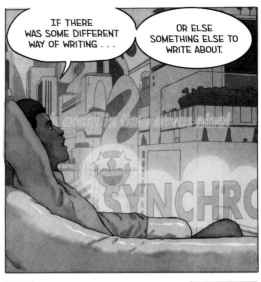

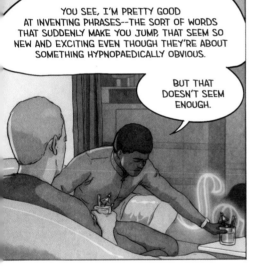

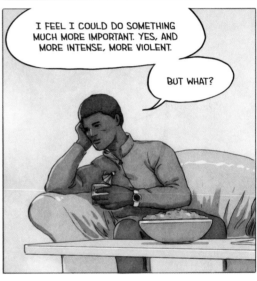

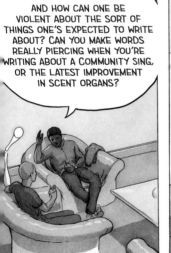

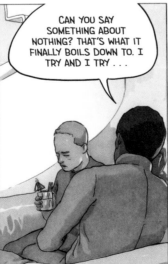

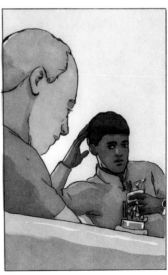

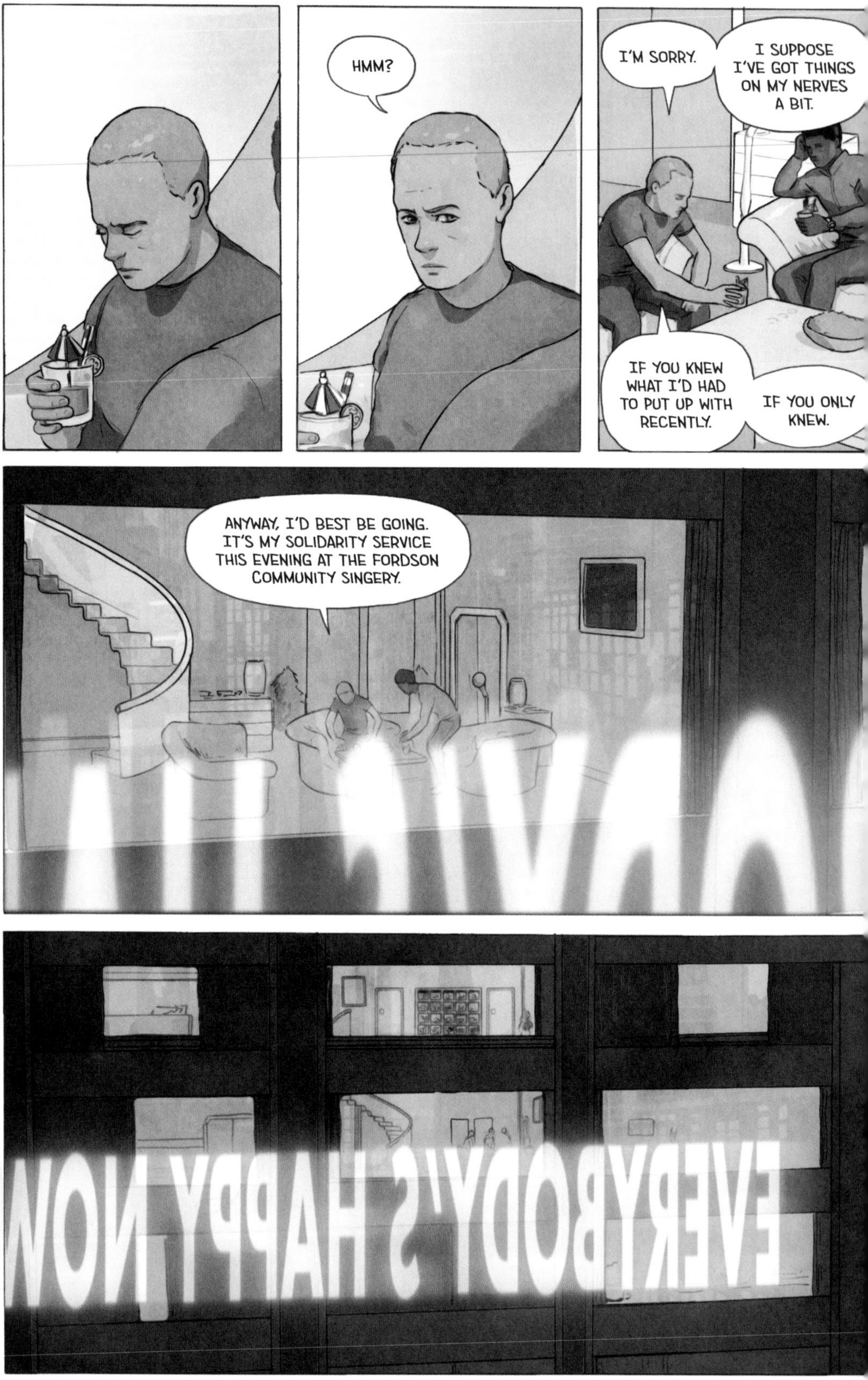
HMM?
I'M SORRY.
I SUPPOSE I'VE GOT THINGS ON MY NERVES A BIT.
IF YOU KNEW WHAT I'D HAD TO PUT UP WITH RECENTLY.
IF YOU ONLY KNEW.
ANYWAY, I'D BEST BE GOING. IT'S MY SOLIDARITY SERVICE THIS EVENING AT THE FORDSON COMMUNITY SINGERY.
EVERYBODY'S HAPPY NOW

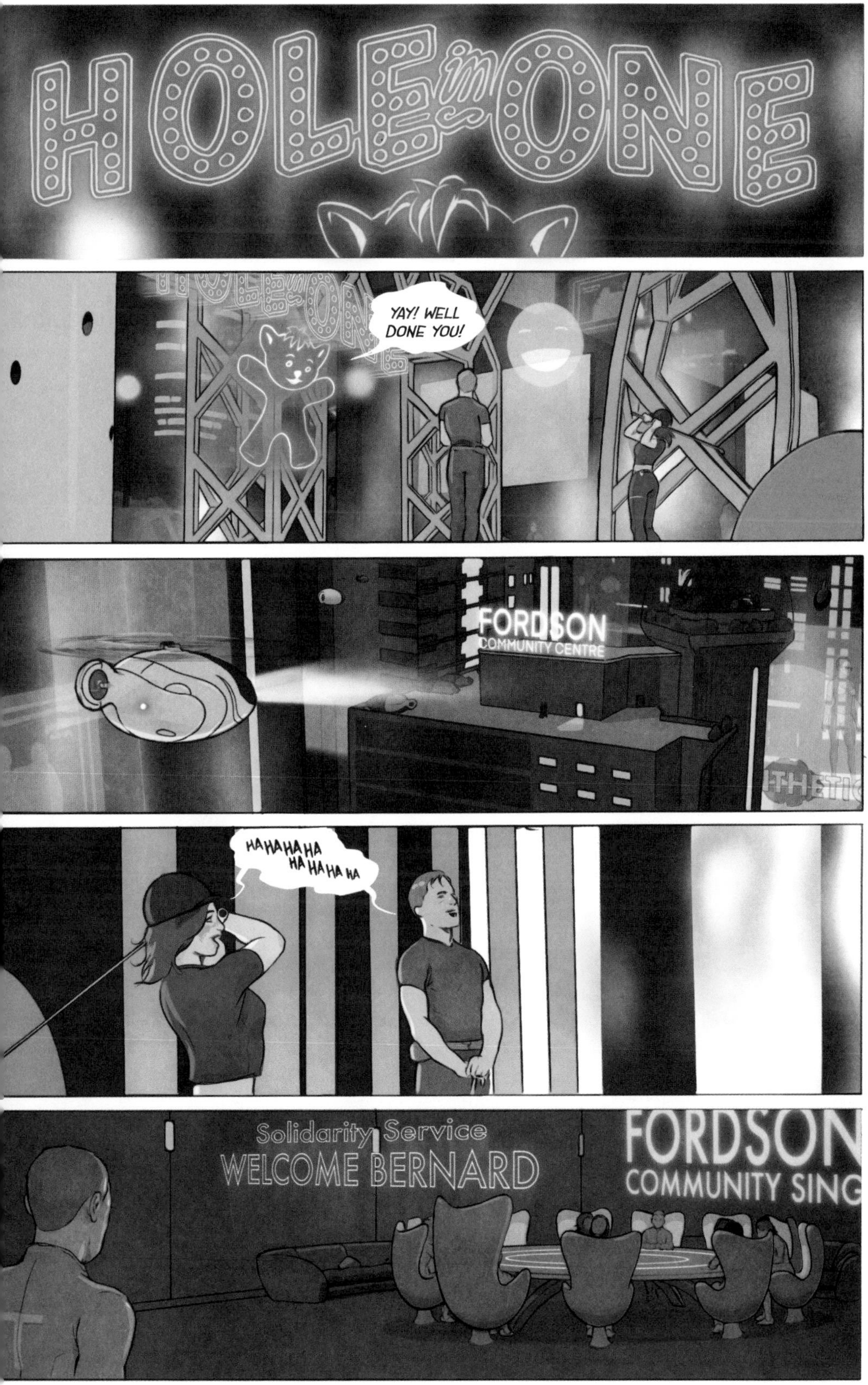
HOLE in ONE
YAY! WELL DONE YOU!
FORDSON
COMMUNITY CENTRE
HA HA HA HA HA
HA HA HA HA HA
Solidarity Service
WELCOME BERNARD
FORDSON
COMMUNITY SING

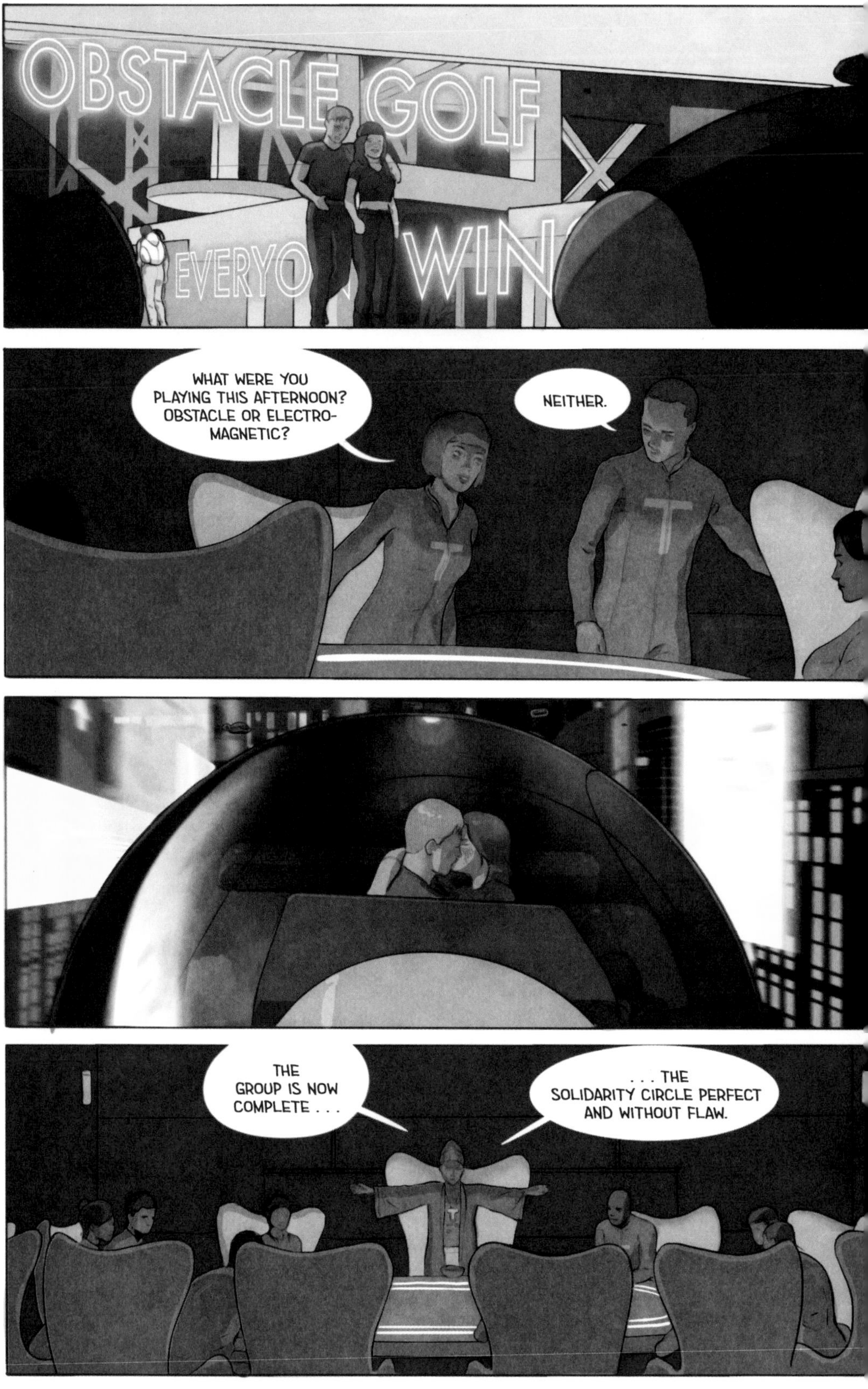
OBSTACLE GOLF
EVERYO WIN
WHAT WERE YOU PLAYING THIS AFTERNOON? OBSTACLE OR ELECTRO-MAGNETIC?
NEITHER.
THE GROUP IS NOW COMPLETE . . .
. . . THE SOLIDARITY CIRCLE PERFECT AND WITHOUT FLAW.

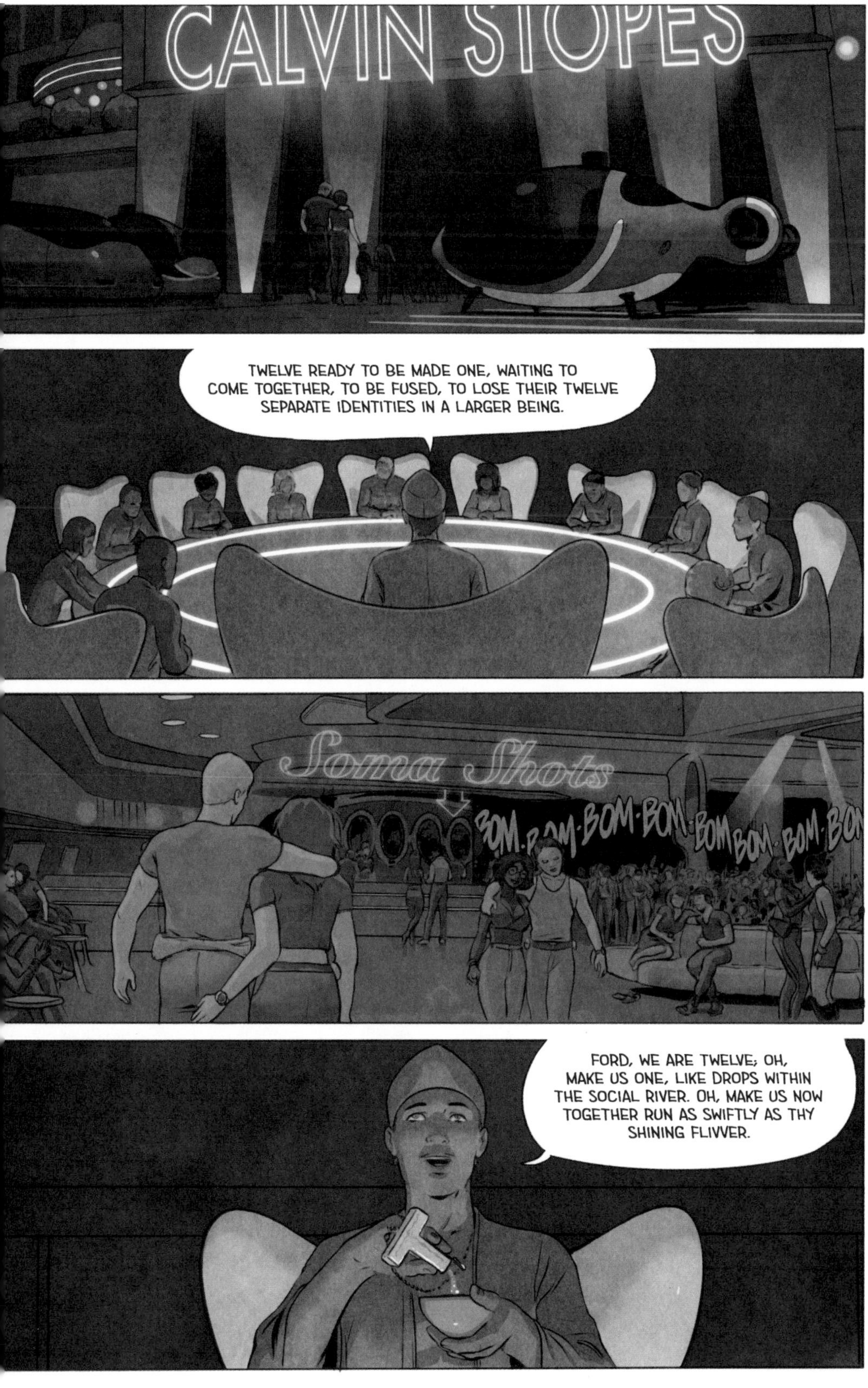
CALVIN STOPES
TWELVE READY TO BE MADE ONE, WAITING TO COME TOGETHER, TO BE FUSED, TO LOSE THEIR TWELVE SEPARATE IDENTITIES IN A LARGER BEING.
Soma Shots
BOM-BOM-BOM-BOM-BOM BOM-BOM
FORD, WE ARE TWELVE; OH, MAKE US ONE, LIKE DROPS WITHIN THE SOCIAL RIVER. OH, MAKE US NOW TOGETHER RUN AS SWIFTLY AS THY SHINING FLIVVER.

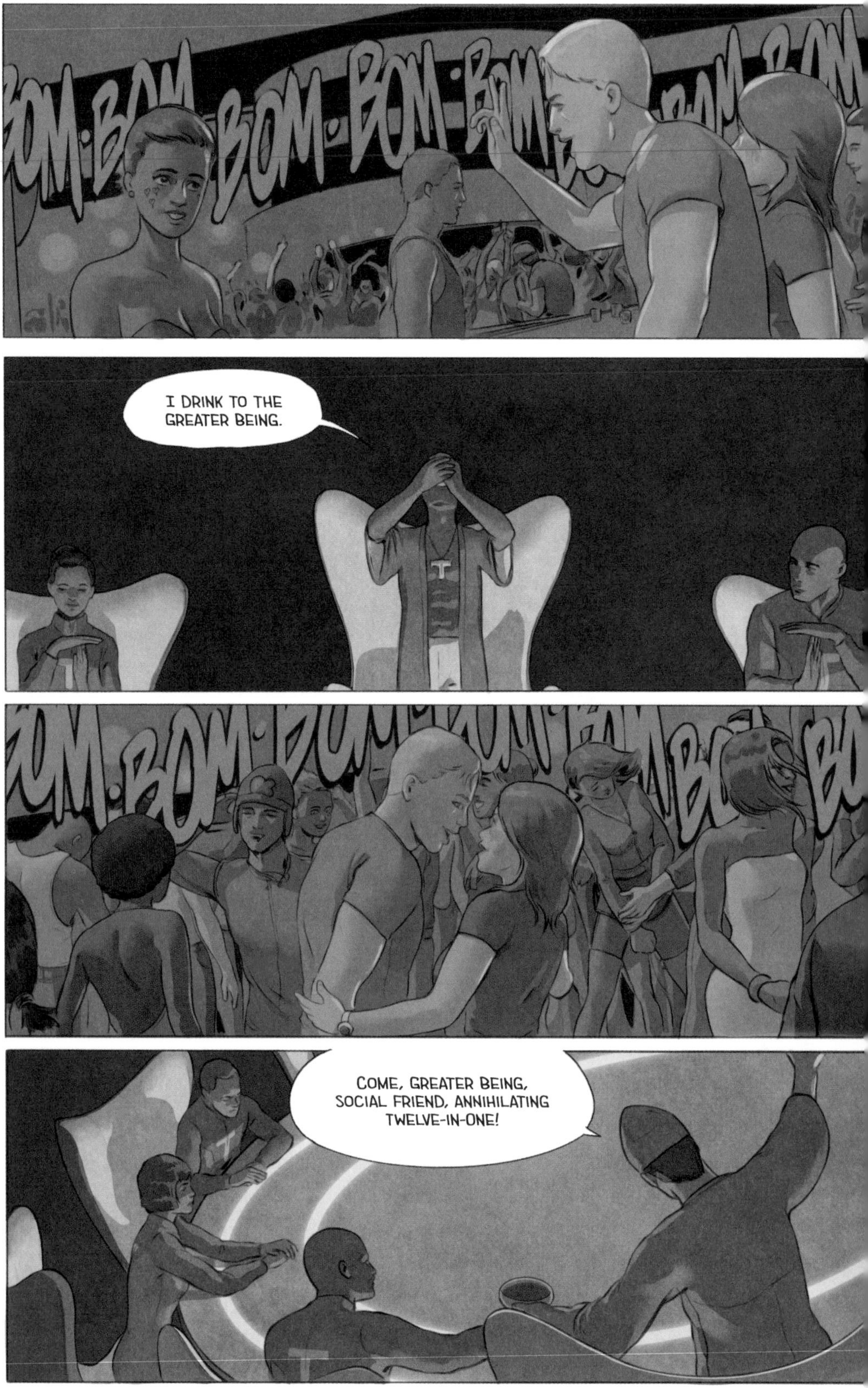
BOM·BOM·BOM·BOM
I DRINK TO THE GREATER BEING.
BOM·BOM
COME, GREATER BEING, SOCIAL FRIEND, ANNIHILATING TWELVE-IN-ONE!

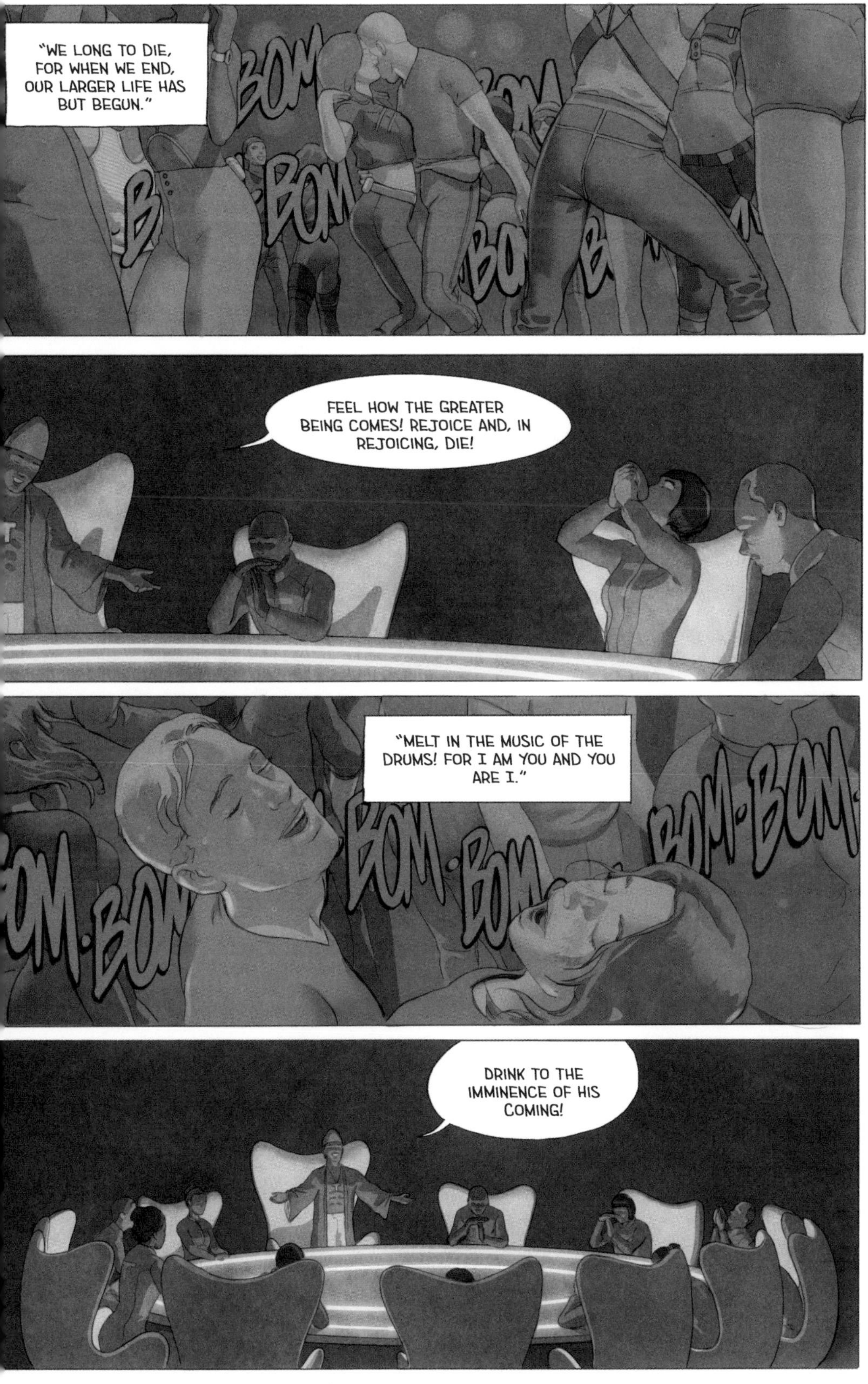
"WE LONG TO DIE, FOR WHEN WE END, OUR LARGER LIFE HAS BUT BEGUN."
BOM
BOM
FEEL HOW THE GREATER BEING COMES! REJOICE AND, IN REJOICING, DIE!
"MELT IN THE MUSIC OF THE DRUMS! FOR I AM YOU AND YOU ARE I."
BOM-BOM
DRINK TO THE IMMINENCE OF HIS COMING!

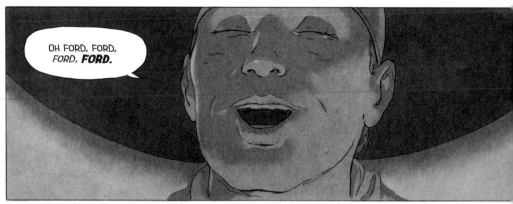

OH FORD, FORD, FORD, **FORD.**

LISTEN! LISTEN! THE FEET OF THE GREATER BEING. THE FEET OF THE GREATER BEING. THE FEET OF THE GREATER BEING ARE ON THE STAIRS.

I HEAR HIM!

HE'S COMING!

YES, HE'S COMING, I HEAR HIM!

OH, OH, OH!

HE'S COMING!

OH, HE'S COMING! *AIE!*

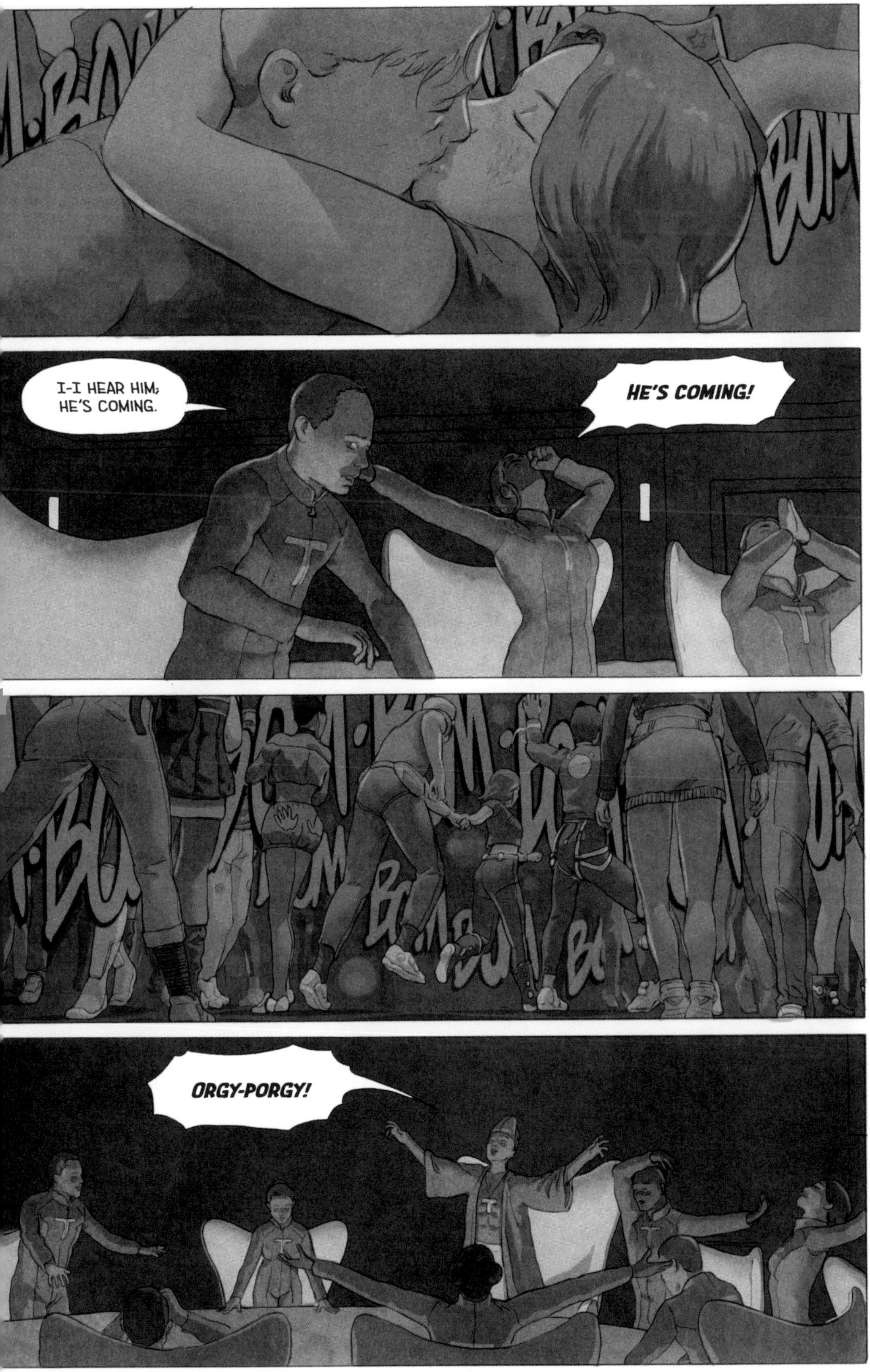
I-I HEAR HIM; HE'S COMING.
HE'S COMING!
ORGY-PORGY!

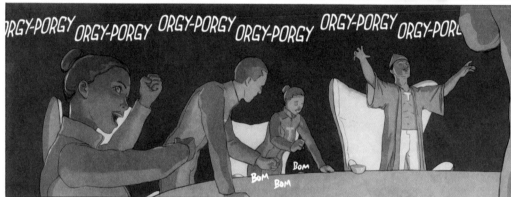

ORGY-PORGY ORGY-PORGY ORGY-PORGY ORGY-PORGY ORGY-PORGY ORGY-POR

SLAP SLAP SLAP

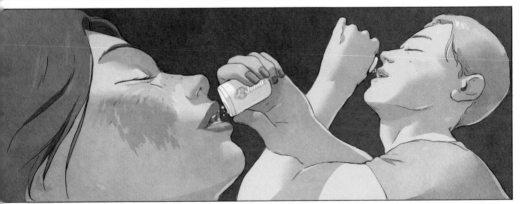

ORGY-PORGY ORGY-PORGY ORGY-PORG

65

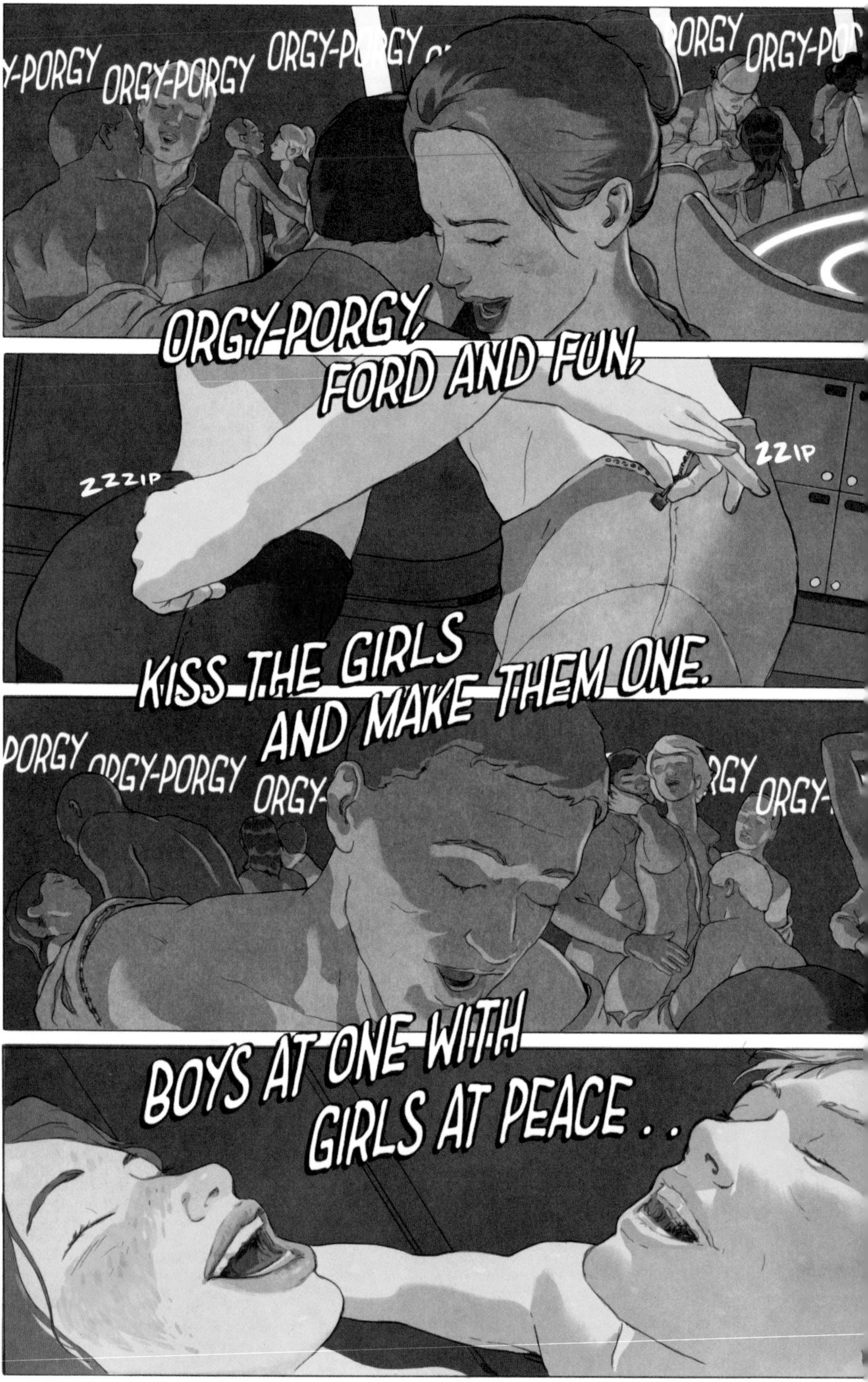

ORGY-PORGY
ORGY-PORGY
ORGY-PORGY,
FORD AND FUN,
ZZZIP
ZZIP
KISS THE GIRLS
AND MAKE THEM ONE.
PORGY
BOYS AT ONE WITH
GIRLS AT PEACE . .

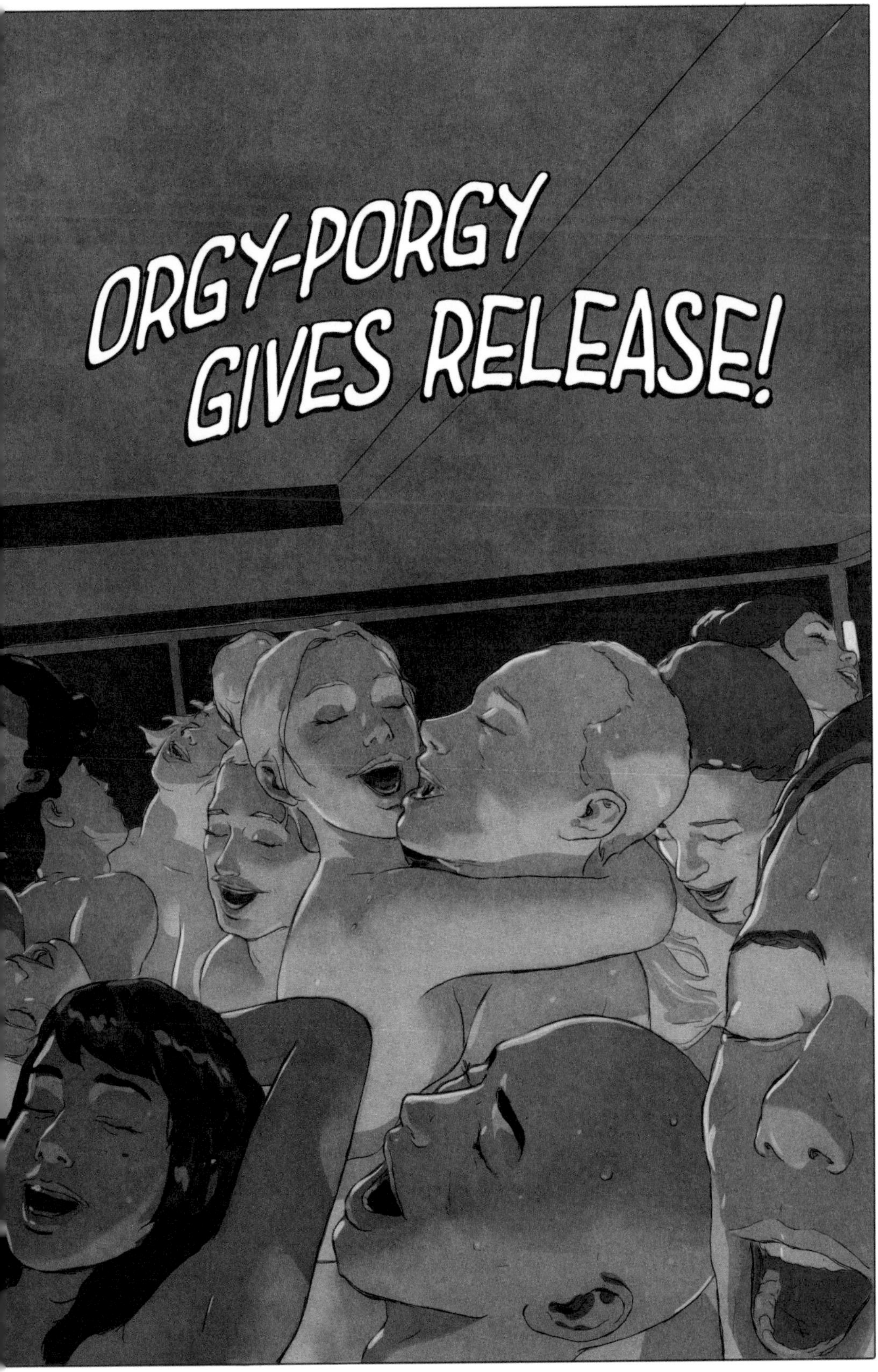
ORGY-PORGY GIVES RELEASE!

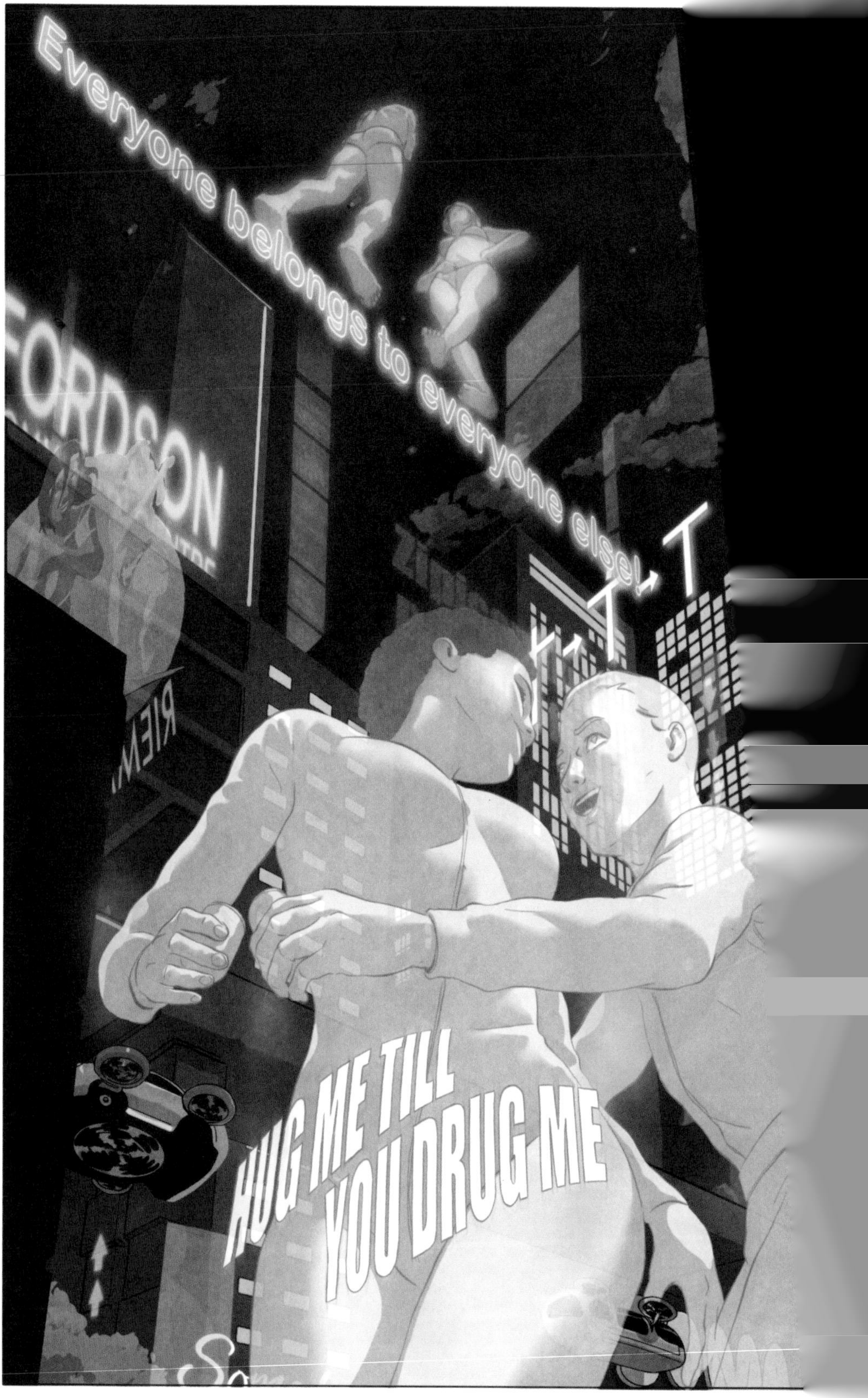
Everyone belongs to everyone else!
FORDSON
HUG ME TILL
YOU DRUG ME

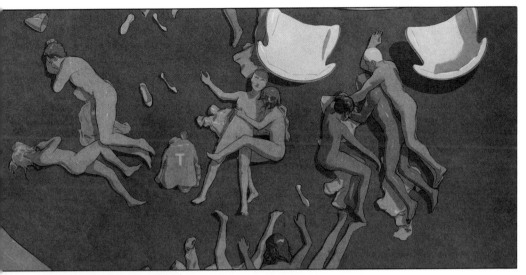

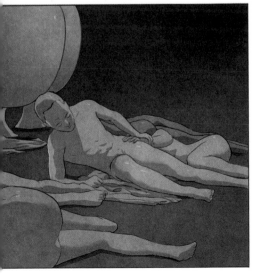

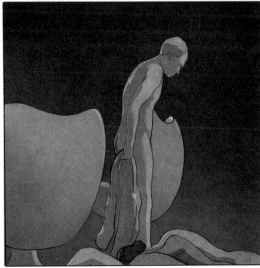

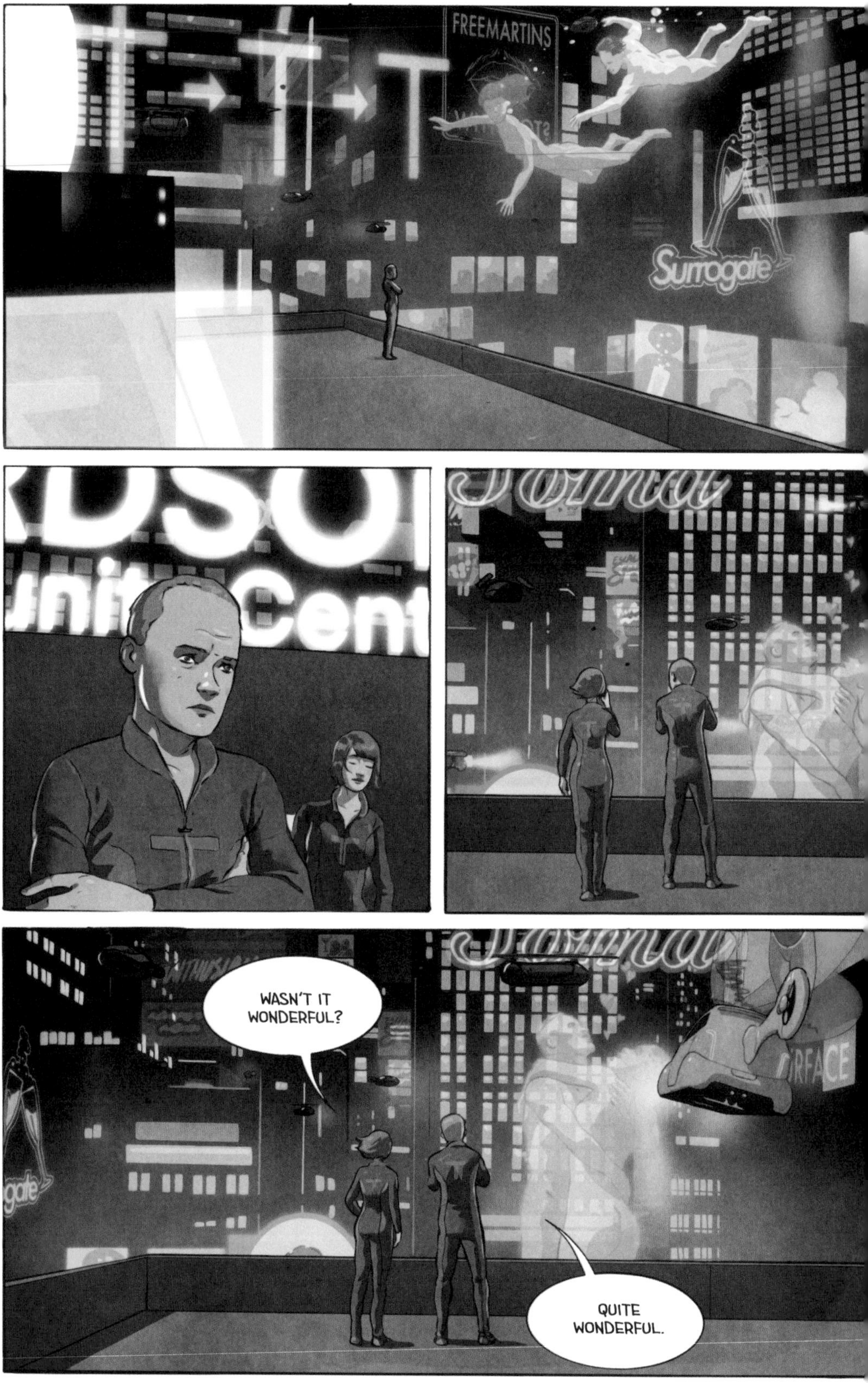
FREEMARTINS
Surrogate
WASN'T IT WONDERFUL?
QUITE WONDERFUL.

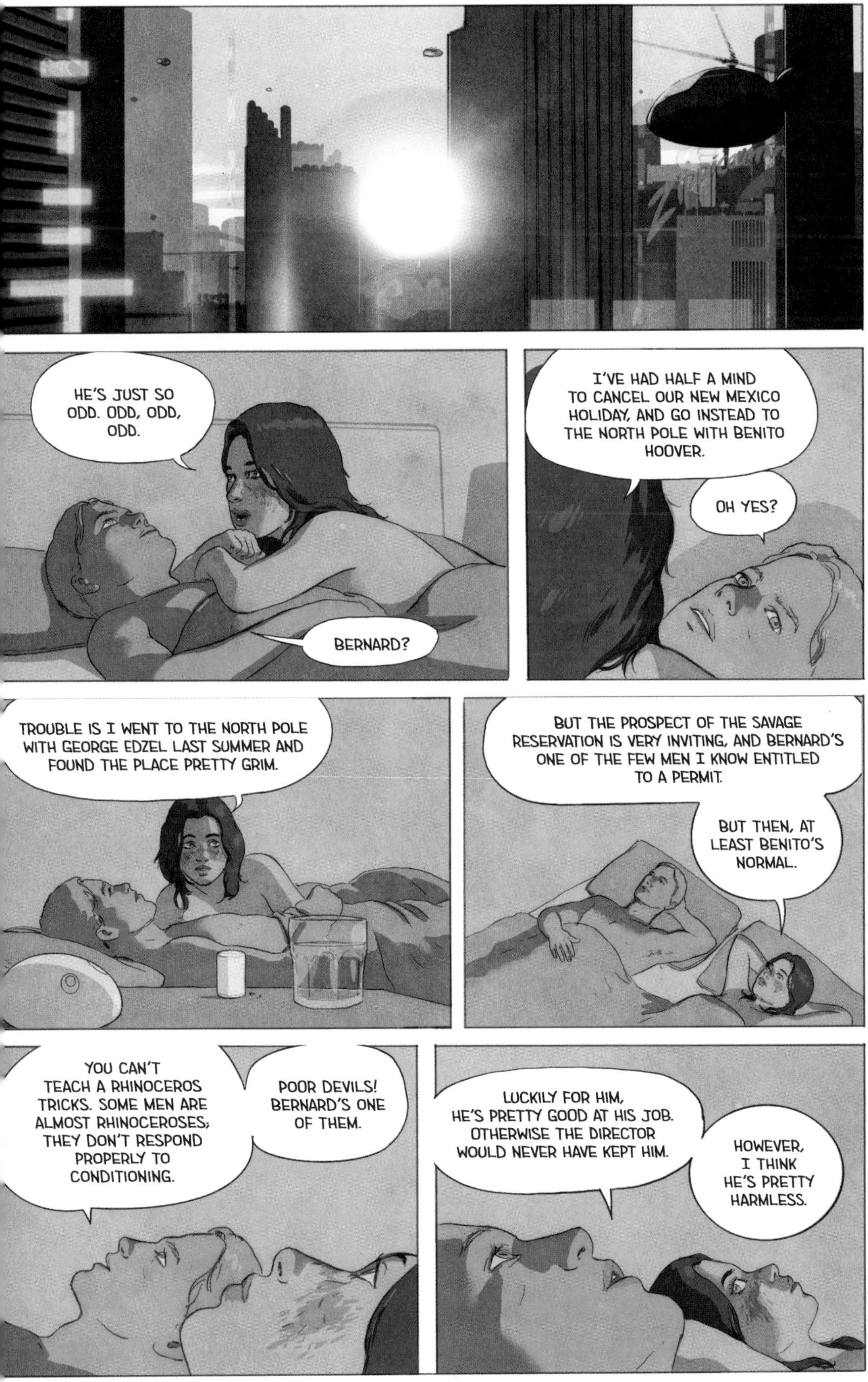
HE'S JUST SO ODD. ODD, ODD, ODD.
BERNARD?
I'VE HAD HALF A MIND TO CANCEL OUR NEW MEXICO HOLIDAY, AND GO INSTEAD TO THE NORTH POLE WITH BENITO HOOVER.
OH YES?
TROUBLE IS I WENT TO THE NORTH POLE WITH GEORGE EDZEL LAST SUMMER AND FOUND THE PLACE PRETTY GRIM.
BUT THE PROSPECT OF THE SAVAGE RESERVATION IS VERY INVITING, AND BERNARD'S ONE OF THE FEW MEN I KNOW ENTITLED TO A PERMIT.
BUT THEN, AT LEAST BENITO'S NORMAL.
YOU CAN'T TEACH A RHINOCEROS TRICKS. SOME MEN ARE ALMOST RHINOCEROSES; THEY DON'T RESPOND PROPERLY TO CONDITIONING.
POOR DEVILS! BERNARD'S ONE OF THEM.
LUCKILY FOR HIM, HE'S PRETTY GOOD AT HIS JOB. OTHERWISE THE DIRECTOR WOULD NEVER HAVE KEPT HIM.
HOWEVER, I THINK HE'S PRETTY HARMLESS.

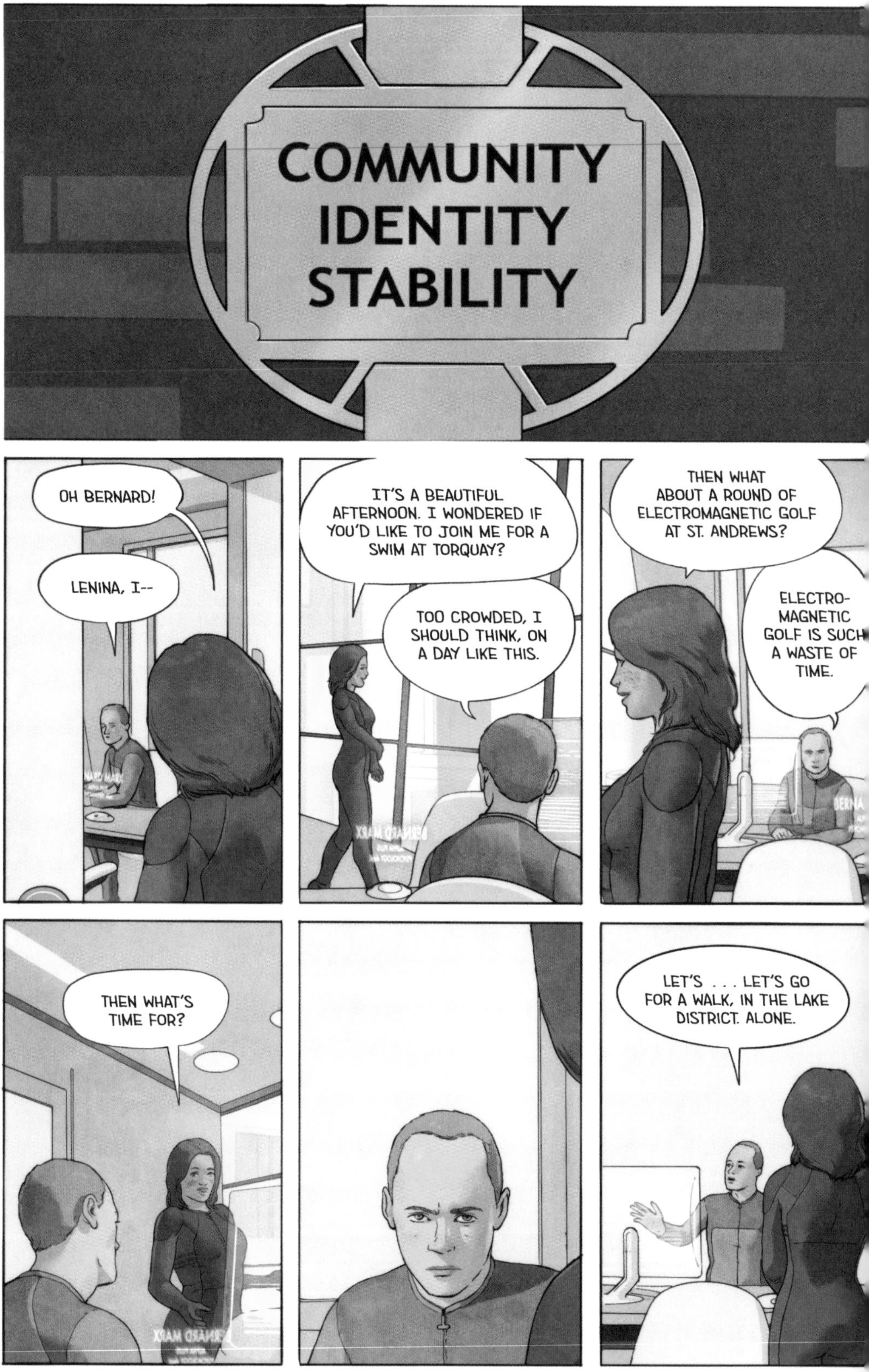
COMMUNITY
IDENTITY
STABILITY
OH BERNARD!
LENINA, I--
IT'S A BEAUTIFUL AFTERNOON. I WONDERED IF YOU'D LIKE TO JOIN ME FOR A SWIM AT TORQUAY?
TOO CROWDED, I SHOULD THINK, ON A DAY LIKE THIS.
THEN WHAT ABOUT A ROUND OF ELECTROMAGNETIC GOLF AT ST. ANDREWS?
ELECTRO-MAGNETIC GOLF IS SUCH A WASTE OF TIME.
THEN WHAT'S TIME FOR?
LET'S . . . LET'S GO FOR A WALK, IN THE LAKE DISTRICT. ALONE.

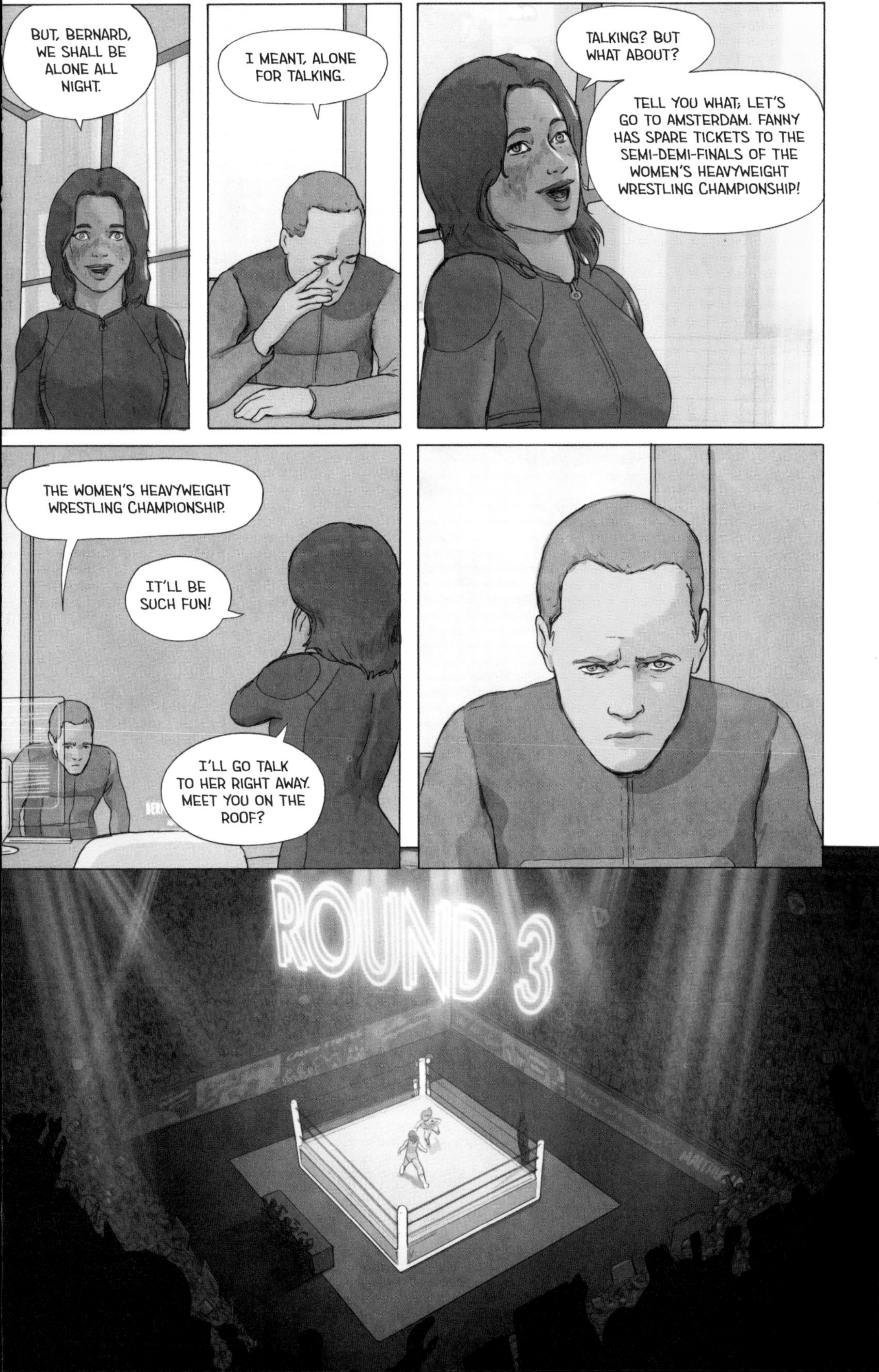
BUT, BERNARD, WE SHALL BE ALONE ALL NIGHT.
I MEANT, ALONE FOR TALKING.
TALKING? BUT WHAT ABOUT?
TELL YOU WHAT; LET'S GO TO AMSTERDAM. FANNY HAS SPARE TICKETS TO THE SEMI-DEMI-FINALS OF THE WOMEN'S HEAVYWEIGHT WRESTLING CHAMPIONSHIP!
THE WOMEN'S HEAVYWEIGHT WRESTLING CHAMPIONSHIP.
IT'LL BE SUCH FUN!
I'LL GO TALK TO HER RIGHT AWAY. MEET YOU ON THE ROOF?
ROUND 3

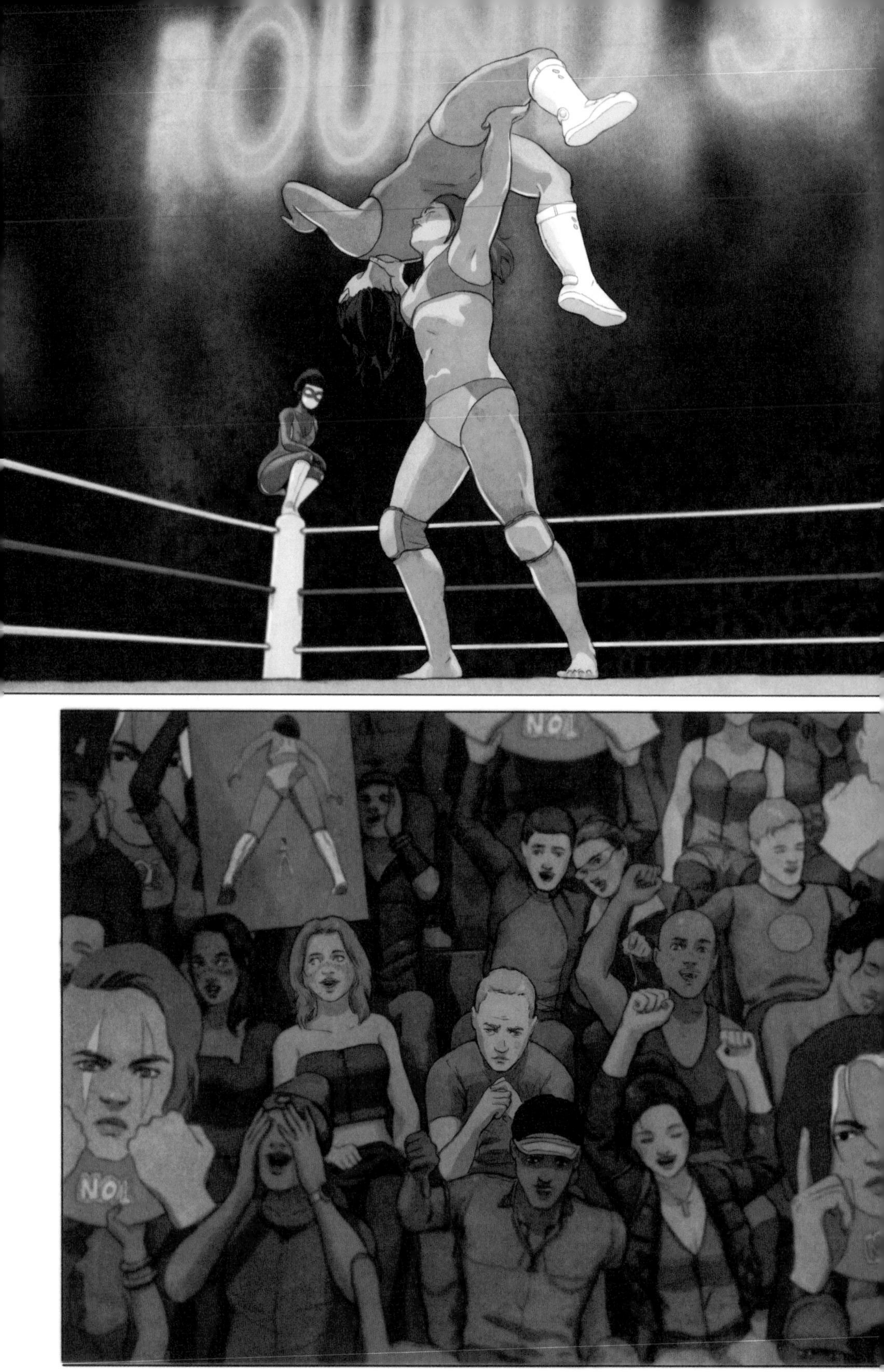

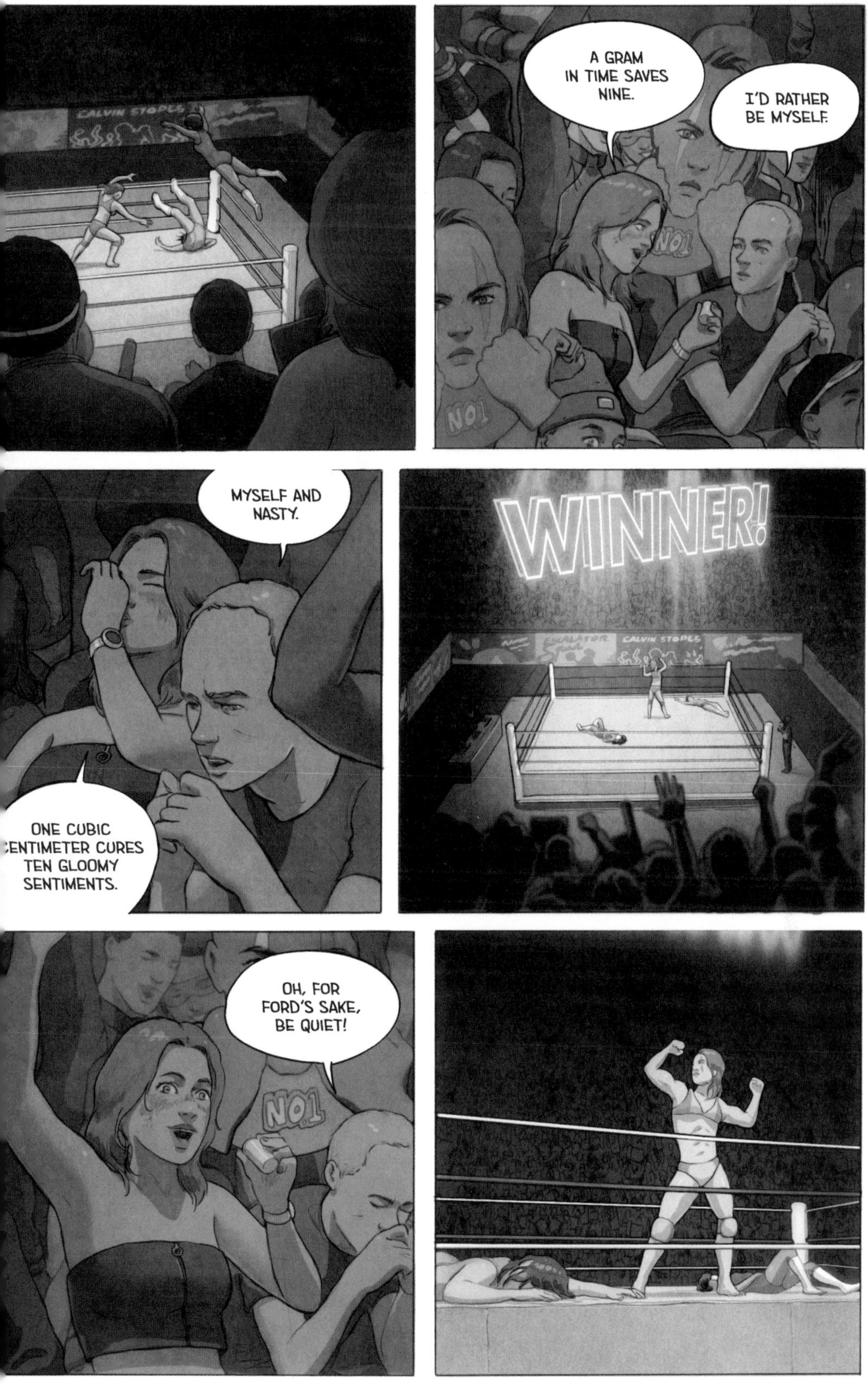
CALVIN STOPES
A GRAM IN TIME SAVES NINE.
I'D RATHER BE MYSELF.
MYSELF AND NASTY.
ONE CUBIC CENTIMETER CURES TEN GLOOMY SENTIMENTS.
WINNER!
CALVIN STOPES
OH, FOR FORD'S SAKE, BE QUIET!

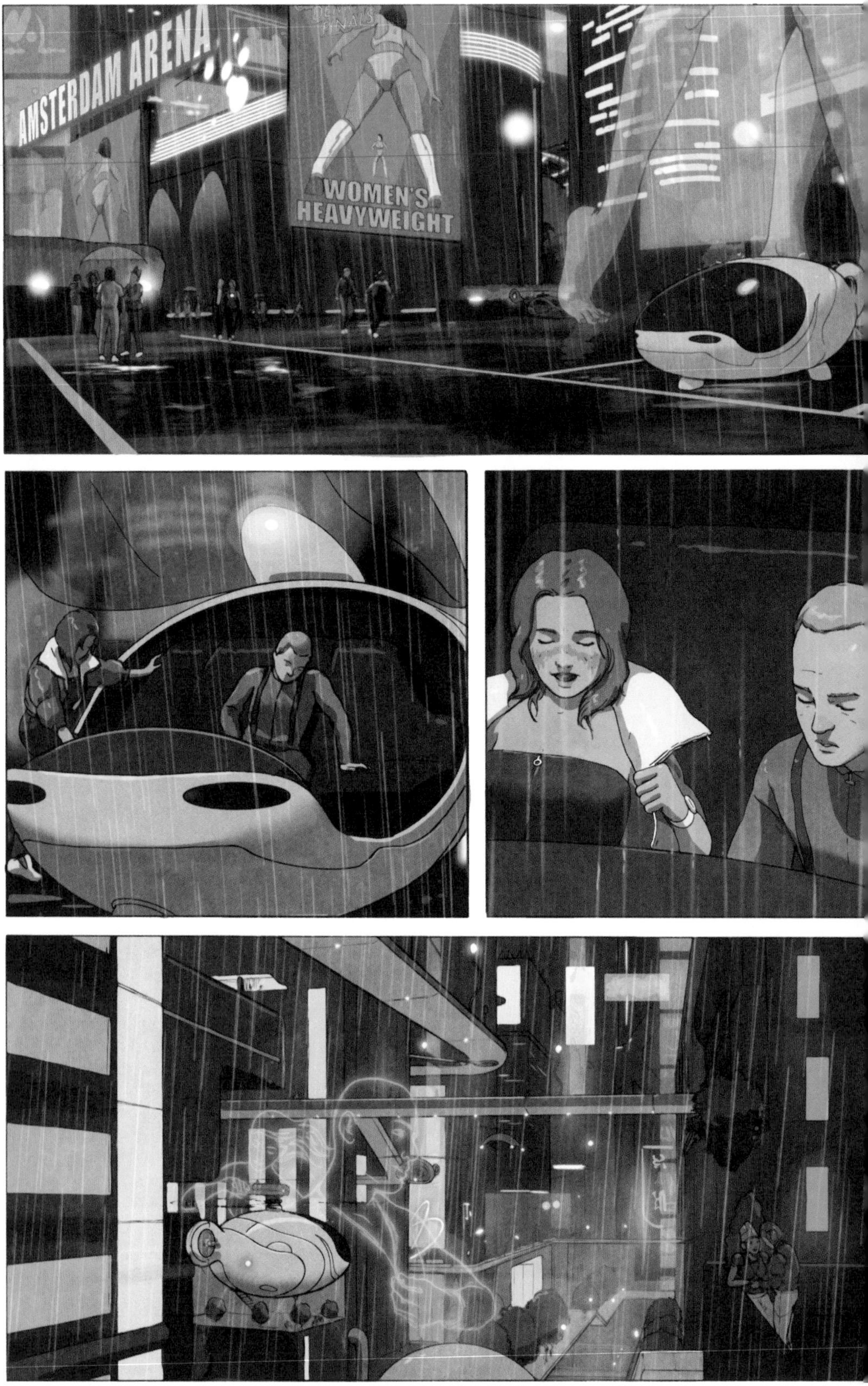
AMSTERDAM ARENA
WOMEN'S HEAVYWEIGHT

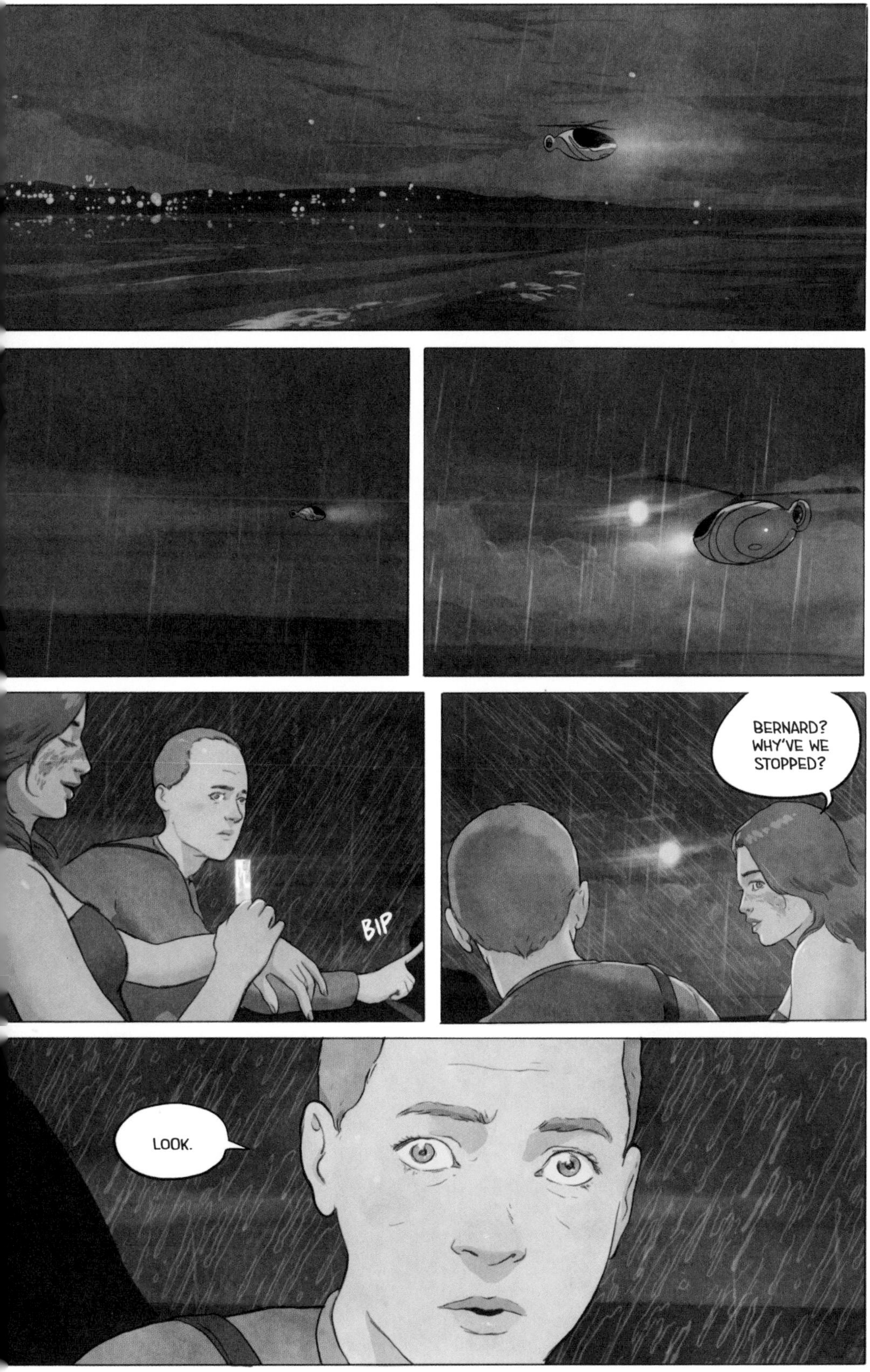
BIP
BERNARD? WHY'VE WE STOPPED?
LOOK.

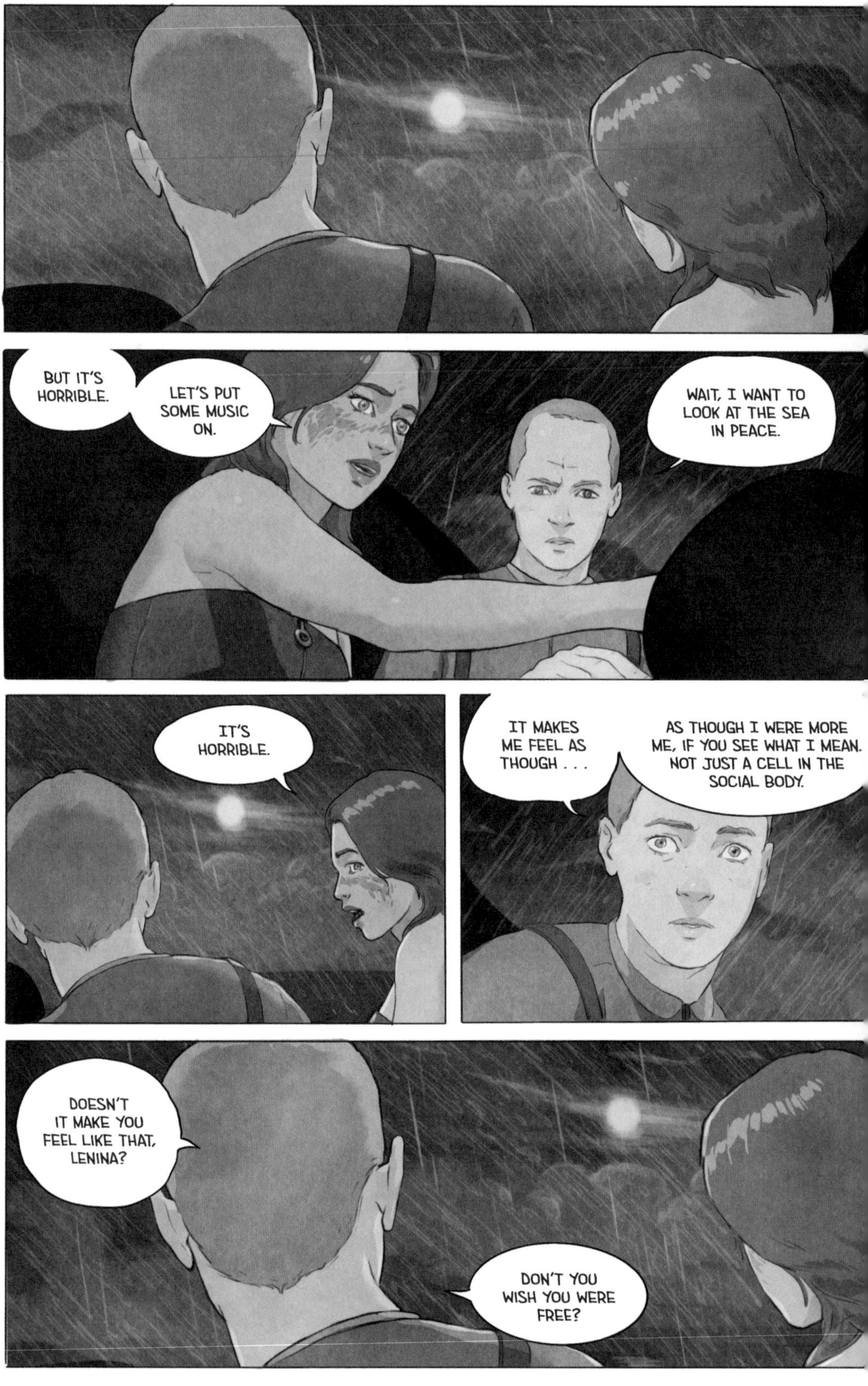
BUT IT'S HORRIBLE.
LET'S PUT SOME MUSIC ON.
WAIT, I WANT TO LOOK AT THE SEA IN PEACE.
IT'S HORRIBLE.
IT MAKES ME FEEL AS THOUGH . . .
AS THOUGH I WERE MORE ME, IF YOU SEE WHAT I MEAN. NOT JUST A CELL IN THE SOCIAL BODY.
DOESN'T IT MAKE YOU FEEL LIKE THAT, LENINA?
DON'T YOU WISH YOU WERE FREE?

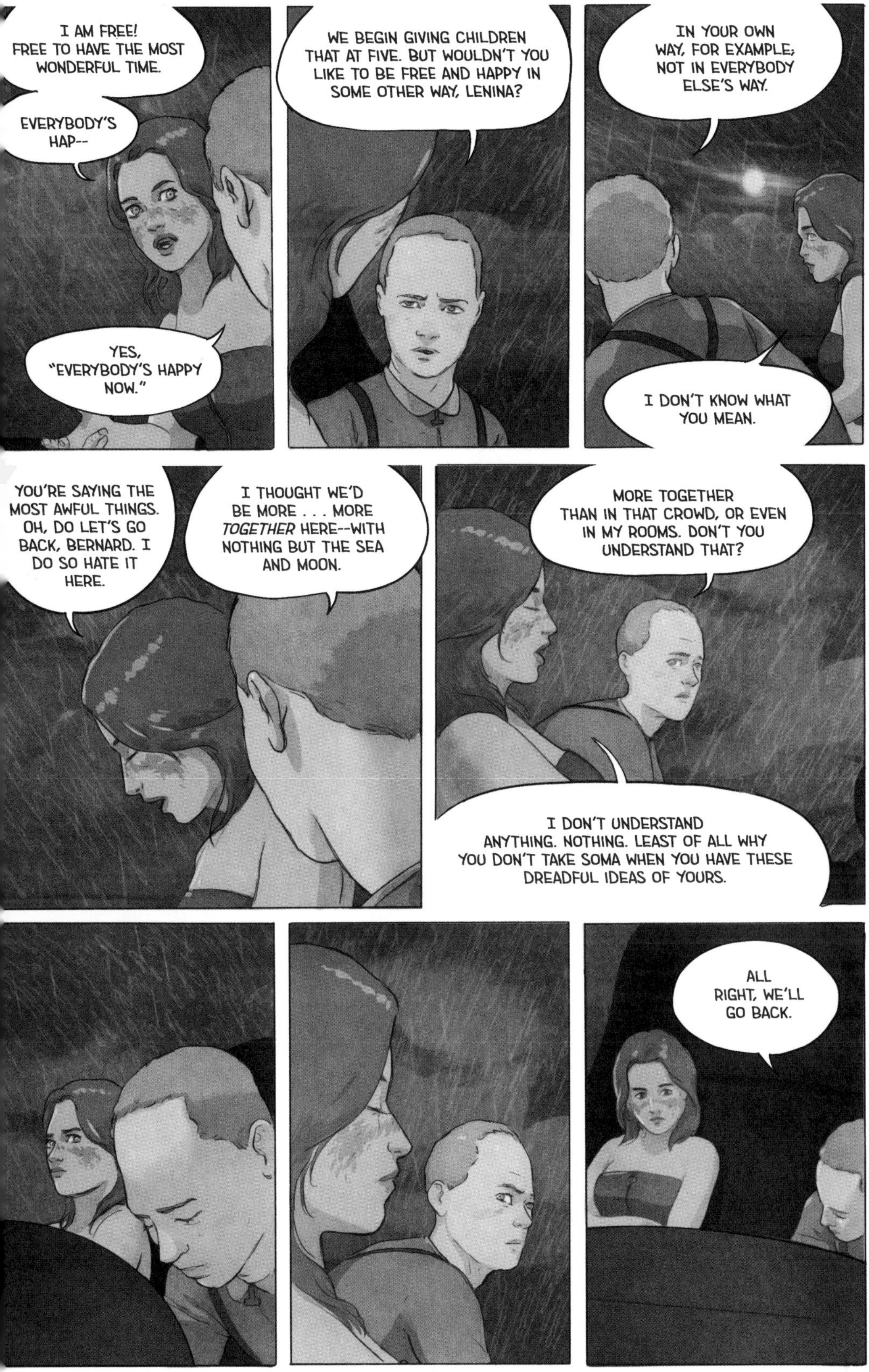
I AM FREE! FREE TO HAVE THE MOST WONDERFUL TIME.
EVERYBODY'S HAP--
YES, "EVERYBODY'S HAPPY NOW."
WE BEGIN GIVING CHILDREN THAT AT FIVE. BUT WOULDN'T YOU LIKE TO BE FREE AND HAPPY IN SOME OTHER WAY, LENINA?
IN YOUR OWN WAY, FOR EXAMPLE; NOT IN EVERYBODY ELSE'S WAY.
I DON'T KNOW WHAT YOU MEAN.
YOU'RE SAYING THE MOST AWFUL THINGS. OH, DO LET'S GO BACK, BERNARD. I DO SO HATE IT HERE.
I THOUGHT WE'D BE MORE . . . MORE *TOGETHER* HERE--WITH NOTHING BUT THE SEA AND MOON.
MORE TOGETHER THAN IN THAT CROWD, OR EVEN IN MY ROOMS. DON'T YOU UNDERSTAND THAT?
I DON'T UNDERSTAND ANYTHING. NOTHING. LEAST OF ALL WHY YOU DON'T TAKE SOMA WHEN YOU HAVE THESE DREADFUL IDEAS OF YOURS.
ALL RIGHT, WE'LL GO BACK.

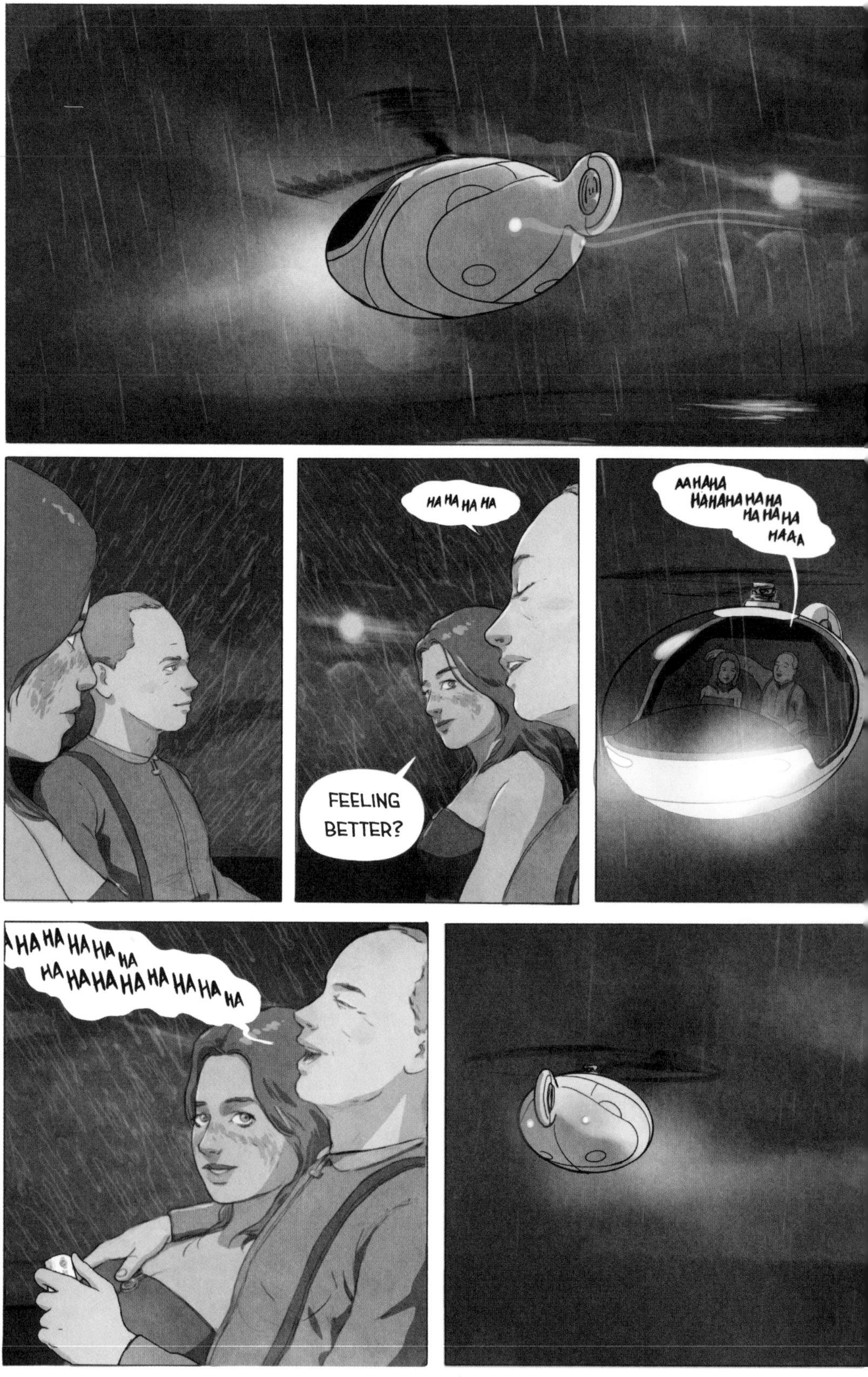
HA HA HA HA
FEELING BETTER?
AAHAHA HAHAHA HAHA HA HA HA HAAA
AHA HA HA HA HA HA
HA HA HA HA HA HA HA HA HA

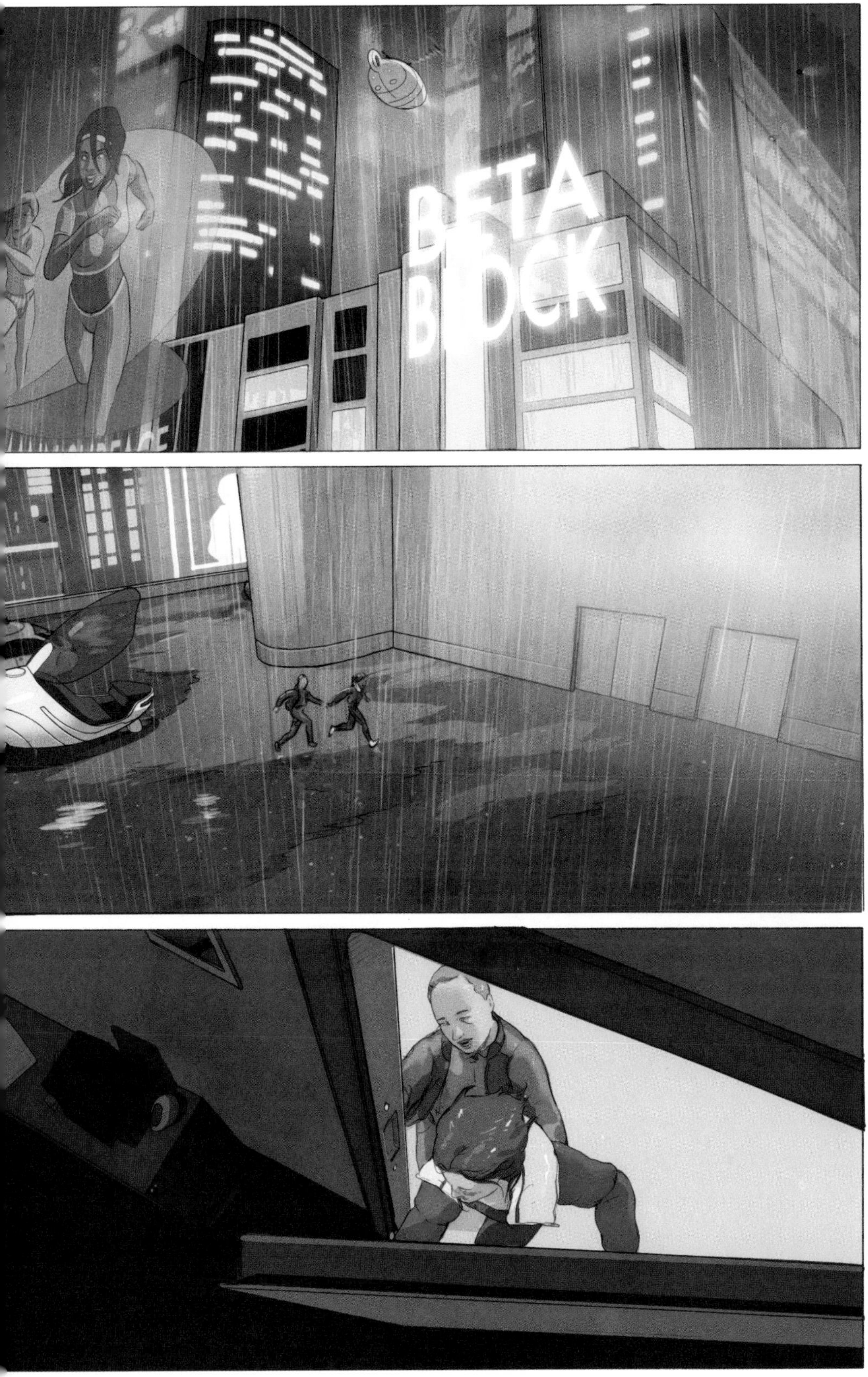
BETA

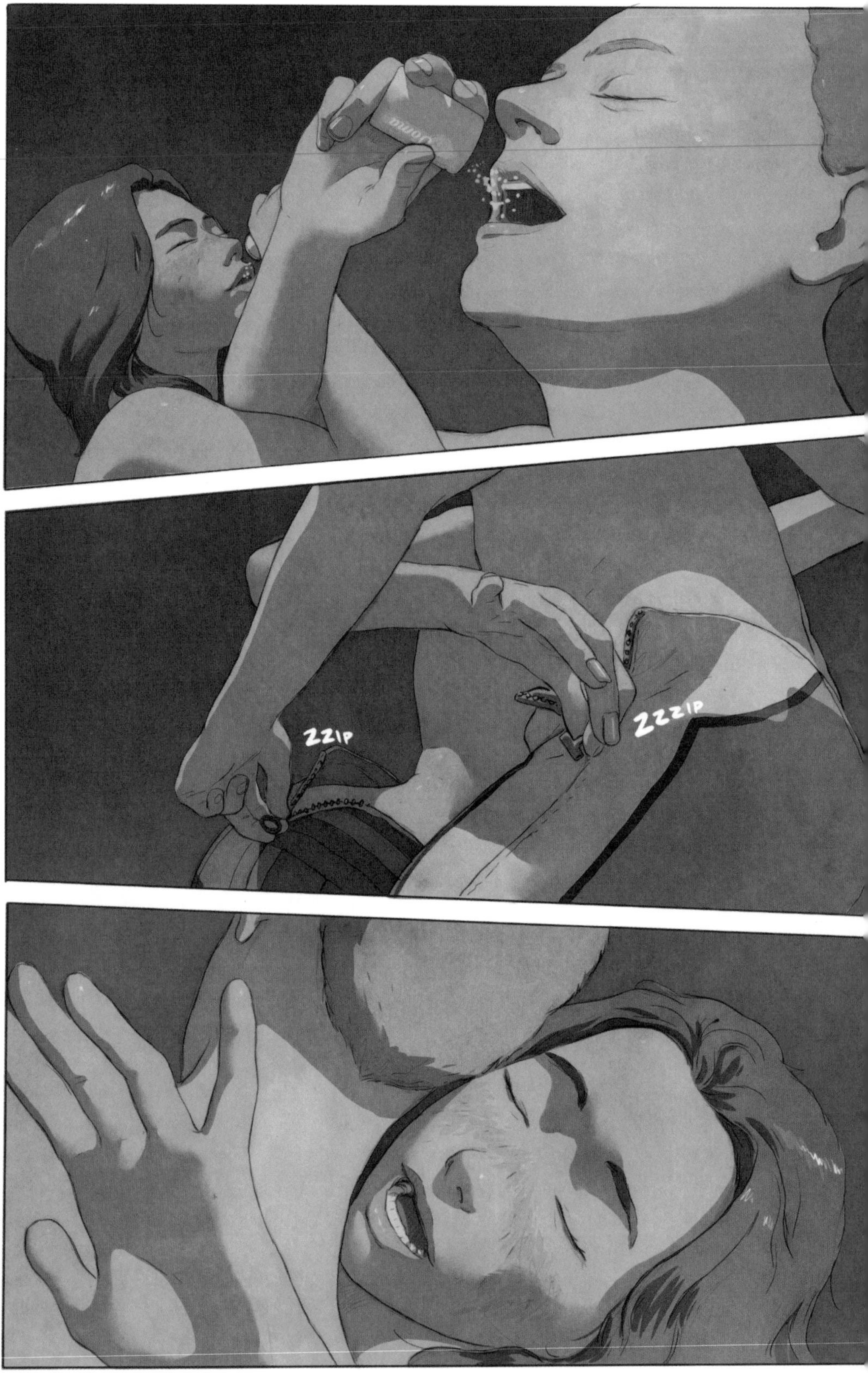
ZZIP
ZZZIP

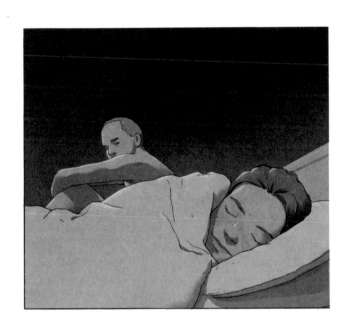

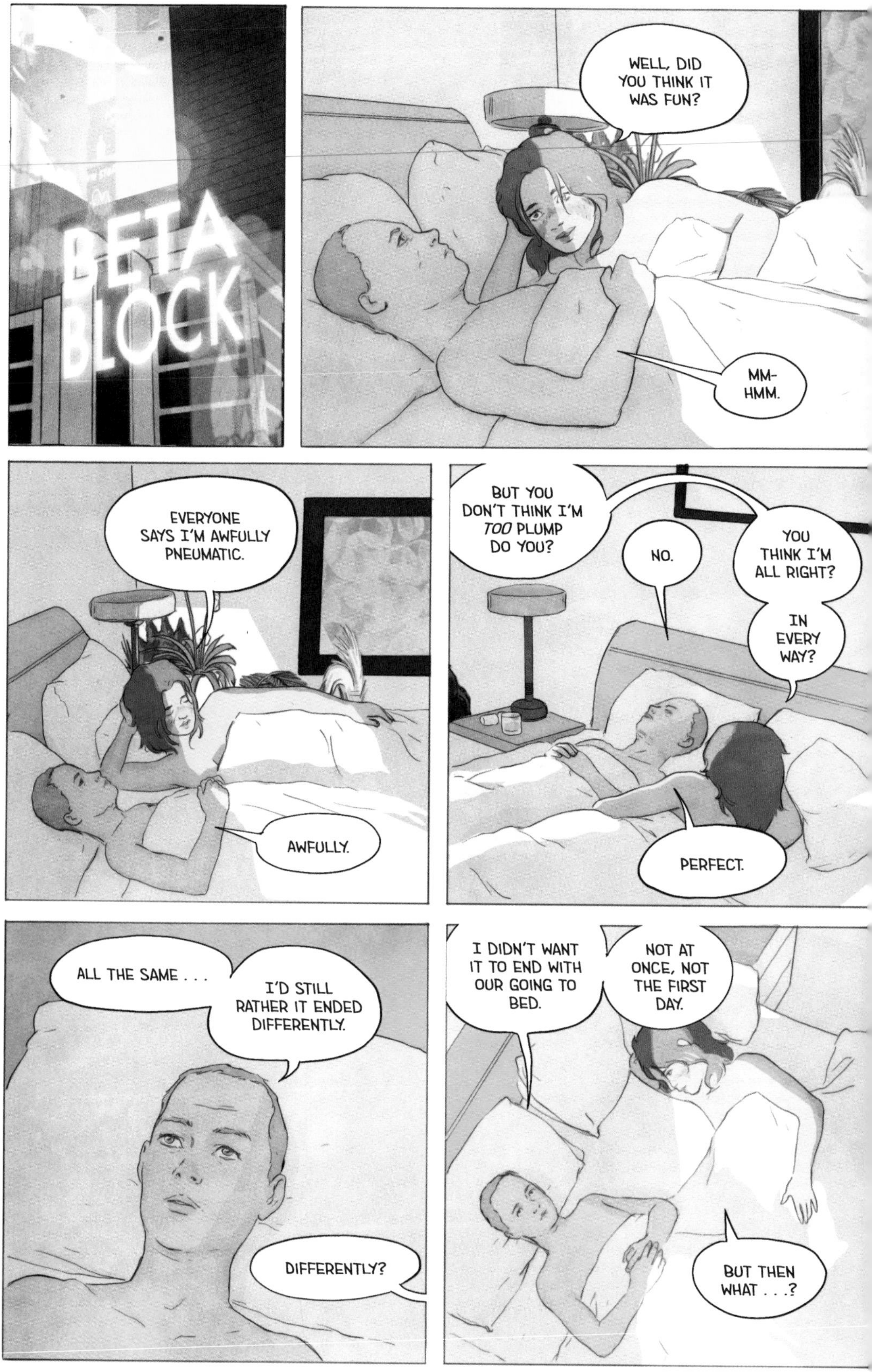
BETA BLOCK
WELL, DID YOU THINK IT WAS FUN?
MM-HMM.
EVERYONE SAYS I'M AWFULLY PNEUMATIC.
AWFULLY.
BUT YOU DON'T THINK I'M *TOO* PLUMP DO YOU?
NO.
YOU THINK I'M ALL RIGHT?
IN EVERY WAY?
PERFECT.
ALL THE SAME . . .
I'D STILL RATHER IT ENDED DIFFERENTLY.
DIFFERENTLY?
I DIDN'T WANT IT TO END WITH OUR GOING TO BED.
NOT AT ONCE, NOT THE FIRST DAY.
BUT THEN WHAT . . .?

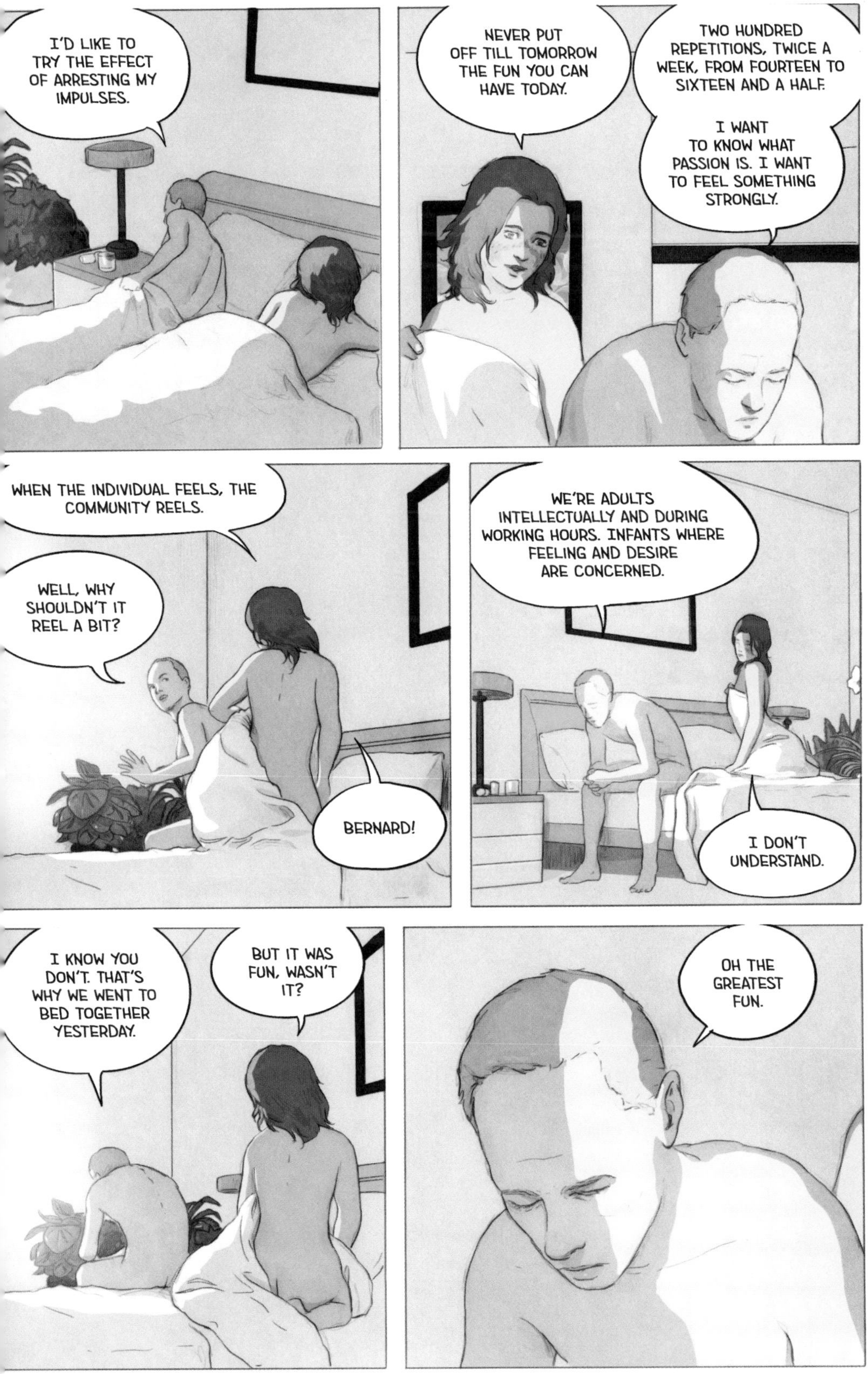
I'D LIKE TO TRY THE EFFECT OF ARRESTING MY IMPULSES.
NEVER PUT OFF TILL TOMORROW THE FUN YOU CAN HAVE TODAY.
TWO HUNDRED REPETITIONS, TWICE A WEEK, FROM FOURTEEN TO SIXTEEN AND A HALF.
I WANT TO KNOW WHAT PASSION IS. I WANT TO FEEL SOMETHING STRONGLY.
WHEN THE INDIVIDUAL FEELS, THE COMMUNITY REELS.
WELL, WHY SHOULDN'T IT REEL A BIT?
BERNARD!
WE'RE ADULTS INTELLECTUALLY AND DURING WORKING HOURS. INFANTS WHERE FEELING AND DESIRE ARE CONCERNED.
I DON'T UNDERSTAND.
I KNOW YOU DON'T. THAT'S WHY WE WENT TO BED TOGETHER YESTERDAY.
BUT IT WAS FUN, WASN'T IT?
OH THE GREATEST FUN.

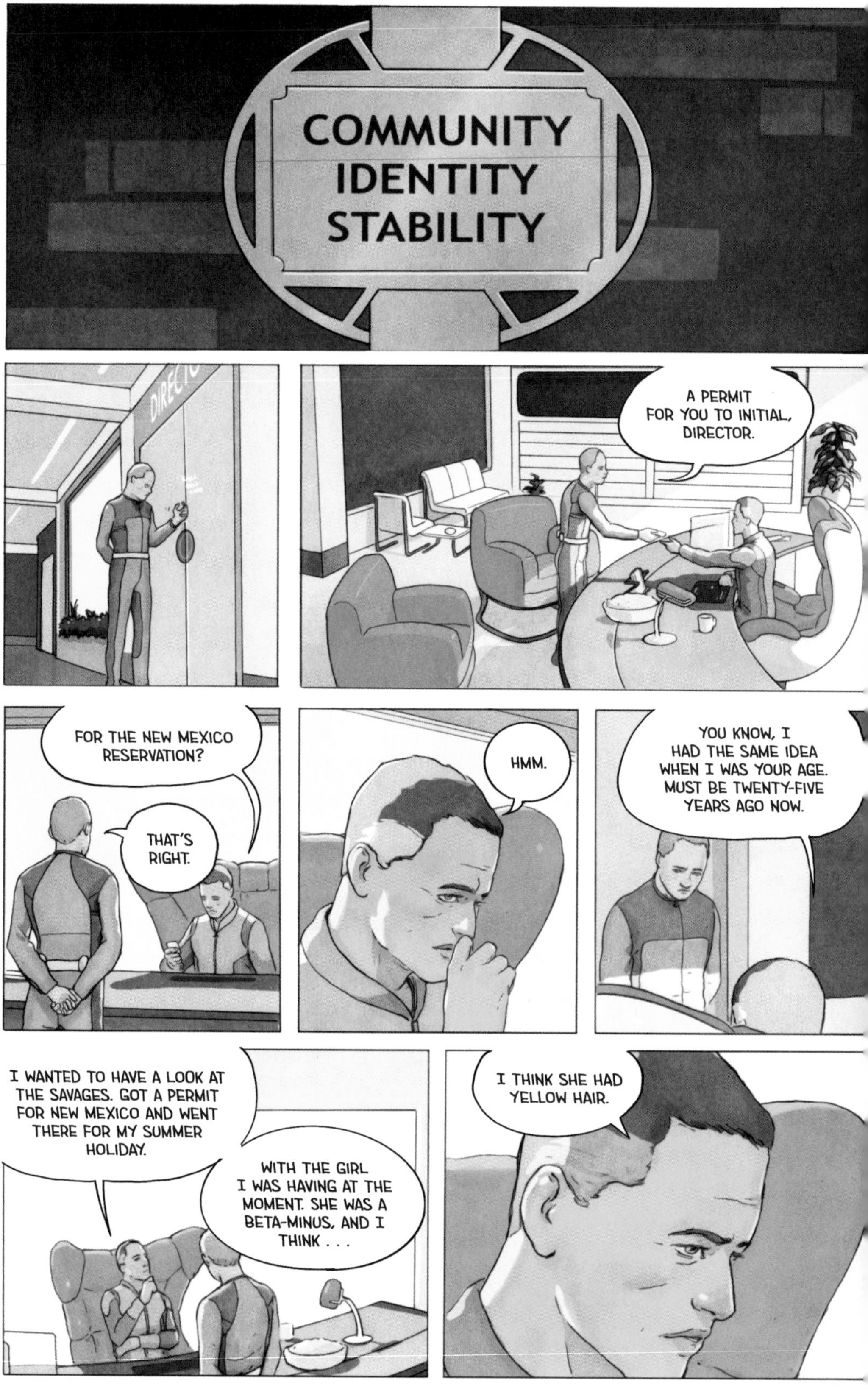
COMMUNITY
IDENTITY
STABILITY
A PERMIT FOR YOU TO INITIAL, DIRECTOR.
FOR THE NEW MEXICO RESERVATION?
THAT'S RIGHT.
HMM.
YOU KNOW, I HAD THE SAME IDEA WHEN I WAS YOUR AGE. MUST BE TWENTY-FIVE YEARS AGO NOW.
I WANTED TO HAVE A LOOK AT THE SAVAGES. GOT A PERMIT FOR NEW MEXICO AND WENT THERE FOR MY SUMMER HOLIDAY.
WITH THE GIRL I WAS HAVING AT THE MOMENT. SHE WAS A BETA-MINUS, AND I THINK . . .
I THINK SHE HAD YELLOW HAIR.

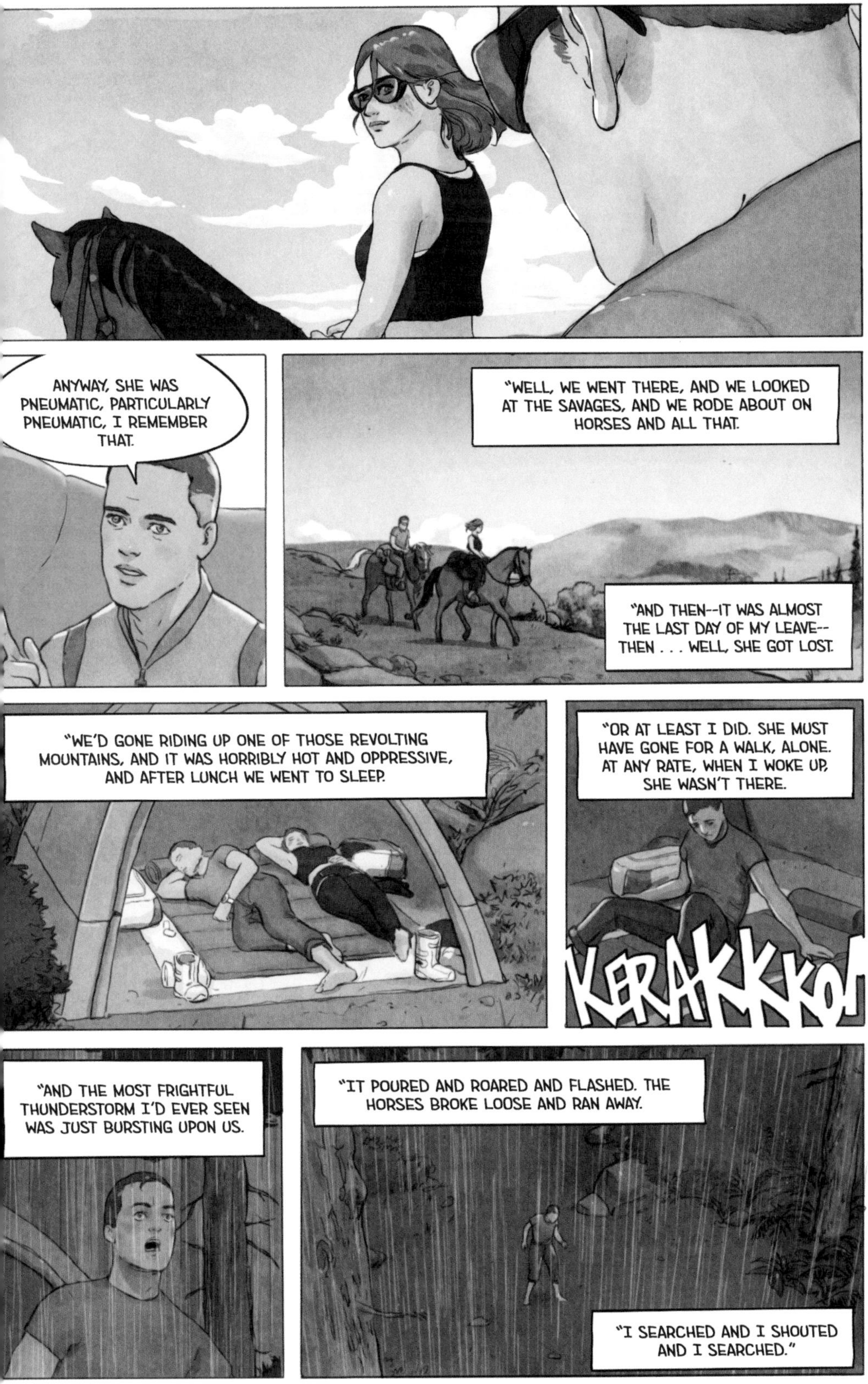
ANYWAY, SHE WAS PNEUMATIC, PARTICULARLY PNEUMATIC, I REMEMBER THAT.
"WELL, WE WENT THERE, AND WE LOOKED AT THE SAVAGES, AND WE RODE ABOUT ON HORSES AND ALL THAT.
"AND THEN--IT WAS ALMOST THE LAST DAY OF MY LEAVE--THEN . . . WELL, SHE GOT LOST.
"WE'D GONE RIDING UP ONE OF THOSE REVOLTING MOUNTAINS, AND IT WAS HORRIBLY HOT AND OPPRESSIVE, AND AFTER LUNCH WE WENT TO SLEEP.
"OR AT LEAST I DID. SHE MUST HAVE GONE FOR A WALK, ALONE. AT ANY RATE, WHEN I WOKE UP, SHE WASN'T THERE.
KERAKKKOO
"AND THE MOST FRIGHTFUL THUNDERSTORM I'D EVER SEEN WAS JUST BURSTING UPON US.
"IT POURED AND ROARED AND FLASHED. THE HORSES BROKE LOOSE AND RAN AWAY.
"I SEARCHED AND I SHOUTED AND I SEARCHED."

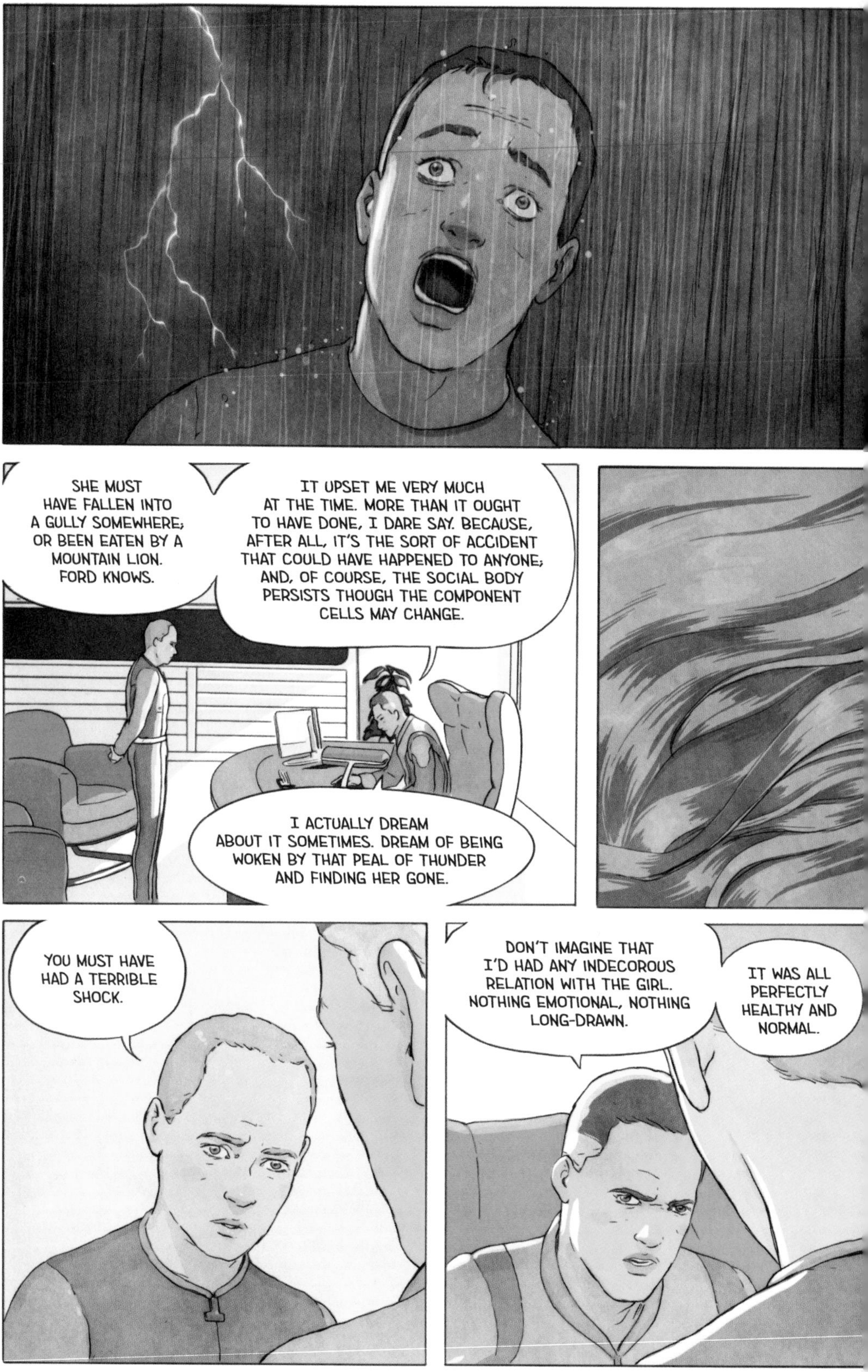
SHE MUST HAVE FALLEN INTO A GULLY SOMEWHERE; OR BEEN EATEN BY A MOUNTAIN LION. FORD KNOWS.
IT UPSET ME VERY MUCH AT THE TIME. MORE THAN IT OUGHT TO HAVE DONE, I DARE SAY. BECAUSE, AFTER ALL, IT'S THE SORT OF ACCIDENT THAT COULD HAVE HAPPENED TO ANYONE; AND, OF COURSE, THE SOCIAL BODY PERSISTS THOUGH THE COMPONENT CELLS MAY CHANGE.
I ACTUALLY DREAM ABOUT IT SOMETIMES. DREAM OF BEING WOKEN BY THAT PEAL OF THUNDER AND FINDING HER GONE.
YOU MUST HAVE HAD A TERRIBLE SHOCK.
DON'T IMAGINE THAT I'D HAD ANY INDECOROUS RELATION WITH THE GIRL. NOTHING EMOTIONAL, NOTHING LONG-DRAWN.
IT WAS ALL PERFECTLY HEALTHY AND NORMAL.

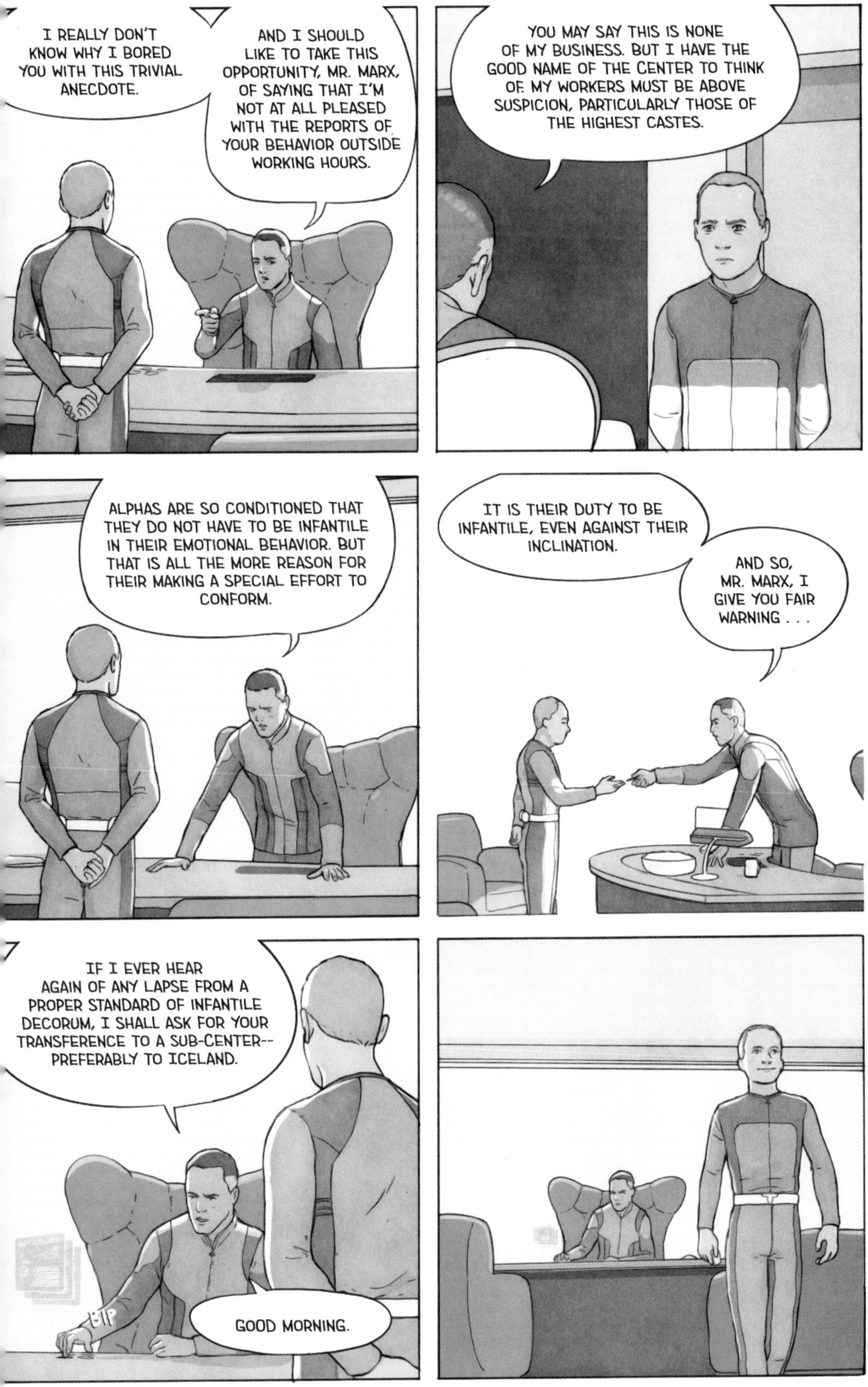
I REALLY DON'T KNOW WHY I BORED YOU WITH THIS TRIVIAL ANECDOTE.
AND I SHOULD LIKE TO TAKE THIS OPPORTUNITY, MR. MARX, OF SAYING THAT I'M NOT AT ALL PLEASED WITH THE REPORTS OF YOUR BEHAVIOR OUTSIDE WORKING HOURS.
YOU MAY SAY THIS IS NONE OF MY BUSINESS. BUT I HAVE THE GOOD NAME OF THE CENTER TO THINK OF. MY WORKERS MUST BE ABOVE SUSPICION, PARTICULARLY THOSE OF THE HIGHEST CASTES.
ALPHAS ARE SO CONDITIONED THAT THEY DO NOT HAVE TO BE INFANTILE IN THEIR EMOTIONAL BEHAVIOR. BUT THAT IS ALL THE MORE REASON FOR THEIR MAKING A SPECIAL EFFORT TO CONFORM.
IT IS THEIR DUTY TO BE INFANTILE, EVEN AGAINST THEIR INCLINATION.
AND SO, MR. MARX, I GIVE YOU FAIR WARNING . . .
IF I EVER HEAR AGAIN OF ANY LAPSE FROM A PROPER STANDARD OF INFANTILE DECORUM, I SHALL ASK FOR YOUR TRANSFERENCE TO A SUB-CENTER-- PREFERABLY TO ICELAND.
BIP
GOOD MORNING.

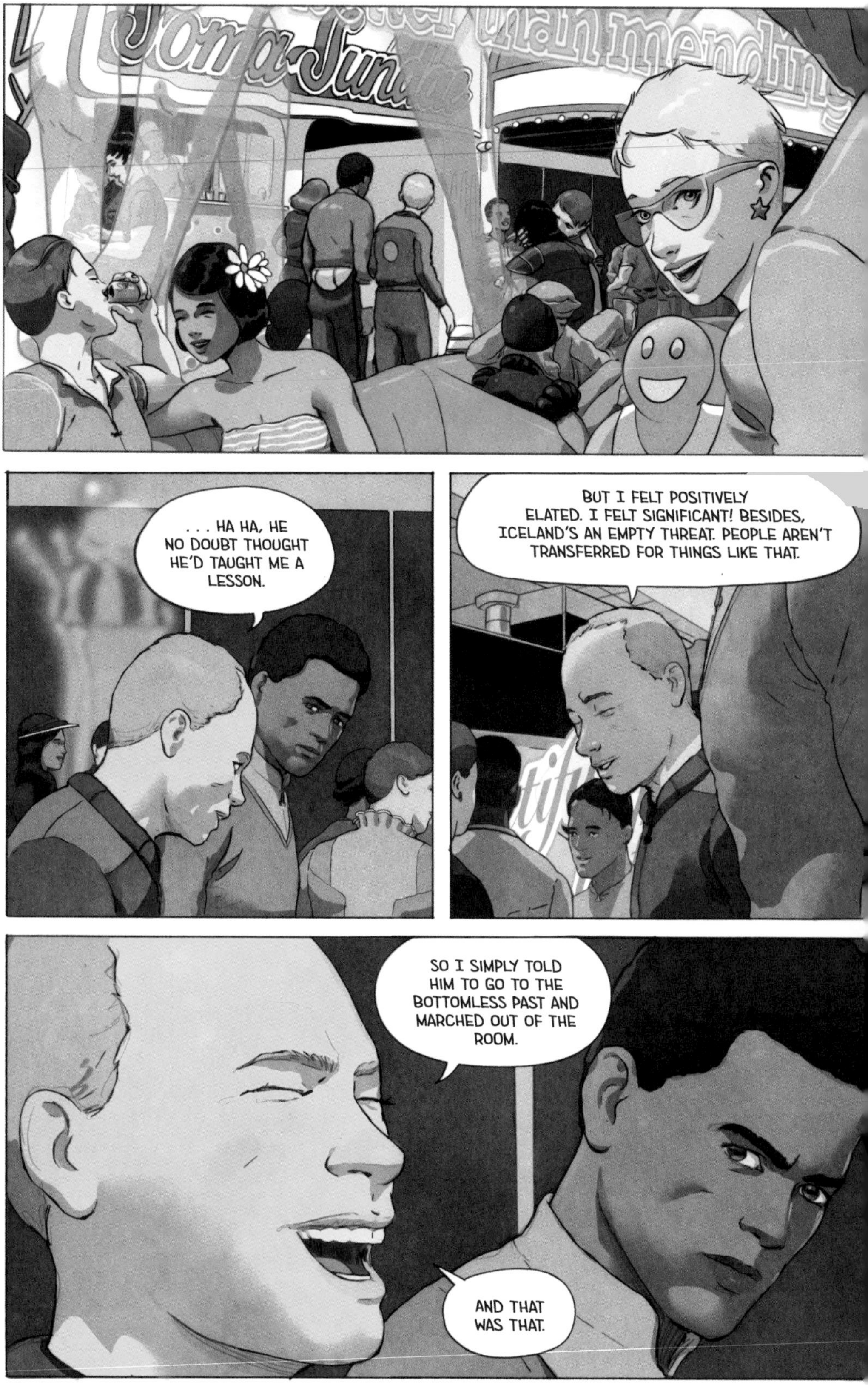
. . . HA HA, HE NO DOUBT THOUGHT HE'D TAUGHT ME A LESSON.
BUT I FELT POSITIVELY ELATED. I FELT SIGNIFICANT! BESIDES, ICELAND'S AN EMPTY THREAT. PEOPLE AREN'T TRANSFERRED FOR THINGS LIKE THAT.
SO I SIMPLY TOLD HIM TO GO TO THE BOTTOMLESS PAST AND MARCHED OUT OF THE ROOM.
AND THAT WAS THAT.

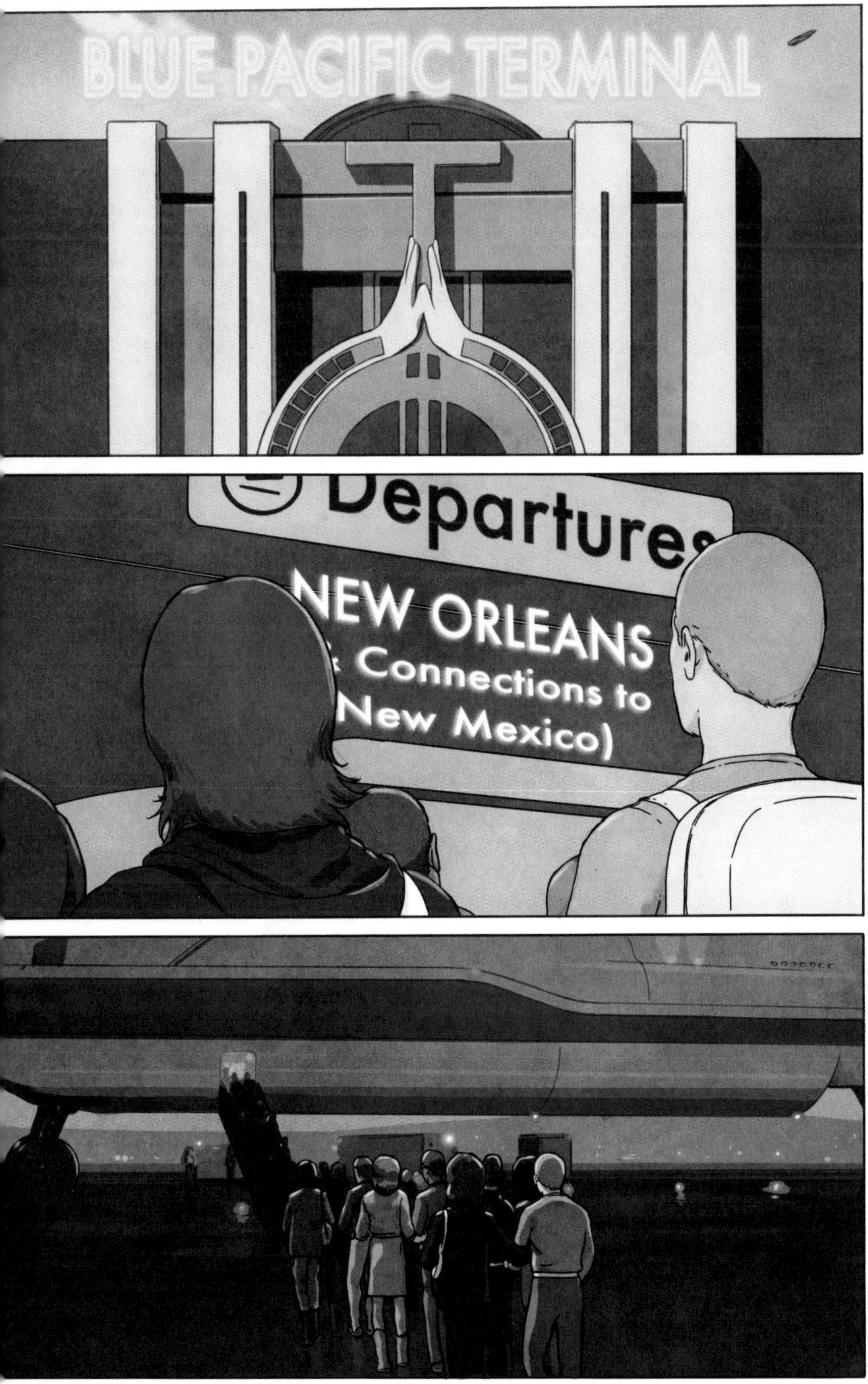
BLUE PACIFIC TERMINAL
Departures
NEW ORLEANS
Connections to
New Mexico)

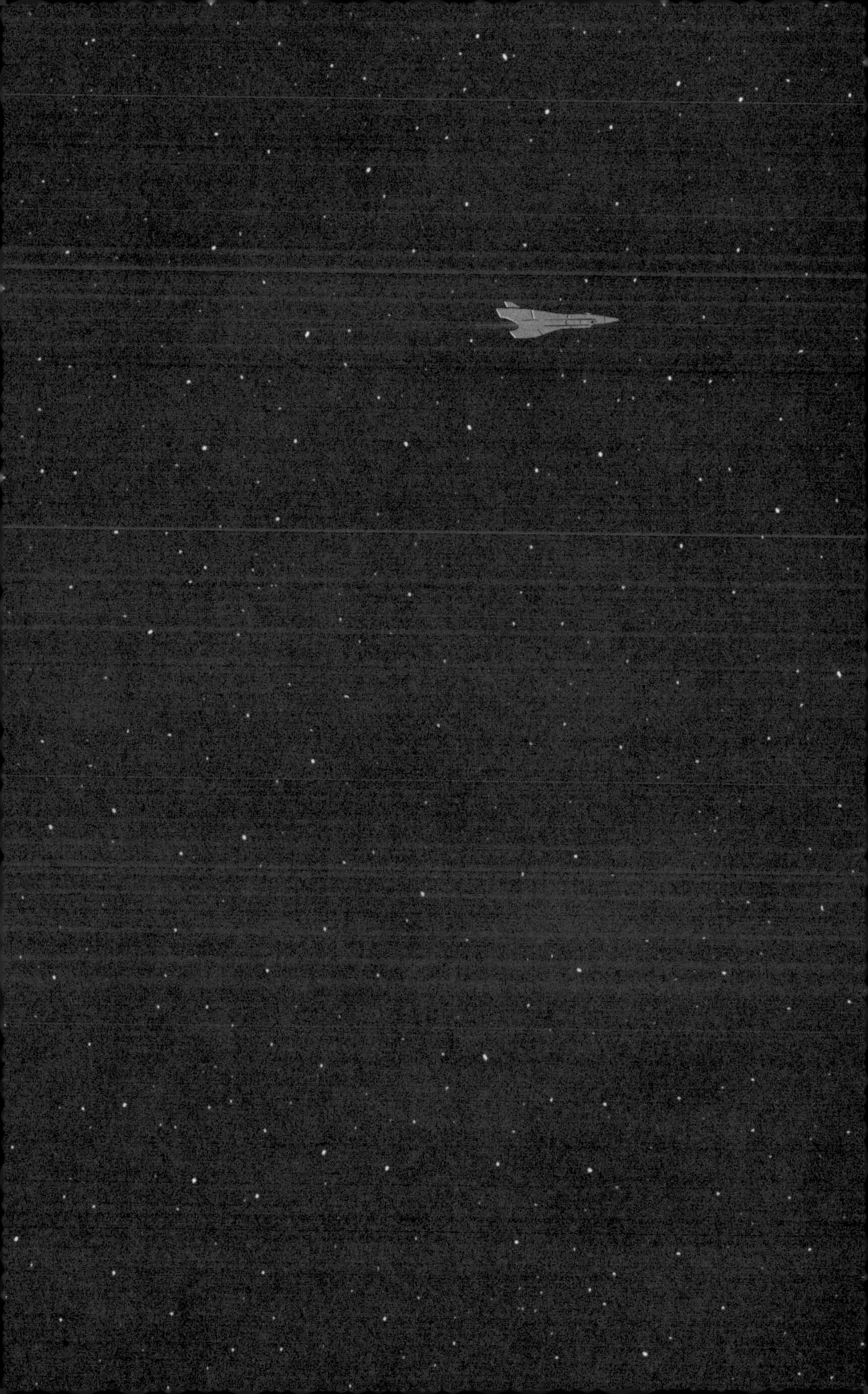

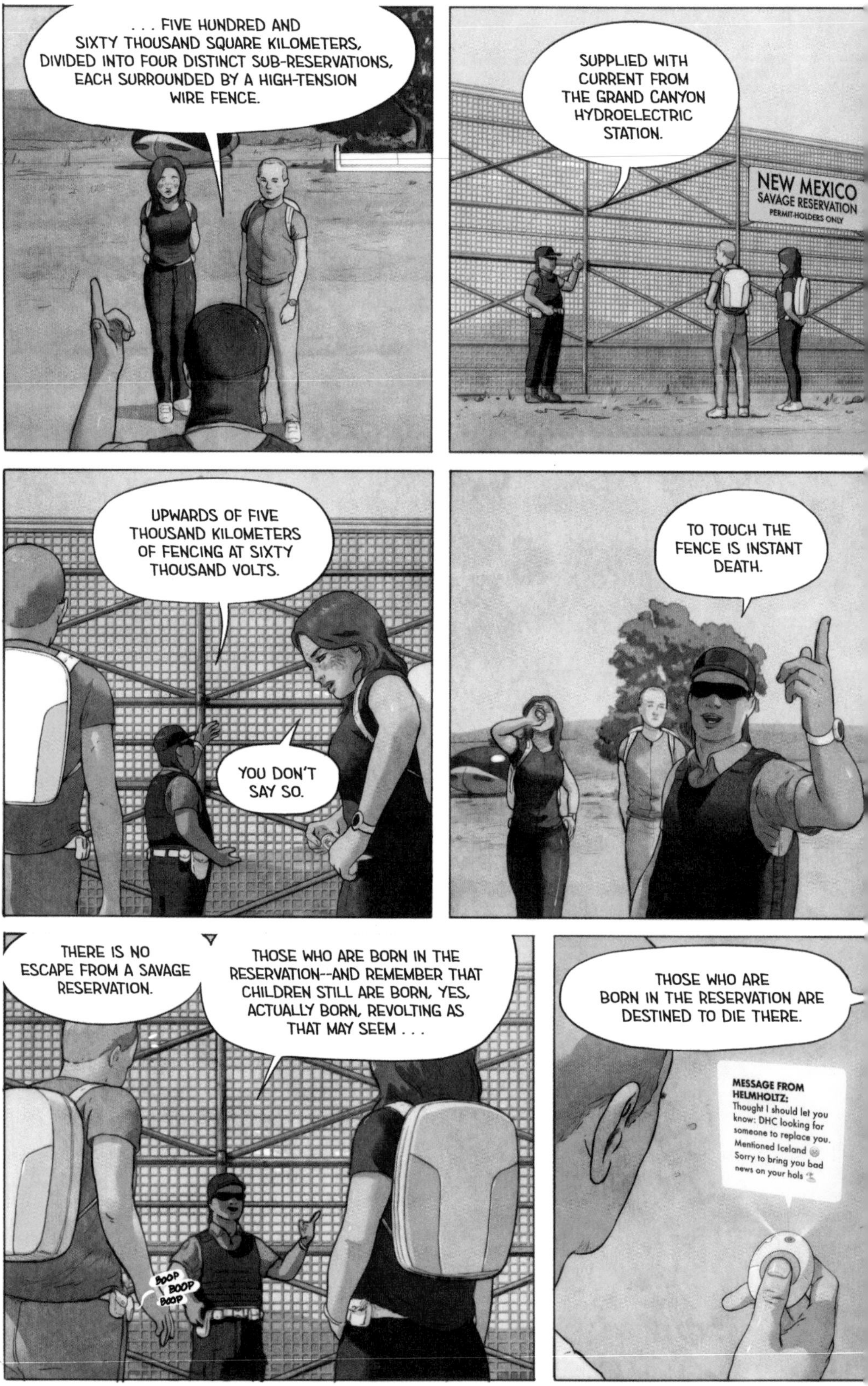
. . . FIVE HUNDRED AND SIXTY THOUSAND SQUARE KILOMETERS, DIVIDED INTO FOUR DISTINCT SUB-RESERVATIONS, EACH SURROUNDED BY A HIGH-TENSION WIRE FENCE.
SUPPLIED WITH CURRENT FROM THE GRAND CANYON HYDROELECTRIC STATION.
NEW MEXICO SAVAGE RESERVATION PERMIT-HOLDERS ONLY
UPWARDS OF FIVE THOUSAND KILOMETERS OF FENCING AT SIXTY THOUSAND VOLTS.
YOU DON'T SAY SO.
TO TOUCH THE FENCE IS INSTANT DEATH.
THERE IS NO ESCAPE FROM A SAVAGE RESERVATION.
THOSE WHO ARE BORN IN THE RESERVATION--AND REMEMBER THAT CHILDREN STILL ARE BORN, YES, ACTUALLY BORN, REVOLTING AS THAT MAY SEEM . . .
BOOP BOOP BOOP
THOSE WHO ARE BORN IN THE RESERVATION ARE DESTINED TO DIE THERE.
MESSAGE FROM HELMHOLTZ:
Thought I should let you know: DHC looking for someone to replace you. Mentioned Iceland
Sorry to bring you bad news on your hols

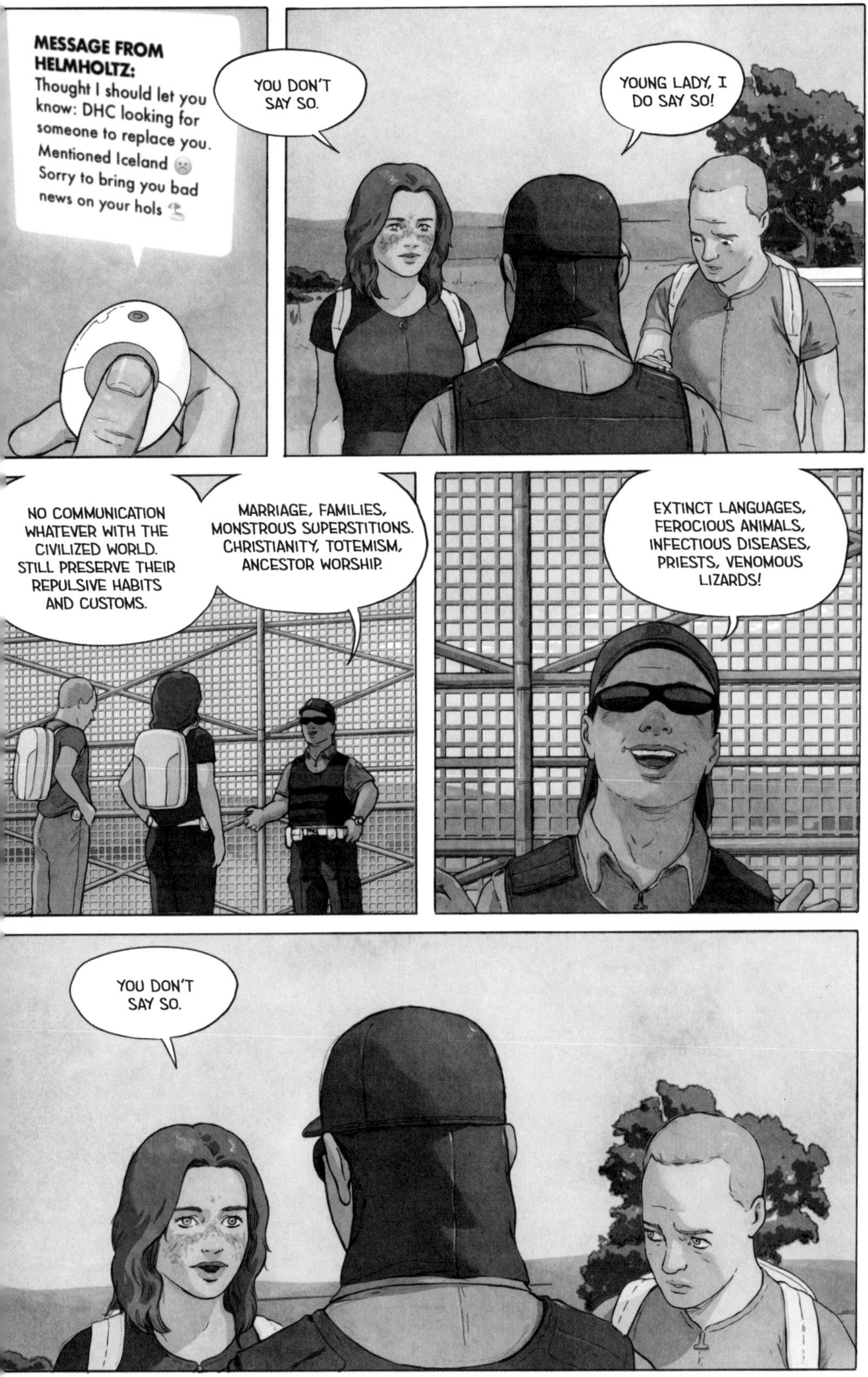

MESSAGE FROM HELMHOLTZ:
Thought I should let you know: DHC looking for someone to replace you. Mentioned Iceland
Sorry to bring you bad news on your hols
YOU DON'T SAY SO.
YOUNG LADY, I DO SAY SO!
NO COMMUNICATION WHATEVER WITH THE CIVILIZED WORLD. STILL PRESERVE THEIR REPULSIVE HABITS AND CUSTOMS.
MARRIAGE, FAMILIES, MONSTROUS SUPERSTITIONS. CHRISTIANITY, TOTEMISM, ANCESTOR WORSHIP.
EXTINCT LANGUAGES, FEROCIOUS ANIMALS, INFECTIOUS DISEASES, PRIESTS, VENOMOUS LIZARDS!
YOU DON'T SAY SO.

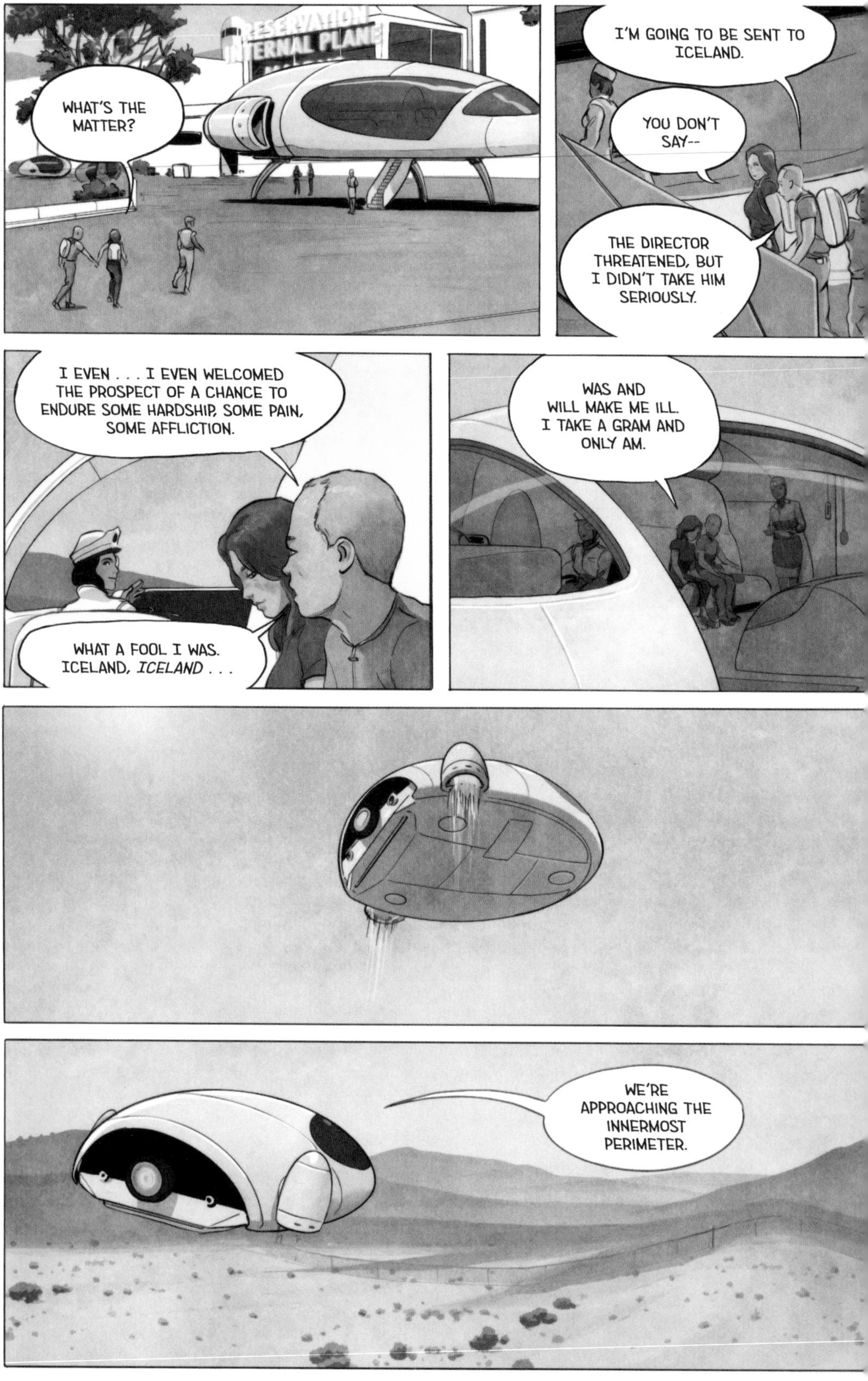
RESERVATION INTERNAL PLANE
WHAT'S THE MATTER?
I'M GOING TO BE SENT TO ICELAND.
YOU DON'T SAY--
THE DIRECTOR THREATENED, BUT I DIDN'T TAKE HIM SERIOUSLY.
I EVEN . . . I EVEN WELCOMED THE PROSPECT OF A CHANCE TO ENDURE SOME HARDSHIP, SOME PAIN, SOME AFFLICTION.
WHAT A FOOL I WAS. ICELAND, *ICELAND* . . .
WAS AND WILL MAKE ME ILL. I TAKE A GRAM AND ONLY AM.
WE'RE APPROACHING THE INNERMOST PERIMETER.

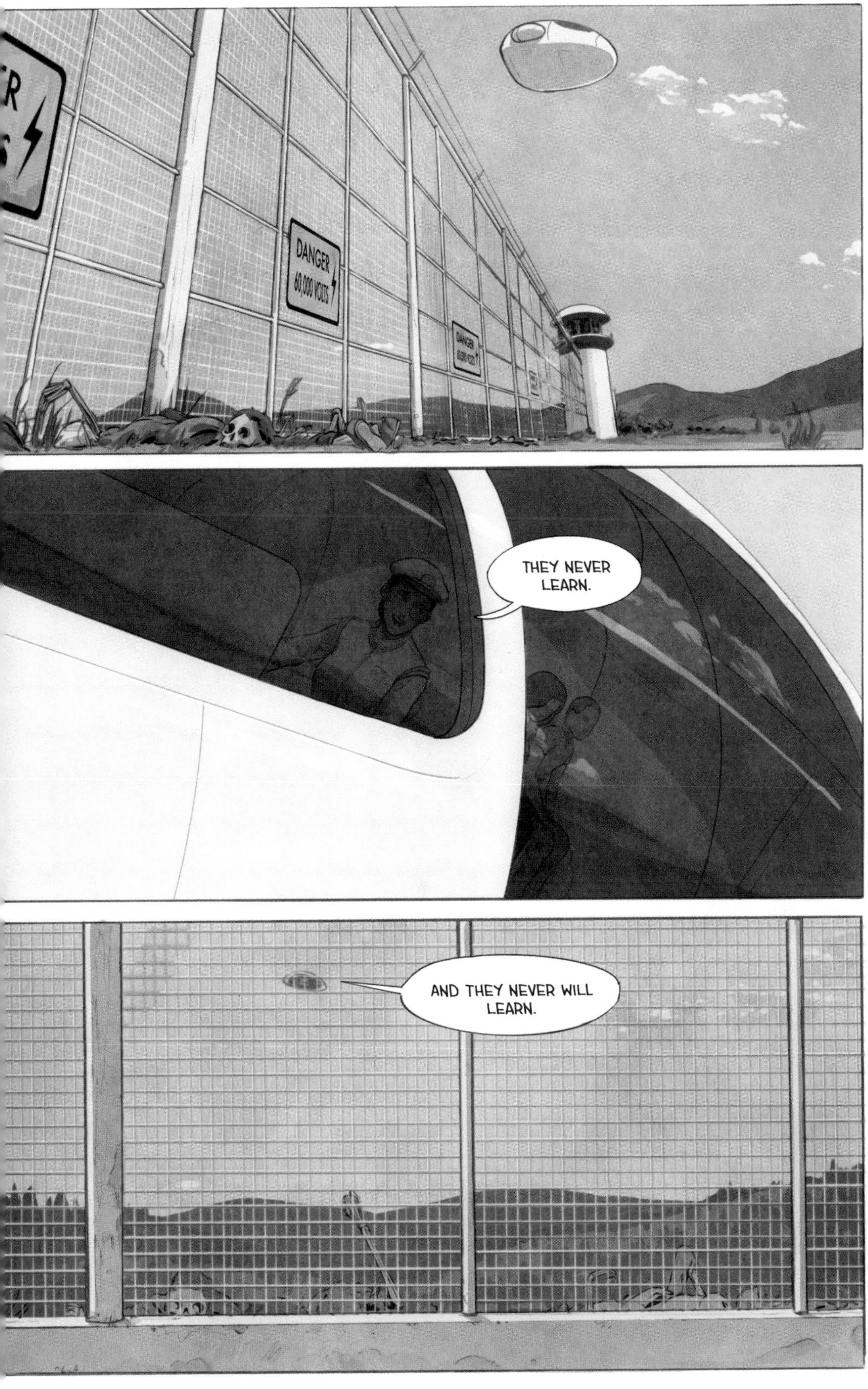
DANGER 60,000 VOLTS
THEY NEVER LEARN.
AND THEY NEVER WILL LEARN.

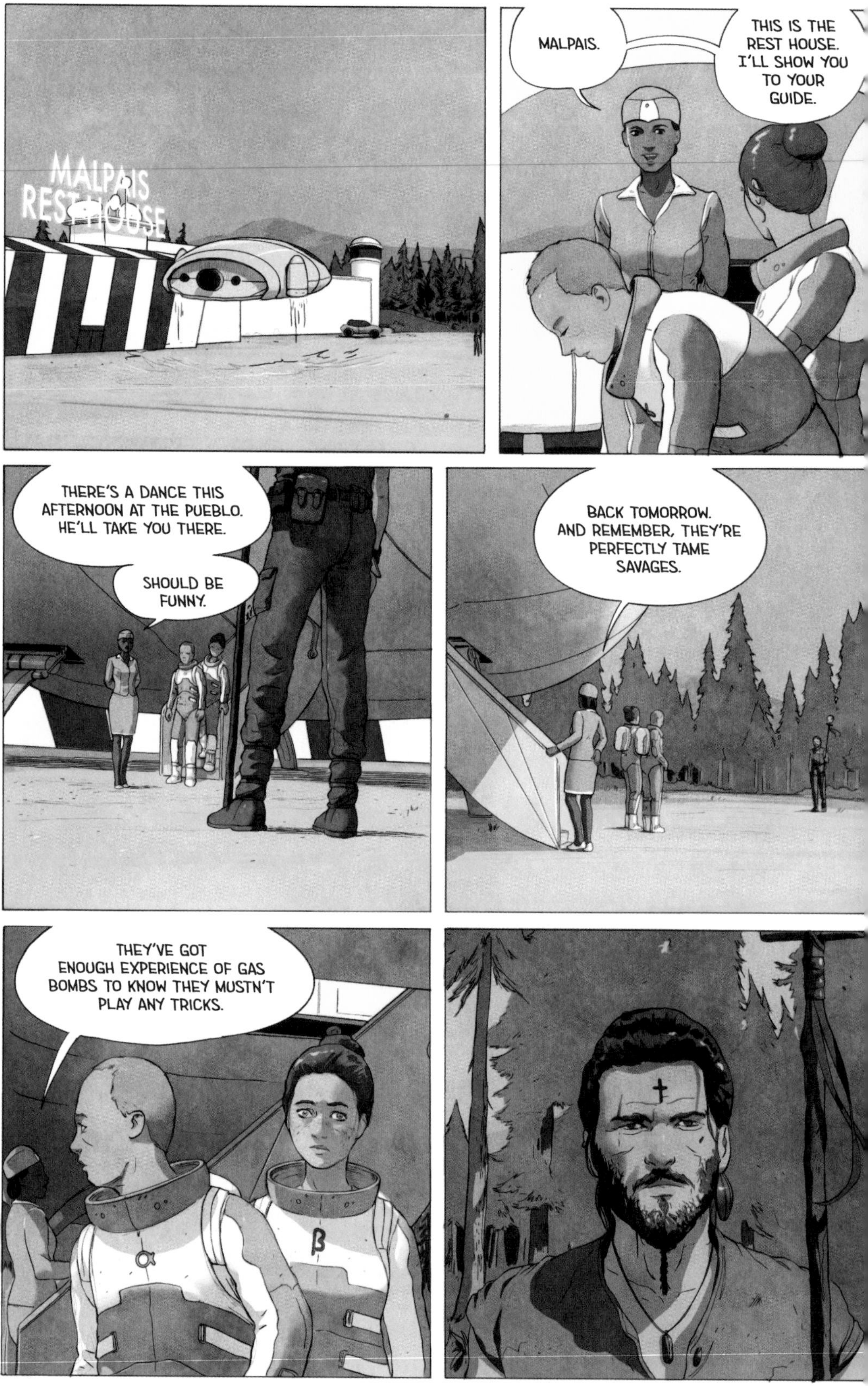
MALPAIS REST HOUSE
MALPAIS.
THIS IS THE REST HOUSE. I'LL SHOW YOU TO YOUR GUIDE.
THERE'S A DANCE THIS AFTERNOON AT THE PUEBLO. HE'LL TAKE YOU THERE.
SHOULD BE FUNNY.
BACK TOMORROW. AND REMEMBER, THEY'RE PERFECTLY TAME SAVAGES.
THEY'VE GOT ENOUGH EXPERIENCE OF GAS BOMBS TO KNOW THEY MUSTN'T PLAY ANY TRICKS.

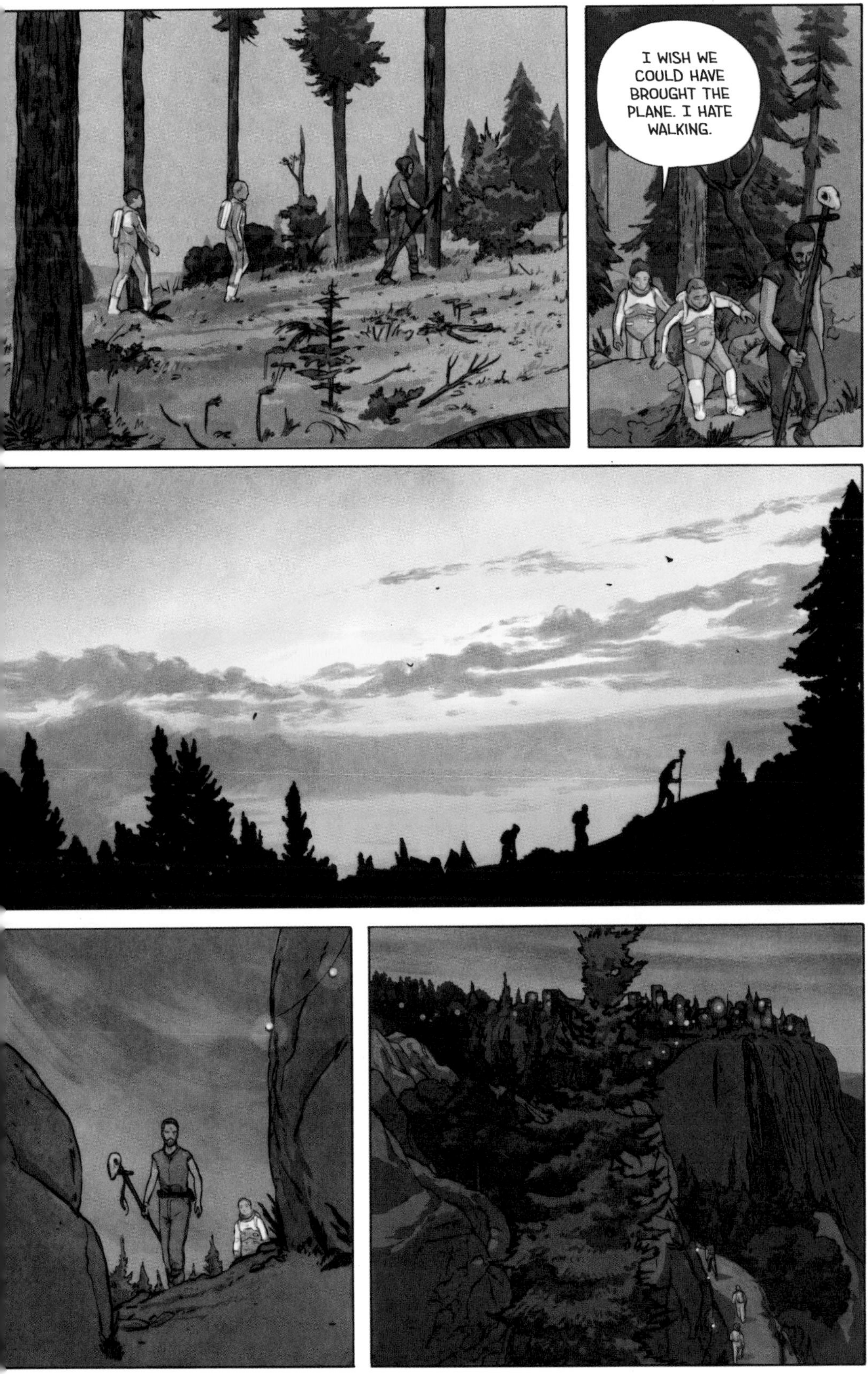
I WISH WE COULD HAVE BROUGHT THE PLANE. I HATE WALKING.

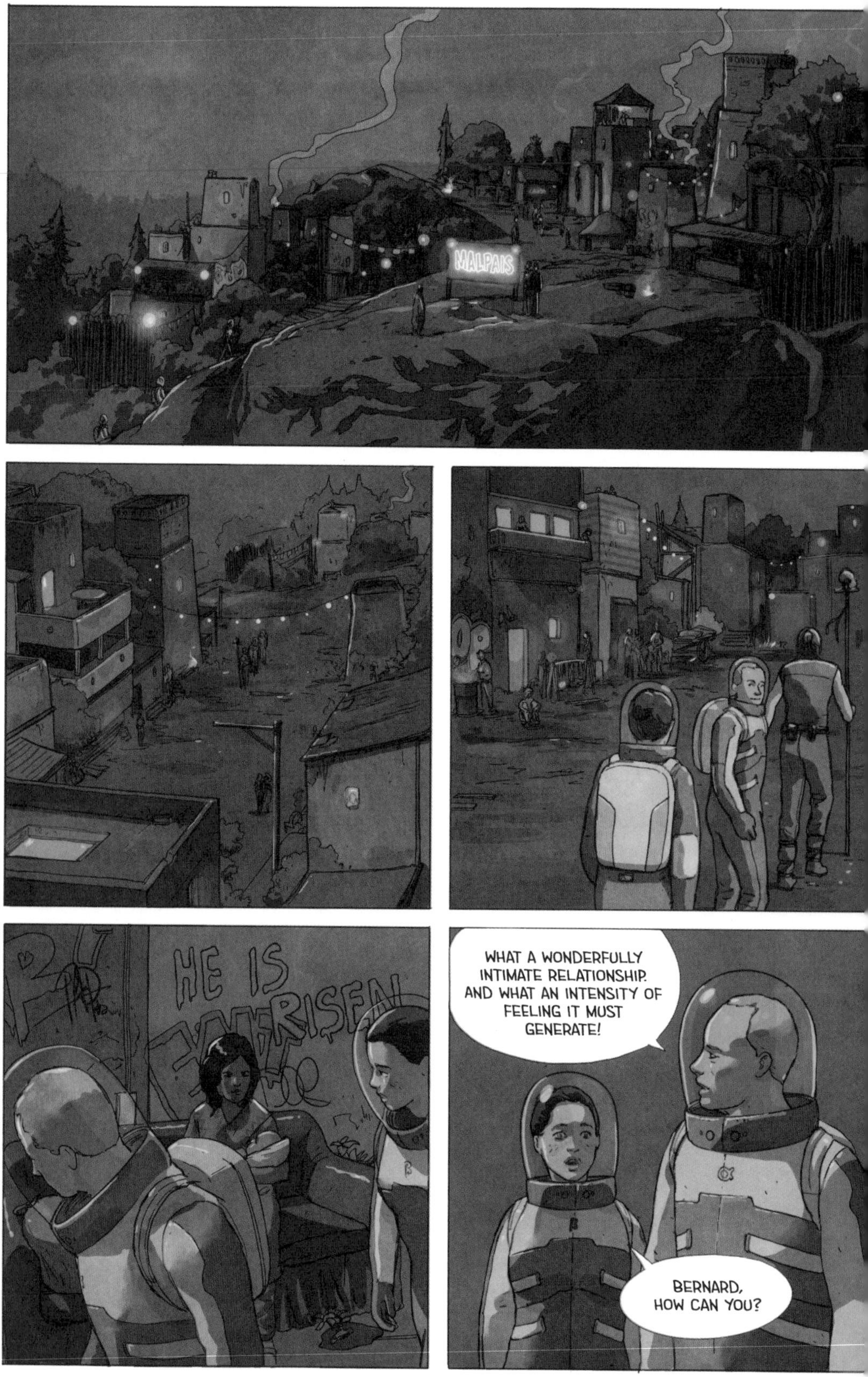
MALPAIS
HE IS RISEN
WHAT A WONDERFULLY INTIMATE RELATIONSHIP. AND WHAT AN INTENSITY OF FEELING IT MUST GENERATE!
BERNARD, HOW CAN YOU?

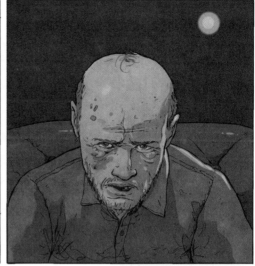

WHAT'S THE MATTER WITH HIM?

HE'S OLD, THAT'S ALL.

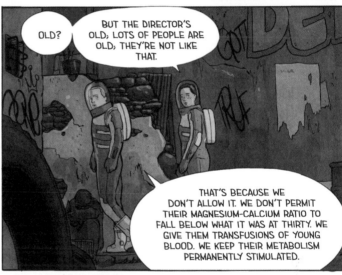

OLD?

BUT THE DIRECTOR'S OLD; LOTS OF PEOPLE ARE OLD; THEY'RE NOT LIKE THAT.

THAT'S BECAUSE WE DON'T ALLOW IT. WE DON'T PERMIT THEIR MAGNESIUM-CALCIUM RATIO TO FALL BELOW WHAT IT WAS AT THIRTY. WE GIVE THEM TRANSFUSIONS OF YOUNG BLOOD. WE KEEP THEIR METABOLISM PERMANENTLY STIMULATED.

YOUTH ALMOST UNIMPAIRED TILL SIXTY, AND THEN, CRACK! THE END.

BUT . . . HOW DO THEY LIVE LIKE THIS?

WE OUGHT NOT TO HAVE COME HERE.

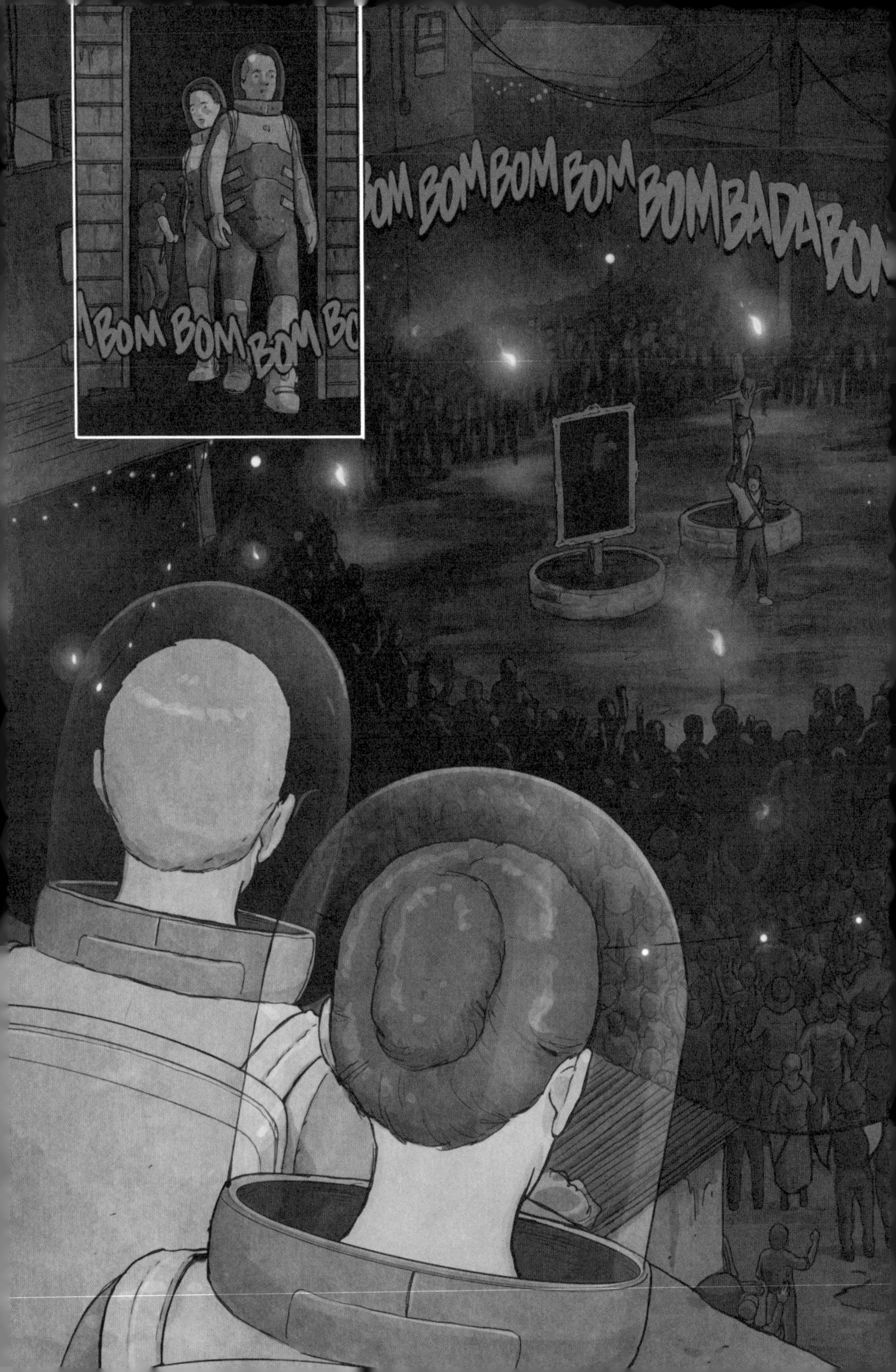
BOM BOM BOM BO
BOM BOM BOM BOM
BOMBADABOM

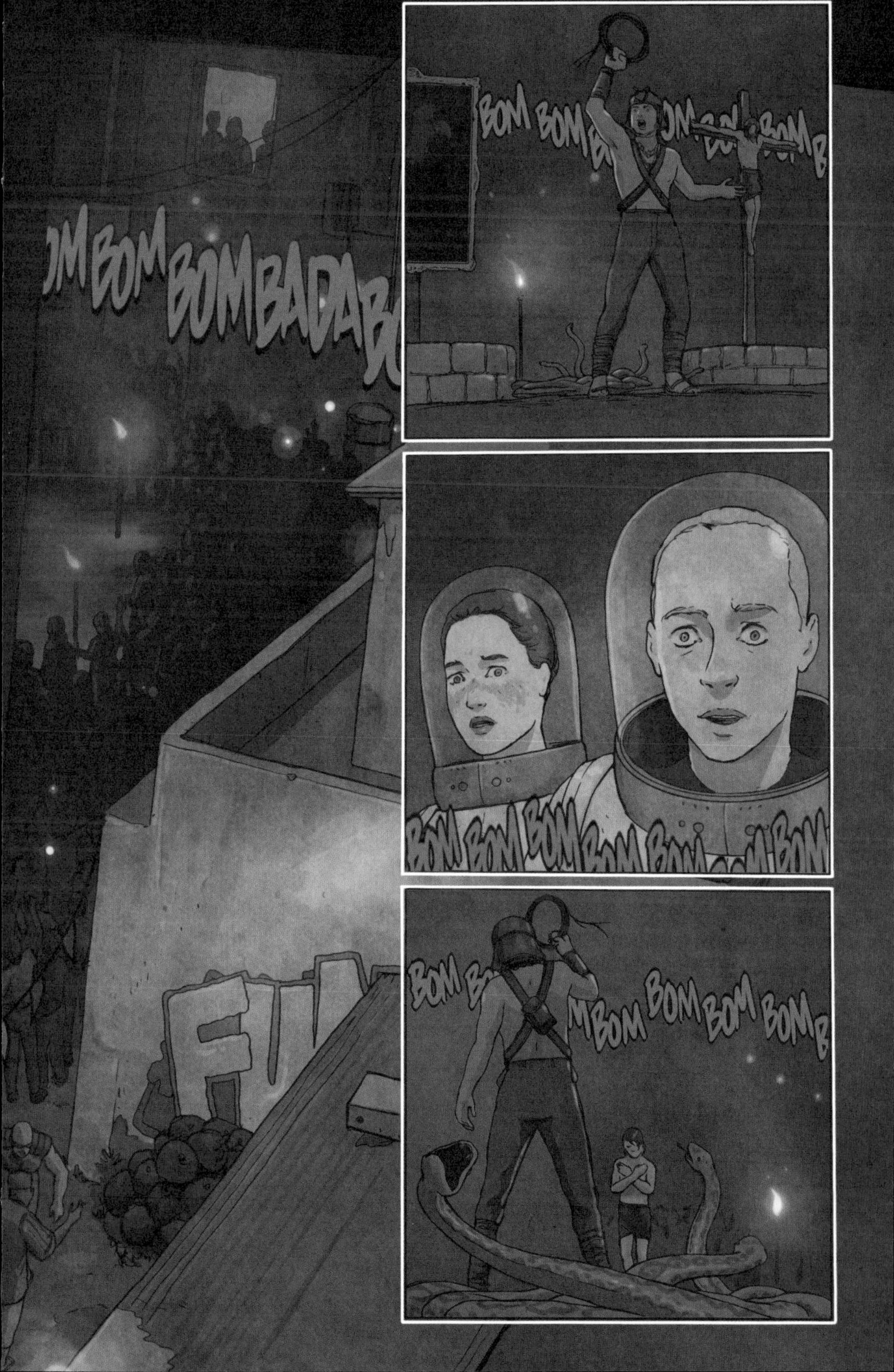
BOM BOMBADA
BOM BOM BOM
BOM BOM BOM BOM
BOM BOM BOM BOM BOM

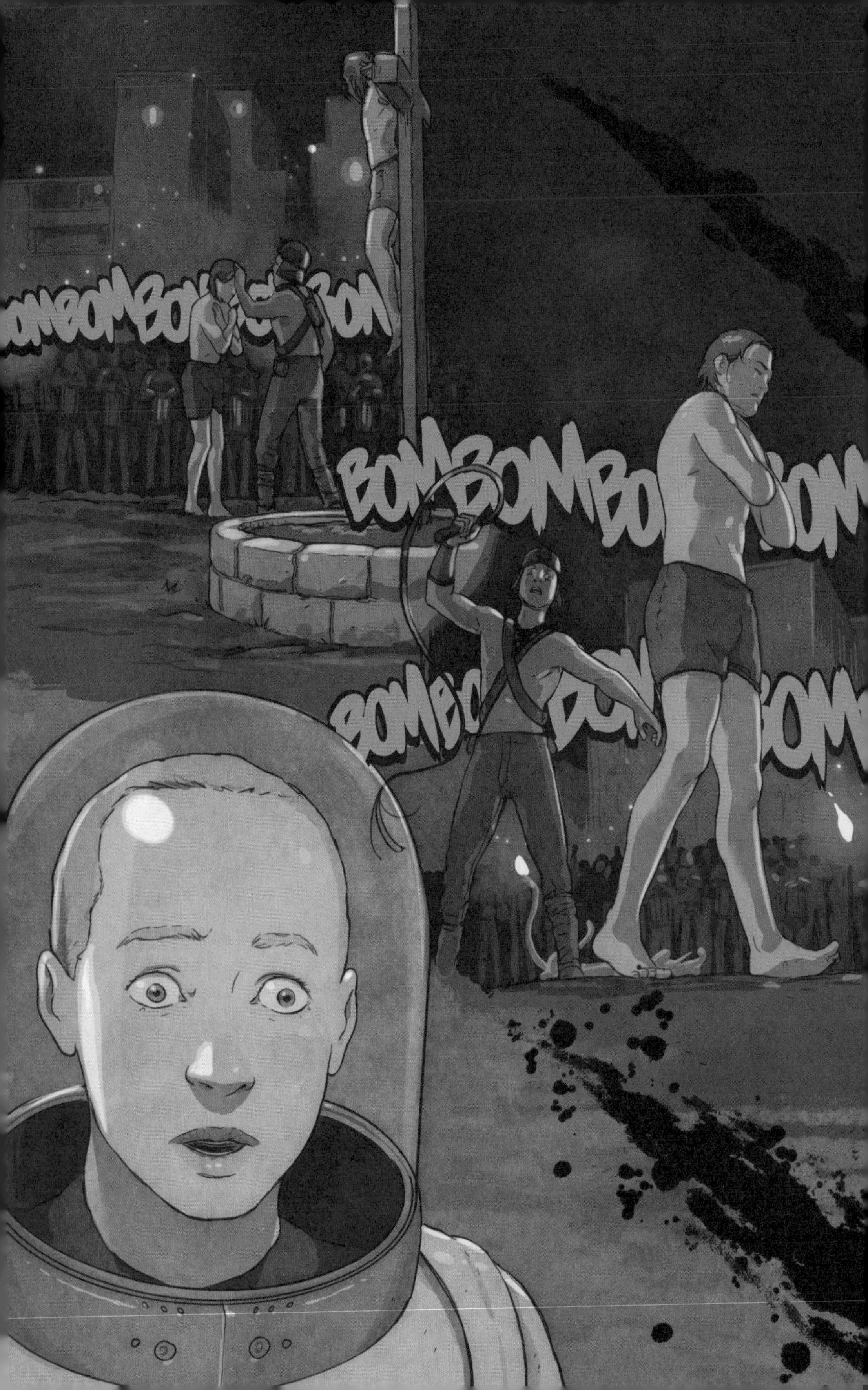

OMBOMBO
BOMBOMBO
BOM
BOMB
BOM

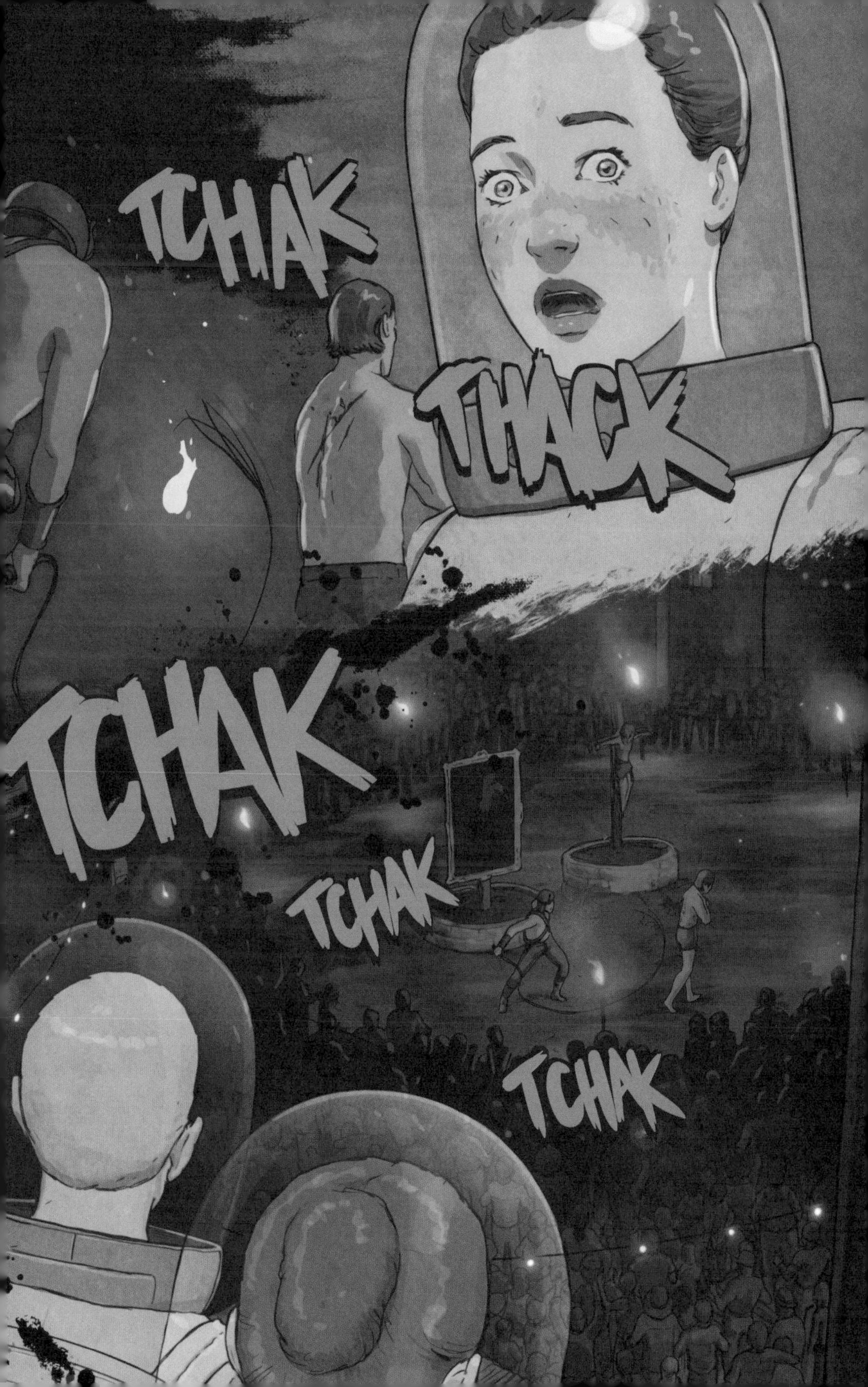
TCHAK
THACK
TCHAK
TCHAK
TCHAK

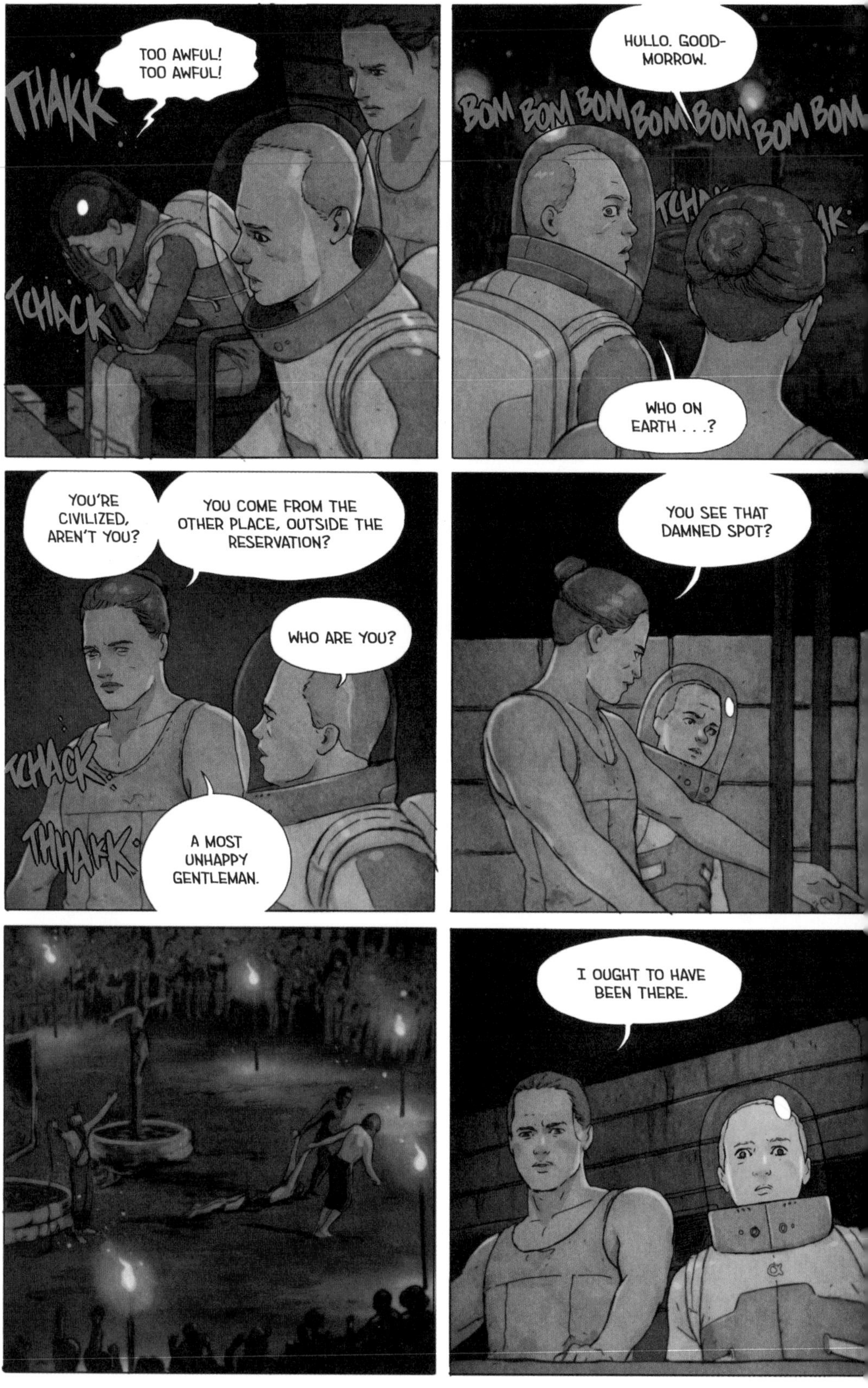
THAKK
TOO AWFUL! TOO AWFUL!
TCHACK
HULLO. GOOD-MORROW.
BOM BOM BOM BOM BOM BOM BOM
WHO ON EARTH . . .?
YOU'RE CIVILIZED, AREN'T YOU?
YOU COME FROM THE OTHER PLACE, OUTSIDE THE RESERVATION?
WHO ARE YOU?
TCHACK
THHAKK
A MOST UNHAPPY GENTLEMAN.
YOU SEE THAT DAMNED SPOT?
I OUGHT TO HAVE BEEN THERE.

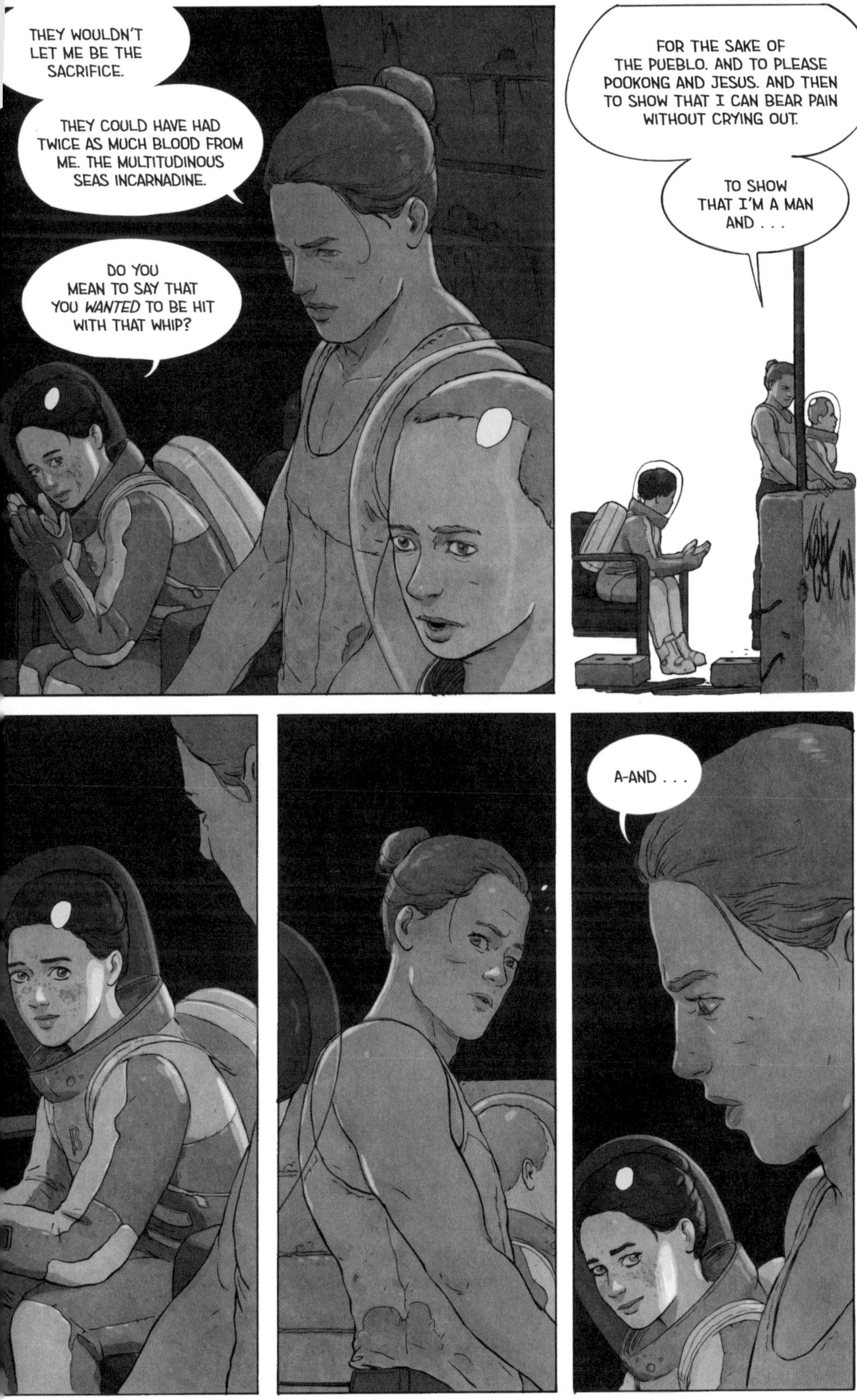
THEY WOULDN'T LET ME BE THE SACRIFICE.
THEY COULD HAVE HAD TWICE AS MUCH BLOOD FROM ME. THE MULTITUDINOUS SEAS INCARNADINE.
DO YOU MEAN TO SAY THAT YOU *WANTED* TO BE HIT WITH THAT WHIP?
FOR THE SAKE OF THE PUEBLO. AND TO PLEASE POOKONG AND JESUS. AND THEN TO SHOW THAT I CAN BEAR PAIN WITHOUT CRYING OUT.
TO SHOW THAT I'M A MAN AND . . .
A-AND . . .

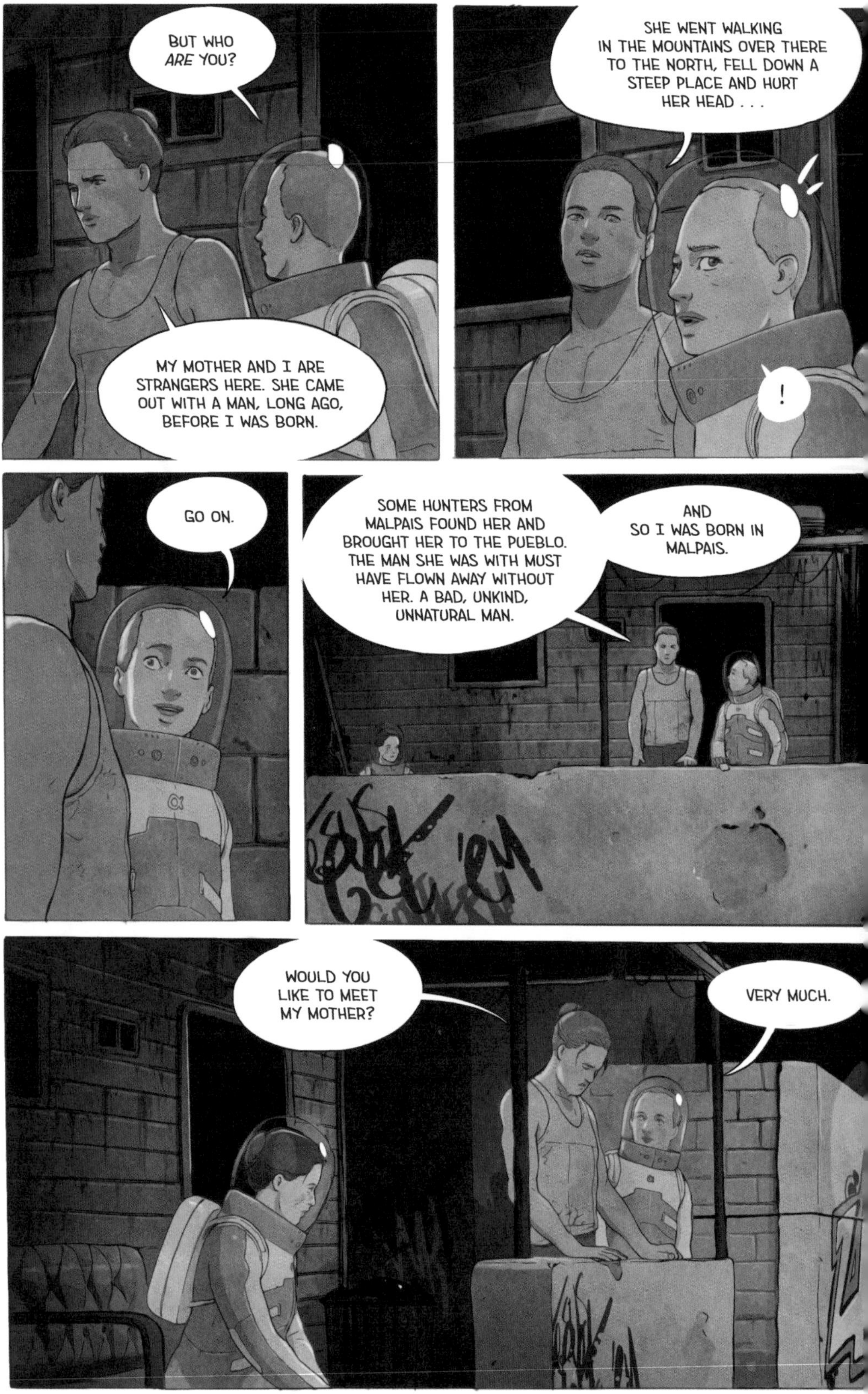
BUT WHO *ARE* YOU?
MY MOTHER AND I ARE STRANGERS HERE. SHE CAME OUT WITH A MAN, LONG AGO, BEFORE I WAS BORN.
SHE WENT WALKING IN THE MOUNTAINS OVER THERE TO THE NORTH, FELL DOWN A STEEP PLACE AND HURT HER HEAD . . .
!
GO ON.
SOME HUNTERS FROM MALPAIS FOUND HER AND BROUGHT HER TO THE PUEBLO. THE MAN SHE WAS WITH MUST HAVE FLOWN AWAY WITHOUT HER. A BAD, UNKIND, UNNATURAL MAN.
AND SO I WAS BORN IN MALPAIS.
WOULD YOU LIKE TO MEET MY MOTHER?
VERY MUCH.

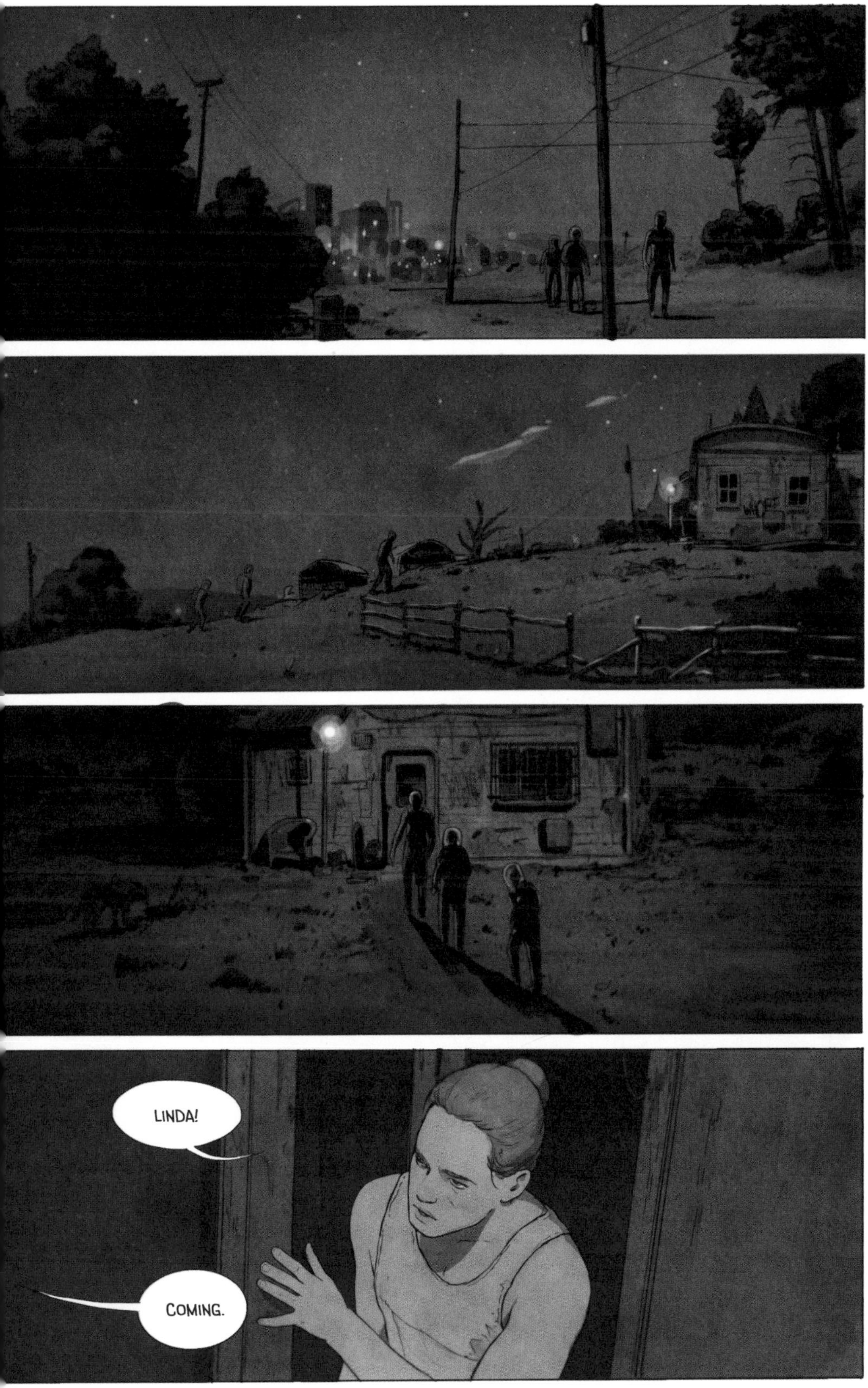
LINDA!
COMING.

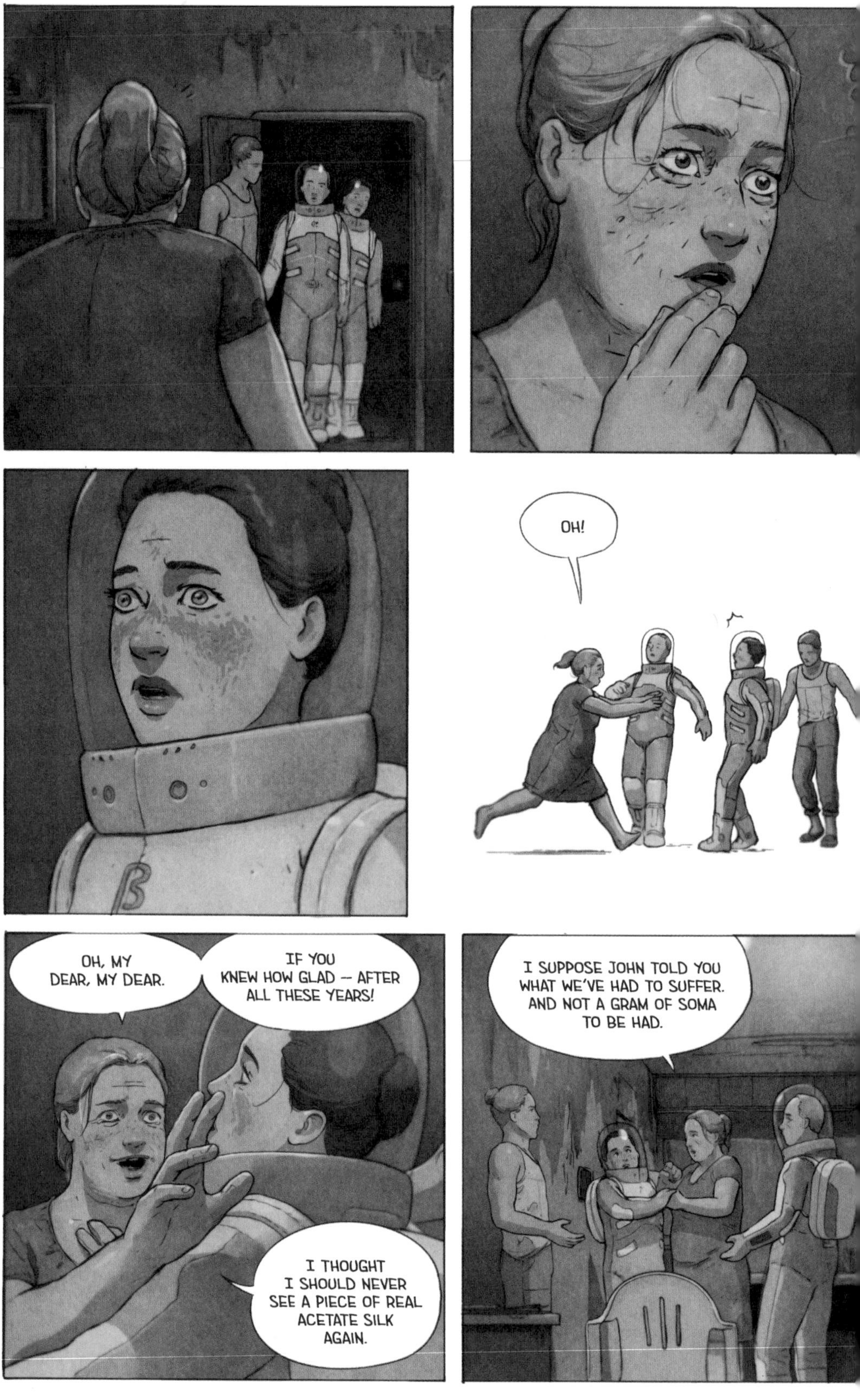
OH!
OH, MY DEAR, MY DEAR.
IF YOU KNEW HOW GLAD -- AFTER ALL THESE YEARS!
I THOUGHT I SHOULD NEVER SEE A PIECE OF REAL ACETATE SILK AGAIN.
I SUPPOSE JOHN TOLD YOU WHAT WE'VE HAD TO SUFFER. AND NOT A GRAM OF SOMA TO BE HAD.

ONLY A DRINK OF MESCAL EVERY NOW AND THEN, WHEN POPÉ USED TO BRING IT. POPÉ IS A BOY I USED TO KNOW.

BUT IT MAKES YOU FEEL SO BAD AFTERWARDS, THE MESCAL DOES.

AND I WAS SO ASHAMED. JUST THINK OF IT: ME, A BETA--HAVING A BABY. PUT YOURSELF IN MY PLACE.

I STILL DON'T KNOW HOW IT HAPPENED, SEEING THAT I DID ALL THE MALTHUSIAN DRILL.

AND OF COURSE THERE WASN'T ANYTHING LIKE THE CHELSEA ABORTION CENTER HERE.

AH, THAT LOVELY PINK GLASS TOWER!

AND THE RIVER AT NIGHT . . .

OH, I'M SO SORRY. I REMEMBER HOW IT USED TO UPSET ME, ALL THAT DIRT, AND NOTHING BEING ASEPTIC.

"CIVILIZATION IS STERILIZATION," I USED TO TELL THEM. AND "STREPTOCOCK-GEE TO BANBURY-T, TO SEE A FINE BATHROOM AND W.C." AS THOUGH THEY WERE CHILDREN.

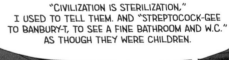

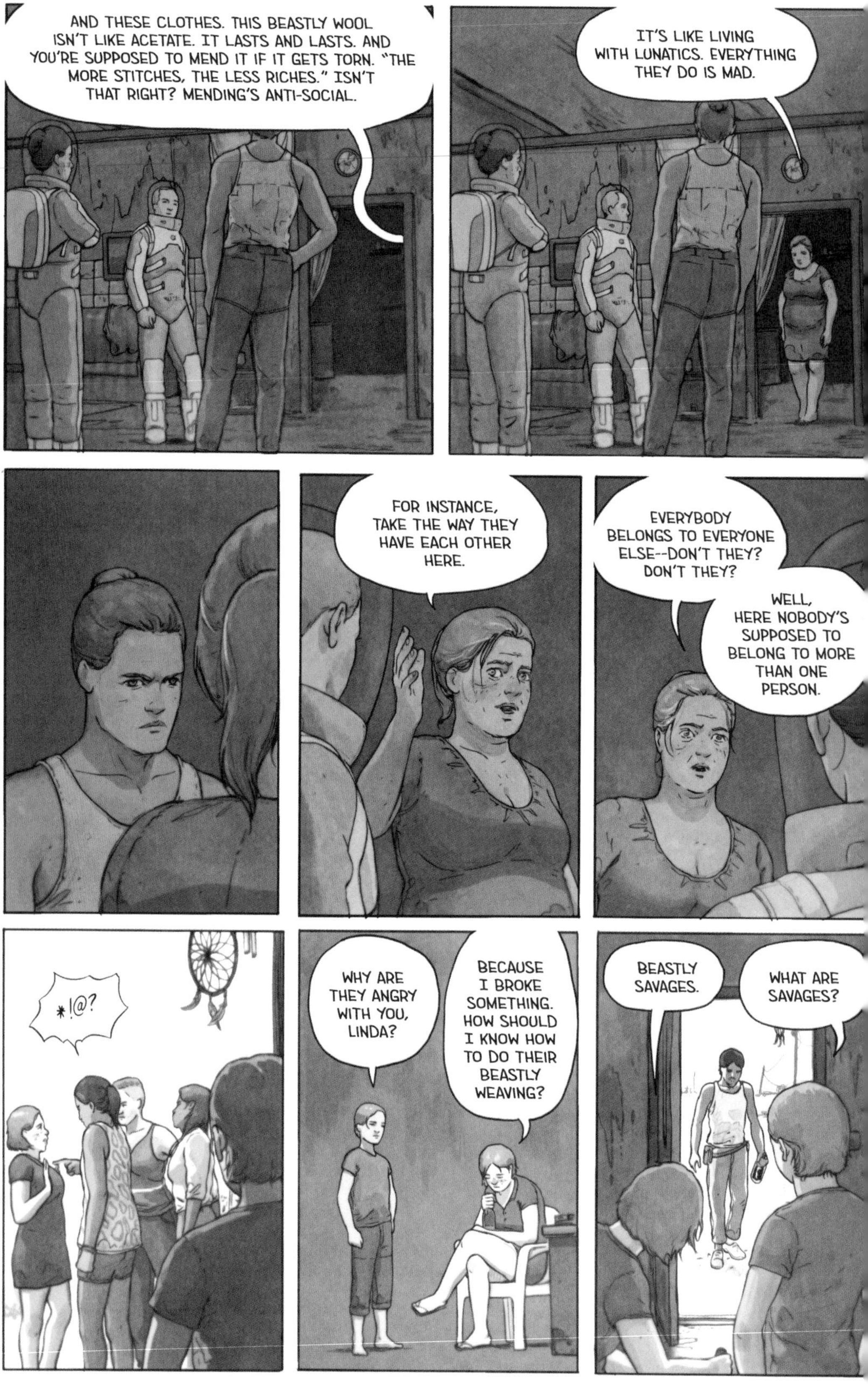

AND THESE CLOTHES. THIS BEASTLY WOOL ISN'T LIKE ACETATE. IT LASTS AND LASTS. AND YOU'RE SUPPOSED TO MEND IT IF IT GETS TORN. "THE MORE STITCHES, THE LESS RICHES." ISN'T THAT RIGHT? MENDING'S ANTI-SOCIAL.
IT'S LIKE LIVING WITH LUNATICS. EVERYTHING THEY DO IS MAD.
FOR INSTANCE, TAKE THE WAY THEY HAVE EACH OTHER HERE.
EVERYBODY BELONGS TO EVERYONE ELSE--DON'T THEY? DON'T THEY?
WELL, HERE NOBODY'S SUPPOSED TO BELONG TO MORE THAN ONE PERSON.
*!@?
WHY ARE THEY ANGRY WITH YOU, LINDA?
BECAUSE I BROKE SOMETHING. HOW SHOULD I KNOW HOW TO DO THEIR BEASTLY WEAVING?
BEASTLY SAVAGES.
WHAT ARE SAVAGES?

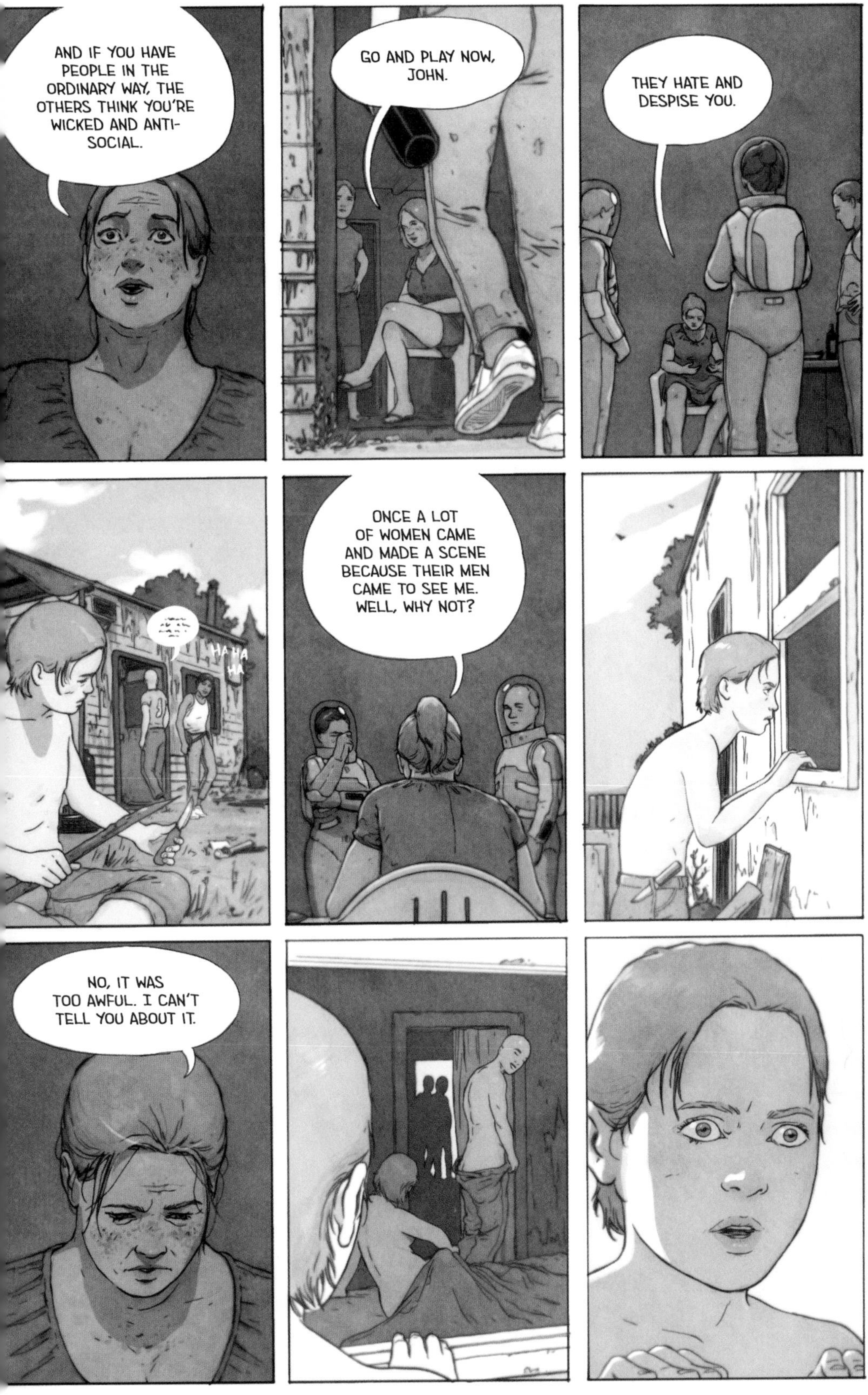
AND IF YOU HAVE PEOPLE IN THE ORDINARY WAY, THE OTHERS THINK YOU'RE WICKED AND ANTI-SOCIAL.
GO AND PLAY NOW, JOHN.
THEY HATE AND DESPISE YOU.
HA HA HA
ONCE A LOT OF WOMEN CAME AND MADE A SCENE BECAUSE THEIR MEN CAME TO SEE ME. WELL, WHY NOT?
NO, IT WAS TOO AWFUL. I CAN'T TELL YOU ABOUT IT.

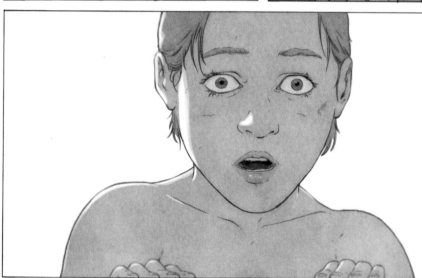

THEY'RE SO HATEFUL, THE WOMEN HERE.

MAD.

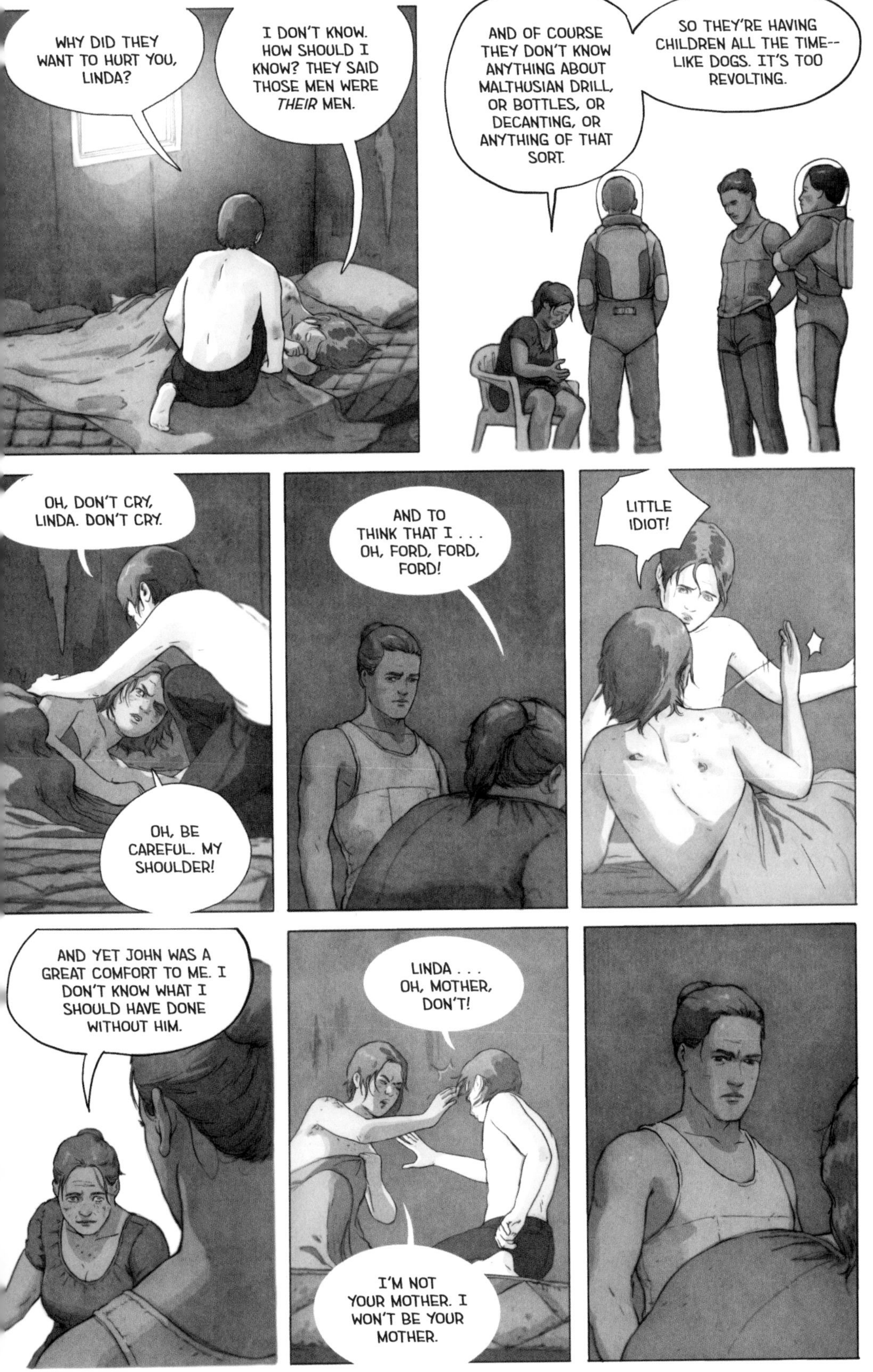

WHY DID THEY WANT TO HURT YOU, LINDA?
I DON'T KNOW. HOW SHOULD I KNOW? THEY SAID THOSE MEN WERE *THEIR* MEN.
AND OF COURSE THEY DON'T KNOW ANYTHING ABOUT MALTHUSIAN DRILL, OR BOTTLES, OR DECANTING, OR ANYTHING OF THAT SORT.
SO THEY'RE HAVING CHILDREN ALL THE TIME-- LIKE DOGS. IT'S TOO REVOLTING.
OH, DON'T CRY, LINDA. DON'T CRY.
OH, BE CAREFUL. MY SHOULDER!
AND TO THINK THAT I . . . OH, FORD, FORD, FORD!
LITTLE IDIOT!
AND YET JOHN WAS A GREAT COMFORT TO ME. I DON'T KNOW WHAT I SHOULD HAVE DONE WITHOUT HIM.
LINDA . . . OH, MOTHER, DON'T!
I'M NOT YOUR MOTHER. I WON'T BE YOUR MOTHER.

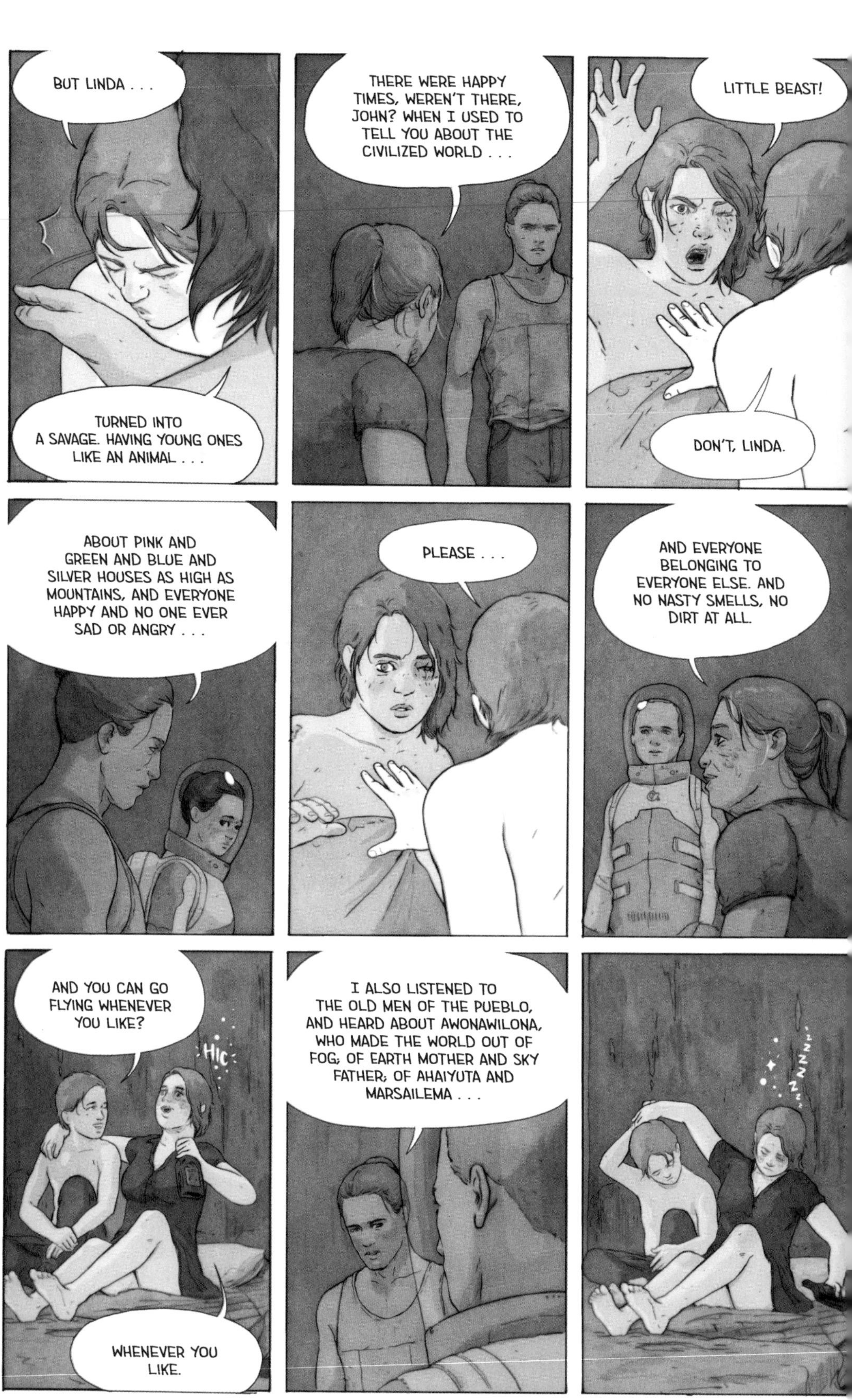
BUT LINDA . . .
TURNED INTO A SAVAGE. HAVING YOUNG ONES LIKE AN ANIMAL . . .
THERE WERE HAPPY TIMES, WEREN'T THERE, JOHN? WHEN I USED TO TELL YOU ABOUT THE CIVILIZED WORLD . . .
LITTLE BEAST!
DON'T, LINDA.
ABOUT PINK AND GREEN AND BLUE AND SILVER HOUSES AS HIGH AS MOUNTAINS, AND EVERYONE HAPPY AND NO ONE EVER SAD OR ANGRY . . .
PLEASE . . .
AND EVERYONE BELONGING TO EVERYONE ELSE. AND NO NASTY SMELLS, NO DIRT AT ALL.
AND YOU CAN GO FLYING WHENEVER YOU LIKE?
HIC
WHENEVER YOU LIKE.
I ALSO LISTENED TO THE OLD MEN OF THE PUEBLO, AND HEARD ABOUT AWONAWILONA, WHO MADE THE WORLD OUT OF FOG; OF EARTH MOTHER AND SKY FATHER; OF AHAIYUTA AND MARSAILEMA . . .
ZZZ

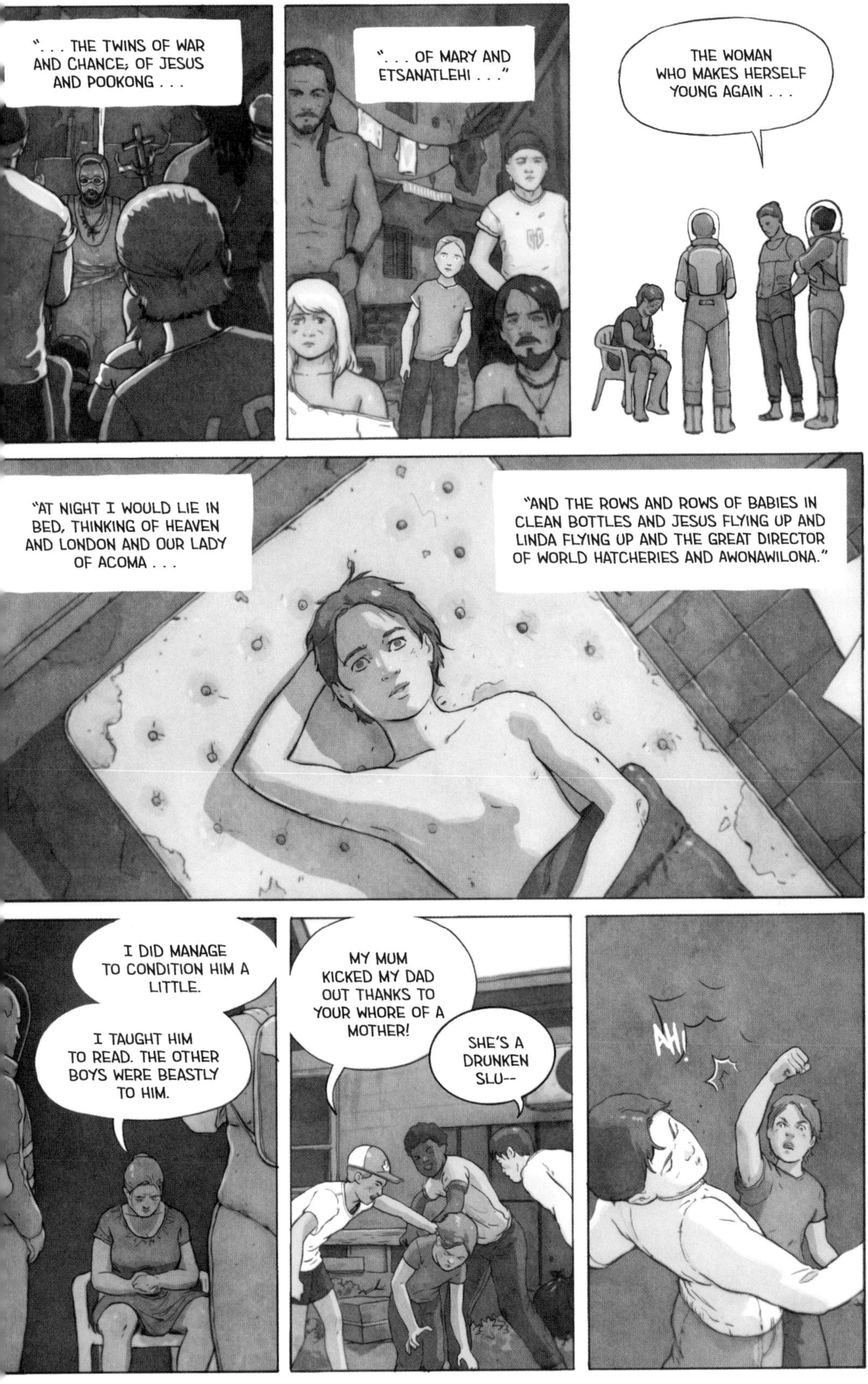
". . . THE TWINS OF WAR AND CHANCE; OF JESUS AND POOKONG . . .
". . . OF MARY AND ETSANATLEHI . . ."
THE WOMAN WHO MAKES HERSELF YOUNG AGAIN . . .
"AT NIGHT I WOULD LIE IN BED, THINKING OF HEAVEN AND LONDON AND OUR LADY OF ACOMA . . .
"AND THE ROWS AND ROWS OF BABIES IN CLEAN BOTTLES AND JESUS FLYING UP AND LINDA FLYING UP AND THE GREAT DIRECTOR OF WORLD HATCHERIES AND AWONAWILONA."
I DID MANAGE TO CONDITION HIM A LITTLE.
I TAUGHT HIM TO READ. THE OTHER BOYS WERE BEASTLY TO HIM.
MY MUM KICKED MY DAD OUT THANKS TO YOUR WHORE OF A MOTHER!
SHE'S A DRUNKEN SLU--
AH!

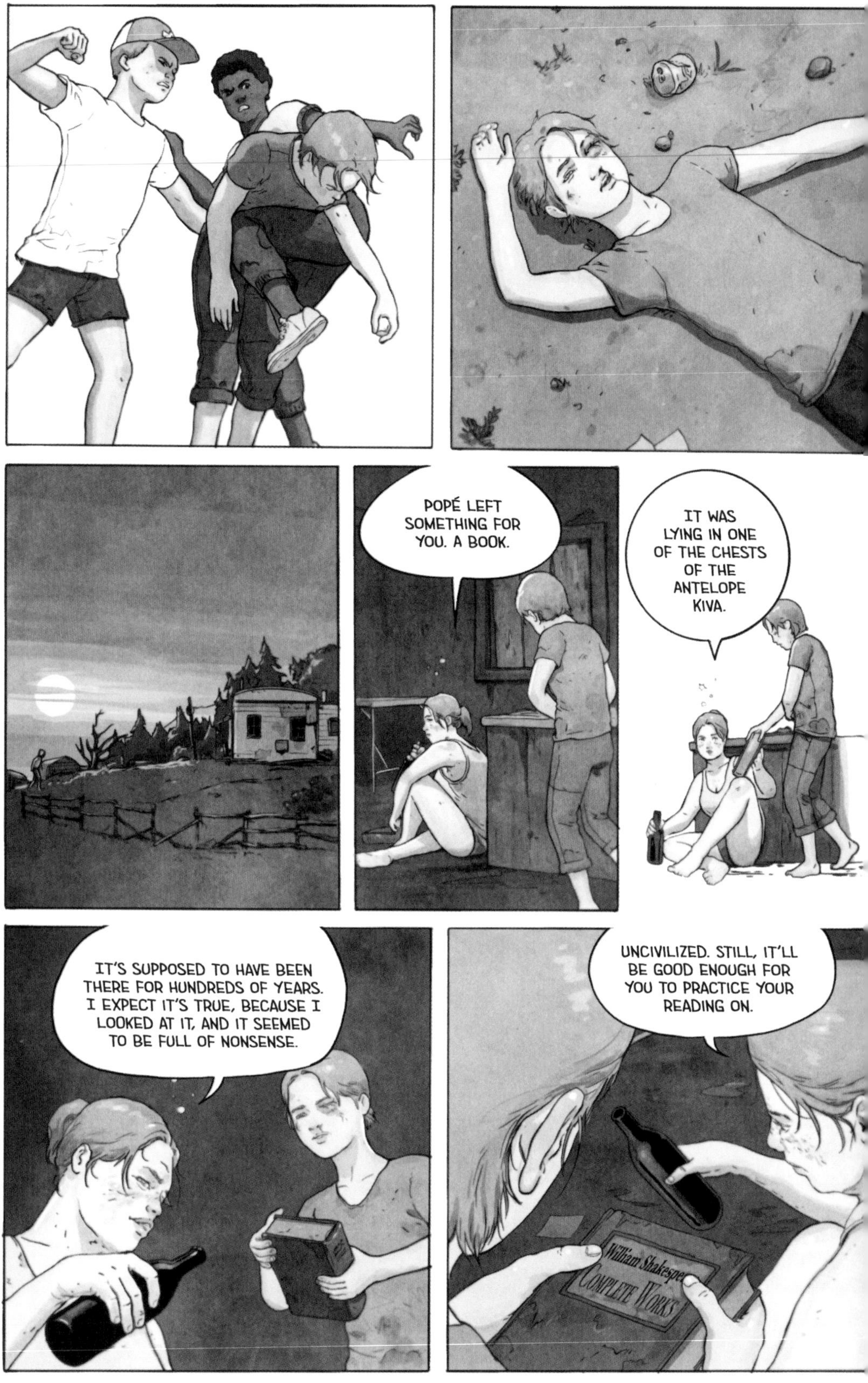
POPÉ LEFT SOMETHING FOR YOU. A BOOK.
IT WAS LYING IN ONE OF THE CHESTS OF THE ANTELOPE KIVA.
IT'S SUPPOSED TO HAVE BEEN THERE FOR HUNDREDS OF YEARS. I EXPECT IT'S TRUE, BECAUSE I LOOKED AT IT, AND IT SEEMED TO BE FULL OF NONSENSE.
UNCIVILIZED. STILL, IT'LL BE GOOD ENOUGH FOR YOU TO PRACTICE YOUR READING ON.
William Shakespe
COMPLETE WORKS

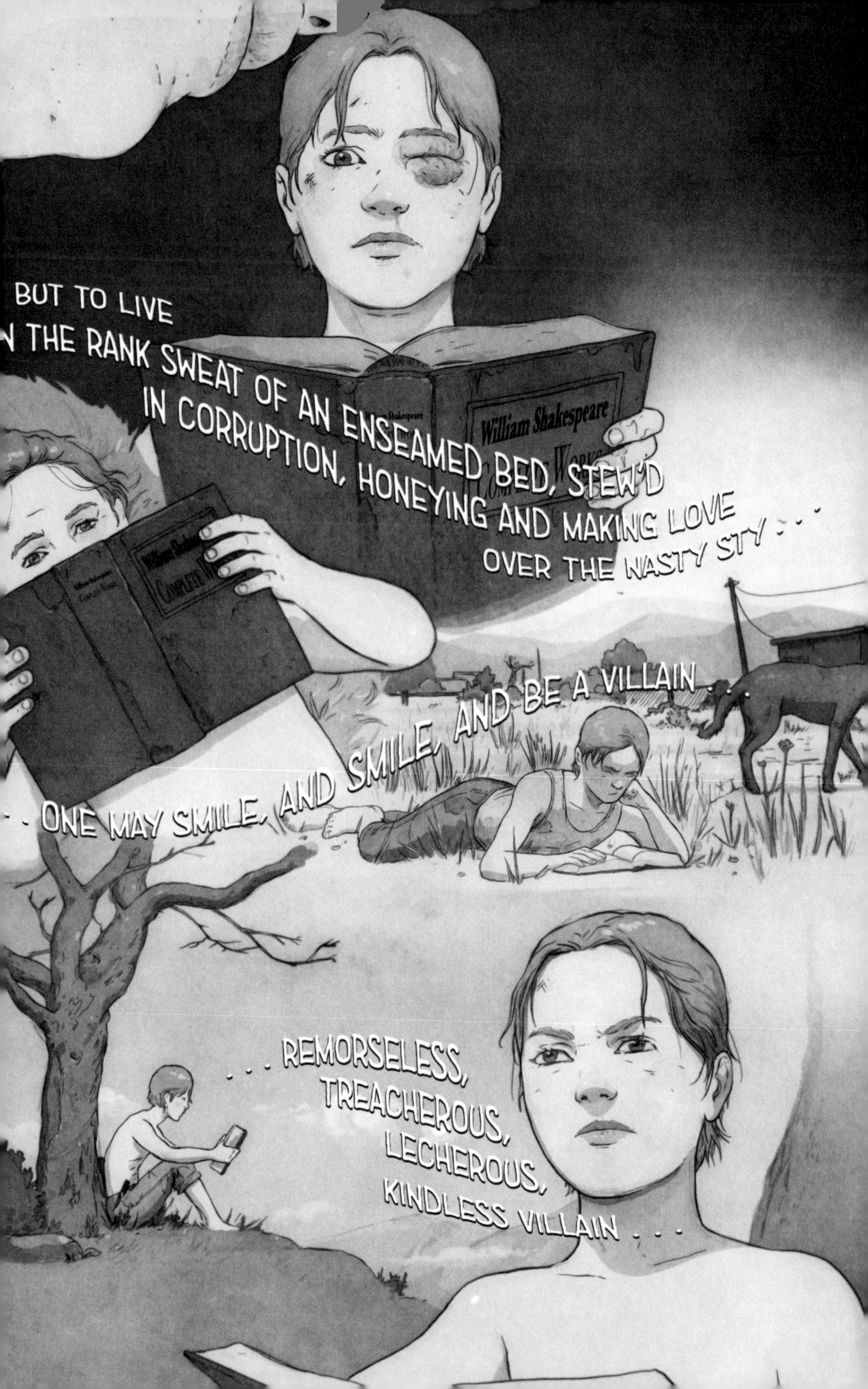
BUT TO LIVE
N THE RANK SWEAT OF AN ENSEAMED BED, STEW'D
IN CORRUPTION, HONEYING AND MAKING LOVE
OVER THE NASTY STY . . .
William Shakespeare
. . . ONE MAY SMILE, AND SMILE, AND BE A VILLAIN . . .
. . . REMORSELESS,
TREACHEROUS,
LECHEROUS,
KINDLESS VILLAIN . . .

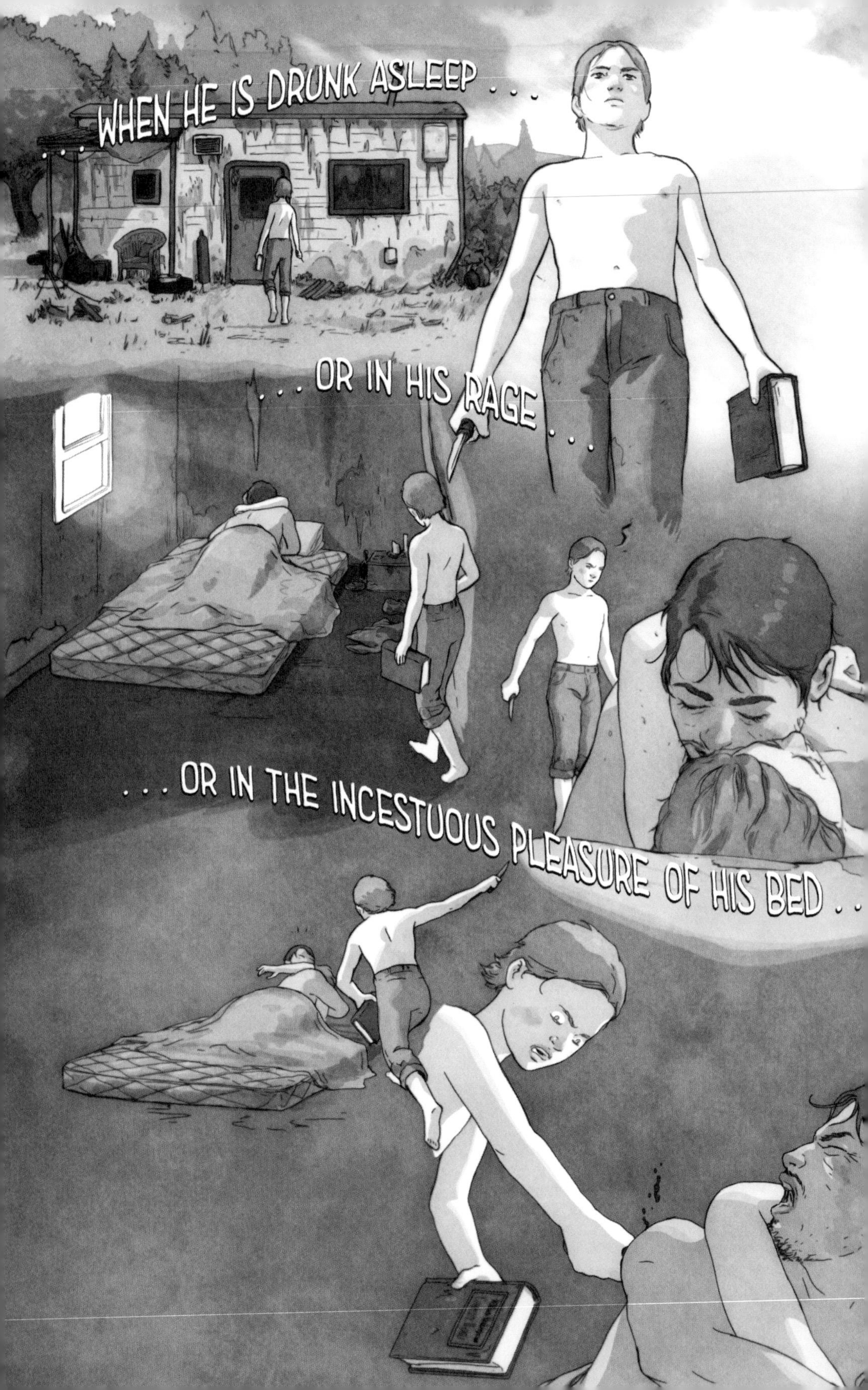
. . . WHEN HE IS DRUNK ASLEEP . . .
. . . OR IN HIS RAGE . . .
. . . OR IN THE INCESTUOUS PLEASURE OF HIS BED . . .

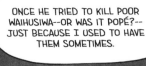

ONCE HE TRIED TO KILL POOR WAIHUSIWA--OR WAS IT POPÉ?-- JUST BECAUSE I USED TO HAVE THEM SOMETIMES.

I NEVER COULD MAKE HIM UNDERSTAND THAT THAT WAS WHAT CIVILIZED PEOPLE OUGHT TO DO.

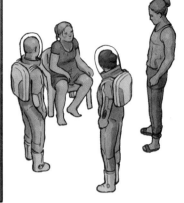

HOW WOULD YOU LIKE TO COME BACK TO LONDON WITH US?

DO YOU REALLY MEAN IT?

OF COURSE, IF I CAN GET PERMISSION, THAT IS.

TO THINK IT SHOULD BE COMING TRUE--WHAT I'VE DREAMED OF ALL MY LIFE.

DO YOU REMEMBER WHAT MIRANDA SAYS?

WHO'S MIRANDA?

O WONDER! HOW MANY GOODLY CREATURES ARE THERE HERE! HOW BEAUTEOUS MANKIND IS!

O BRAVE NEW WORLD. O BRAVE NEW WORLD THAT HAS SUCH PEOPLE IN IT!

YOU HAVE A MOST PECULIAR WAY OF TALKING SOMETIMES. AND, ANYHOW, HADN'T YOU BETTER WAIT TILL YOU ACTUALLY SEE THE NEW WORLD?

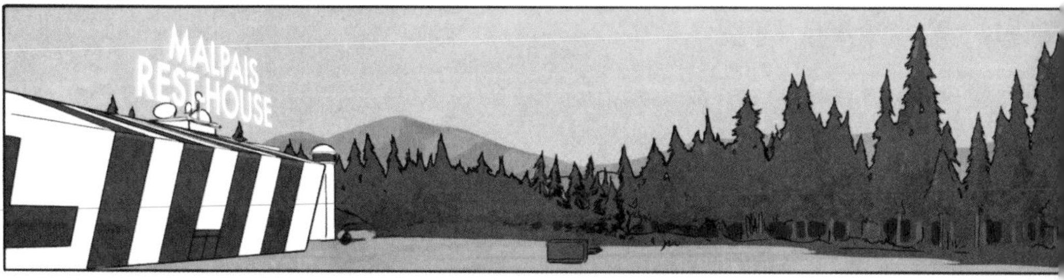
MALPAIS REST-HOUSE

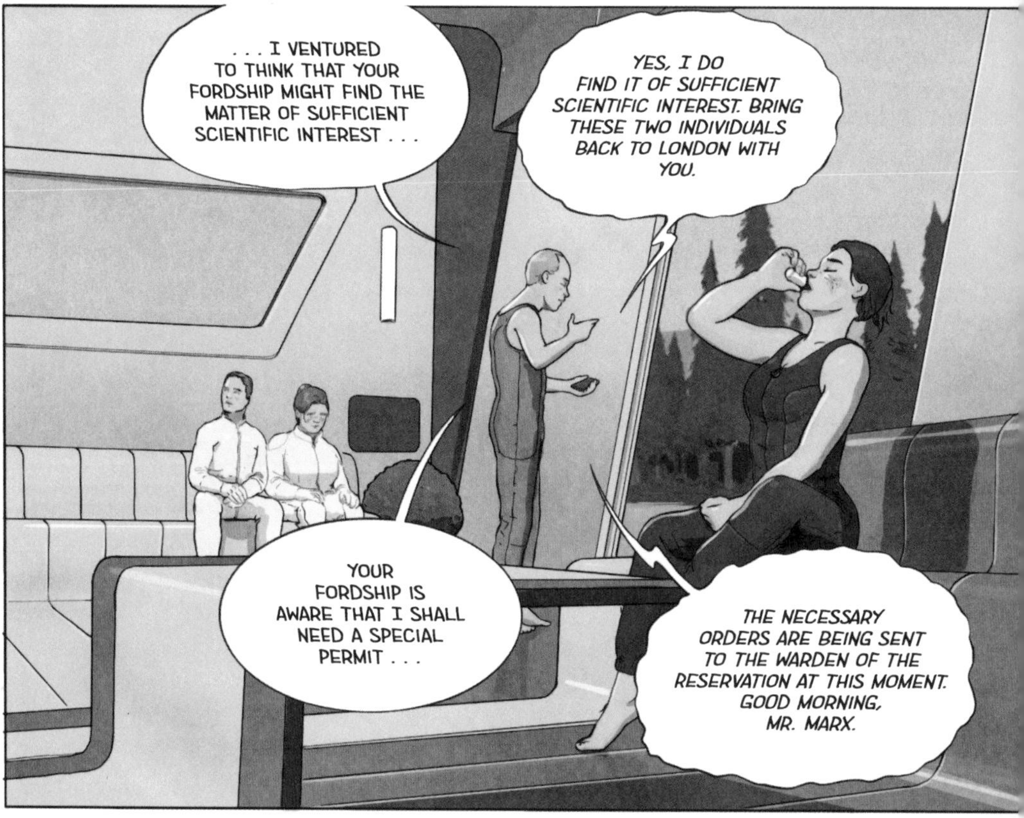
. . . I VENTURED TO THINK THAT YOUR FORDSHIP MIGHT FIND THE MATTER OF SUFFICIENT SCIENTIFIC INTEREST . . .
YES, I DO FIND IT OF SUFFICIENT SCIENTIFIC INTEREST. BRING THESE TWO INDIVIDUALS BACK TO LONDON WITH YOU.
YOUR FORDSHIP IS AWARE THAT I SHALL NEED A SPECIAL PERMIT . . .
THE NECESSARY ORDERS ARE BEING SENT TO THE WARDEN OF THE RESERVATION AT THIS MOMENT. GOOD MORNING, MR. MARX.

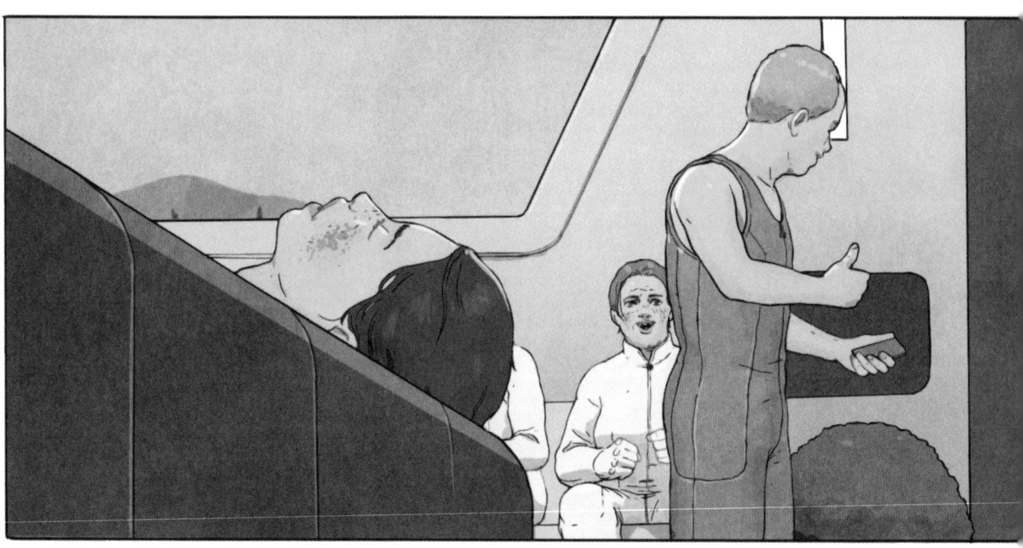

MR. MARX, WE HAVE JUST RECEIVED SPECIAL ORDERS . . .

I KNOW, I WAS TALKING TO THE CONTROLLER A MOMENT AGO.

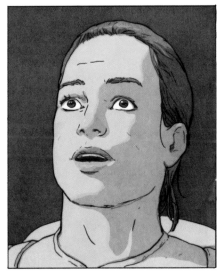

MISS CROWNE'S GONE ON SOMA HOLIDAY. CAN HARDLY BE BACK BEFORE FIVE.

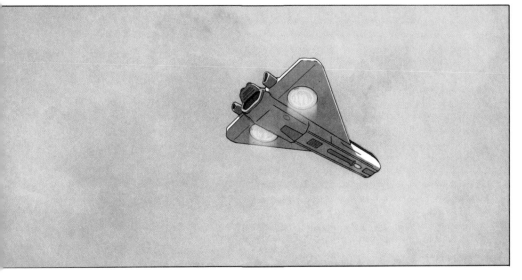

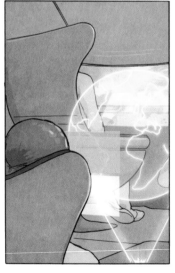

YOU ARE FIFTEEN. NOW I MAY TEACH YOU TO WORK THE CLAY.

FIRST OF ALL, WE MAKE A LITTLE MOON.

A MOON, A CUP, AND NOW A SNAKE. THEN ANOTHER SNAKE. AND ANOTHER.

HA HA HA HA HA HA HA HA HA

THE NEXT ONE WILL BE BETTER.

NEXT WINTER I WILL TEACH YOU TO MAKE THE BOW.

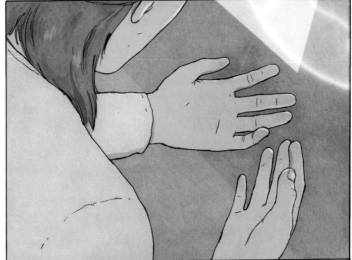

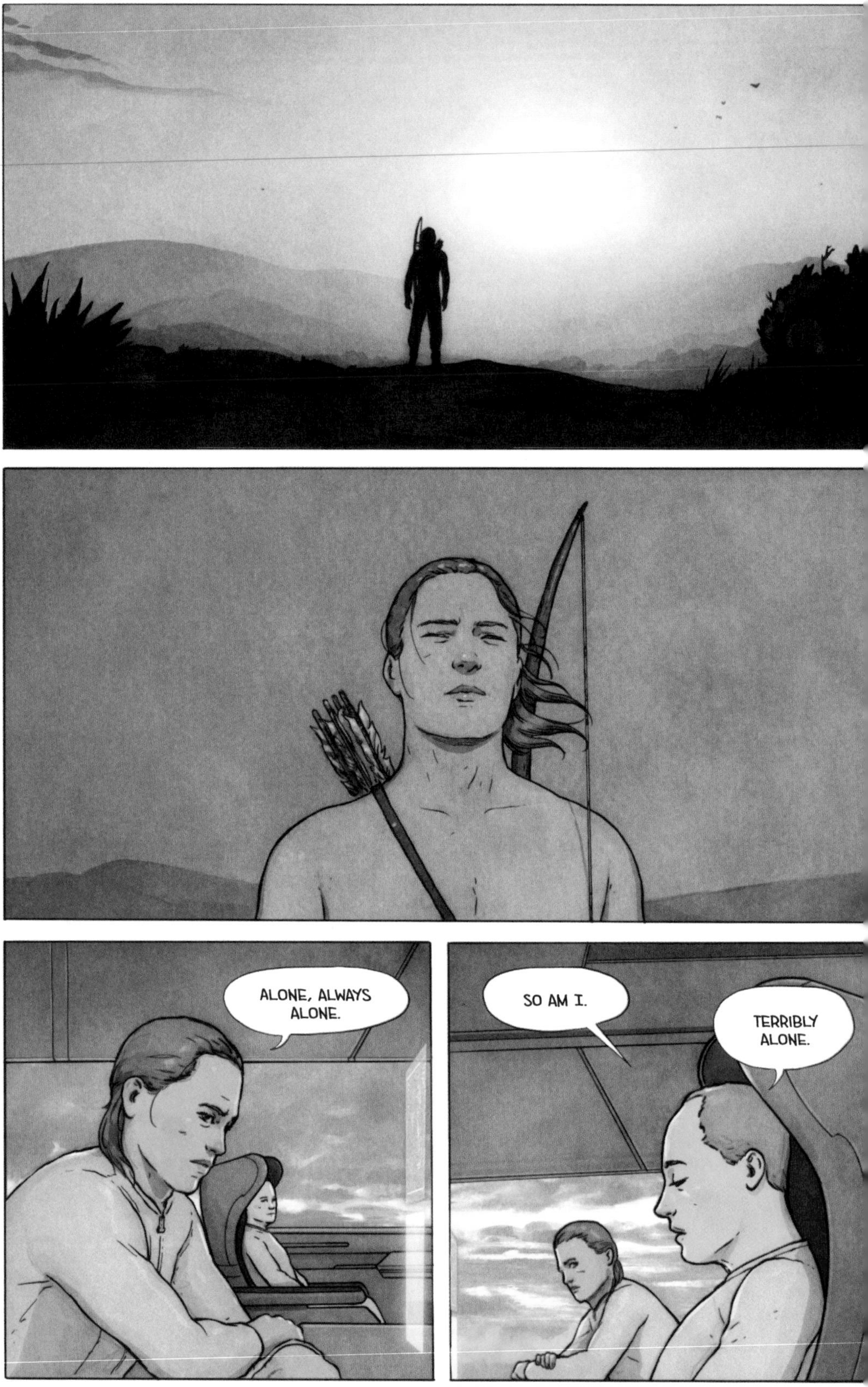
ALONE, ALWAYS ALONE.
SO AM I.
TERRIBLY ALONE.

ARE YOU?

I THOUGHT THAT IN THE OTHER PLACE . . . I MEAN, LINDA ALWAYS SAID THAT NOBODY WAS EVER ALONE THERE.

I'M . . . RATHER DIFFERENT FROM MOST PEOPLE, I SUPPOSE.

IF ONE HAPPENS TO BE DECANTED DIFFERENT . . .

YES, THAT'S JUST IT. IF ONE'S DIFFERENT, ONE'S BOUND TO BE LONELY.

WHEN THE OTHER BOYS WERE SENT OUT TO SPEND THE NIGHT ON THE MOUNTAINS--YOU KNOW, WHEN YOU HAVE TO DREAM WHICH YOUR SACRED ANIMAL IS--THEY WOULDN'T LET ME GO.

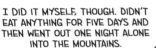

I DID IT MYSELF, THOUGH. DIDN'T EAT ANYTHING FOR FIVE DAYS AND THEN WENT OUT ONE NIGHT ALONE INTO THE MOUNTAINS.

AND DID YOU DREAM OF ANYTHING?

YES. BUT I MUSTN'T TELL YOU WHAT.

ONCE I DID SOMETHING THAT NONE OF THE OTHERS DID: I STOOD ON A ROCK IN THE MIDDLE OF THE DAY, IN SUMMER, WITH MY ARMS OUT, LIKE JESUS ON THE CROSS.

WHAT ON EARTH FOR?

I WANTED TO KNOW WHAT IT WAS LIKE BEING CRUCIFIED. HANGING THERE IN THE SUN.

BUT WHY?

WHY? WELL . . . BECAUSE I FELT I OUGHT TO. IF JESUS COULD STAND IT.

BESIDES, I WAS UNHAPPY; THAT WAS ANOTHER REASON.

IT SEEMS A FUNNY WAY OF CURING YOUR UNHAPPINESS . . .

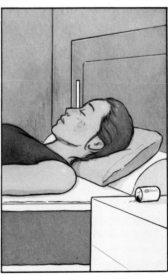

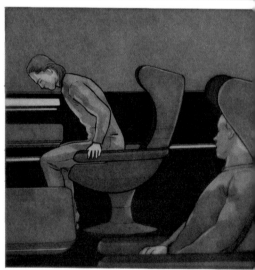

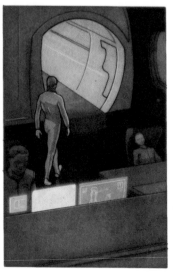

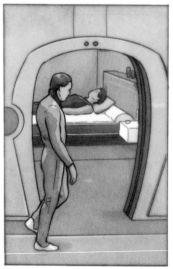

HER EYES . . .

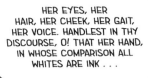

HER EYES, HER HAIR, HER CHEEK, HER GAIT, HER VOICE. HANDLEST IN THY DISCOURSE, O! THAT HER HAND, IN WHOSE COMPARISON ALL WHITES ARE INK . . .

WRITING THEIR OWN REPROACH; TO WHOSE SOFT SEIZURE THE CYGNET'S DOWN IS HARSH . . .

ON THE WHITE WONDER OF DEAR JULIET'S HAND, MAY SEIZE AND STEAL IMMORTAL BLESSING FROM HER LIPS . . .

WHO, EVEN IN PURE AND VESTAL MODESTY, STILL BLUSH, AS THINKING THEIR OWN KISSES SIN.

HOW BEAUTIFUL SHE IS.

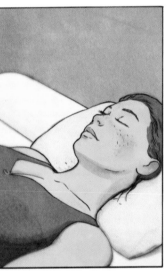

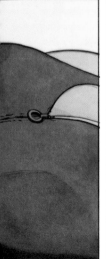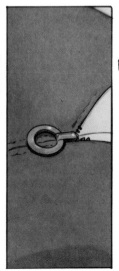

Z I P

DETESTABLE THOUGHT!

129

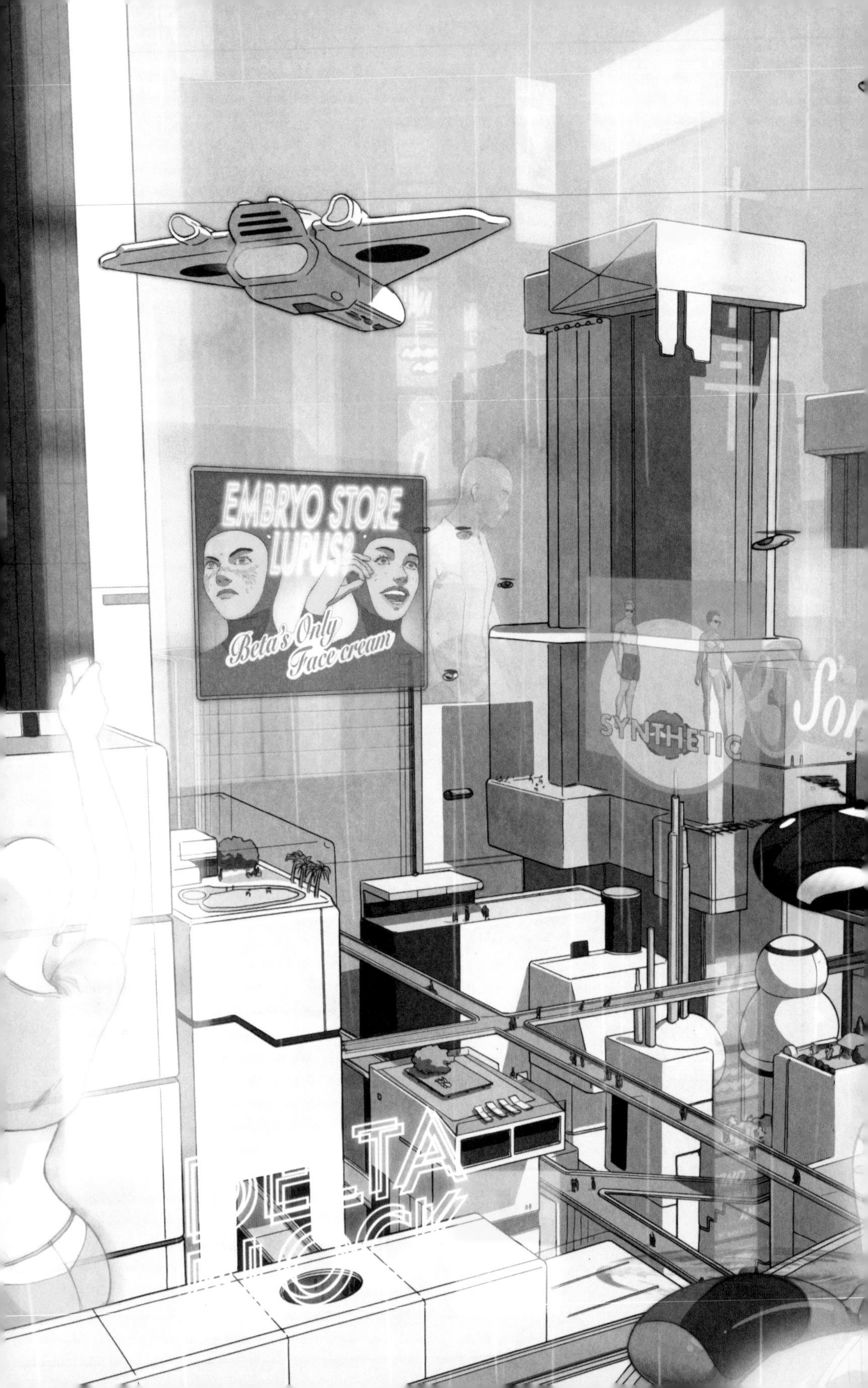
EMBRYO STORE
LUPUS?
Beta's Only
Face cream
SYNTHETIC

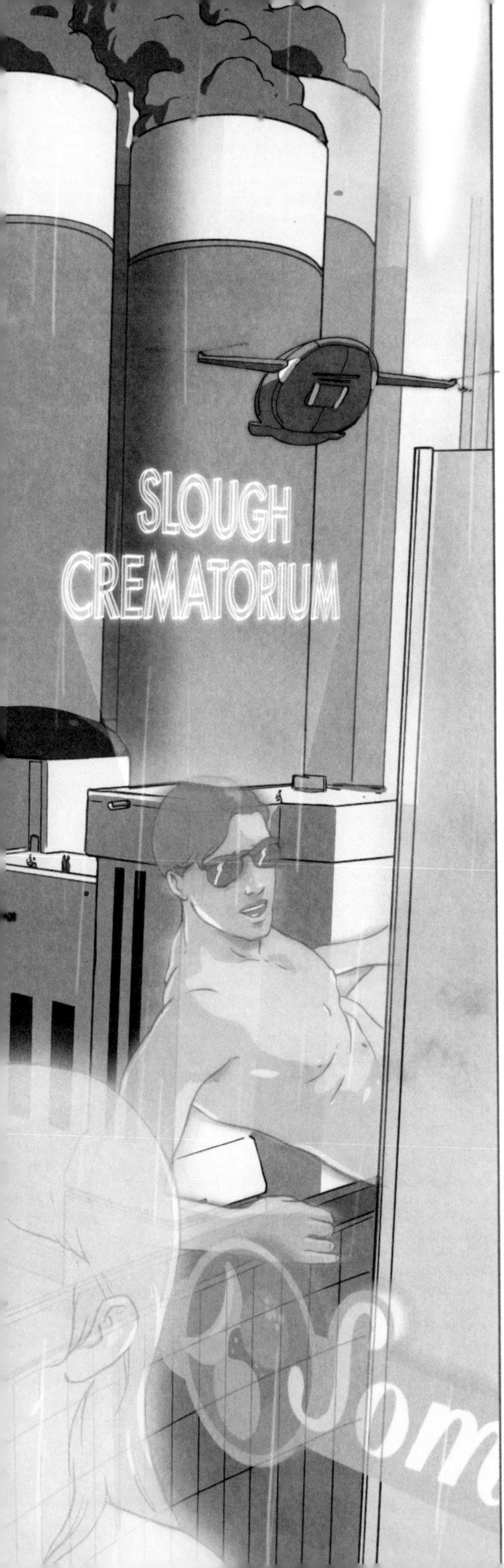
SLOUGH
CREMATORIUM

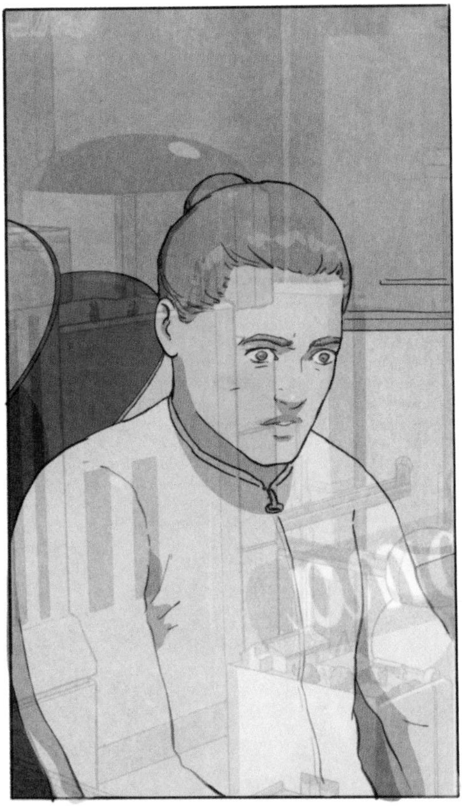

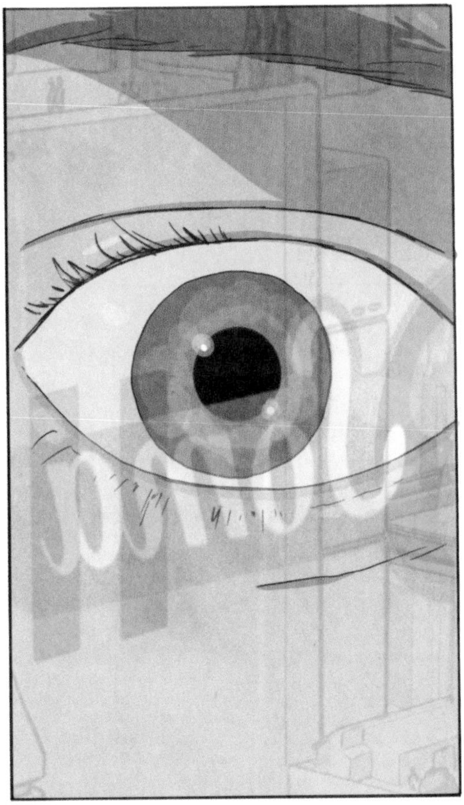

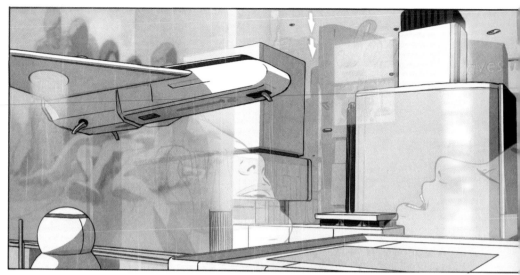

TWELVE HUNDRED AND FIFTY KILOMETERS AN HOUR. WHAT DO YOU THINK OF THAT, MR. SAVAGE?

VERY NICE.

STILL, ARIEL COULD PUT A GIRDLE ROUND THE EARTH IN FORTY MINUTES.

EH?

NOTHING.

MESSAGE FROM THE DIRECTOR OF HATCHERIES: MR. MARX TO REPORT TO THE FERTILIZING ROOM TOMORROW AT TWO THIRTY P.M. TO MEET WITH THE DHC. MESSAGE ENDS. HAVE A GREAT DAY!

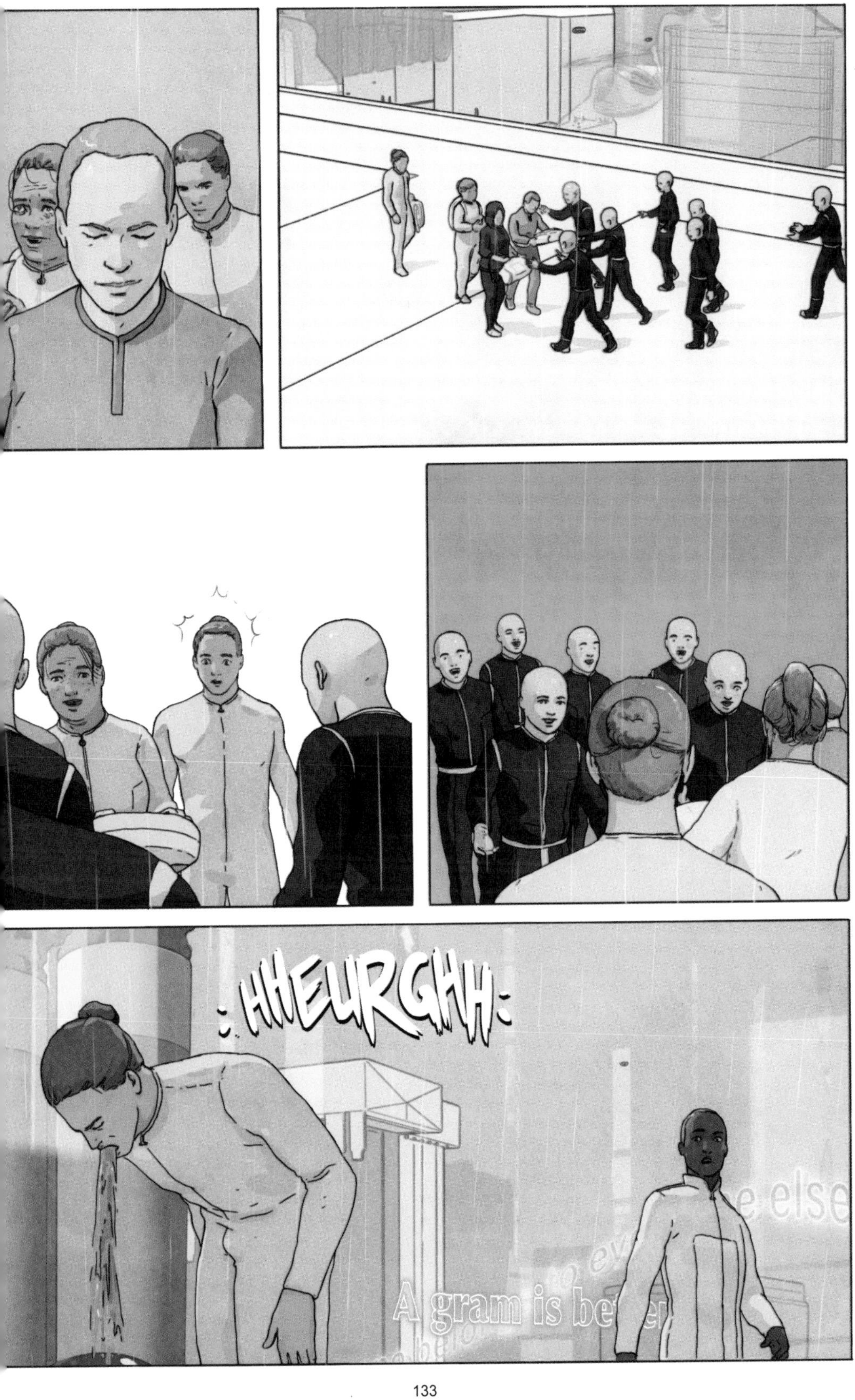
HHEURGHH
A gram is bet
e else

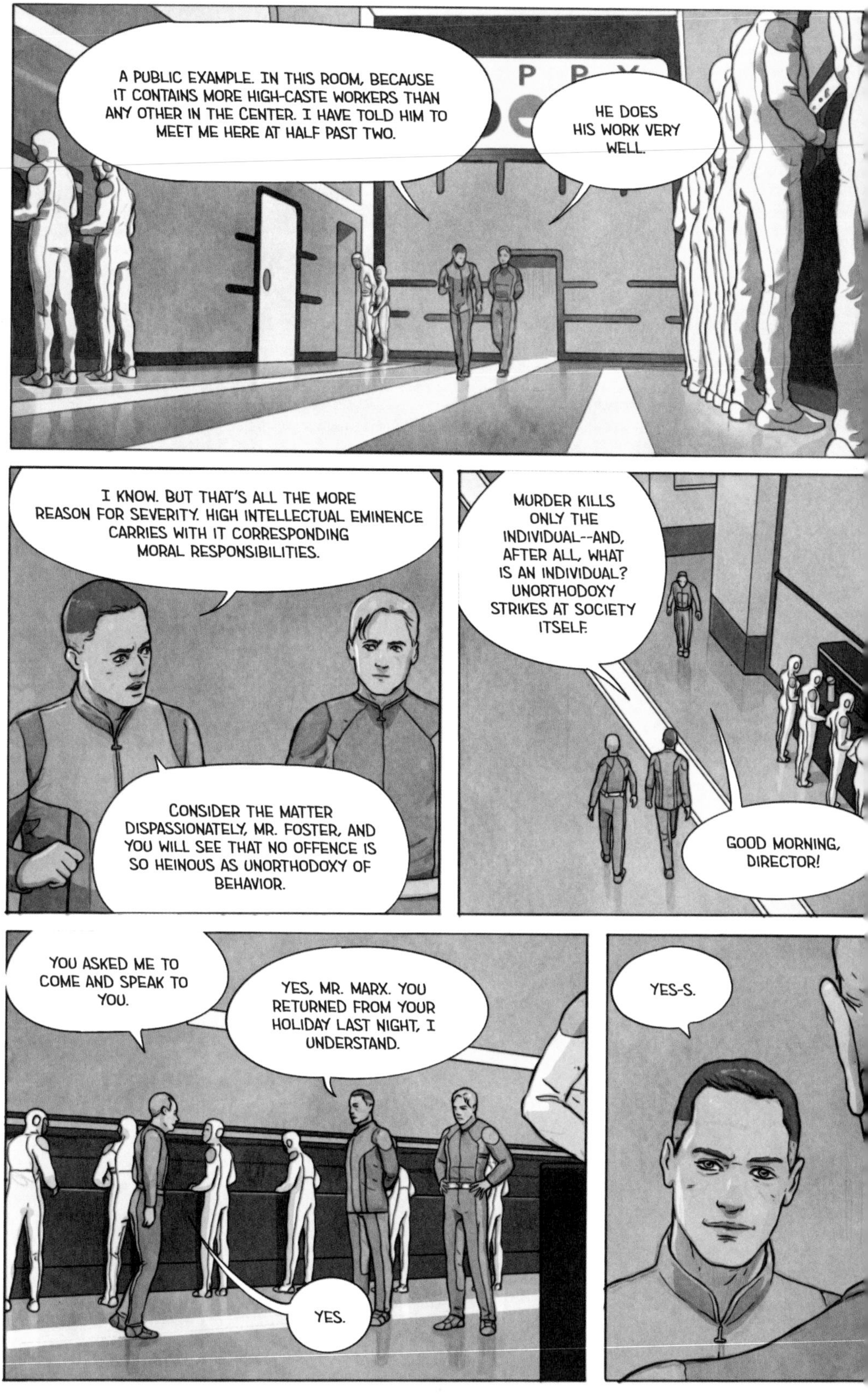
A PUBLIC EXAMPLE. IN THIS ROOM, BECAUSE IT CONTAINS MORE HIGH-CASTE WORKERS THAN ANY OTHER IN THE CENTER. I HAVE TOLD HIM TO MEET ME HERE AT HALF PAST TWO.
HE DOES HIS WORK VERY WELL.
I KNOW. BUT THAT'S ALL THE MORE REASON FOR SEVERITY. HIGH INTELLECTUAL EMINENCE CARRIES WITH IT CORRESPONDING MORAL RESPONSIBILITIES.
CONSIDER THE MATTER DISPASSIONATELY, MR. FOSTER, AND YOU WILL SEE THAT NO OFFENCE IS SO HEINOUS AS UNORTHODOXY OF BEHAVIOR.
MURDER KILLS ONLY THE INDIVIDUAL--AND, AFTER ALL, WHAT IS AN INDIVIDUAL? UNORTHODOXY STRIKES AT SOCIETY ITSELF.
GOOD MORNING, DIRECTOR!
YOU ASKED ME TO COME AND SPEAK TO YOU.
YES, MR. MARX. YOU RETURNED FROM YOUR HOLIDAY LAST NIGHT, I UNDERSTAND.
YES.
YES-S.

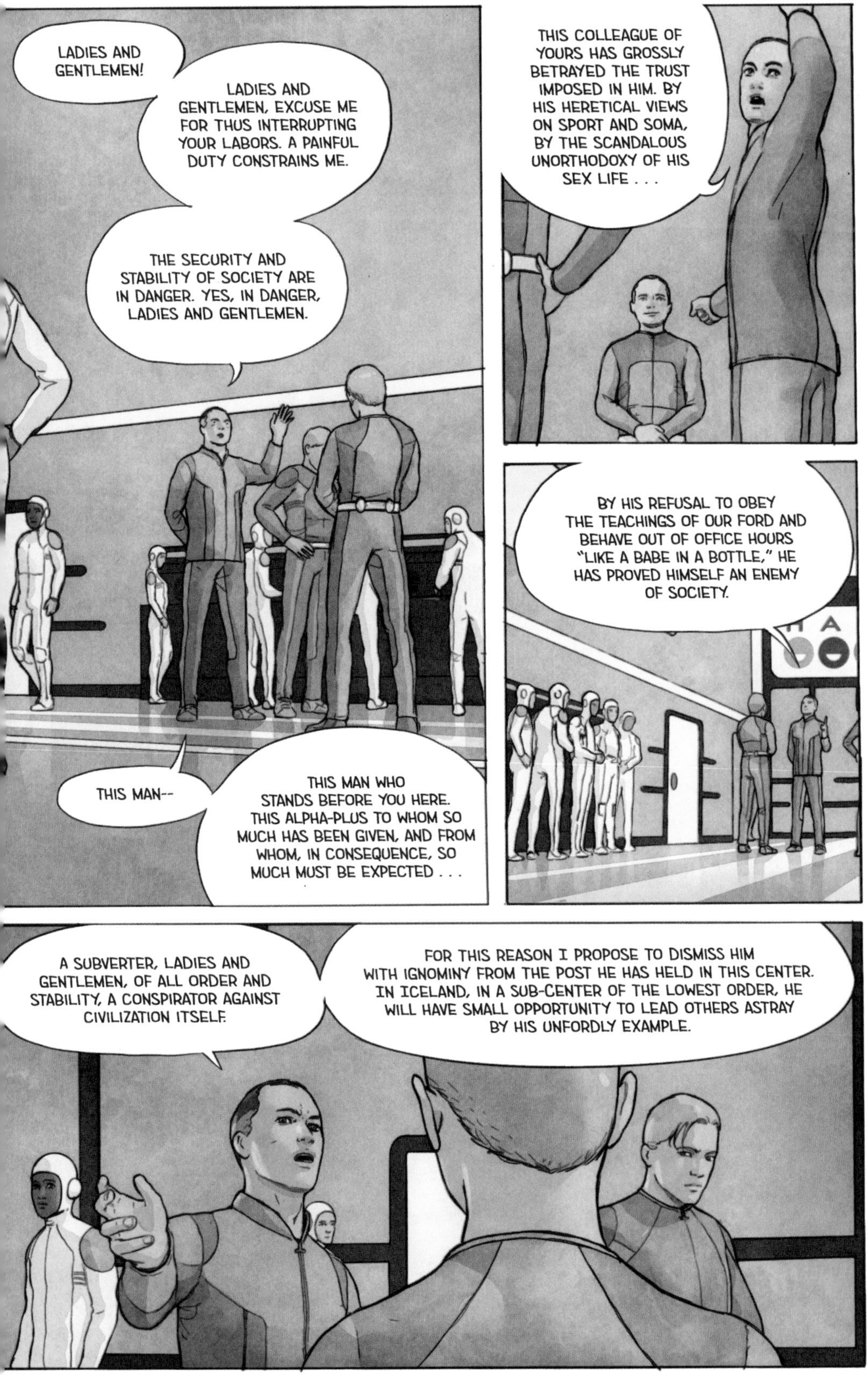
LADIES AND GENTLEMEN!
LADIES AND GENTLEMEN, EXCUSE ME FOR THUS INTERRUPTING YOUR LABORS. A PAINFUL DUTY CONSTRAINS ME.
THE SECURITY AND STABILITY OF SOCIETY ARE IN DANGER. YES, IN DANGER, LADIES AND GENTLEMEN.
THIS MAN--
THIS MAN WHO STANDS BEFORE YOU HERE. THIS ALPHA-PLUS TO WHOM SO MUCH HAS BEEN GIVEN, AND FROM WHOM, IN CONSEQUENCE, SO MUCH MUST BE EXPECTED . . .
THIS COLLEAGUE OF YOURS HAS GROSSLY BETRAYED THE TRUST IMPOSED IN HIM. BY HIS HERETICAL VIEWS ON SPORT AND SOMA, BY THE SCANDALOUS UNORTHODOXY OF HIS SEX LIFE . . .
BY HIS REFUSAL TO OBEY THE TEACHINGS OF OUR FORD AND BEHAVE OUT OF OFFICE HOURS "LIKE A BABE IN A BOTTLE," HE HAS PROVED HIMSELF AN ENEMY OF SOCIETY.
A SUBVERTER, LADIES AND GENTLEMEN, OF ALL ORDER AND STABILITY, A CONSPIRATOR AGAINST CIVILIZATION ITSELF.
FOR THIS REASON I PROPOSE TO DISMISS HIM WITH IGNOMINY FROM THE POST HE HAS HELD IN THIS CENTER. IN ICELAND, IN A SUB-CENTER OF THE LOWEST ORDER, HE WILL HAVE SMALL OPPORTUNITY TO LEAD OTHERS ASTRAY BY HIS UNFORDLY EXAMPLE.

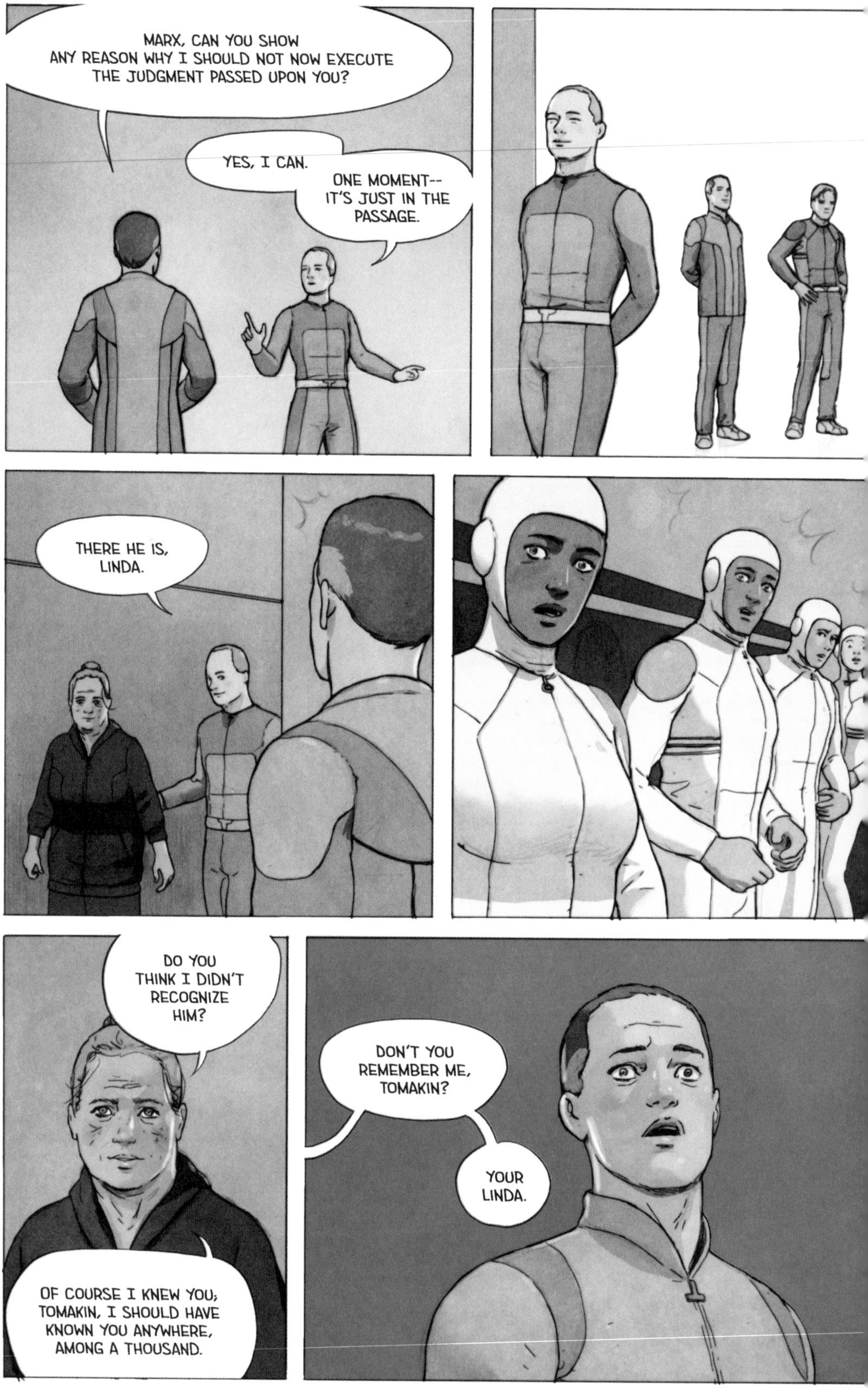
MARX, CAN YOU SHOW ANY REASON WHY I SHOULD NOT NOW EXECUTE THE JUDGMENT PASSED UPON YOU?
YES, I CAN.
ONE MOMENT-- IT'S JUST IN THE PASSAGE.
THERE HE IS, LINDA.
DO YOU THINK I DIDN'T RECOGNIZE HIM?
OF COURSE I KNEW YOU; TOMAKIN, I SHOULD HAVE KNOWN YOU ANYWHERE, AMONG A THOUSAND.
DON'T YOU REMEMBER ME, TOMAKIN?
YOUR LINDA.

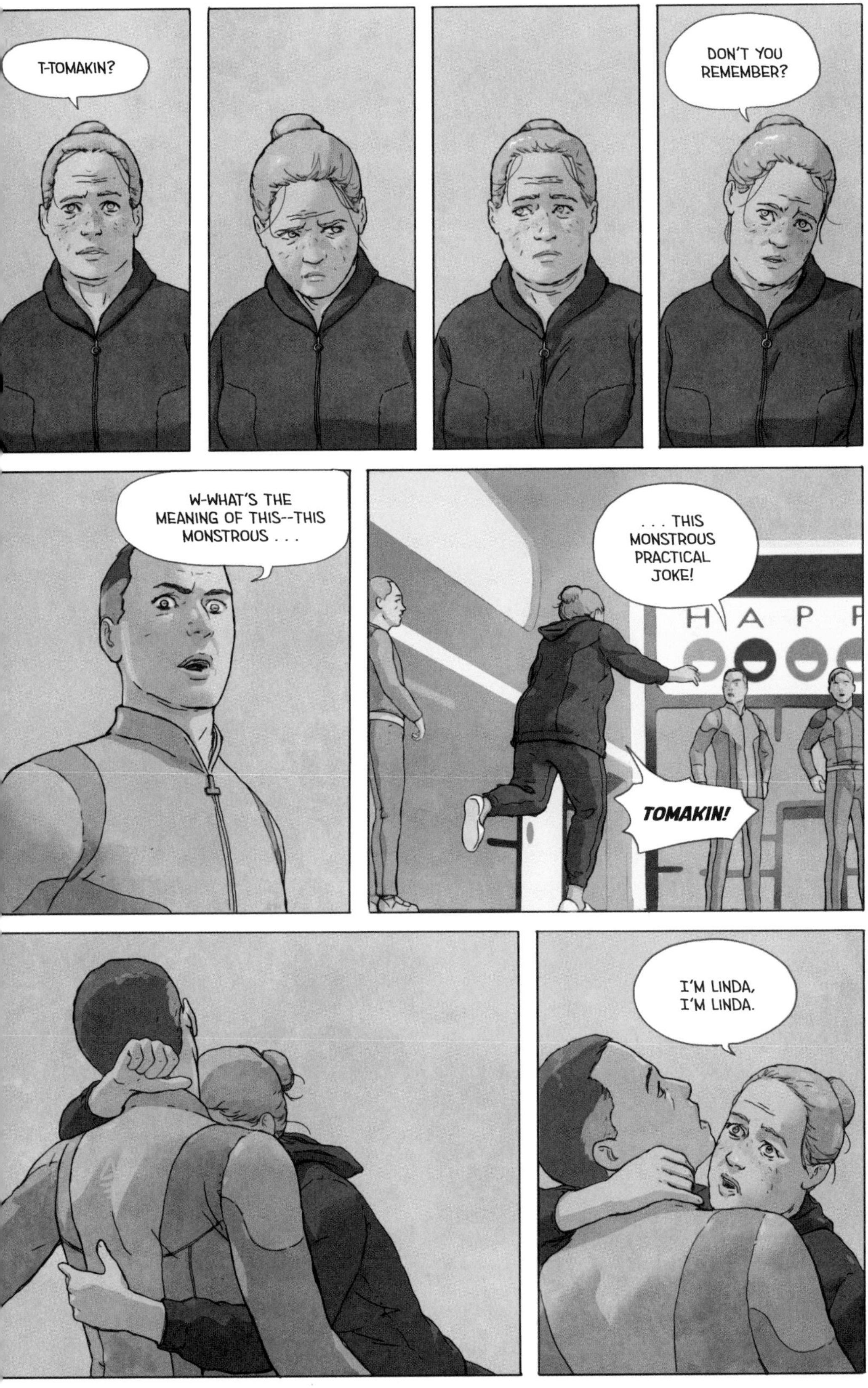
T-TOMAKIN?
DON'T YOU REMEMBER?
W-WHAT'S THE MEANING OF THIS--THIS MONSTROUS . . .
. . . THIS MONSTROUS PRACTICAL JOKE!
TOMAKIN!
I'M LINDA, I'M LINDA.

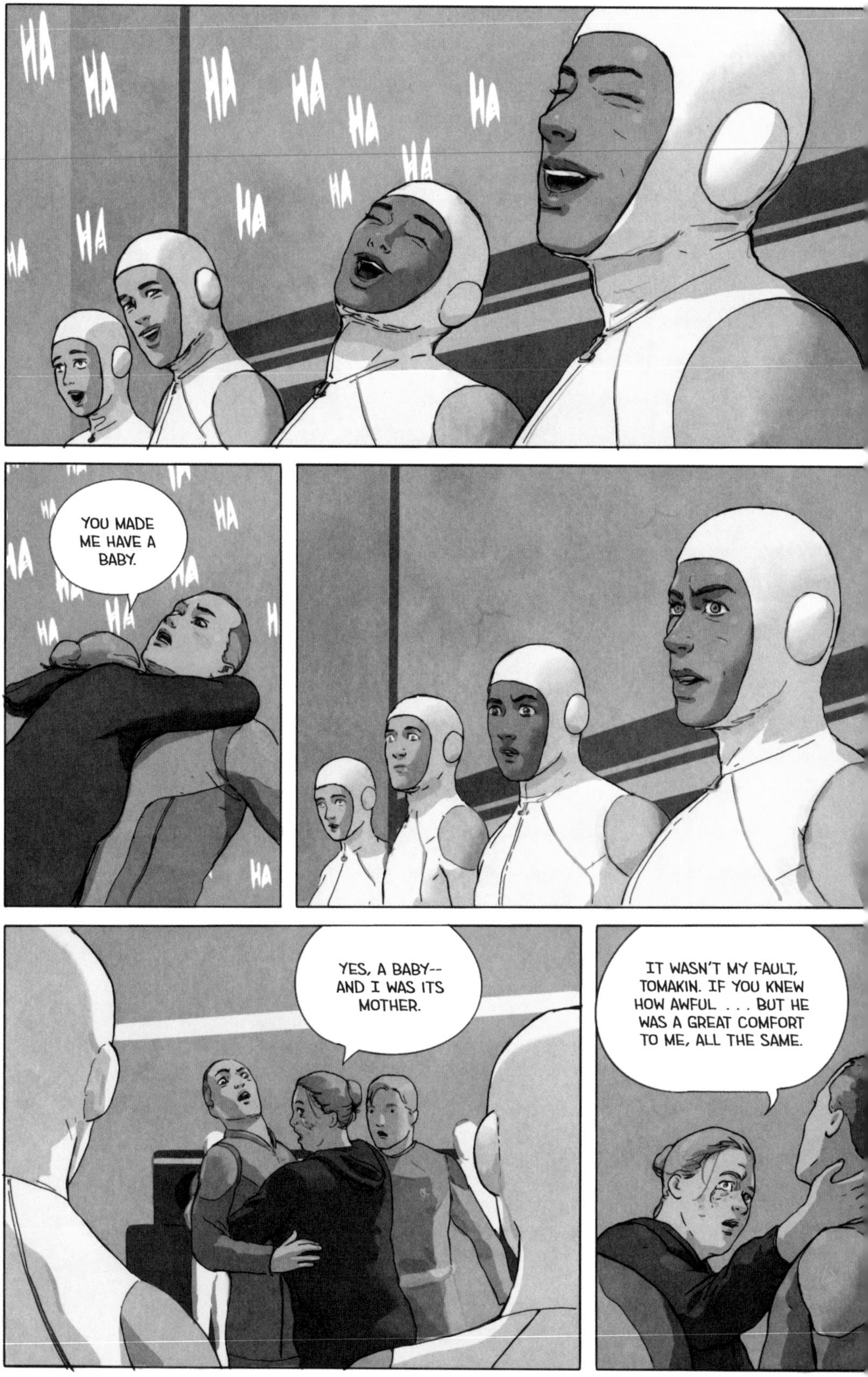
HA HA HA HA HA HA HA HA HA HA HA HA
YOU MADE ME HAVE A BABY.
YES, A BABY-- AND I WAS ITS MOTHER.
IT WASN'T MY FAULT, TOMAKIN. IF YOU KNEW HOW AWFUL . . . BUT HE WAS A GREAT COMFORT TO ME, ALL THE SAME.

JOHN!

JOHN!

MOTHER. . .

LINDA!

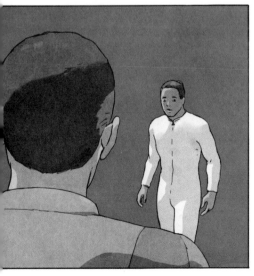

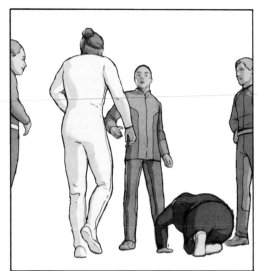

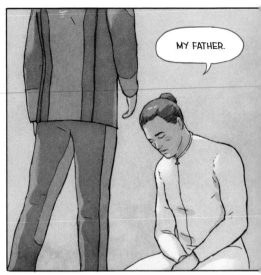

MY FATHER.

HA HA HA HA HA HA HA HA HA HA HA

MY FATHER!

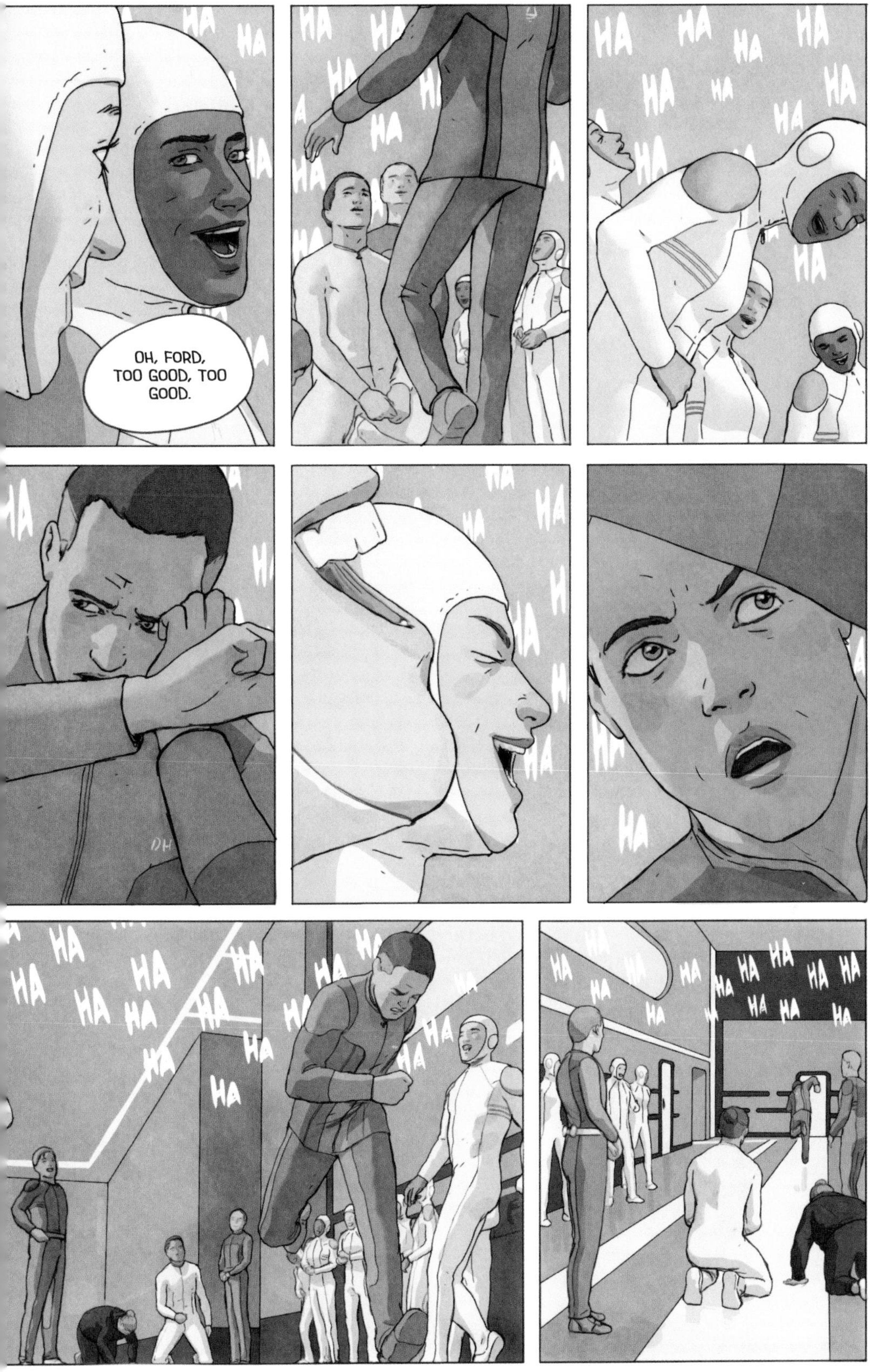
HA HA
OH, FORD, TOO GOOD, TOO GOOD.
HA HA HA HA HA HA HA HA HA HA HA HA
HA HA HA HA
HA HA HA HA HA HA HA HA HA HA HA HA HA HA HA HA HA HA HA HA HA HA HA HA HA HA HA HA HA HA

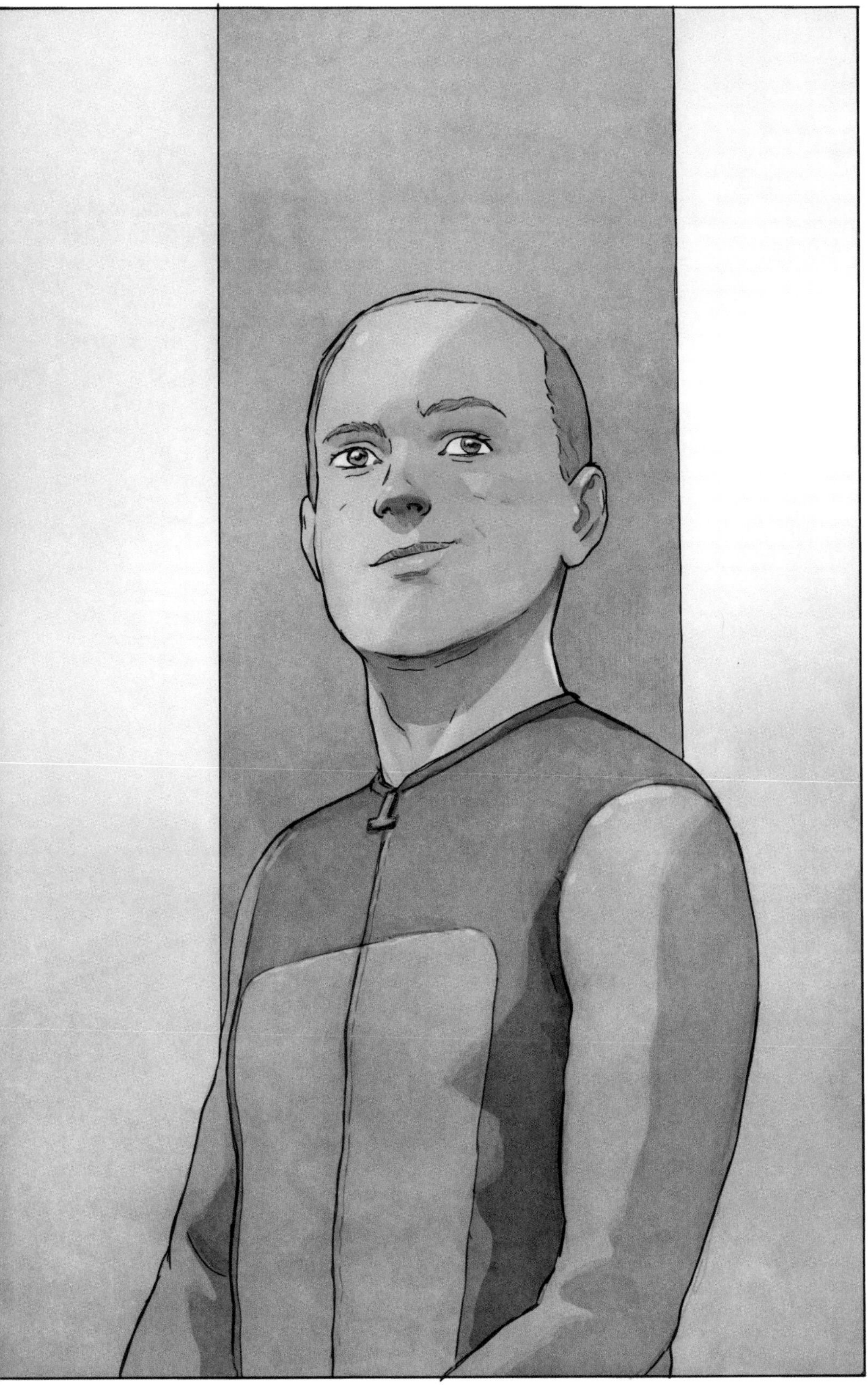

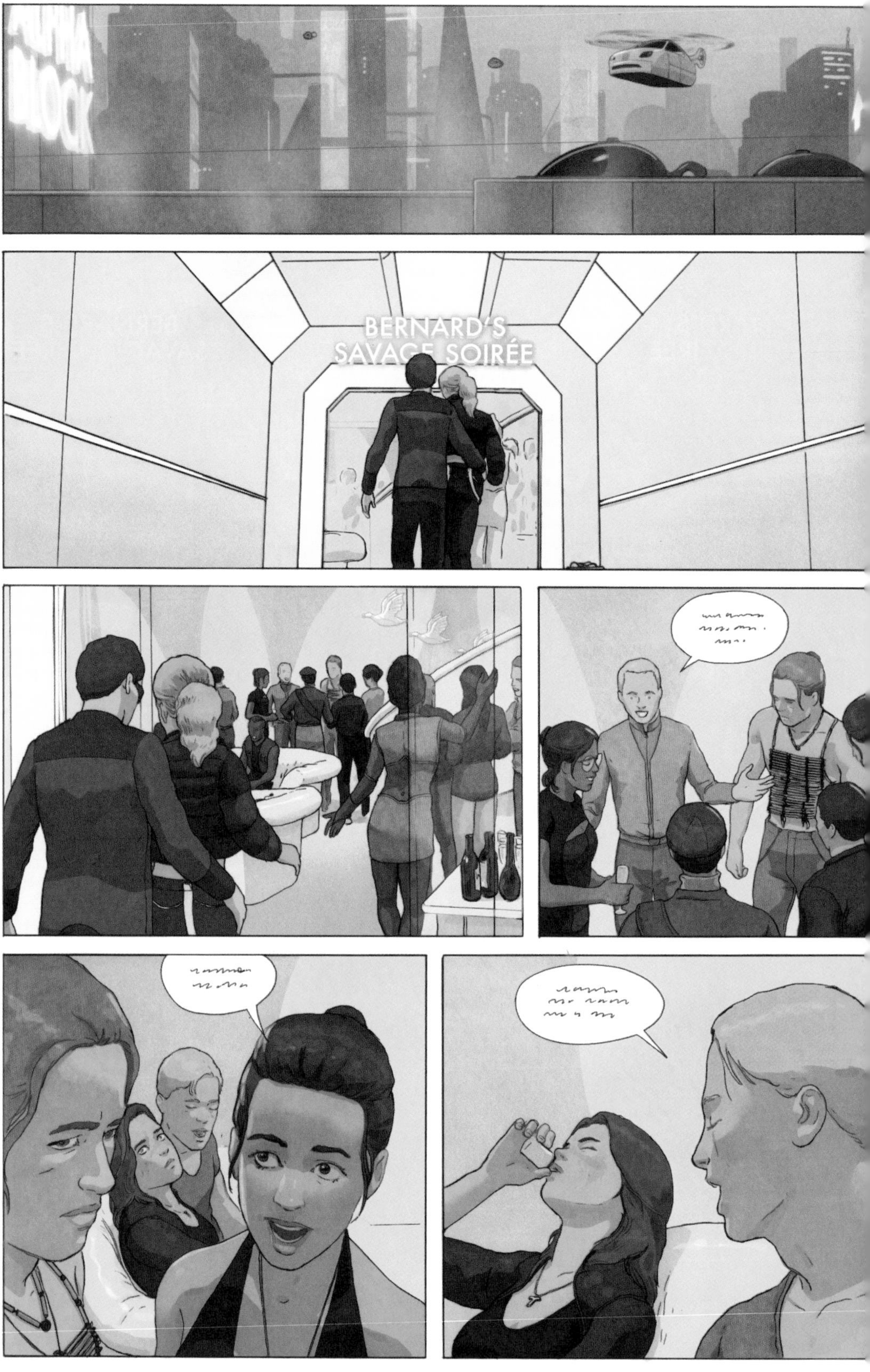
BERNARD'S
SAVAGE SOIRÉE

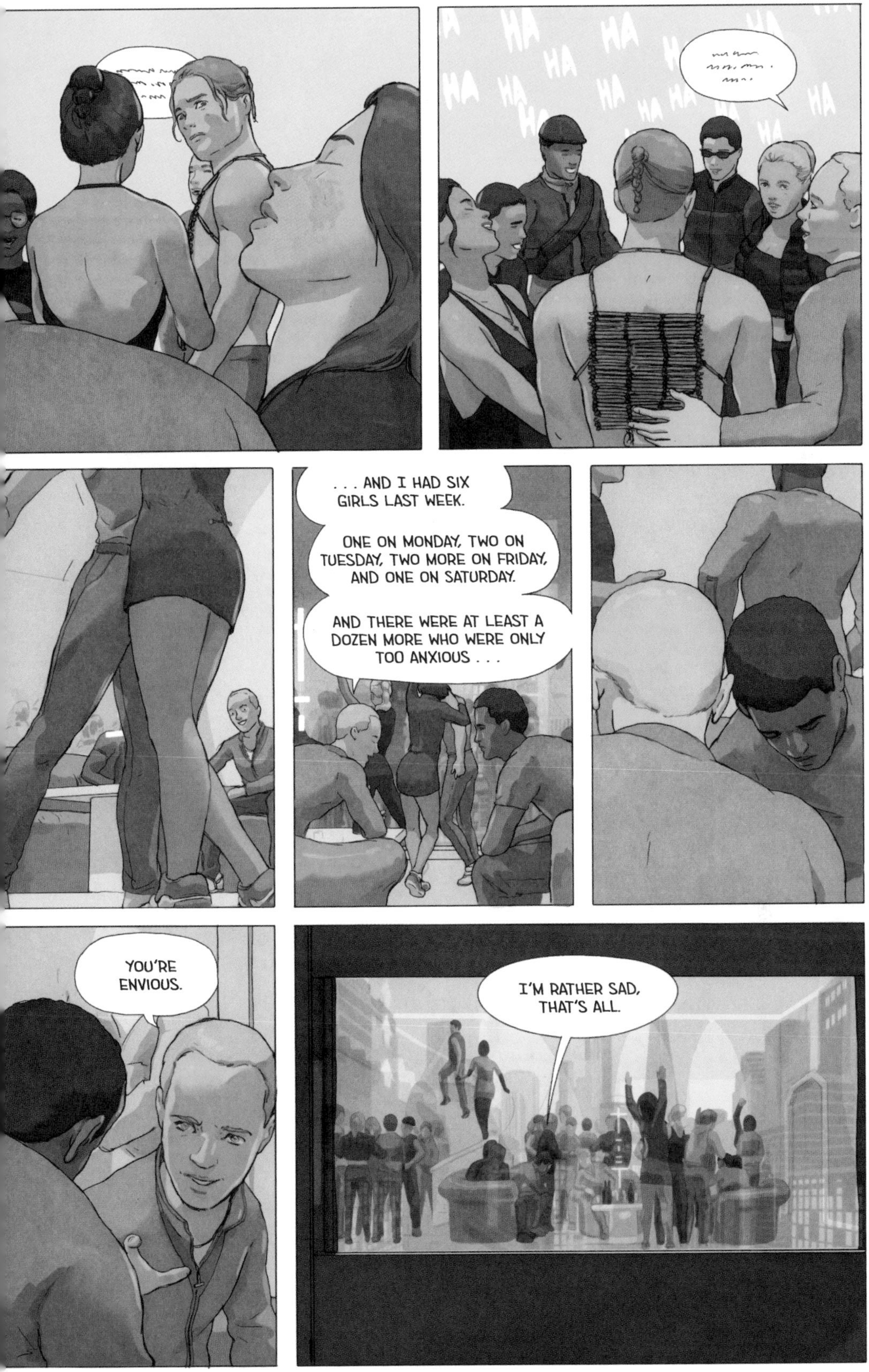
HA HA HA HA HA HA HA HA HA HA HA HA HA HA
. . . AND I HAD SIX GIRLS LAST WEEK.
ONE ON MONDAY, TWO ON TUESDAY, TWO MORE ON FRIDAY, AND ONE ON SATURDAY.
AND THERE WERE AT LEAST A DOZEN MORE WHO WERE ONLY TOO ANXIOUS . . .
YOU'RE ENVIOUS.
I'M RATHER SAD, THAT'S ALL.

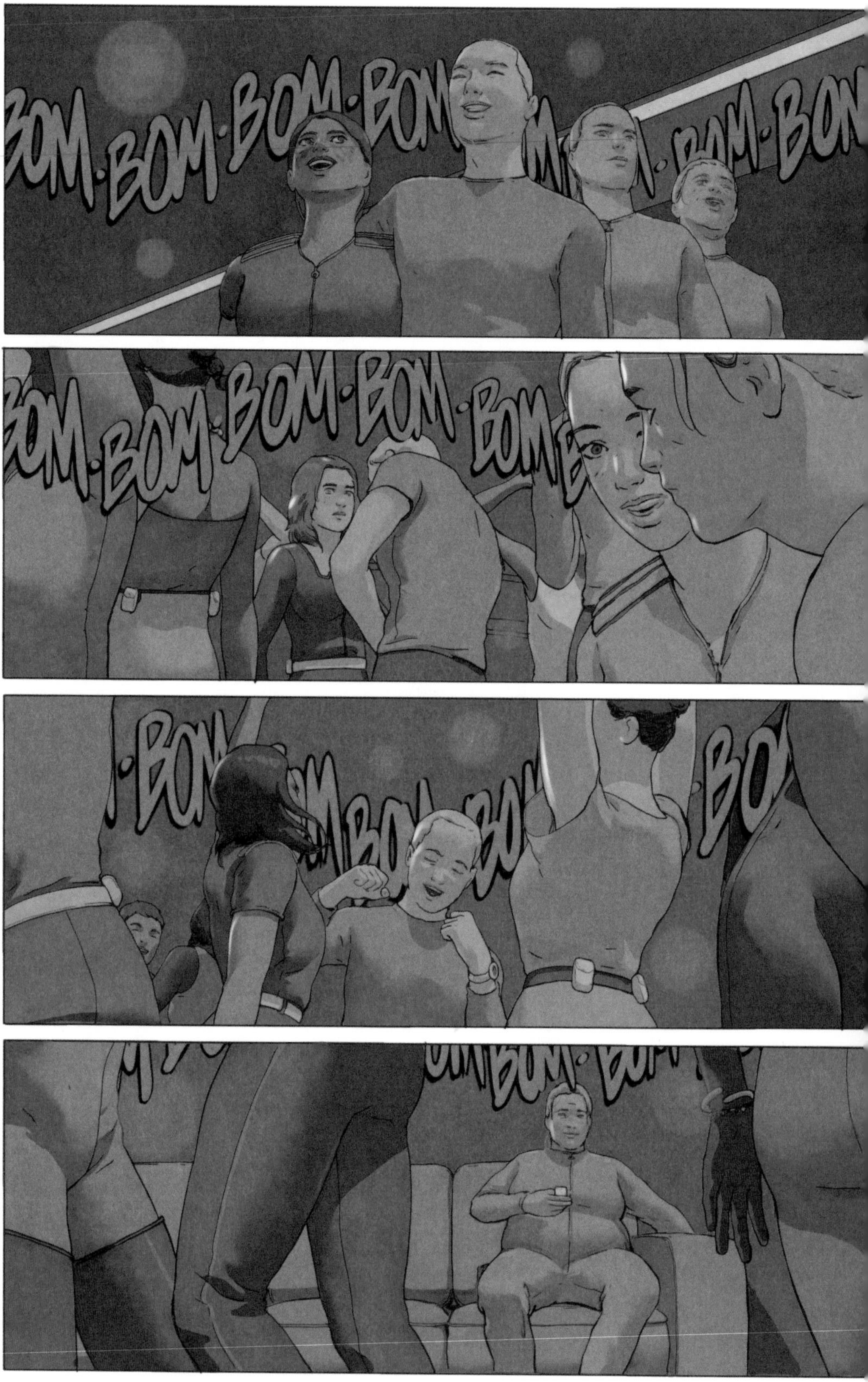
BOM·BOM·BOM·BOM
BOM·BOM·BOM·BOM·BOM
BOM
BOM·

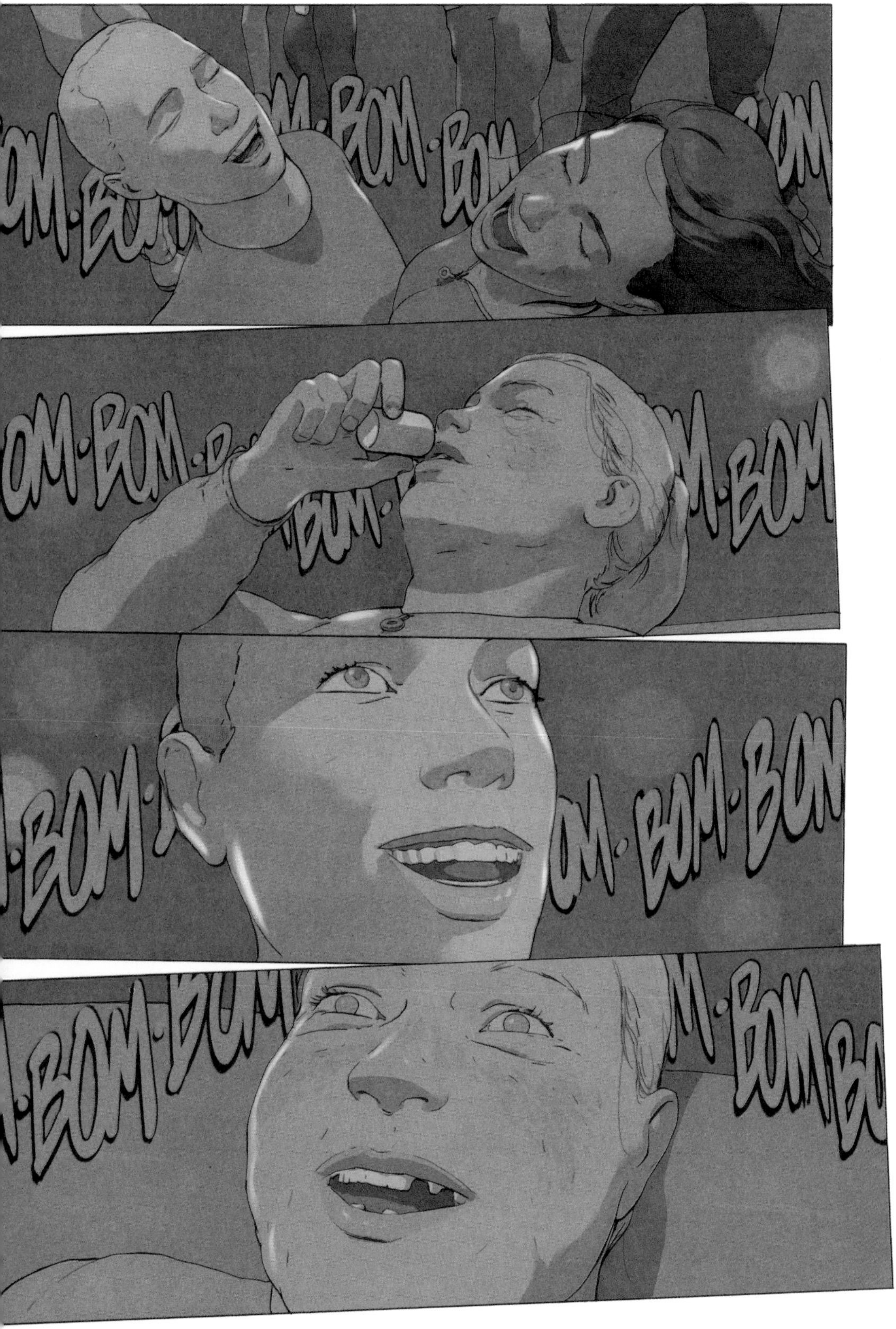
OM·BOM
M·BOM·BOM
OM
OM·BOM·B
BOM
M·BOM
·BOM·
OM·BOM·BO
·BOM·BOM
M·BOM
BO

UP TO TWENTY GRAMS A DAY YOU SAY SHE'S BEEN TAKING?

WHO'S TO BLAME HER? HER SON'S BEEN A TREMENDOUS HIT, OF COURSE, BUT LINDA--WELL, WHO WANTS TO SEE A FAT, BLOTCHY OLD THING WITH MISSING TEETH? A MOTHER!

SHE'S NOT EVEN STRICTLY A REAL SAVAGE--SHE WAS HATCHED FROM A BOTTLE AND CONDITIONED JUST LIKE EVERYONE ELSE.

SO HER RETURN TO CIVILIZATION'S BEEN ONE LONG SOMA HOLIDAY, HAS IT?

WELL, IT'LL FINISH HER OFF IN A MONTH OR TWO. ONE DAY THE RESPIRATORY CENTER WILL BE PARALYZED. NO MORE BREATHING.

GOOD THING, TOO.

IN ANY CASE, UPPING HER DOSAGE IS ONLY SHORTENING HER LIFE IN ONE SENSE.

EVERY SOMA HOLIDAY IS A BIT OF WHAT OUR ANCESTORS USED TO CALL ETERNITY.

SOMA MAY MAKE YOU LOSE A FEW YEARS IN TIME, BUT THINK OF THE ENORMOUS, IMMEASURABLE DURATIONS IT CAN GIVE YOU OUT OF TIME.

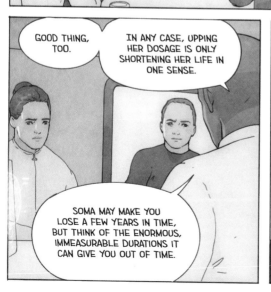

I'M VERY GLAD TO HAVE HAD THIS OPPORTUNITY TO SEE AN EXAMPLE OF SENILITY IN A HUMAN BEING. THANK YOU SO MUCH FOR COMING IN.

For the attention of his fordship, Mustapha Mond: A report concerning the discovery of the Savage, John, and his m—, Linda, by Bernard Marx.

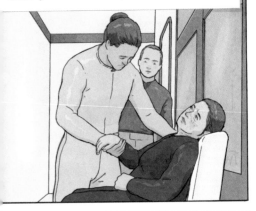

The Savage shows surprisingly little astonishment at, or awe of, civilized inventions. This is partly due, no doubt, to the fact that he has heard them talked about by the woman Linda, his m—.

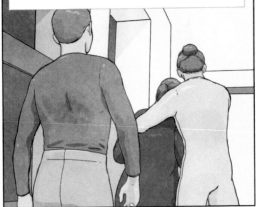

The Savage refuses to take soma and seems much distressed because the woman Linda remains permanently on soma holiday.

It is worthy of note that in spite of his m—'s senility and the extreme repulsiveness of her appearance, the Savage frequently goes to see her and appears to be much attached to her.

An interesting example of the way in which early conditioning can be made to modify and even run counter to natural impulses (in this case, the impulse to recoil from an unpleasant object).

DOES THE FOOL THINK I'M TOO SQUEAMISH TO SEE THE WORD "MOTHER" WRITTEN OUT AT FULL LENGTH?

Partly on his interest being focused on what he calls "the soul," which he persists as regarding as an entity independent of the physical environment; whereas, as I tried to point out to him . . .

HA! NOW LISTEN TO THIS: "I MUST ADMIT THAT I AGREE WITH THE SAVAGE IN FINDING CIVILIZED INFANTILITY TOO EASY OR, AS HE PUTS IT, NOT EXPENSIVE ENOUGH."

THE IDEA OF THIS CREATURE SOLEMNLY LECTURING YOU--YOU-- ABOUT THE SOCIAL ORDER REALLY IS TOO GROTESQUE.

Everybody belongs to everybody else

YOU SEEM VERY PLEASED WITH YOURSELF.

I *AM* PLEASED. BERNARD HAS AN UNEXPECTED ENGAGEMENT AND HE'S ASKED ME IF I'D TAKE THE SAVAGE TO THE FEELIES THIS EVENING.

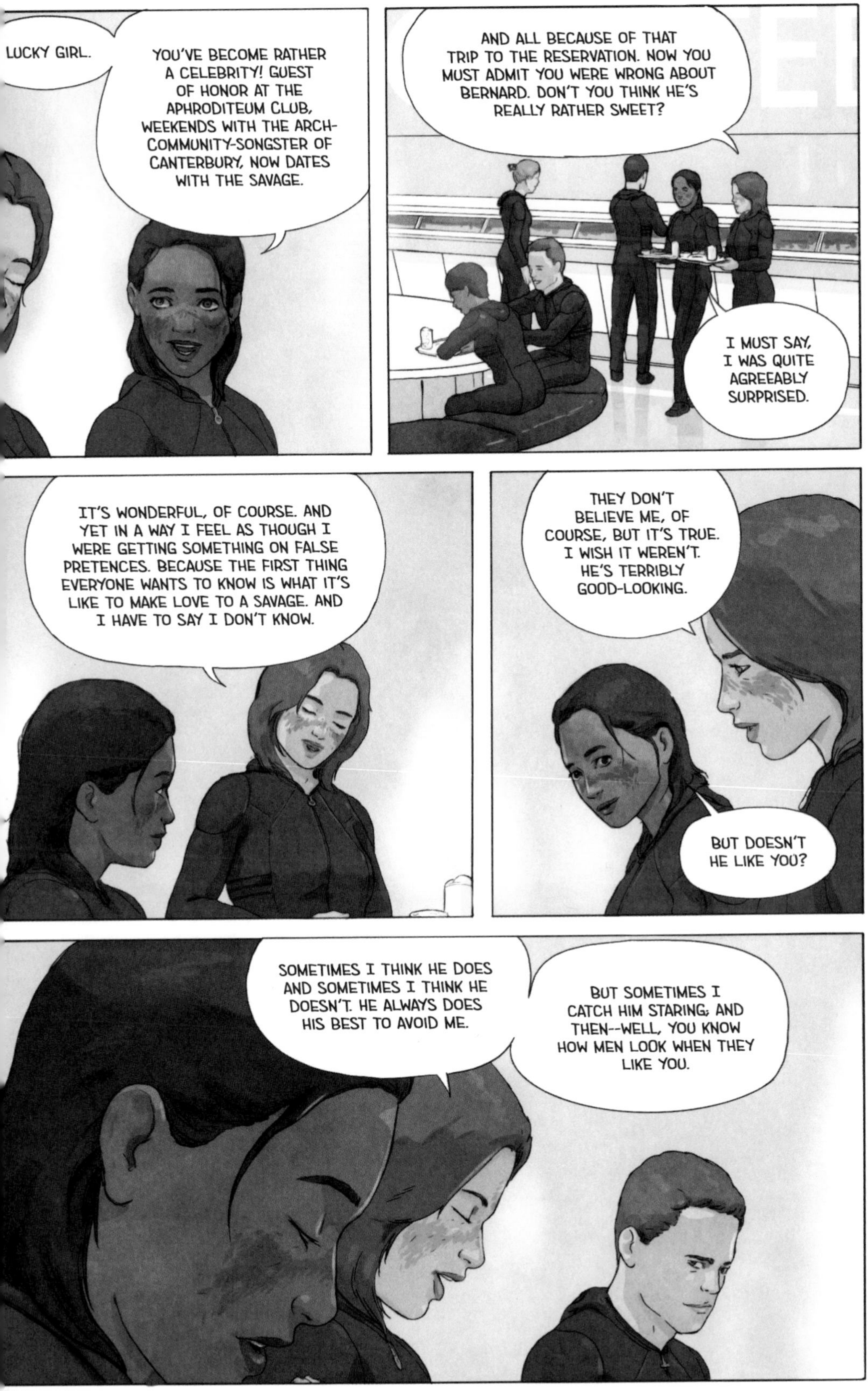
LUCKY GIRL.
YOU'VE BECOME RATHER A CELEBRITY! GUEST OF HONOR AT THE APHRODITEUM CLUB, WEEKENDS WITH THE ARCH-COMMUNITY-SONGSTER OF CANTERBURY, NOW DATES WITH THE SAVAGE.
AND ALL BECAUSE OF THAT TRIP TO THE RESERVATION. NOW YOU MUST ADMIT YOU WERE WRONG ABOUT BERNARD. DON'T YOU THINK HE'S REALLY RATHER SWEET?
I MUST SAY, I WAS QUITE AGREEABLY SURPRISED.
IT'S WONDERFUL, OF COURSE. AND YET IN A WAY I FEEL AS THOUGH I WERE GETTING SOMETHING ON FALSE PRETENCES. BECAUSE THE FIRST THING EVERYONE WANTS TO KNOW IS WHAT IT'S LIKE TO MAKE LOVE TO A SAVAGE. AND I HAVE TO SAY I DON'T KNOW.
THEY DON'T BELIEVE ME, OF COURSE, BUT IT'S TRUE. I WISH IT WEREN'T. HE'S TERRIBLY GOOD-LOOKING.
BUT DOESN'T HE LIKE YOU?
SOMETIMES I THINK HE DOES AND SOMETIMES I THINK HE DOESN'T. HE ALWAYS DOES HIS BEST TO AVOID ME.
BUT SOMETIMES I CATCH HIM STARING; AND THEN--WELL, YOU KNOW HOW MEN LOOK WHEN THEY LIKE YOU.

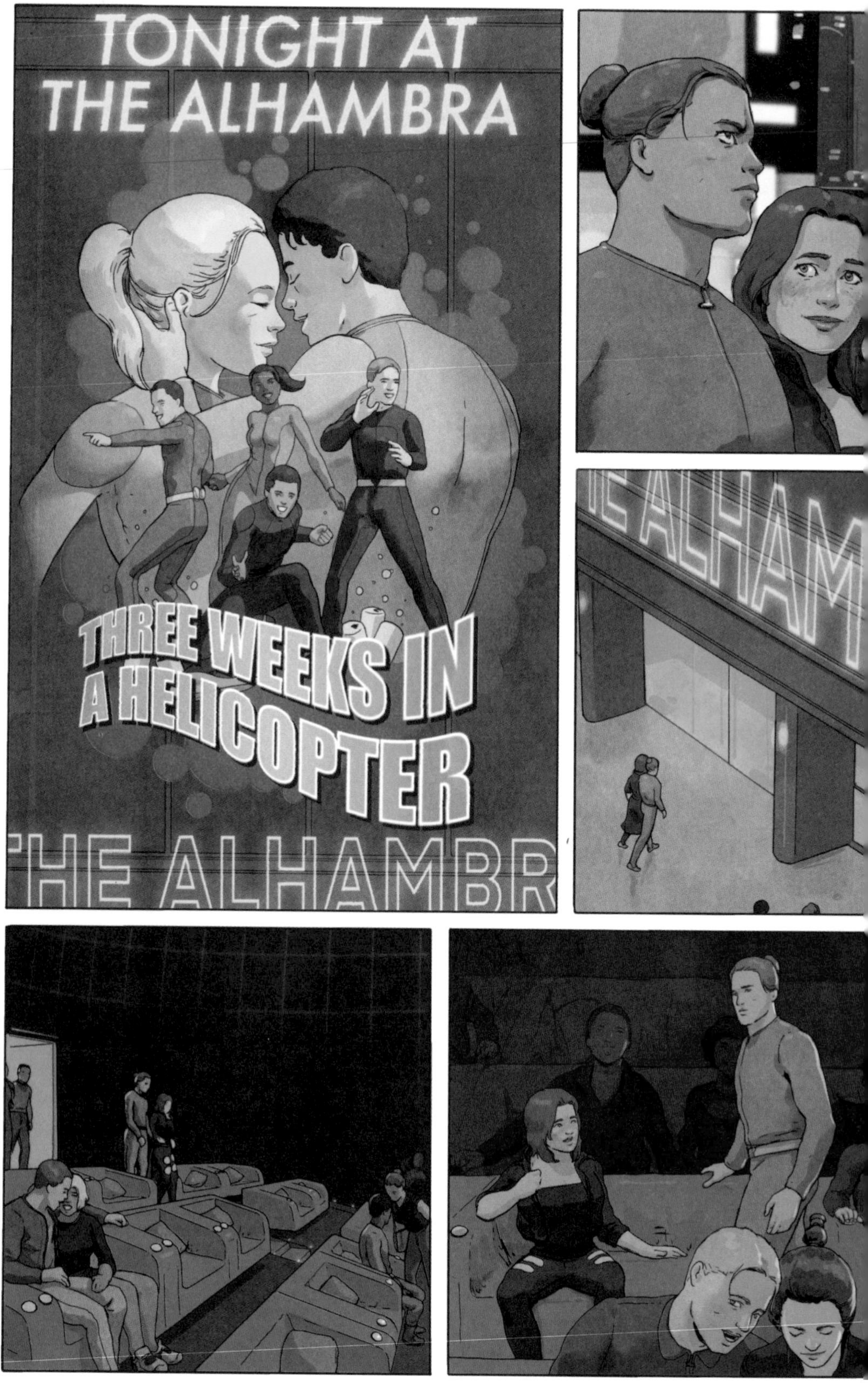
TONIGHT AT THE ALHAMBRA
THREE WEEKS IN A HELICOPTER

TAKE HOLD OF THOSE METAL KNOBS ON THE ARMS OF YOUR CHAIR OR YOU WON'T GET ANY OF THE FEELY EFFECTS.

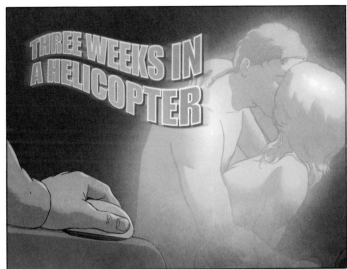

THREE WEEKS IN A HELICOPTER

?!

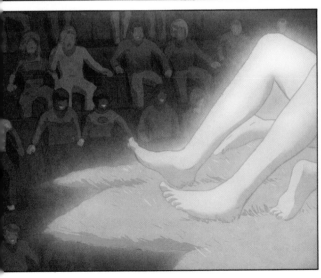

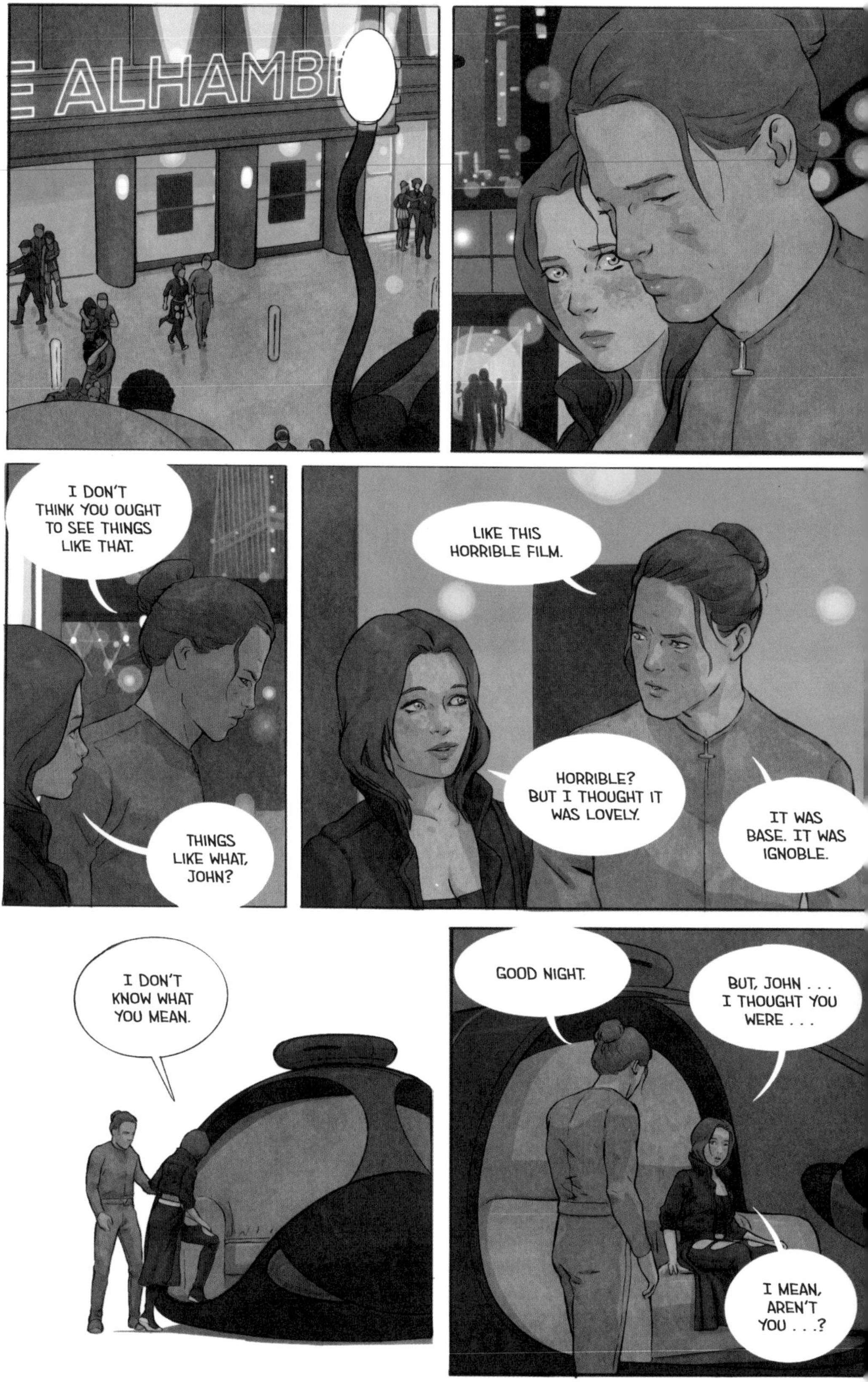
ALHAMBR
I DON'T THINK YOU OUGHT TO SEE THINGS LIKE THAT.
THINGS LIKE WHAT, JOHN?
LIKE THIS HORRIBLE FILM.
HORRIBLE? BUT I THOUGHT IT WAS LOVELY.
IT WAS BASE. IT WAS IGNOBLE.
I DON'T KNOW WHAT YOU MEAN.
GOOD NIGHT.
BUT, JOHN . . . I THOUGHT YOU WERE . . .
I MEAN, AREN'T YOU . . .?

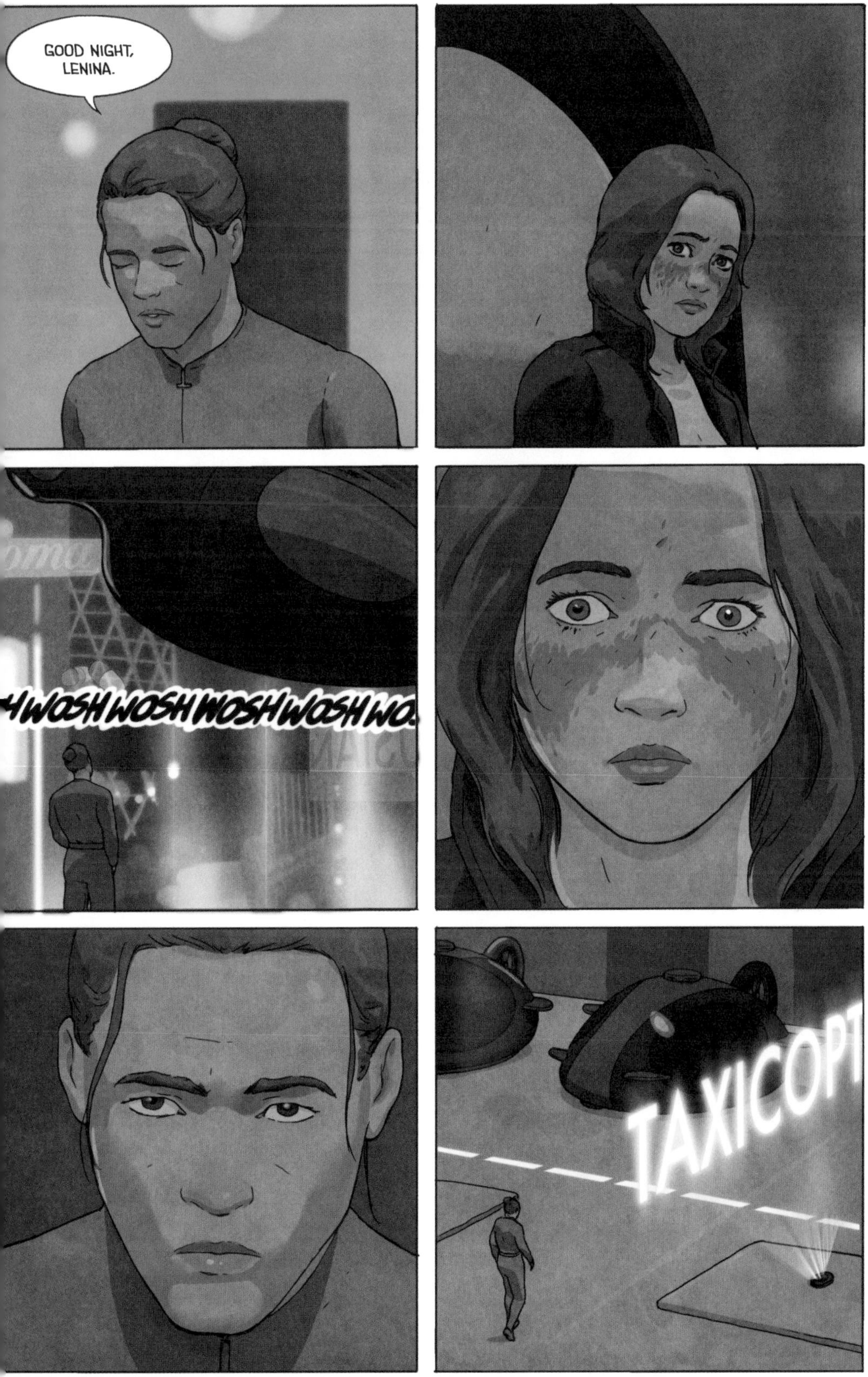
GOOD NIGHT, LENINA.
WOSH WOSH WOSH WOSH
TAXICOPT

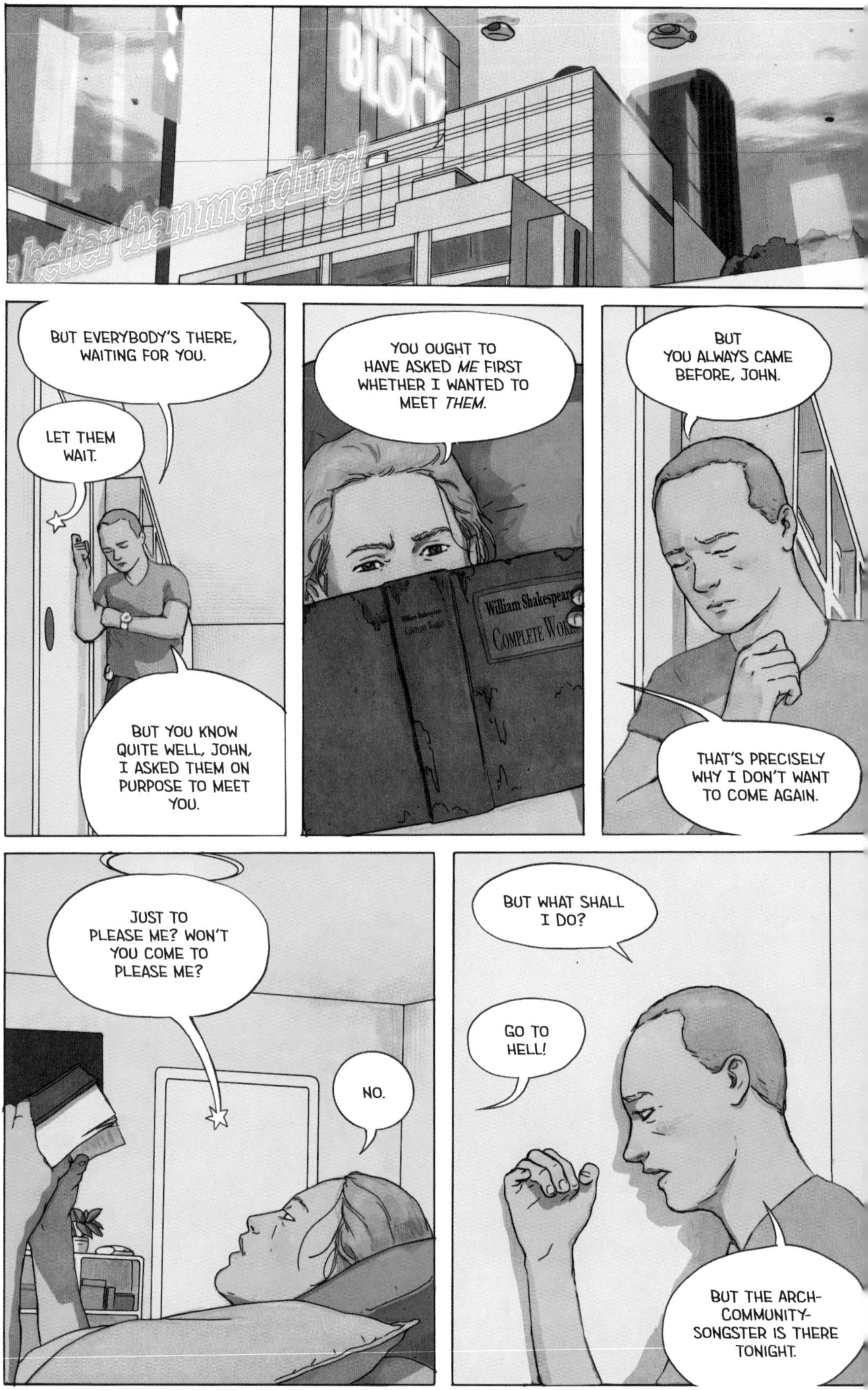
better than mending!
ALPHA BLOCK
BUT EVERYBODY'S THERE, WAITING FOR YOU.
LET THEM WAIT.
BUT YOU KNOW QUITE WELL, JOHN, I ASKED THEM ON PURPOSE TO MEET YOU.
YOU OUGHT TO HAVE ASKED *ME* FIRST WHETHER I WANTED TO MEET *THEM*.
William Shakespeare
COMPLETE WORK
BUT YOU ALWAYS CAME BEFORE, JOHN.
THAT'S PRECISELY WHY I DON'T WANT TO COME AGAIN.
JUST TO PLEASE ME? WON'T YOU COME TO PLEASE ME?
NO.
BUT WHAT SHALL I DO?
GO TO HELL!
BUT THE ARCH-COMMUNITY-SONGSTER IS THERE TONIGHT.

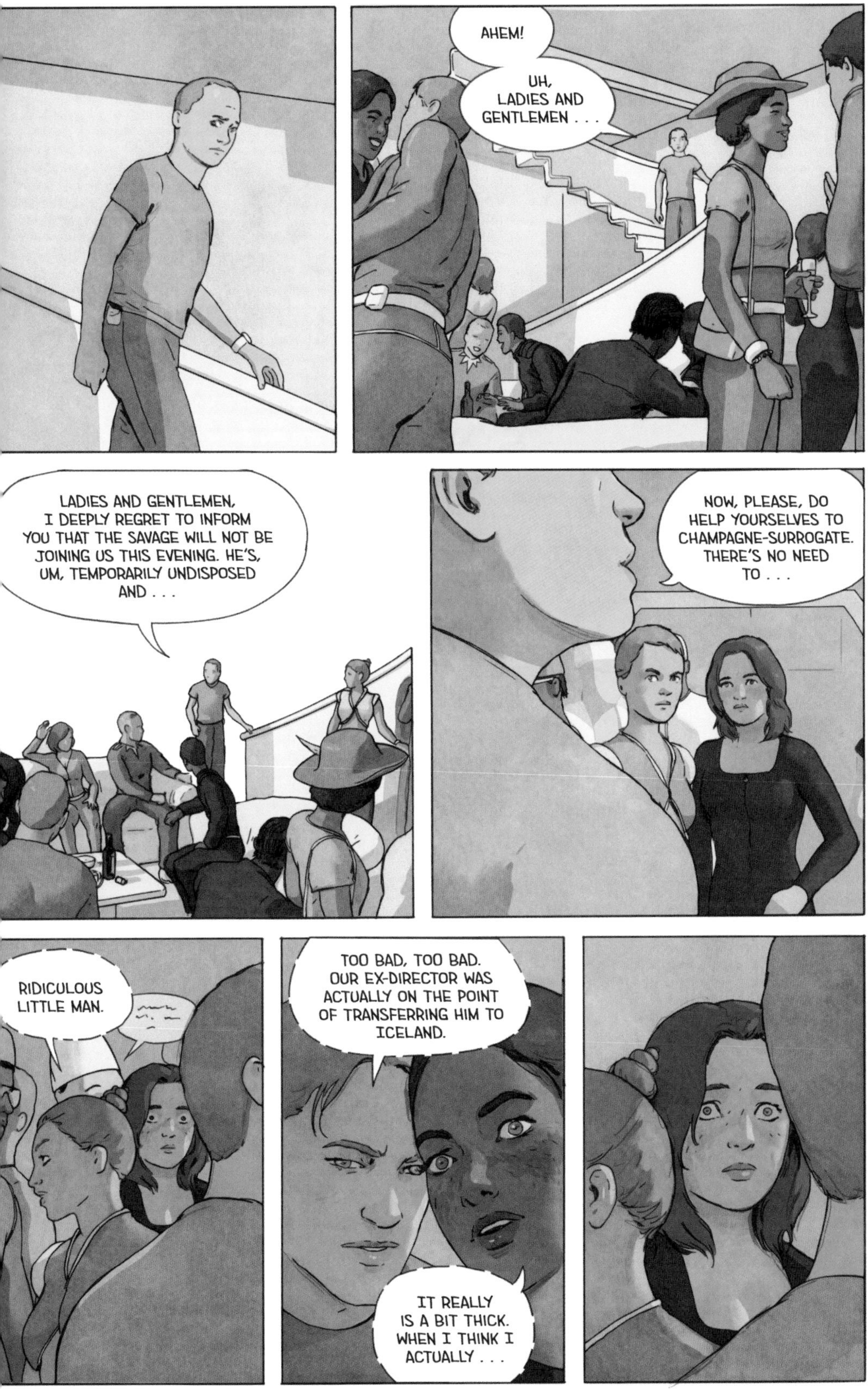
AHEM!
UH, LADIES AND GENTLEMEN . . .
LADIES AND GENTLEMEN, I DEEPLY REGRET TO INFORM YOU THAT THE SAVAGE WILL NOT BE JOINING US THIS EVENING. HE'S, UM, TEMPORARILY UNDISPOSED AND . . .
NOW, PLEASE, DO HELP YOURSELVES TO CHAMPAGNE-SURROGATE. THERE'S NO NEED TO . . .
RIDICULOUS LITTLE MAN.
TOO BAD, TOO BAD. OUR EX-DIRECTOR WAS ACTUALLY ON THE POINT OF TRANSFERRING HIM TO ICELAND.
IT REALLY IS A BIT THICK. WHEN I THINK I ACTUALLY . . .

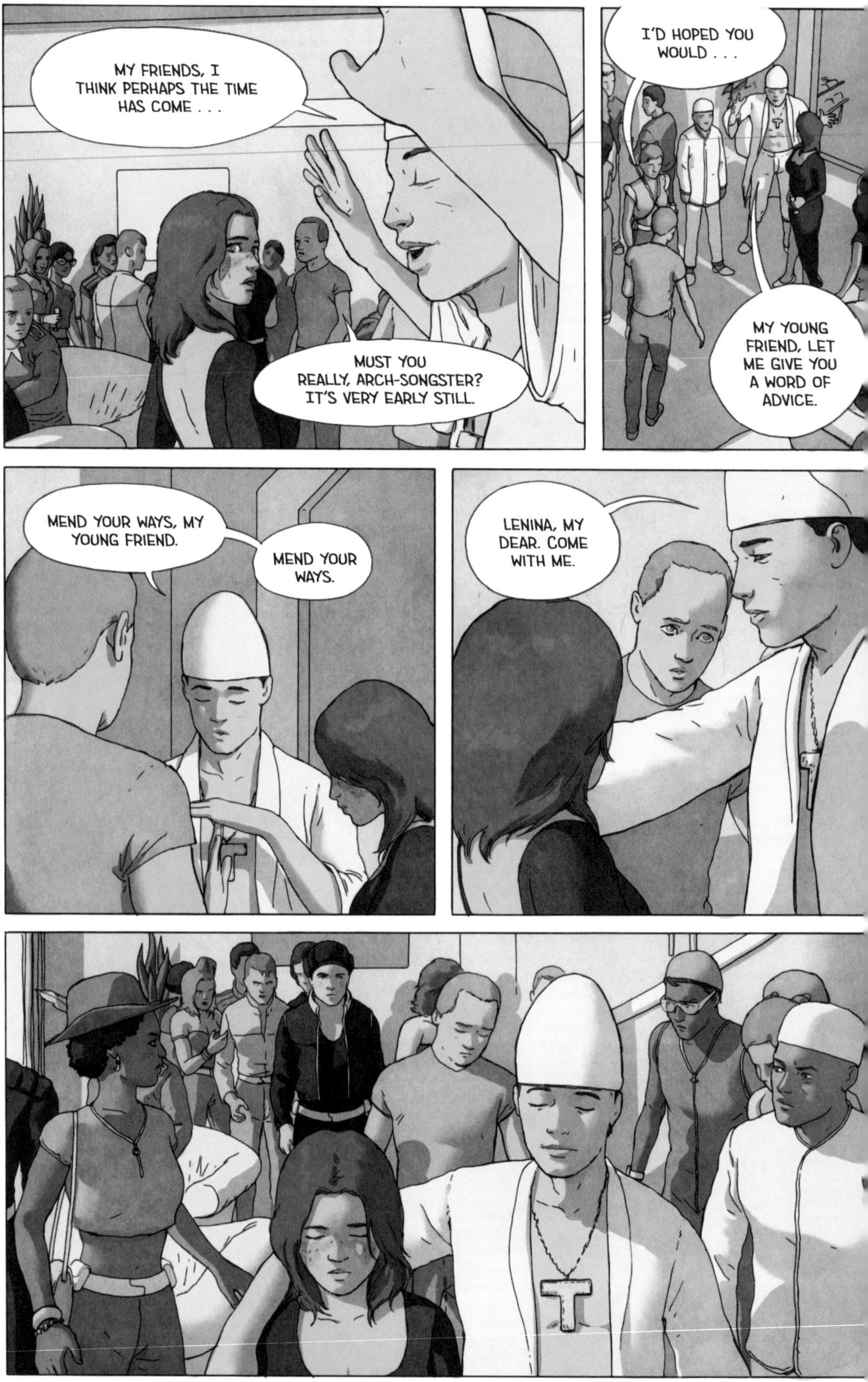
MY FRIENDS, I THINK PERHAPS THE TIME HAS COME . . .
MUST YOU REALLY, ARCH-SONGSTER? IT'S VERY EARLY STILL.
I'D HOPED YOU WOULD . . .
MY YOUNG FRIEND, LET ME GIVE YOU A WORD OF ADVICE.
MEND YOUR WAYS, MY YOUNG FRIEND.
MEND YOUR WAYS.
LENINA, MY DEAR. COME WITH ME.

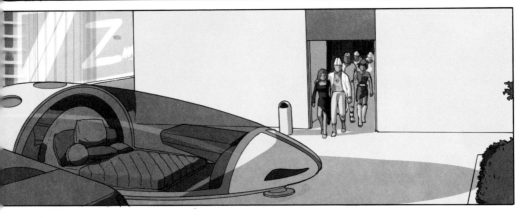

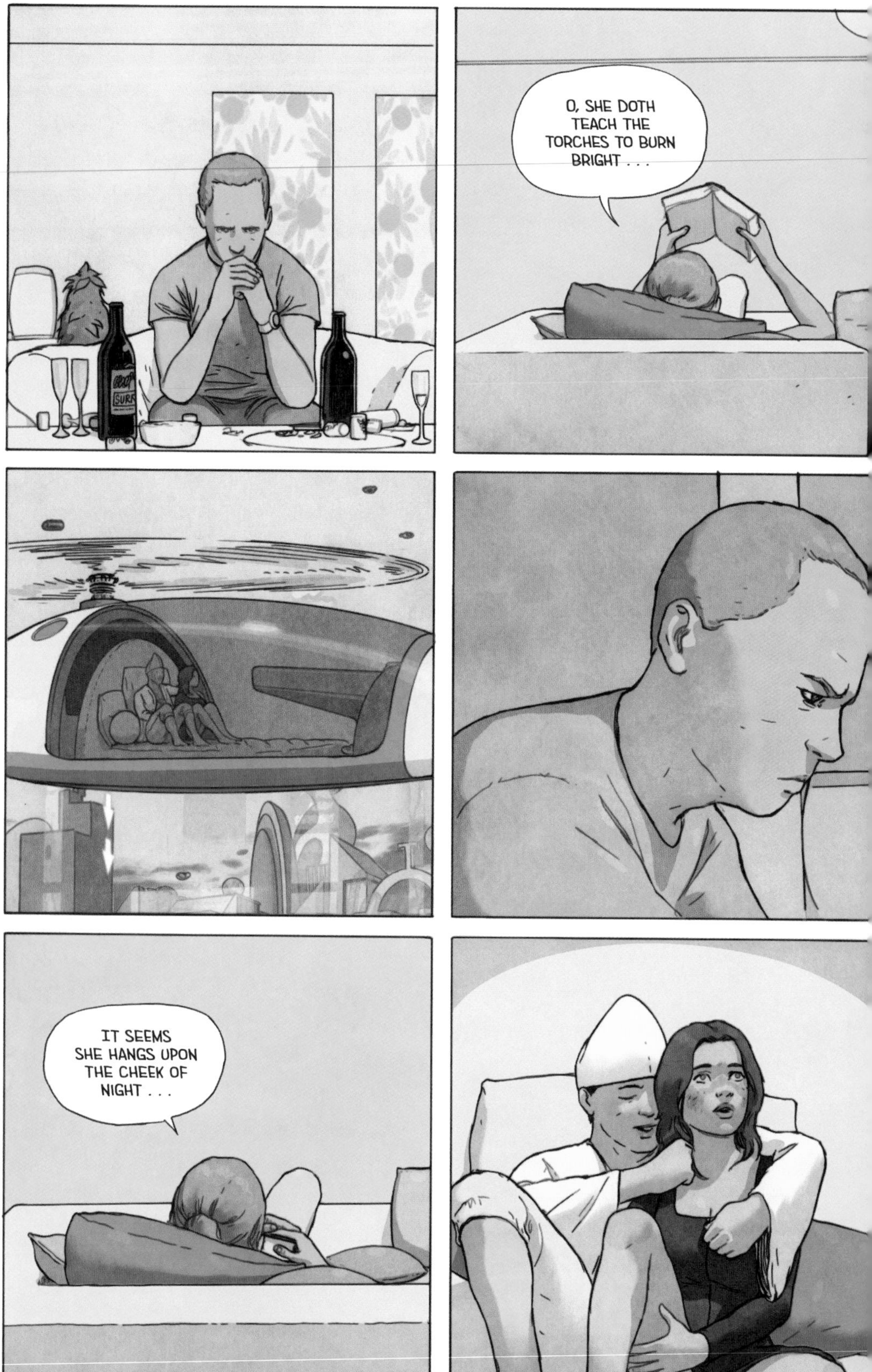
SURF
O, SHE DOTH TEACH THE TORCHES TO BURN BRIGHT . . .
IT SEEMS SHE HANGS UPON THE CHEEK OF NIGHT . . .

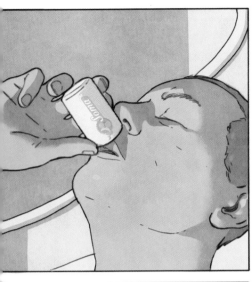

LIKE A RICH JEWEL IN AN ETHIOP'S EAR . . .

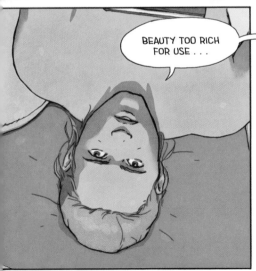

BEAUTY TOO RICH FOR USE . . .

FOR EARTH TOO DEAR.

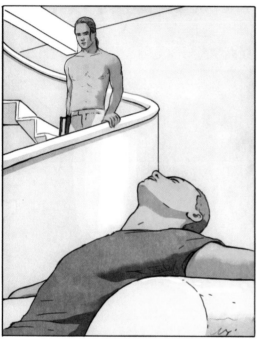

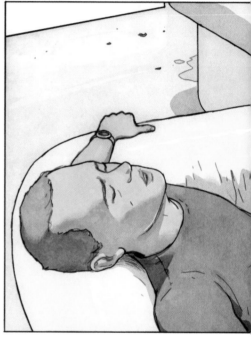

YOU'RE MORE LIKE YOU WERE AT MALPAIS. DO YOU REMEMBER WHEN WE FIRST TALKED TOGETHER?

YOU'RE LIKE WHAT YOU WERE THEN.

BECAUSE I'M UNHAPPY AGAIN, THAT'S WHY.

WELL, I'D RATHER BE UNHAPPY THAN HAVE THE SORT OF FALSE, LYING HAPPINESS YOU WERE HAVING HERE.

I LIKE THAT! WHEN IT'S YOU WHO WERE THE CAUSE OF IT ALL. REFUSING TO COME TO MY PARTY AND SO TURNING THEM ALL AGAINST ME!

I'VE ASKED MY ESTRANGED FRIEND HELMHOLTZ OVER. I THINK YOU'LL GET ON--HE, TOO, DISAPPROVES OF MY RECENT . . . WELL . . .

HE APPEARS TO HAVE FORGIVEN ME, IN ANY CASE. HE AT LEAST WAS SYMPATHETIC TO MY MISERABLE TALE.

TAP TAP TAP

TAP TAP

BOOP

HELMHOLTZ, YOU'VE MET JOHN THE SAVAGE.

GOOD TO SEE YOU AGAIN, JOHN.

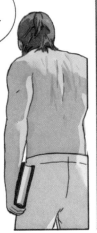

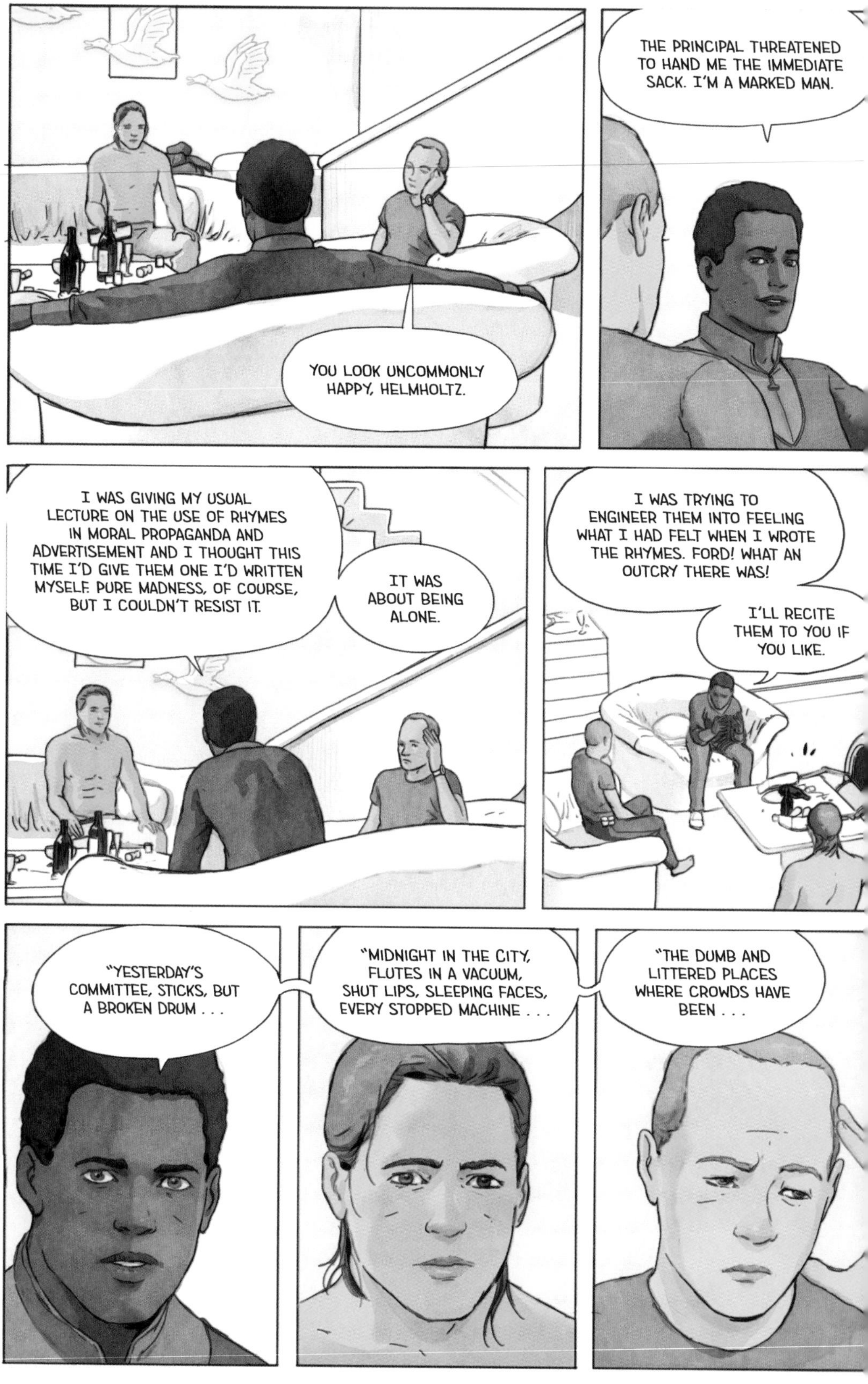
YOU LOOK UNCOMMONLY HAPPY, HELMHOLTZ.
THE PRINCIPAL THREATENED TO HAND ME THE IMMEDIATE SACK. I'M A MARKED MAN.
I WAS GIVING MY USUAL LECTURE ON THE USE OF RHYMES IN MORAL PROPAGANDA AND ADVERTISEMENT AND I THOUGHT THIS TIME I'D GIVE THEM ONE I'D WRITTEN MYSELF. PURE MADNESS, OF COURSE, BUT I COULDN'T RESIST IT.
IT WAS ABOUT BEING ALONE.
I WAS TRYING TO ENGINEER THEM INTO FEELING WHAT I HAD FELT WHEN I WROTE THE RHYMES. FORD! WHAT AN OUTCRY THERE WAS!
I'LL RECITE THEM TO YOU IF YOU LIKE.
"YESTERDAY'S COMMITTEE, STICKS, BUT A BROKEN DRUM . . .
"MIDNIGHT IN THE CITY, FLUTES IN A VACUUM, SHUT LIPS, SLEEPING FACES, EVERY STOPPED MACHINE . . .
"THE DUMB AND LITTERED PLACES WHERE CROWDS HAVE BEEN . . .

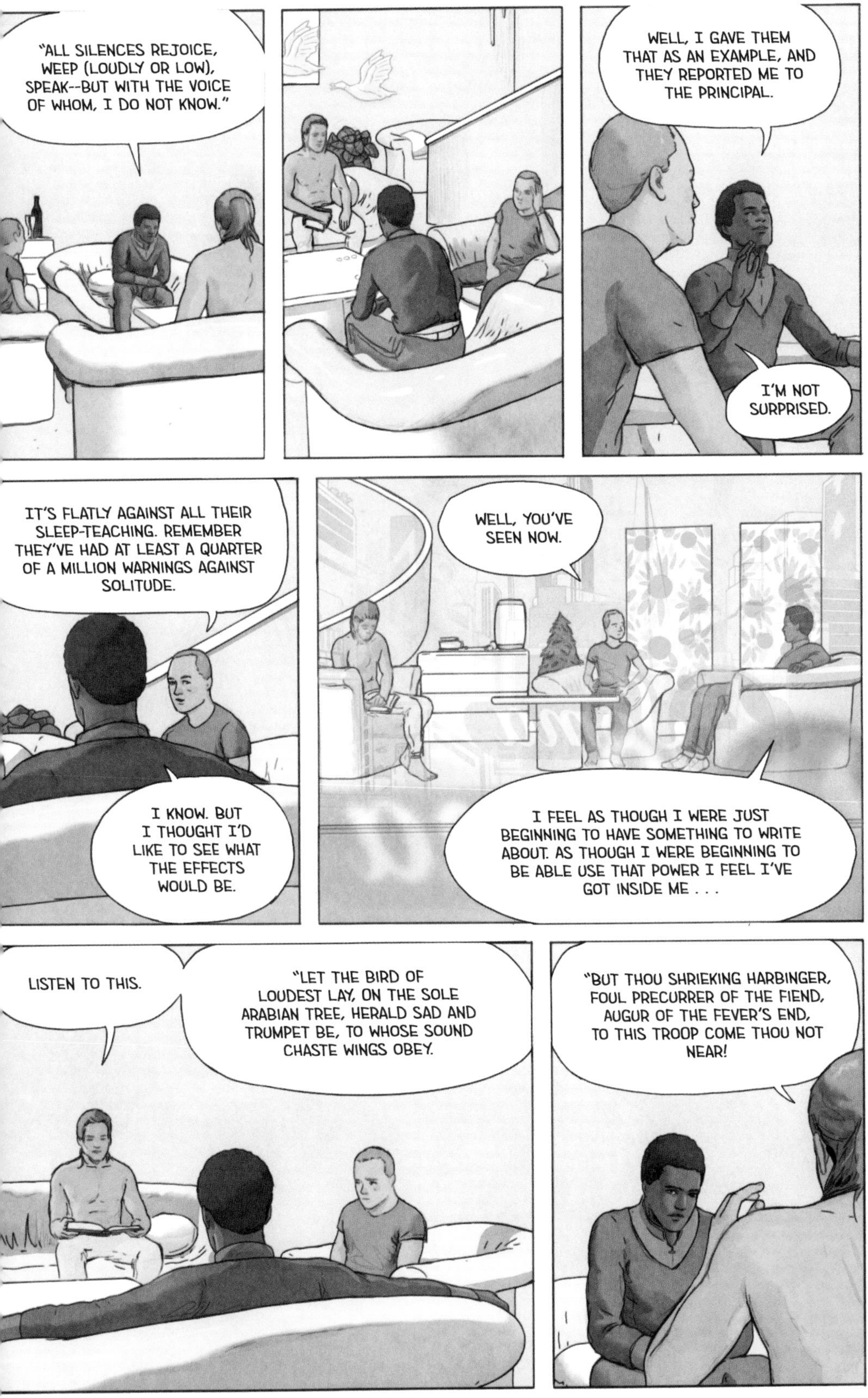
"ALL SILENCES REJOICE, WEEP (LOUDLY OR LOW), SPEAK--BUT WITH THE VOICE OF WHOM, I DO NOT KNOW."
WELL, I GAVE THEM THAT AS AN EXAMPLE, AND THEY REPORTED ME TO THE PRINCIPAL.
I'M NOT SURPRISED.
IT'S FLATLY AGAINST ALL THEIR SLEEP-TEACHING. REMEMBER THEY'VE HAD AT LEAST A QUARTER OF A MILLION WARNINGS AGAINST SOLITUDE.
I KNOW. BUT I THOUGHT I'D LIKE TO SEE WHAT THE EFFECTS WOULD BE.
WELL, YOU'VE SEEN NOW.
I FEEL AS THOUGH I WERE JUST BEGINNING TO HAVE SOMETHING TO WRITE ABOUT. AS THOUGH I WERE BEGINNING TO BE ABLE USE THAT POWER I FEEL I'VE GOT INSIDE ME . . .
LISTEN TO THIS.
"LET THE BIRD OF LOUDEST LAY, ON THE SOLE ARABIAN TREE, HERALD SAD AND TRUMPET BE, TO WHOSE SOUND CHASTE WINGS OBEY.
"BUT THOU SHRIEKING HARBINGER, FOUL PRECURRER OF THE FIEND, AUGUR OF THE FEVER'S END, TO THIS TROOP COME THOU NOT NEAR!

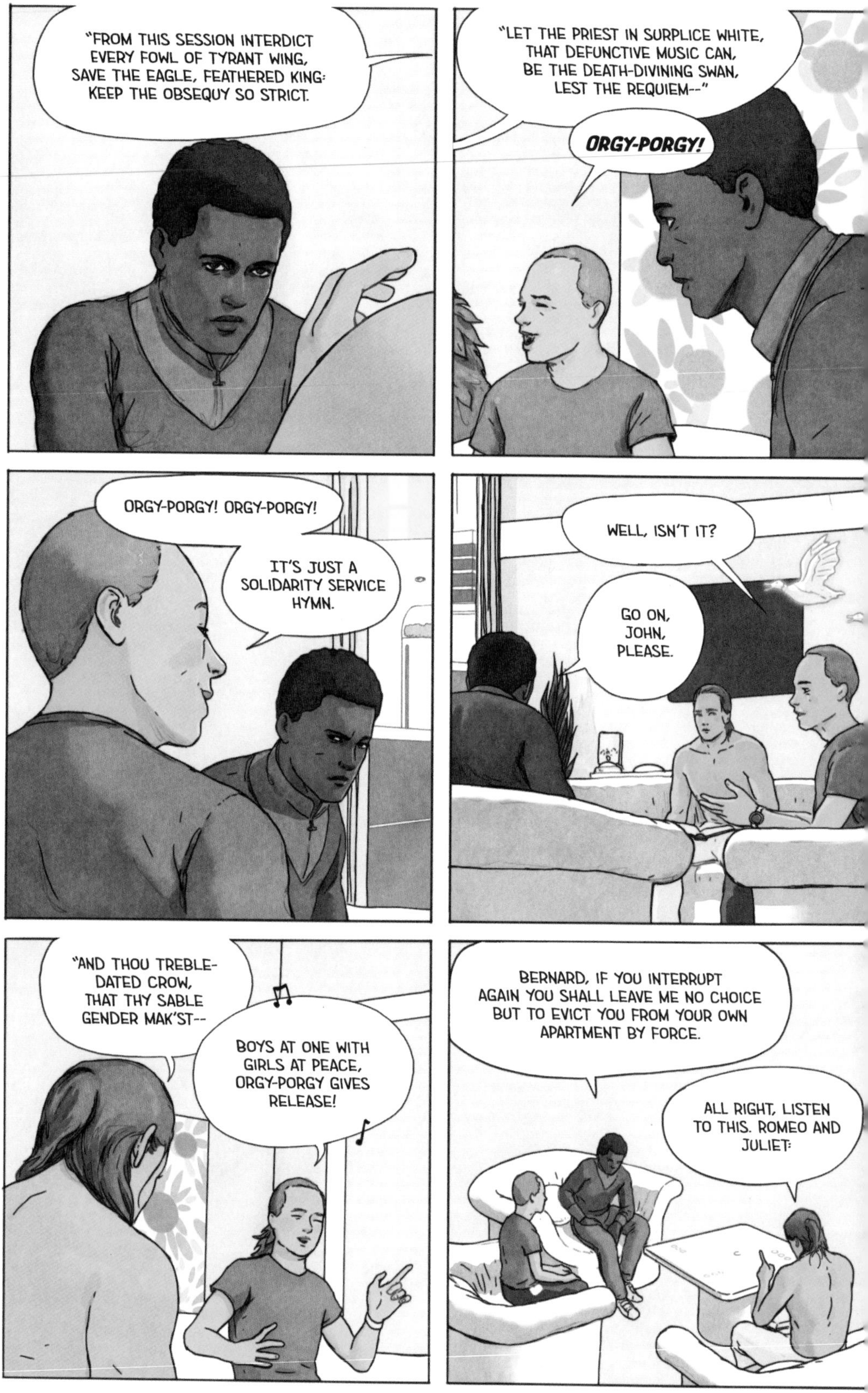
"FROM THIS SESSION INTERDICT EVERY FOWL OF TYRANT WING, SAVE THE EAGLE, FEATHERED KING: KEEP THE OBSEQUY SO STRICT.
"LET THE PRIEST IN SURPLICE WHITE, THAT DEFUNCTIVE MUSIC CAN, BE THE DEATH-DIVINING SWAN, LEST THE REQUIEM--"
ORGY-PORGY!
ORGY-PORGY! ORGY-PORGY!
IT'S JUST A SOLIDARITY SERVICE HYMN.
WELL, ISN'T IT?
GO ON, JOHN, PLEASE.
"AND THOU TREBLE-DATED CROW, THAT THY SABLE GENDER MAK'ST--
BOYS AT ONE WITH GIRLS AT PEACE, ORGY-PORGY GIVES RELEASE!
BERNARD, IF YOU INTERRUPT AGAIN YOU SHALL LEAVE ME NO CHOICE BUT TO EVICT YOU FROM YOUR OWN APARTMENT BY FORCE.
ALL RIGHT, LISTEN TO THIS. ROMEO AND JULIET:

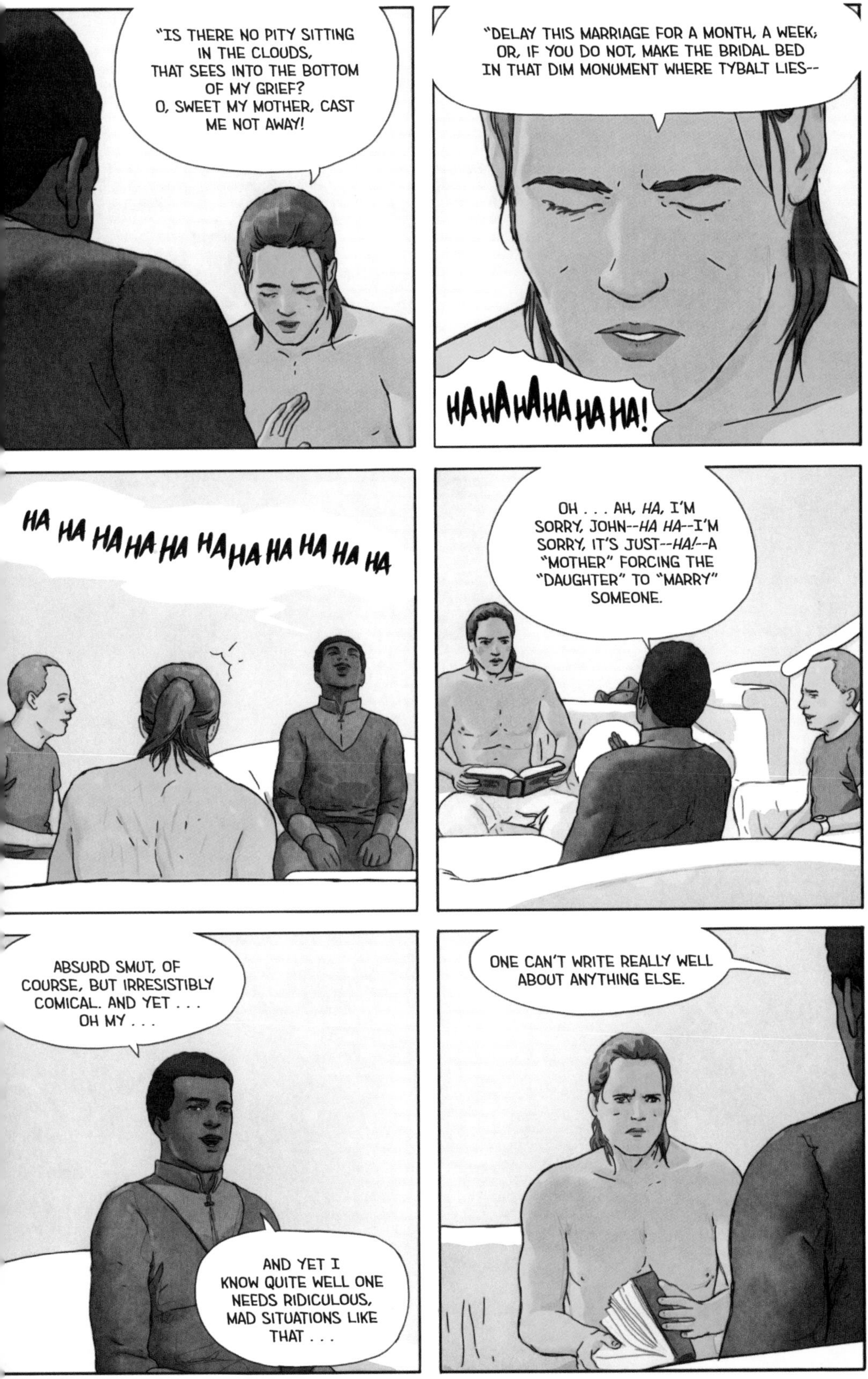
"IS THERE NO PITY SITTING IN THE CLOUDS, THAT SEES INTO THE BOTTOM OF MY GRIEF? O, SWEET MY MOTHER, CAST ME NOT AWAY!
"DELAY THIS MARRIAGE FOR A MONTH, A WEEK; OR, IF YOU DO NOT, MAKE THE BRIDAL BED IN THAT DIM MONUMENT WHERE TYBALT LIES--
HA HA HA HA HA HA!
HA HA HA HA HA HA HA HA HA HA HA HA
OH . . . AH, *HA*, I'M SORRY, JOHN--*HA HA*--I'M SORRY, IT'S JUST--*HA!*--A "MOTHER" FORCING THE "DAUGHTER" TO "MARRY" SOMEONE.
ABSURD SMUT, OF COURSE, BUT IRRESISTIBLY COMICAL. AND YET . . . OH MY . . .
AND YET I KNOW QUITE WELL ONE NEEDS RIDICULOUS, MAD SITUATIONS LIKE THAT . . .
ONE CAN'T WRITE REALLY WELL ABOUT ANYTHING ELSE.

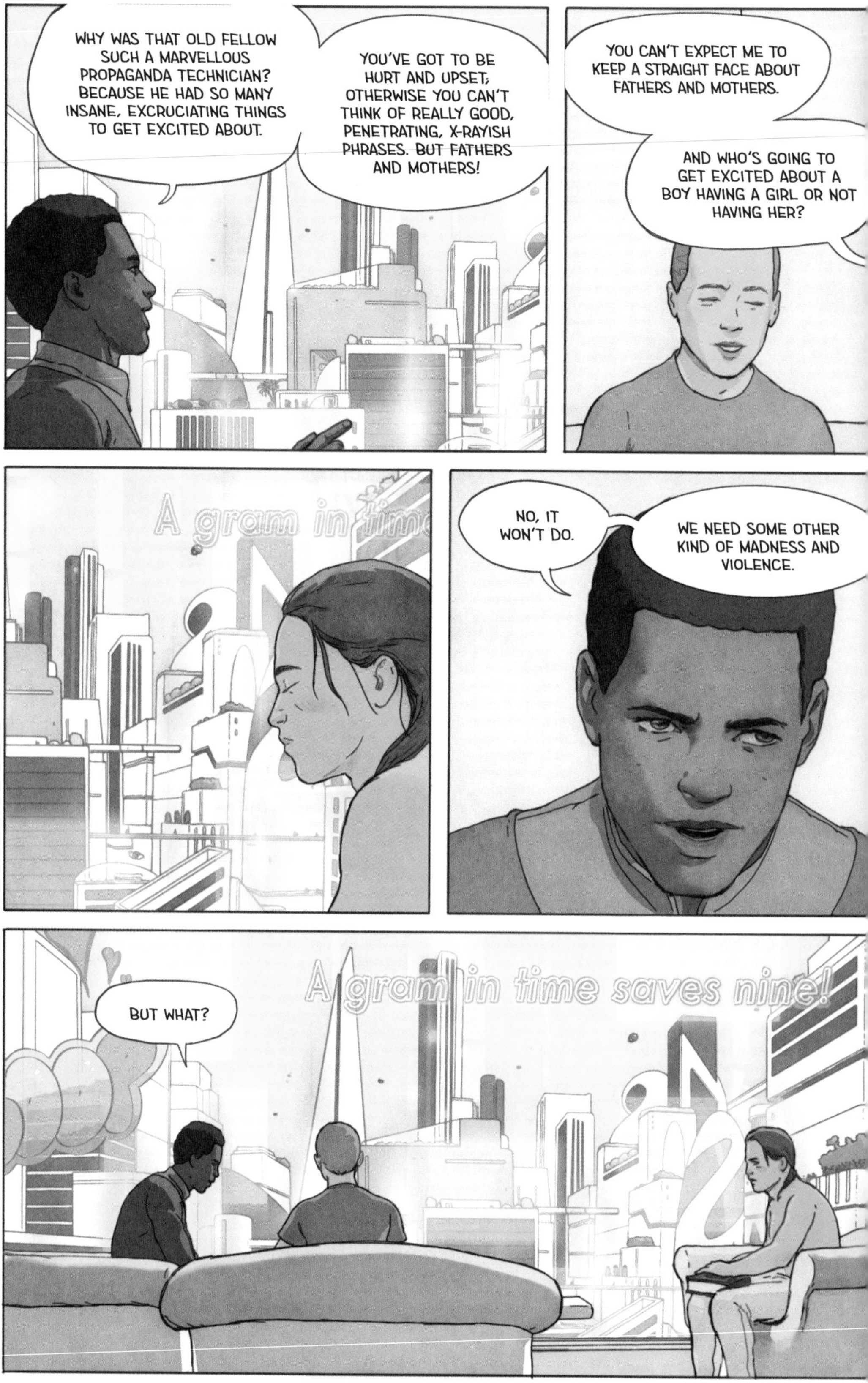
WHY WAS THAT OLD FELLOW SUCH A MARVELLOUS PROPAGANDA TECHNICIAN? BECAUSE HE HAD SO MANY INSANE, EXCRUCIATING THINGS TO GET EXCITED ABOUT.
YOU'VE GOT TO BE HURT AND UPSET; OTHERWISE YOU CAN'T THINK OF REALLY GOOD, PENETRATING, X-RAYISH PHRASES. BUT FATHERS AND MOTHERS!
YOU CAN'T EXPECT ME TO KEEP A STRAIGHT FACE ABOUT FATHERS AND MOTHERS.
AND WHO'S GOING TO GET EXCITED ABOUT A BOY HAVING A GIRL OR NOT HAVING HER?
A gram in time
NO, IT WON'T DO.
WE NEED SOME OTHER KIND OF MADNESS AND VIOLENCE.
A gram in time saves nine!
BUT WHAT?

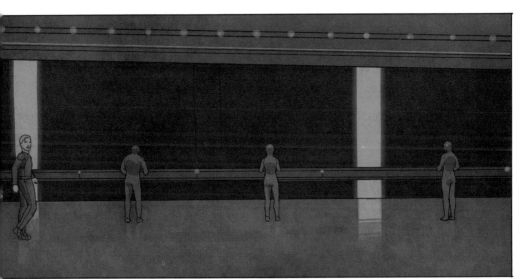

LIKE TO COME TO A FEELY THIS EVENING, LENINA?

NOT THIS EVENING.

GOING OUT WITH SOMEONE ELSE?

NO.

YOU'RE NOT FEELING ILL, ARE YOU?

NO.

ANYHOW, YOU OUGHT TO GO AND SEE THE DOCTOR.

YOU MAY NEED A PREGNANCY SUBSTITUTE. OR ELSE AN EXTRA STRONG VPS TREATMENT.

SOMETIMES, YOU KNOW, THE STANDARD PASSION SURROGATE ISN'T QUITE--

OH, FOR FORD'S SAKE, SHUT UP!

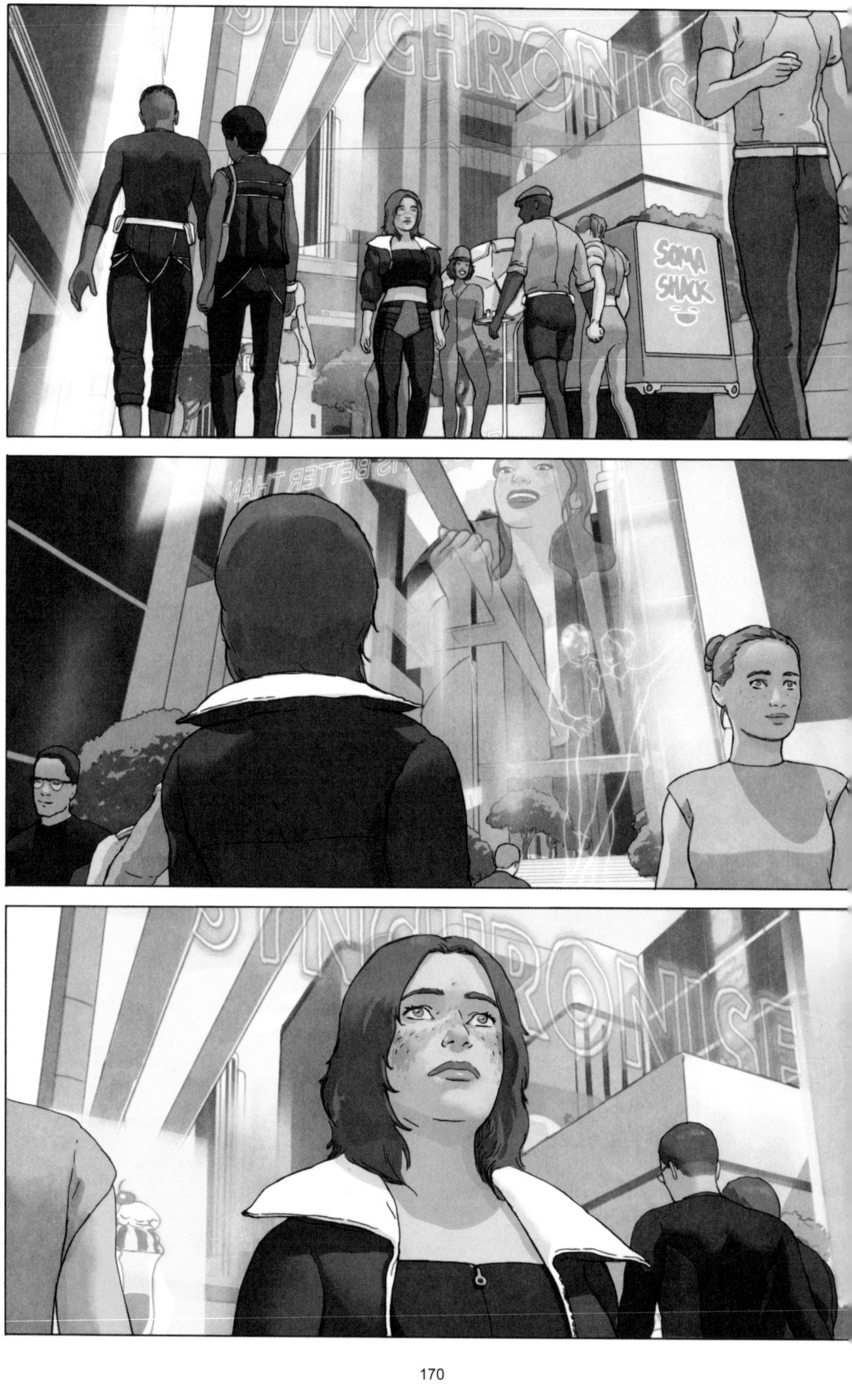
SOMA SHACK

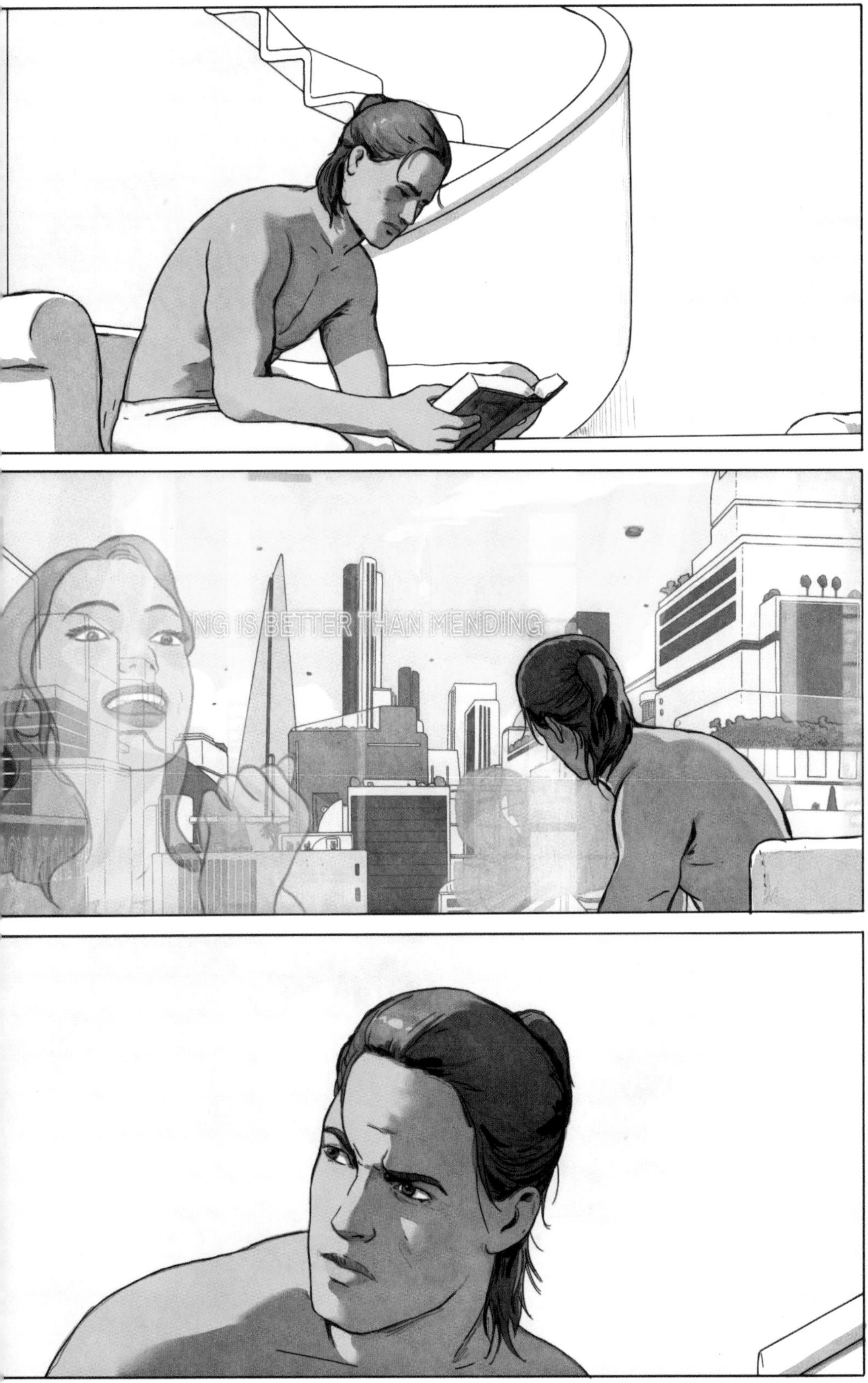
NG IS BETTER THAN MENDING

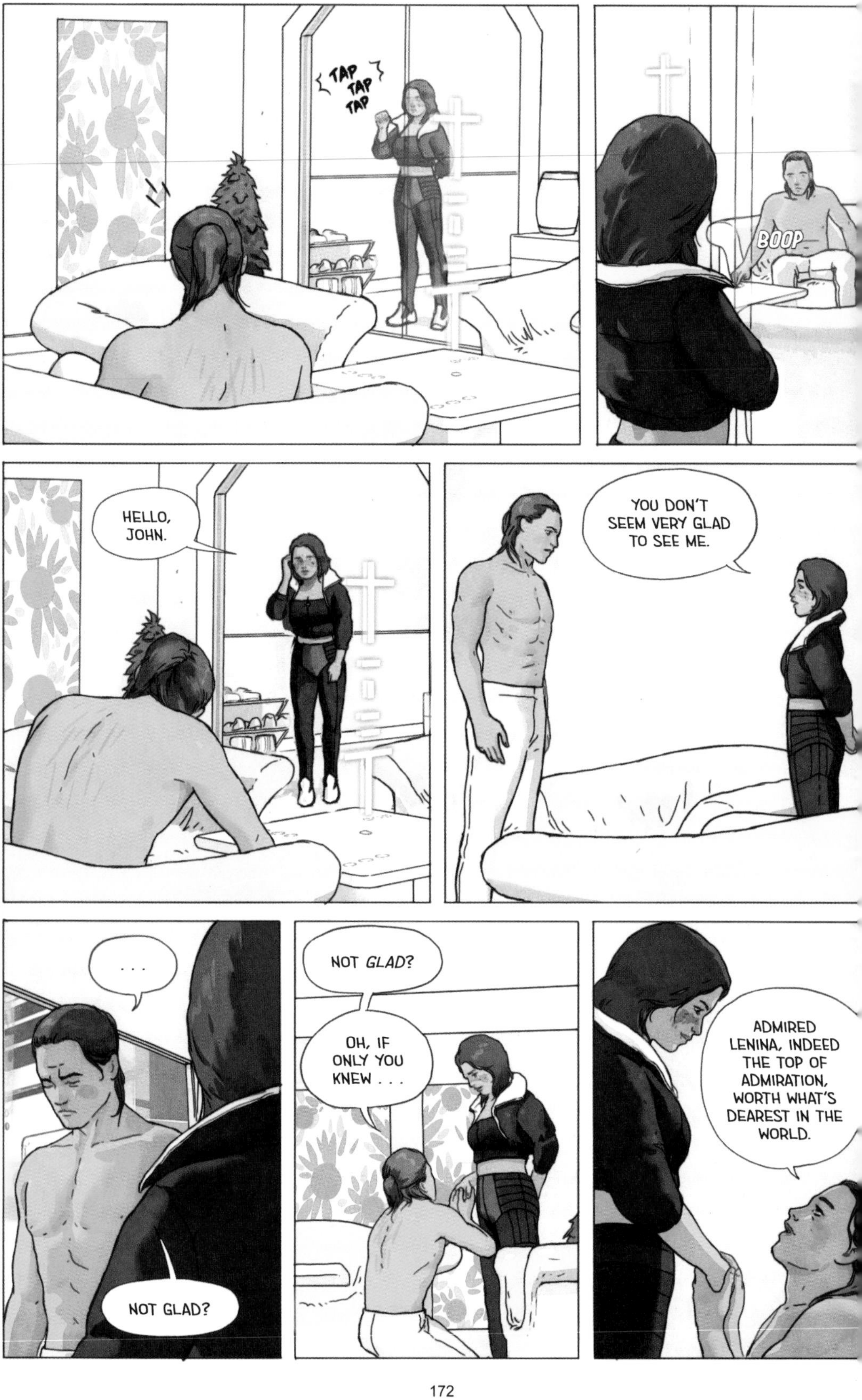
TAP TAP TAP
BOOP
HELLO, JOHN.
YOU DON'T SEEM VERY GLAD TO SEE ME.
. . .
NOT GLAD?
NOT *GLAD*?
OH, IF ONLY YOU KNEW . . .
ADMIRED LENINA, INDEED THE TOP OF ADMIRATION, WORTH WHAT'S DEAREST IN THE WORLD.

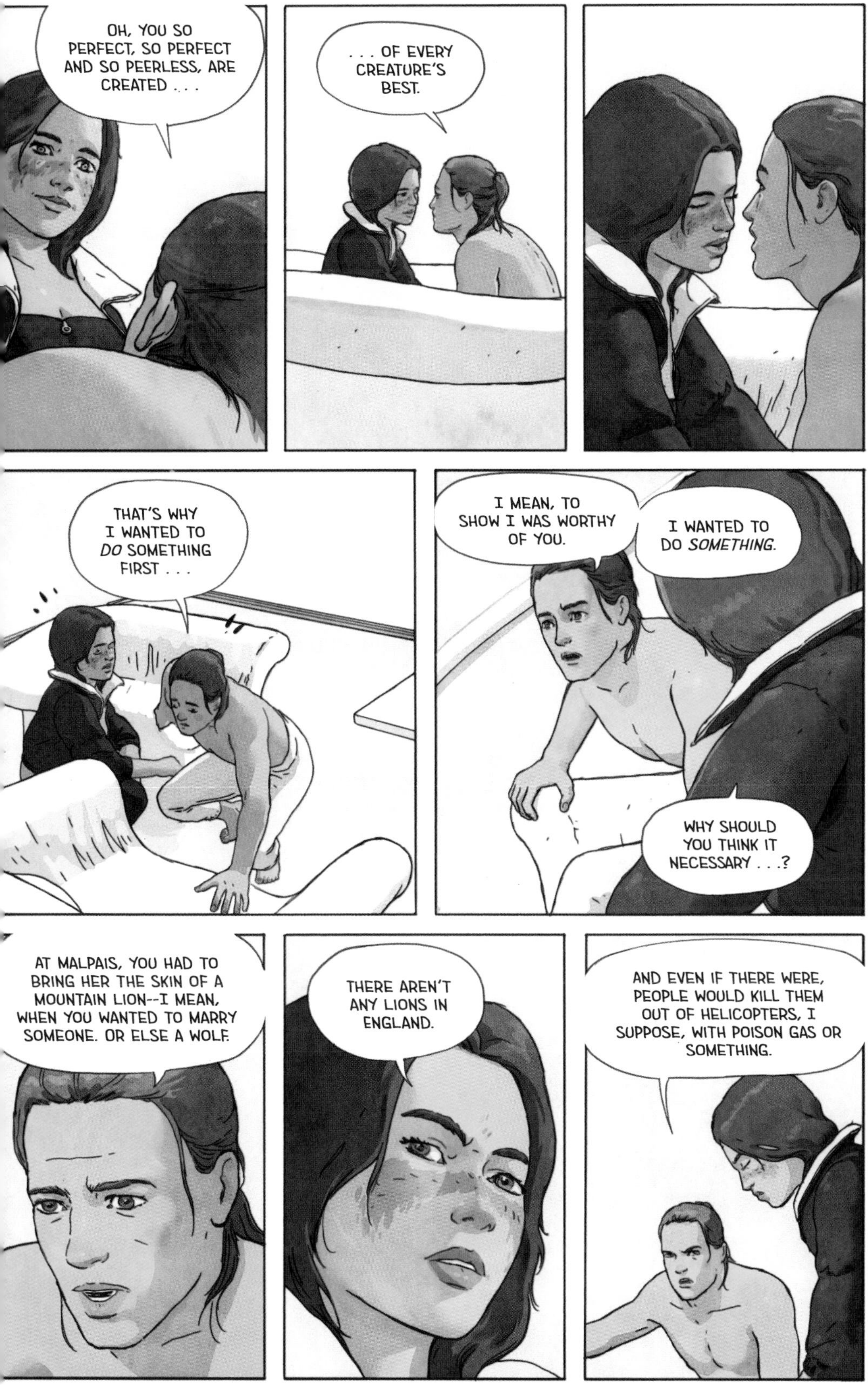
OH, YOU SO PERFECT, SO PERFECT AND SO PEERLESS, ARE CREATED . . .
. . . OF EVERY CREATURE'S BEST.
THAT'S WHY I WANTED TO *DO* SOMETHING FIRST . . .
I MEAN, TO SHOW I WAS WORTHY OF YOU.
I WANTED TO DO *SOMETHING.*
WHY SHOULD YOU THINK IT NECESSARY . . .?
AT MALPAIS, YOU HAD TO BRING HER THE SKIN OF A MOUNTAIN LION--I MEAN, WHEN YOU WANTED TO MARRY SOMEONE. OR ELSE A WOLF.
THERE AREN'T ANY LIONS IN ENGLAND.
AND EVEN IF THERE WERE, PEOPLE WOULD KILL THEM OUT OF HELICOPTERS, I SUPPOSE, WITH POISON GAS OR SOMETHING.

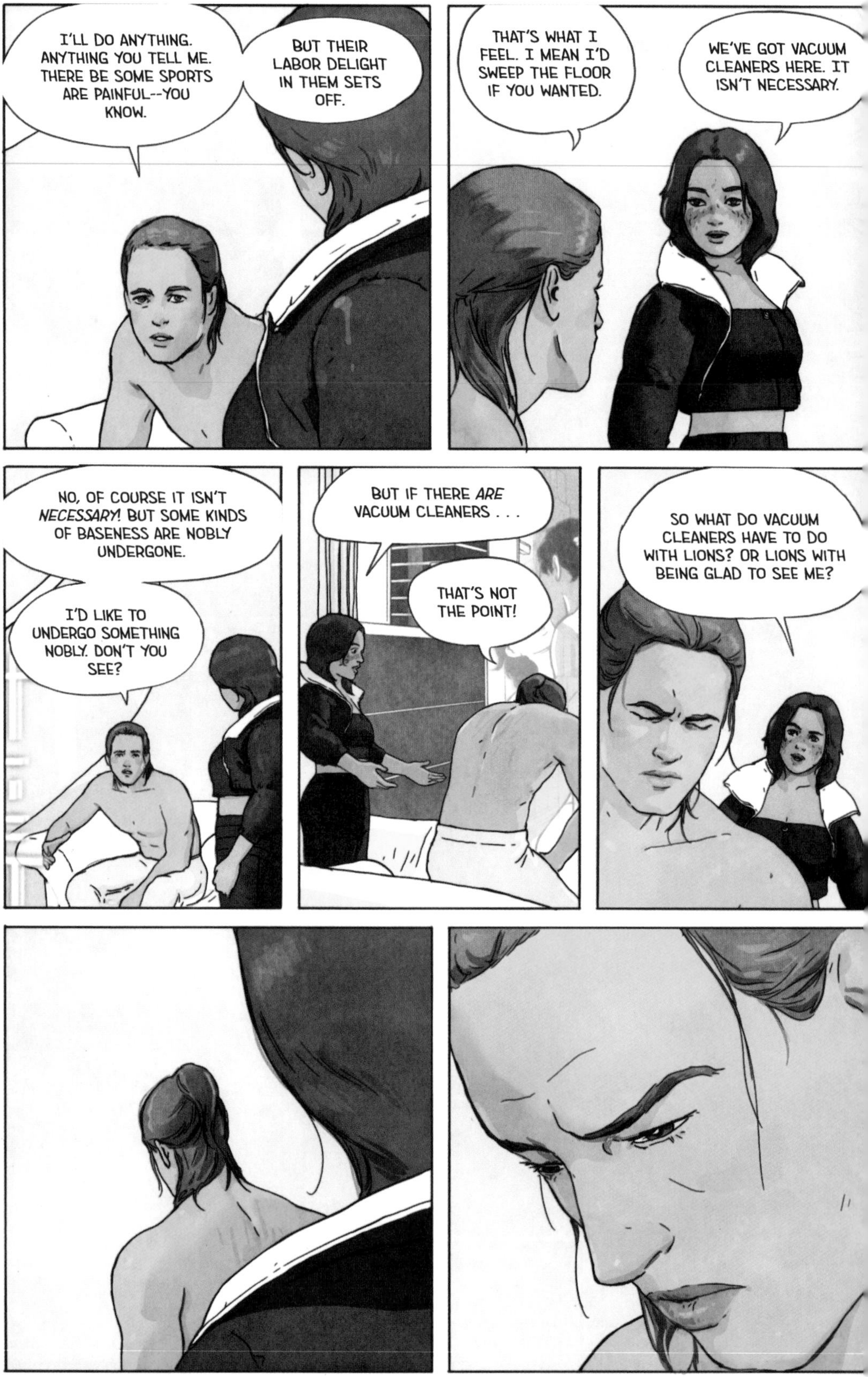
I'LL DO ANYTHING. ANYTHING YOU TELL ME. THERE BE SOME SPORTS ARE PAINFUL--YOU KNOW.
BUT THEIR LABOR DELIGHT IN THEM SETS OFF.
THAT'S WHAT I FEEL. I MEAN I'D SWEEP THE FLOOR IF YOU WANTED.
WE'VE GOT VACUUM CLEANERS HERE. IT ISN'T NECESSARY.
NO, OF COURSE IT ISN'T *NECESSARY*! BUT SOME KINDS OF BASENESS ARE NOBLY UNDERGONE.
I'D LIKE TO UNDERGO SOMETHING NOBLY. DON'T YOU SEE?
BUT IF THERE *ARE* VACUUM CLEANERS . . .
THAT'S NOT THE POINT!
SO WHAT DO VACUUM CLEANERS HAVE TO DO WITH LIONS? OR LIONS WITH BEING GLAD TO SEE ME?

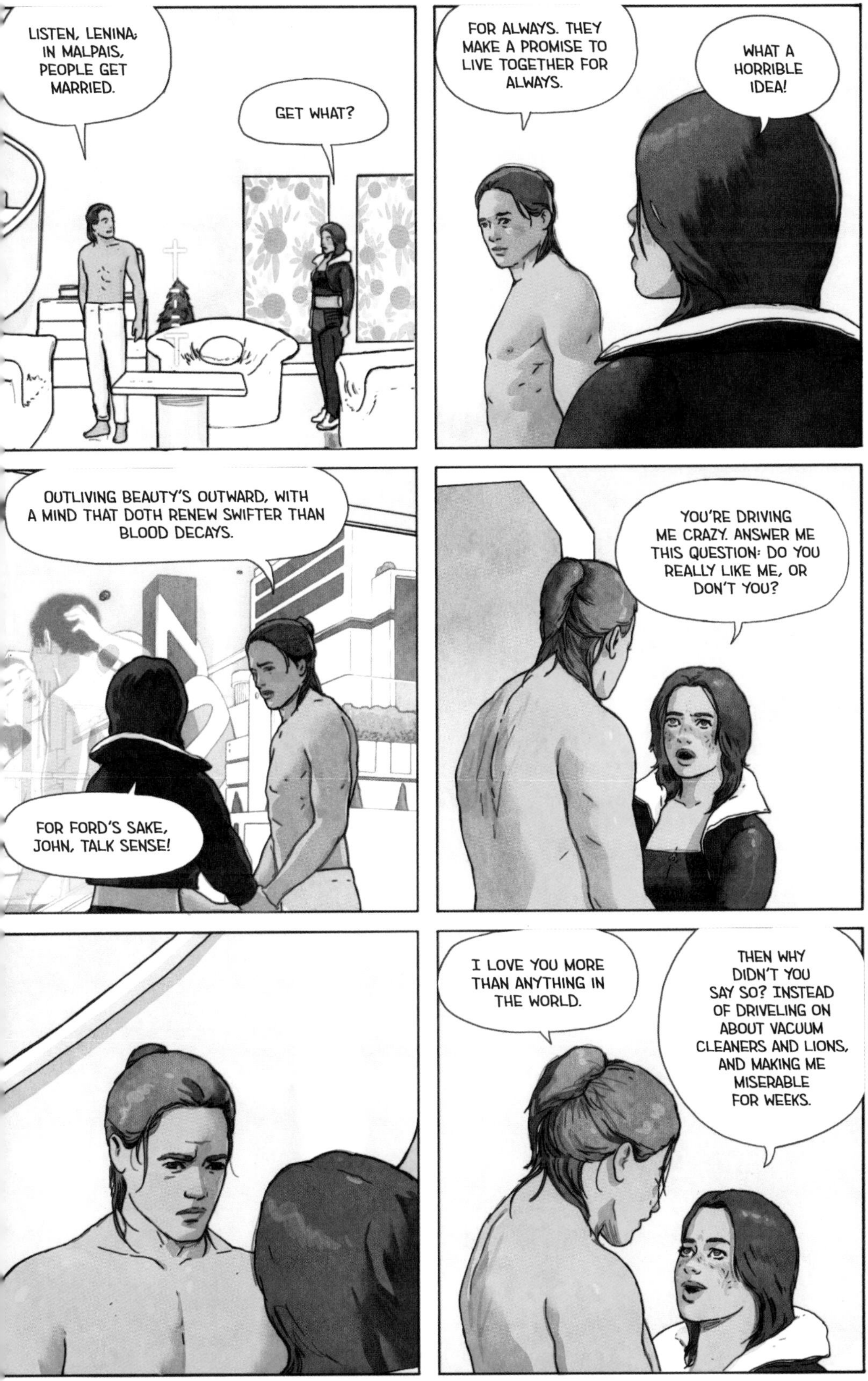
LISTEN, LENINA; IN MALPAIS, PEOPLE GET MARRIED.
GET WHAT?
FOR ALWAYS. THEY MAKE A PROMISE TO LIVE TOGETHER FOR ALWAYS.
WHAT A HORRIBLE IDEA!
OUTLIVING BEAUTY'S OUTWARD, WITH A MIND THAT DOTH RENEW SWIFTER THAN BLOOD DECAYS.
FOR FORD'S SAKE, JOHN, TALK SENSE!
YOU'RE DRIVING ME CRAZY. ANSWER ME THIS QUESTION: DO YOU REALLY LIKE ME, OR DON'T YOU?
I LOVE YOU MORE THAN ANYTHING IN THE WORLD.
THEN WHY DIDN'T YOU SAY SO? INSTEAD OF DRIVELING ON ABOUT VACUUM CLEANERS AND LIONS, AND MAKING ME MISERABLE FOR WEEKS.

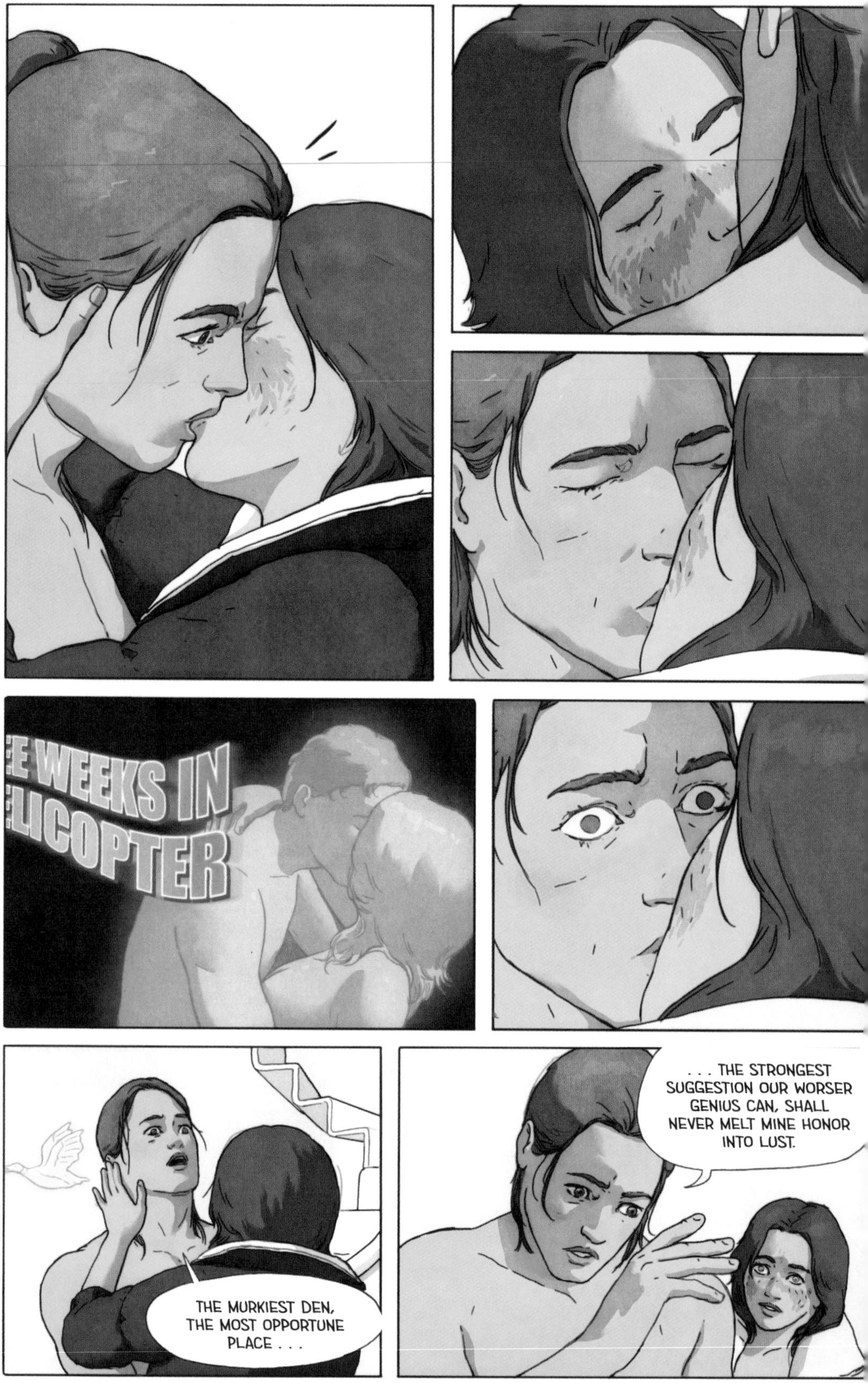

EE WEEKS IN
ELICOPTER
THE MURKIEST DEN, THE MOST OPPORTUNE PLACE . . .
. . . THE STRONGEST SUGGESTION OUR WORSER GENIUS CAN, SHALL NEVER MELT MINE HONOR INTO LUST.

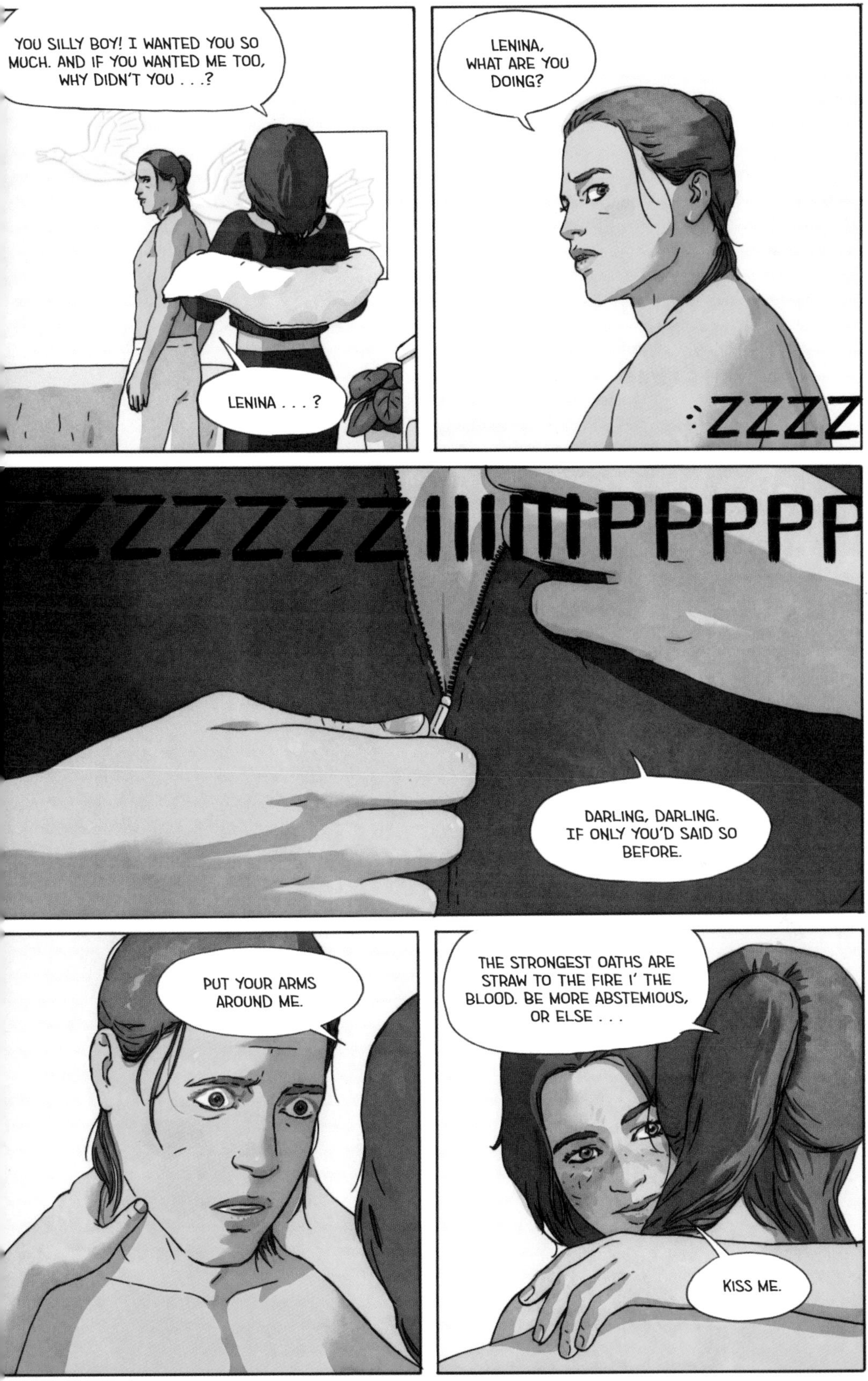

YOU SILLY BOY! I WANTED YOU SO MUCH. AND IF YOU WANTED ME TOO, WHY DIDN'T YOU . . .?
LENINA . . . ?
LENINA, WHAT ARE YOU DOING?
ZZZZ
ZZZZZZZIIIIIPPPPP
DARLING, DARLING. IF ONLY YOU'D SAID SO BEFORE.
PUT YOUR ARMS AROUND ME.
THE STRONGEST OATHS ARE STRAW TO THE FIRE I' THE BLOOD. BE MORE ABSTEMIOUS, OR ELSE . . .
KISS ME.

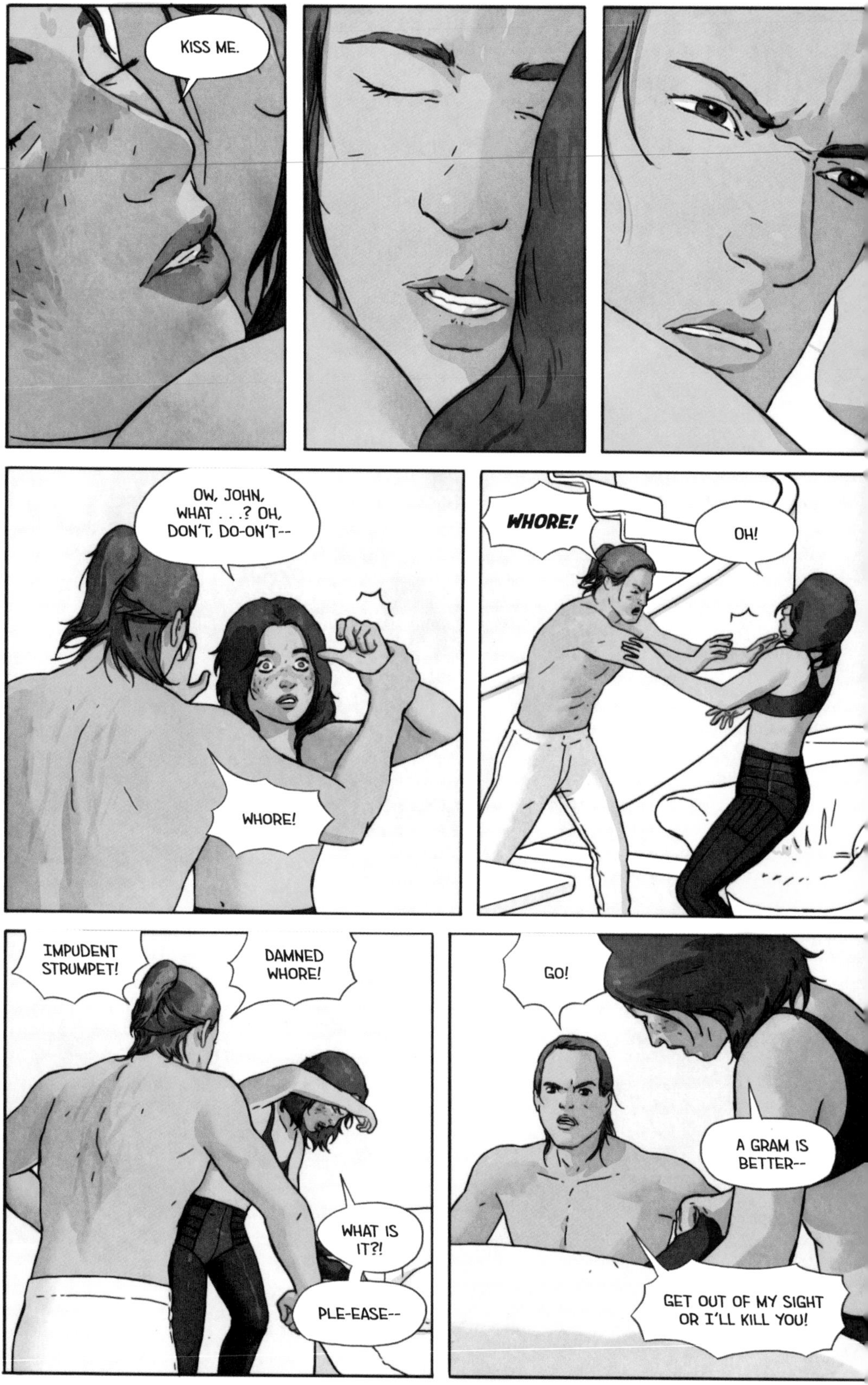
KISS ME.
OW, JOHN, WHAT . . .? OH, DON'T, DO-ON'T--
WHORE!
WHORE!
OH!
IMPUDENT STRUMPET!
DAMNED WHORE!
WHAT IS IT?!
PLE-EASE--
GO!
A GRAM IS BETTER--
GET OUT OF MY SIGHT OR I'LL KILL YOU!

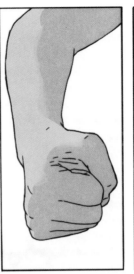

CLICK
CLICK
CLICK

BING

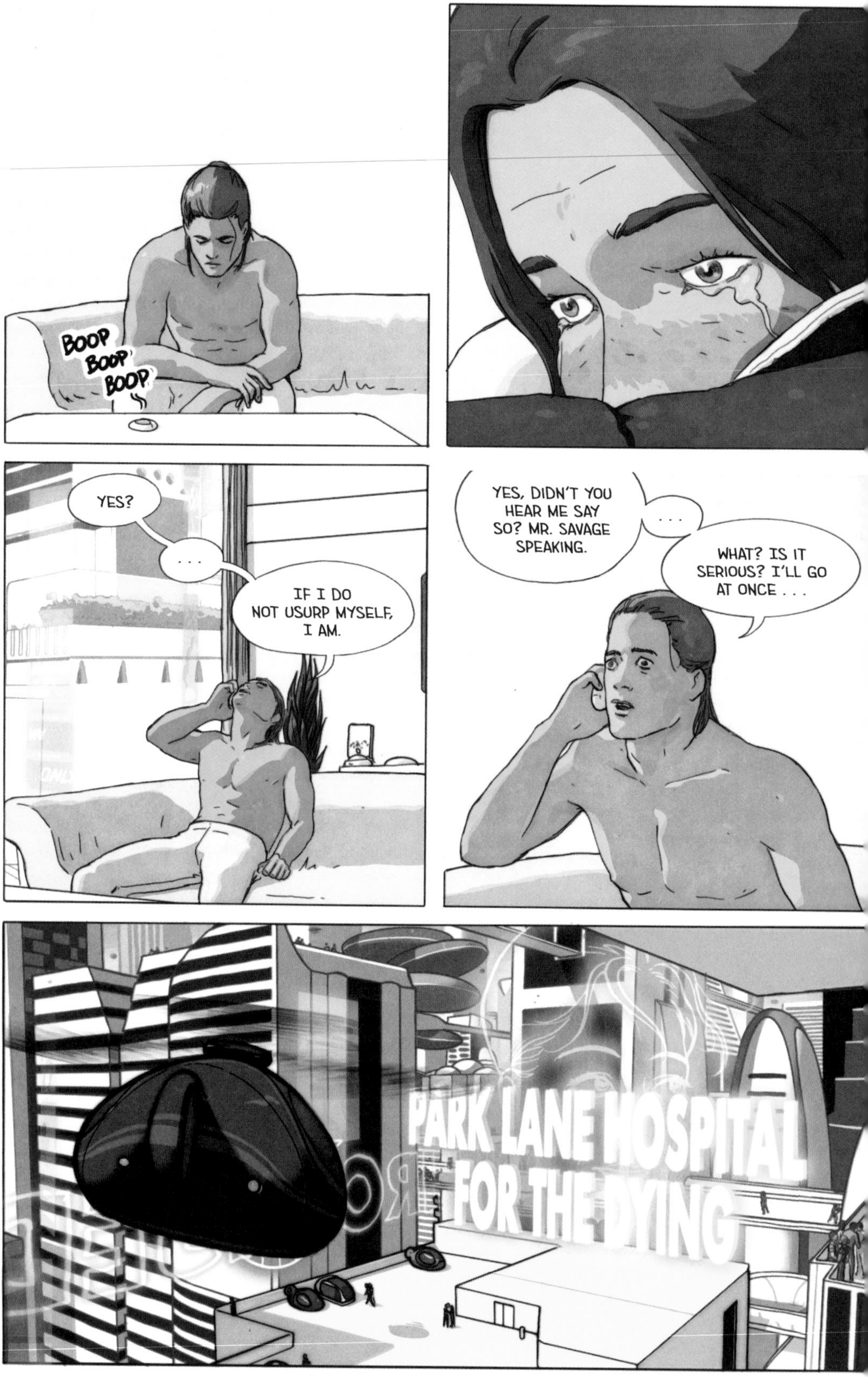
BOOP BOOP BOOP
YES?
. . .
IF I DO NOT USURP MYSELF, I AM.
YES, DIDN'T YOU HEAR ME SAY SO? MR. SAVAGE SPEAKING.
. . .
WHAT? IS IT SERIOUS? I'LL GO AT ONCE . . .
PARK LANE HOSPITAL FOR THE DYING

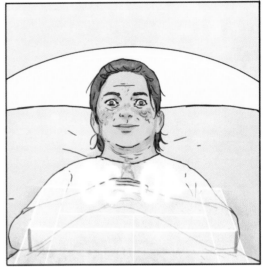

LINDA . . .

MOTHER . . .

A, B, C, VITAMIN D:
THE FAT'S IN THE LIVER,
THE COD'S IN THE
SEA.

. . .

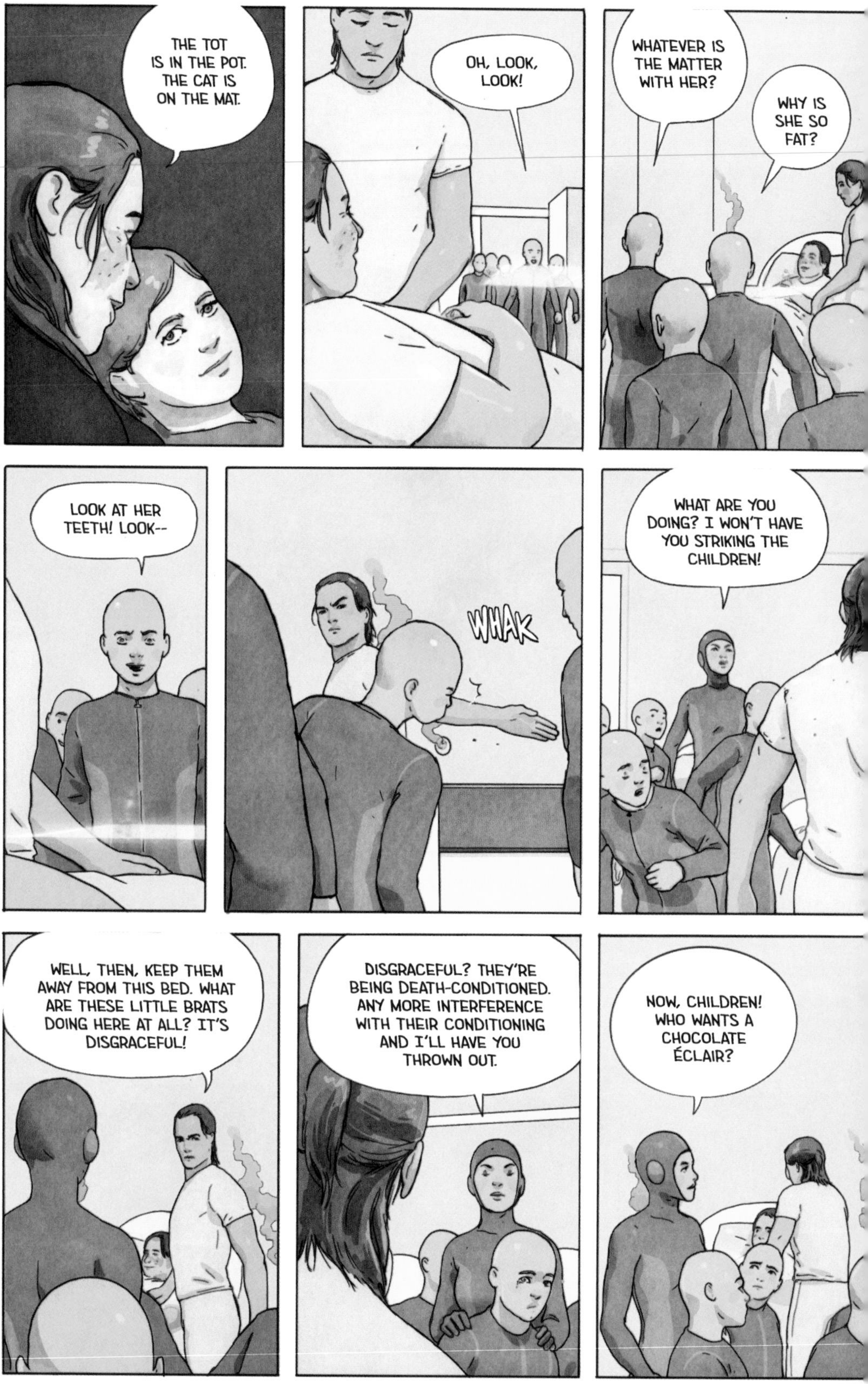
THE TOT IS IN THE POT. THE CAT IS ON THE MAT.
OH, LOOK, LOOK!
WHATEVER IS THE MATTER WITH HER?
WHY IS SHE SO FAT?
LOOK AT HER TEETH! LOOK--
WHAK
WHAT ARE YOU DOING? I WON'T HAVE YOU STRIKING THE CHILDREN!
WELL, THEN, KEEP THEM AWAY FROM THIS BED. WHAT ARE THESE LITTLE BRATS DOING HERE AT ALL? IT'S DISGRACEFUL!
DISGRACEFUL? THEY'RE BEING DEATH-CONDITIONED. ANY MORE INTERFERENCE WITH THEIR CONDITIONING AND I'LL HAVE YOU THROWN OUT.
NOW, CHILDREN! WHO WANTS A CHOCOLATE ÉCLAIR?

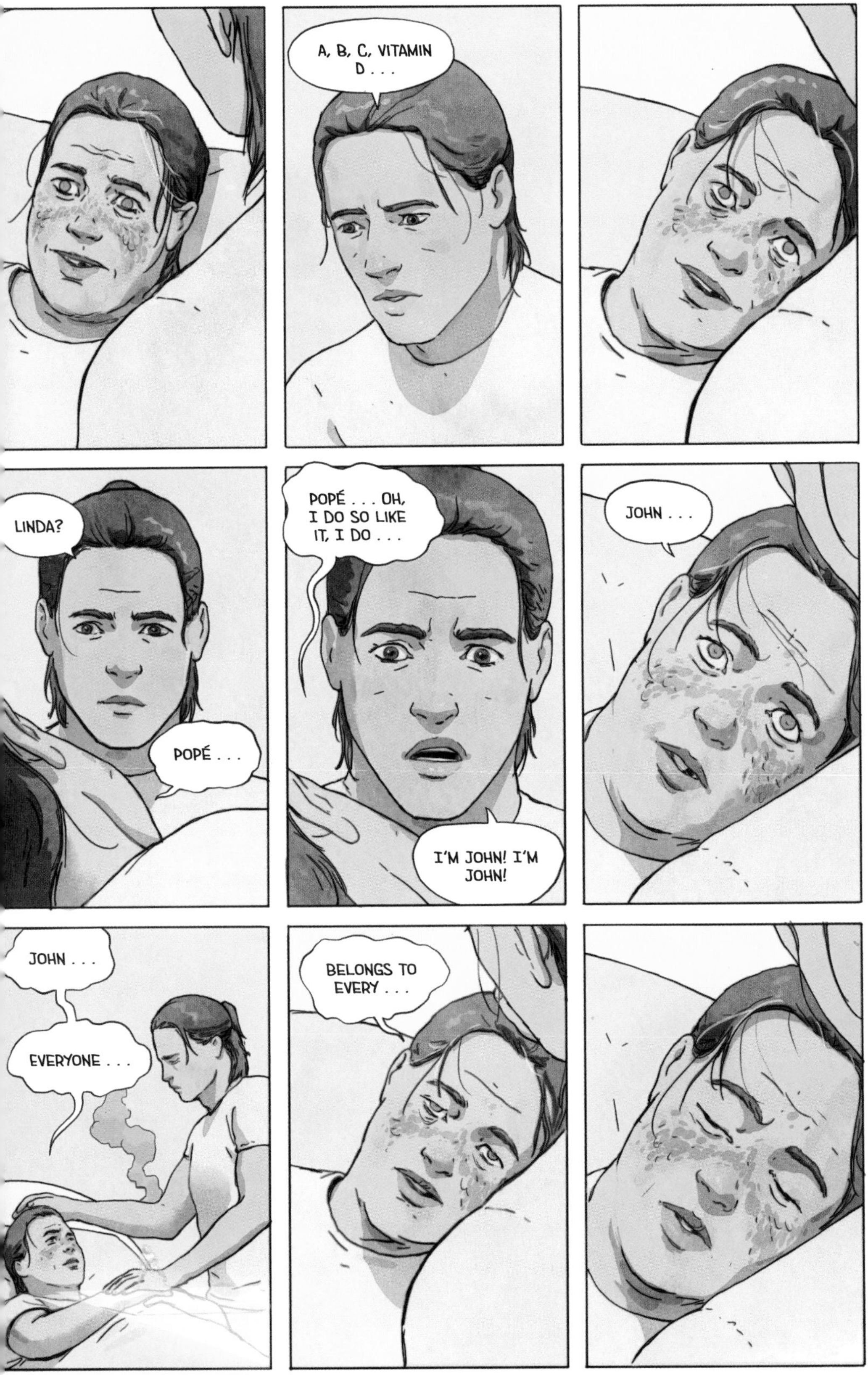
A, B, C, VITAMIN D . . .
LINDA?
POPÉ . . .
POPÉ . . . OH, I DO SO LIKE IT, I DO . . .
I'M JOHN! I'M JOHN!
JOHN . . .
JOHN . . .
EVERYONE . . .
BELONGS TO EVERY . . .

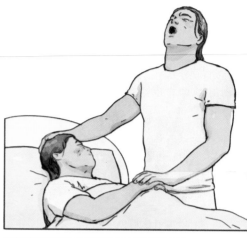

CAN'T YOU BEHAVE?

YOU'LL HAVE SET THESE POOR CHILDREN'S DEATH-CONDITIONING BACK MONTHS WITH THIS SCANDALOUS EXHIBITION.

DISGUSTING OUTCRY, AS THOUGH ANYONE MATTERED AS MUCH AS ALL THAT.

GIVE THEM THE MOST DISASTROUS IDEAS ABOUT THE SUBJECT. MIGHT UPSET THEM INTO REACTING IN THE ENTIRELY WRONG, UTTERLY ANTI-SOCIAL WAY.

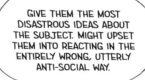
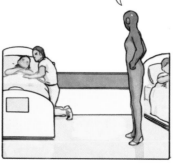

NOT IN HIS OWN ROOMS, NOT IN MINE. WHERE CAN HE HAVE GOT TO?

WE'LL GIVE HIM FIVE MORE MINUTES. IF HE DOESN'T TURN UP BY THEN, WE'LL . . .

BOOP BOOP BOOP

HELLO . . . SPEAKING . . .

FORD IN FLIVVER! I'LL COME AT ONCE.

WHAT IS IT?

I KNOW A FELLOW AT THE PARK LANE HOSPITAL. THE SAVAGE IS THERE. SEEMS TO HAVE GONE MAD.

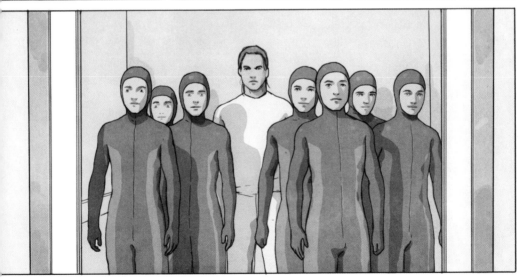

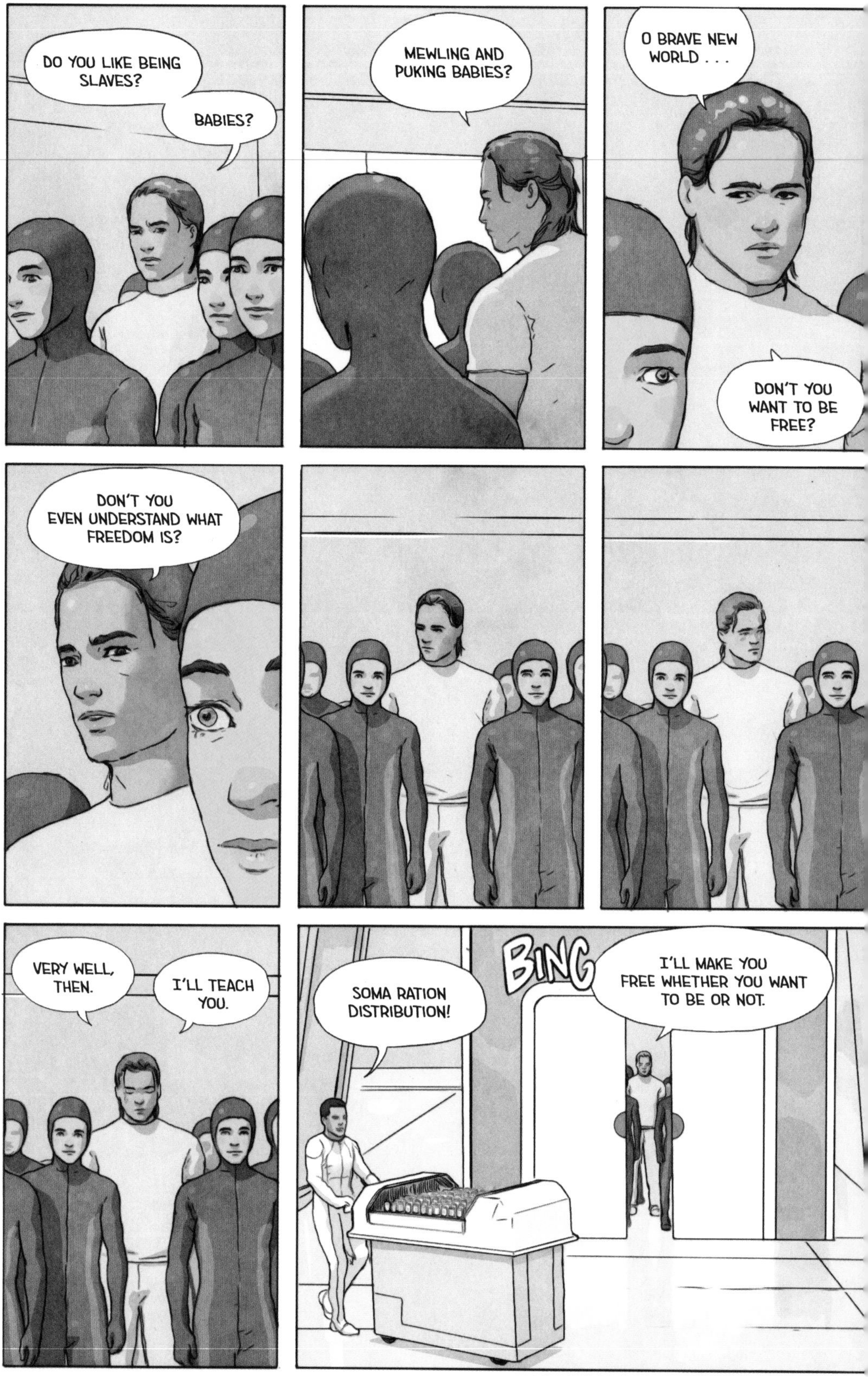
DO YOU LIKE BEING SLAVES?
BABIES?
MEWLING AND PUKING BABIES?
O BRAVE NEW WORLD . . .
DON'T YOU WANT TO BE FREE?
DON'T YOU EVEN UNDERSTAND WHAT FREEDOM IS?
VERY WELL, THEN.
I'LL TEACH YOU.
SOMA RATION DISTRIBUTION!
BING
I'LL MAKE YOU FREE WHETHER YOU WANT TO BE OR NOT.

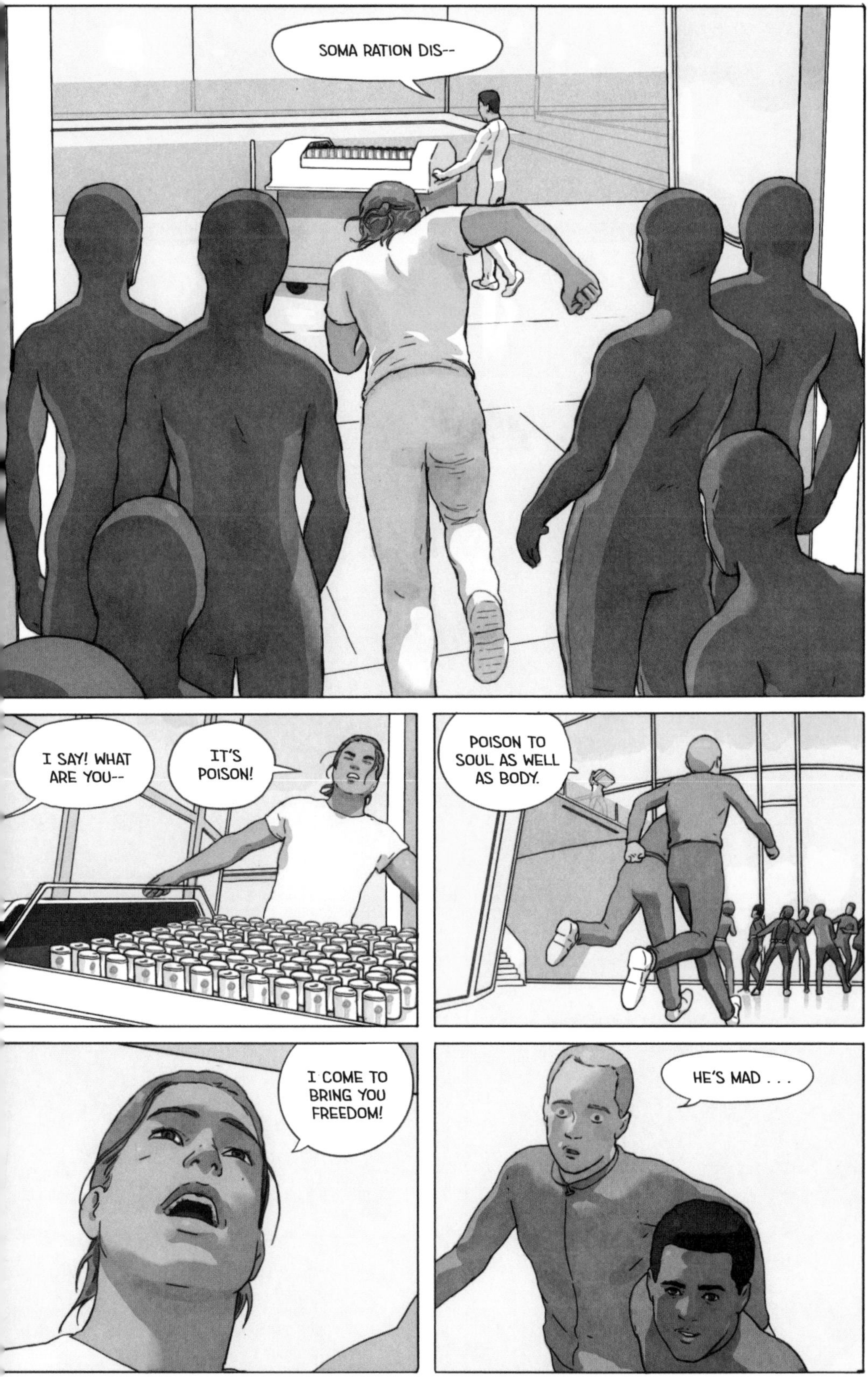
SOMA RATION DIS--
I SAY! WHAT ARE YOU--
IT'S POISON!
POISON TO SOUL AS WELL AS BODY.
I COME TO BRING YOU FREEDOM!
HE'S MAD . . .

FREEDOM!

THEY'LL KILL HIM. THEY'LL . . .

FORD HELP HIM.

FORD HELPS THOSE WHO HELP THEMSELVES!

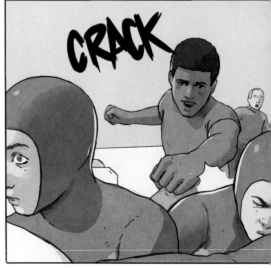

CRACK

FREE, HELMHOLTZ, FREE!
MEN AT LAST!
SOMA SOAKER!
POLICE
POLICE
POLICE
POLICE
POLICE
POLICE
POLICE
BIP
MY FRIENDS, MY FRIENDS!
SED SOMA

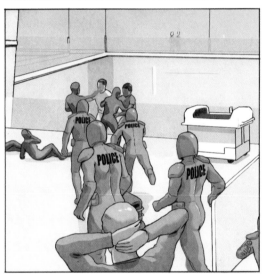

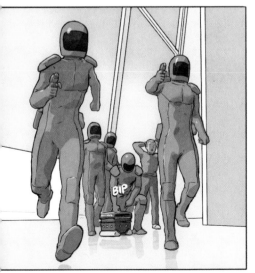

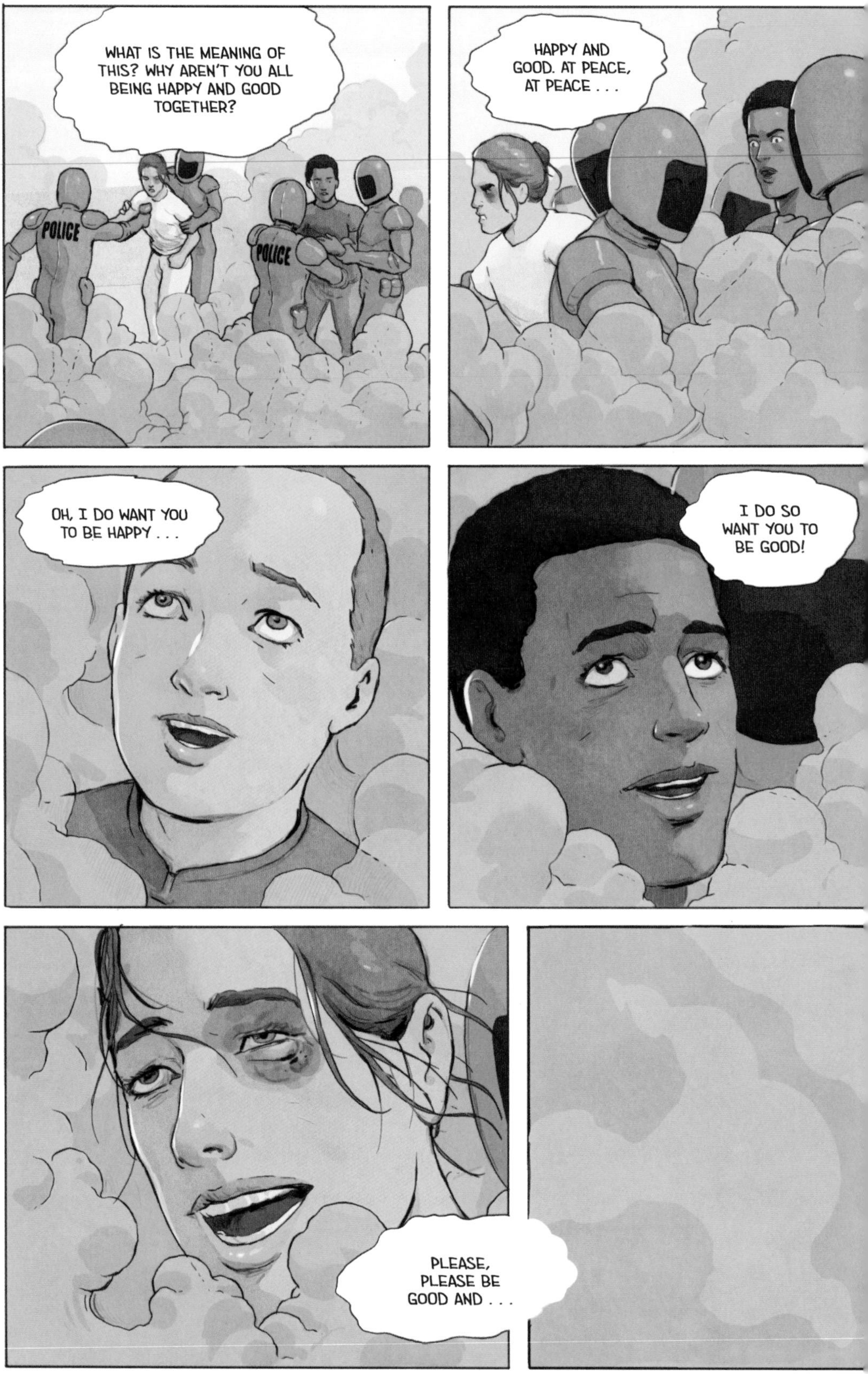
WHAT IS THE MEANING OF THIS? WHY AREN'T YOU ALL BEING HAPPY AND GOOD TOGETHER?
POLICE
POLICE
HAPPY AND GOOD. AT PEACE, AT PEACE . . .
OH, I DO WANT YOU TO BE HAPPY . . .
I DO SO WANT YOU TO BE GOOD!
PLEASE, PLEASE BE GOOD AND . . .

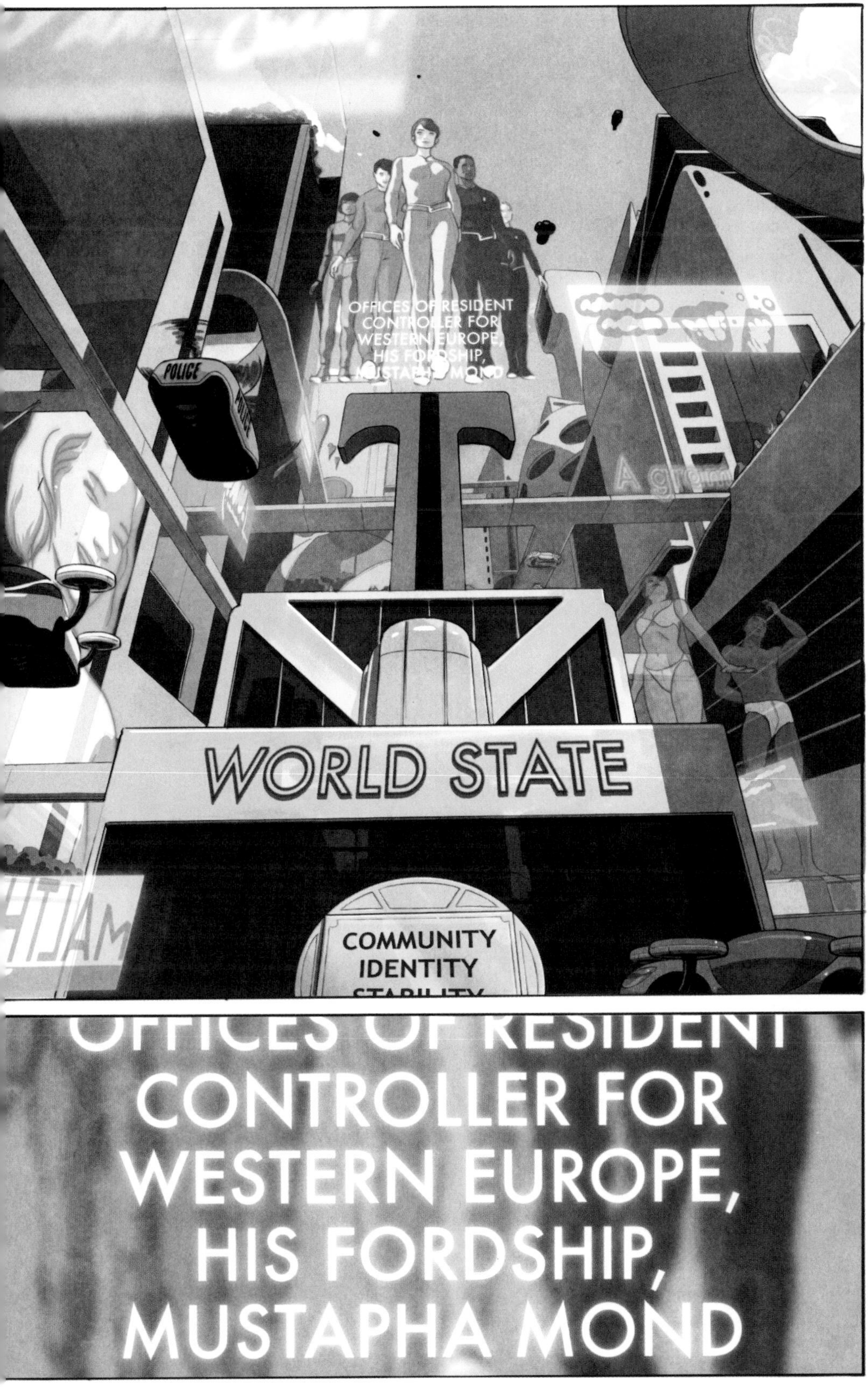
POLICE
WORLD STATE
COMMUNITY
IDENTITY
OFFICES OF RESIDENT
CONTROLLER FOR
WESTERN EUROPE,
HIS FORDSHIP,
MUSTAPHA MOND

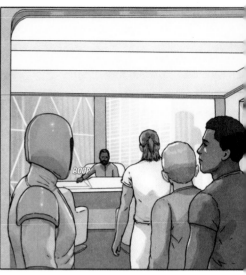

BOOP

IT'S MORE LIKE A CAFFEINE SOLUTION PARTY THAN A TRIAL.

CHEER UP, BERNARD.

SO.

YOU DON'T MUCH LIKE CIVILIZATION, MR. SAVAGE.

NO.

BUT, JOHN--

THAT WILL DO, MR. MARX.

OF COURSE, THERE ARE SOME VERY NICE THINGS. ALL THAT MUSIC IN THE AIR, FOR INSTANCE . . .

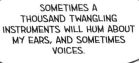

SOMETIMES A THOUSAND TWANGLING INSTRUMENTS WILL HUM ABOUT MY EARS, AND SOMETIMES VOICES.

YOU'VE READ SHAKESPEARE? I THOUGHT NOBODY KNEW ABOUT IT HERE IN ENGLAND.

ALMOST NOBODY. I'M ONE OF THE VERY FEW. IT'S PROHIBITED, YOU SEE.

BUT AS I MAKE THE LAWS HERE, I CAN ALSO BREAK THEM.

WITH IMPUNITY, MR. MARX. WHICH I'M AFRAID YOU *CAN'T* DO.

BUT WHY IS IT PROHIBITED?

BECAUSE IT'S OLD.

WE HAVEN'T ANY USE FOR OLD THINGS HERE.

EVEN WHEN THEY'RE BEAUTIFUL?

PARTICULARLY WHEN THEY'RE BEAUTIFUL. BEAUTY'S ATTRACTIVE, AND WE DON'T WANT PEOPLE TO BE ATTRACTED BY OLD THINGS.

WE WANT THEM TO LIKE NEW ONES.

BUT THE NEW ONES ARE STUPID AND HORRIBLE. WHY DON'T YOU LET THEM SEE *OTHELLO* INSTEAD?

I'VE TOLD YOU; IT'S OLD.

BESIDES, THEY COULDN'T UNDERSTAND IT.

WELL, THAT'S TRUE.

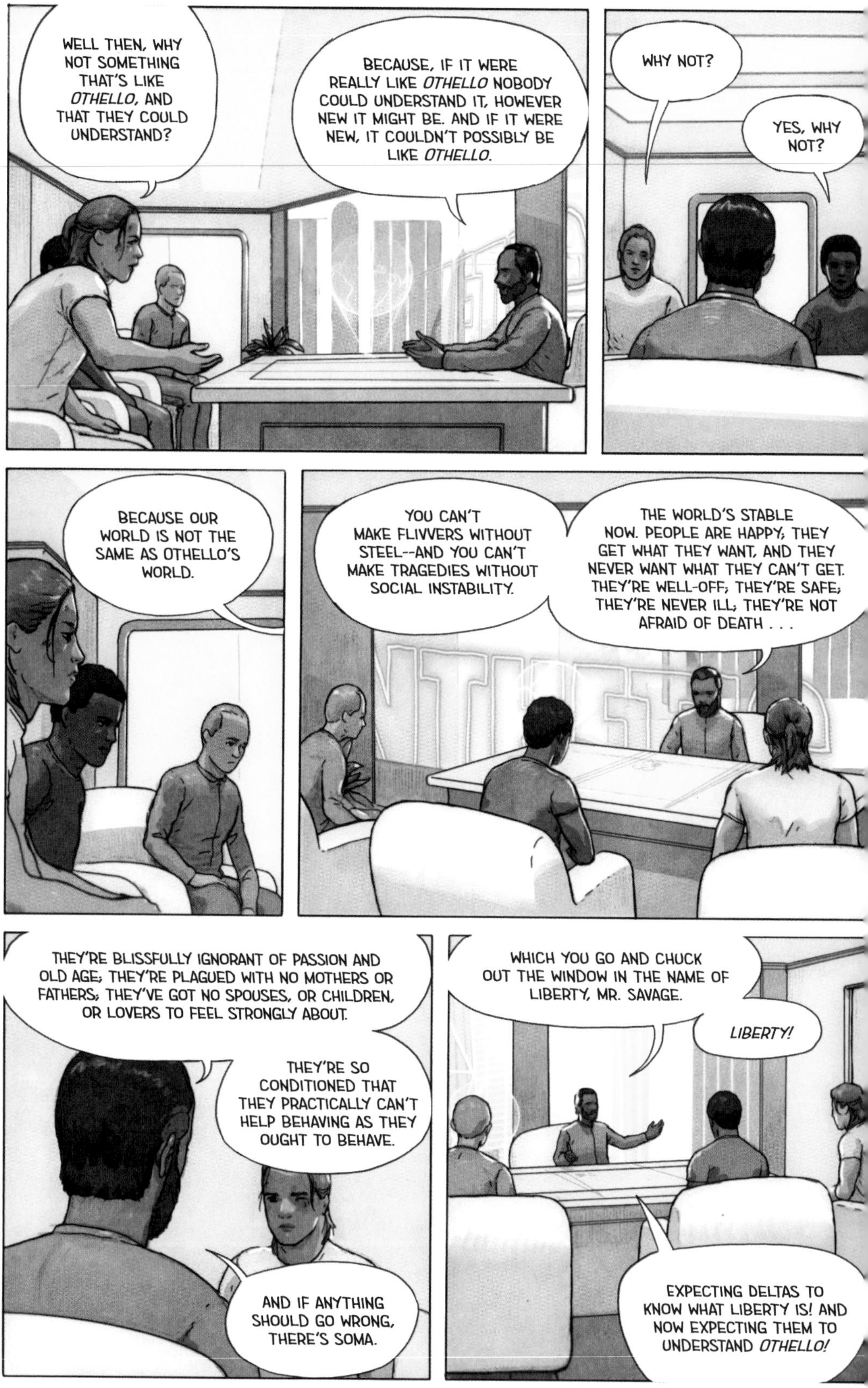
WELL THEN, WHY NOT SOMETHING THAT'S LIKE *OTHELLO*, AND THAT THEY COULD UNDERSTAND?
BECAUSE, IF IT WERE REALLY LIKE *OTHELLO* NOBODY COULD UNDERSTAND IT, HOWEVER NEW IT MIGHT BE. AND IF IT WERE NEW, IT COULDN'T POSSIBLY BE LIKE *OTHELLO*.
WHY NOT?
YES, WHY NOT?
BECAUSE OUR WORLD IS NOT THE SAME AS OTHELLO'S WORLD.
YOU CAN'T MAKE FLIVVERS WITHOUT STEEL--AND YOU CAN'T MAKE TRAGEDIES WITHOUT SOCIAL INSTABILITY.
THE WORLD'S STABLE NOW. PEOPLE ARE HAPPY; THEY GET WHAT THEY WANT, AND THEY NEVER WANT WHAT THEY CAN'T GET. THEY'RE WELL-OFF; THEY'RE SAFE; THEY'RE NEVER ILL; THEY'RE NOT AFRAID OF DEATH . . .
THEY'RE BLISSFULLY IGNORANT OF PASSION AND OLD AGE; THEY'RE PLAGUED WITH NO MOTHERS OR FATHERS; THEY'VE GOT NO SPOUSES, OR CHILDREN, OR LOVERS TO FEEL STRONGLY ABOUT.
THEY'RE SO CONDITIONED THAT THEY PRACTICALLY CAN'T HELP BEHAVING AS THEY OUGHT TO BEHAVE.
AND IF ANYTHING SHOULD GO WRONG, THERE'S SOMA.
WHICH YOU GO AND CHUCK OUT THE WINDOW IN THE NAME OF LIBERTY, MR. SAVAGE.
LIBERTY!
EXPECTING DELTAS TO KNOW WHAT LIBERTY IS! AND NOW EXPECTING THEM TO UNDERSTAND *OTHELLO!*

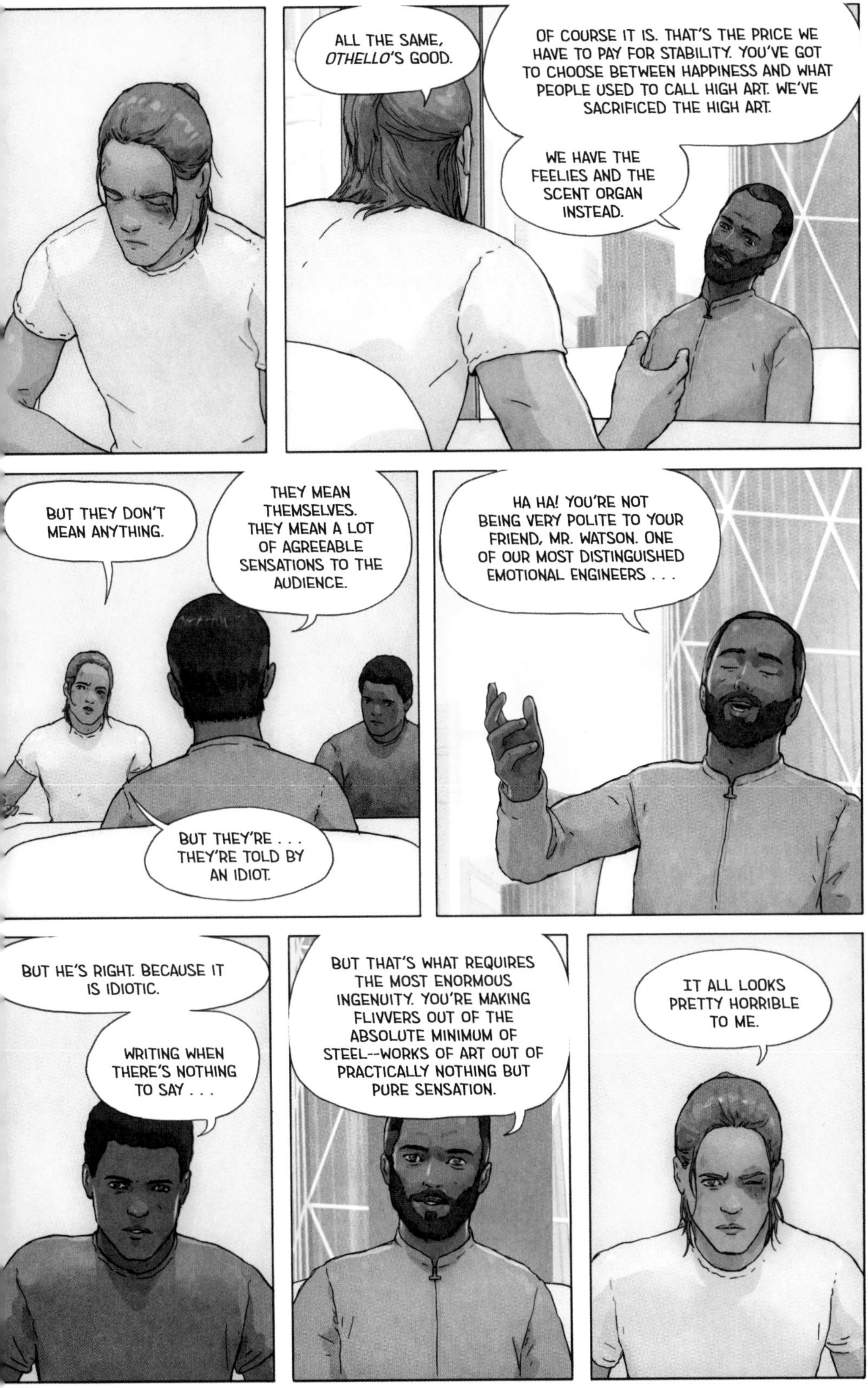
ALL THE SAME, OTHELLO'S GOOD.
OF COURSE IT IS. THAT'S THE PRICE WE HAVE TO PAY FOR STABILITY. YOU'VE GOT TO CHOOSE BETWEEN HAPPINESS AND WHAT PEOPLE USED TO CALL HIGH ART. WE'VE SACRIFICED THE HIGH ART.
WE HAVE THE FEELIES AND THE SCENT ORGAN INSTEAD.
BUT THEY DON'T MEAN ANYTHING.
THEY MEAN THEMSELVES. THEY MEAN A LOT OF AGREEABLE SENSATIONS TO THE AUDIENCE.
BUT THEY'RE . . . THEY'RE TOLD BY AN IDIOT.
HA HA! YOU'RE NOT BEING VERY POLITE TO YOUR FRIEND, MR. WATSON. ONE OF OUR MOST DISTINGUISHED EMOTIONAL ENGINEERS . . .
BUT HE'S RIGHT. BECAUSE IT IS IDIOTIC.
WRITING WHEN THERE'S NOTHING TO SAY . . .
BUT THAT'S WHAT REQUIRES THE MOST ENORMOUS INGENUITY. YOU'RE MAKING FLIVVERS OUT OF THE ABSOLUTE MINIMUM OF STEEL--WORKS OF ART OUT OF PRACTICALLY NOTHING BUT PURE SENSATION.
IT ALL LOOKS PRETTY HORRIBLE TO ME.

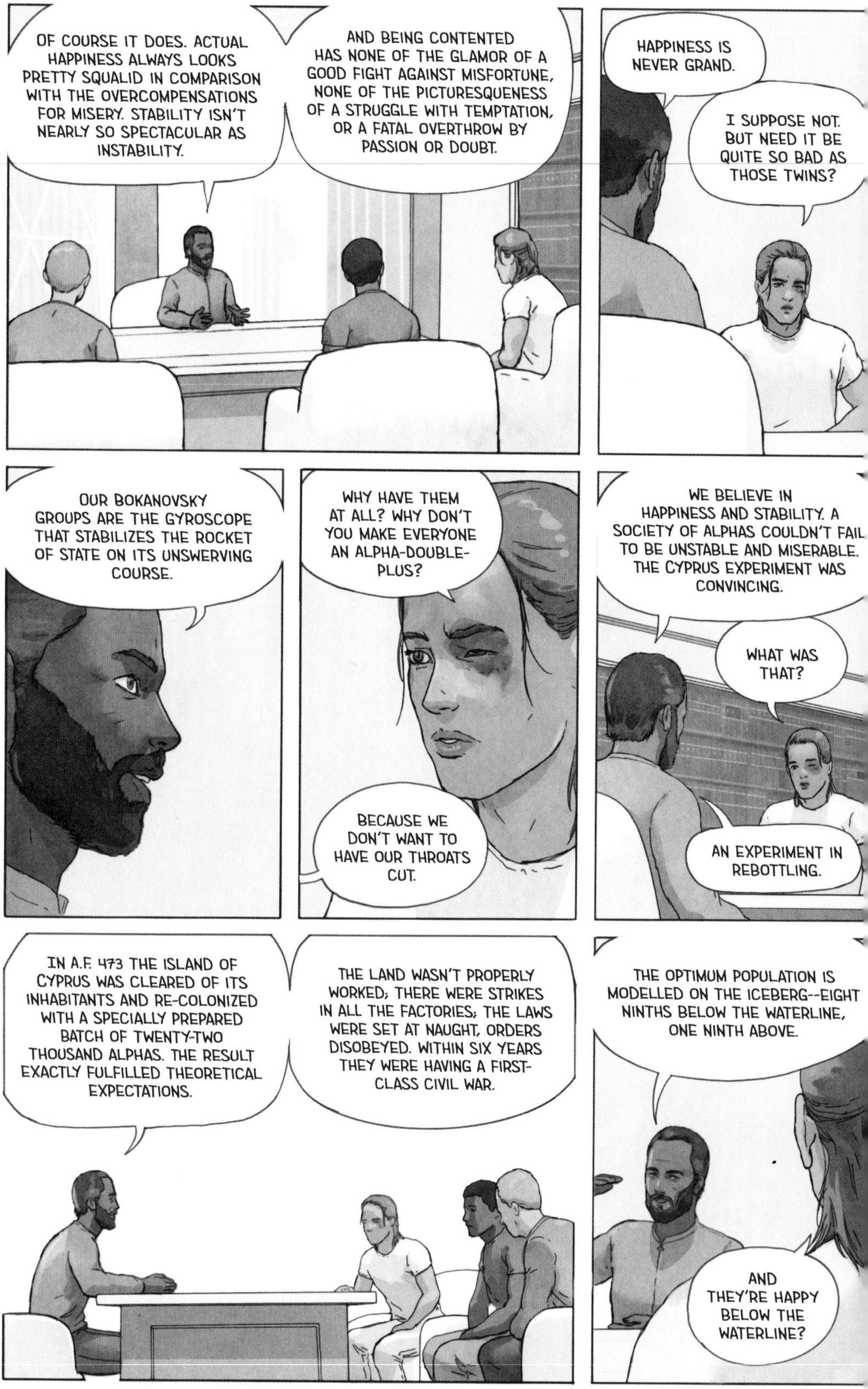
OF COURSE IT DOES. ACTUAL HAPPINESS ALWAYS LOOKS PRETTY SQUALID IN COMPARISON WITH THE OVERCOMPENSATIONS FOR MISERY. STABILITY ISN'T NEARLY SO SPECTACULAR AS INSTABILITY.
AND BEING CONTENTED HAS NONE OF THE GLAMOR OF A GOOD FIGHT AGAINST MISFORTUNE, NONE OF THE PICTURESQUENESS OF A STRUGGLE WITH TEMPTATION, OR A FATAL OVERTHROW BY PASSION OR DOUBT.
HAPPINESS IS NEVER GRAND.
I SUPPOSE NOT. BUT NEED IT BE QUITE SO BAD AS THOSE TWINS?
OUR BOKANOVSKY GROUPS ARE THE GYROSCOPE THAT STABILIZES THE ROCKET OF STATE ON ITS UNSWERVING COURSE.
WHY HAVE THEM AT ALL? WHY DON'T YOU MAKE EVERYONE AN ALPHA-DOUBLE-PLUS?
BECAUSE WE DON'T WANT TO HAVE OUR THROATS CUT.
WE BELIEVE IN HAPPINESS AND STABILITY. A SOCIETY OF ALPHAS COULDN'T FAIL TO BE UNSTABLE AND MISERABLE. THE CYPRUS EXPERIMENT WAS CONVINCING.
WHAT WAS THAT?
AN EXPERIMENT IN REBOTTLING.
IN A.F. 473 THE ISLAND OF CYPRUS WAS CLEARED OF ITS INHABITANTS AND RE-COLONIZED WITH A SPECIALLY PREPARED BATCH OF TWENTY-TWO THOUSAND ALPHAS. THE RESULT EXACTLY FULFILLED THEORETICAL EXPECTATIONS.
THE LAND WASN'T PROPERLY WORKED; THERE WERE STRIKES IN ALL THE FACTORIES; THE LAWS WERE SET AT NAUGHT, ORDERS DISOBEYED. WITHIN SIX YEARS THEY WERE HAVING A FIRST-CLASS CIVIL WAR.
THE OPTIMUM POPULATION IS MODELLED ON THE ICEBERG--EIGHT NINTHS BELOW THE WATERLINE, ONE NINTH ABOVE.
AND THEY'RE HAPPY BELOW THE WATERLINE?

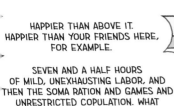

HAPPIER THAN ABOVE IT. HAPPIER THAN YOUR FRIENDS HERE, FOR EXAMPLE.

SEVEN AND A HALF HOURS OF MILD, UNEXHAUSTING LABOR, AND THEN THE SOMA RATION AND GAMES AND UNRESTRICTED COPULATION. WHAT MORE CAN THEY ASK FOR?

TRUE, THEY MIGHT ASK FOR SHORTER HOURS. BUT THAT EXPERIMENT WAS TRIED. THE RESULT? SOCIAL UNREST AND A LARGE INCREASE IN THE CONSUMPTION OF SOMA. THOSE EXTRA HOURS OF LEISURE WERE SO FAR FROM BEING A SOURCE OF HAPPINESS THAT PEOPLE FELT CONSTRAINED TO TAKE A HOLIDAY FROM THEM. IT'S SHEER CRUELTY TO AFFLICT THEM WITH EXCESSIVE LEISURE.

IT'S THE SAME WITH AGRICULTURE. WE COULD SYNTHESIZE EVERY MORSEL OF FOOD IF WE WANTED TO. BUT WE PREFER TO KEEP A THIRD OF THE POPULATION ON THE LAND. FOR THEIR OWN SAKES.

THAT'S WHY WE'RE SO CHARY OF APPLYING NEW INVENTIONS. EVERY DISCOVERY IN PURE SCIENCE IS POTENTIALLY SUBVERSIVE. THAT'S ANOTHER ITEM IN THE COST OF STABILITY. IT ISN'T ONLY ART THAT'S INCOMPATIBLE WITH HAPPINESS; IT'S ALSO SCIENCE.

WHAT? BUT WE'RE ALWAYS SAYING SCIENCE IS EVERYTHING. IT'S A HYPNOPAEDIC PLATITUDE.

THREE TIMES A WEEK BETWEEN THIRTEEN AND SEVENTEEN.

YES, BUT WHAT SORT OF SCIENCE? YOU HAD NO SCIENTIFIC TRAINING, SO YOU CAN'T JUDGE. I WAS A PRETTY GOOD PHYSICIST IN MY TIME. GOOD ENOUGH TO REALIZE THAT ALL OUR SCIENCE IS JUST A COOKERY BOOK.

IT HAS A LIST OF RECIPES THAT MUSTN'T BE ADDED TO EXCEPT BY SPECIAL PERMISSION FROM THE HEAD COOK. I'M THE HEAD COOK NOW. BUT I WAS AN INQUISITIVE YOUNG SCULLION ONCE.

I STARTED DOING A BIT OF COOKING ON MY OWN. UNORTHODOX COOKING, ILLICIT COOKING. A BIT OF REAL SCIENCE, IN FACT.

WHAT HAPPENED?

VERY NEARLY WHAT'S GOING TO HAPPEN TO YOU YOUNG MEN. I WAS ON THE POINT OF BEING SENT TO AN ISLAND.

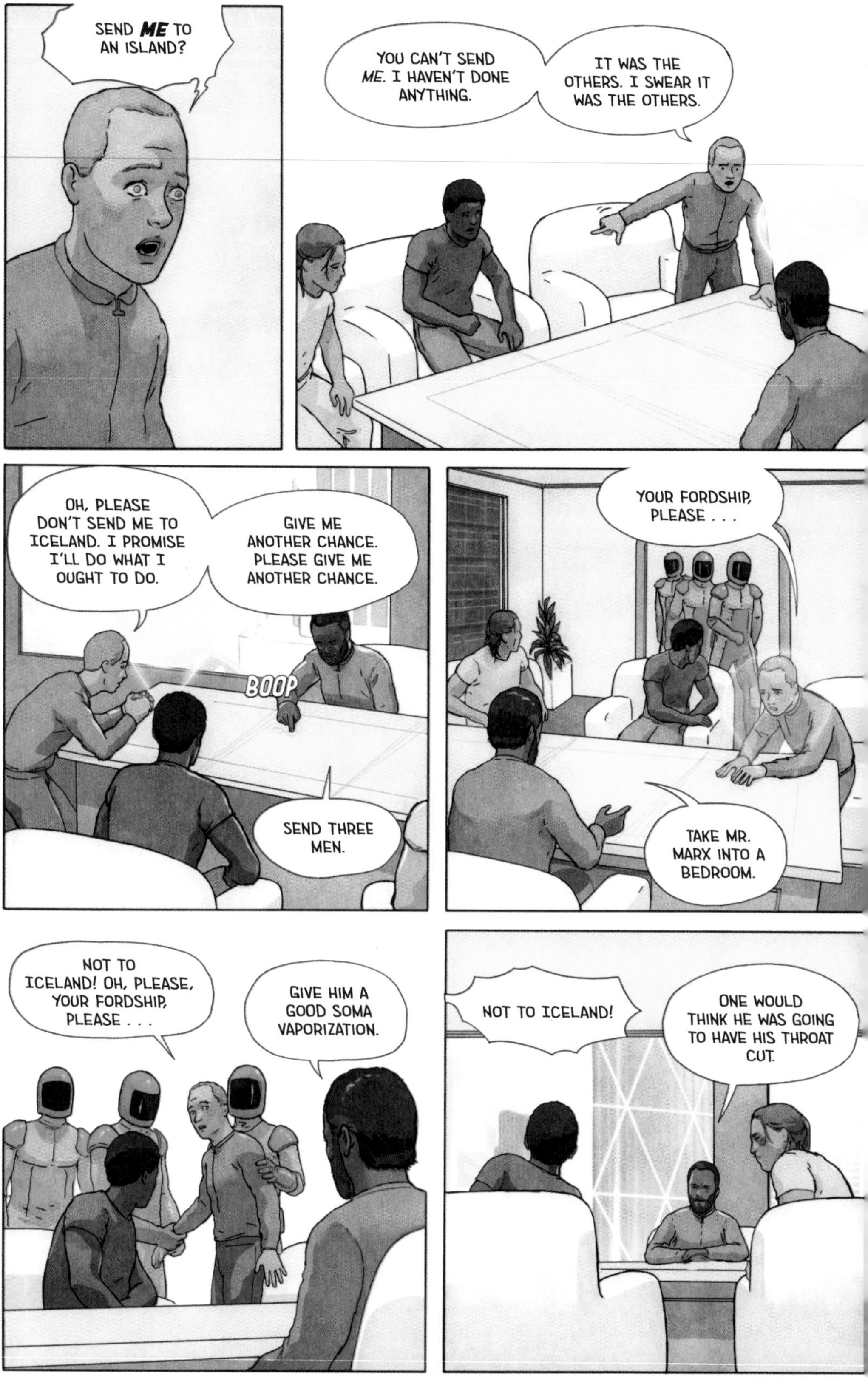
SEND ME TO AN ISLAND?
YOU CAN'T SEND ME. I HAVEN'T DONE ANYTHING.
IT WAS THE OTHERS. I SWEAR IT WAS THE OTHERS.
OH, PLEASE DON'T SEND ME TO ICELAND. I PROMISE I'LL DO WHAT I OUGHT TO DO.
GIVE ME ANOTHER CHANCE. PLEASE GIVE ME ANOTHER CHANCE.
BOOP
SEND THREE MEN.
YOUR FORDSHIP, PLEASE . . .
TAKE MR. MARX INTO A BEDROOM.
NOT TO ICELAND! OH, PLEASE, YOUR FORDSHIP, PLEASE . . .
GIVE HIM A GOOD SOMA VAPORIZATION.
NOT TO ICELAND!
ONE WOULD THINK HE WAS GOING TO HAVE HIS THROAT CUT.

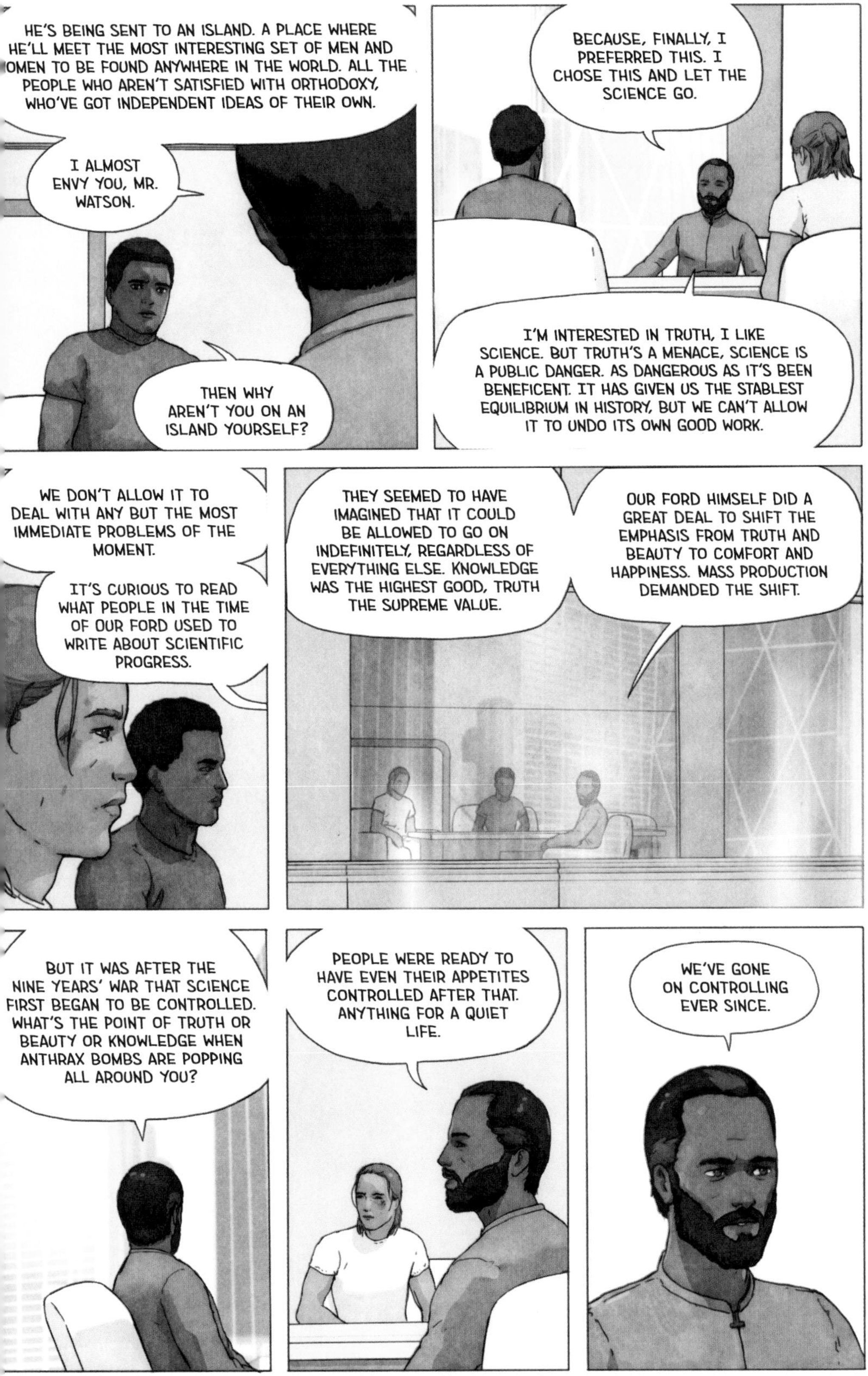
HE'S BEING SENT TO AN ISLAND. A PLACE WHERE HE'LL MEET THE MOST INTERESTING SET OF MEN AND OMEN TO BE FOUND ANYWHERE IN THE WORLD. ALL THE PEOPLE WHO AREN'T SATISFIED WITH ORTHODOXY, WHO'VE GOT INDEPENDENT IDEAS OF THEIR OWN.
I ALMOST ENVY YOU, MR. WATSON.
THEN WHY AREN'T YOU ON AN ISLAND YOURSELF?
BECAUSE, FINALLY, I PREFERRED THIS. I CHOSE THIS AND LET THE SCIENCE GO.
I'M INTERESTED IN TRUTH, I LIKE SCIENCE. BUT TRUTH'S A MENACE, SCIENCE IS A PUBLIC DANGER. AS DANGEROUS AS IT'S BEEN BENEFICENT. IT HAS GIVEN US THE STABLEST EQUILIBRIUM IN HISTORY, BUT WE CAN'T ALLOW IT TO UNDO ITS OWN GOOD WORK.
WE DON'T ALLOW IT TO DEAL WITH ANY BUT THE MOST IMMEDIATE PROBLEMS OF THE MOMENT.
IT'S CURIOUS TO READ WHAT PEOPLE IN THE TIME OF OUR FORD USED TO WRITE ABOUT SCIENTIFIC PROGRESS.
THEY SEEMED TO HAVE IMAGINED THAT IT COULD BE ALLOWED TO GO ON INDEFINITELY, REGARDLESS OF EVERYTHING ELSE. KNOWLEDGE WAS THE HIGHEST GOOD, TRUTH THE SUPREME VALUE.
OUR FORD HIMSELF DID A GREAT DEAL TO SHIFT THE EMPHASIS FROM TRUTH AND BEAUTY TO COMFORT AND HAPPINESS. MASS PRODUCTION DEMANDED THE SHIFT.
BUT IT WAS AFTER THE NINE YEARS' WAR THAT SCIENCE FIRST BEGAN TO BE CONTROLLED. WHAT'S THE POINT OF TRUTH OR BEAUTY OR KNOWLEDGE WHEN ANTHRAX BOMBS ARE POPPING ALL AROUND YOU?
PEOPLE WERE READY TO HAVE EVEN THEIR APPETITES CONTROLLED AFTER THAT. ANYTHING FOR A QUIET LIFE.
WE'VE GONE ON CONTROLLING EVER SINCE.

ONE CAN'T HAVE SOMETHING FOR NOTHING. HAPPINESS HAS GOT TO BE PAID FOR. YOU'RE PAYING FOR IT, MR. WATSON, BECAUSE YOU HAPPEN TO BE TOO MUCH INTERESTED IN BEAUTY. I WAS TOO MUCH INTERESTED IN TRUTH; I PAID TOO.

BUT YOU DIDN'T GO TO AN ISLAND.

THAT'S HOW I PAID: BY CHOOSING TO SERVE HAPPINESS. OTHER PEOPLE'S-- NOT MINE.

IT'S A GOOD THING THERE ARE SO MANY ISLANDS IN THE WORLD. I DON'T KNOW WHAT WE'D DO WITHOUT THEM. PUT YOU ALL IN THE LETHAL CHAMBER, I SUPPOSE!

BY THE WAY, MR. WATSON, WOULD YOU LIKE A TROPICAL CLIMATE? OR SOMETHING MORE BRACING?

I SHOULD LIKE A THOROUGHLY BAD CLIMATE. I BELIEVE ONE WOULD WRITE BETTER IF THE CLIMATE WERE BAD.

IF THERE WERE A LOT OF WIND AND STORMS, FOR EXAMPLE.

I LIKE YOUR SPIRIT, MR. WATSON. I LIKE IT VERY MUCH INDEED. AS MUCH AS I OFFICIALLY DISAPPROVE OF IT.

HOW ABOUT THE FALKLAND ISLANDS?

YES, I THINK THAT WILL DO.

AND NOW, IF YOU DON'T MIND, I'LL GO AND SEE HOW POOR BERNARD'S GETTING ON.

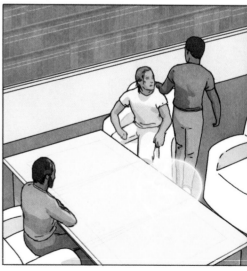

ART, SCIENCE--YOU SEEM TO HAVE PAID A FAIRLY HIGH PRICE FOR YOUR HAPPINESS. ANYTHING ELSE?

WELL, RELIGION, OF COURSE.

THERE USED TO BE SOMETHING CALLED GOD--BEFORE THE NINE YEARS' WAR.

BOOP

IT'S A SUBJECT THAT HAS ALWAYS HAD A GREAT INTEREST FOR ME.

I'VE GOT PLENTY MORE. A WHOLE COLLECTION OF PORNOGRAPHIC BOOKS.

The Imitation of Christ

The Holy Bible

THE VARIETIES OF RELIGIOUS EXPERIENCE
WILLIAM JAMES

GOD IN THE SAFE, FORD ON THE SHELVES.

IF YOU KNOW ABOUT GOD, WHY DON'T YOU TELL THEM? WHY DON'T YOU GIVE THEM THESE BOOKS ABOUT GOD?

FOR THE SAME REASON WE DON'T GIVE THEM *OTHELLO*: THEY'RE OLD. THEY'RE ABOUT GOD HUNDREDS OF YEARS AGO, NOT ABOUT GOD NOW.

BUT GOD DOESN'T CHANGE.

MEN DO, THOUGH.

ONE OF THE NUMEROUS THINGS IN HEAVEN AND EARTH THAT THE PHILOSOPHERS DIDN'T DREAM ABOUT WAS *THIS*.

US, THE MODERN WORLD.

"YOU CAN ONLY BE INDEPENDENT OF GOD WHILE YOU'VE GOT YOUTH AND PROSPERITY; INDEPENDENCE WON'T TAKE YOU RIGHT UP TO THE END." WELL, WE'VE NOW GOT YOUTH AND PROSPERITY RIGHT UP TO THE END.

"THE RELIGIOUS SENTIMENT WILL COMPENSATE US FOR ALL OUR LOSSES." BUT THERE AREN'T ANY LOSSES FOR US TO COMPENSATE.

AND WHY SHOULD WE GO HUNTING FOR A SUBSTITUTE FOR YOUTHFUL DESIRES, WHEN YOUTHFUL DESIRES NEVER FAIL?

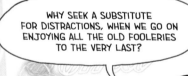

WHY SEEK A SUBSTITUTE FOR DISTRACTIONS, WHEN WE GO ON ENJOYING ALL THE OLD FOOLERIES TO THE VERY LAST?

WHAT NEED HAVE WE OF REPOSE WHEN OUR MINDS AND BODIES CONTINUE TO DELIGHT IN ACTIVITY? OF CONSOLATION WHEN WE HAVE SOMA? OF SOMETHING IMMOVABLE WHEN THERE IS THE SOCIAL ORDER?

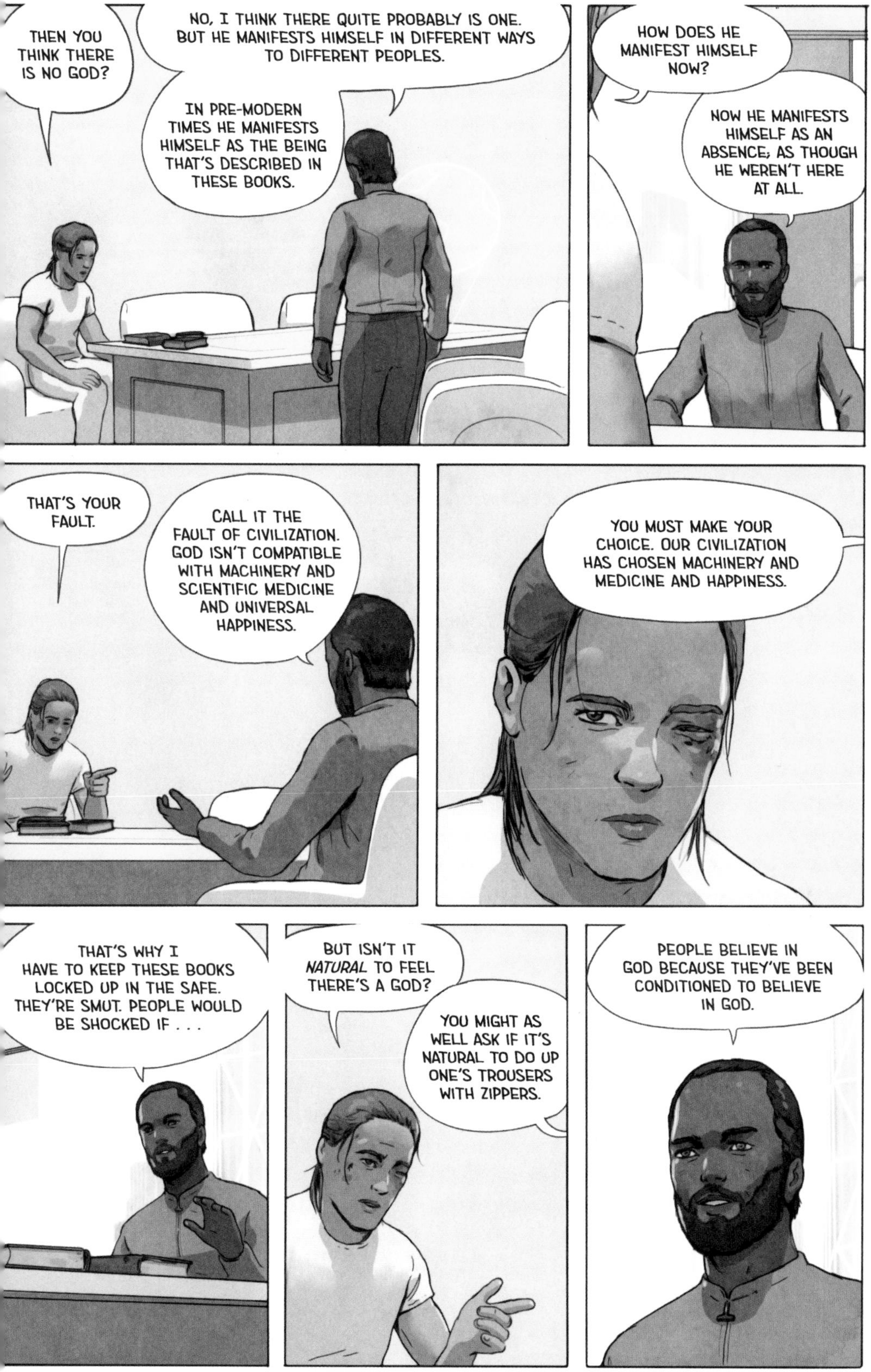
THEN YOU THINK THERE IS NO GOD?
NO, I THINK THERE QUITE PROBABLY IS ONE. BUT HE MANIFESTS HIMSELF IN DIFFERENT WAYS TO DIFFERENT PEOPLES.
IN PRE-MODERN TIMES HE MANIFESTS HIMSELF AS THE BEING THAT'S DESCRIBED IN THESE BOOKS.
HOW DOES HE MANIFEST HIMSELF NOW?
NOW HE MANIFESTS HIMSELF AS AN ABSENCE; AS THOUGH HE WEREN'T HERE AT ALL.
THAT'S YOUR FAULT.
CALL IT THE FAULT OF CIVILIZATION. GOD ISN'T COMPATIBLE WITH MACHINERY AND SCIENTIFIC MEDICINE AND UNIVERSAL HAPPINESS.
YOU MUST MAKE YOUR CHOICE. OUR CIVILIZATION HAS CHOSEN MACHINERY AND MEDICINE AND HAPPINESS.
THAT'S WHY I HAVE TO KEEP THESE BOOKS LOCKED UP IN THE SAFE. THEY'RE SMUT. PEOPLE WOULD BE SHOCKED IF . . .
BUT ISN'T IT *NATURAL* TO FEEL THERE'S A GOD?
YOU MIGHT AS WELL ASK IF IT'S NATURAL TO DO UP ONE'S TROUSERS WITH ZIPPERS.
PEOPLE BELIEVE IN GOD BECAUSE THEY'VE BEEN CONDITIONED TO BELIEVE IN GOD.

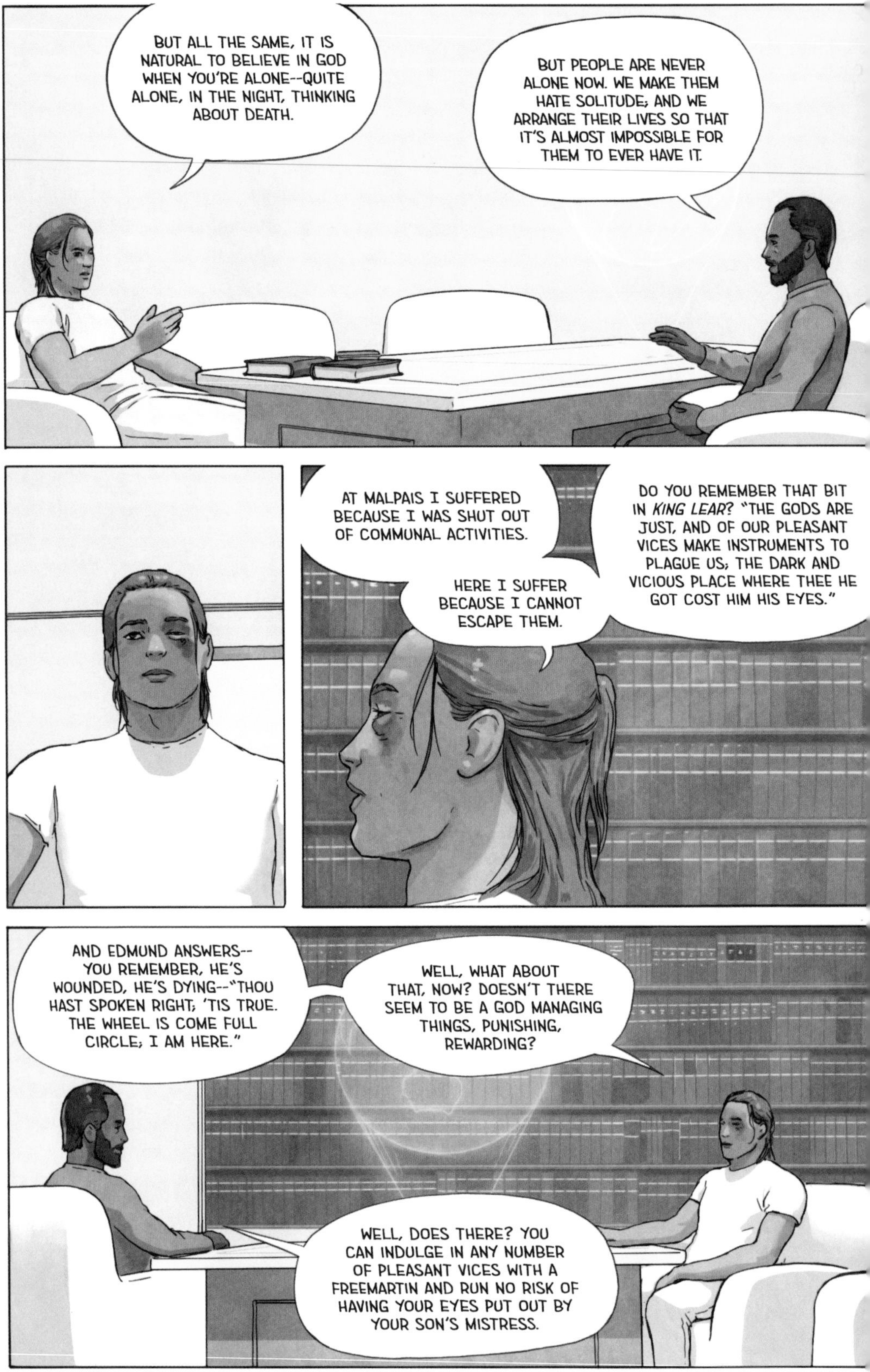
BUT ALL THE SAME, IT IS NATURAL TO BELIEVE IN GOD WHEN YOU'RE ALONE--QUITE ALONE, IN THE NIGHT, THINKING ABOUT DEATH.
BUT PEOPLE ARE NEVER ALONE NOW. WE MAKE THEM HATE SOLITUDE; AND WE ARRANGE THEIR LIVES SO THAT IT'S ALMOST IMPOSSIBLE FOR THEM TO EVER HAVE IT.
AT MALPAIS I SUFFERED BECAUSE I WAS SHUT OUT OF COMMUNAL ACTIVITIES.
HERE I SUFFER BECAUSE I CANNOT ESCAPE THEM.
DO YOU REMEMBER THAT BIT IN *KING LEAR*? "THE GODS ARE JUST, AND OF OUR PLEASANT VICES MAKE INSTRUMENTS TO PLAGUE US; THE DARK AND VICIOUS PLACE WHERE THEE HE GOT COST HIM HIS EYES."
AND EDMUND ANSWERS-- YOU REMEMBER, HE'S WOUNDED, HE'S DYING--"THOU HAST SPOKEN RIGHT; 'TIS TRUE. THE WHEEL IS COME FULL CIRCLE; I AM HERE."
WELL, WHAT ABOUT THAT, NOW? DOESN'T THERE SEEM TO BE A GOD MANAGING THINGS, PUNISHING, REWARDING?
WELL, DOES THERE? YOU CAN INDULGE IN ANY NUMBER OF PLEASANT VICES WITH A FREEMARTIN AND RUN NO RISK OF HAVING YOUR EYES PUT OUT BY YOUR SON'S MISTRESS.

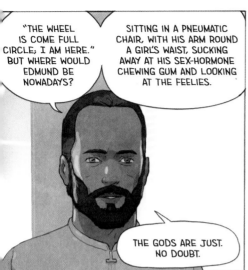

"THE WHEEL IS COME FULL CIRCLE; I AM HERE." BUT WHERE WOULD EDMUND BE NOWADAYS?

SITTING IN A PNEUMATIC CHAIR, WITH HIS ARM ROUND A GIRL'S WAIST, SUCKING AWAY AT HIS SEX-HORMONE CHEWING GUM AND LOOKING AT THE FEELIES.

THE GODS ARE JUST. NO DOUBT.

BUT THEIR CODE OF LAW IS DICTATED, IN THE LAST RESORT, BY THE PEOPLE WHO ORGANIZE SOCIETY. PROVIDENCE TAKES ITS CUE FROM MEN.

ARE YOU QUITE SURE THAT THE EDMUND IN THAT PNEUMATIC CHAIR HASN'T BEEN JUST AS HEAVILY PUNISHED AS THE EDMUND WHO'S BLEEDING TO DEATH?

THE GODS ARE JUST. HAVEN'T THEY USED HIS PLEASANT VICES AS AN INSTRUMENT TO DEGRADE HIM?

DEGRADE HIM FROM WHAT POSITION? AS A HAPPY, HARDWORKING, GOODS-CONSUMING CITIZEN, HE'S PERFECT. OF COURSE, IF YOU CHOOSE SOME OTHER STANDARD THAN OURS, THEN PERHAPS YOU MIGHT SAY HE WAS DEGRADED.

BUT YOU'VE GOT TO STICK TO ONE SET OF POSTULATES. YOU CAN'T PLAY ELECTROMAGNETIC GOLF ACCORDING TO THE RULES OF CENTRIFUGAL BUMBLE-PUPPY.

IF YOU ALLOWED YOURSELVES TO THINK OF GOD, YOU WOULDN'T ALLOW YOURSELVES TO BE DEGRADED BY PLEASANT VICES.

YOU'D HAVE A REASON FOR BEARING THINGS PATIENTLY, FOR DOING THINGS WITH COURAGE. YOU'D HAVE A REASON FOR SELF-DENIAL.

YOU'D HAVE A REASON FOR CHASTITY.

BUT CHASTITY MEANS PASSION. AND PASSION MEANS INSTABILITY. AND INSTABILITY MEANS THE END OF CIVILIZATION.

NOBILITY AND HEROISM ARE SYMPTOMS OF POLITICAL INEFFICIENCY.

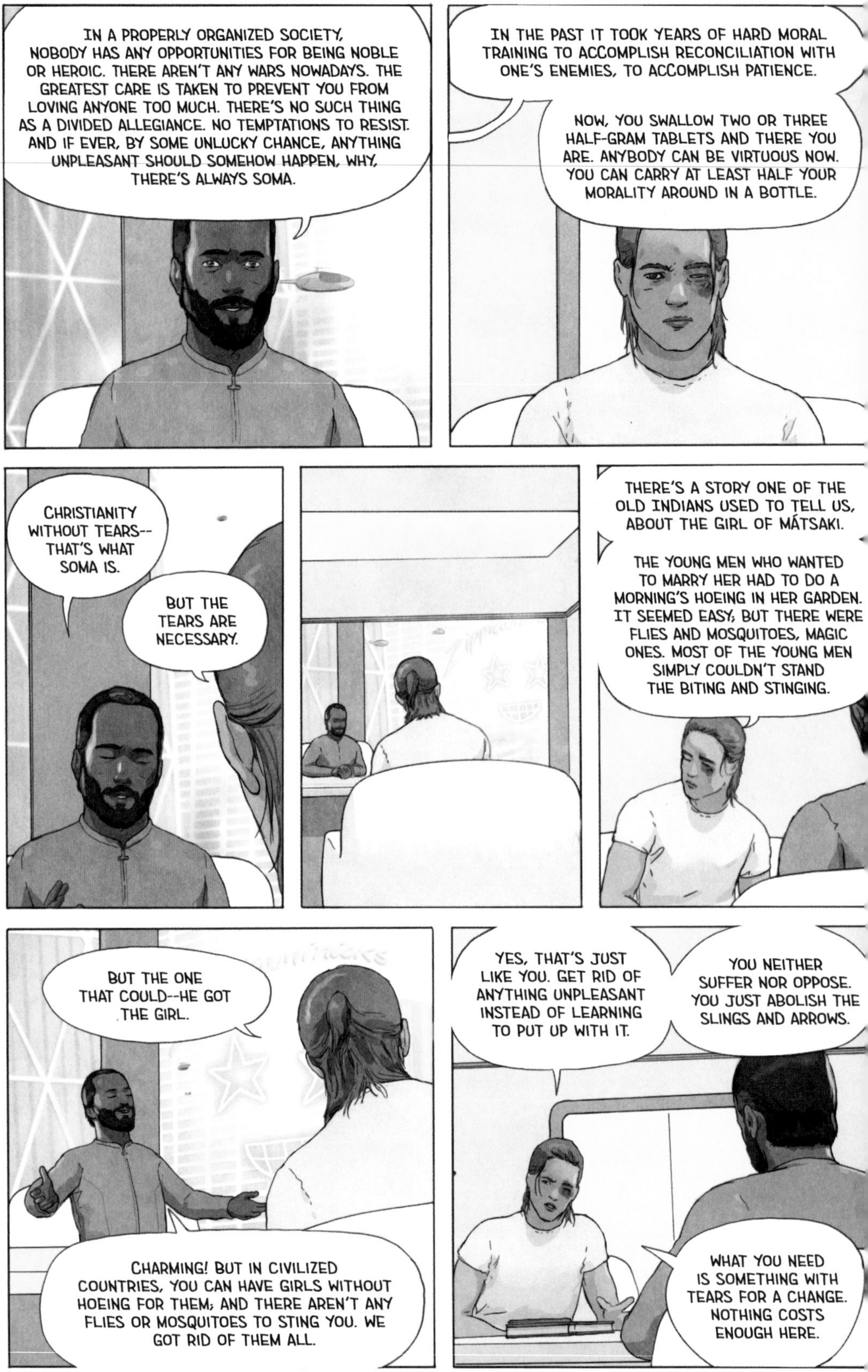

IN A PROPERLY ORGANIZED SOCIETY, NOBODY HAS ANY OPPORTUNITIES FOR BEING NOBLE OR HEROIC. THERE AREN'T ANY WARS NOWADAYS. THE GREATEST CARE IS TAKEN TO PREVENT YOU FROM LOVING ANYONE TOO MUCH. THERE'S NO SUCH THING AS A DIVIDED ALLEGIANCE. NO TEMPTATIONS TO RESIST. AND IF EVER, BY SOME UNLUCKY CHANCE, ANYTHING UNPLEASANT SHOULD SOMEHOW HAPPEN, WHY, THERE'S ALWAYS SOMA.
IN THE PAST IT TOOK YEARS OF HARD MORAL TRAINING TO ACCOMPLISH RECONCILIATION WITH ONE'S ENEMIES, TO ACCOMPLISH PATIENCE.
NOW, YOU SWALLOW TWO OR THREE HALF-GRAM TABLETS AND THERE YOU ARE. ANYBODY CAN BE VIRTUOUS NOW. YOU CAN CARRY AT LEAST HALF YOUR MORALITY AROUND IN A BOTTLE.
CHRISTIANITY WITHOUT TEARS--THAT'S WHAT SOMA IS.
BUT THE TEARS ARE NECESSARY.
THERE'S A STORY ONE OF THE OLD INDIANS USED TO TELL US, ABOUT THE GIRL OF MÁTSAKI.
THE YOUNG MEN WHO WANTED TO MARRY HER HAD TO DO A MORNING'S HOEING IN HER GARDEN. IT SEEMED EASY; BUT THERE WERE FLIES AND MOSQUITOES, MAGIC ONES. MOST OF THE YOUNG MEN SIMPLY COULDN'T STAND THE BITING AND STINGING.
BUT THE ONE THAT COULD--HE GOT THE GIRL.
CHARMING! BUT IN CIVILIZED COUNTRIES, YOU CAN HAVE GIRLS WITHOUT HOEING FOR THEM; AND THERE AREN'T ANY FLIES OR MOSQUITOES TO STING YOU. WE GOT RID OF THEM ALL.
YES, THAT'S JUST LIKE YOU. GET RID OF ANYTHING UNPLEASANT INSTEAD OF LEARNING TO PUT UP WITH IT.
YOU NEITHER SUFFER NOR OPPOSE. YOU JUST ABOLISH THE SLINGS AND ARROWS.
WHAT YOU NEED IS SOMETHING WITH TEARS FOR A CHANGE. NOTHING COSTS ENOUGH HERE.

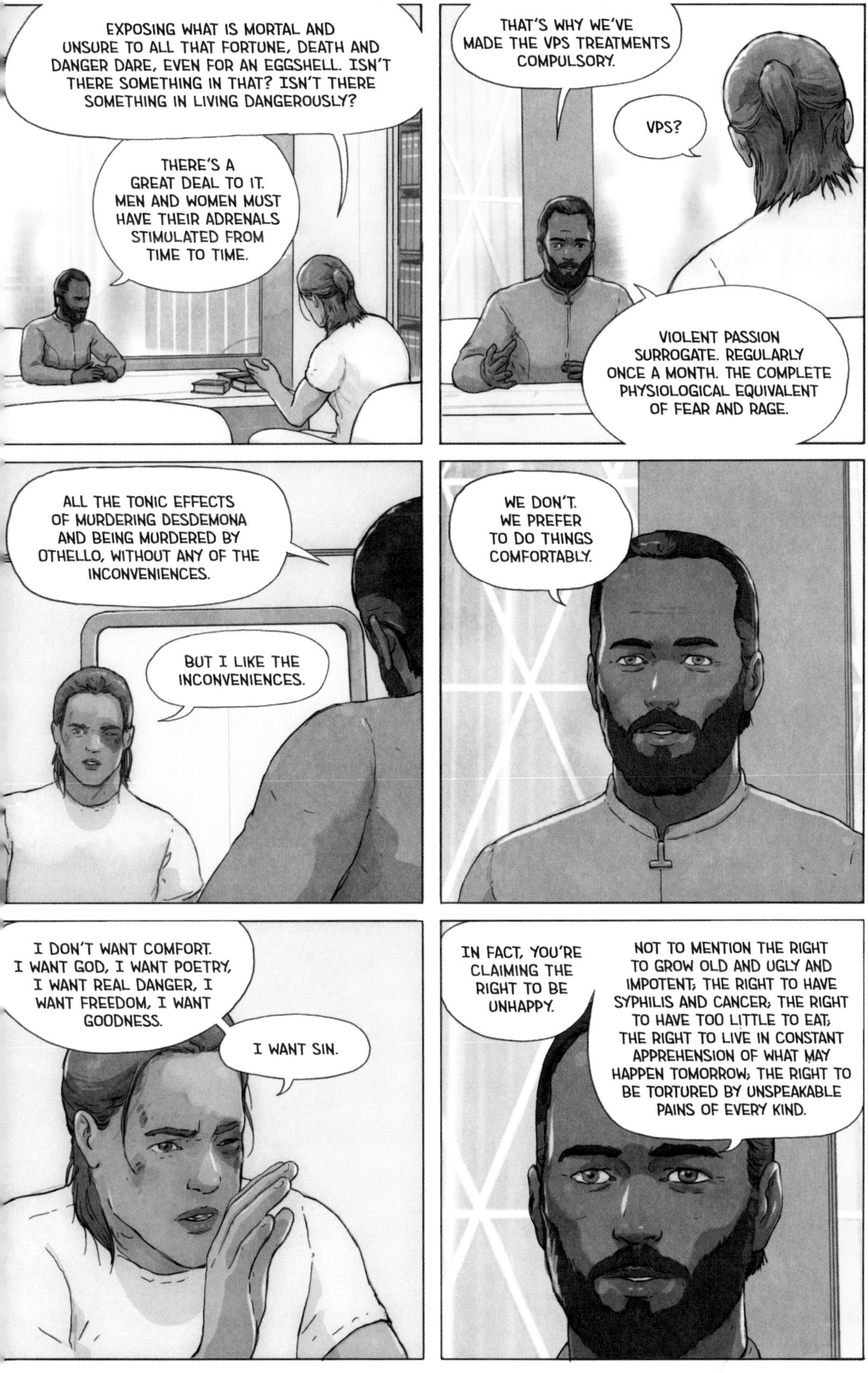
EXPOSING WHAT IS MORTAL AND UNSURE TO ALL THAT FORTUNE, DEATH AND DANGER DARE, EVEN FOR AN EGGSHELL. ISN'T THERE SOMETHING IN THAT? ISN'T THERE SOMETHING IN LIVING DANGEROUSLY?
THERE'S A GREAT DEAL TO IT. MEN AND WOMEN MUST HAVE THEIR ADRENALS STIMULATED FROM TIME TO TIME.
THAT'S WHY WE'VE MADE THE VPS TREATMENTS COMPULSORY.
VPS?
VIOLENT PASSION SURROGATE. REGULARLY ONCE A MONTH. THE COMPLETE PHYSIOLOGICAL EQUIVALENT OF FEAR AND RAGE.
ALL THE TONIC EFFECTS OF MURDERING DESDEMONA AND BEING MURDERED BY OTHELLO, WITHOUT ANY OF THE INCONVENIENCES.
BUT I LIKE THE INCONVENIENCES.
WE DON'T. WE PREFER TO DO THINGS COMFORTABLY.
I DON'T WANT COMFORT. I WANT GOD, I WANT POETRY, I WANT REAL DANGER, I WANT FREEDOM, I WANT GOODNESS.
I WANT SIN.
IN FACT, YOU'RE CLAIMING THE RIGHT TO BE UNHAPPY.
NOT TO MENTION THE RIGHT TO GROW OLD AND UGLY AND IMPOTENT; THE RIGHT TO HAVE SYPHILIS AND CANCER; THE RIGHT TO HAVE TOO LITTLE TO EAT; THE RIGHT TO LIVE IN CONSTANT APPREHENSION OF WHAT MAY HAPPEN TOMORROW; THE RIGHT TO BE TORTURED BY UNSPEAKABLE PAINS OF EVERY KIND.

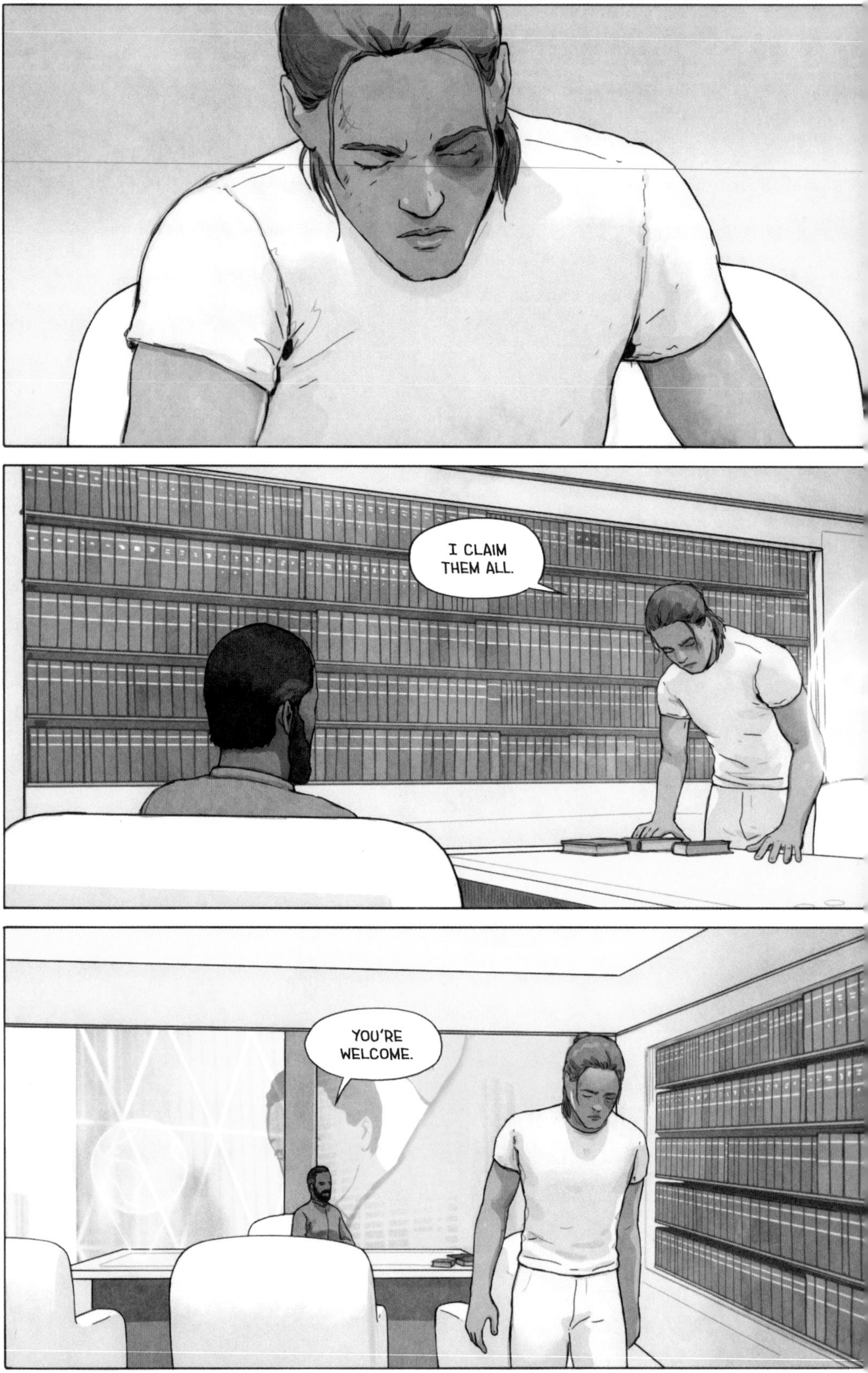
I CLAIM THEM ALL.
YOU'RE WELCOME.

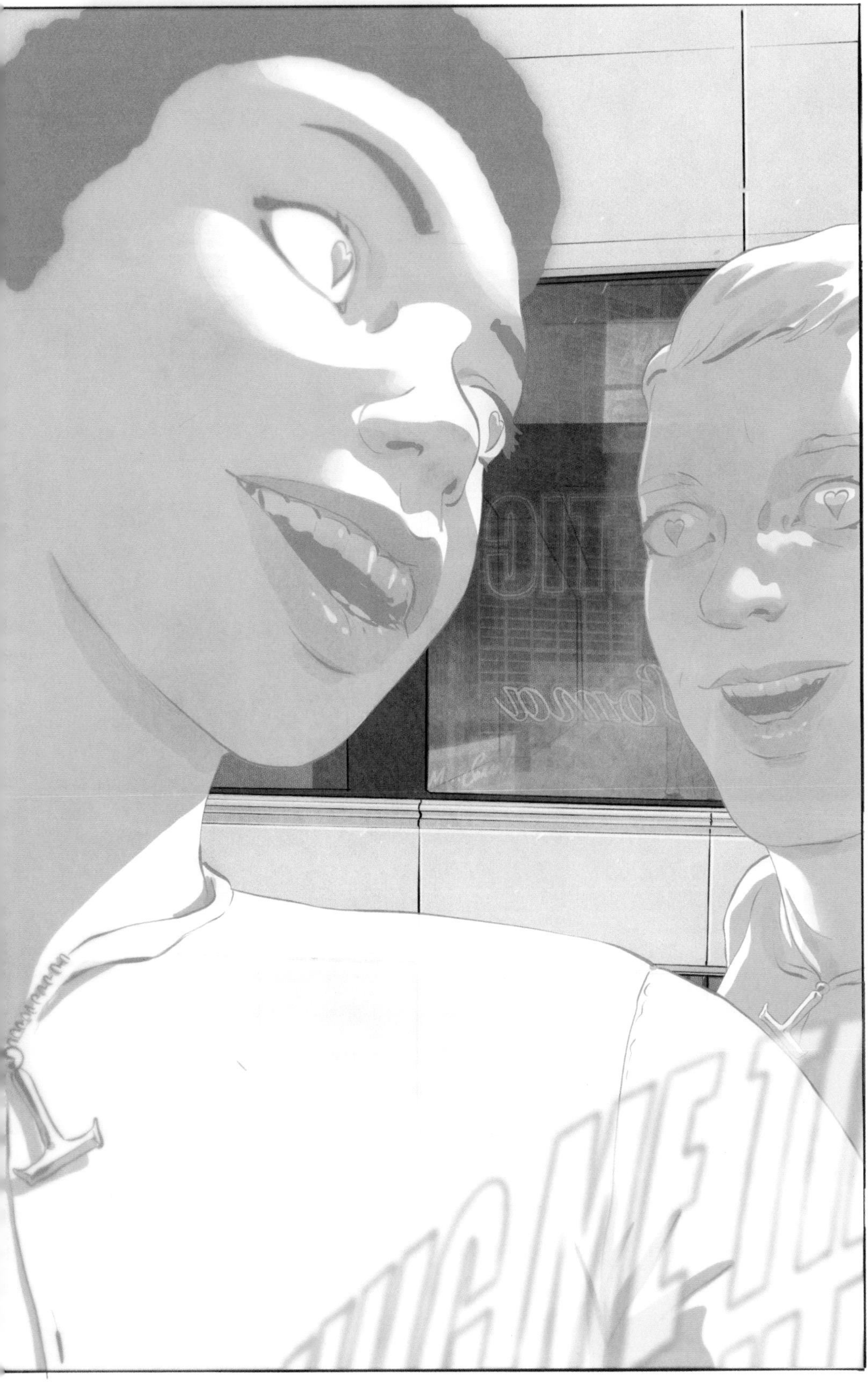

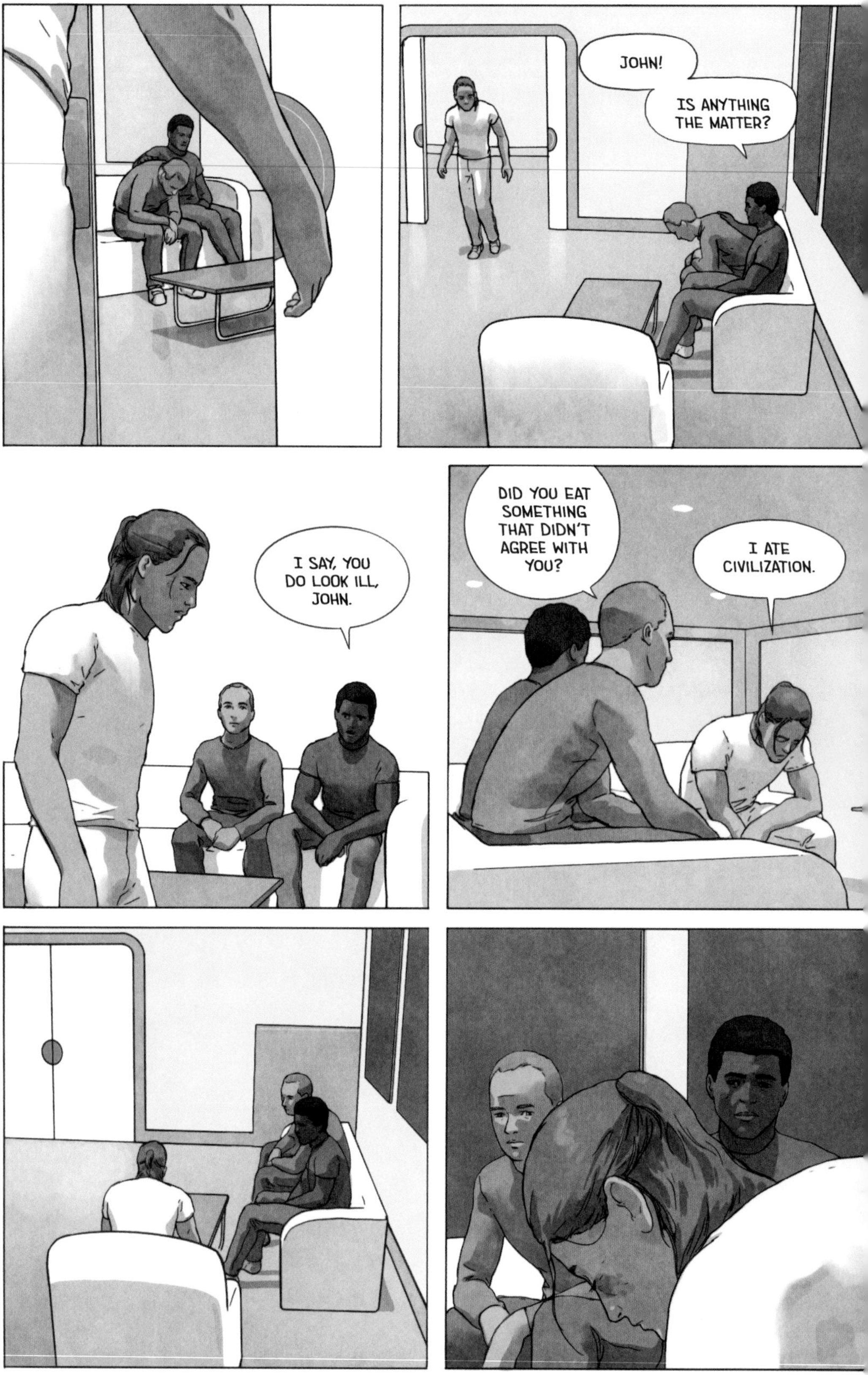
JOHN!
IS ANYTHING THE MATTER?
I SAY, YOU DO LOOK ILL, JOHN.
DID YOU EAT SOMETHING THAT DIDN'T AGREE WITH YOU?
I ATE CIVILIZATION.

WE'RE OFF TOMORROW MORNING.

BY THE WAY, JOHN, I WANT TO SAY HOW SORRY I AM ABOUT EVERYTHING THAT HAPPENED . . .

HOW ASHAMED. HOW REALLY . . .

HELMHOLTZ WAS WONDERFUL TO ME. IF IT HADN'T BEEN FOR HIM, I SHOULD . . .

NOW, NOW.

I ASKED IF I MIGHTN'T GO TO THE ISLANDS WITH YOU.

AND?

HE WOULDN'T LET ME. HE SAID HE WANTED TO GO ON WITH THE EXPERIMENT.

I'M DAMNED IF I'LL GO ON BEING EXPERIMENTED WITH.

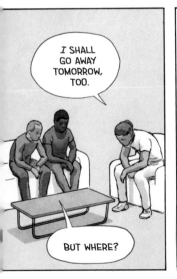

I SHALL GO AWAY TOMORROW, TOO.

BUT WHERE?

ANYWHERE. I DON'T CARE.

SO LONG AS I CAN BE ALONE.

SOMA SUNDAE
EVERYBODY'S HAPPY

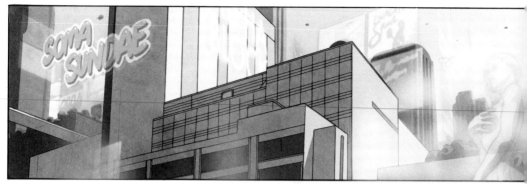

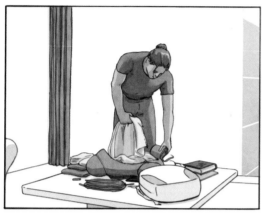

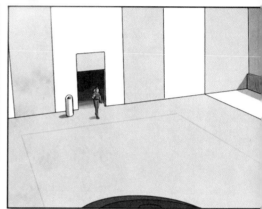

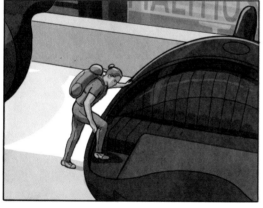

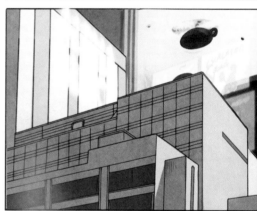

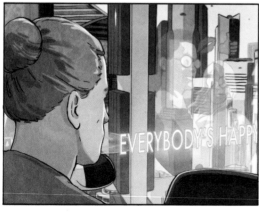

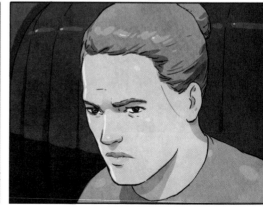

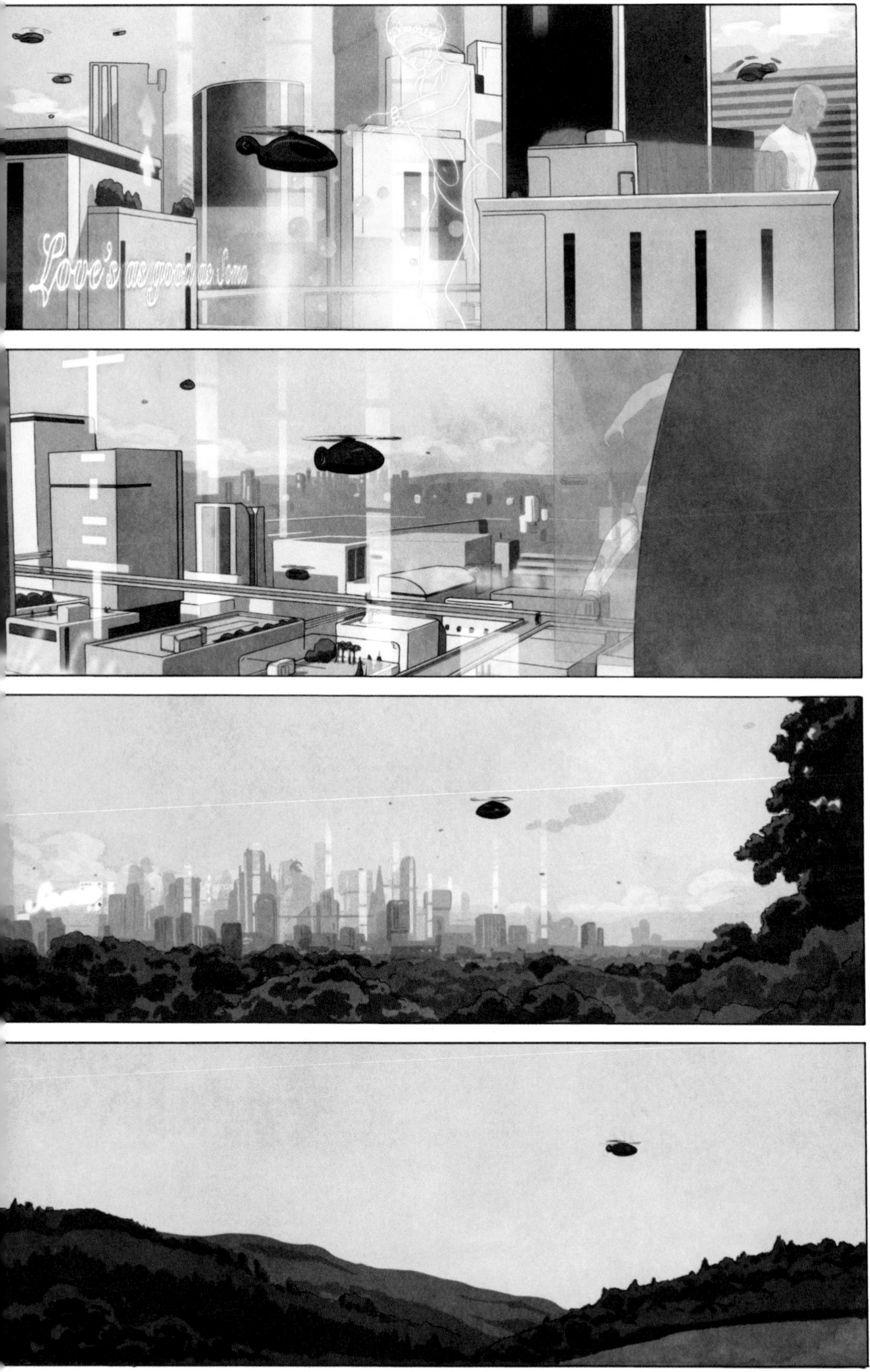
Love's as good as Soma

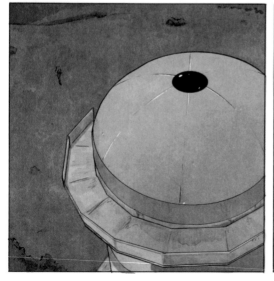

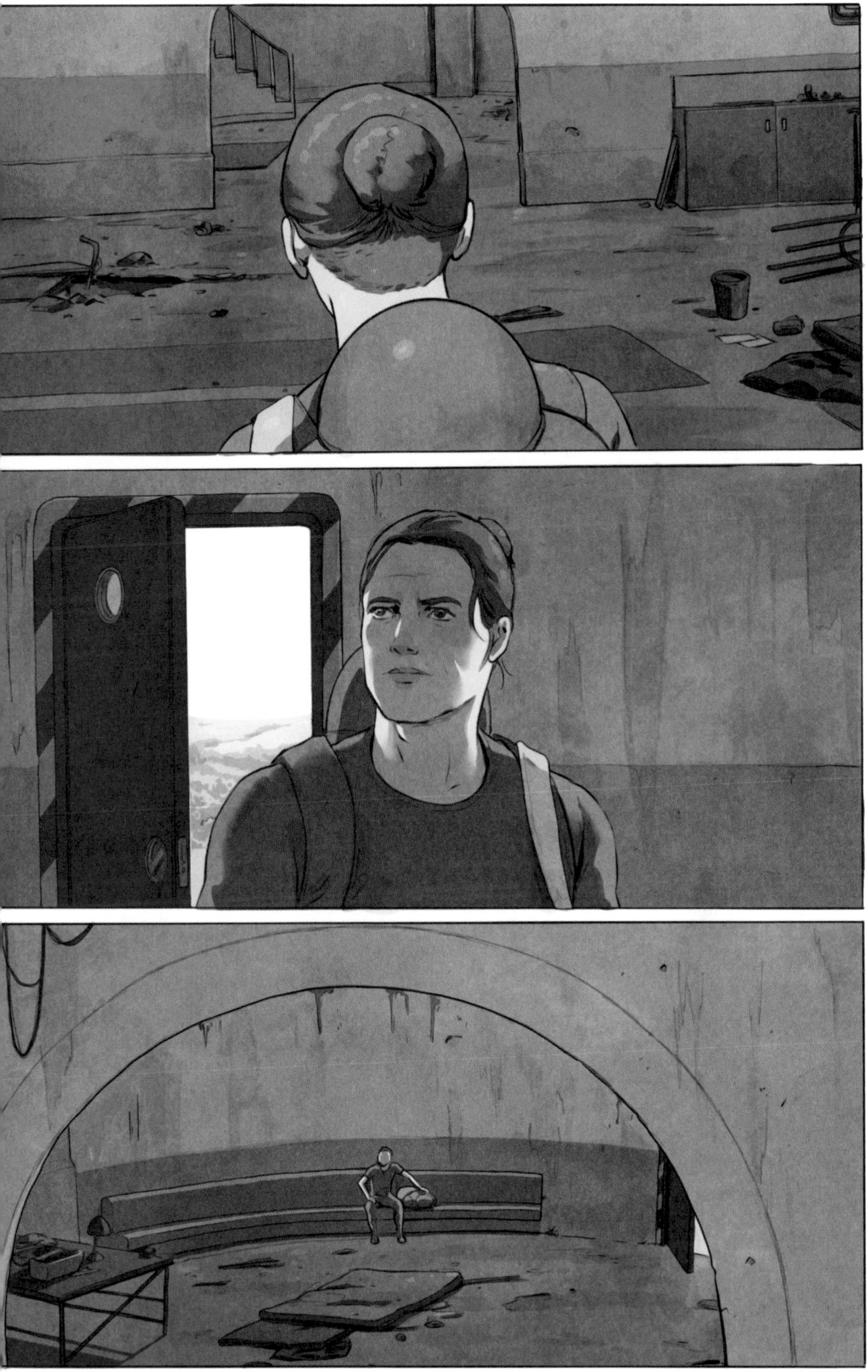

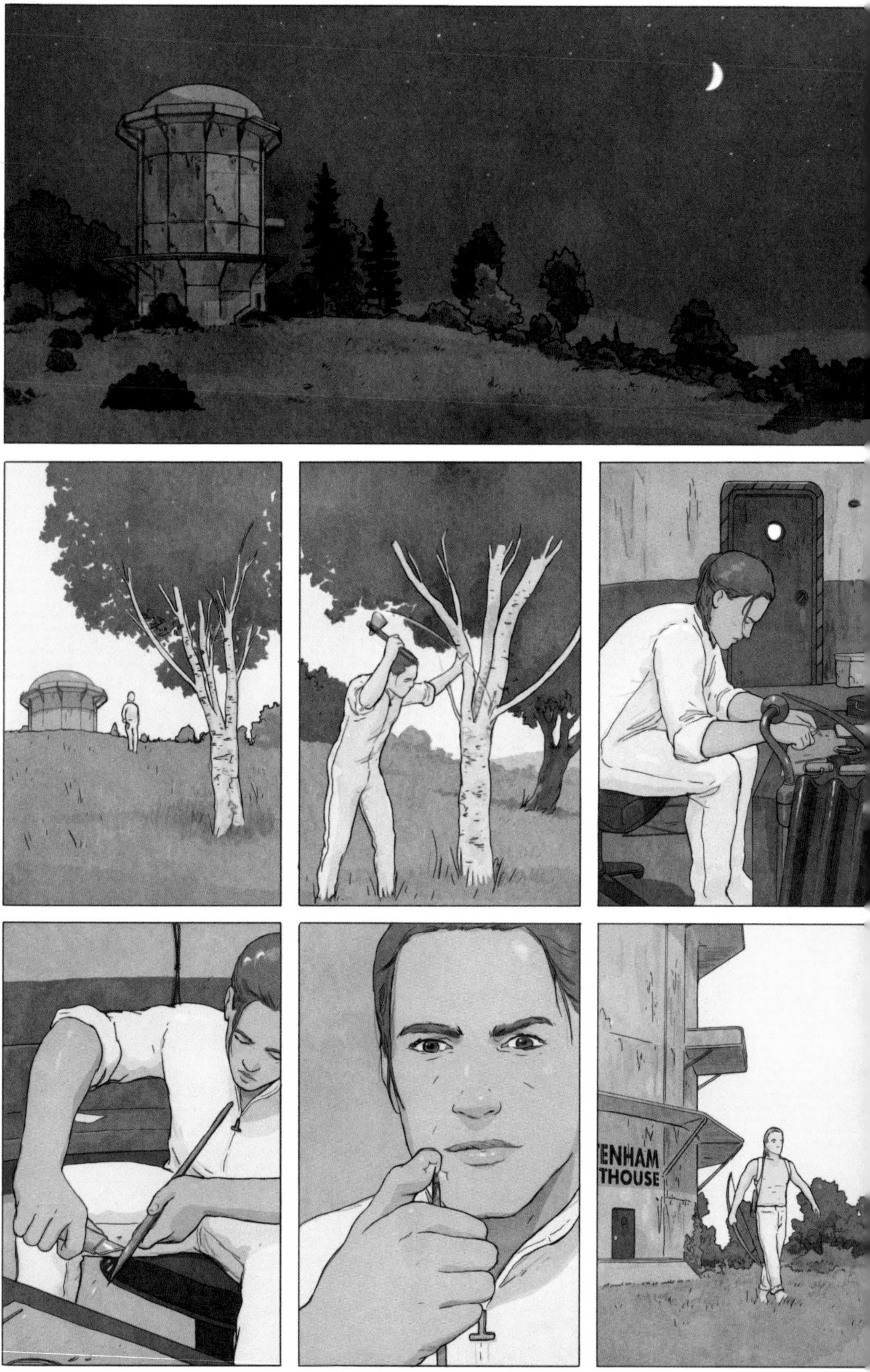
ENHAM
THOUSE

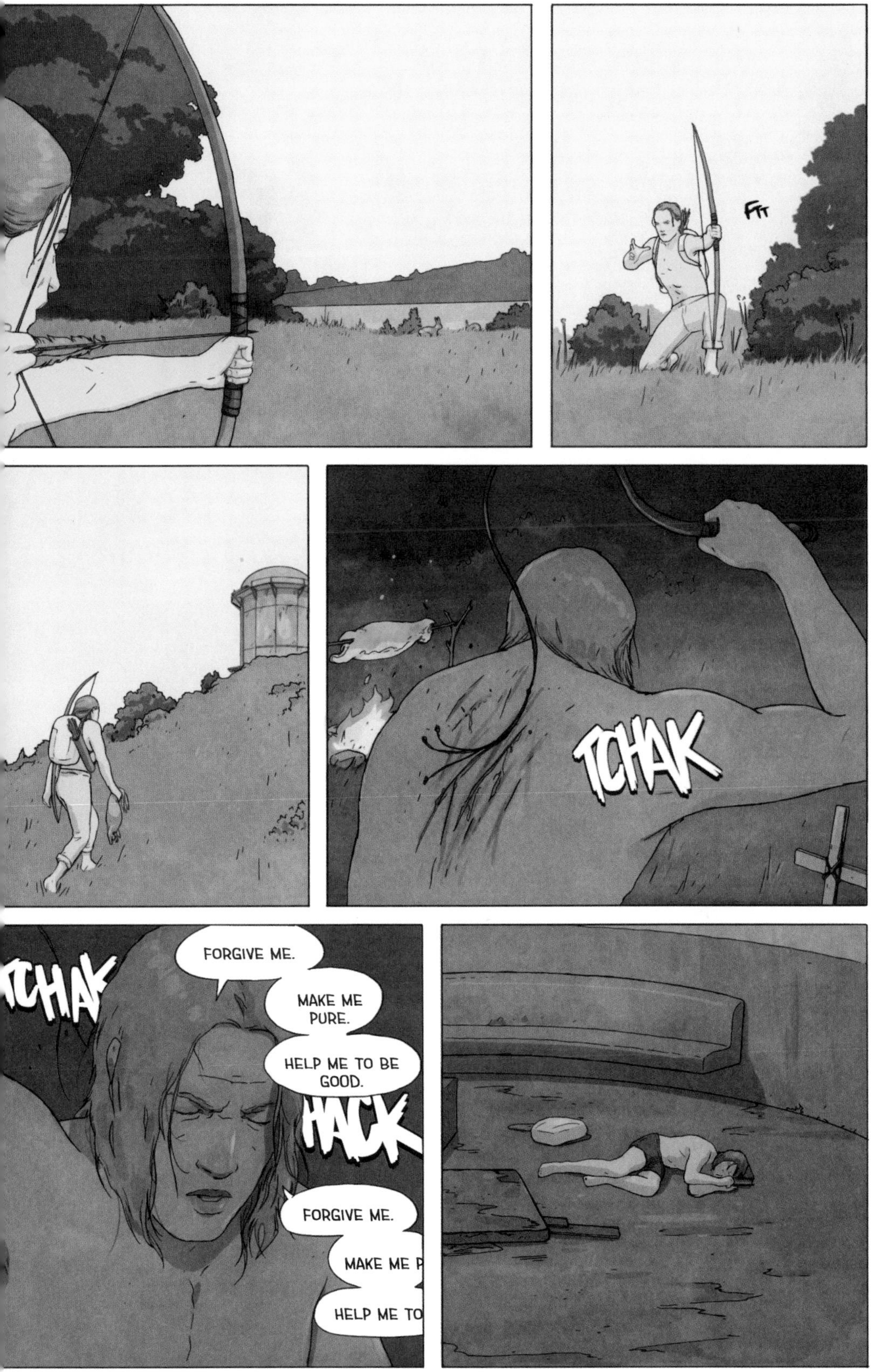
FFT
TCHAK
TCHAK
FORGIVE ME.
MAKE ME PURE.
HELP ME TO BE GOOD.
HACK
FORGIVE ME.
MAKE ME P
HELP ME TO

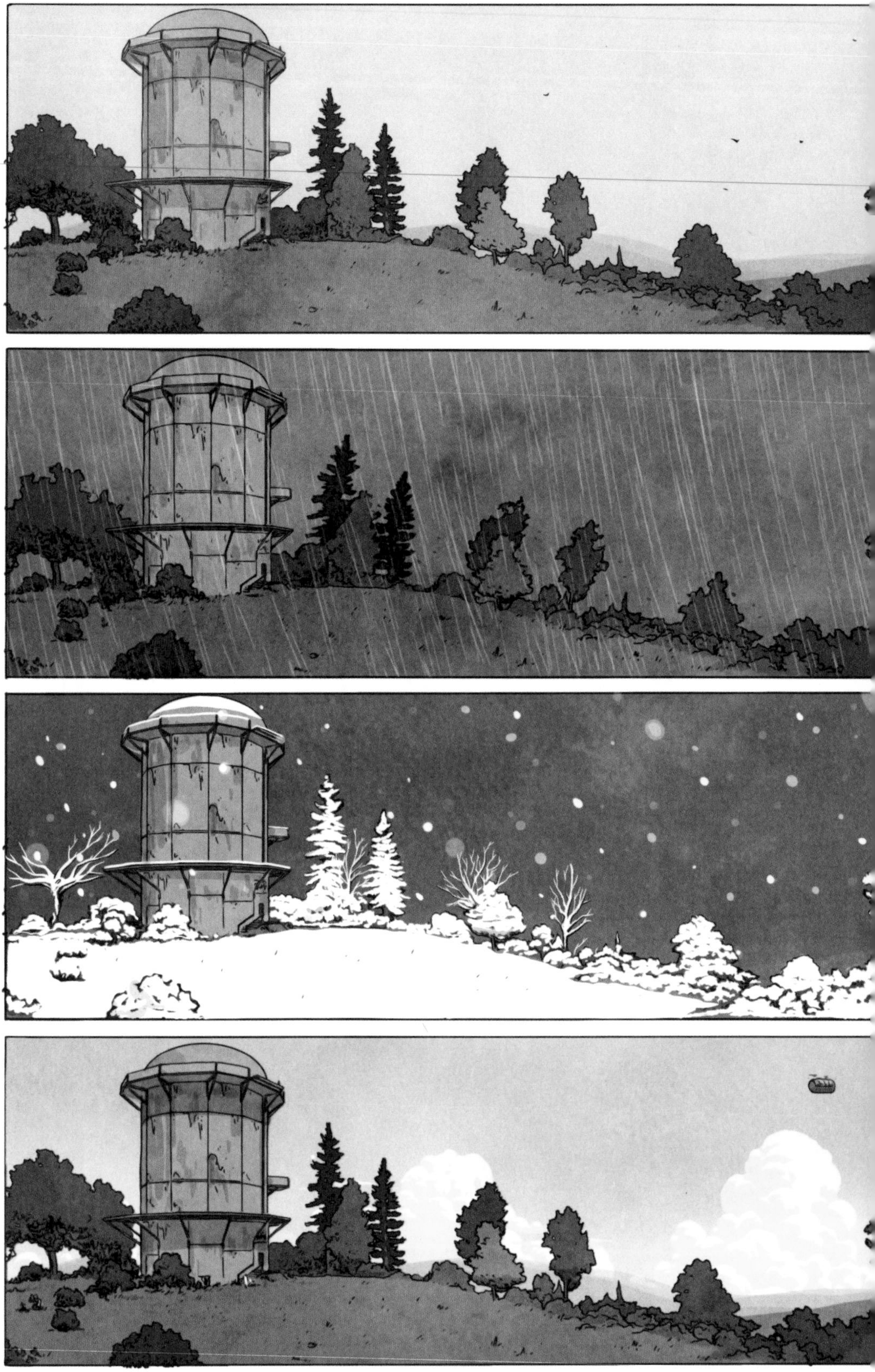

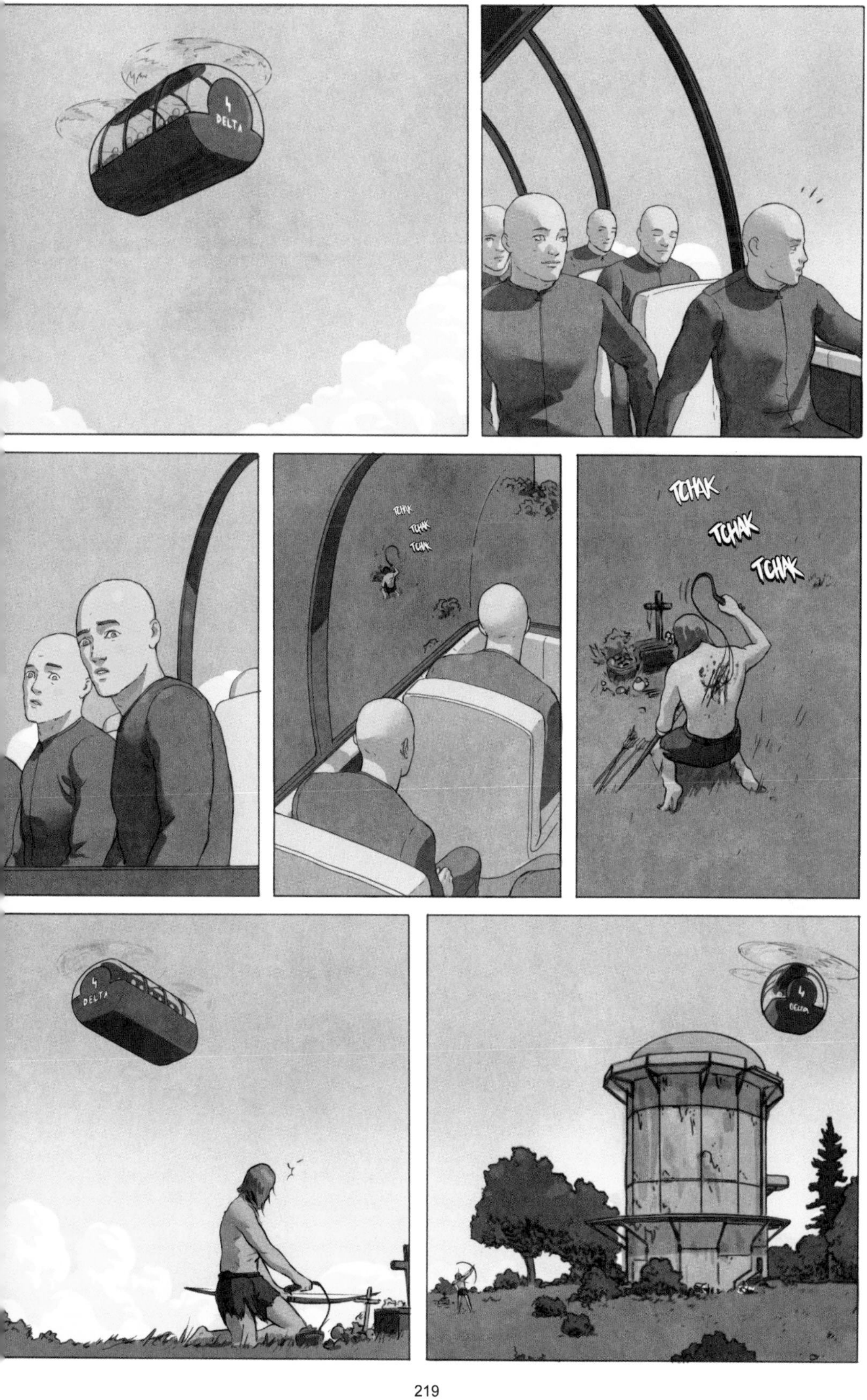
4
DELTA
TCHAK
TCHAK
TCHAK
TCHAK
TCHAK
TCHAK
4
DELTA
4
DELTA

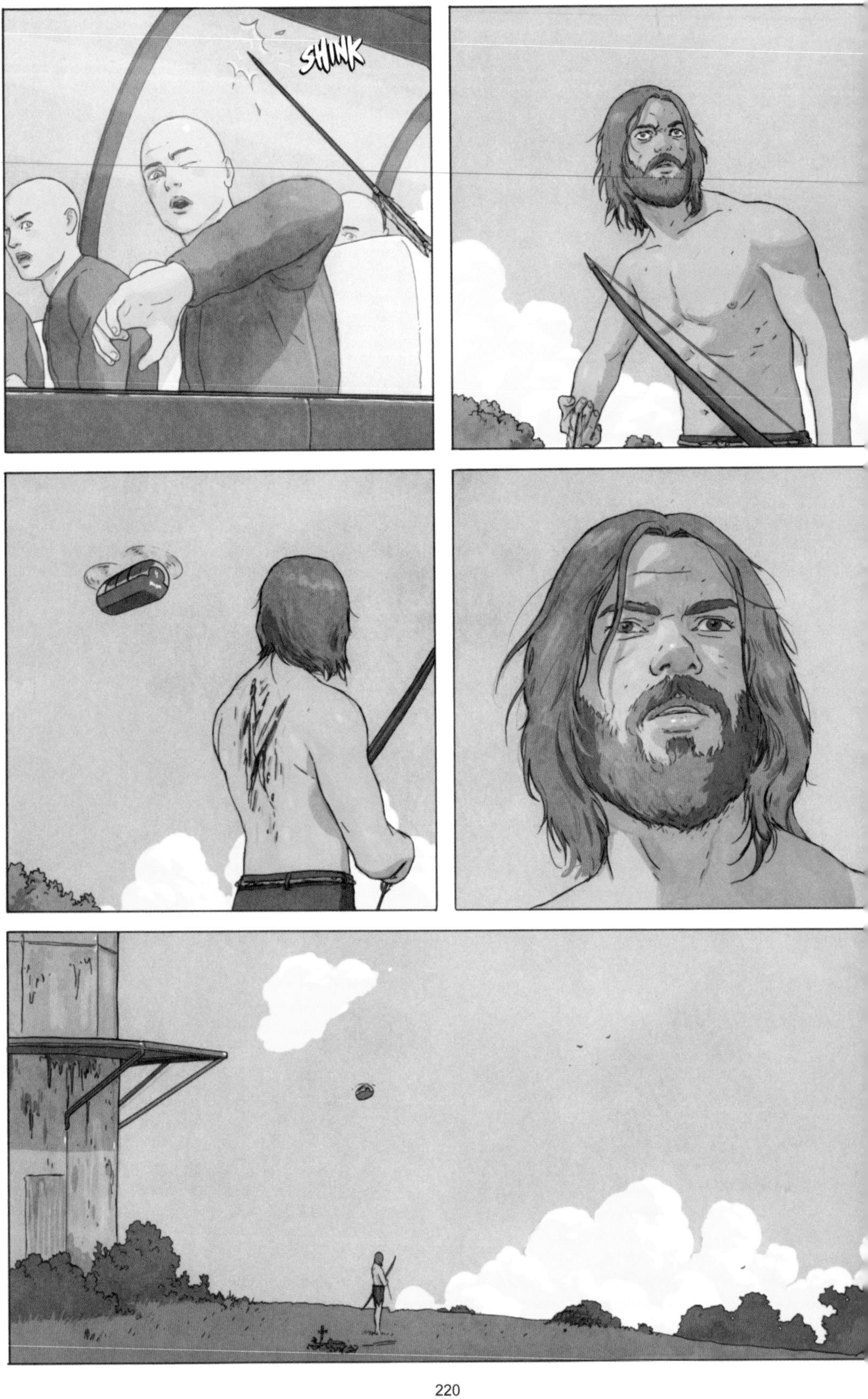
SHINK

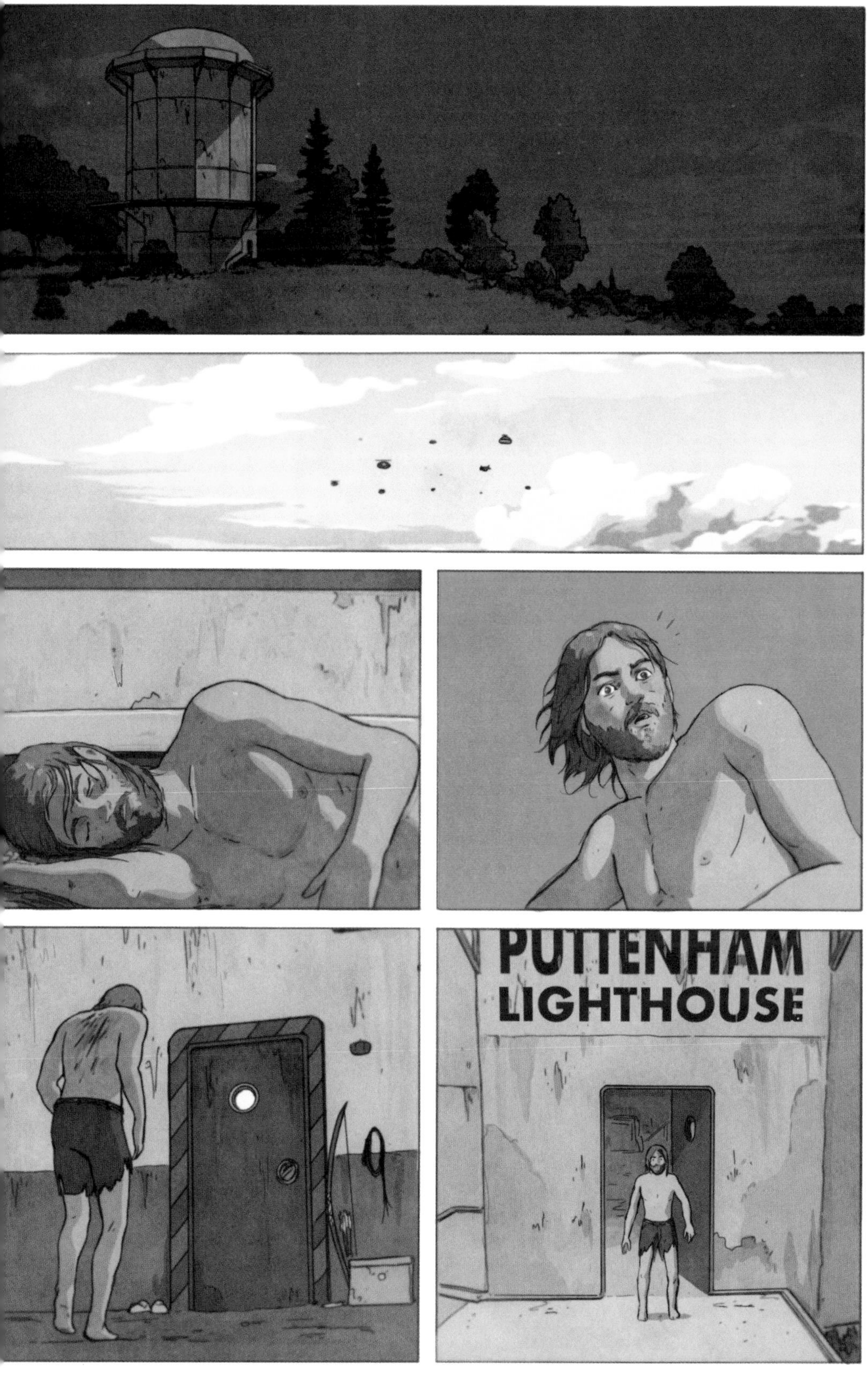
PUTTENHAM
LIGHTHOUSE

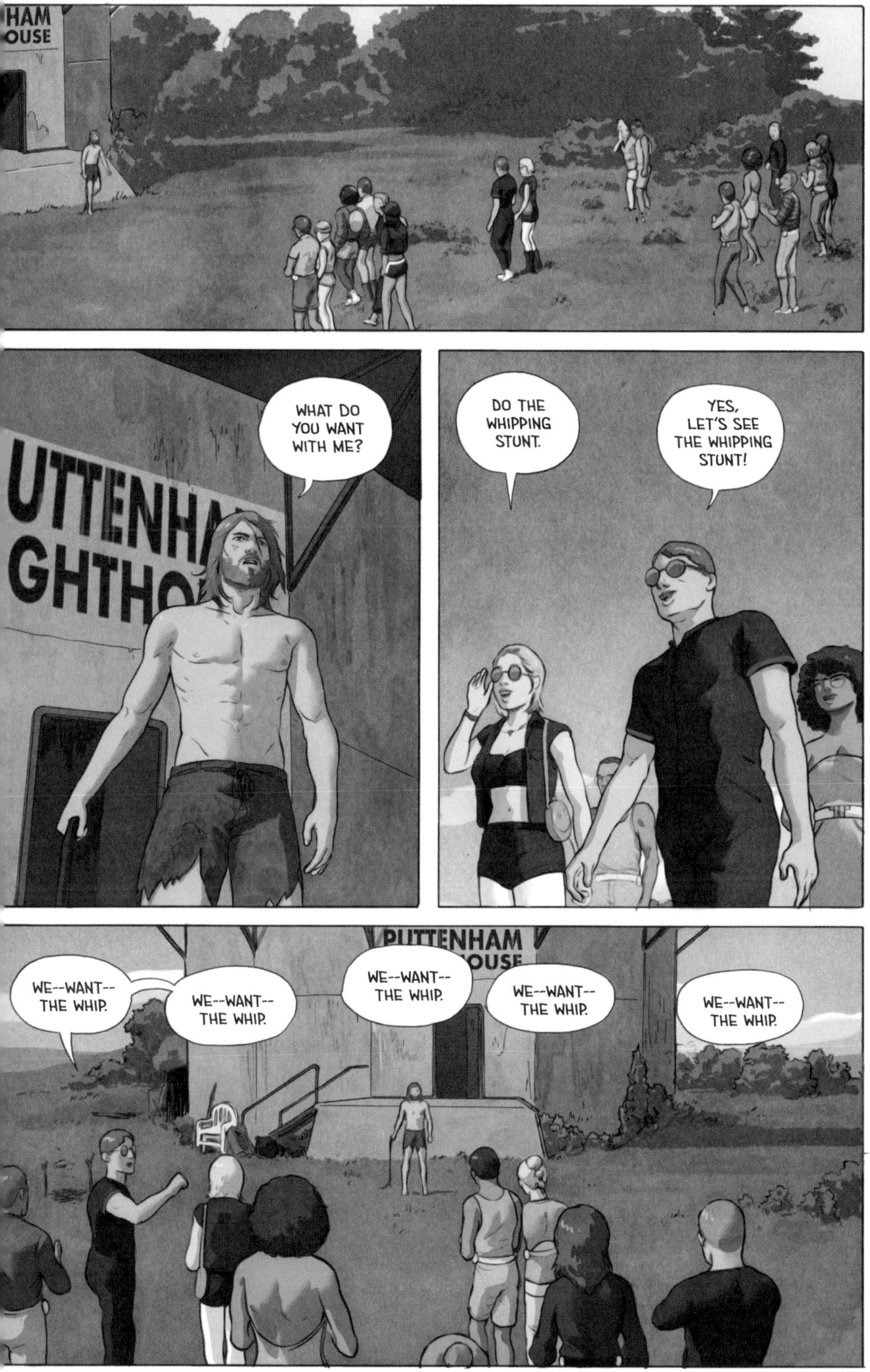
HAM
OUSE
UTTENHA
GHTHO
WHAT DO YOU WANT WITH ME?
DO THE WHIPPING STUNT.
YES, LET'S SEE THE WHIPPING STUNT!
PUTTENHAM
OUSE
WE--WANT-- THE WHIP.
WE--WANT-- THE WHIP.
WE--WANT-- THE WHIP.
WE--WANT-- THE WHIP.
WE--WANT-- THE WHIP.

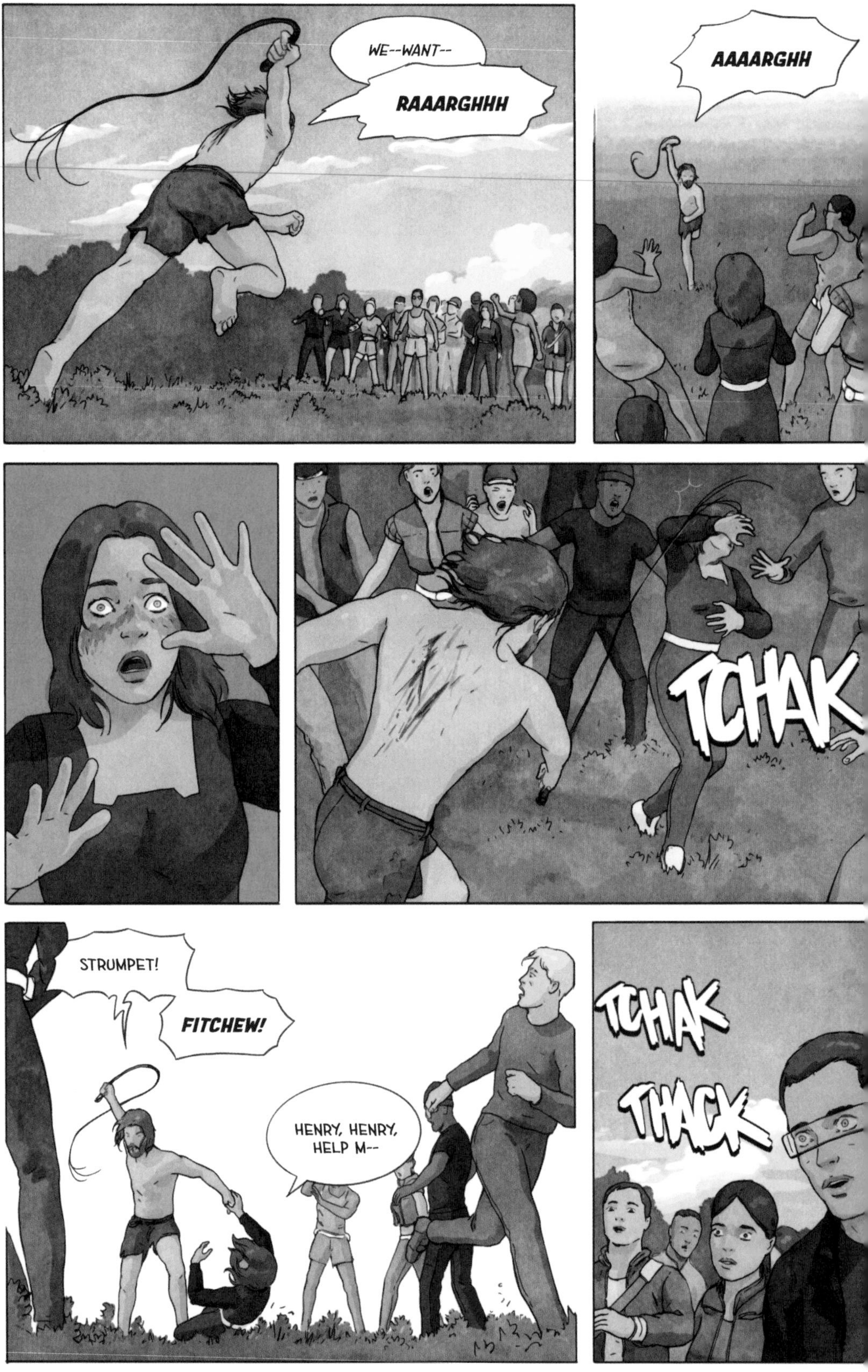
WE--WANT--
RAAARGHHH
AAAARGHH
TCHAK
STRUMPET!
FITCHEW!
HENRY, HENRY, HELP M--
TCHAK
THACK

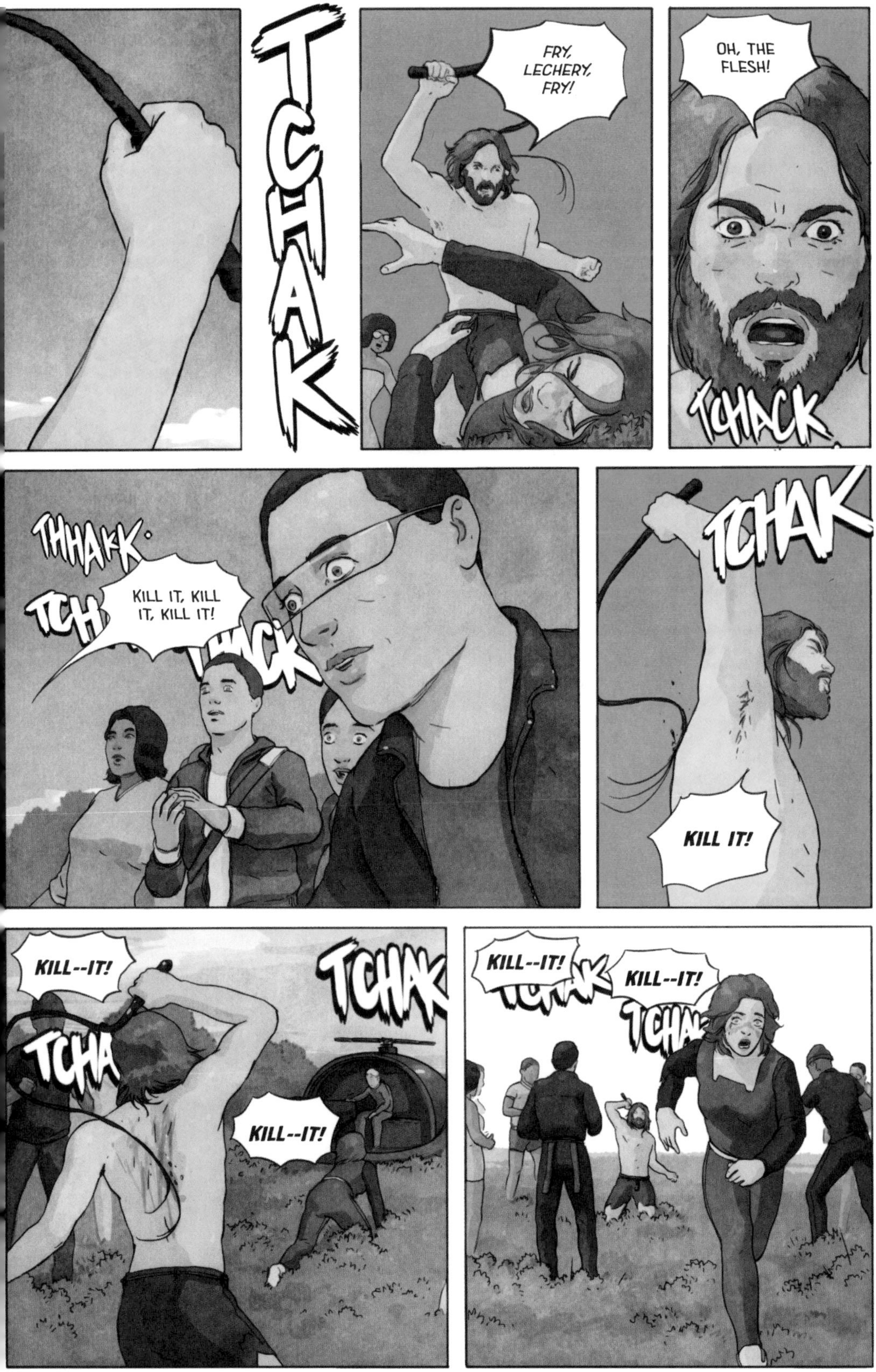
TCHAK
FRY, LECHERY, FRY!
OH, THE FLESH!
TCHACK
THHAKK
TCH
KILL IT, KILL IT, KILL IT!
THACK
TCHAK
KILL IT!
KILL--IT!
TCHAK
TCHA
KILL--IT!
KILL--IT!
TCHAK
KILL--IT!
TCHA

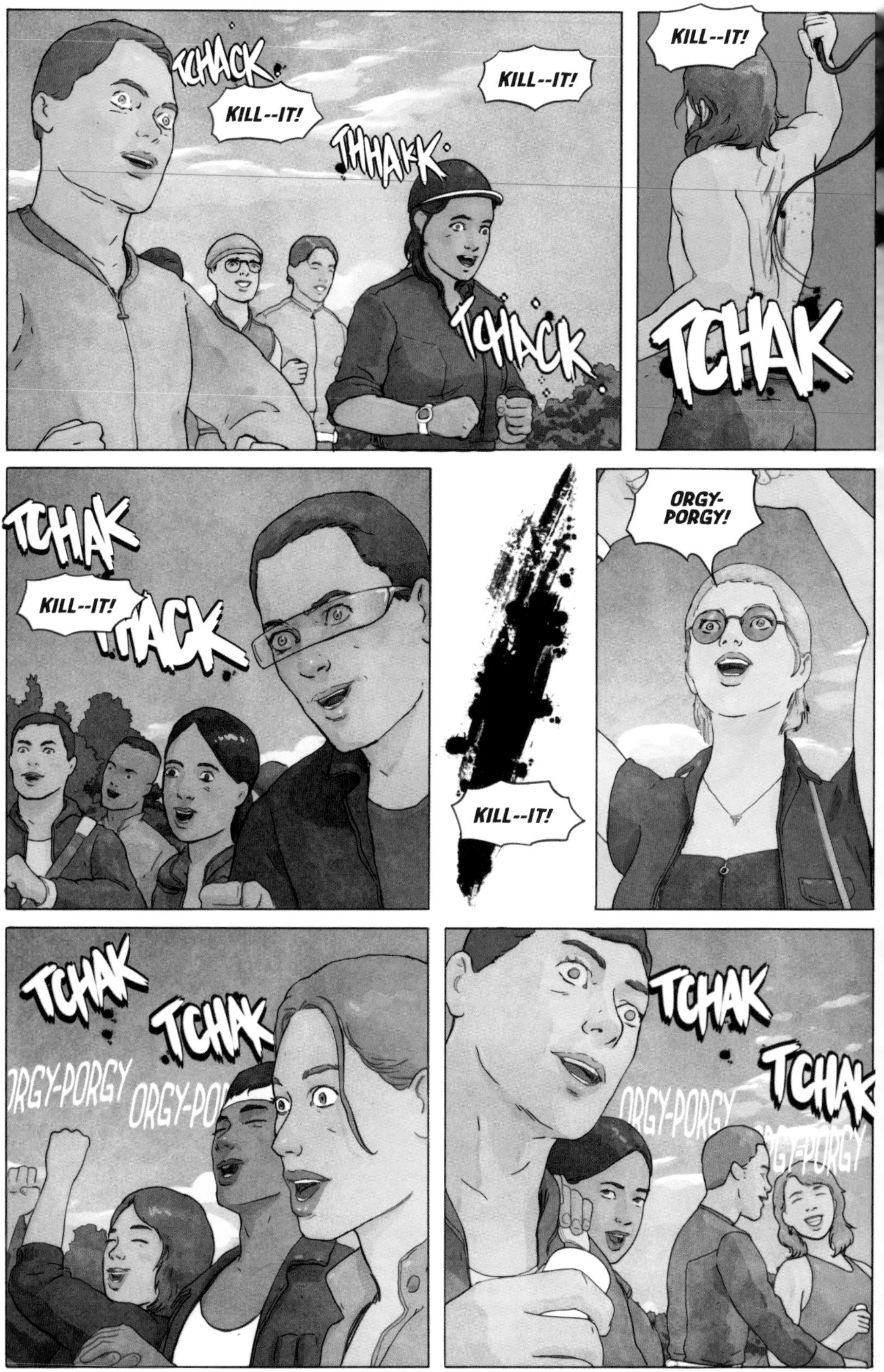
TCHACK
KILL--IT!
KILL--IT!
THHAKK
TCHACK
KILL--IT!
TCHAK
TCHAK
KILL--IT!
THACK
KILL--IT!
ORGY-
PORGY!
TCHAK
TCHAK
ORGY-PORGY
ORGY-PO
TCHAK
TCHAK
ORGY-PORGY
ORGY-PORGY

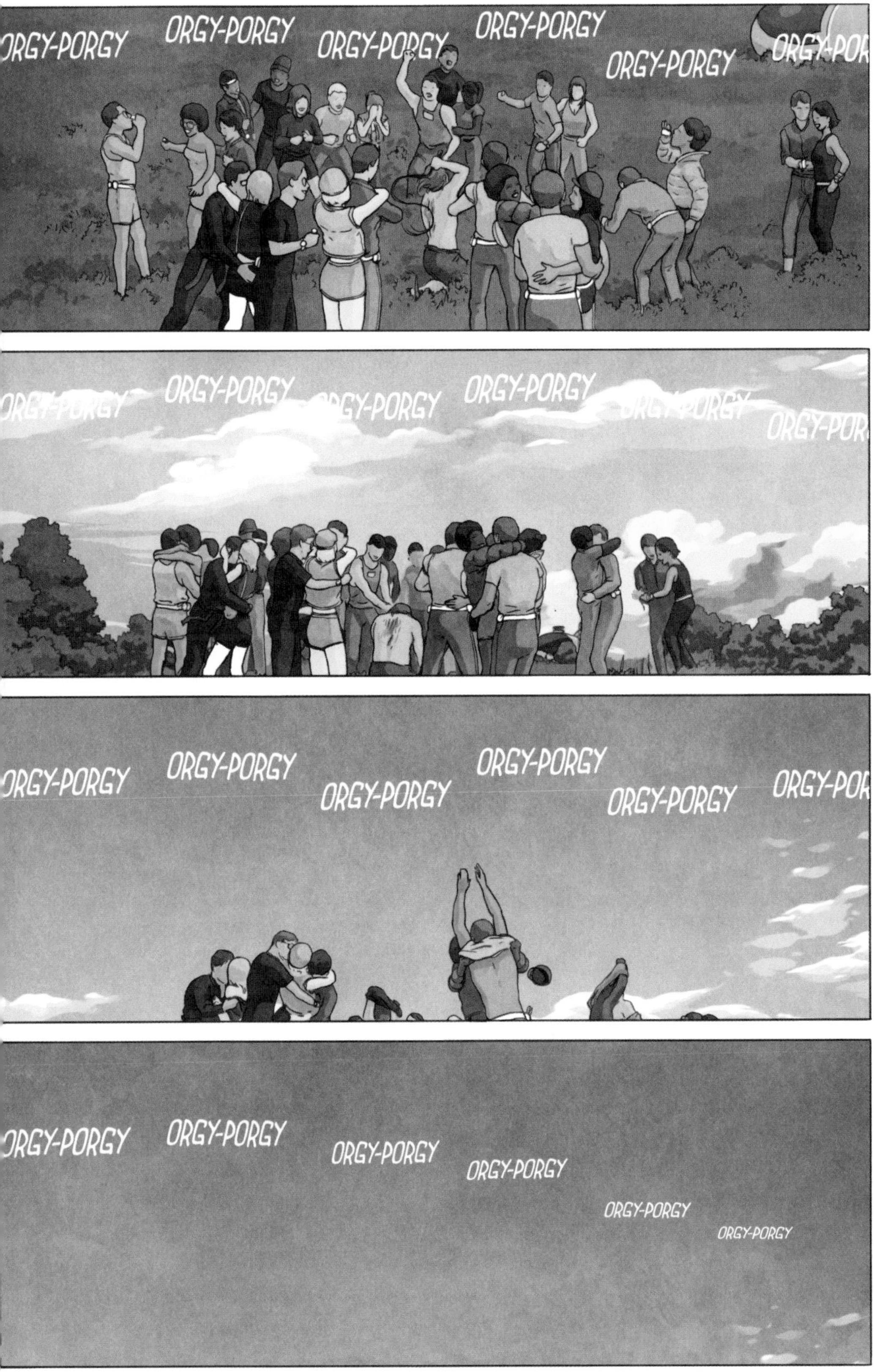
ORGY-PORGY
ORGY-PORGY
ORGY-PORGY
ORGY-PORGY
ORGY-PORGY
ORGY-PORGY
ORGY-PORGY
ORGY-PORGY
ORGY-PORGY
ORGY-PORGY
ORGY-PORGY
ORGY-PORGY
ORGY-PORGY
ORGY-PORGY
ORGY-PORGY

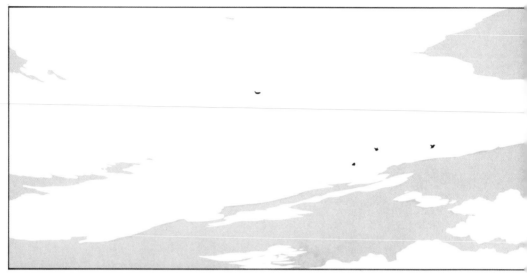

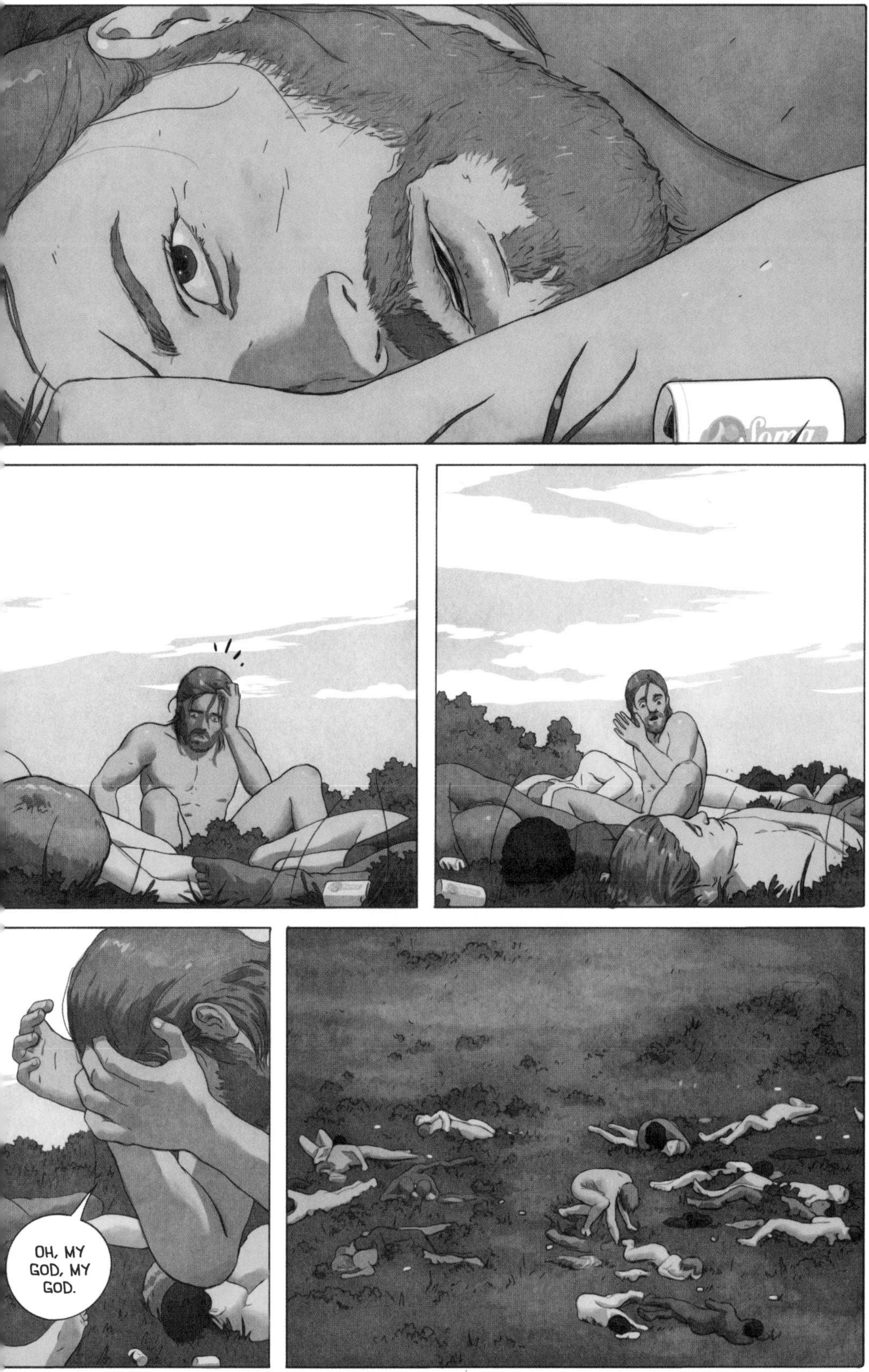
OH, MY GOD, MY GOD.

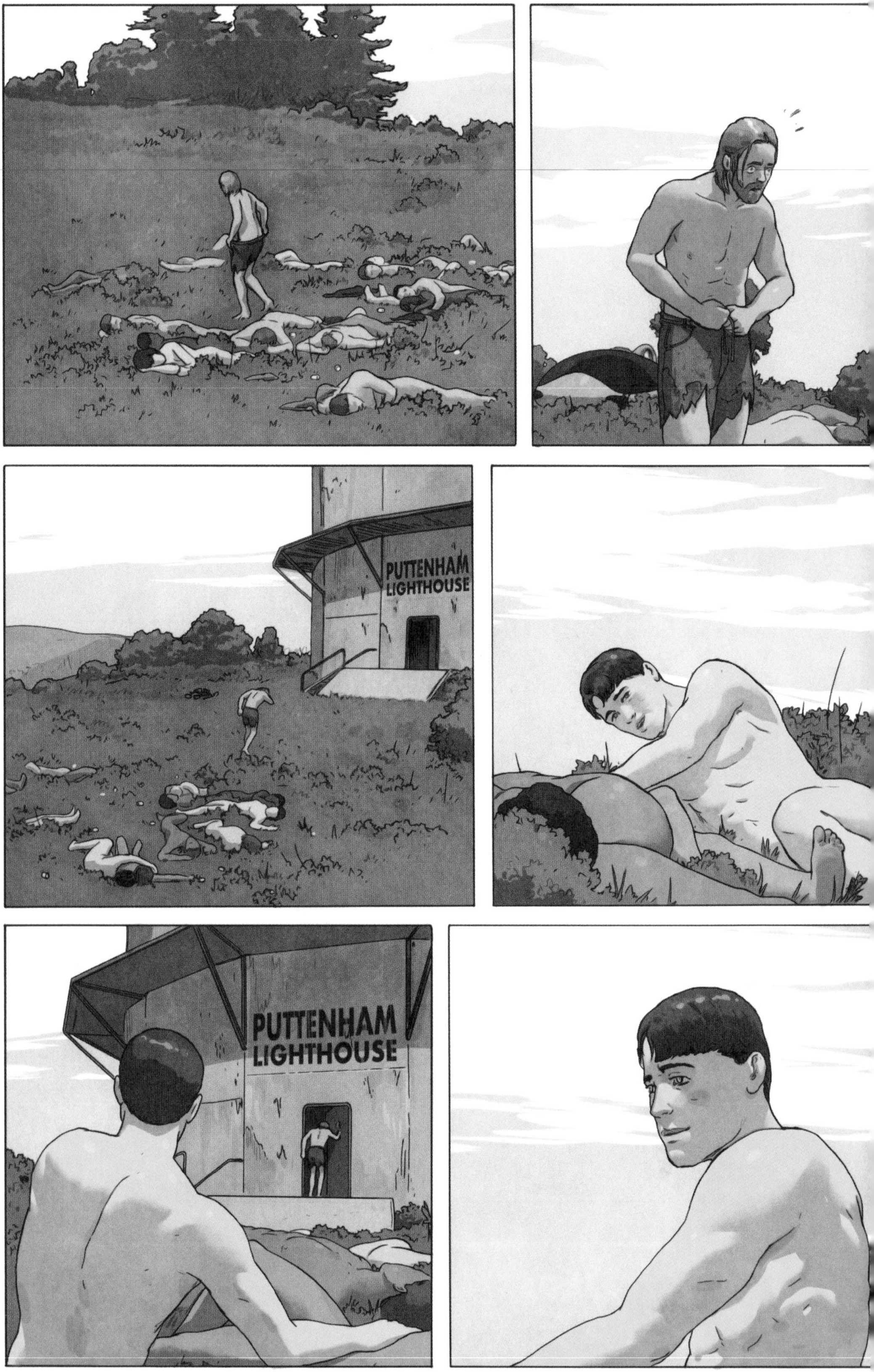
PUTTENHAM
LIGHTHOUSE
PUTTENHAM
LIGHTHOUSE

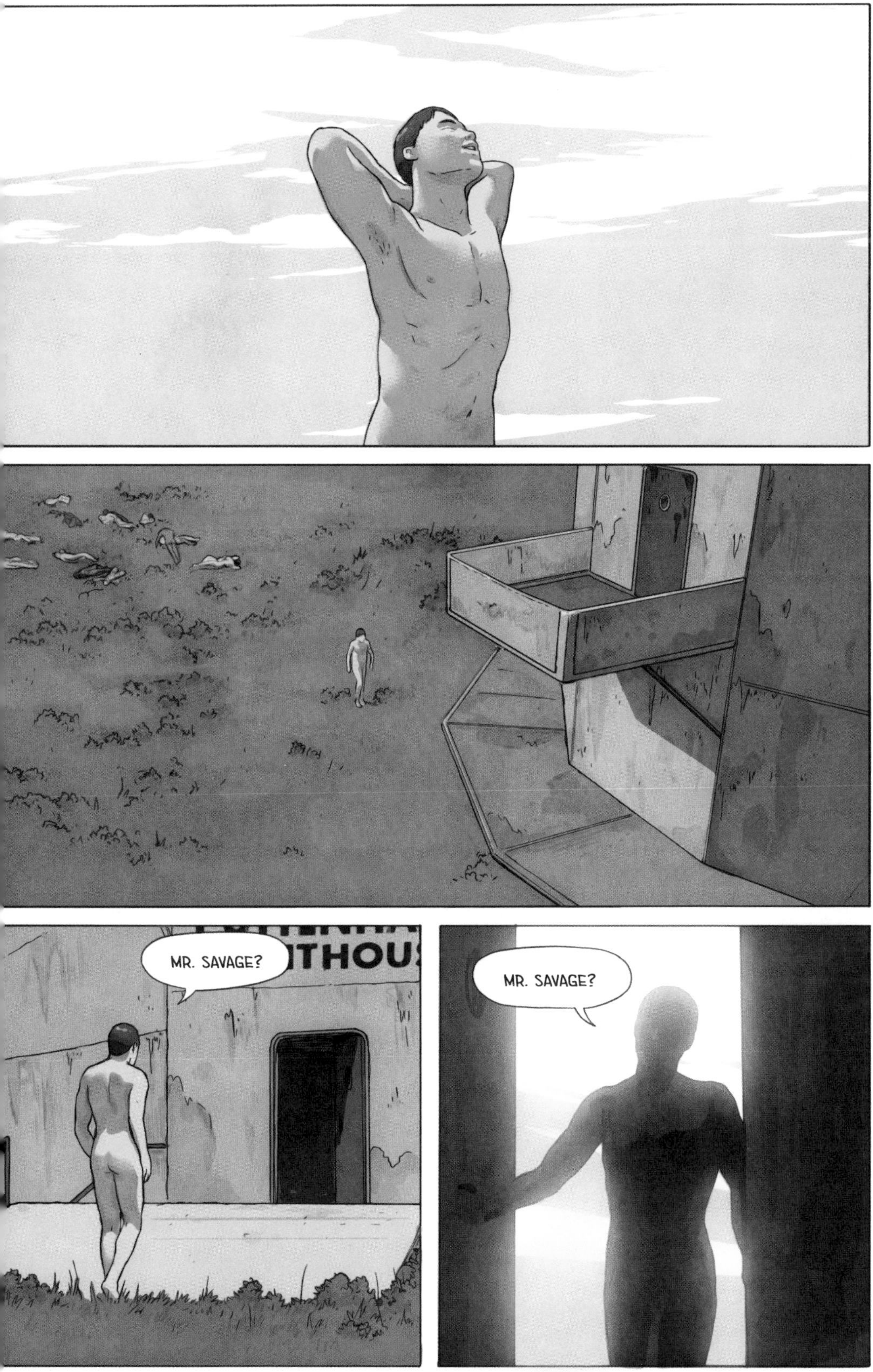
MR. SAVAGE?
MR. SAVAGE?

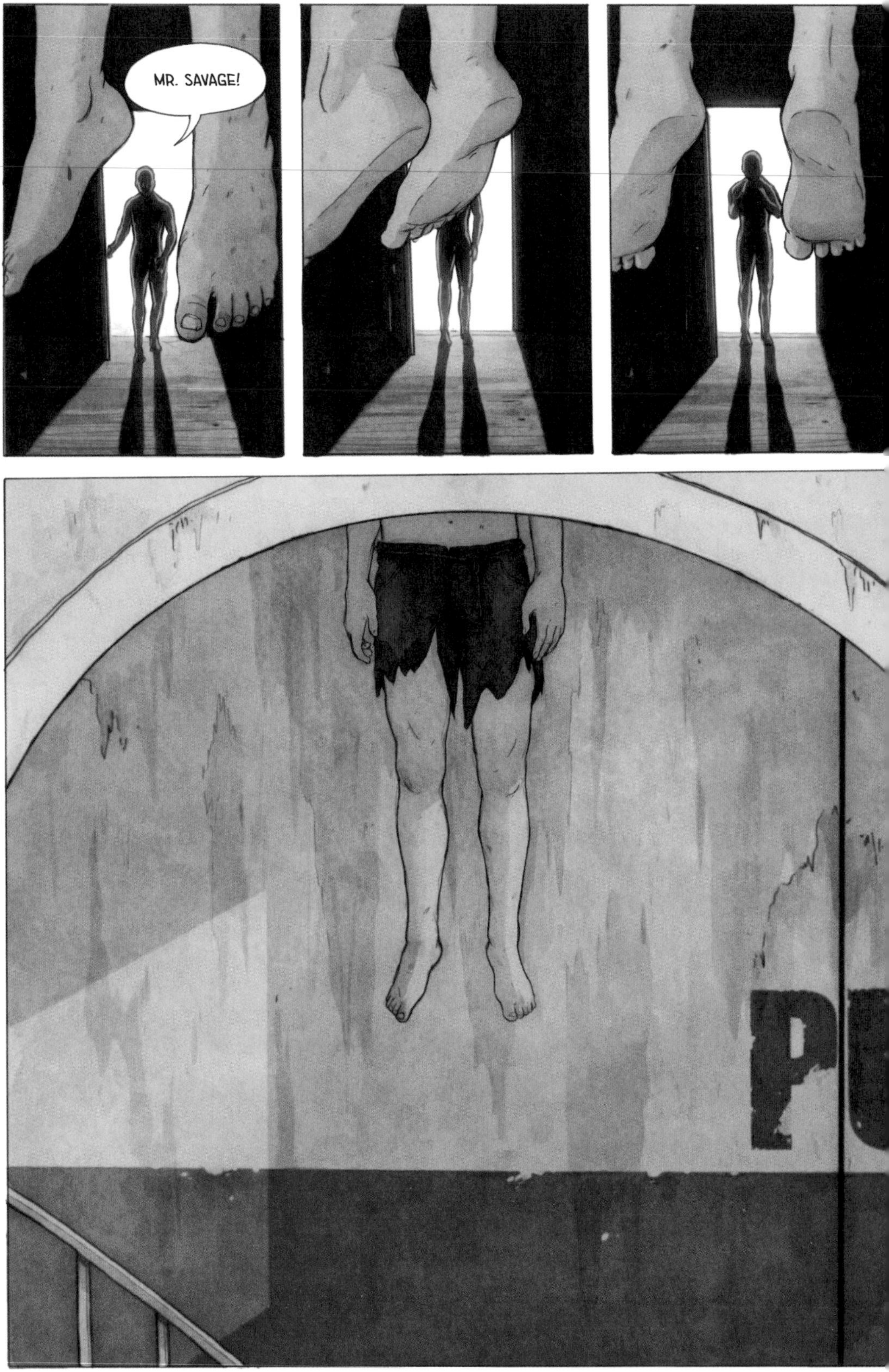
MR. SAVAGE!

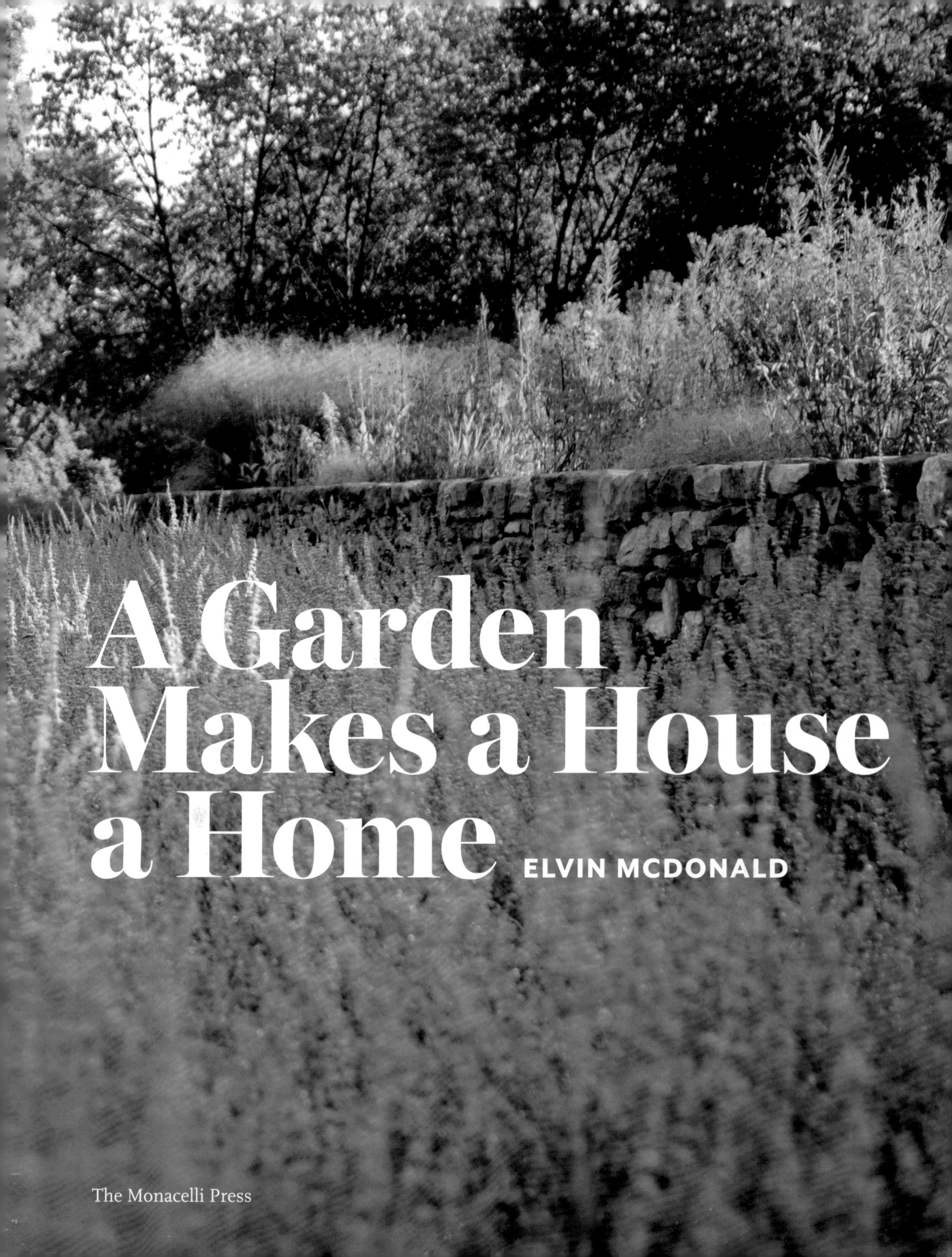

A Garden Makes a House a Home

ELVIN MCDONALD

The Monacelli Press

For C. Z. Guest, who for nearly thirty years, until her death in 2003,
called me her gardening husband, and Karol Nickell, who brought me
to Des Moines in 1995 to be garden editor of *Traditional Home*.

Copyright © 2012 by The Monacelli Press

All rights reserved. Published in the United States
by The Monacelli Press, LLC, New York.

Library of Congress
Cataloging-in-Publication Data

McDonald, Elvin.
A garden makes a house a home / by Elvin McDonald.—1st ed. p. cm.
ISBN 978-1-58093-330-8 (hardcover)
1. Gardens, American. 2. Gardens—United States— Design.
3. Gardens, American— Pictorial works.
4. Gardens—United States— Design—Pictorial works. I. Title.
SB457.53.M37 2012
635.90973—dc23   2012008431

10 9 8 7 6 5 4 3 2 1
First Edition

www.monacellipress.com

Printed in China

Designed by Michelle Leong

contents

preface

WHEN I MOVED TO IOWA in 1995 to become garden editor of *Traditional Home* magazine, I first lived in an apartment. It included a detached garage where I could stockpile the makings of a future garden—furniture and objects. It was 1997 before I found a more permanent situation, an "executive rental." Afternoon sunlight streamed into the kitchen, and its large dining and great rooms instantly sold me. I also liked the landlady and got no resistance to my off-the-cuff ideas for transforming the yard. Renting meant I could spend my cash on gardening.

The "contemporary" description of the house, constructed in 1974, was euphemistic. An architect friend of mine defined it more appropriately as "Mediterranean Tudor two-story ranch with touches of Prairie School." What couldn't be changed, I embraced and embellished. The bricked arch at the entry is a motif now repeated twice, in lattice arches leading to and from the front and back gardens and in a Chinese moon gate along the north lot line that echoes an Edwardian seat arbor opposite, 150 feet across the yard, on the south lot line.

A 5-foot square of "Tudor" timbering on the upper story inspired the layout of the front gardens. When I moved in, there was lawn, a red maple at the southeast corner, and some meaningless foundation plantings. I left the tree and pulled out the rest. Using the 5-by-5 module, I sectioned off the lawn, planting a flowering crab apple tree with daffodils in every other square and French landscape roses in the squares between.

This framing reduced the amount of lawn and added a serene vest-pocket park in front of the house. Matching blue garden benches face each other at either end. The entry walk, which bisects this parklike setting, is lined by raised planting beds filled with seasonal flowers. Removal of the foundation plantings

OPPOSITE, CLOCKWISE FROM TOP LEFT Lilies add color to the driveway; a table set for a late summer dinner on the deck, with a backdrop of autumn clematis; a blue bench overlooks the parklike front garden; lavender-colored sweet rocket grows in tufts next to an arbor; a Chinese moon gate; simple café furniture replicates the feel of a front porch.

BELOW, CLOCKWISE FROM TOP LEFT Yellow mums and white autumn clematis add color to the front lawn; a shed-cum-tea house with sweet potato vines and coleus; a walk created with simple pavers; apple espaliers in terra-cotta pots; a faux rug painted on the back deck; an arch and path leading from the front to the back yard, lined with white impatiens.

made room for an entry "hall" from the driveway to the front door and beyond. A golden *chamaecyparis* stops the eye at one end, and a potted weeping Siberian pea-tree at the other. A setback overlooked by a bay window in the living room is now outfitted with garden furniture, to represent a welcoming front porch. Boston ivy also clothes most of the house's brick facade.

The narrow side yard at the south end of the house hosts an allée of Colonnade apple trees in raised beds otherwise devoted to ferns, white narcissus, hyacinths, 'Casa Blanca' lilies, white begonias, and impatiens. Pine needles carpet the walkway.

A deck overlooks the back gardens. Opposite, at the back lot line, I added a latticed dining pavilion fronted by a four-square garden framed by overturned clay pots arranged decoratively and colored with spring bulbs, alpine strawberries, sage, coleus, plectranthus, ornamental sweet potatoes, and hardy mums.

A windowless tool shed at the southwest corner of the lot became a tea house with the addition of windows and French doors, sisal carpeting, and paint for the walls. A rose garden with raised beds and an 8-foot obelisk that climbing roses can cling to covers the space between it and the main house. Two existing green ash trees have burgeoned with the watering and fertilizing of the roses and have recently been limbed up so they shade the upper-story rooms but permit more sun to reach the garden.

My overall goal was to create numerous places where I could feel as though I had left the house, but without having to get in the car. These gardens have not only transformed a rental house—which I later purchased—into a home, they have also become a place where teachers from the neighborhood school bring students to study art and plant science, an unexpected source of great pleasure for me.

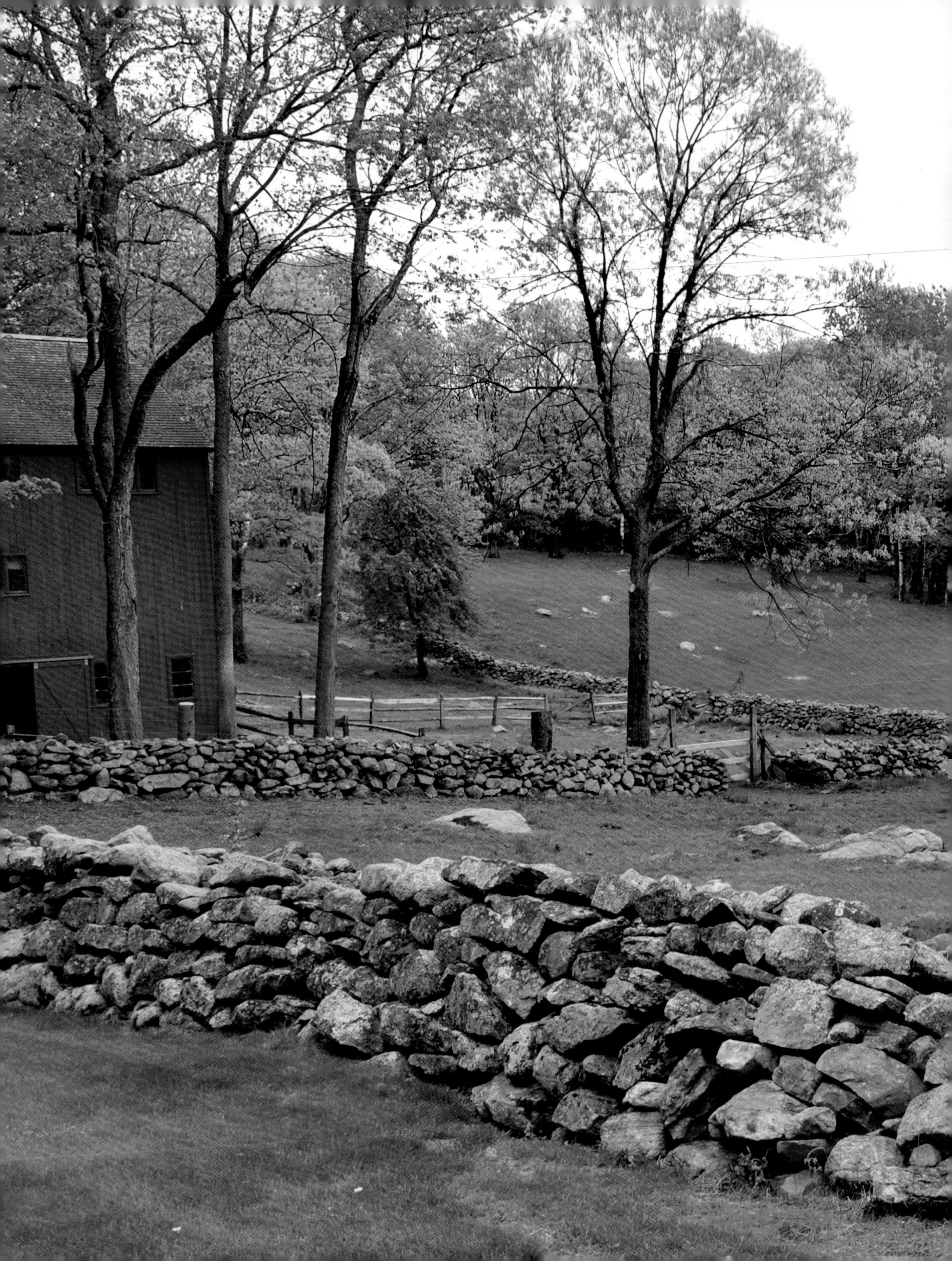

northeast

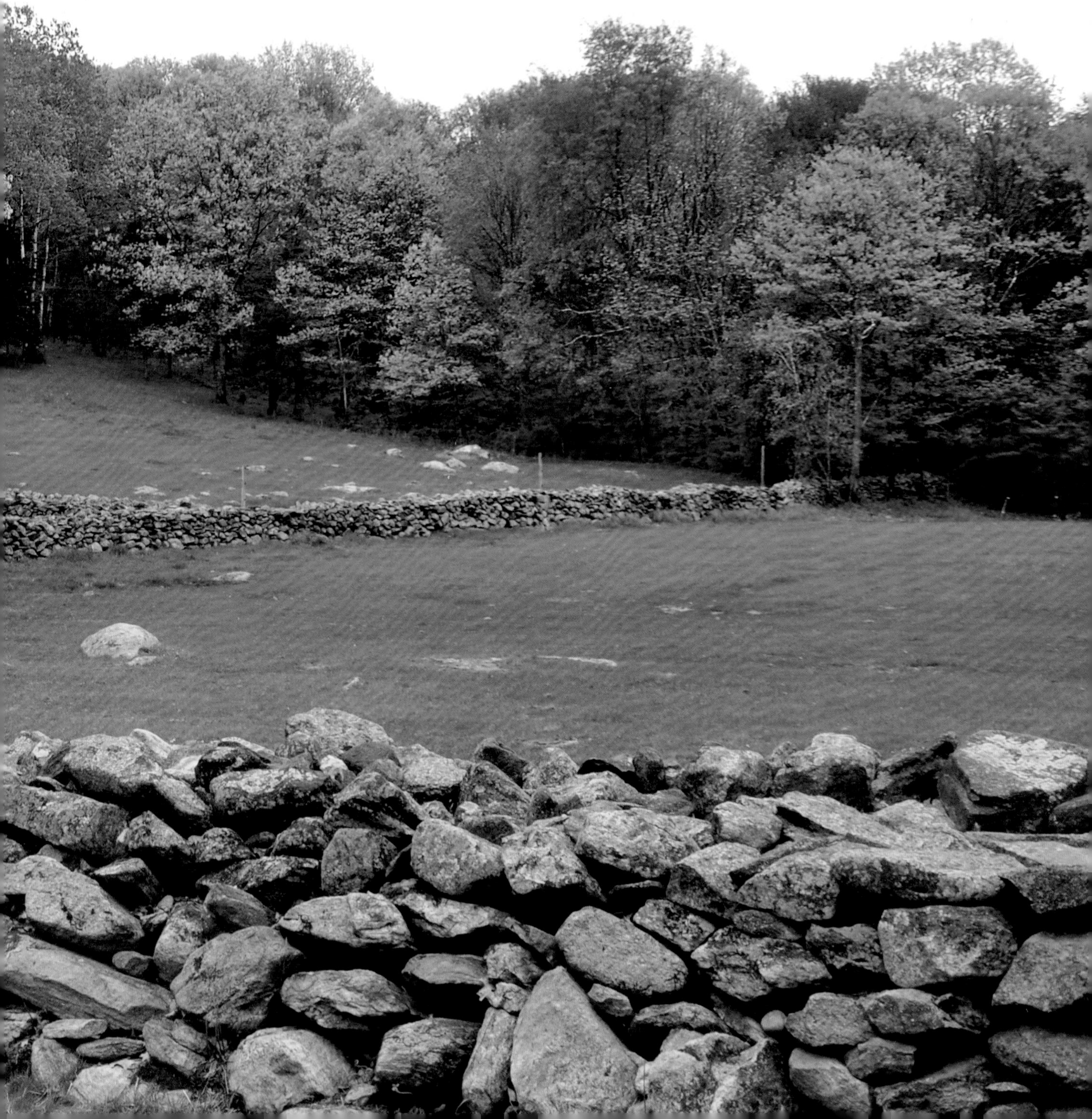

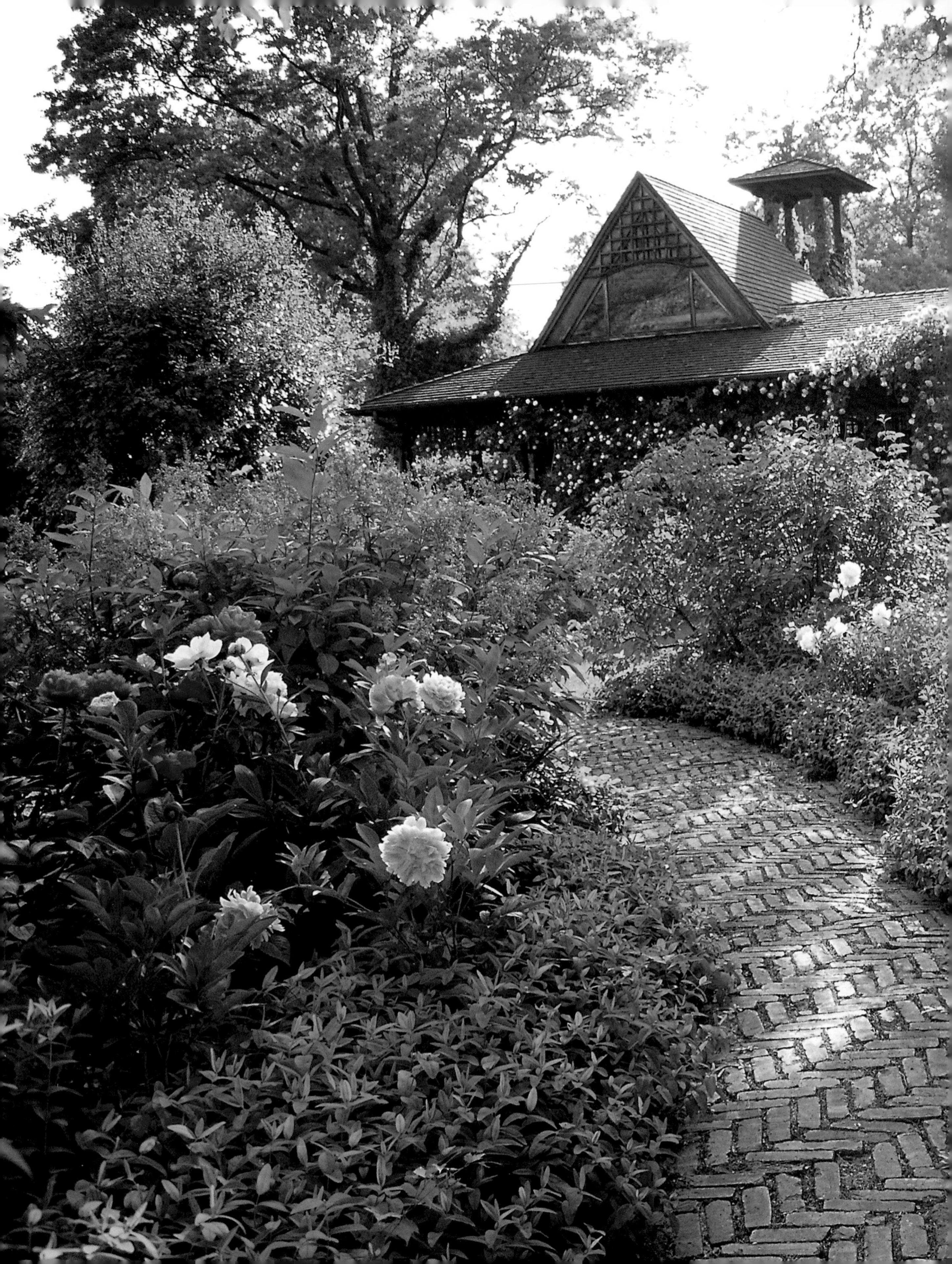

S uzy and Carter Bales purchased this property on the north shore of Long Island in 1978, complete with a 1908 Tudor house in desperate need of renovation. After cutting back the honeysuckle vines and English ivy covering the walls—and most of the windows—sunlight flooded into every room and made it warm and inviting.

Although the grounds had been well planted at the outset, the first spring Suzy was disappointed there were so few flowers. "Snowdrops, iris, a climbing rose, and a wild rose or two," she recalls. "I was hoping for lilacs and peonies to cut for the house." In the fall Suzy discovered that autumn crocus, a treasure too little planted in American gardens, had naturalized; she divided the plants and distributed them across the property, even into distant corners of the woods.

In the early 1980s, the Baleses engaged landscape architect Alice Recknagel Ireys to help them design a comprehensive plan for the property. One of her earliest comments, directed at Carter's newly planted bed of hostas and azaleas in all the loudest colors, was: "It looks like a motel planting. Take it out!" Suzy says he planted only white azaleas for years afterward. Despite being opinionated and outspoken, Ireys also believed strongly in educating her clients. "She taught me the importance of designing with nature while paying attention to the classic principles of scale, proportion, unity, balance, and rhythm," Suzy says. "A garden must not look contrived or too planned, but as if it came into being on its site as an act of nature."

Ireys divided the property into several garden "rooms." At the entrance to the property, she added an orchard of a dozen fruit trees inside a living fence of espaliered apples and pears, for example, while a dying apple orchard in the rear was replaced by a crescent-shaped formal perennial and rose garden. This in turn connects to a kitchen garden via a walk lined with lilacs and peonies. A small pond at the back of the house empties into a stream that meanders down a hill, spilling over as a waterfall into a larger pond, and a pump returns the water to the top in a closed cycle. In time a swimming pool and tennis court were also added. Flagstones loosely laid over the carriage house courtyard are bordered by creeping thyme, and miniature bulbs are planted between them.

These many years later, Suzy can say with authority, "I have never finished a garden." She does have help and a loving, supportive family that cheers her on and occasionally pulls weeds. "I'm in love with the garden's mysteries and the pure joy of sharing with others. Some visitors insist on walking the property, others gravitate to the seating and dining areas. My children and their friends can play croquet on the front lawn, and we made room for a basketball court, too."

Suzy's gardens have served as the source of her many books' content and of the wisdom she shares in her magazine articles for many years. Her most important piece of advice is: "Work with a long-range plan, concentrate on one thing at a time—and don't think the plan can't be changed for the better."

RIGHT AND BELOW Brick walkways carry visitors from garden room to garden room; seating is always close by for a moment of rest or conversation.

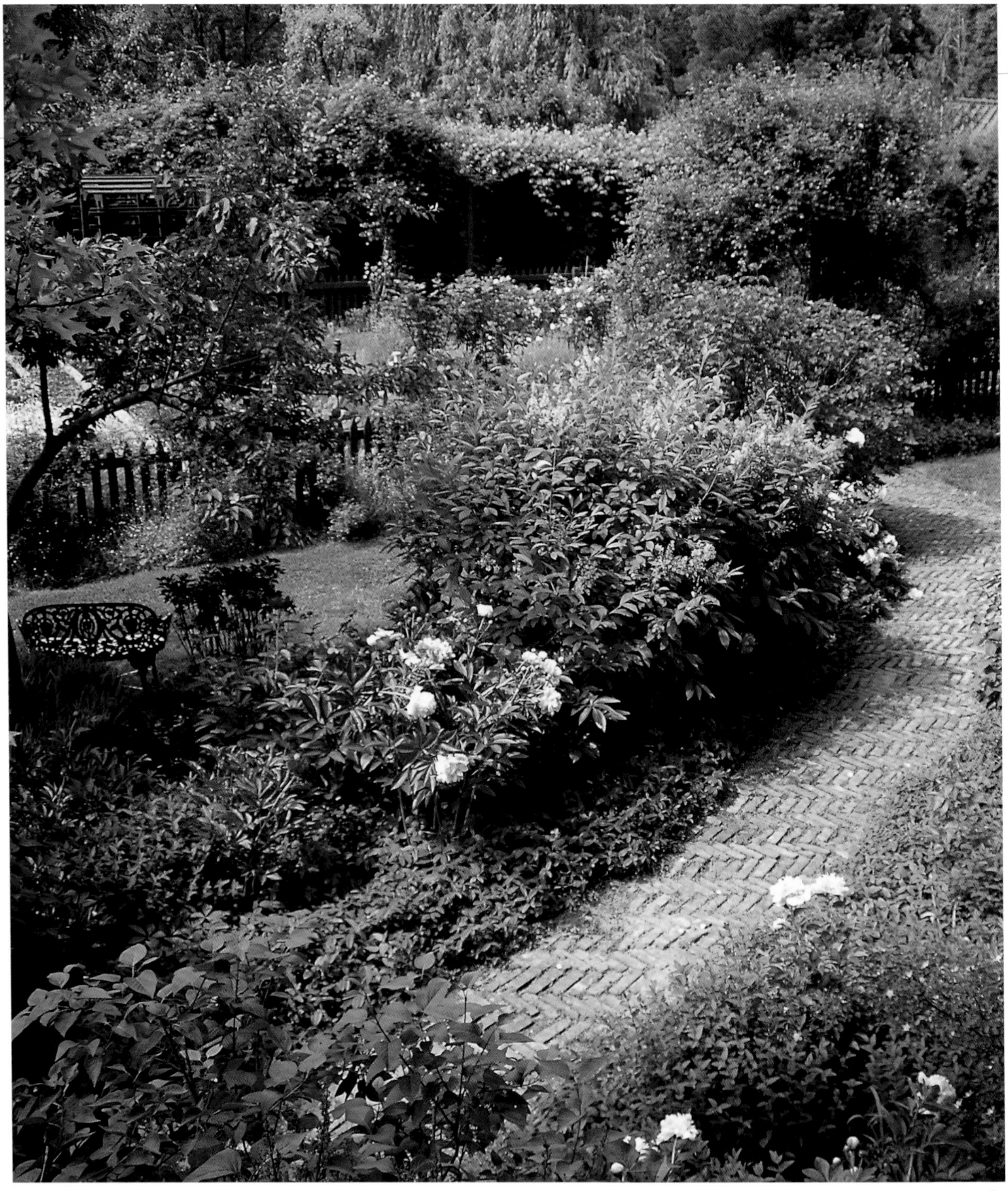

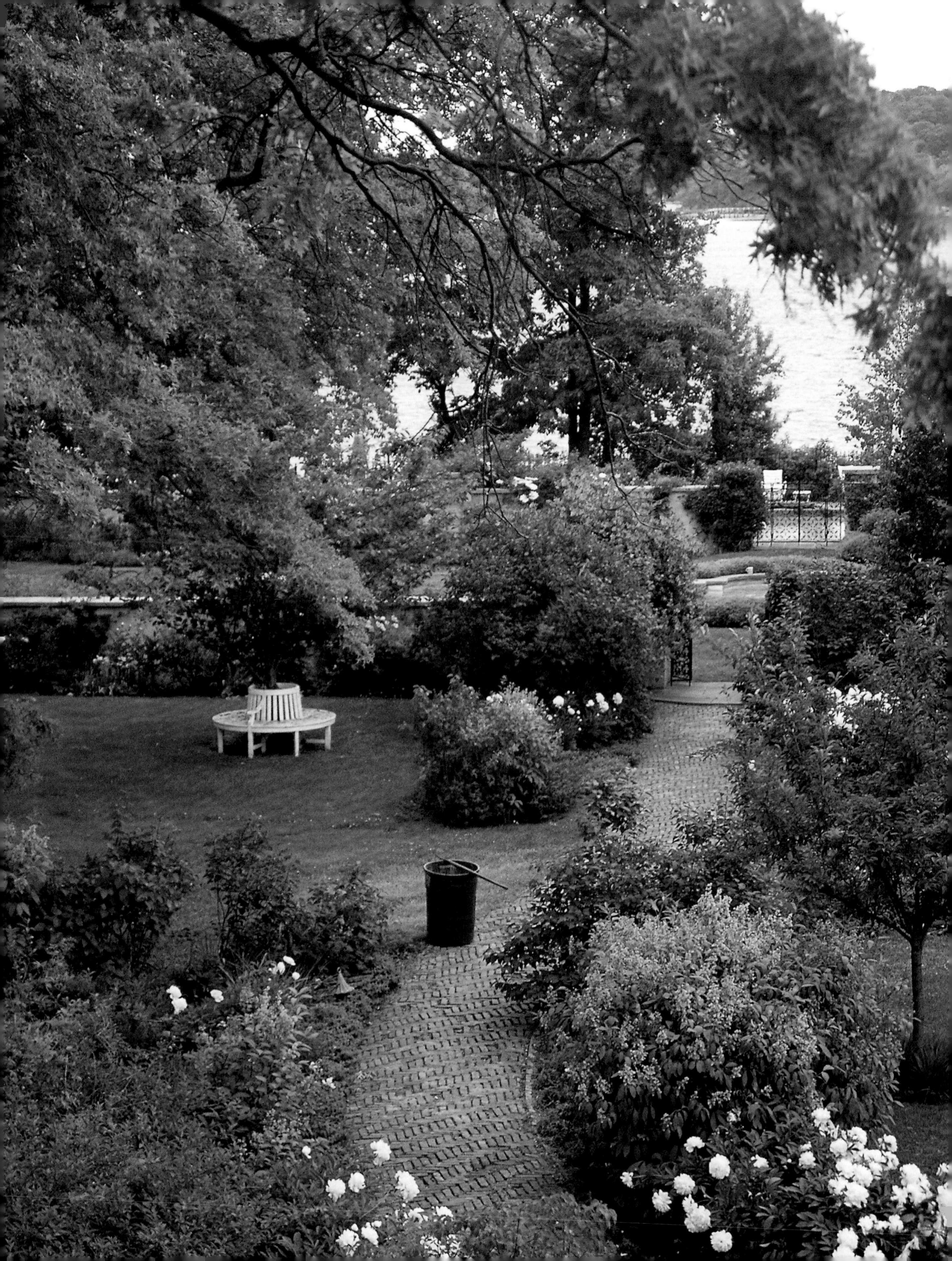

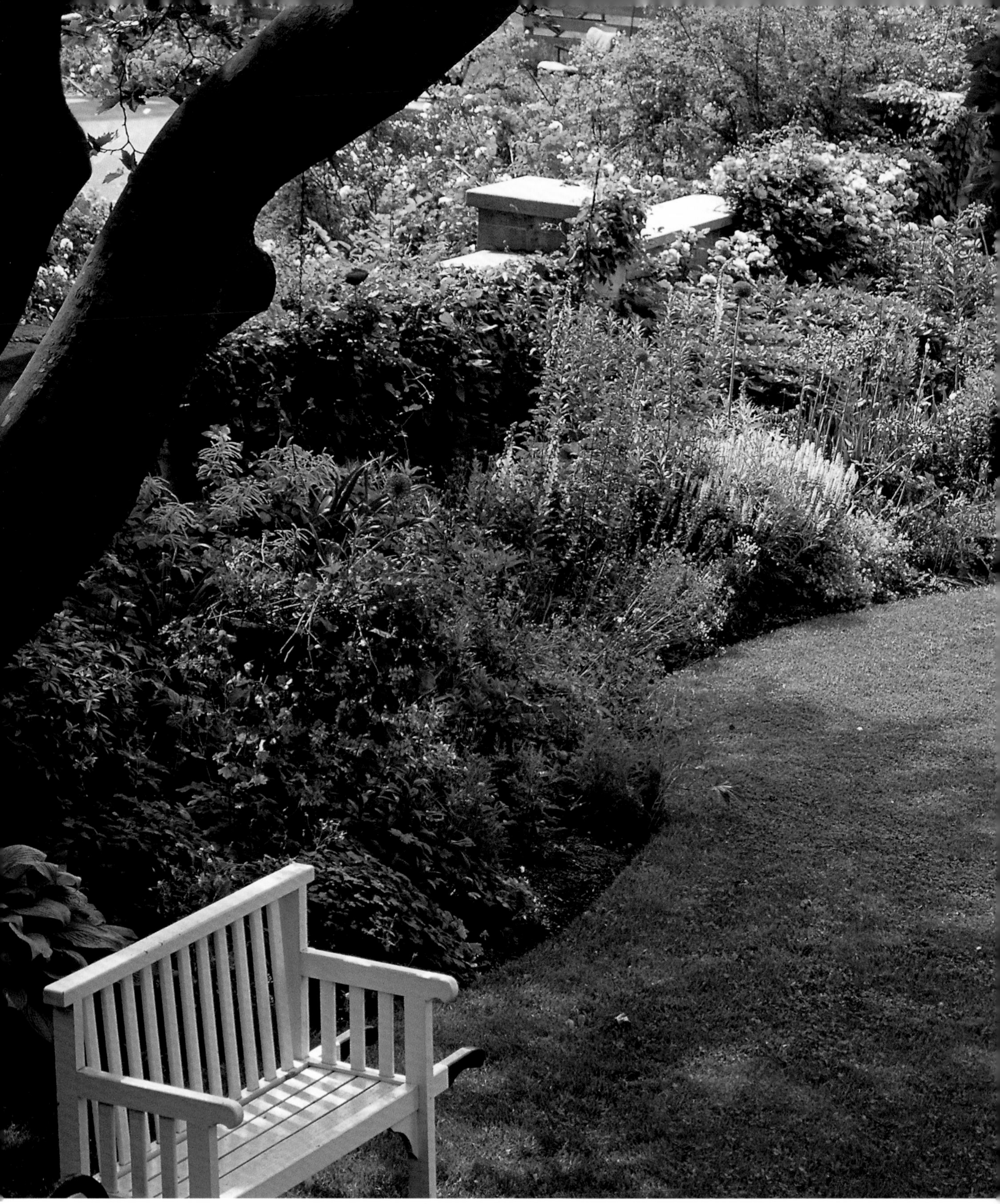

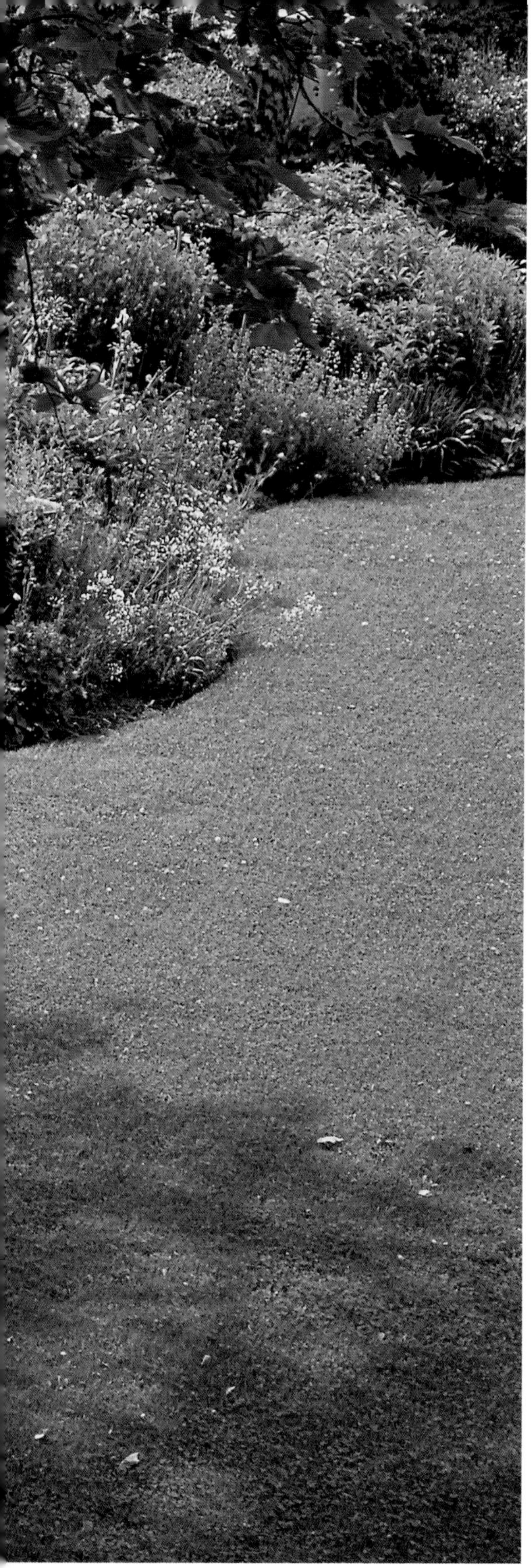

LEFT Perennial borders adjusted and reworked over the course of many years create an ever-changing display of seasonal color and texture. **BELOW** 'Sombreuil,' an intensely fragrant white heirloom rose dating from 1850, cascades over one of the garden's many arbors. **OVERLEAF** A gazebo discreetly tucked into a glen of rhododendrons and dogwoods.

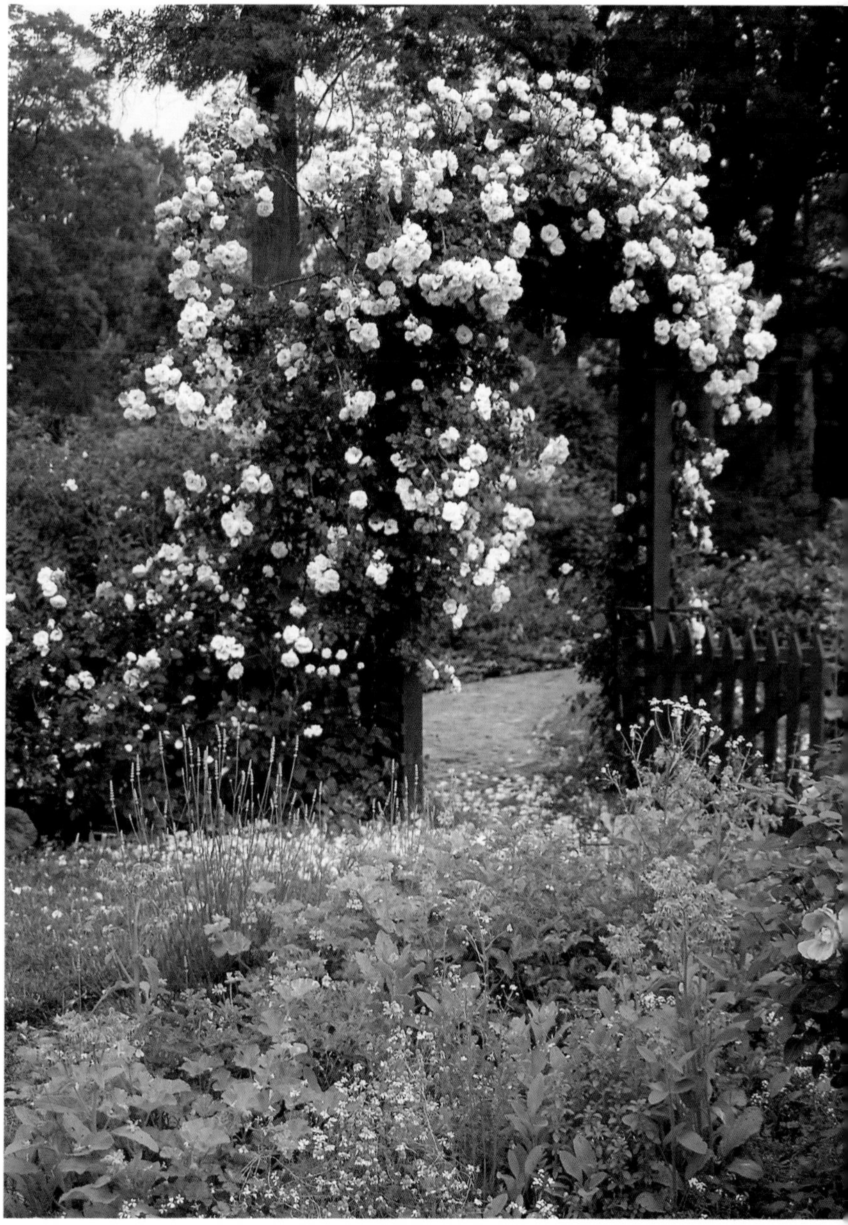

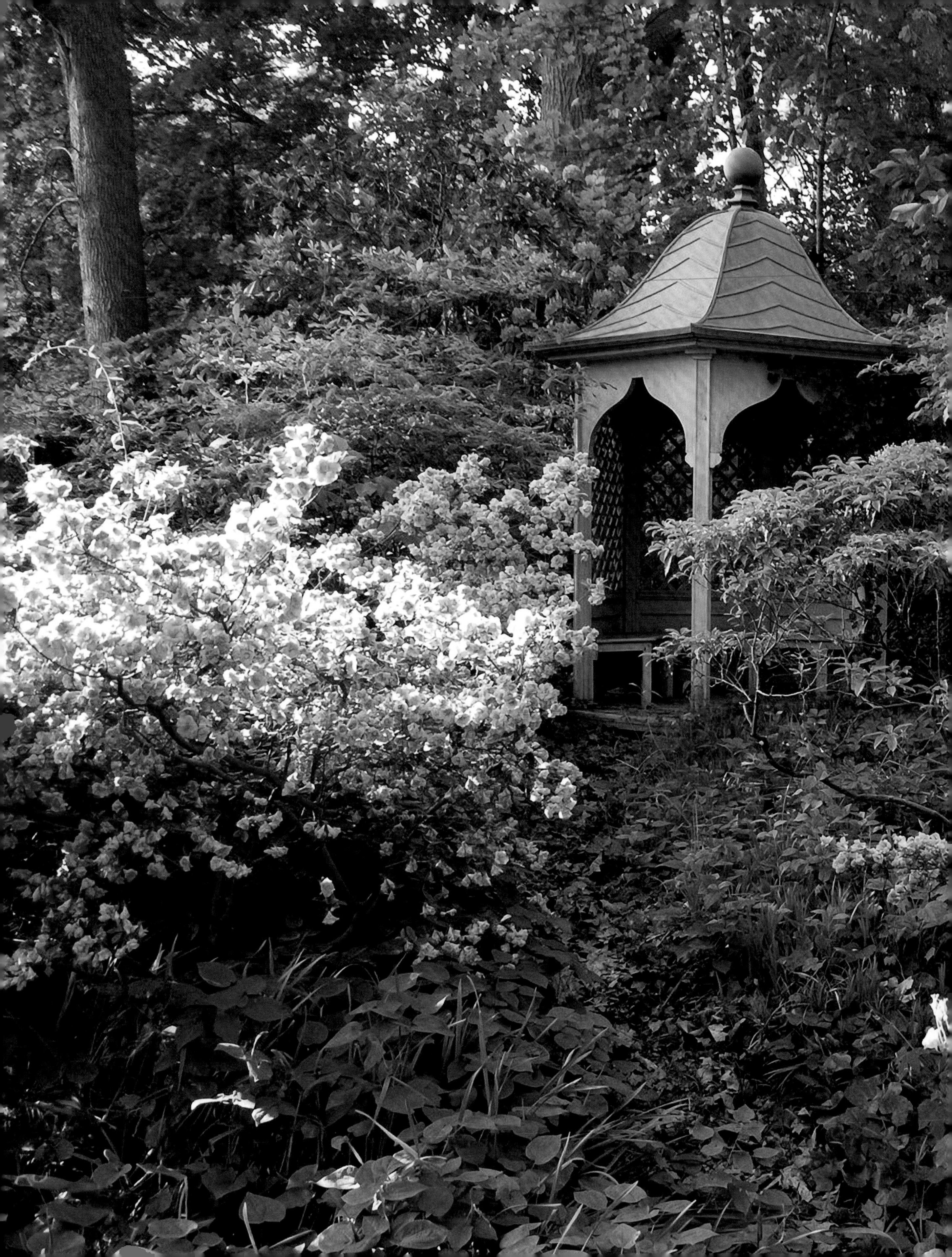

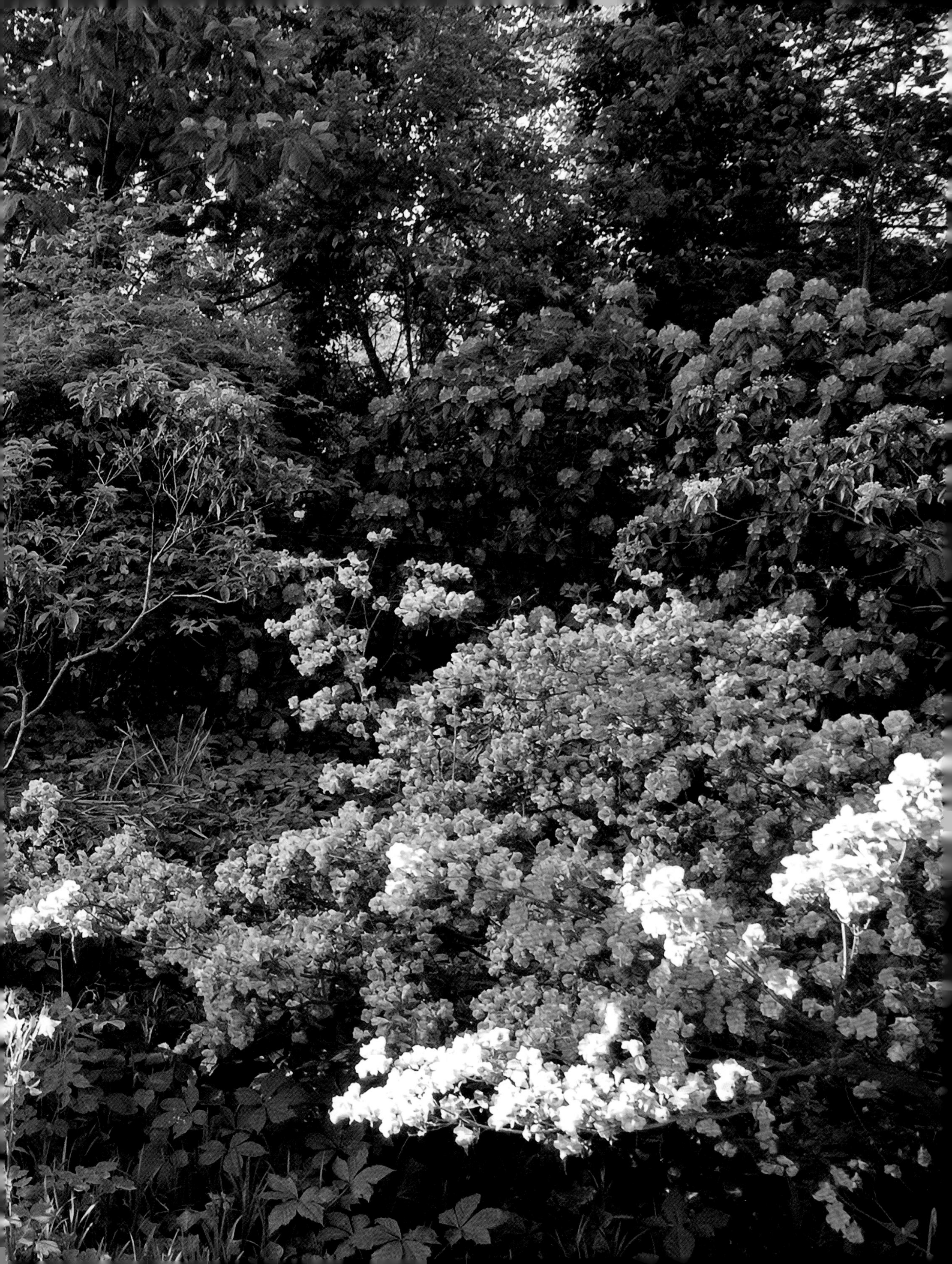

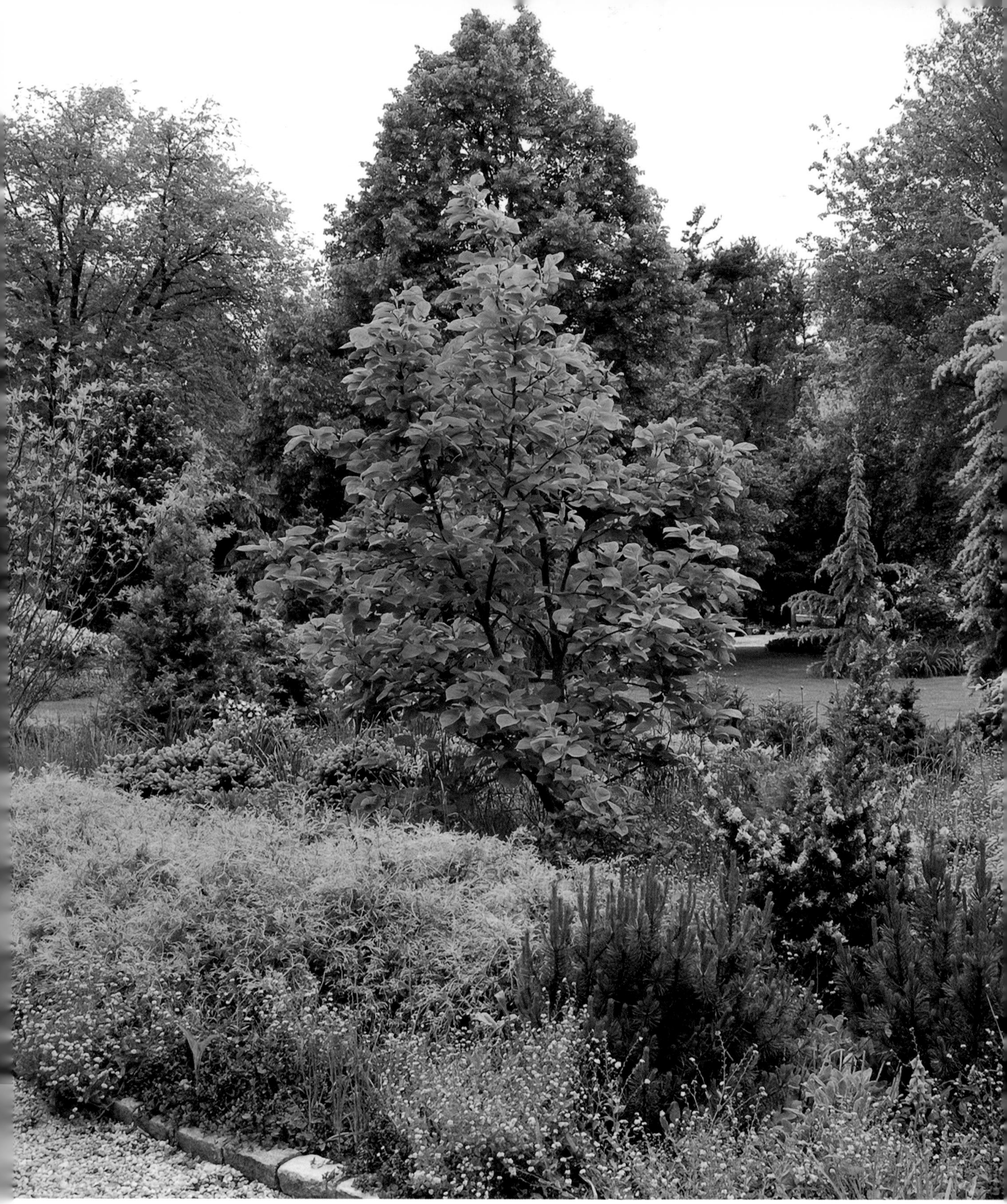

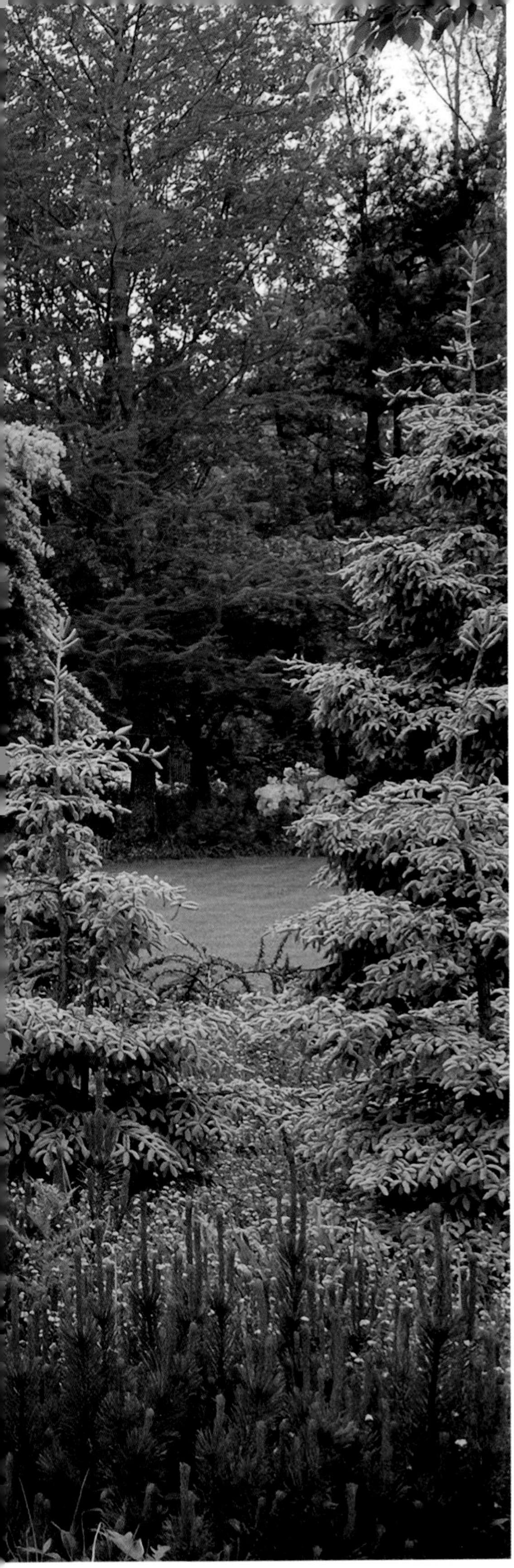

OPPOSITE Plantings varied in color, texture, and height combine to create a rich border. **BELOW** Teddy guards against chipmunks and squirrels near a bench encircling a tree.

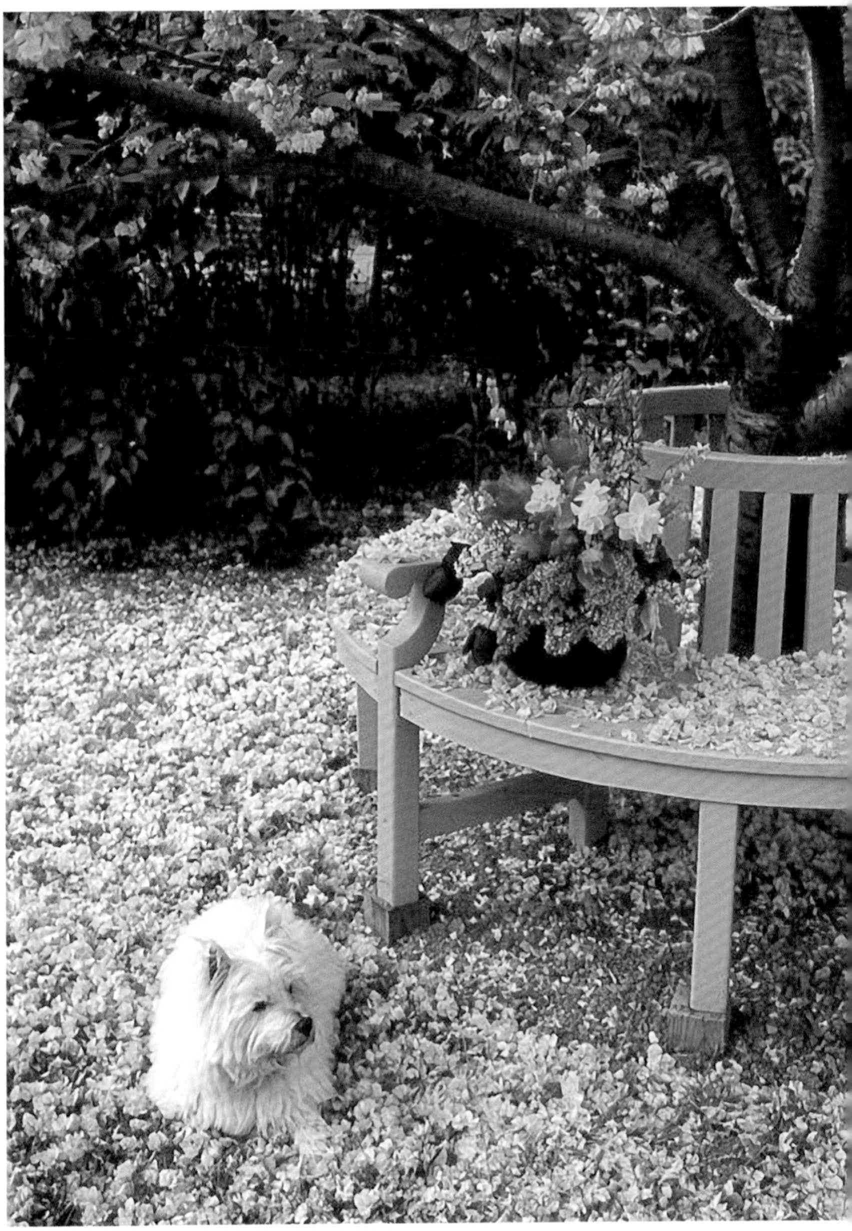

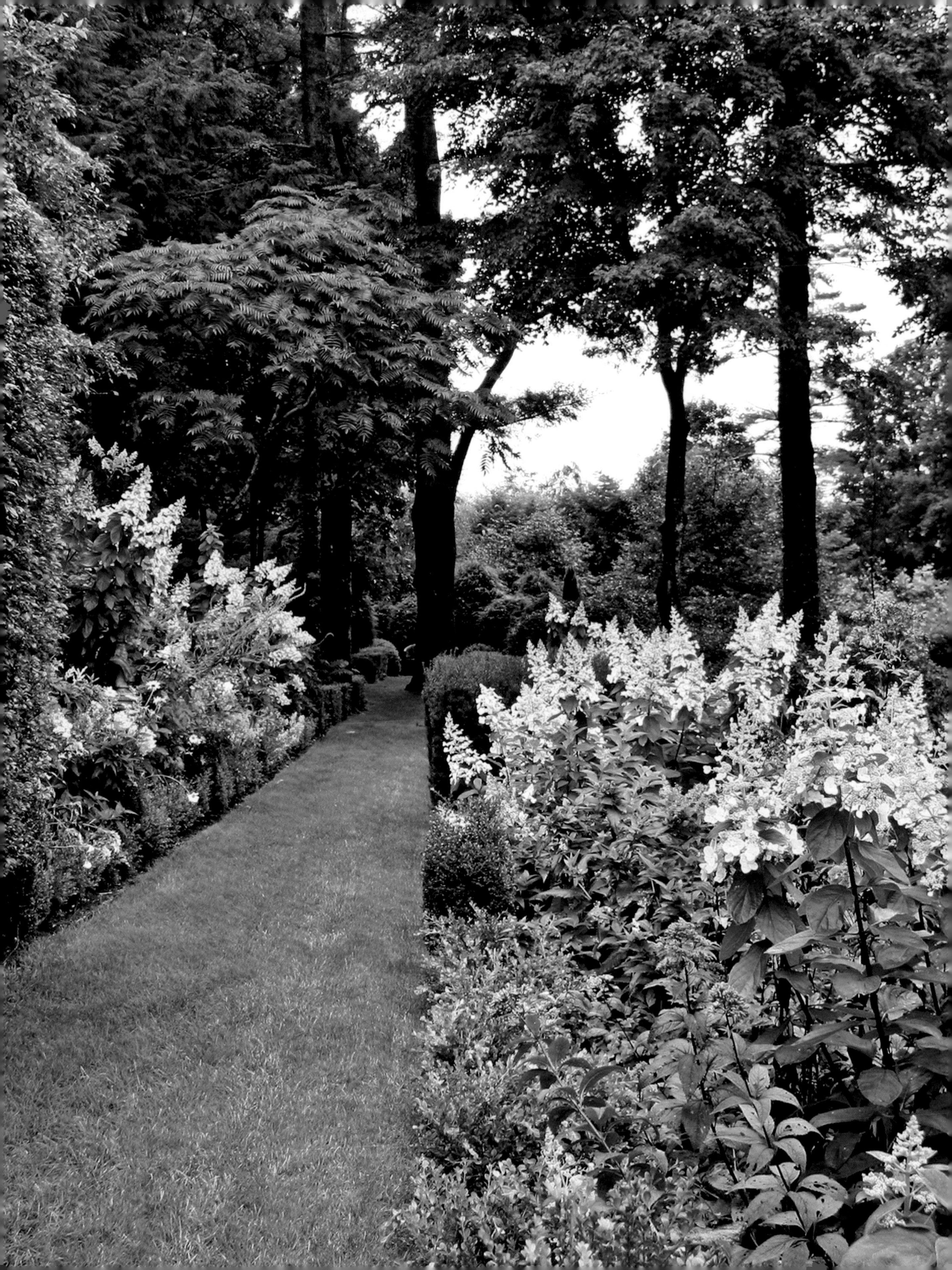

Most people wouldn't survey twelve acres of land in rocky, hilly New Hampshire—legendary for its bone-chilling winters and abbreviated growing season—and think of it as the ideal site for an Edwardian-style garden. Most people aren't Stan Fry. The garden, actually a series of separate but linked and unified gardens, is his obsession.

Fry's gardening odyssey began in late 1990 when he and his wife, Cheri, purchased the main house and property complete with overgrown shrubs and impenetrable brambles. In time they also bought two lots across the street—one containing a guesthouse—plus the adjacent property to the south, which included a nineteenth-century Cape Cod house where extended family members now live.

"The first few years we spent removing brush and brambles. Today we have an expansive lawn area that was previously field-mowed," says Fry, who owns several high-tech businesses and has an office in a cottage behind the main barn. "The half-acre perennial garden around it was all weeds and was nearly unnavigable due to prickle bushes. After the areas were cleared, we started to do some minimal landscaping."

At that juncture, Fry brought in garden designer Gordon Hayward. Together they began to lay the plans that are today realized in some forty distinct gardens connected by pebbled or grassed walkways. "Gordon knew what would grow here," Stan says, "and I knew what I wanted in terms of formality."

At the outset, elevation changes—nearly 110 feet between street level and the ponds below—were a major consideration. "I advocated terracing to create level spaces and garden areas," Hayward says. "For example, a 300-foot-long allée of sycamores linking two of the properties is supported by a pair of native stone retaining walls." He also recommended keeping areas close to the house formal, and those at a distance less structured. The gardens in front of the Frys' main residence follow that guideline but are also the simplest—ground covers and evergreens—so as not to detract from the early Federal-style architecture.

Asked what motivates him, Fry says, "It's not the garden-tour visitors; I do it for the pleasure of doing it. I like the science and the labor involved and the satisfaction of a project completed. My parents were gardeners—it must have worn off on me. Working with the dirt is relaxing and stress-reducing." He typically works in the garden from dawn until 9 a.m. and takes no calls, preferring to remain focused on the task at hand.

When Fry's not gardening, he shops for classic garden benches, statuary, and antique urns in the local area. "Especially lead," he says. "It's sort of a side hobby. I also build the plinths for the urns and cast statues from molds we have made."

Stan Fry's stewardship of the land strikes a reassuring note—a thoroughly modern businessman living life to the fullest in the gentlemanly pursuit of gardenmaking. Thomas Jefferson had Monticello; Lawrence Johnston, an American by birth, had Hidcote Manor in England; and steel magnate Howard Phipps had his rhododendrons.

BELOW A series of terraces negotiates the property's steep hillside, which drops 110 feet between street level and the ponds below. **RIGHT** A 300-foot-long allée of sycamores connects semicircular retaining walls off the house's main deck to the studio at its terminus. **OVERLEAF** Pebbled and turf walkways connect the forty different gardens on the property.

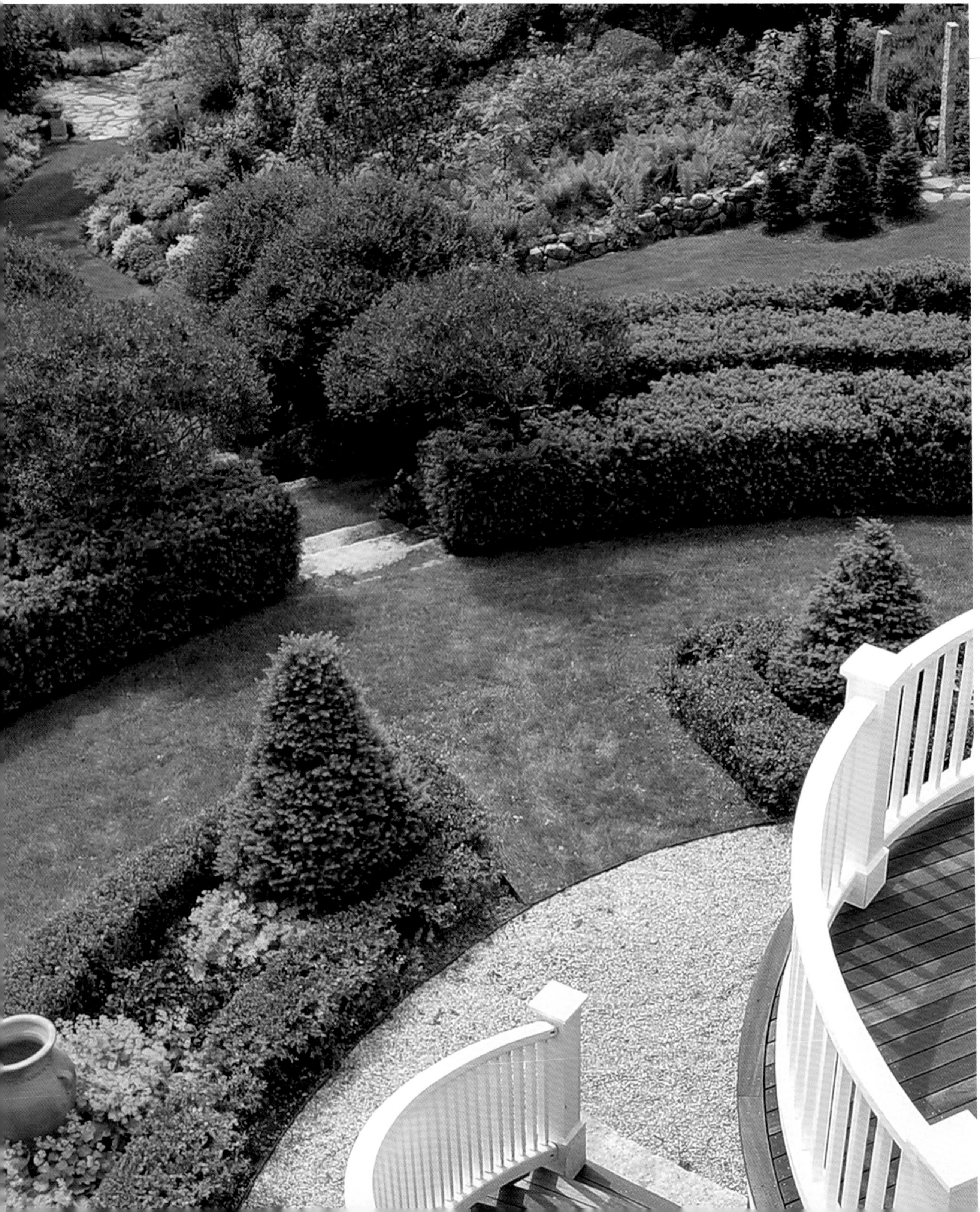

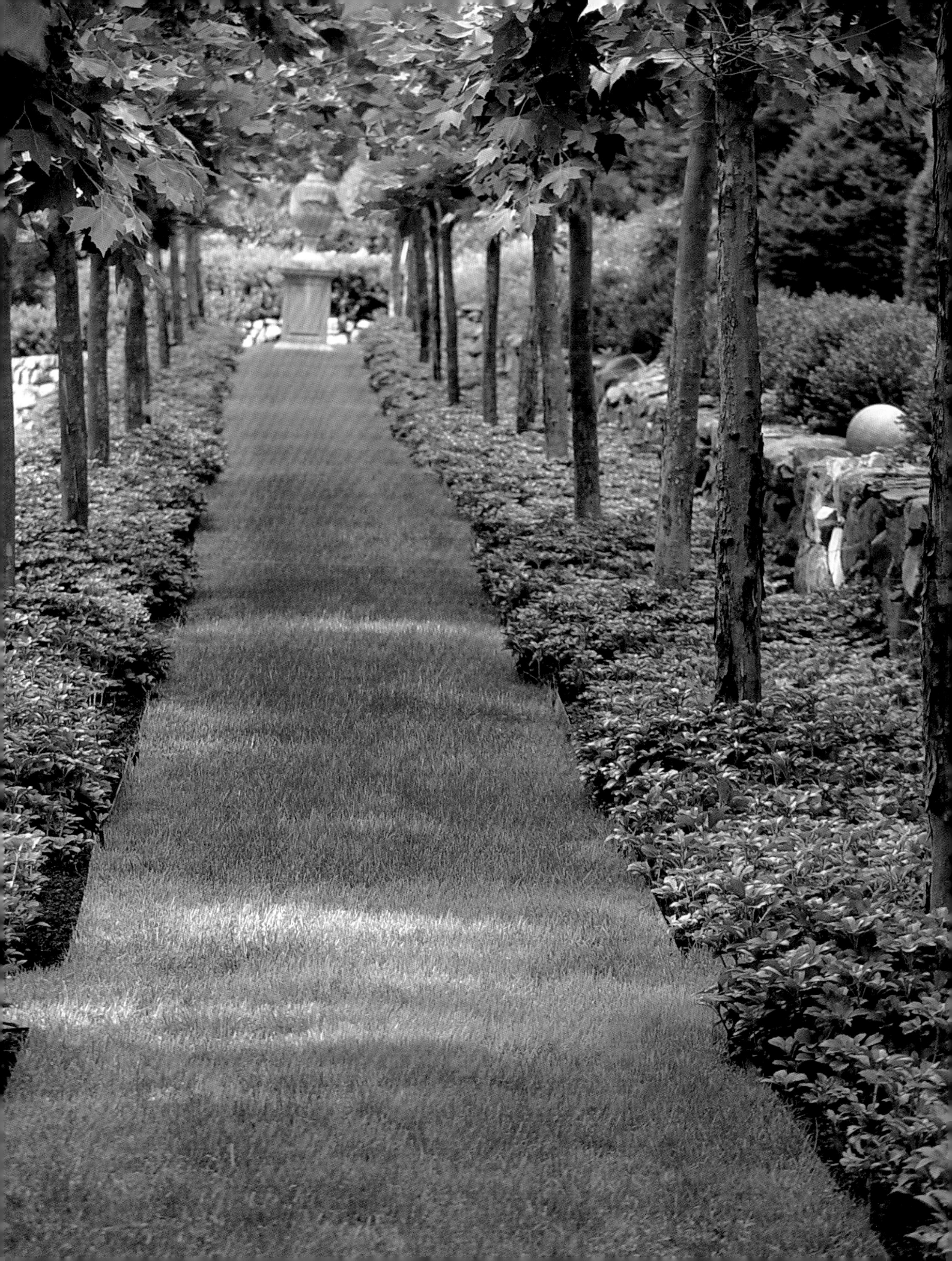

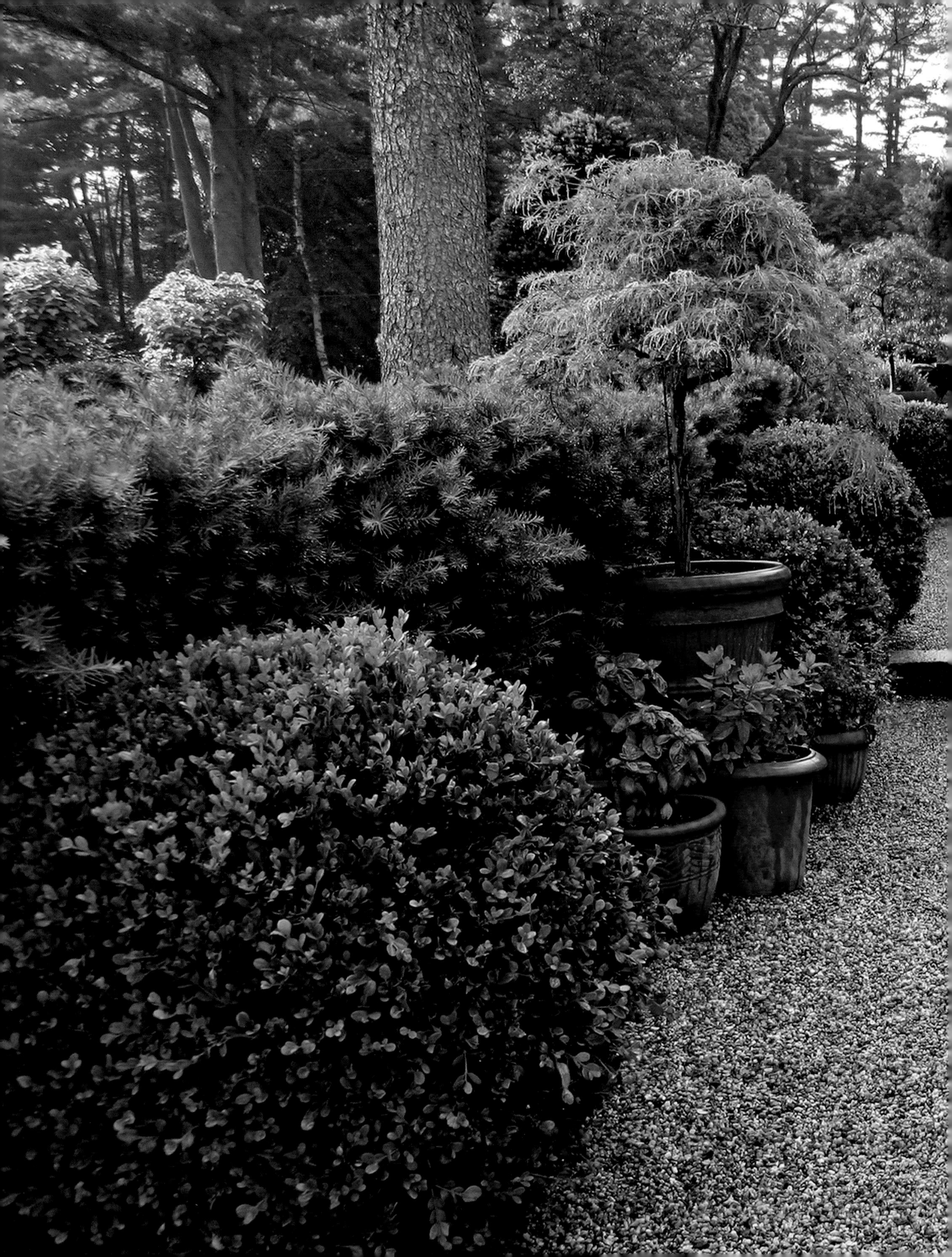

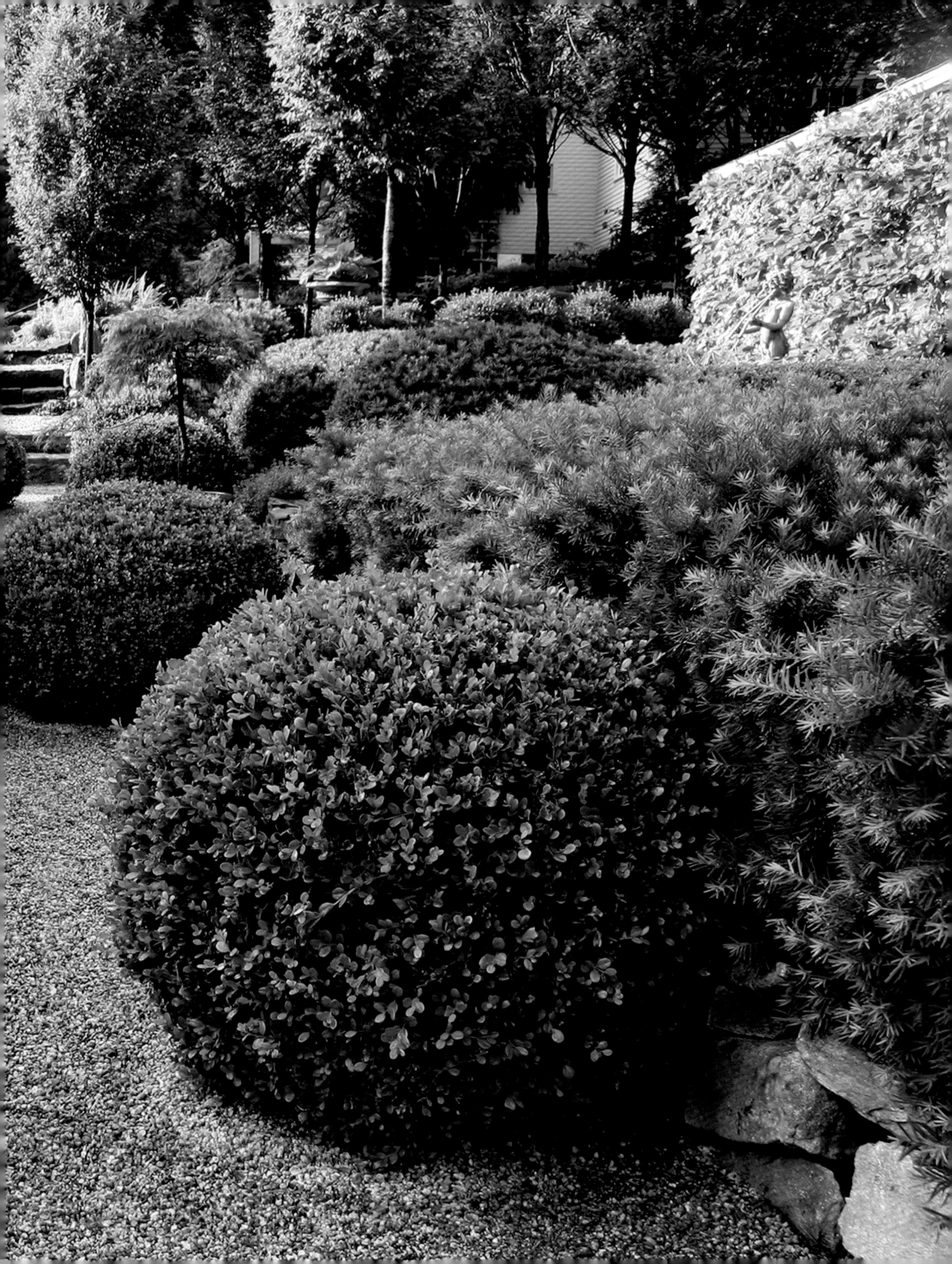

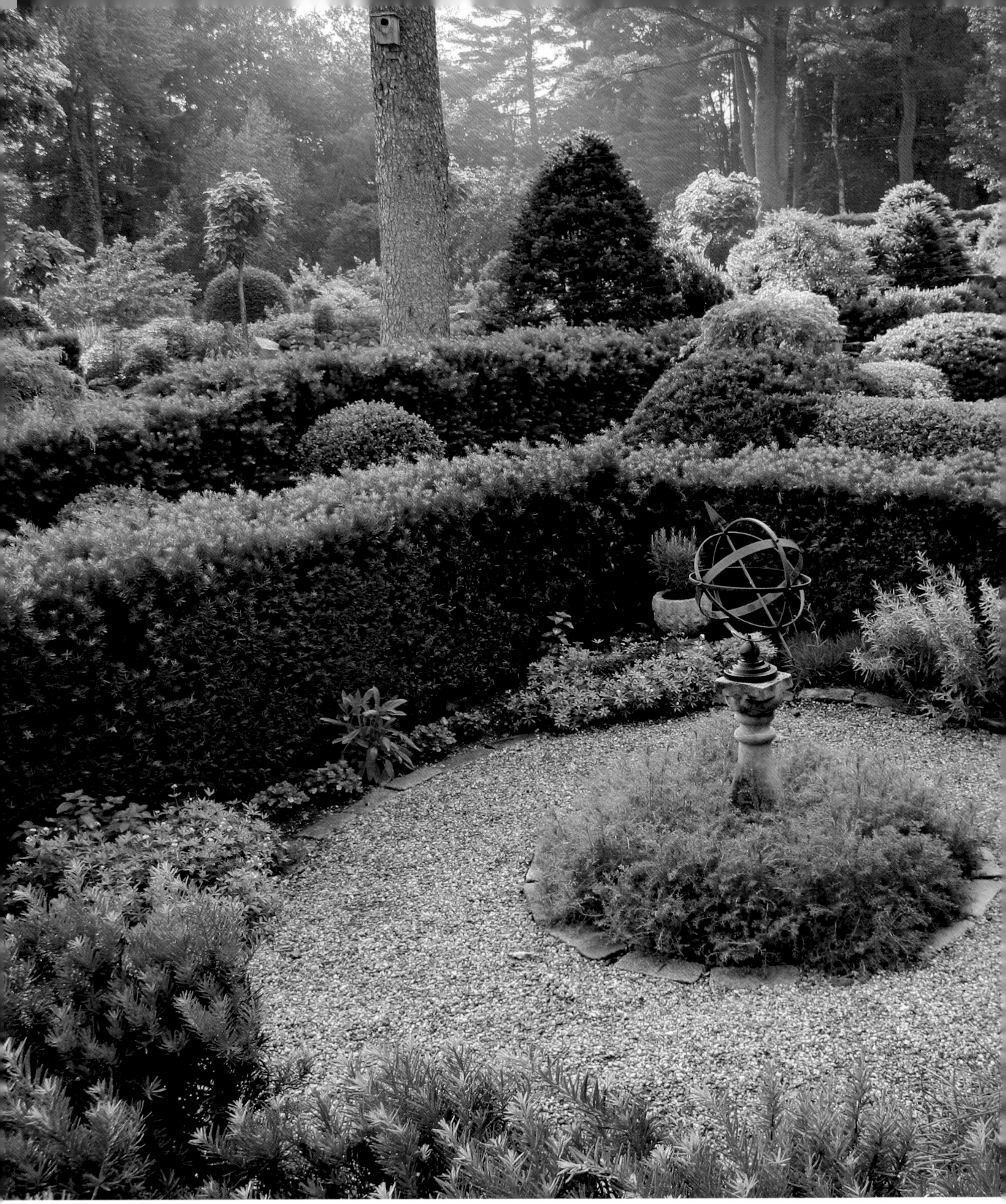

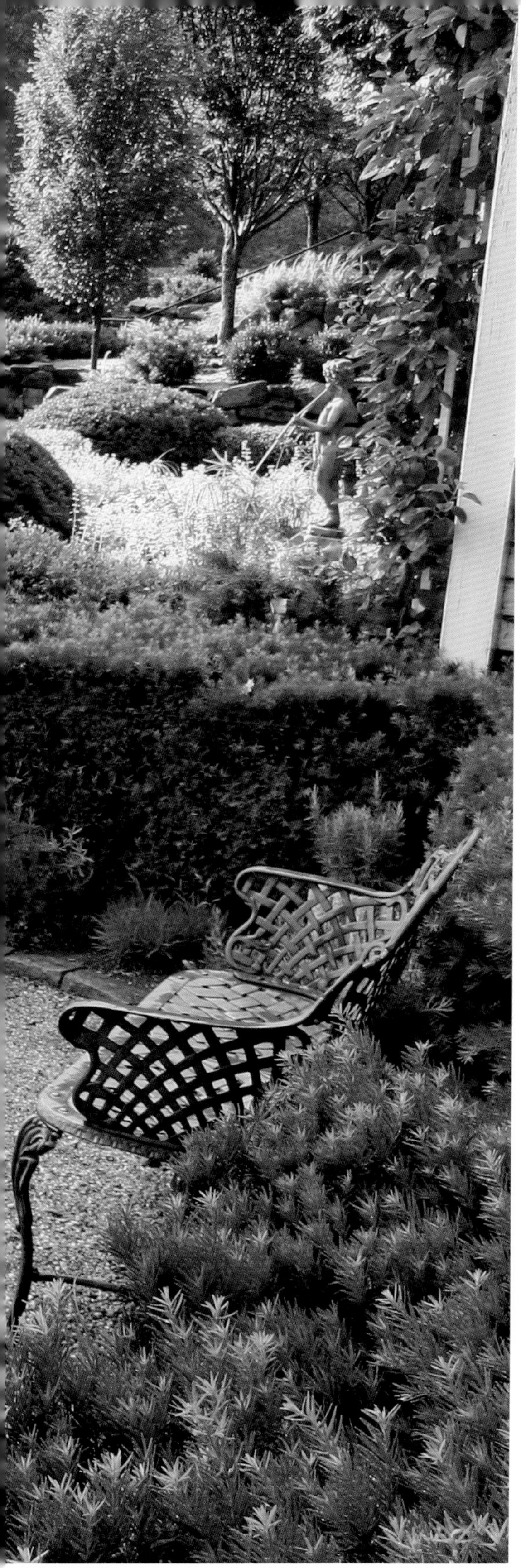

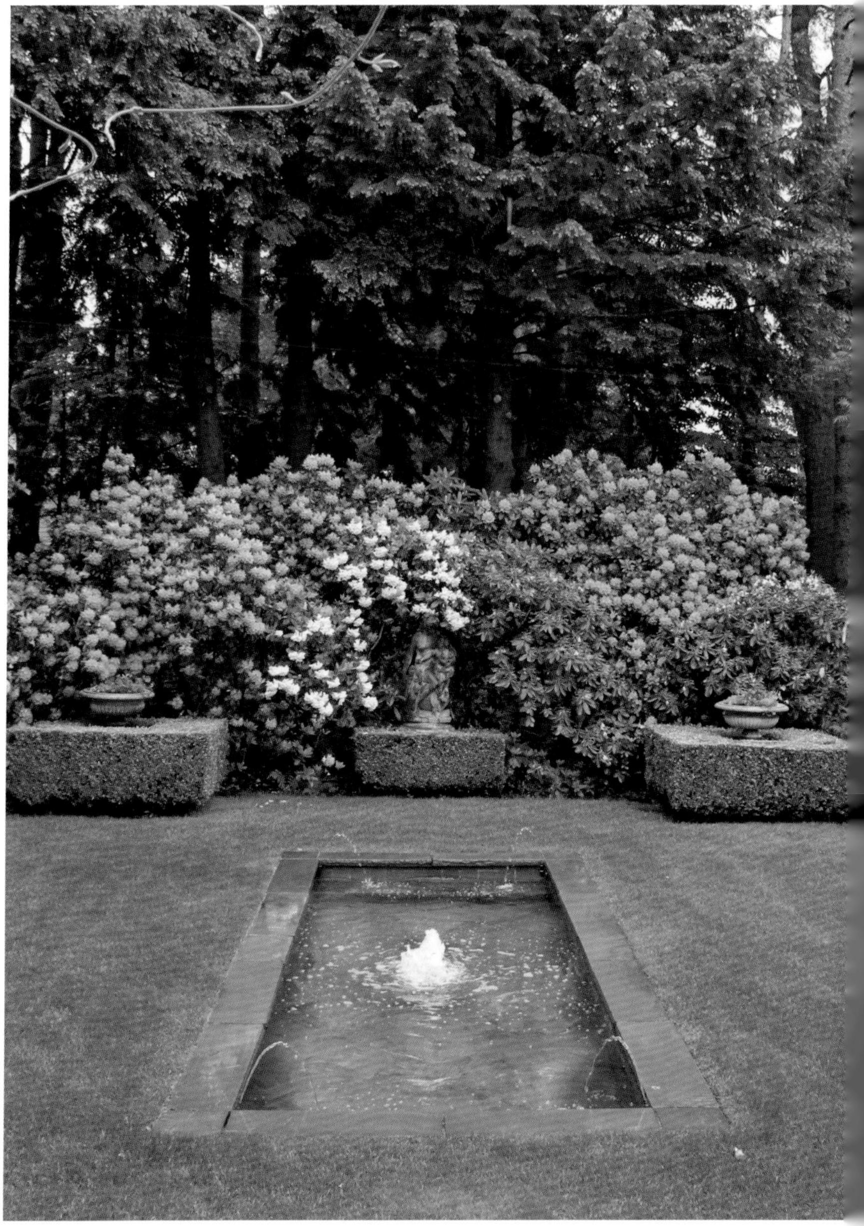

LEFT Pollarded and coppiced woody plants animate many of Fry's gardens and provide a unifying design element from one garden to the next. **BELOW** Sharply clipped boxwood hedges seem to float above the ground behind a formal pool.

BELOW Hawthorns and dogwoods provide flashy color displays in late spring. **RIGHT** Stan Fry's daily commute is an enviable walk from the house through densely wooded grounds to his office, just visible at the top of this photograph. **OVERLEAF** French lilacs pollarded into tree forms spill down the hillside in front of Fry's office, where his employees often eat lunch.

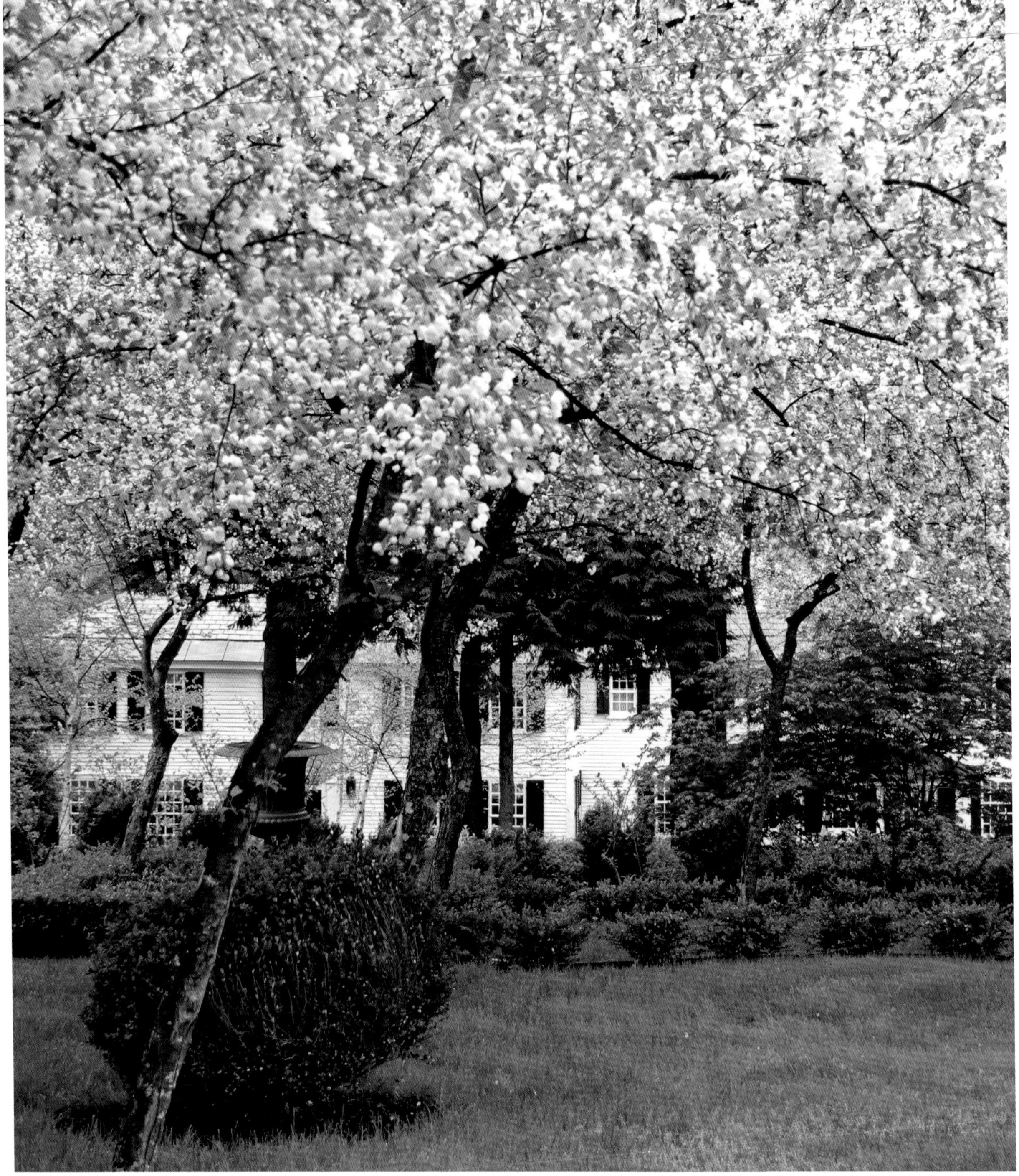

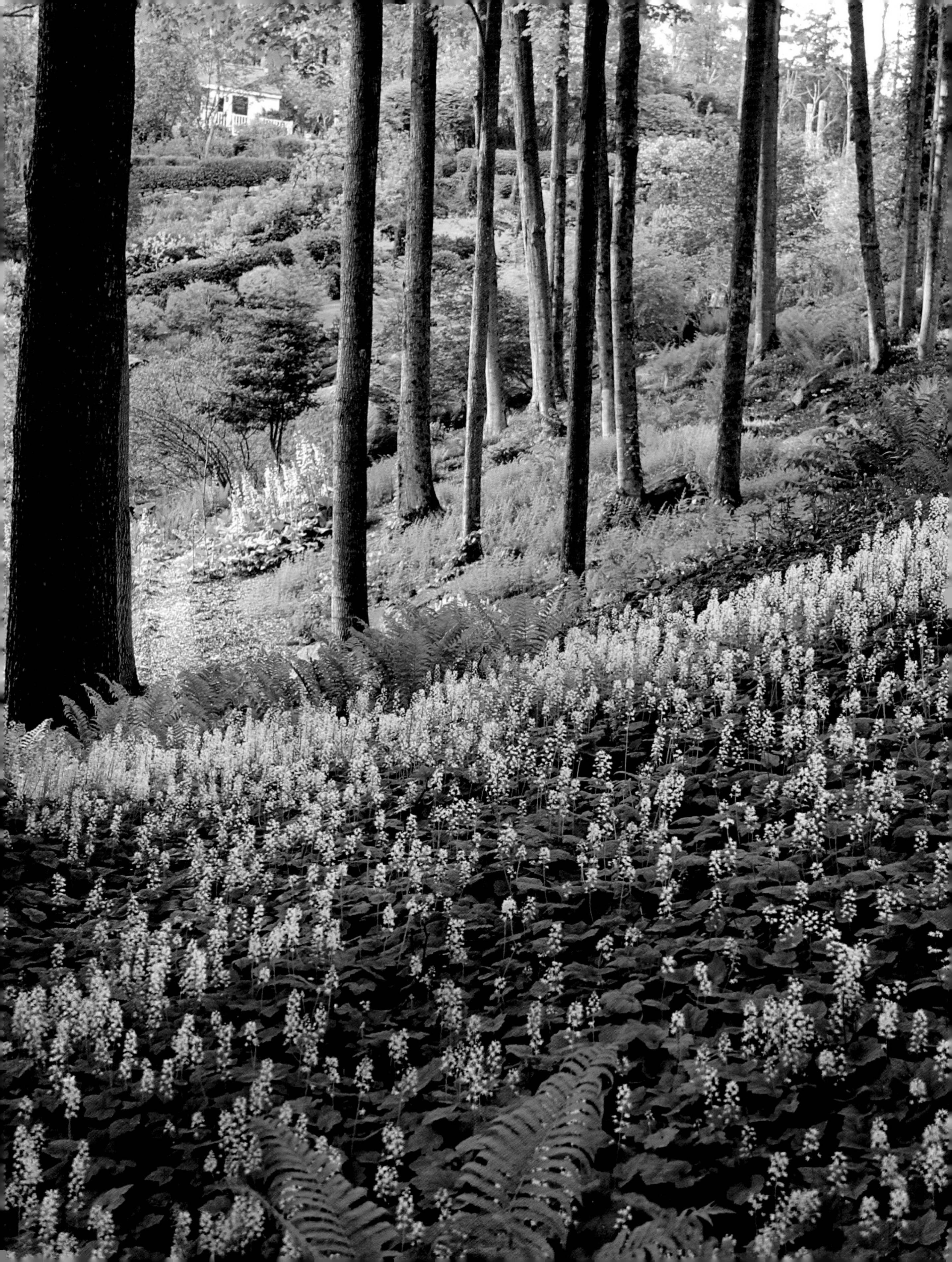

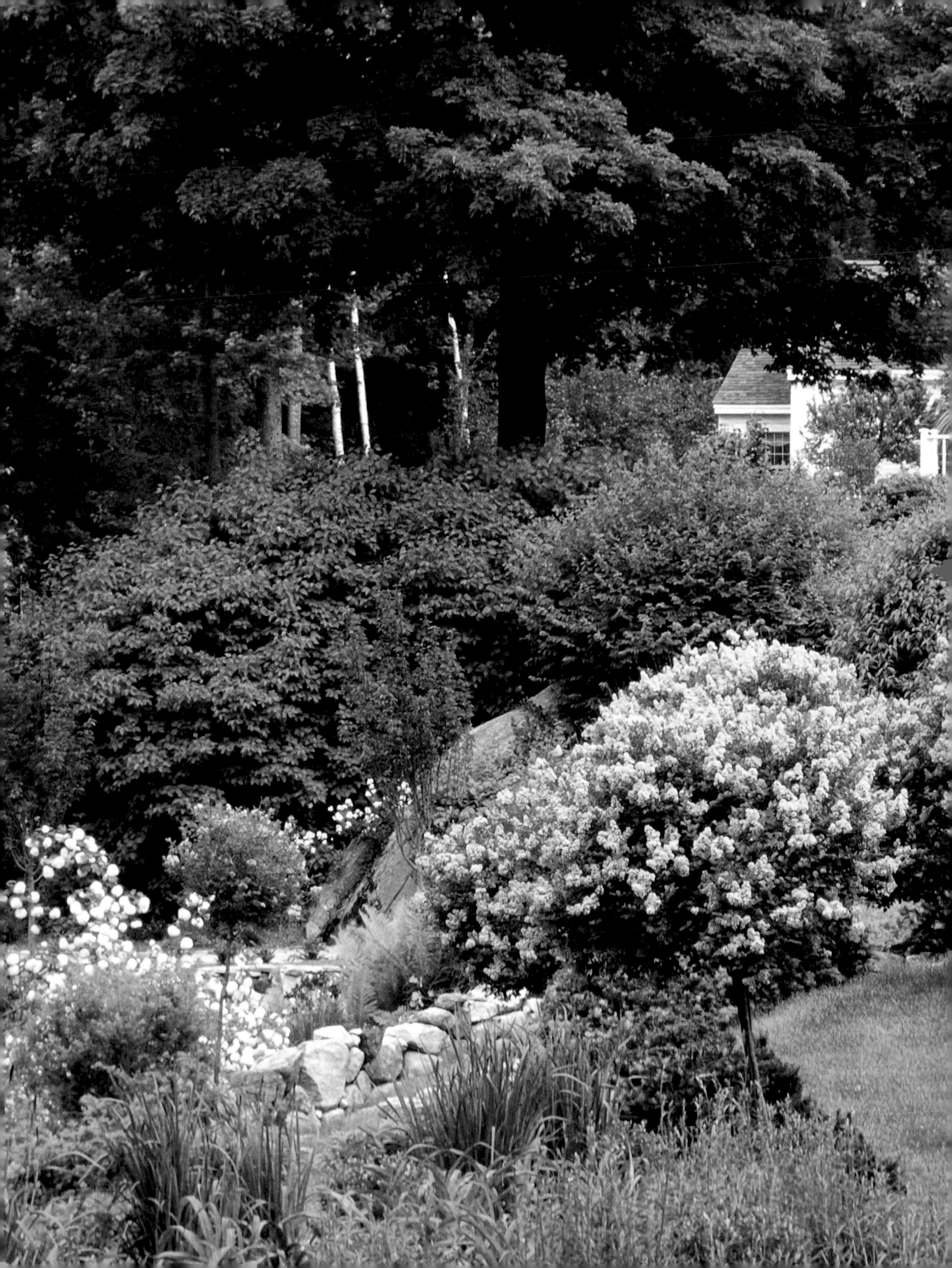

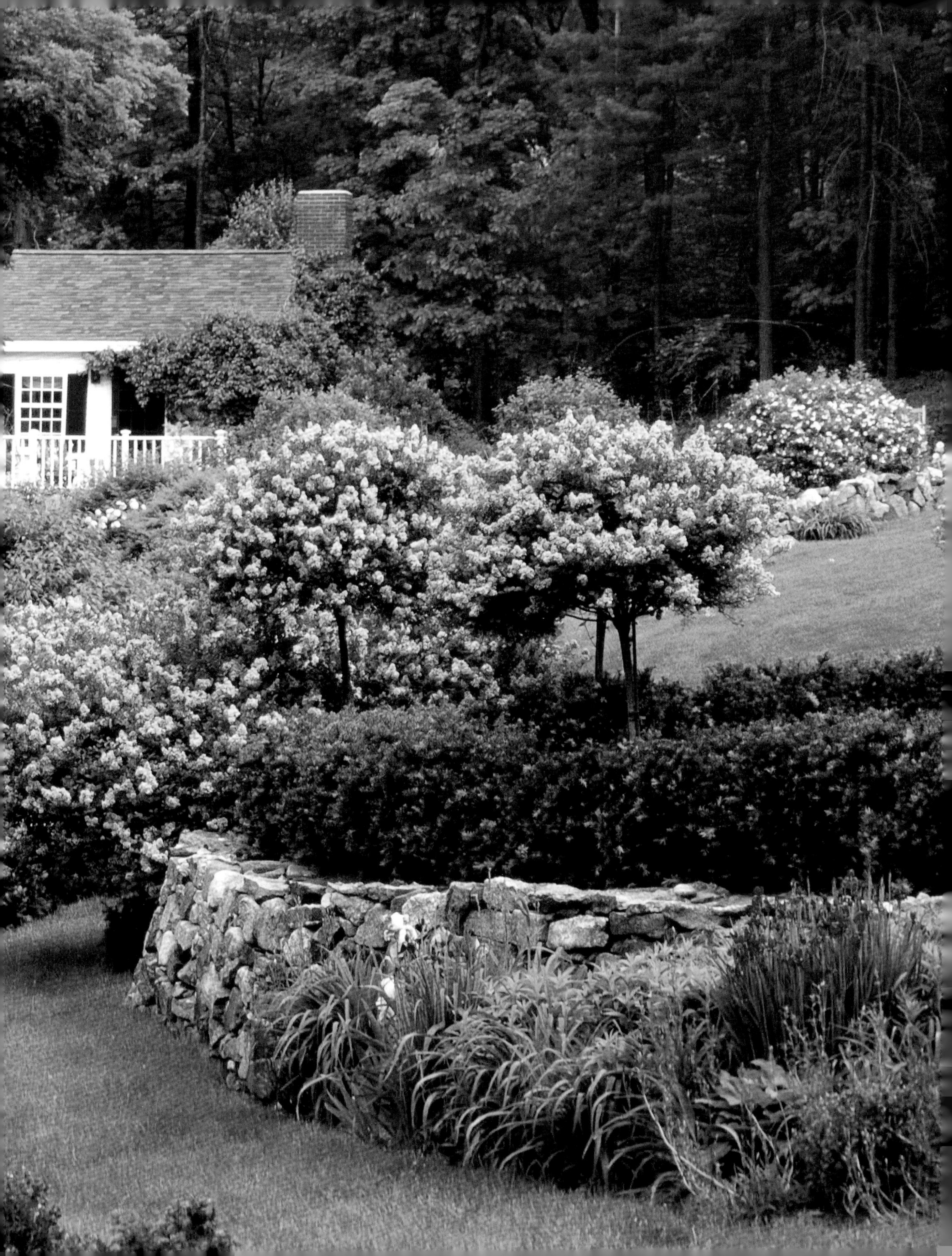

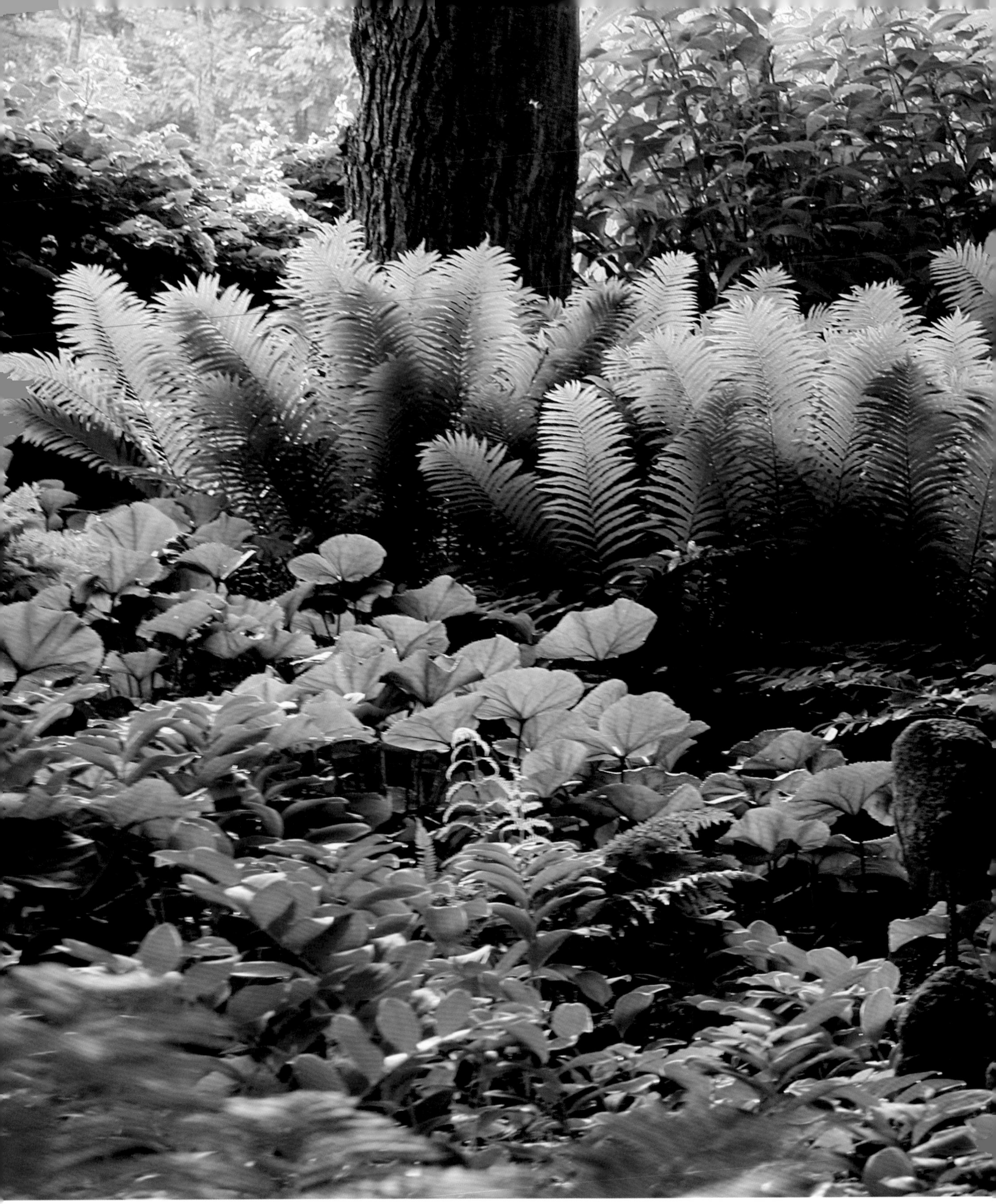

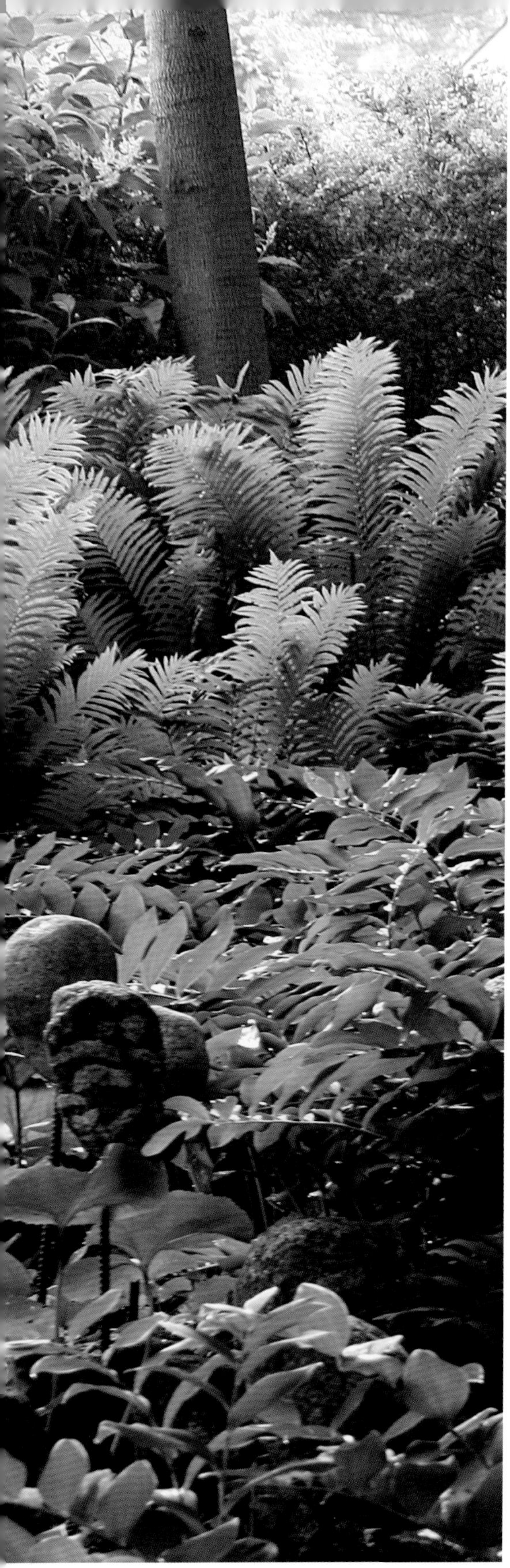

LEFT Rustic sculptures emerge just above naturalistic plantings of ostrich fern, *Ligularia*, and Solomon's seal in a woodland glen at the bottom of the property's ravine. **BELOW** Statuesque foxgloves have naturalized through the lower shade gardens.

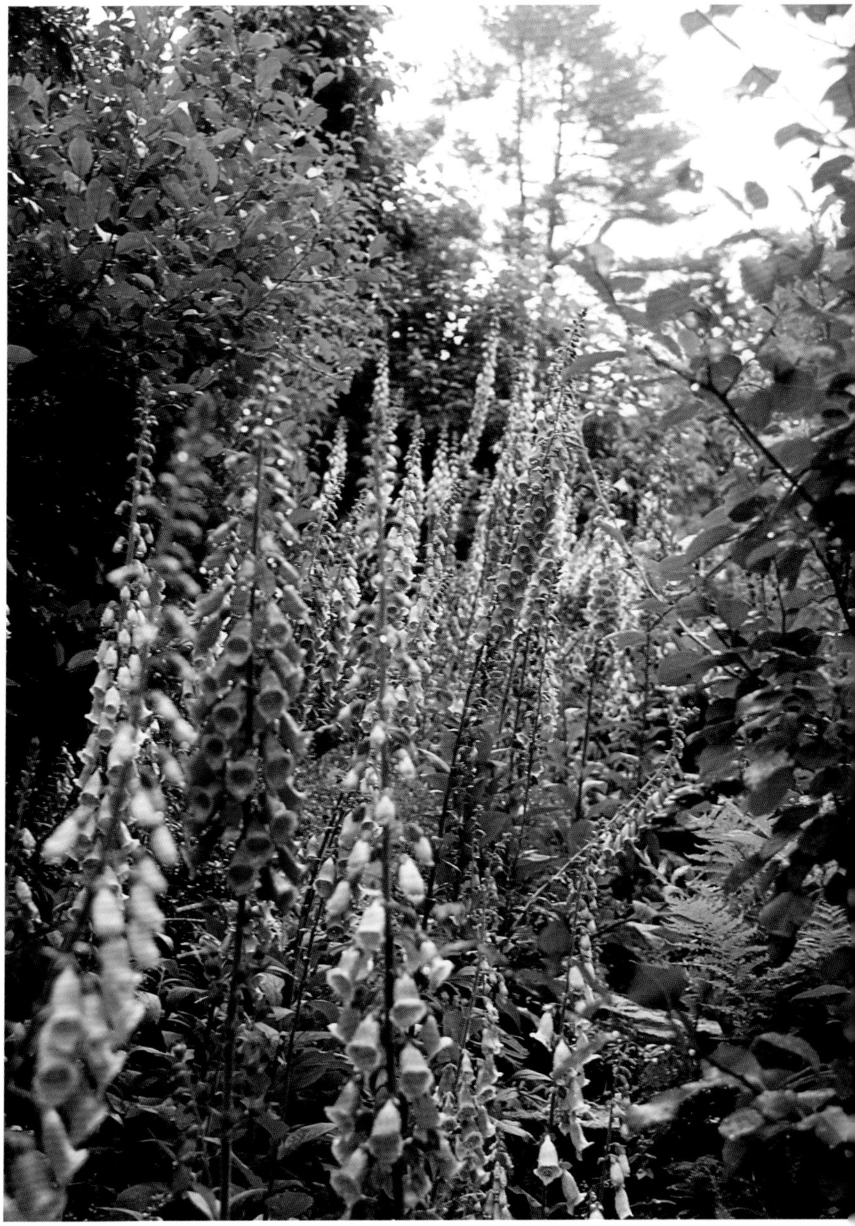

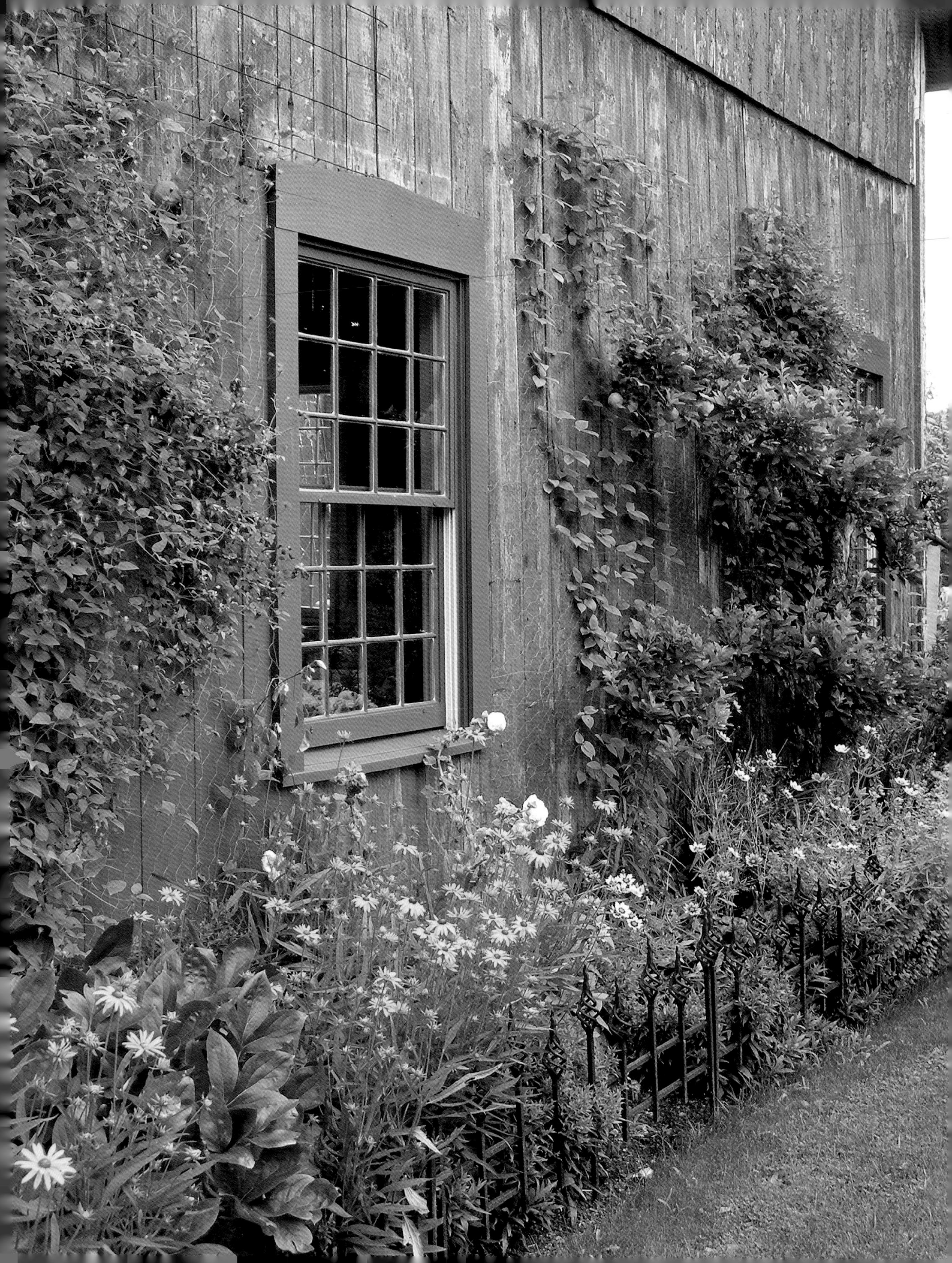

J udy Murphy, a graduate of the landscape architecture program at Cornell University, and her husband, Pat, have been designing and building gardens for decades. They worked first in Greenbrier County, West Virginia, then moved to Lakeville, Connecticut, in the late 1980s. "We wanted to raise our boys in New England, near our families," Judy says, "and the country-side here reminded us of West Virginia."

Their farmhouse, gardens, and nursery occupy 15 acres surrounded by fields. The road runs close to the front of the house, so all activity takes place behind it, and the views and gardens face north across hay fields, ponds, and woods, and finally the Berkshires in the distance.

The property came with a cornfield, a pond, some stone walls, an old house, and outbuildings—assorted barns and silos. "We removed several barns, fixed up the remaining ones, turned the cornfield into a vegetable garden, fenced in areas to keep our small boys safe, and went to work landscaping," Judy says. "We expanded the gardens slowly. Initially I just planted any tree that arrived at the nursery damaged. I also appropriated any plants left over at the end of the selling season."

As time went by and their business became more successful, the gardens benefited by becoming more structured. "We began to install plants we actually wanted to cultivate, not just what fell our way," Judy says. "We created rooms where one garden led to another, changing styles as inspiration struck." An adjacent barn was subsequently renovated into a multi-purpose structure to expand the nursery's offerings of garden ornaments as well. "I have always enjoyed them, so we established an area where ornaments purchased in France and England can be displayed," she says. After several years, the couple also added a swimming pool in what they call the "secret" garden.

A deck off the back of the house is resplendent with container plantings that bring color and fragrance up close to the outdoor living and dining area. More often than not, what is served is grown on the property. "We live off the garden and orchards as much as we can," Judy says. "From March to December we work seven days a week and also entertain. The gardens are an extension of what we do professionally as well as personally. Our kids have been involved in helping clients, working on the landscape crew, helping make gardening decisions. I think they feel this is their place as much as ours, although both now live and work in New York City."

Even the most casual visitor to Old Farm Nursery cannot escape noticing the synergy created from a dynamic marriage of industry and pleasure. "Our gardens are our work, our home, and our life," Judy says. "Working outside all the time allows us to connect intimately with what we do. We spend our working lives creating gardens for others, and it gives us great pleasure to come home to our own. They give us a sense of wonder that we appreciate every time we look out a window or walk out the door. They belong to all the clients and gardeners that walk through by day, but at dawn, when we're the only ones here, they belong to us alone."

BELOW AND RIGHT The garden's "hot border" features perennials in orange and China red complemented by cool purples and blues, which appear particularly vibrant against a backdrop of evergreens.

BOTTOM Hostas, maidenhair ferns, and *Rodgersias* form lush underplantings that relate to the tones of white pine trees in the woodland garden.

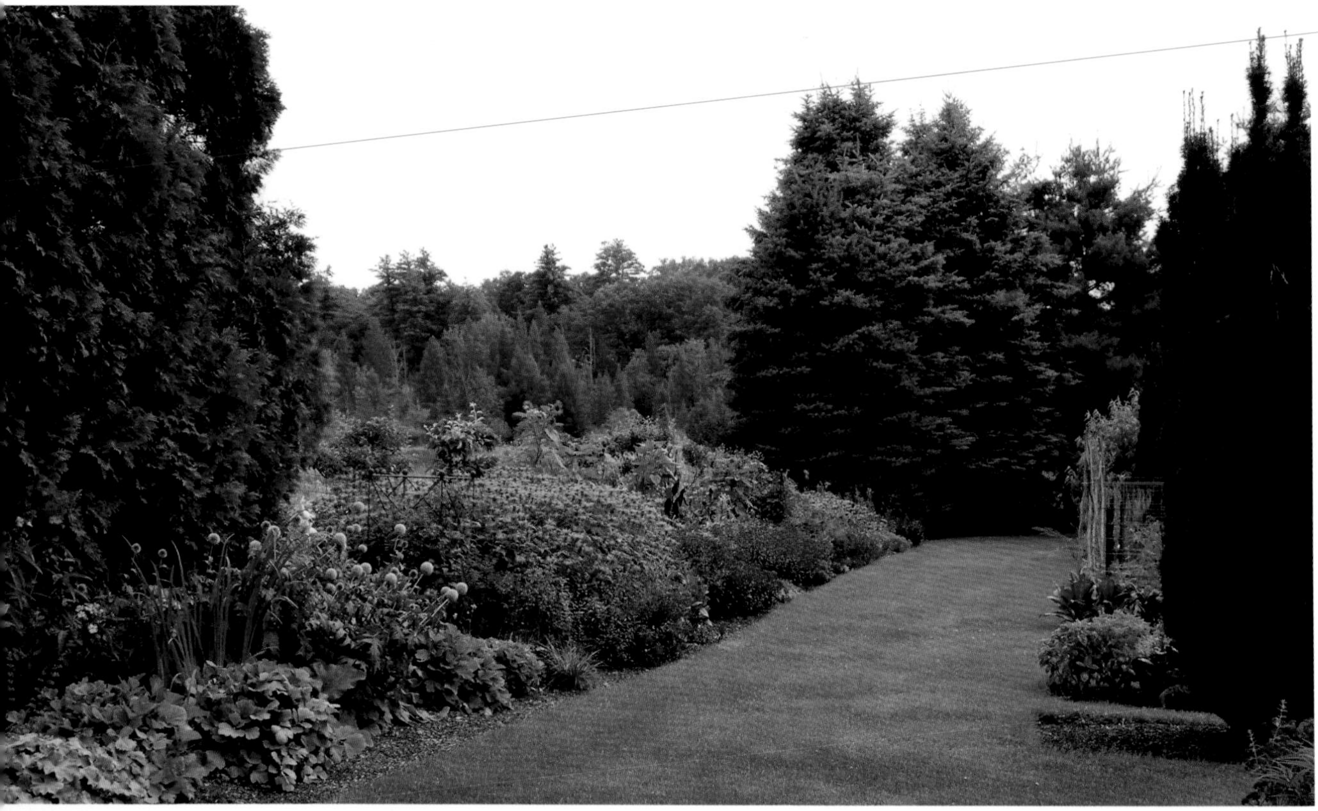

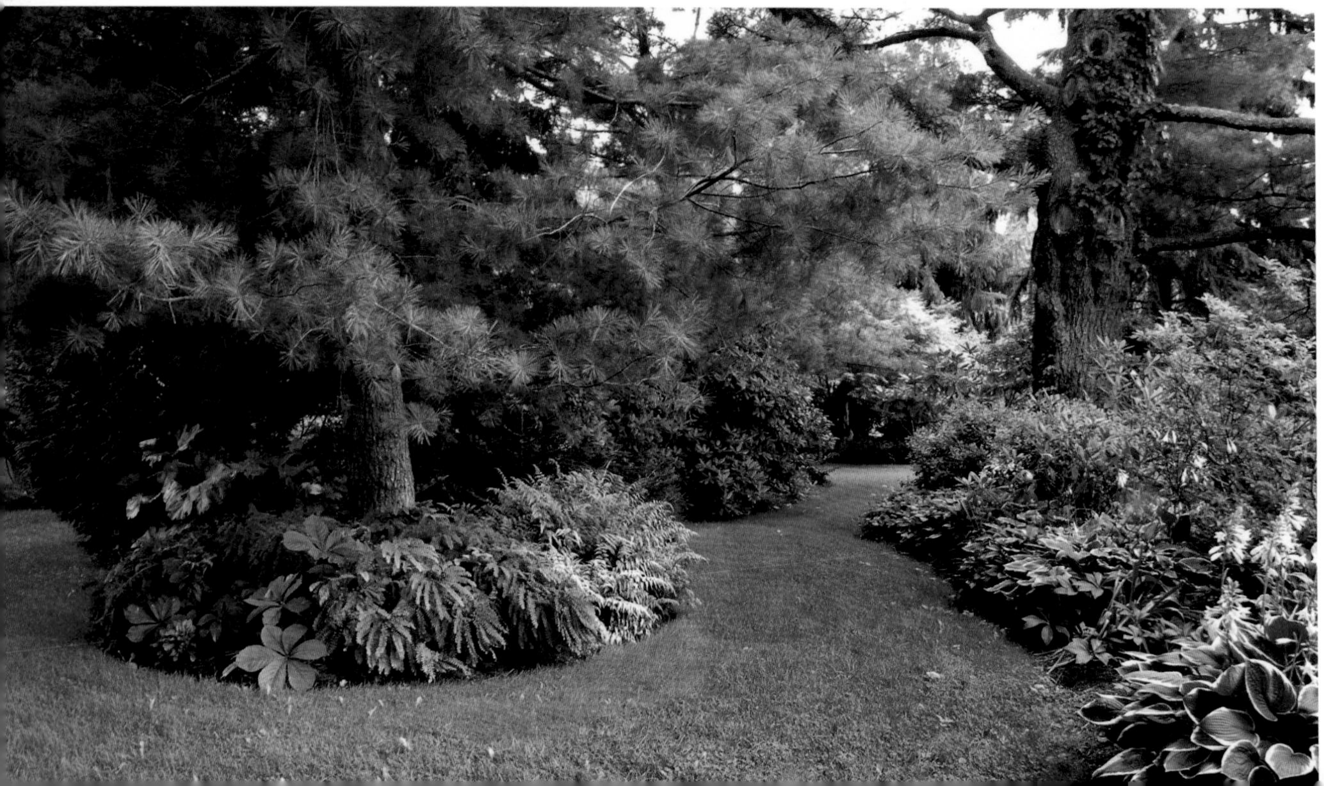

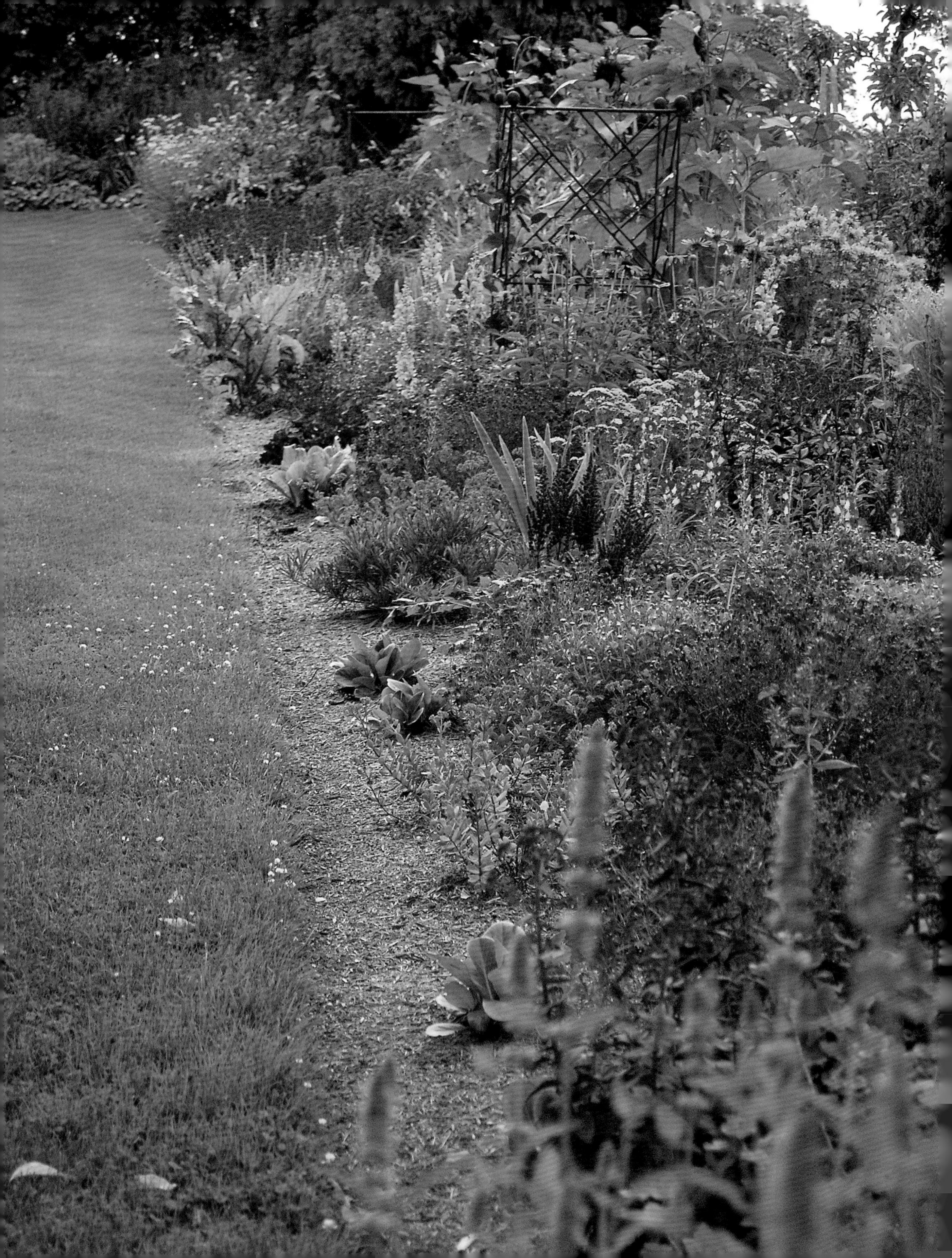

BELOW Simple timber-and-bamboo frames support an abundance of tomato plants in the vegetable garden. **RIGHT, ABOVE AND BELOW** Flagstone and turf paths lead visitors out into the landscape adjoining the house, which is filled with perennials, shrubs, and garden ornaments. **OVERLEAF** Afternoon sun streams across the perennial border, vegetable garden, nursery, and out to marshes and mountains in the Connecticut landscape beyond.

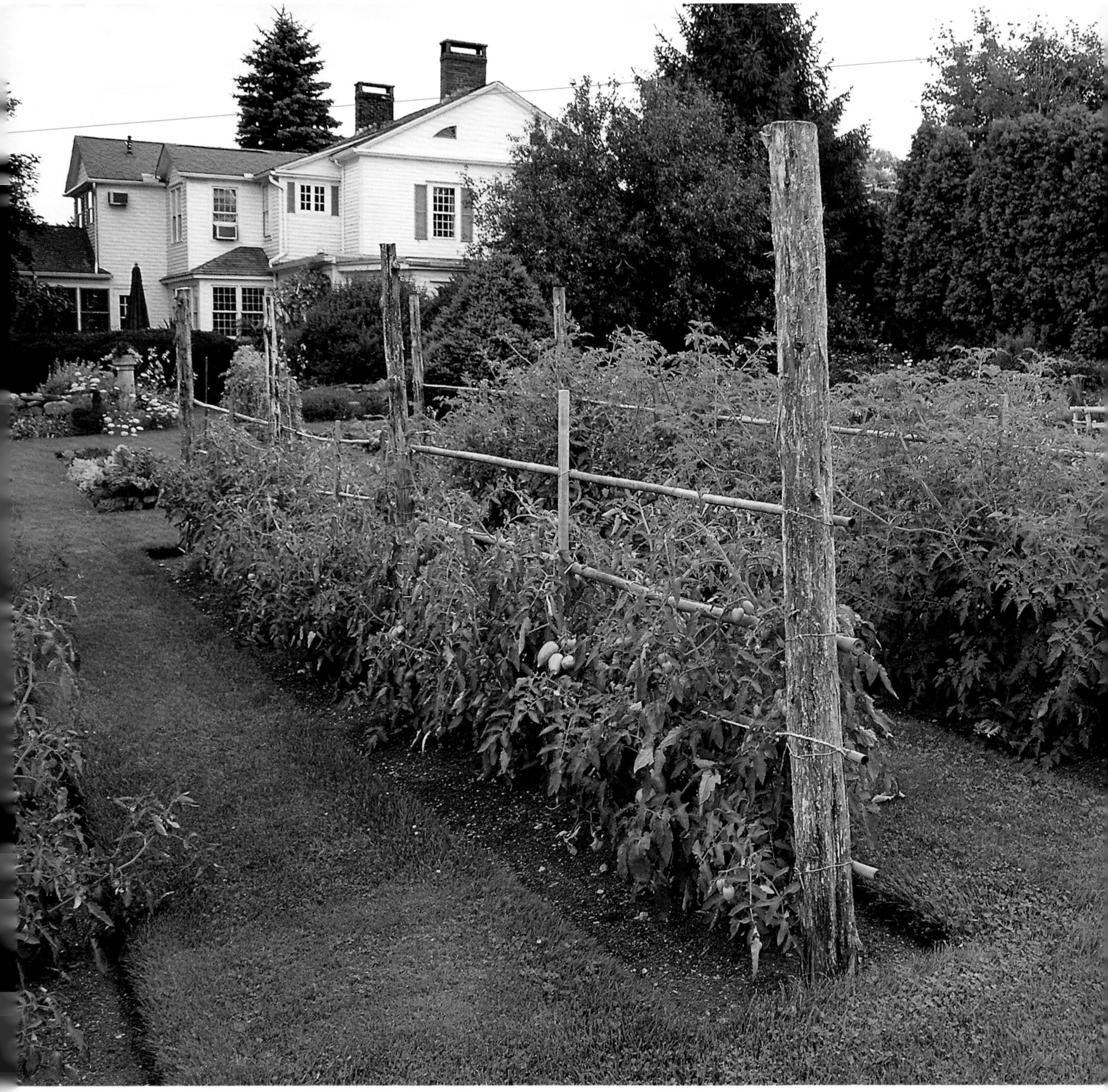

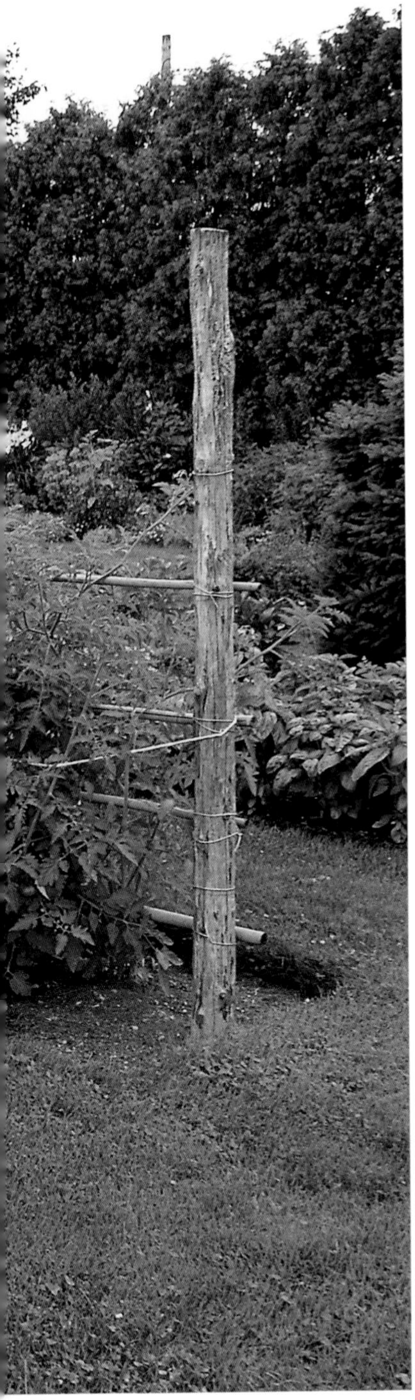

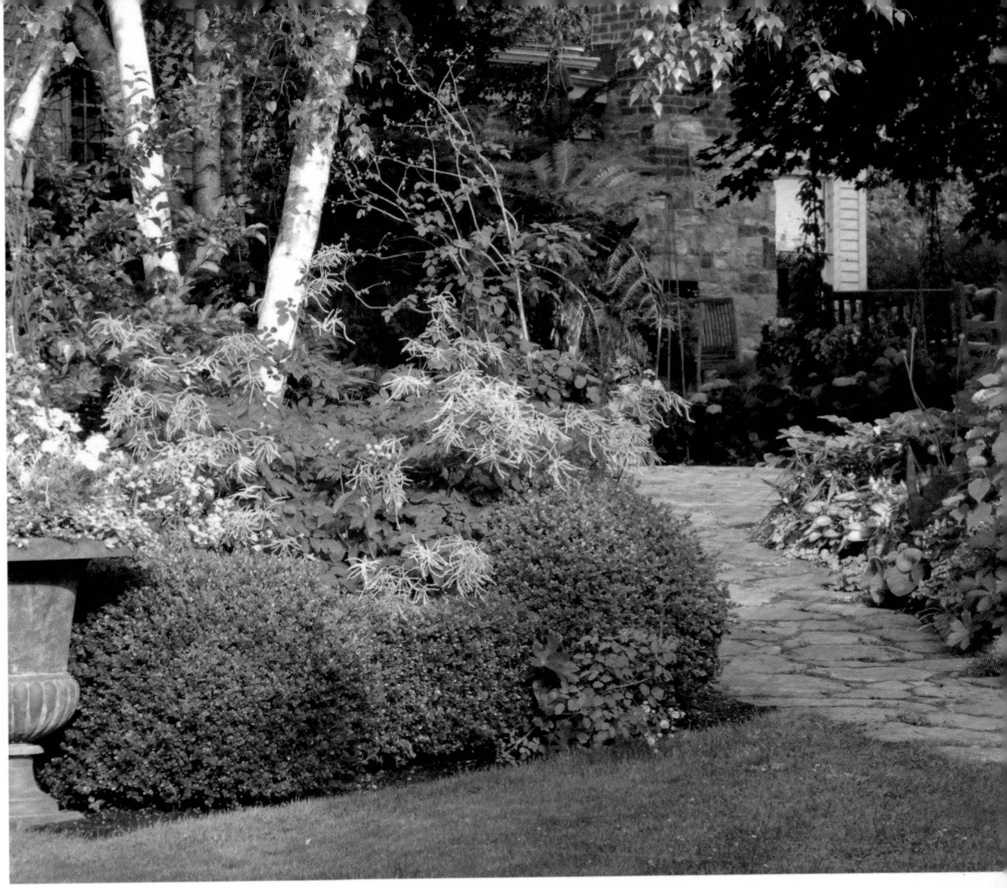

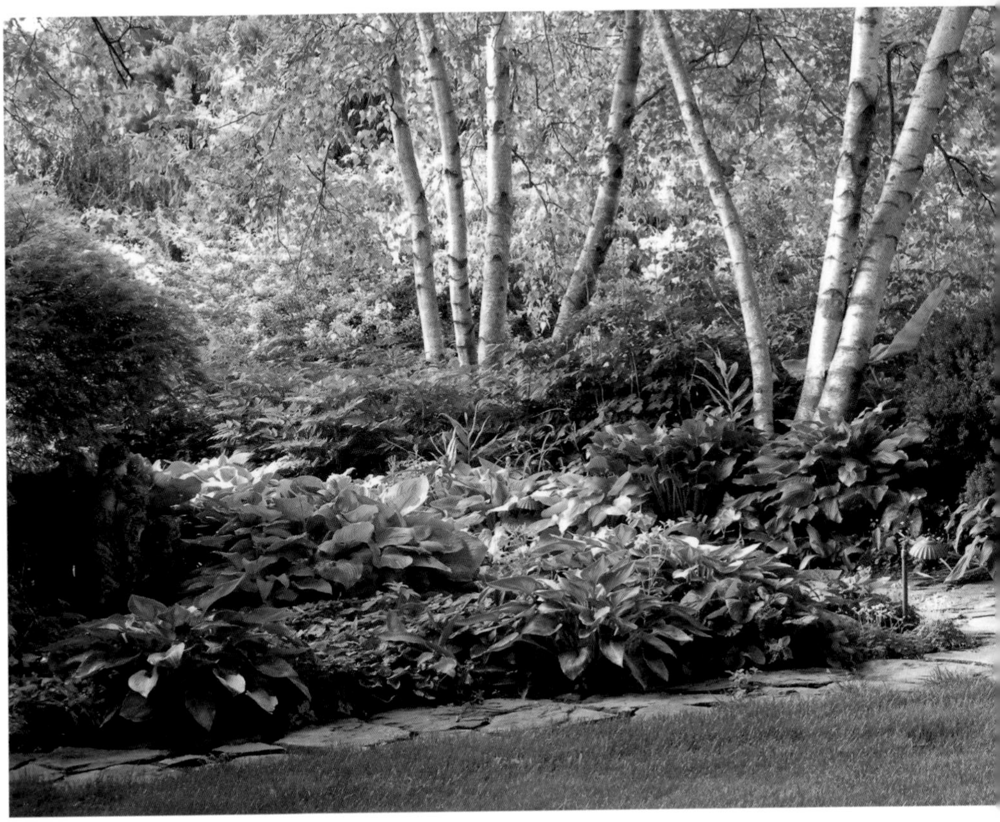

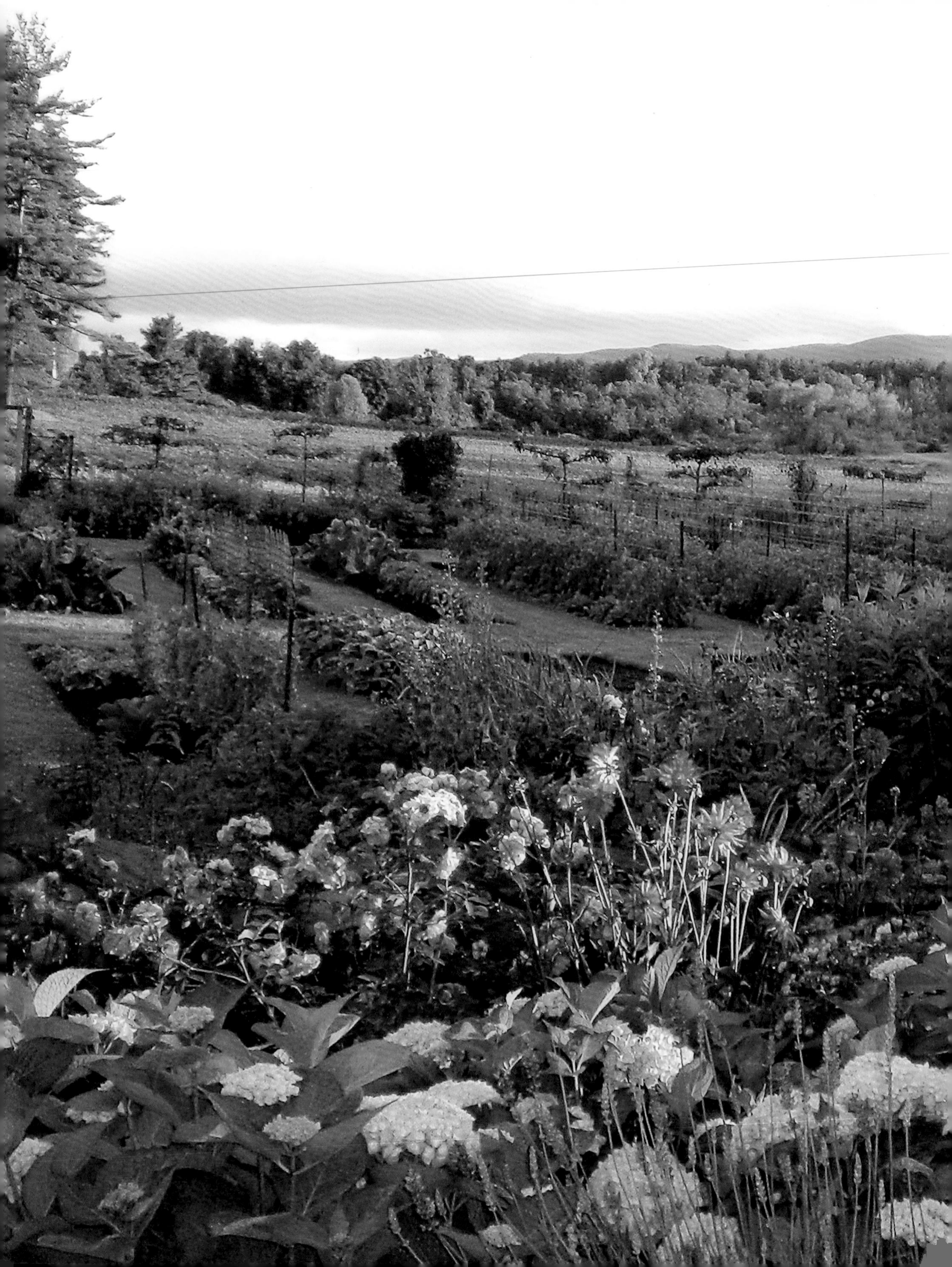

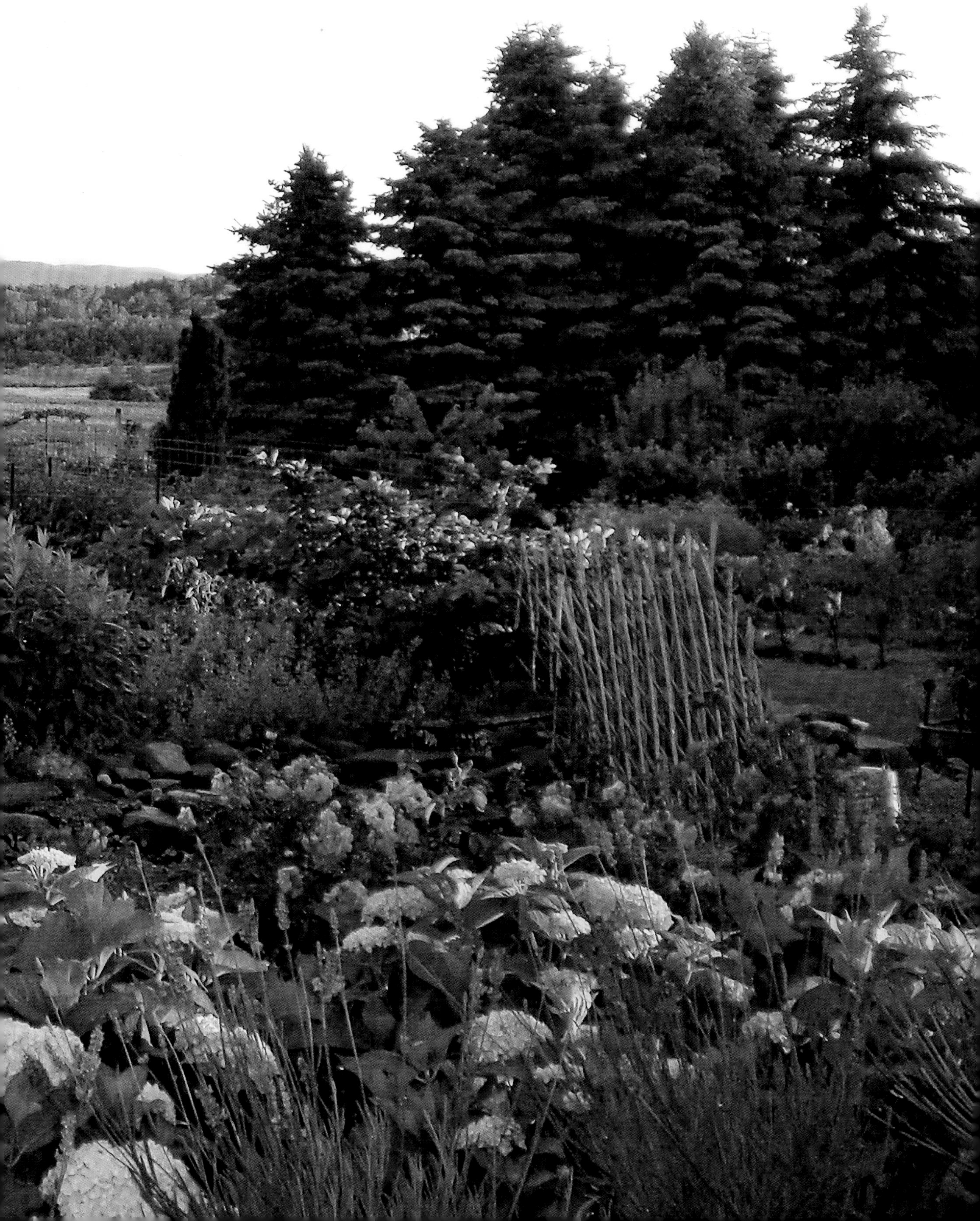

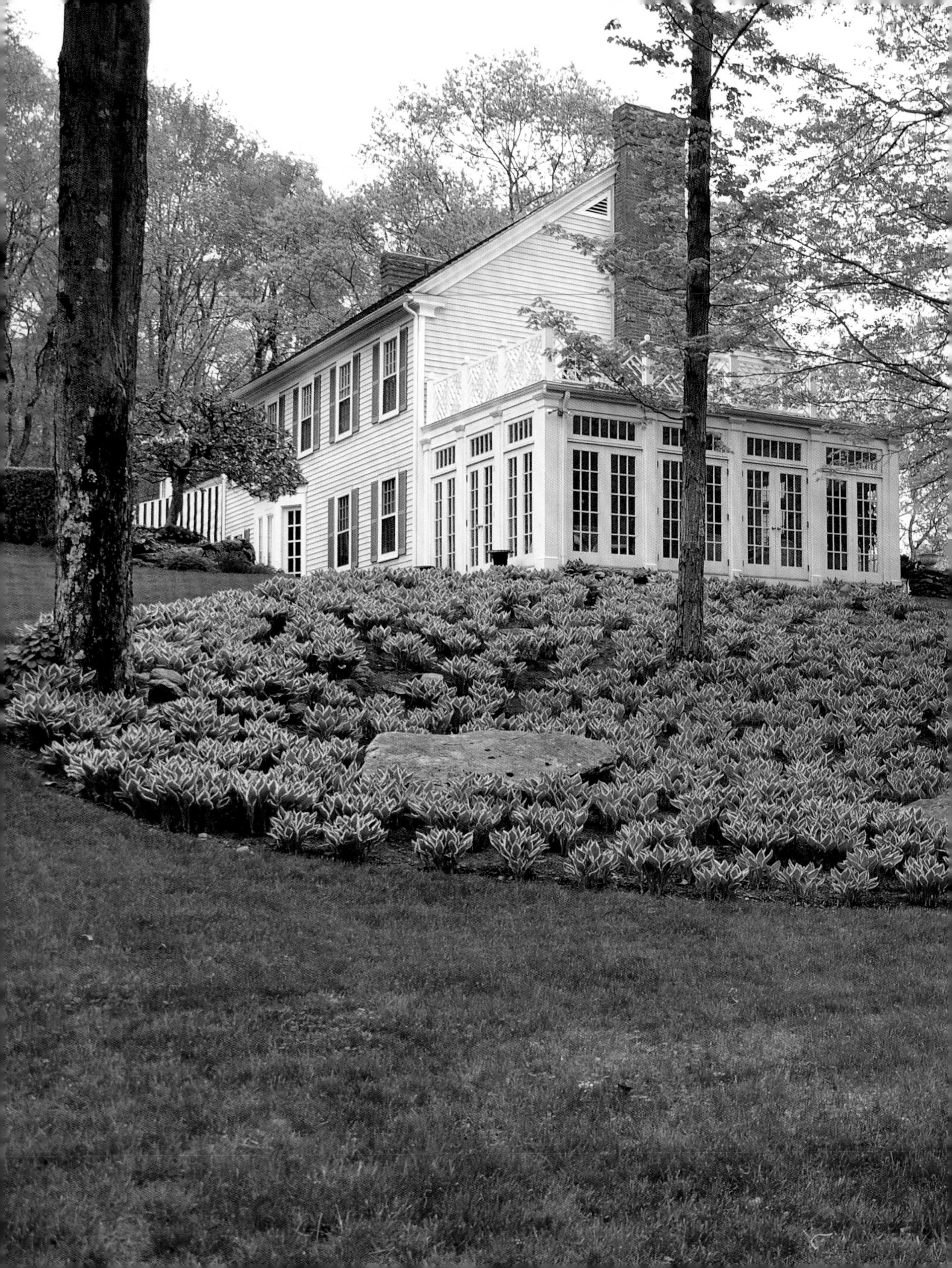

In 1980, when Larry Power and Lea Davies purchased their 45 acres in Sharon, Connecticut, the only access was by foot. Wild plums they encountered blooming on the banks of a stream meandering through the property inspired them to name it Plum Creek Farm. What began as a weekend retreat from busy lives in New York City has now become the couple's primary residence.

After choosing the sites on which to build a house, and a barn with a caretaker's apartment, they created a long entry drive and added two bridges to cross the spring-fed stream. Pristine white gates announce arrival at the three cultivated acres that surround the house; the rest of the property is comprised of fields, horse pastures, and native woods transected by riding trails.

An early project involved digging two ponds near the entrance—one upper, one lower—and creating a water cascade between them. Thirty daylilies originally planted by the lower pond were divided over the course of five years, until they completely covered the hillside. "The lower wet field with large boulders and tall trees was always a problem area we didn't know what to do with," Davies says. "After a trip to England, we were inspired to transform it into a three-tiered, formal garden that incorporates seating areas and views into the surrounding woods and the pond with a geyser. We had to use bulldozers to clear the dense trees and boulders from the area."

After entering through the front gates, visitors pass the ponds and waterfall, extensive rhododendron plantings, and horse pastures as they approach the house. The view extends to a 100-foot-long perennial border and rock garden. The border is planted for summer-long flowering interest as well as variations in color and texture. Walking paths invite strollers to a fern and woodland walk, or down to the three-tiered formal garden with vistas to the upper pond and its geyser, and finally a columned classical folly in the woods.

The formal garden features flowering crab apples, tree-form standard Korean lilacs, and hydrangeas, in addition to columnar and shrub arborvitaes, ivy, and pachysandra that provide visual interest in the long winters. Two areas designed for outdoor living include a terrace off the main house's sun room—which has creeping thymes planted between the flagstones—and a large awning-covered terrace off the kitchen that overlooks a border of perennials backed by a hedge.

Great gardens often represent the passions of two distinct personalities, one focused on structure, the other on content. Just as Sir Edwin Lutyens gave structure to the plantings provided by Gertrude Jekyll, Davies says that at Plum Creek Farm, "Larry is the idea person who also trims the hedges—sometimes weekly in the summer—and I'm the plantsman who maintains the borders, divides, transplants, and deadheads, with a little help from a one-day-a-week gardener. Being actively involved in all aspects of the gardens brings us happiness. We see them from every room in the house and, especially with the geyser lighted at night, they provide a perfect backdrop for parties large and small."

RIGHT One side of the formal garden contains a classical, columned garden folly in the woods.
BELOW The three-tiered formal garden incorporates dramatic views of the upper pond and its geyser.

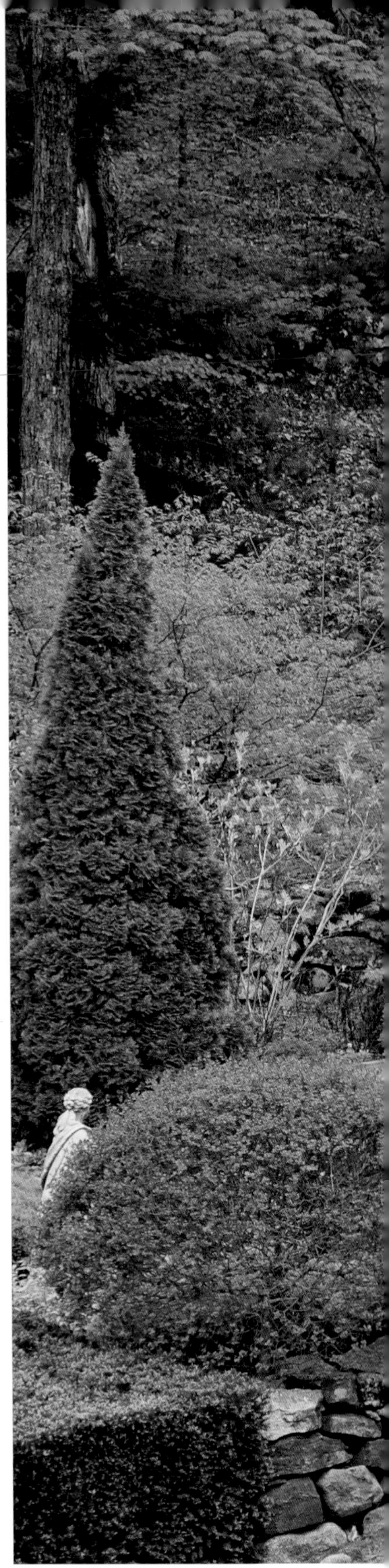

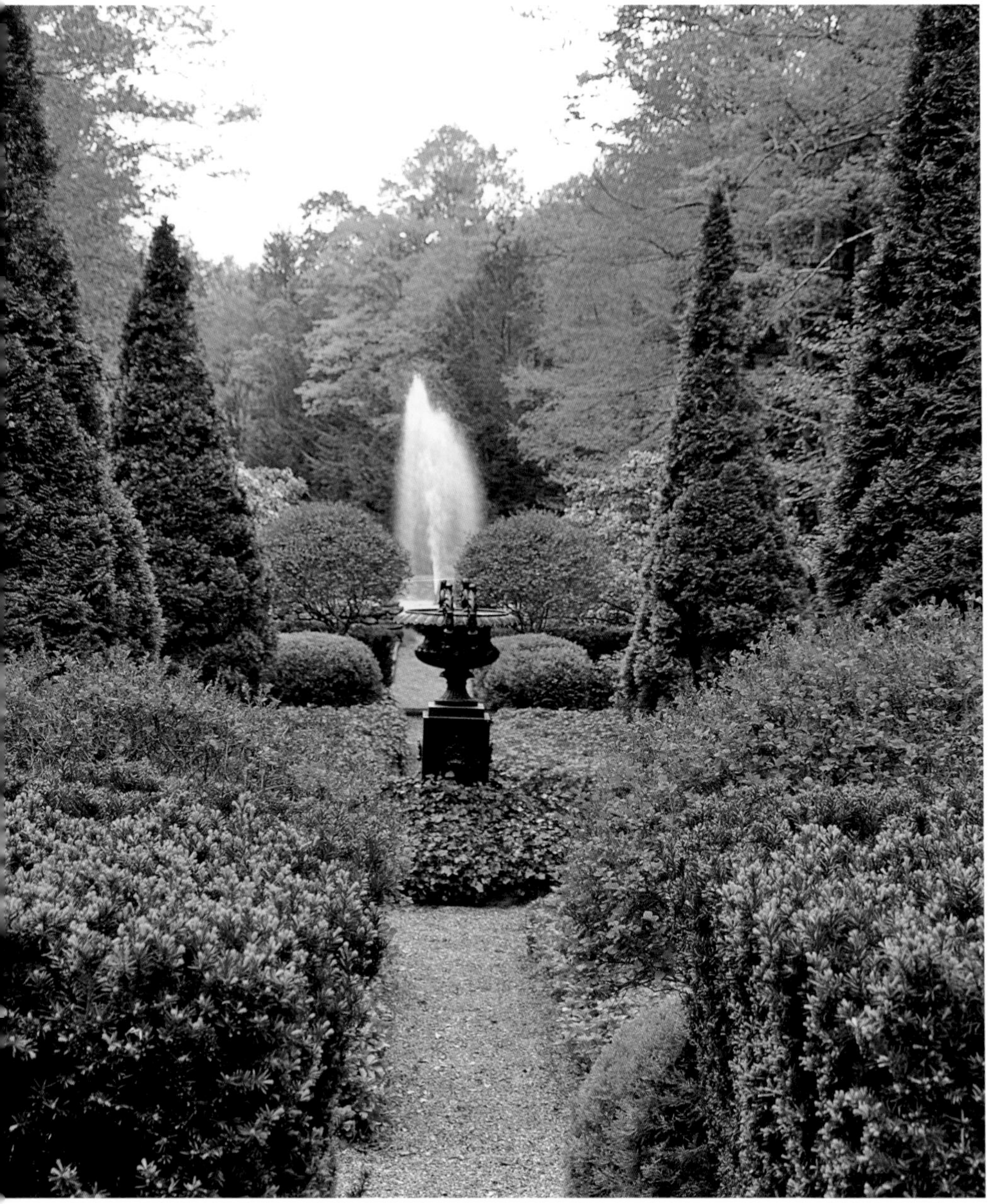

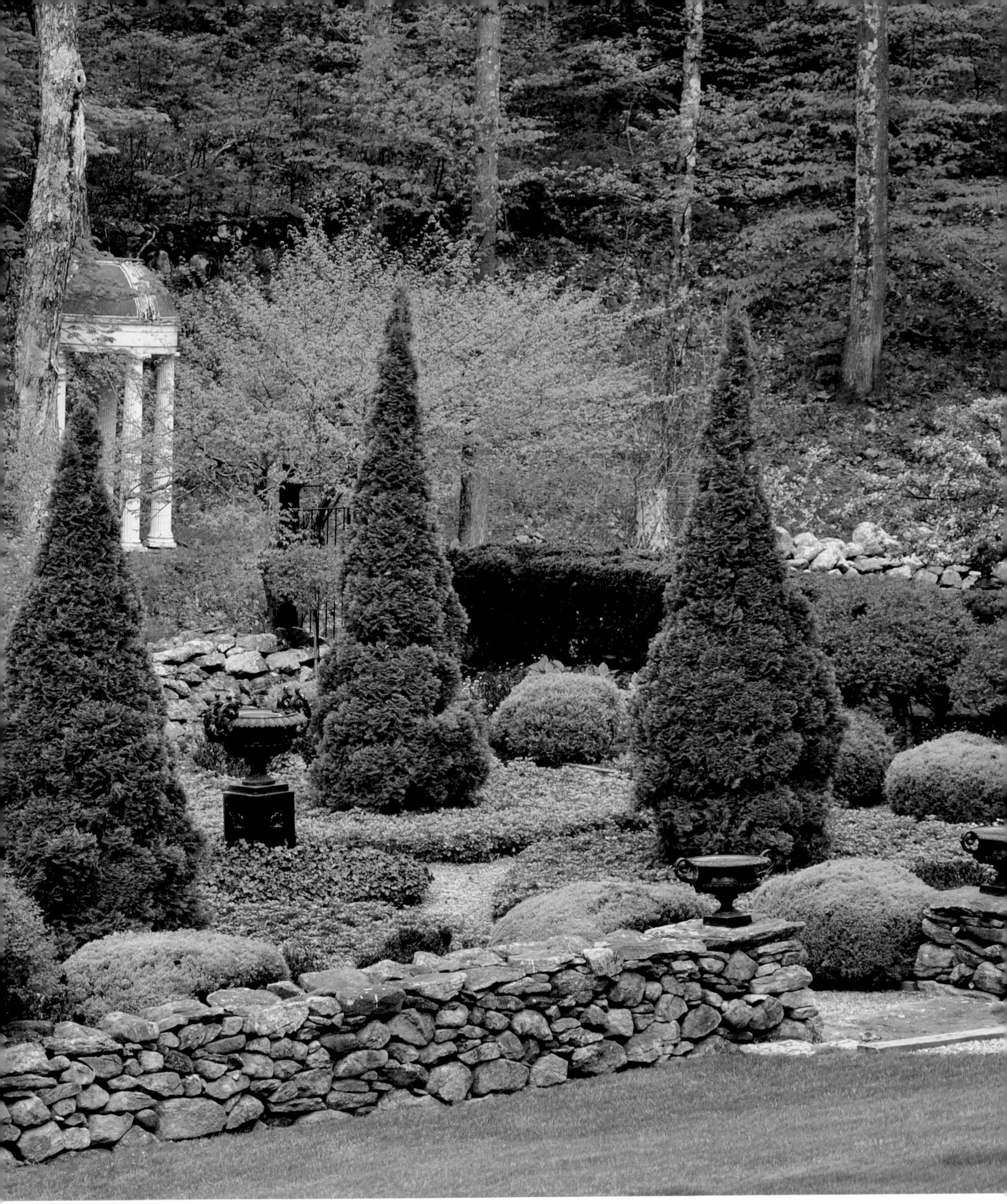

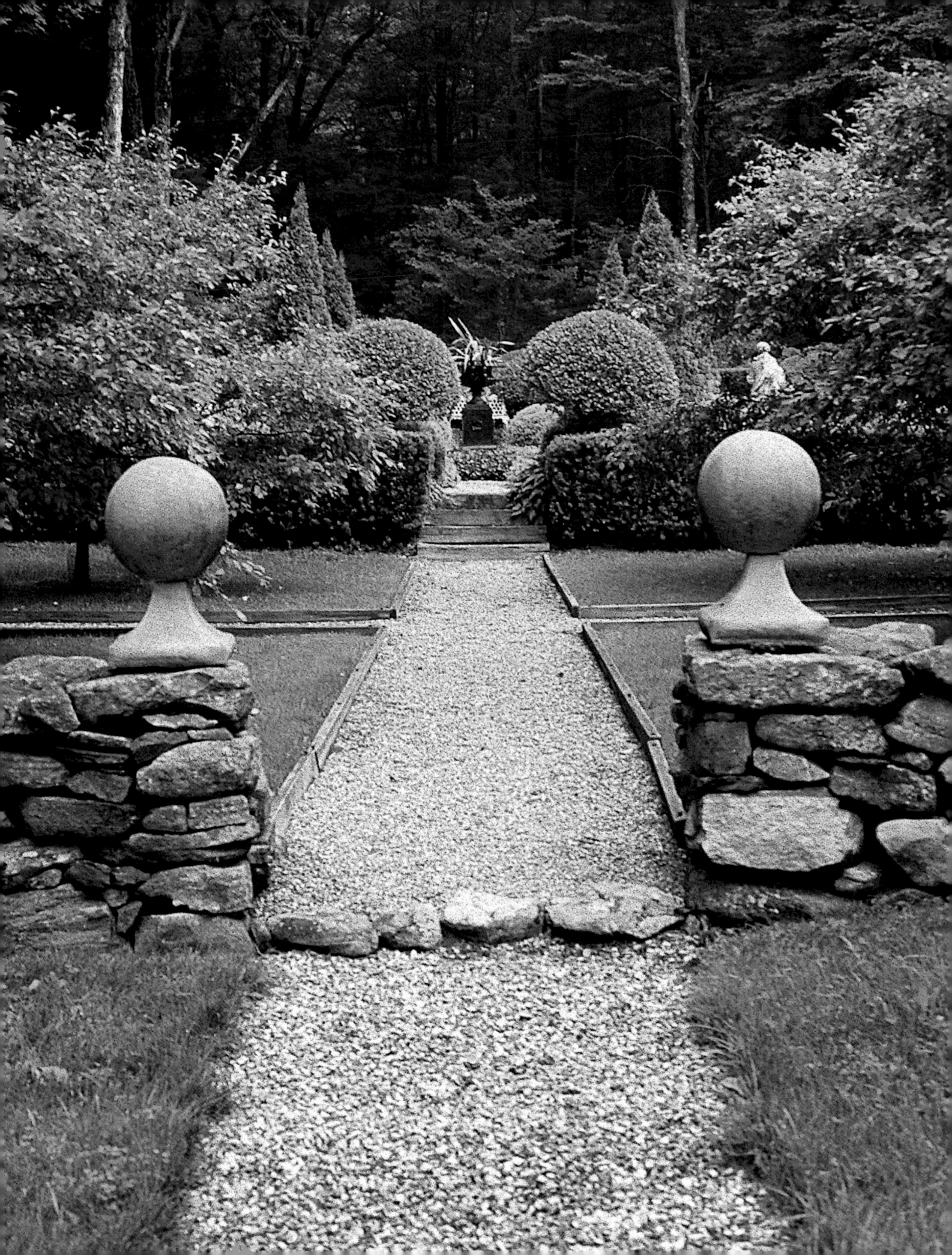

LEFT Formal finials lead the way toward formal gardens. **BELOW** The awning-covered terrace provides outdoor living space and overlooks an elaborate perennial border.

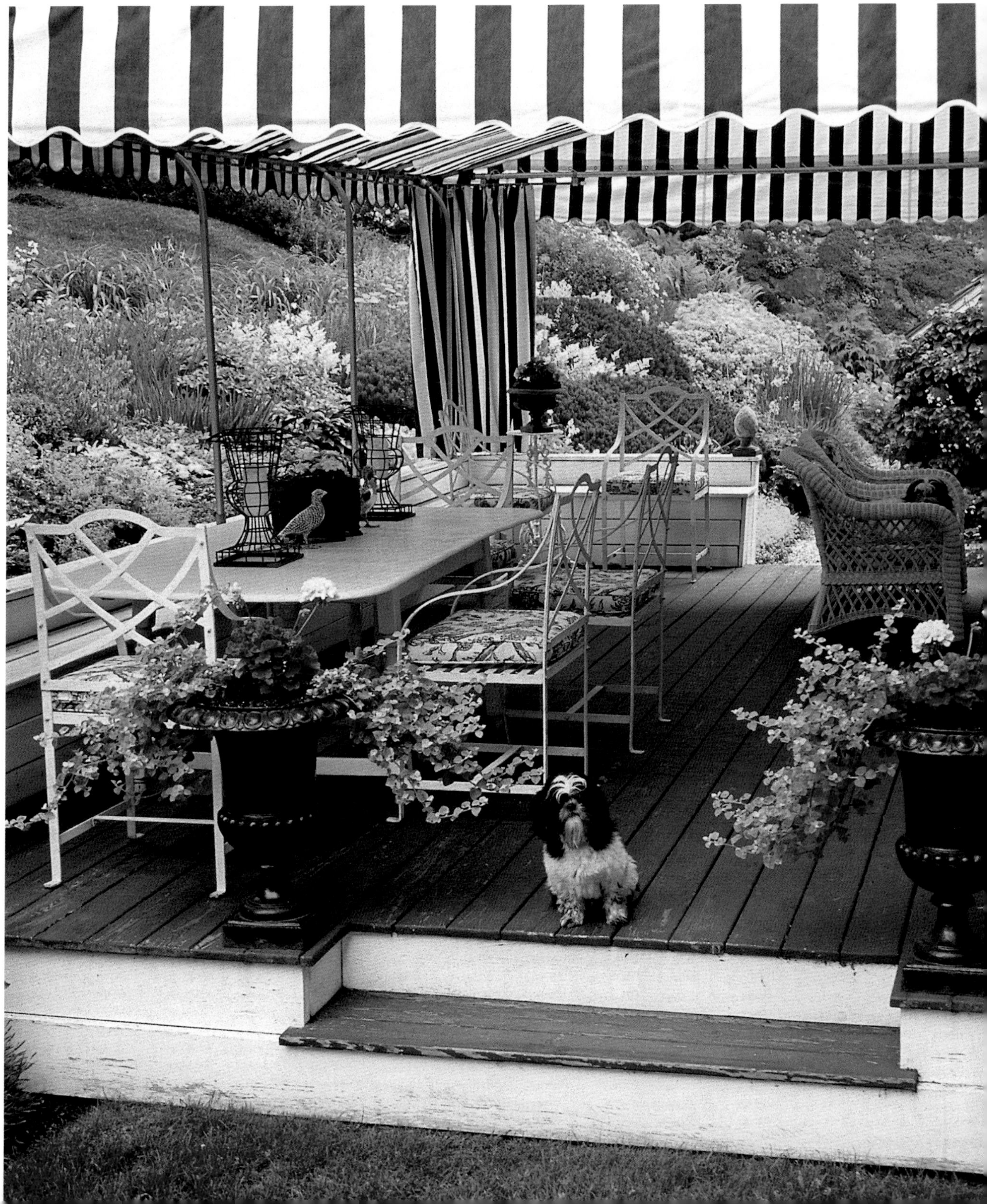

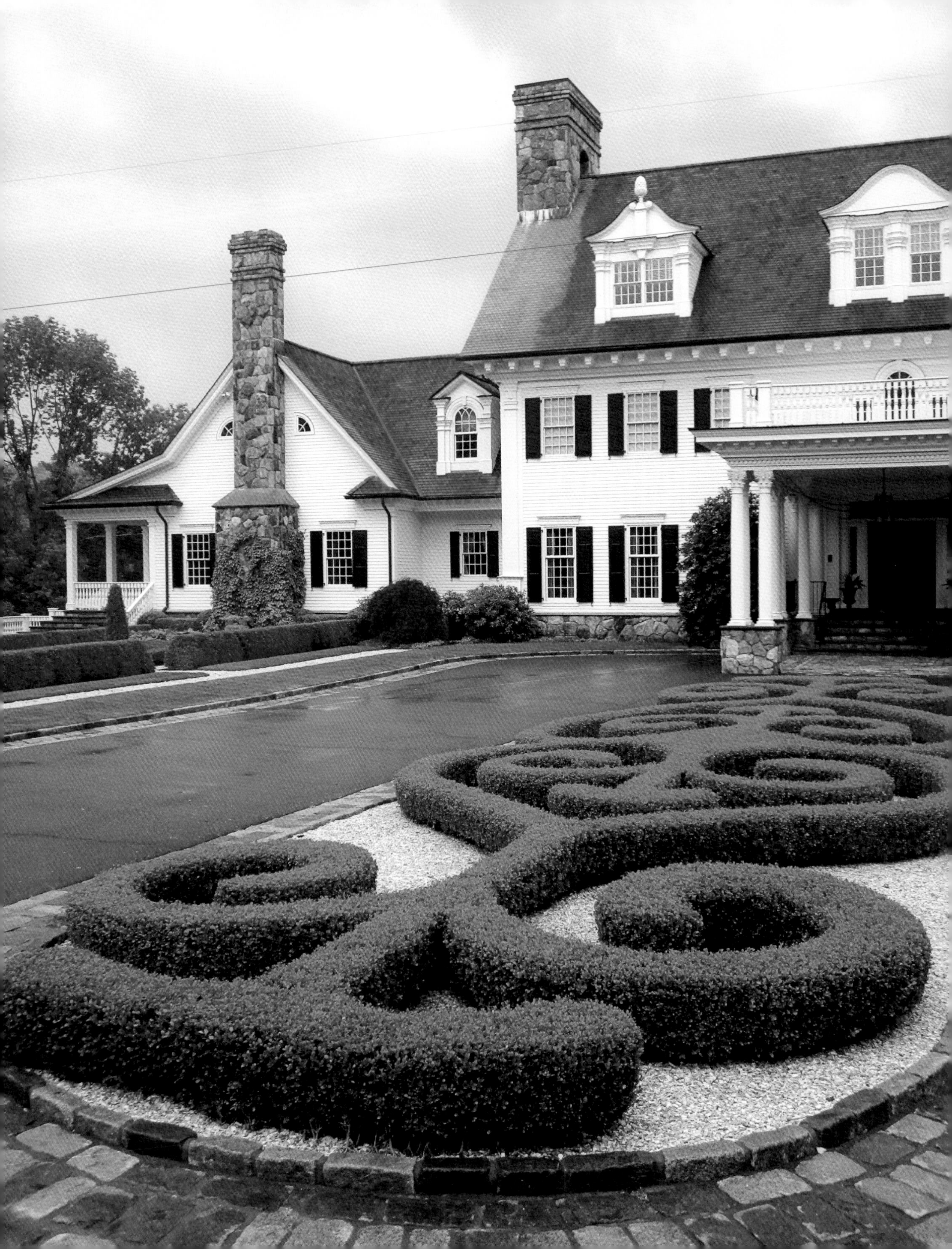

Garden designer Phillip Watson's first suggestion to the owners of this 10-acre property in the back country near Greenwich, Connecticut, was that the classically proportioned dwelling would make an ideal backdrop for Versailles-type parterres. Two months later they called him and said, "We're at Versailles. We like them. Please proceed."

On entering the property through the front gates, a corridor of little-leaf linden trees and a large parterre of clipped boxwood on a field of quarried white shells greet visitors. The carefully shaped motif is reminiscent of anchors—meant to symbolize the clients' love of the sea, yacht races, and lanai deck cocktail parties. "That bit of whimsy is tempered by the strict geometry of the flanking rectilinear parterres," Watson says. "They brim in summer with frothy white 'Diamond Frost' euphorbia."

On any particular day, the view to the right of the house may include couples playing doubles on the tennis court, which is surrounded by weeping white birches and the perennial red hibiscus 'Lord Baltimore.' In the rear, children can play in the 45-by-45-foot black-bottomed pool surrounded by clipped yew walls that serve as a backdrop to long borders of annuals, perennials, and seasonal bulbs.

Colorful chairs and lounges provide ample seating in front of the pool house and around the pool. Their fabrics mirror colors of the furniture on the home's rear porch, thanks to the work of interior designer Richard Keith Langham. The pool house itself, designed by architect Paul Marchese, relates in shape to the cupola atop the main house. A favorite spot for summer dining, it purposely evokes an orangery—a second reference to Versailles.

To the right of the pool house, two further structures with distinct purposes await. The first, referred to as the "party barn," is a former Quaker meetinghouse that was once located elsewhere on the property. Its foundation plants are common species: *Pieris japonica* in the fore, and lanky lilacs at the rear. The pathway leading to its front door is simple fieldstone set into the lawn. The tall, ragged stones that flank the start of the path were formerly hitching posts for horses. Just to the side of the barn is a guesthouse that barely escaped being torn down; it has been transformed into a cozy place set within a garden dell of white 'Annabelle' hydrangeas. The pathway to the cottage meanders through a shade garden filled with hostas, ferns, lily of the valley, and Lenten rose hellebores. The path itself is composed of fieldstone brightened by golden *Lysimachia*, which creeps over and between the stones.

The garden was designed and installed six years ago, and was a blank slate except for an allée of lindens at the entrance and mature trees dotting the property. "After the late bloomers have finished the season," Watson says, "the clipped parterres and the sculpted greenery walls and topiaries take center stage and provide beautiful patterns to enjoy throughout the winter. These architectural plantings are arranged as extensions of the home and offer spectacular views from inside, especially when dusted with frost or light snow."

RIGHT Big, bold 'Annabelle' hydrangeas frame the entrance to the guesthouse. **BELOW** An antique French urn near the main house's porte cochère is planted to complement the silver-and-yellow tones of the parterres; hostas and *Lysimachia* fill the curvilinear bed.

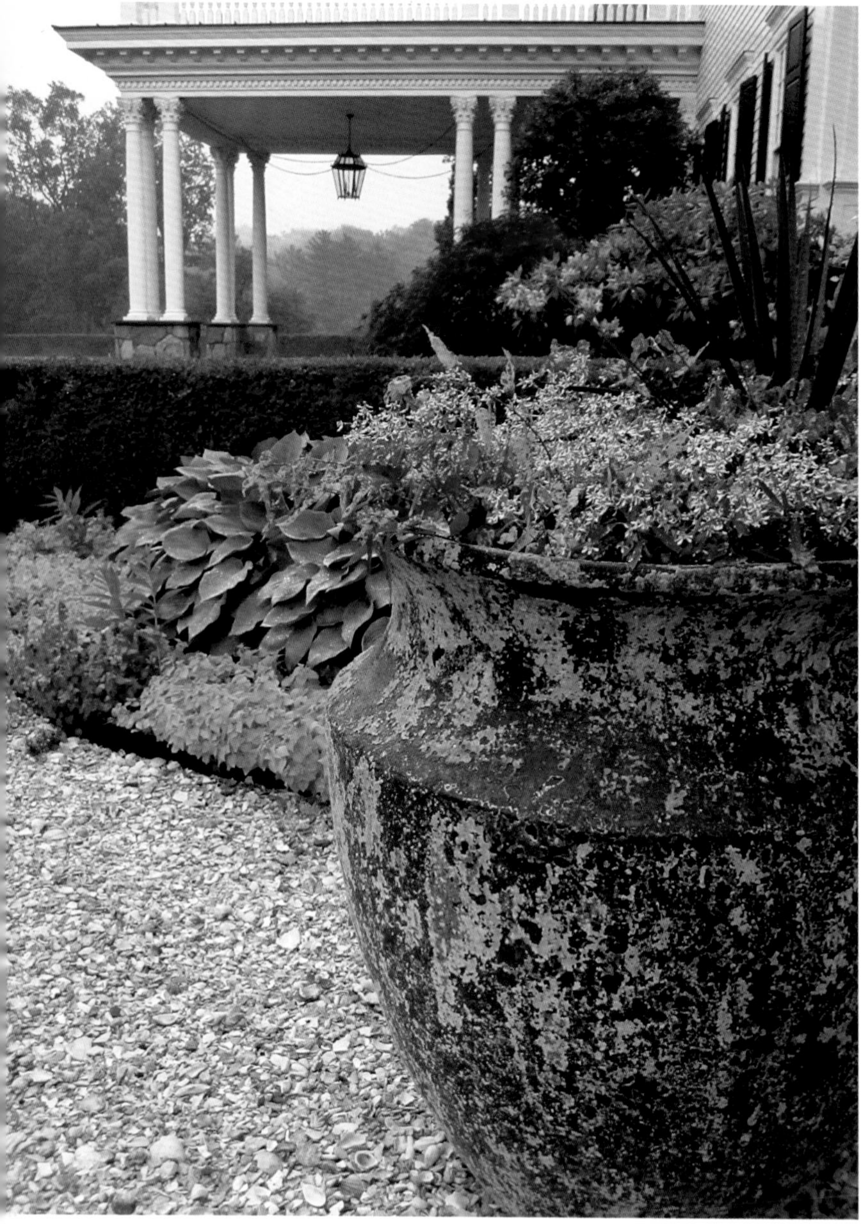

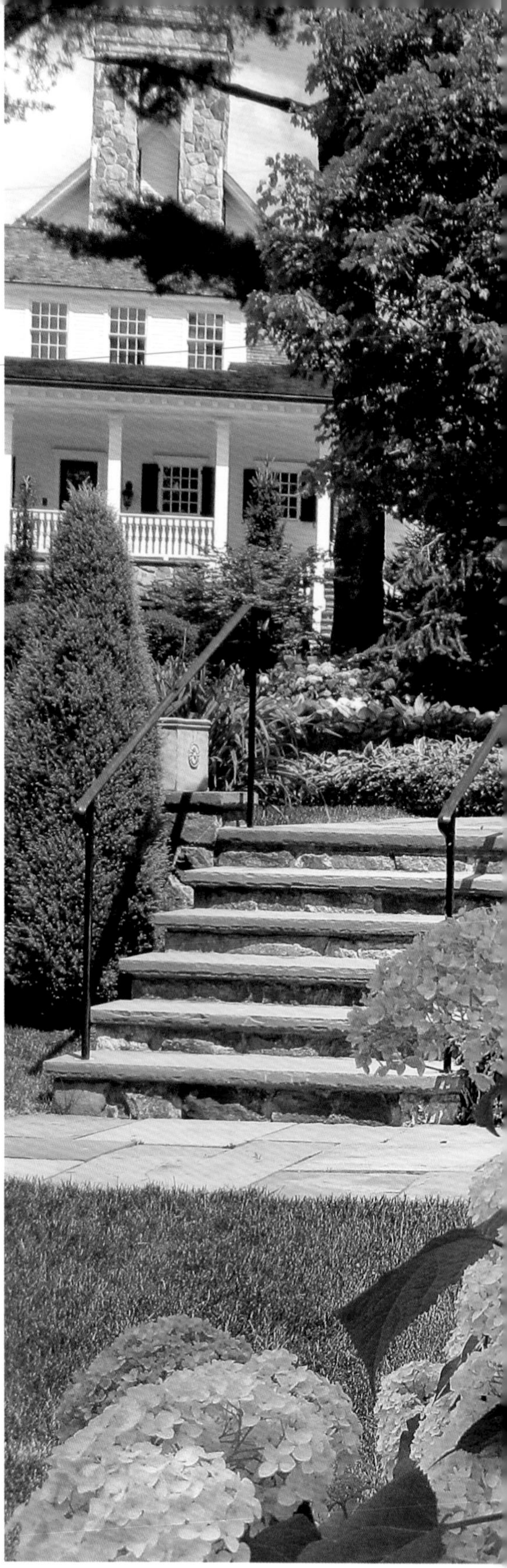

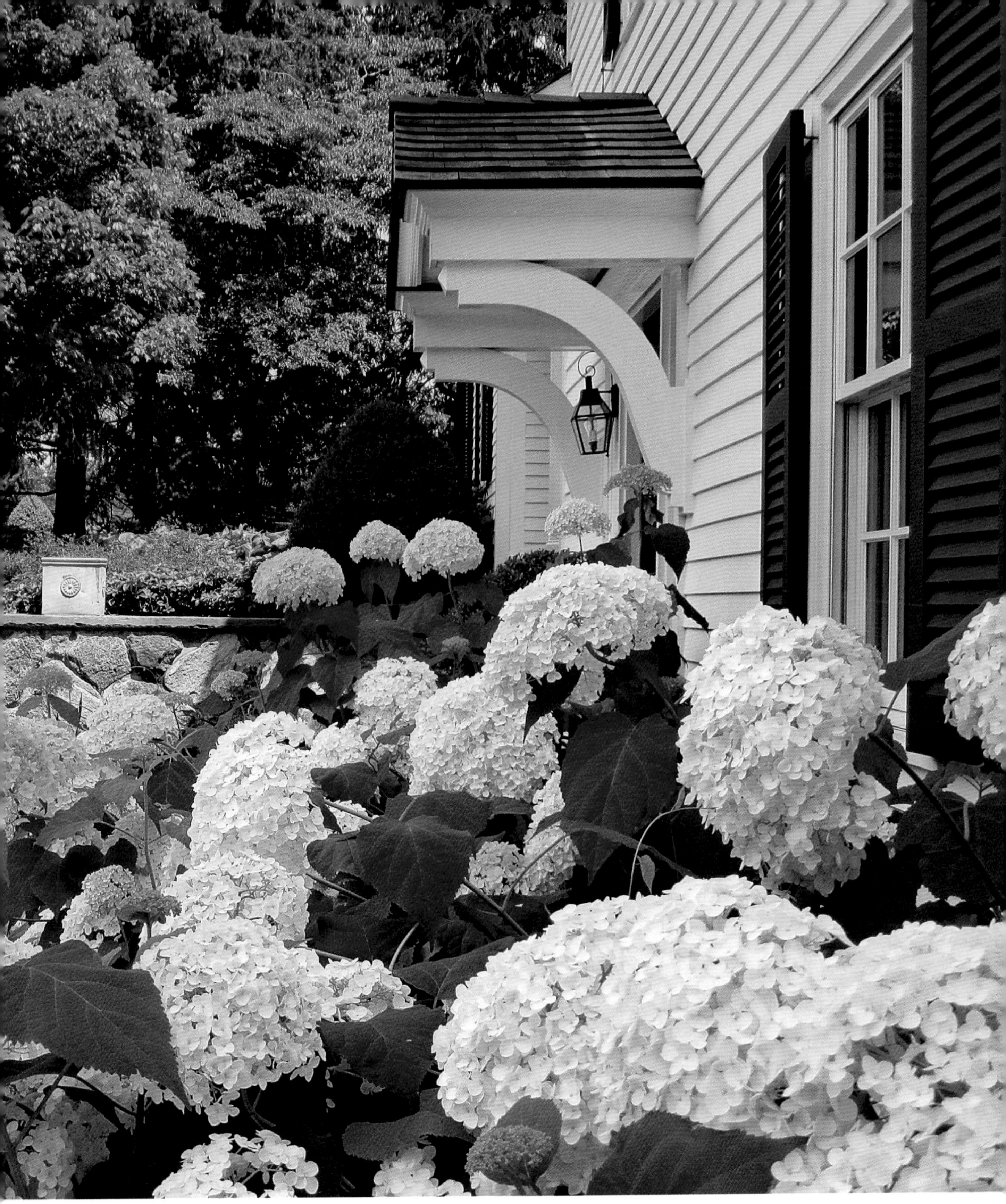

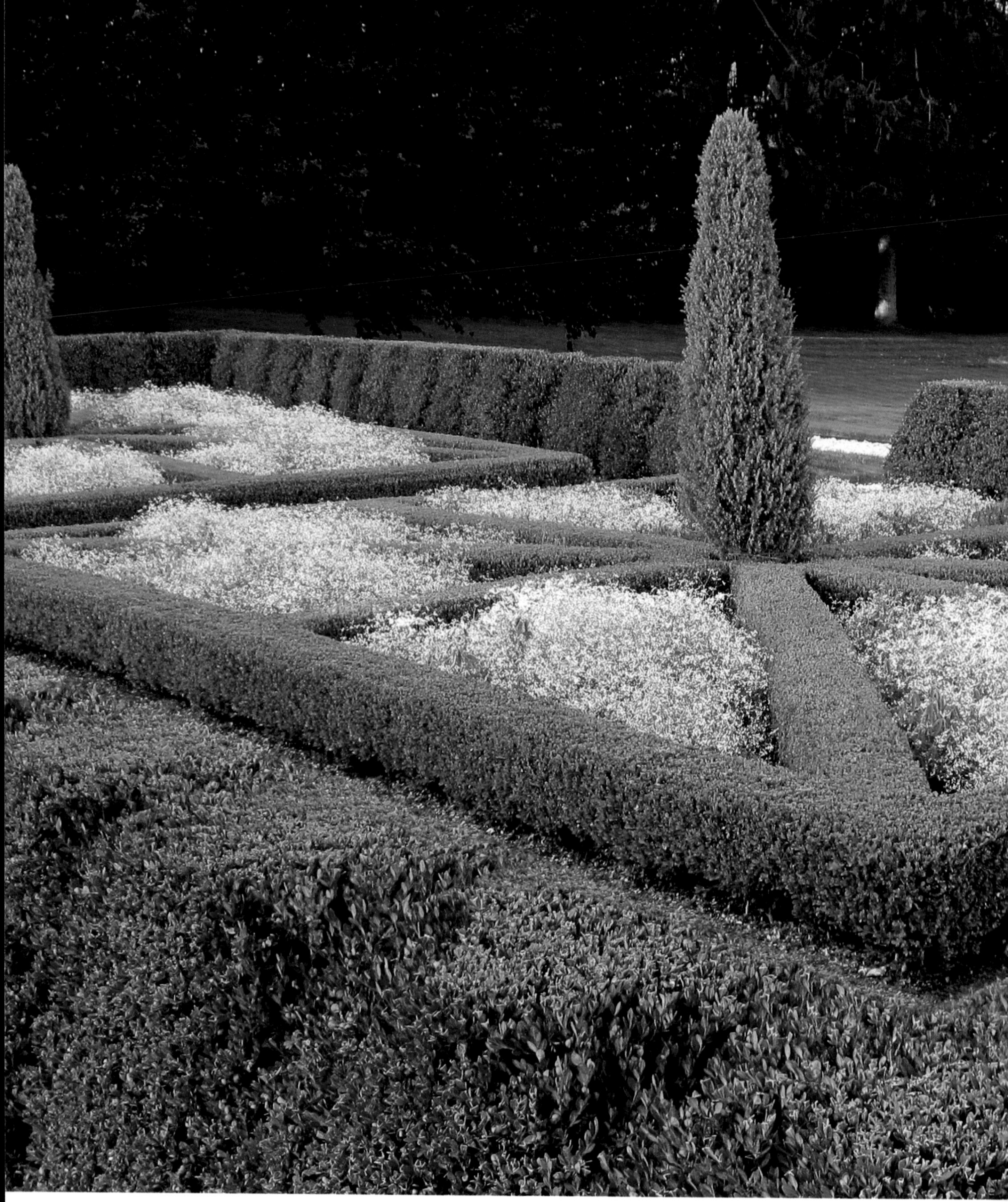

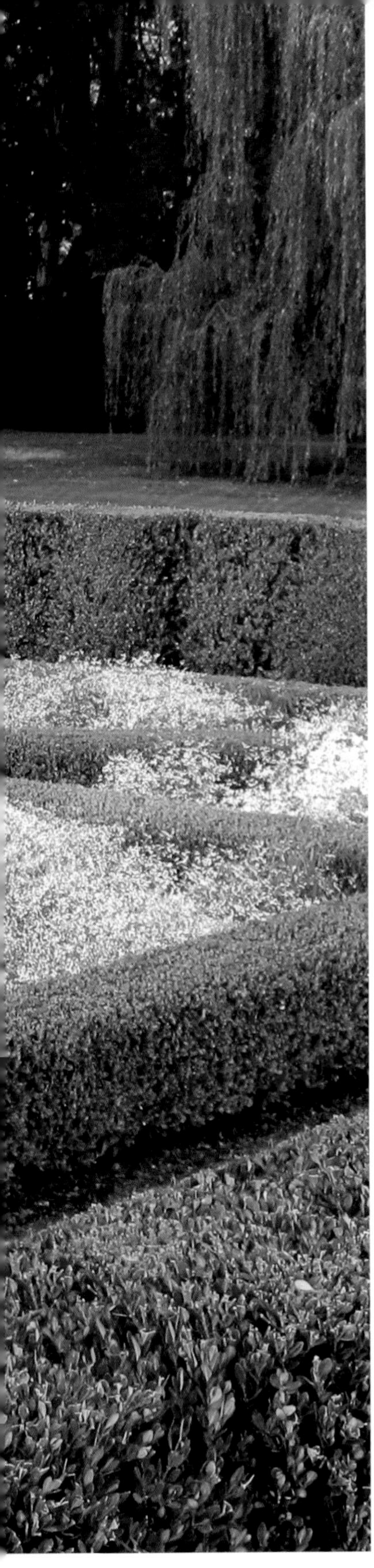

LEFT Formal, rectilinear parterres flank either side of the entrance drive; their groomed boxwood hedges contain clouds of 'Diamond Frost' euphorbia that blooms all summer. **BELOW** Golden *Lysimachia* lines flagstone pavers that lead the way to the guesthouse; shade gardens filled with hostas, ferns, lily of the valley, and hellebores lie to either side.

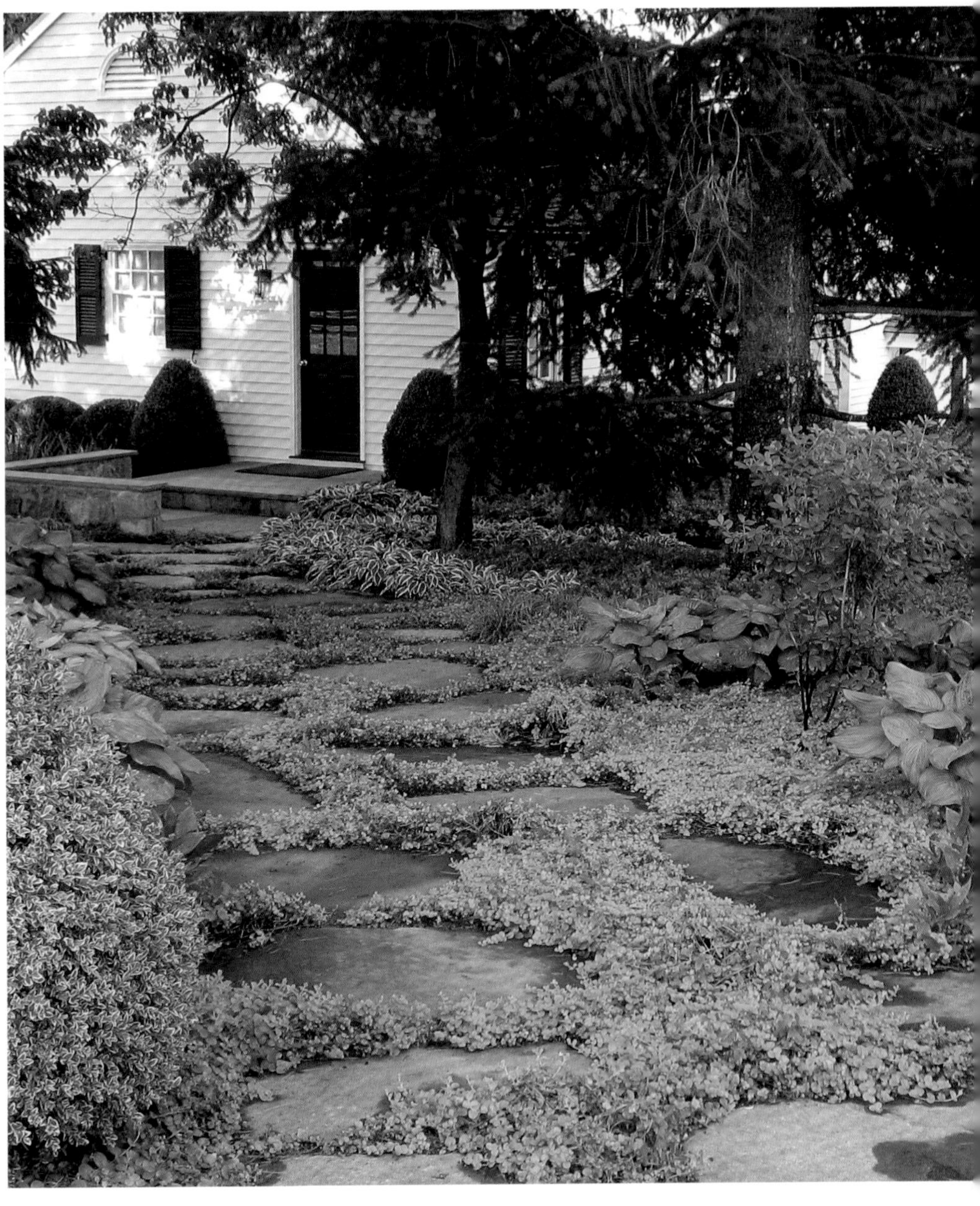

RIGHT AND BELOW Meadow plantings of gloriosa daisies and *Verbena bonariensis* surround the pool house; their colors complement the fabric on the furniture, by interior designer Richard Keith Langham, while the pool house itself, designed by architect Paul Marchese, is meant to evoke an orangery in reference to Versailles.

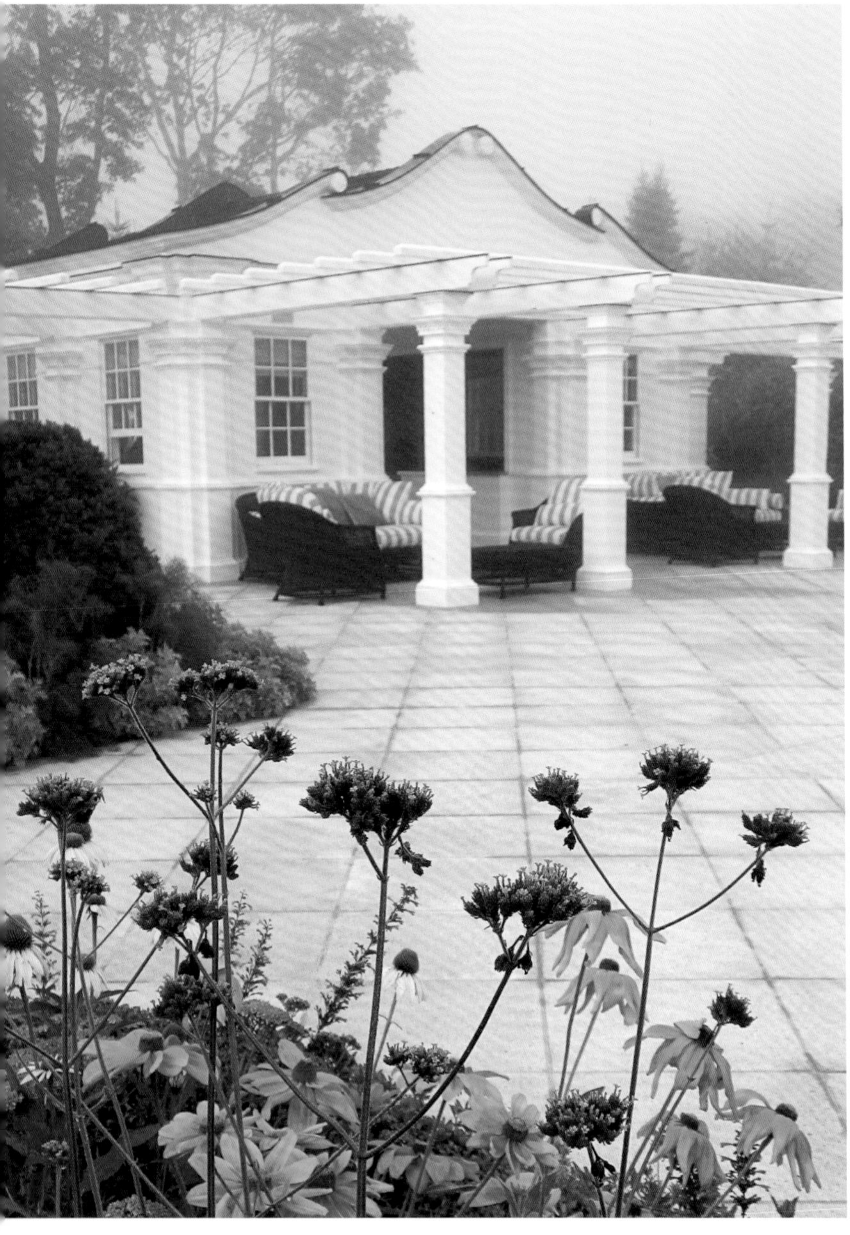

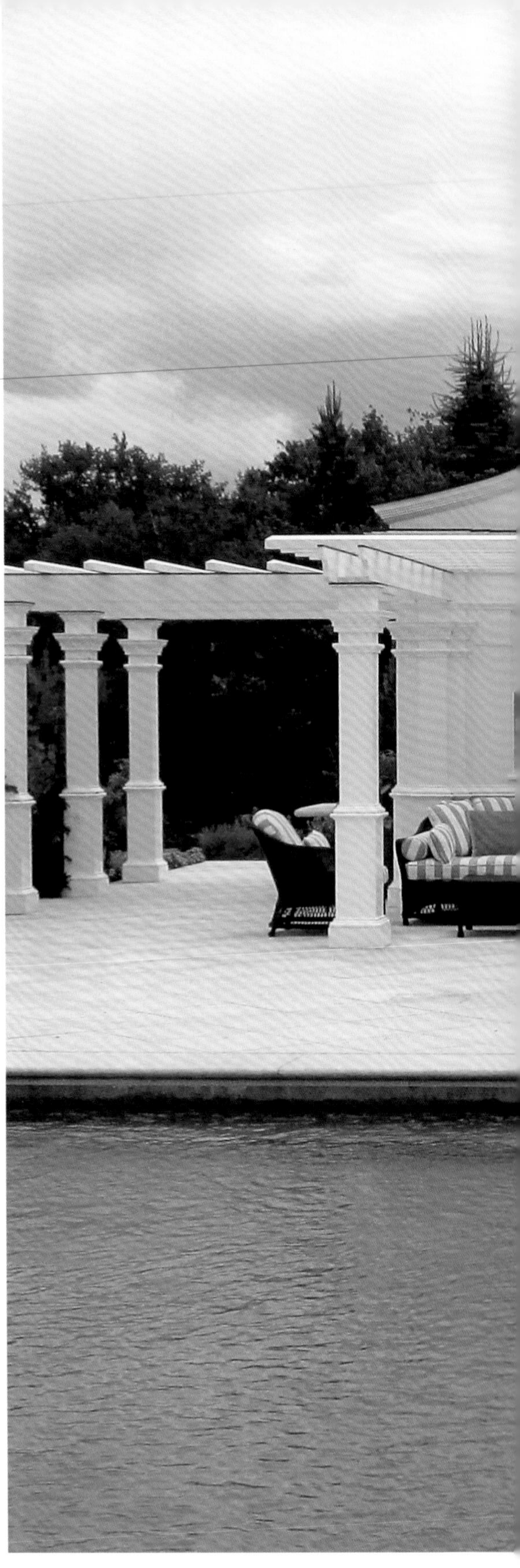

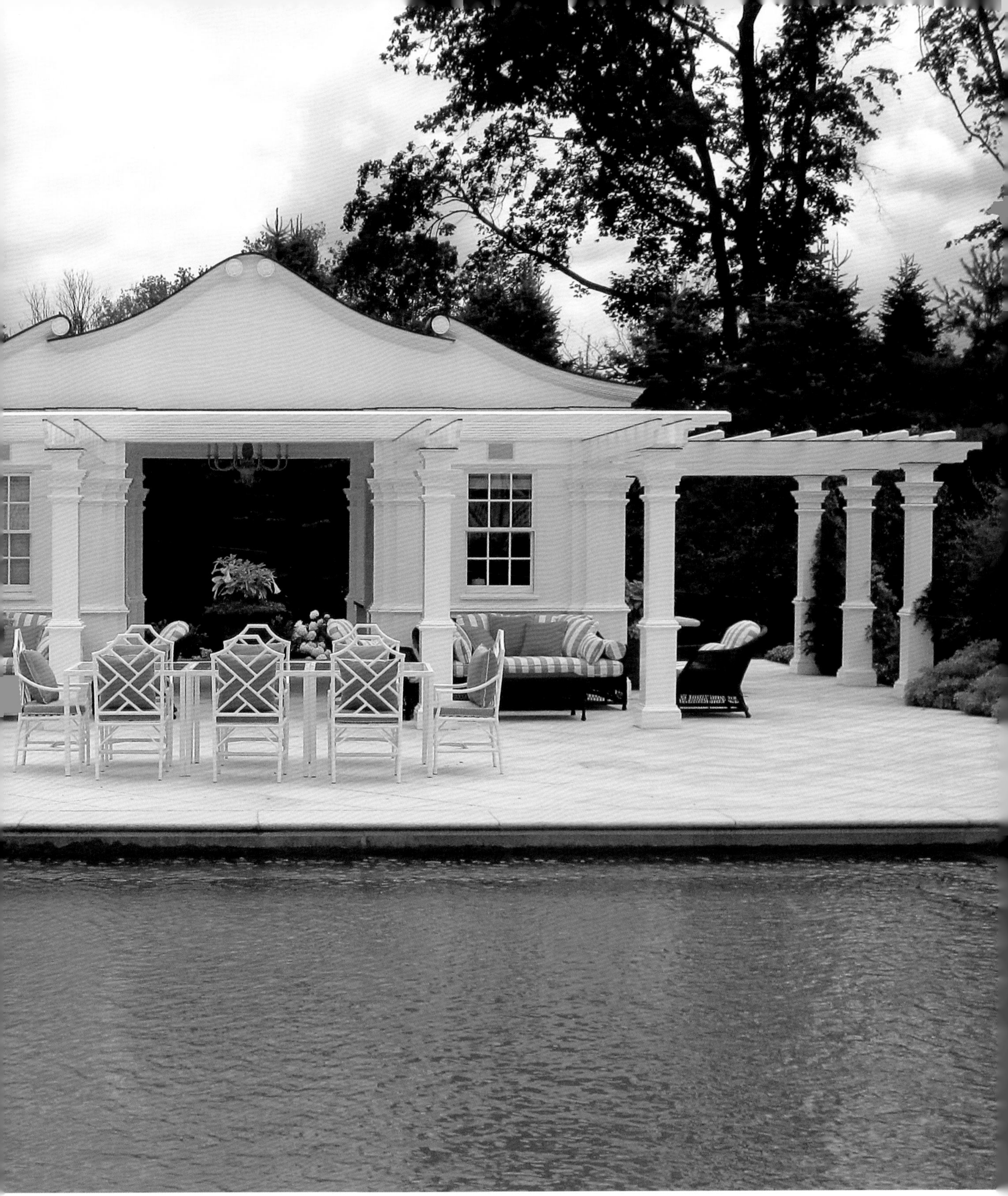

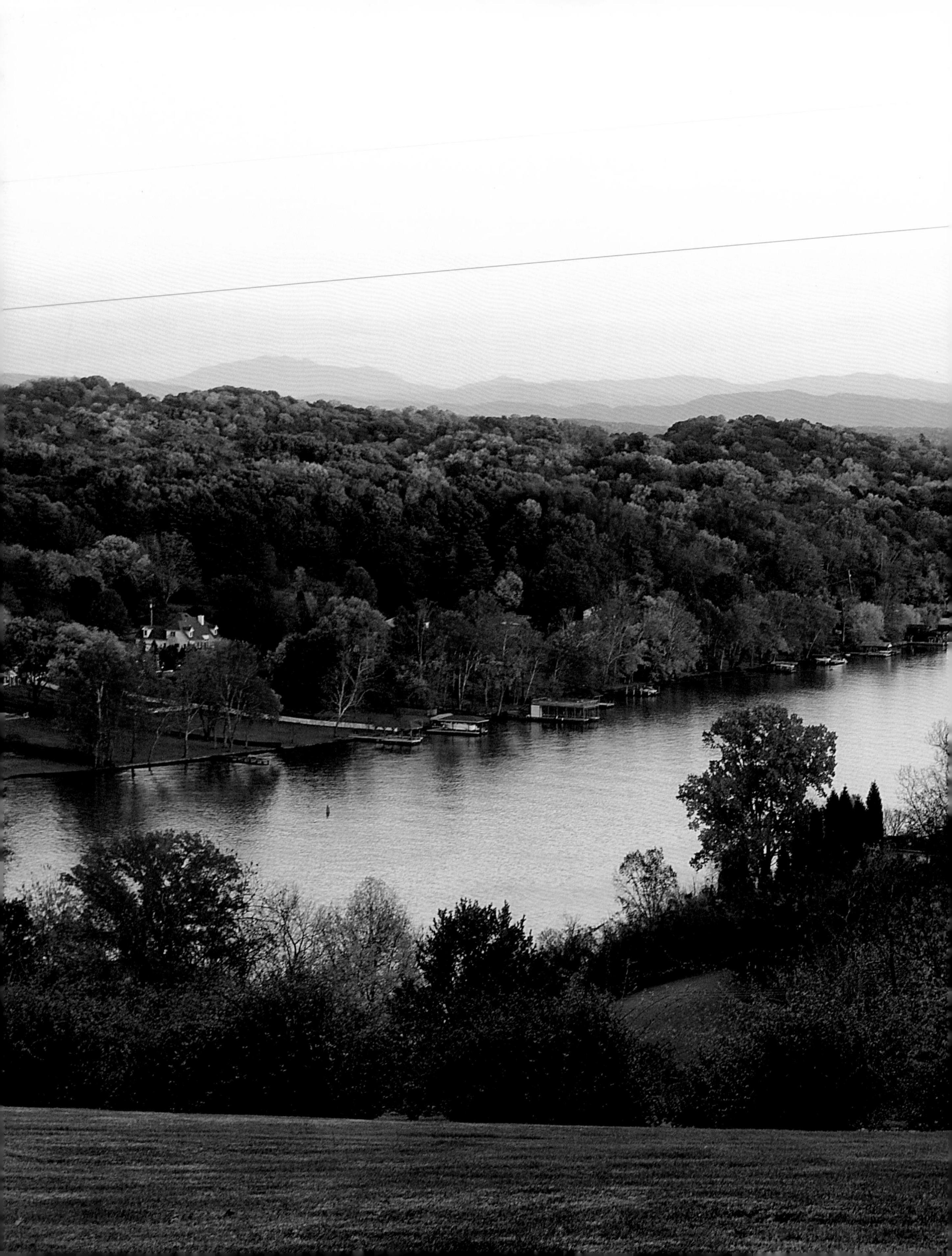

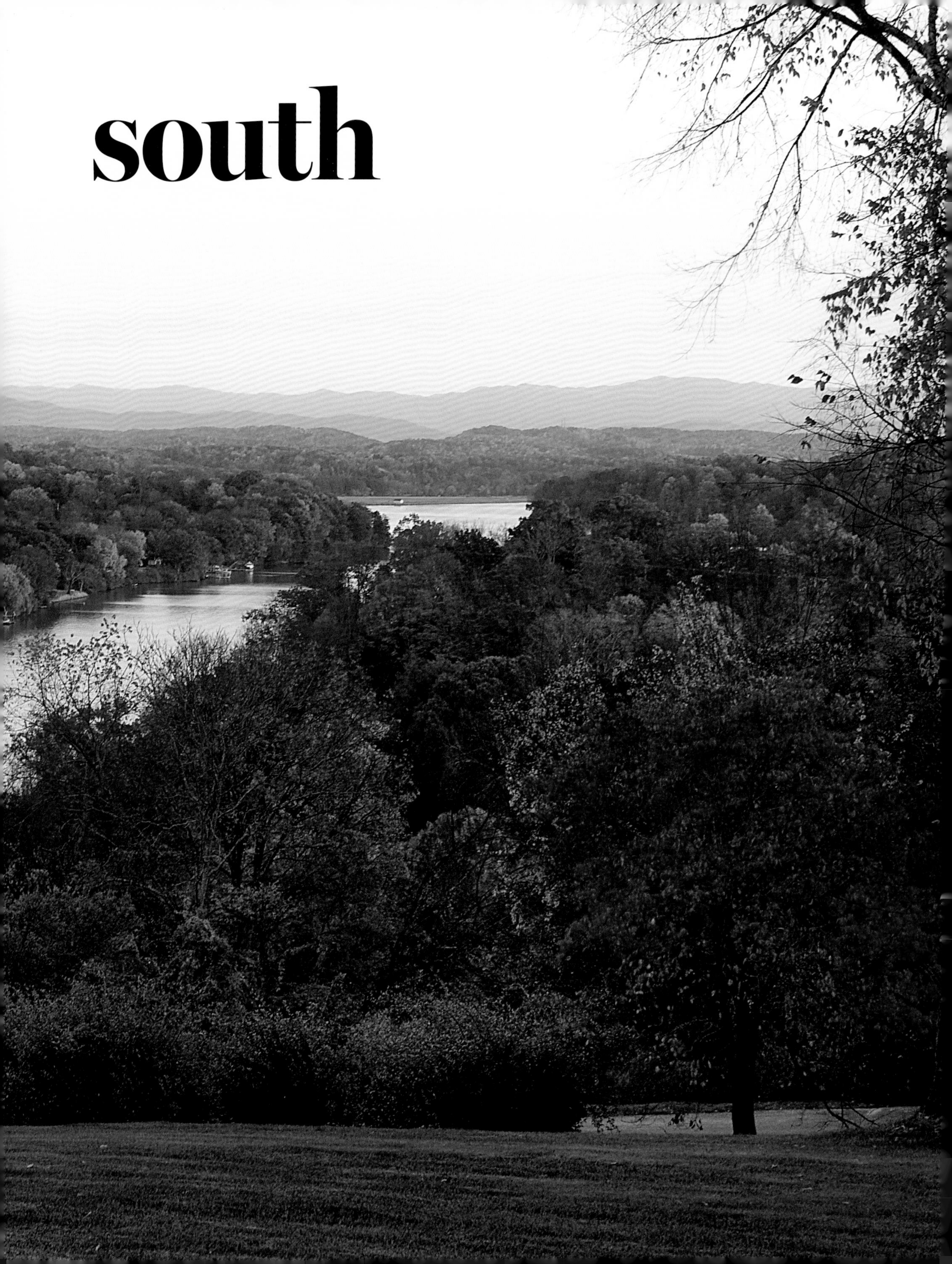
south

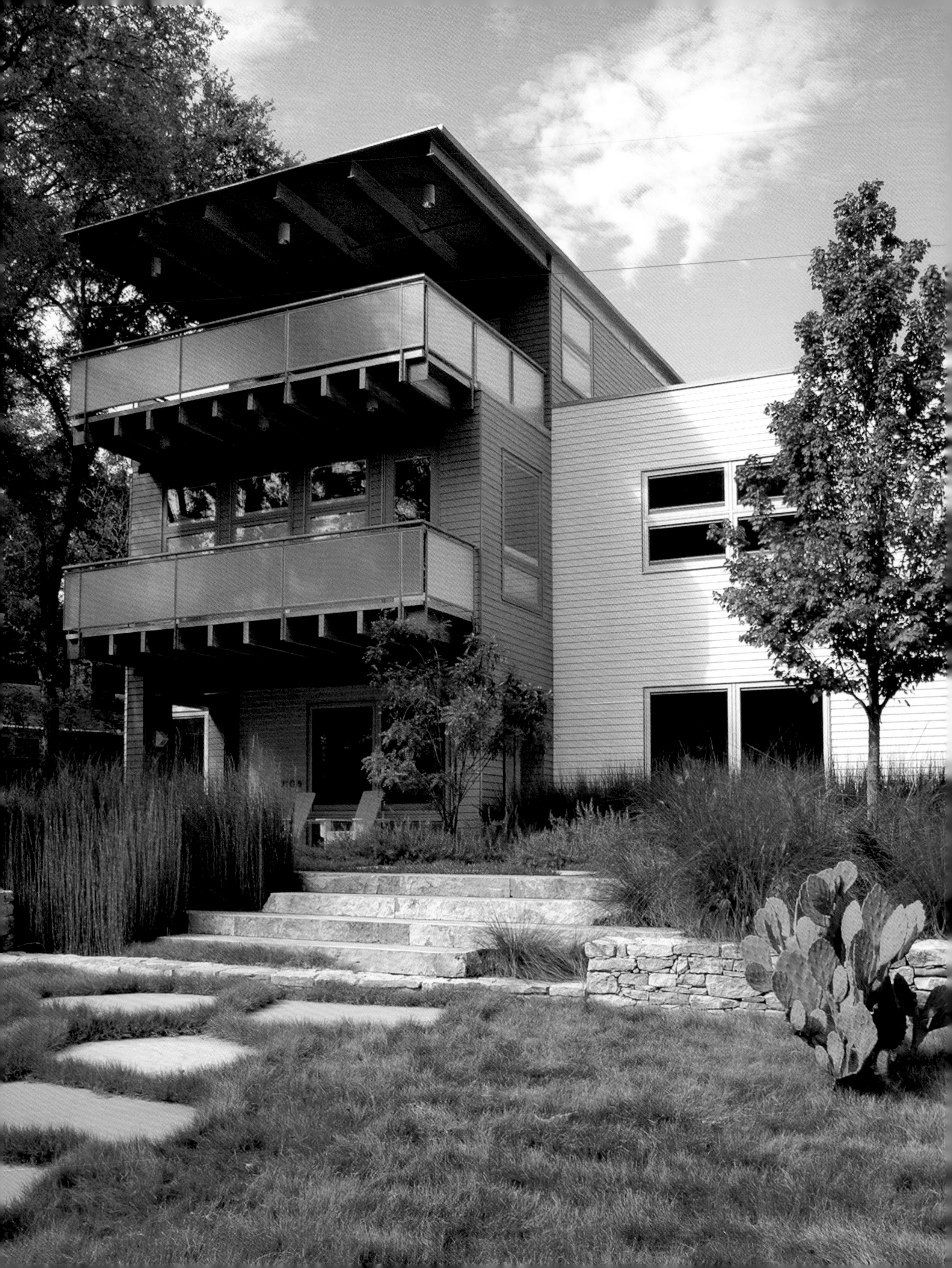

Landscape architect David Hocker's design challenge for this property on Dallas's White Rock Lake, a 1,015-acre reservoir, was to revitalize a vacant lot as it was replaced with the first ground-up construction in this small neighborhood in over fifty years. "The landscape was the catalyst to create a positive dialogue between the modernist house designed by architect Gary Cunningham and the surrounding community," Hocker says. "My goal was to create a landscape that complements the park and lake beyond with native and adaptive plantings."

Oversized Lueders limestone slabs punctuate the landscape and form pathways that provide guidance and direction throughout the garden; a subtle mow path also defines the connection from front to rear. Hocker used a low fieldstone wall to suggest an informal sense of separation and boundary. A break in the wall guides walkers to solid limestone block steps leading up to a grassy plinth. This plinth creates an extension of the entry porch and provides a gathering place in front of the house. A limestone block bench completes the space by adding intimacy and human scale.

A screened porch behind the house provides a retreat within a contemplative rear garden. A serene oval trough of a pool is tucked into the landscaped terrace outside the porch, and a Laminar jet hidden in a grove of golden bamboo nearby shoots water into it, masking noise from the neighborhood beyond with its own gentle sound as it breaks the surface of the water. The pool is surrounded by large, irregularly shaped limestone slabs fitted together with grass joints that highlight their unexpected forms.

The fence enclosing the backyard is a modernist interpretation of the iconic picket fence—it substitutes steel pipe for wood in a sculptural, serpentine line that weaves in and out of the landscape. The seamless rhythmic appearance of the fence is broken by a large pivot gate allowing entrance to the garden.

Hocker's landscape studies at Texas A&M University were enriched by two semesters in Italy studying design and architecture. While there, he met and married his wife, from Lucignano, in Tuscany. The couple regularly returns to her home, and Hocker continues to study and be inspired by the region's vegetation and landscaping. He says this project "was informed mainly by the classical influence of formal Italian gardens, but was softened by Tuscany's rustic agricultural heritage, and is reinterpreted with the plant life and aesthetics of Texas."

Hocker made a point to utilize native and adapted specimens to limit water use and keep the garden as low-maintenance as possible. Strong seasonal interest keeps the garden colorful and full of wildlife all year.

Hocker says he grew up working with plants and the outdoor environment, which led him to devote his life to becoming a landscape architect. "My philosophy—or obsession—follows Mies van der Rohe's statement 'God is in the details,' and by keeping it always top of mind, I hope to never lose my constant curiosity about how things work or are put together."

BELOW The rear garden features a tranquil oval pool with a delicate jet of water that emerges from a bamboo grove, creating a contemplative mood. **RIGHT** Leuders limestone pavers in free-form shapes make a pathway from the rear garden, where grass is kept clipped, to the outside of the fence, where the turf evolves into a lawn of natural buffalograss. **OVERLEAF** The area between the street and the fieldstone wall is dotted with colonies of *Yucca pallida*, echoing the grasslands of the natural lakeside setting.

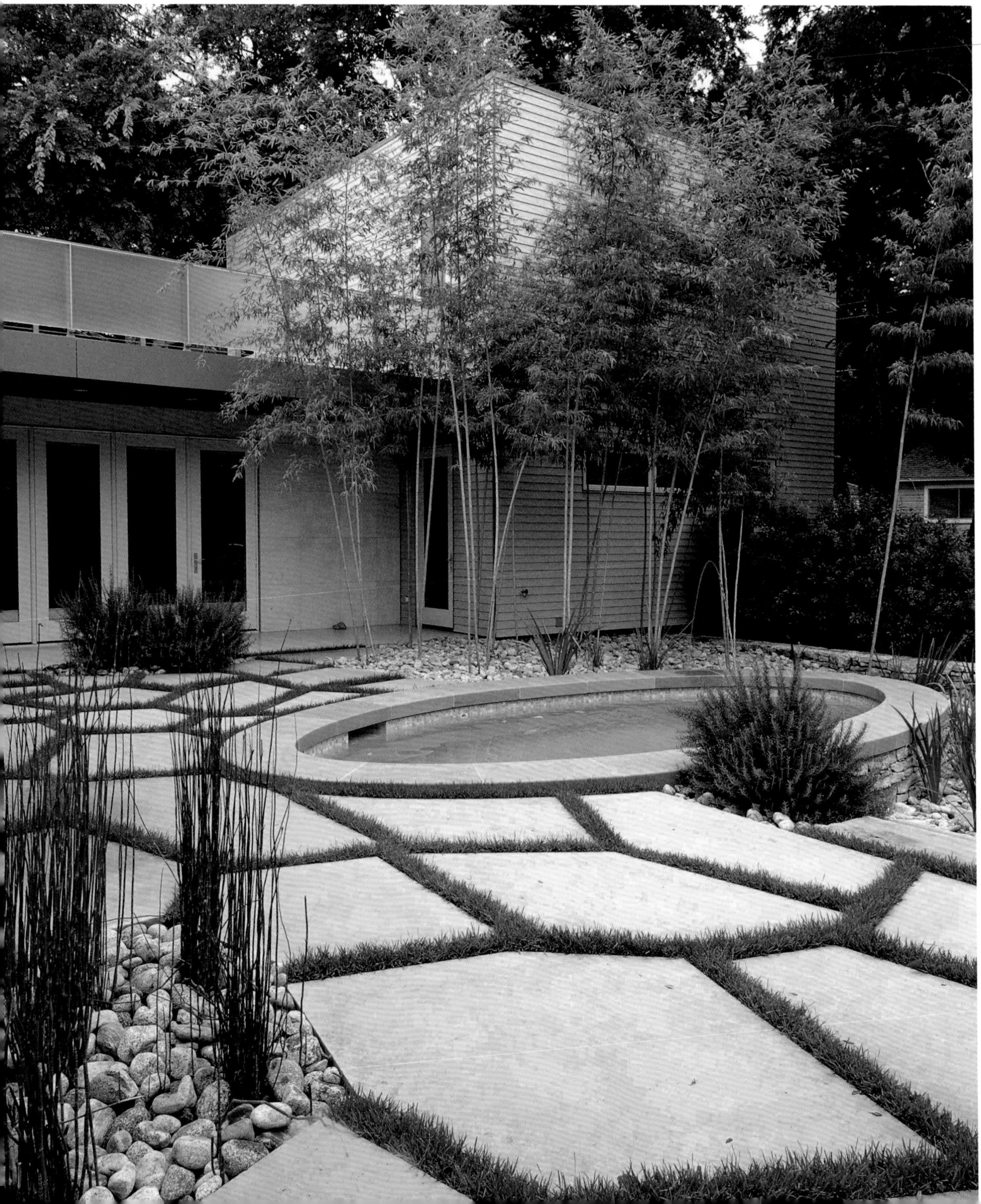

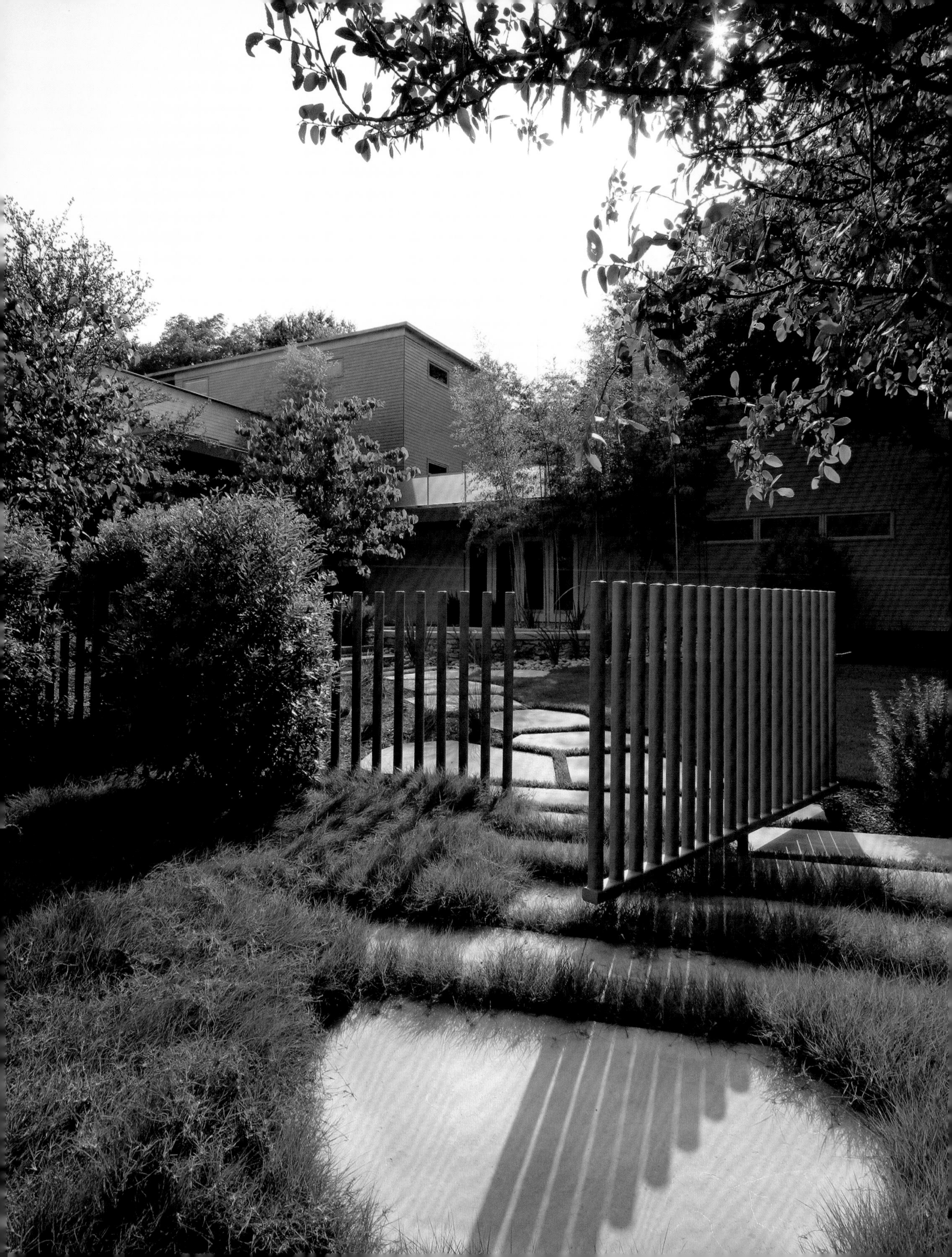

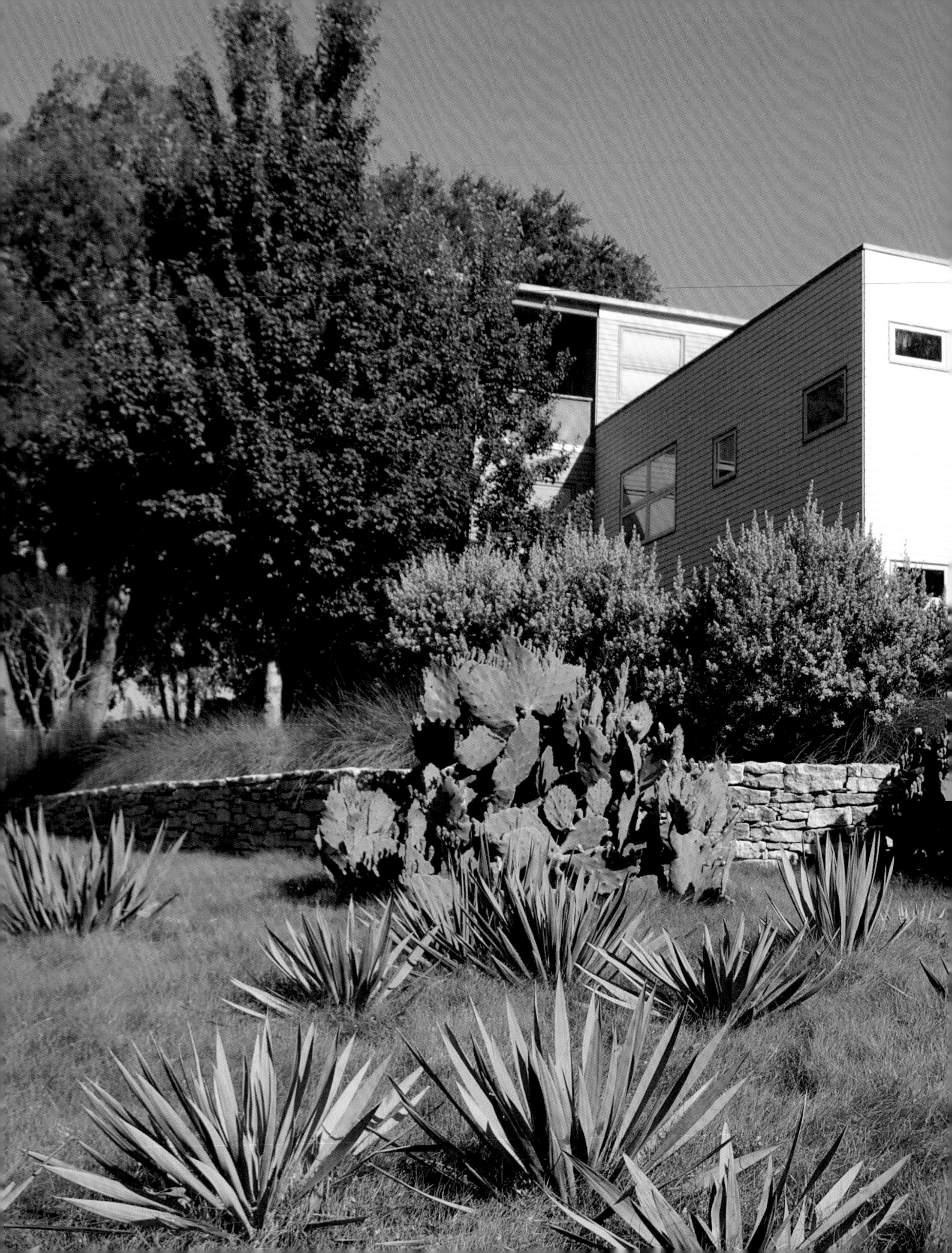

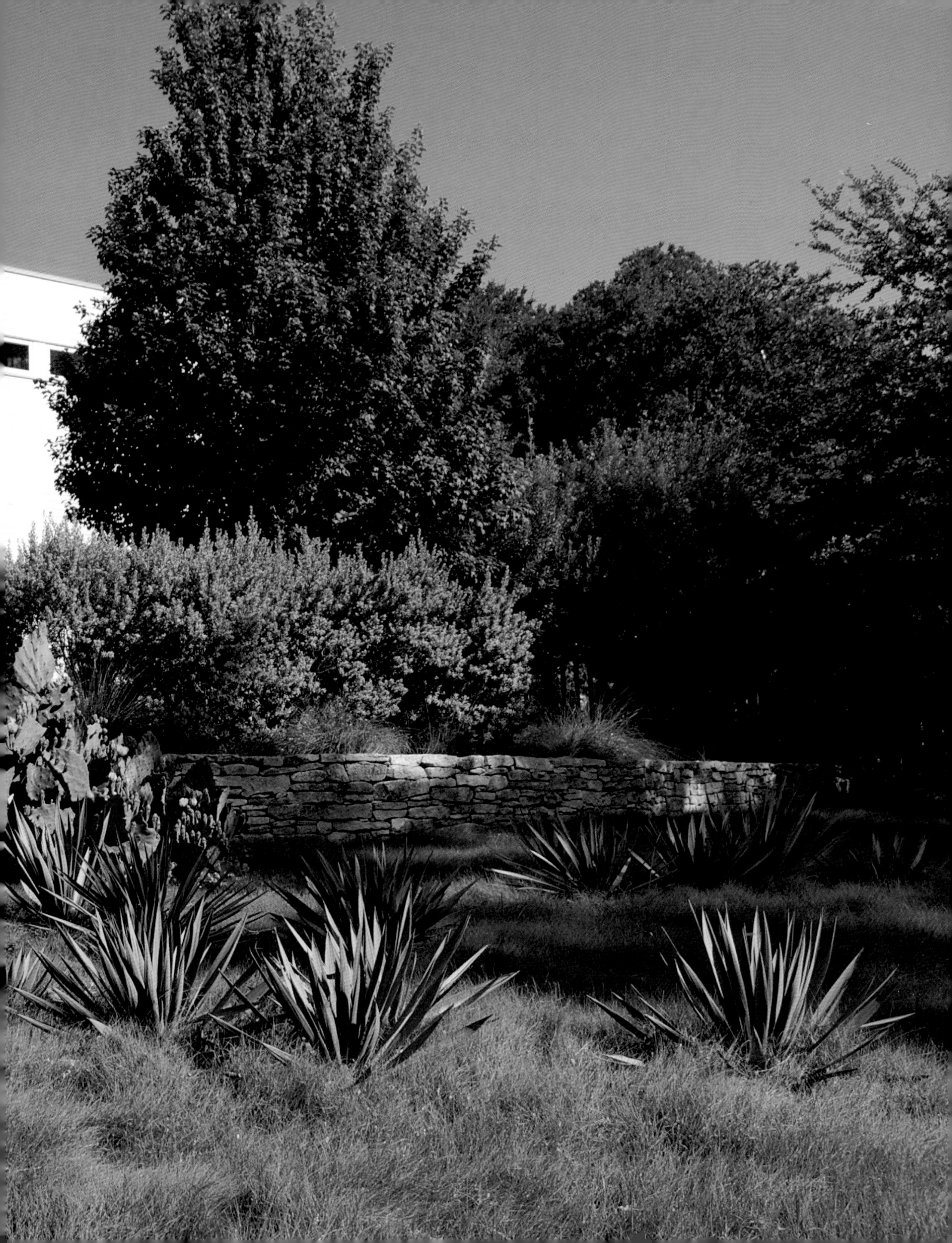

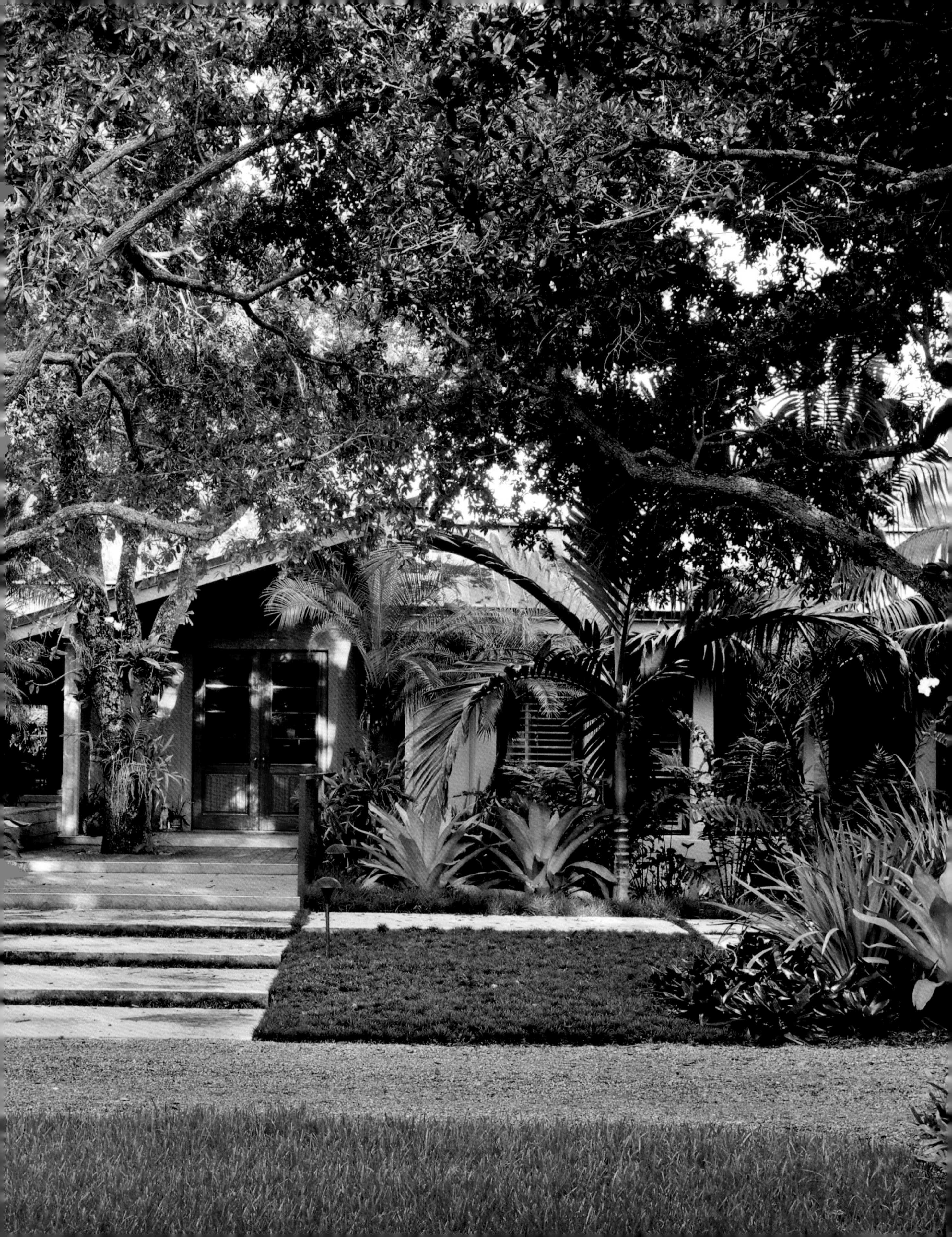

Architect Mark Hampton brought in landscape architect Raymond Jungles as his partner to design a seamlessly fused indoor-outdoor living environment for this Miami property, knowing that Jungles's sensitivity to architecture and his work—widely admired for its simplicity—would fit well with the site's modern house.

What was an outdated 1960s South Miami home with no remarkable landscaping to speak of is updated with contemporary touches and a Zen-inspired garden. There is also better accommodation for parking, greater privacy from the neighbors, and outdoor living spaces have been created in areas of the yard that previously went unused.

Shadows from branches of mature live oak trees paint a playful, moving texture on the new drive, which replaced an existing suburban-like circular iteration that previously crowded the house and placed parking in unpleasantly close proximity to the front door. "I pushed the driveway farther away in order to create a ceremonial garden entry to the home," Jungles says. "This was achieved by building a wooden deck around an existing mahogany tree and adding elevated, asymmetric concrete steps pressed with rock salt, to give depth and texture. Sand screens installed along the driveway also create a softer, more natural appearance."

The clients desired ample open lawn areas, which Jungles achieved while maintaining privacy by creating a dense, verdant background of native plantings along the periphery of the garden. Staghorn ferns thrive in the crooks of the mature live oaks, and color-rich clusters of bromeliads spread underneath. This thick border also creates habitat for wildlife.

The existing swimming pool was in a less-than-desirable location in relation to the redesigned house, so Jungles created a new outdoor entertaining area, swimming pool, and barbecue to link the garden hardscape with the house's floor plan. After conducting a series of site studies, he replaced the existing swimming pool with a sculptural, bubbling water feature to enliven the outside dining area and to shield this corner lot from the noise generated on the surrounding streets. The outdoor areas now present many different views into the garden, where a meditative aura reigns. "A play of scale and texture of leaf and plant forms was a predominant design element," Jungles says. "Color is interspersed as if by an artist. Within the streams of color, hypnotic sounds echo throughout the garden from the water element."

The swimming pool was extended out onto a previously unused part of the site, thus increasing the potential for enjoying the property. "The swimming pool is not only inviting for swimming," Jungles notes, "it becomes the visual focal point for the most heavily used areas of the residence—the kitchen and living room. Much thought was given as to what forms the pool's surface would reflect in the daytime, what natural and artificial light would reflect at night, and how the reflections would fall."

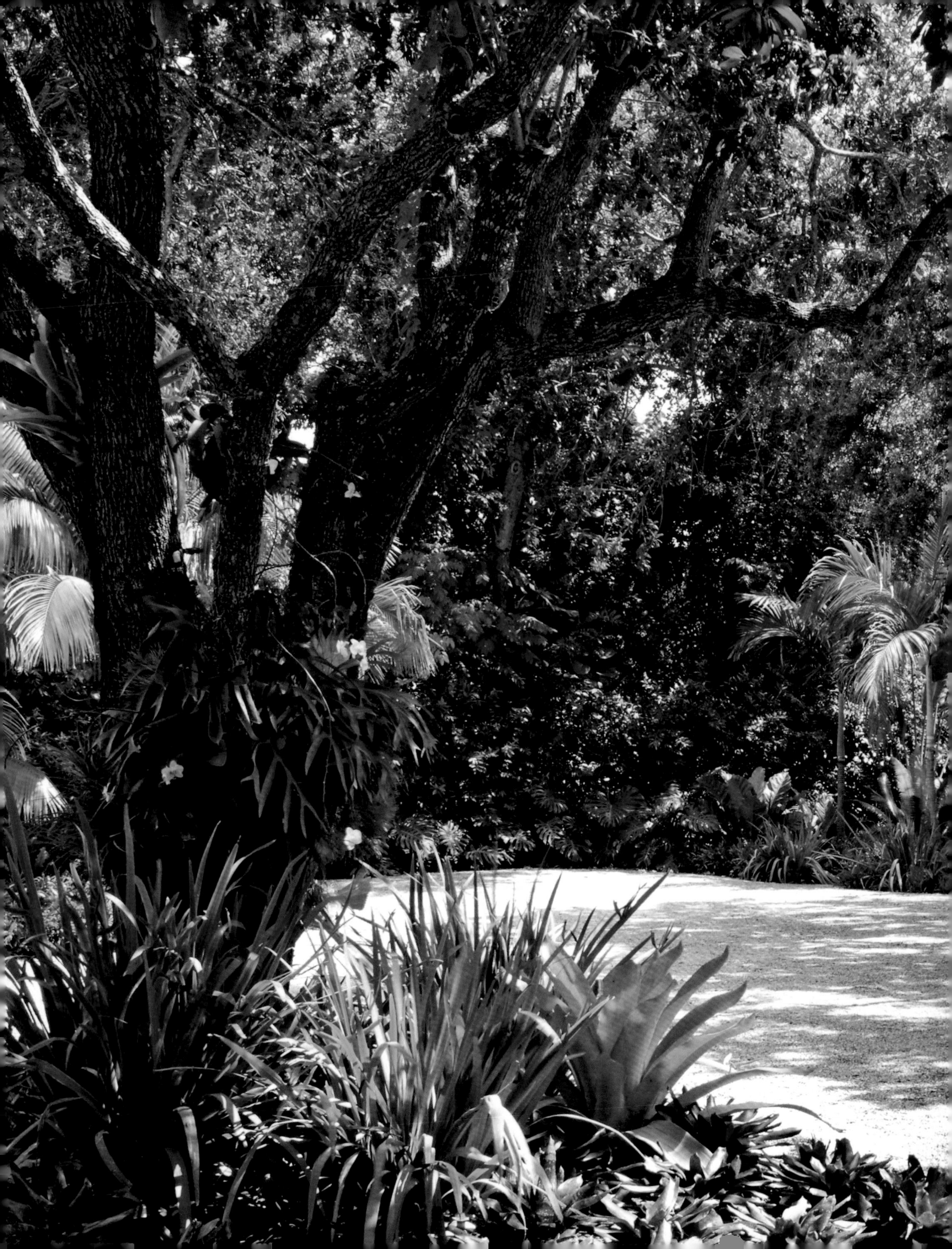

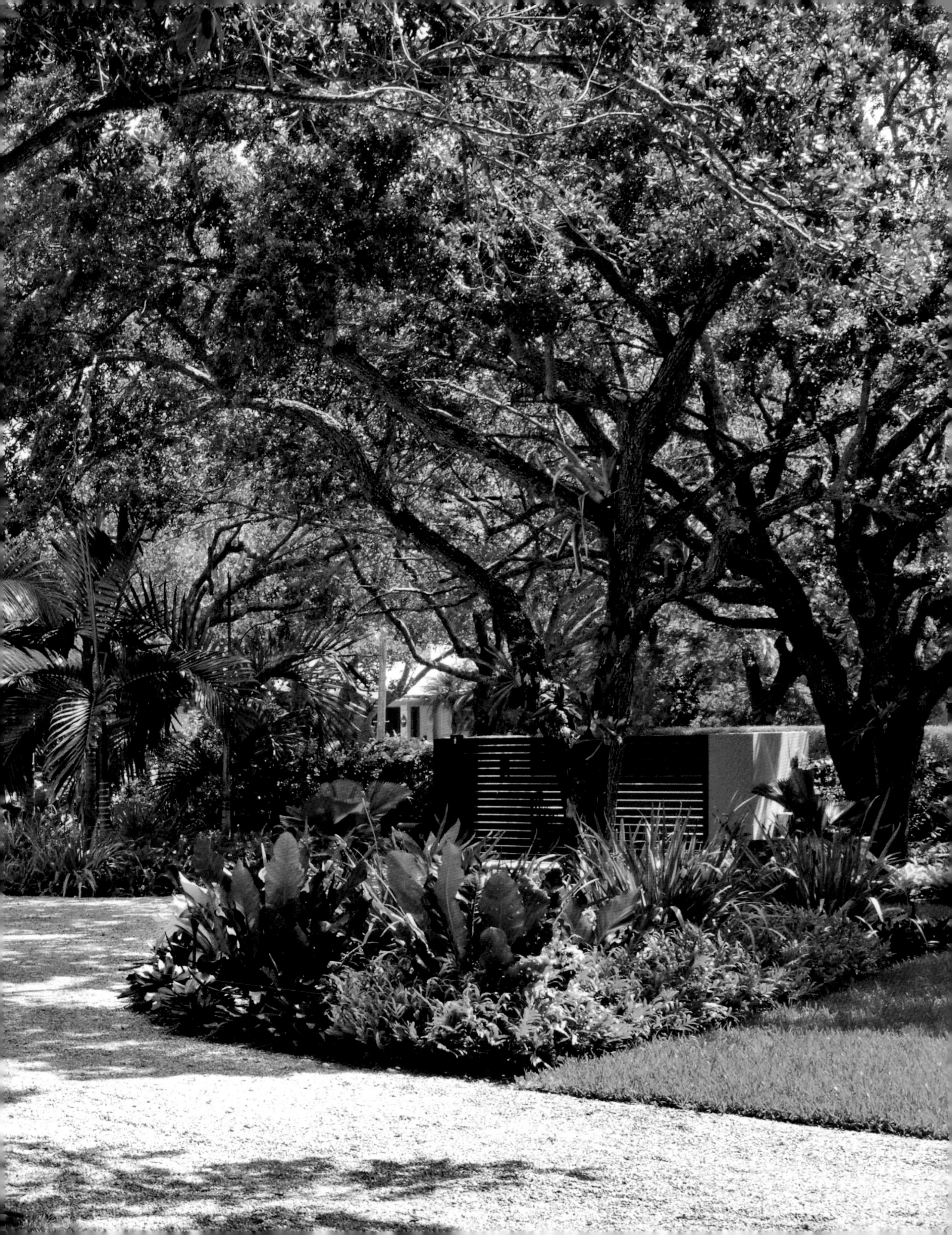

RIGHT A modernist water feature installed on the site of a former swimming pool makes hypnotic sounds that echo throughout the garden as water trickles down its rough stone sides. **BELOW** The walk from the drive to the house is planted with tropical specimens that yield much close-up interest. **PREVIOUS PAGES** A shady ceremonial entrance to the house, created by pushing the path of the original driveway away from the house during remodeling.

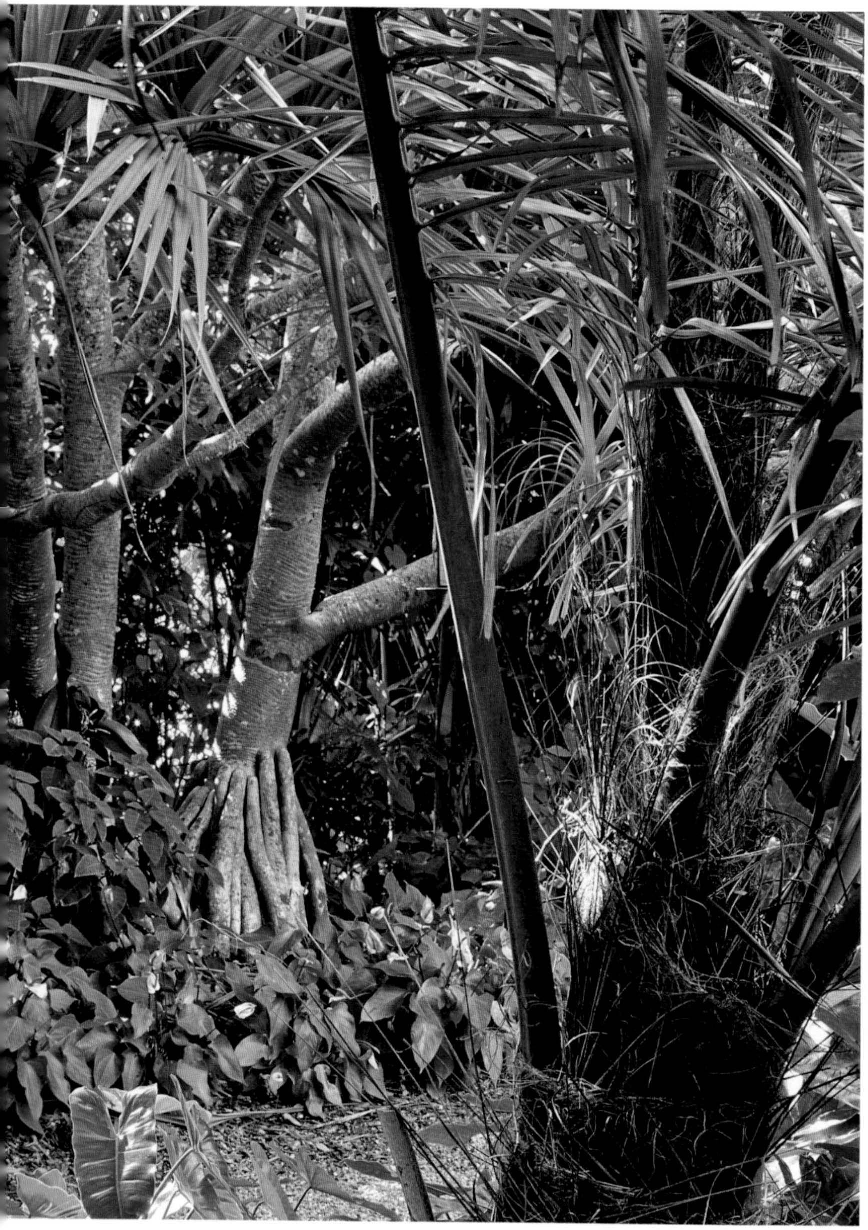

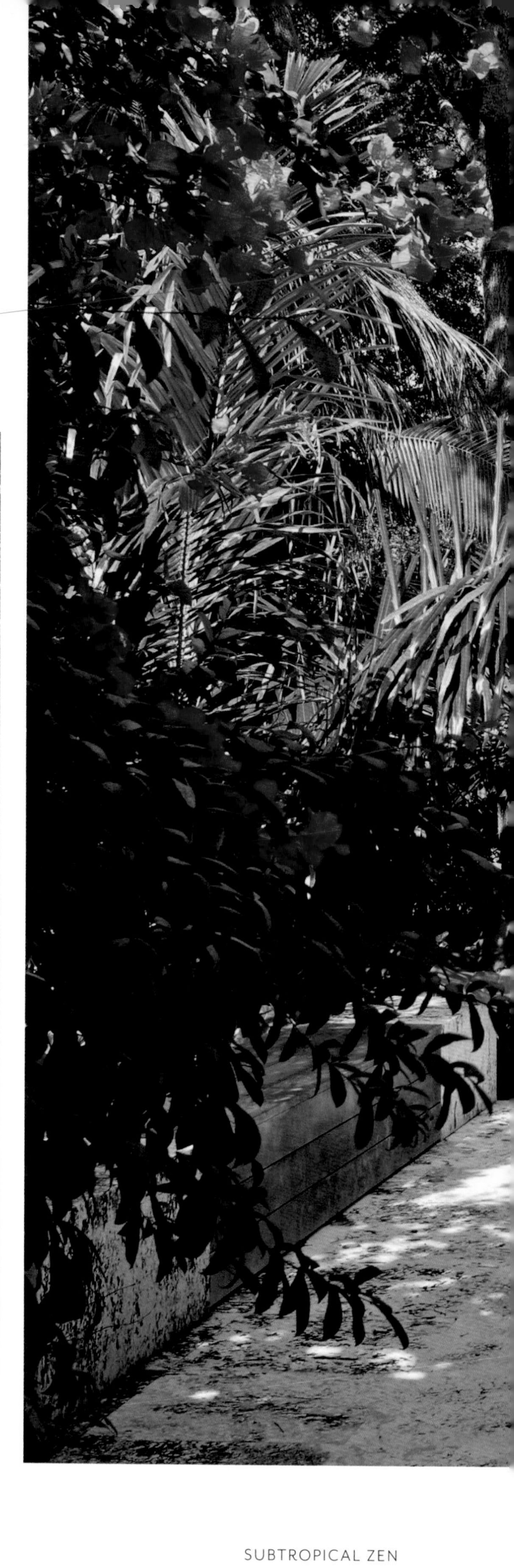

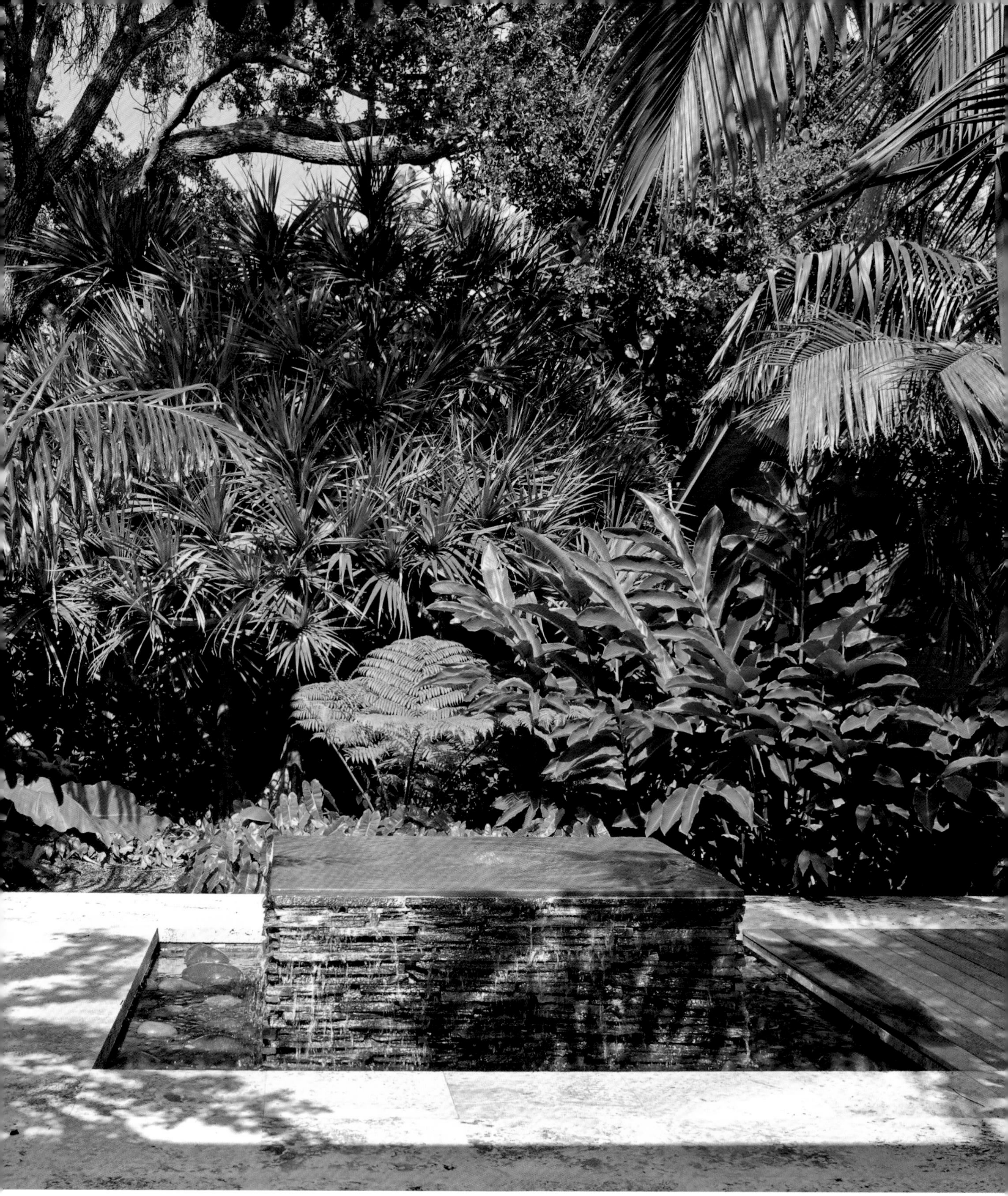

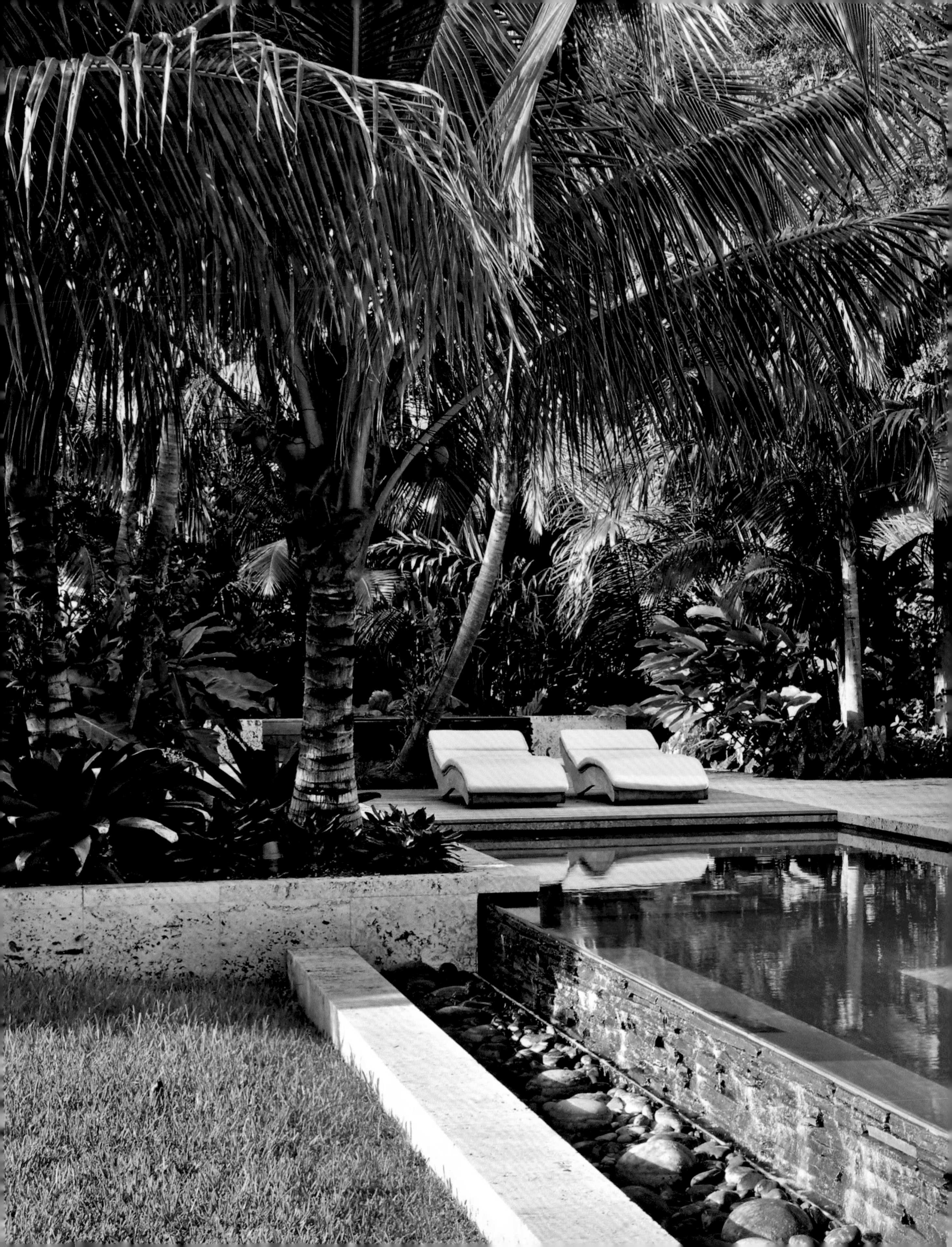

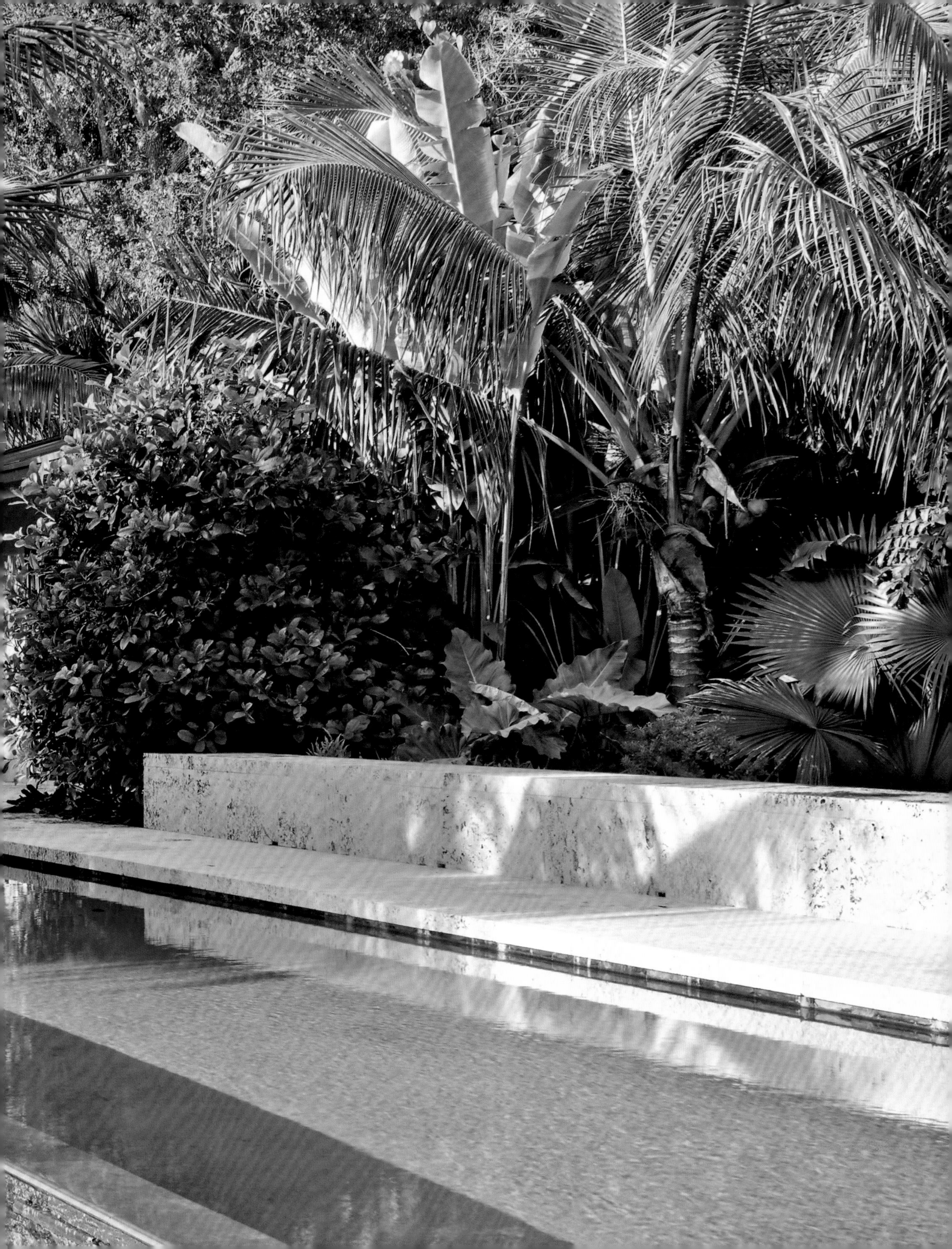

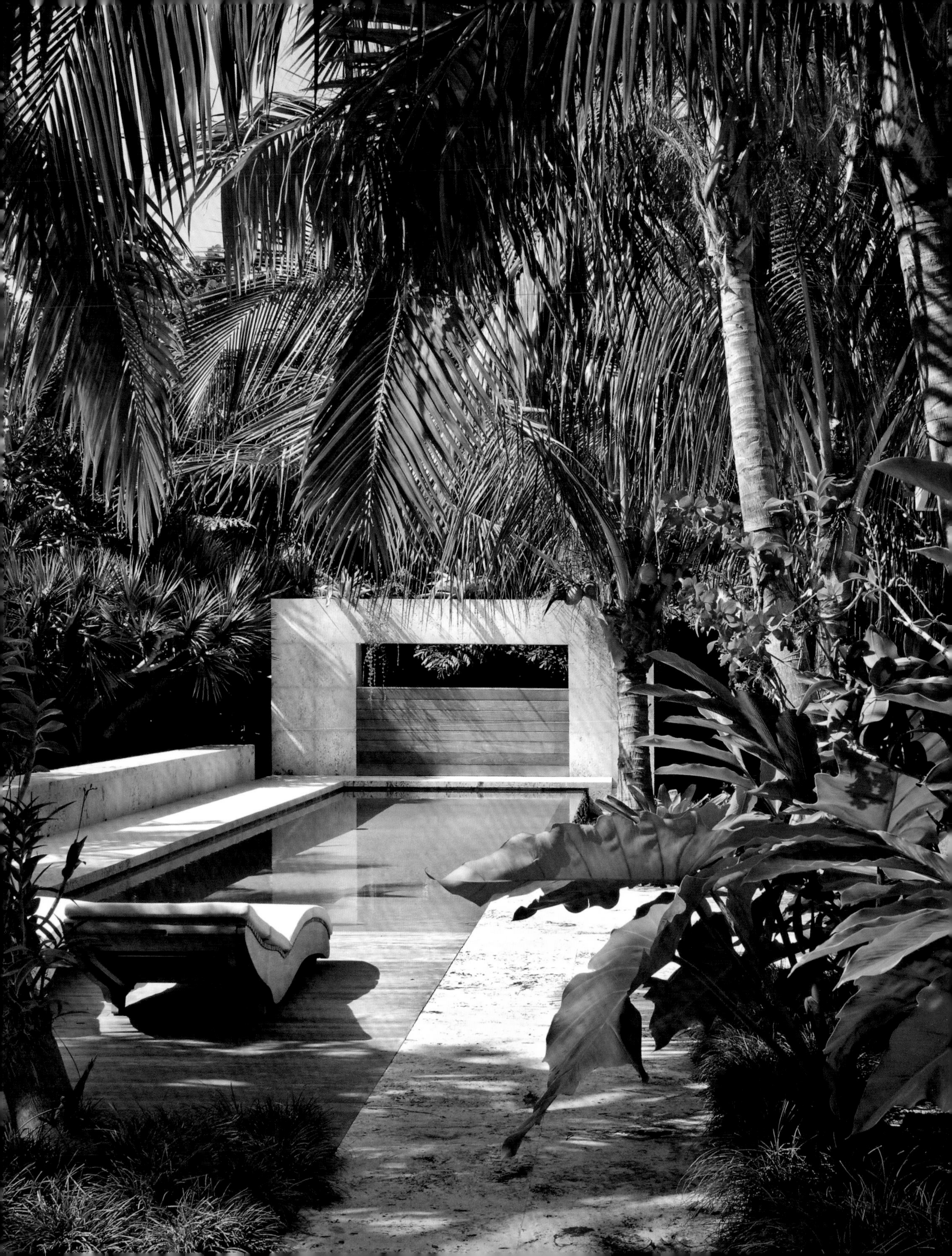

BELOW Lush tropical plantings, including arum, a grove of palms, bird-of-paradise, and ginger, create an intimate entry path. **LEFT** Strong, simple architectural forms complement the bold textures and colors of tropical plants in the backyard, including palms, gingers, bromeliads, and orchids. **PREVIOUS PAGES** Dramatic foliage, the play of shadow and light, and ever-changing reflections help to make the swimming pool the yard's visual focal point.

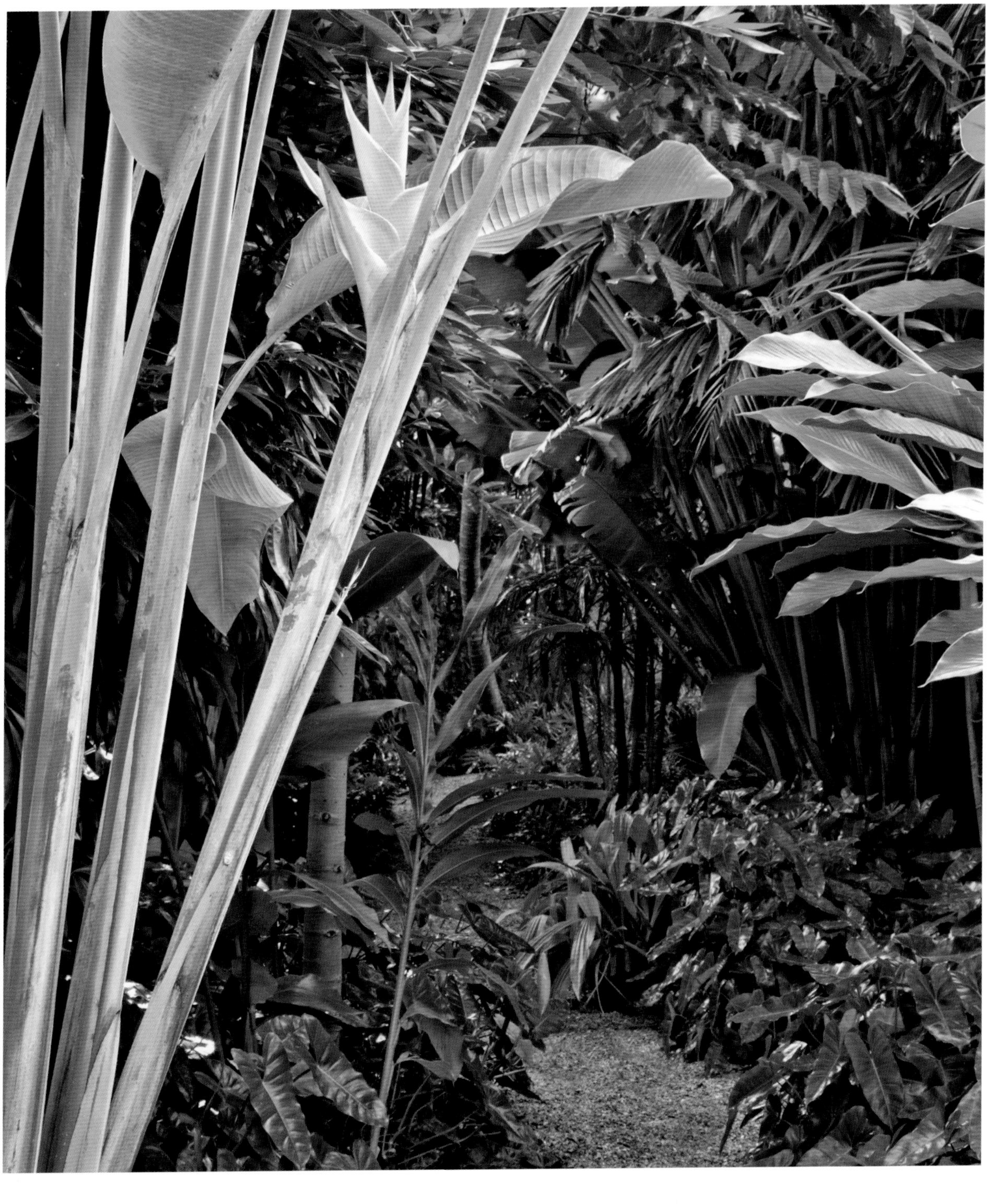

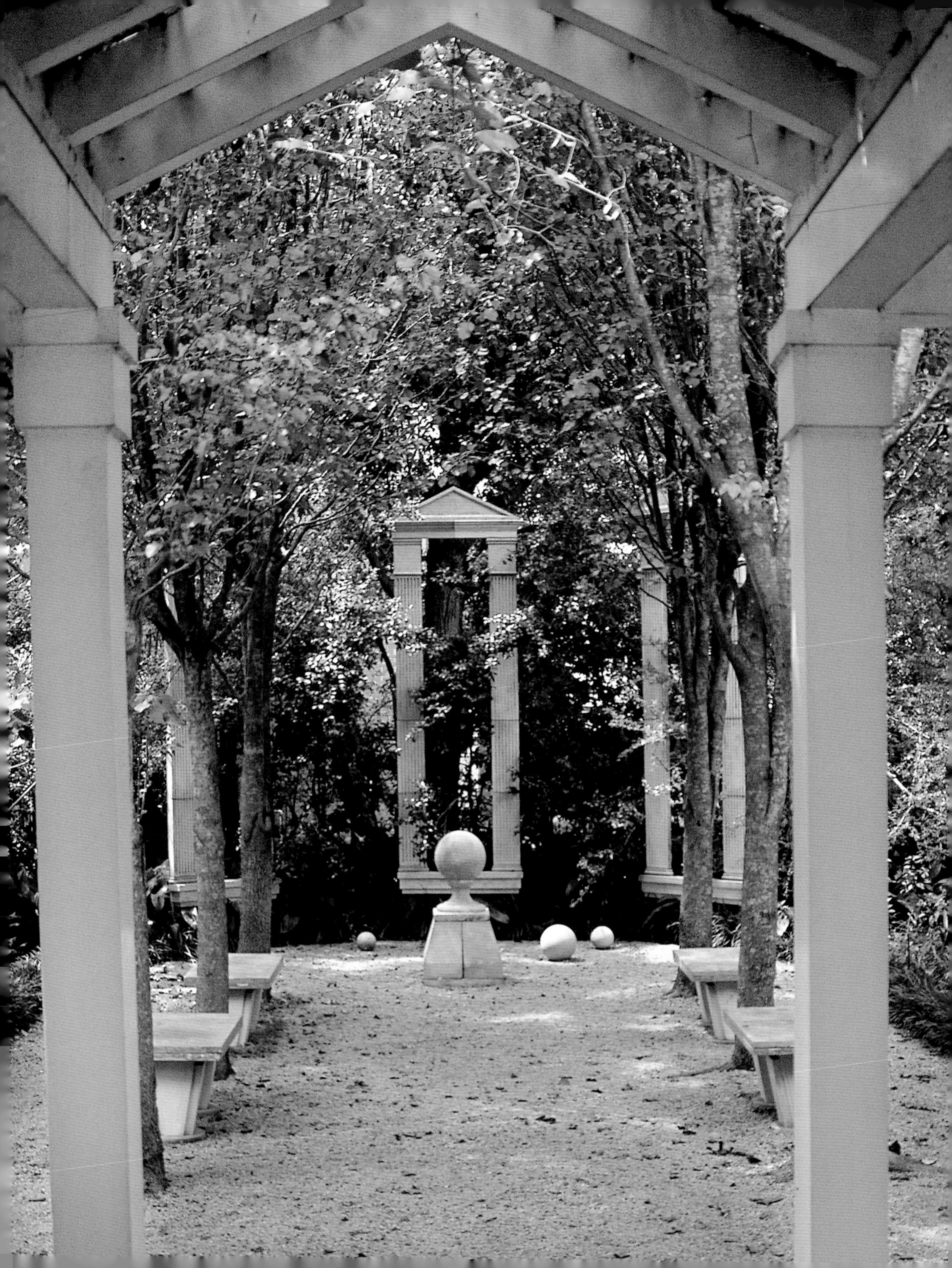

H ouston architect R. Michael Lee purchased his 1937 Colonial house in 1976. To gain a sense of arrival, he added brick pillars flanking the front walk, topped with concrete planters, which he says were "designed under the influence of Frank Lloyd Wright and his Prairie School." Instead of a solid surface for the front walk, Lee envisioned something "softer," a desire that eventually led him to consider a pile of unused clay tiles behind the garage. After counting and measuring, it became apparent he had just enough to stretch from the street to the porch. He finally decided to create a grid pattern, with open spaces for planting dwarf mondo or monkey grass. "It looks high maintenance but is virtually no maintenance," he says.

A porch and arbor on the south side of the house are the point of departure for an allée of Bradford pear trees. Architectural follies in the form of oversized window frames that seem to float in a semicircle mark its end. Immediately west of the allée, custom-designed bonsai stands lift the little trees to chest height—ideal for appreciating their character. "I wanted something simple that would not compete with the bonsai," Lee says. "The trays have a rim so they hold water, which helps provide the humidity woody tropicals need. I have a ficus from China that is close to a hundred years old and a Korean hornbeam that is even older."

A meandering path leads west from the bonsai to another of the garden's main features, a pond with floating blue glass balls and koi. "The fish are very large and all have Japanese names," Lee says. "They are like pets to me." Along the path and at other strategic points in the garden, the Japanese motif continues with granite lanterns filled with candles, whose gentle light is the only source of illumination in the evenings.

The aviary node, one of the garden's most prominent features, is directly behind the house. Its roundness formalizes the garden's curvilinear components hinted at in the meandering pathways, a satisfying counterpoint to the rectilinear lines of the house and the allée. The aviary itself, home in warm weather to a collection of tropical birds, stands 12 feet tall by 12 feet in diameter. It is designed so that when temperatures drop to freezing the structure can be wrapped in plastic to protect the tropical plants inside.

A railroad right-of-way that abuts the back of the property constitutes a quasi-public garden. "It was derelict and unloved," Lee says. "I gradually cleaned it up and began planting—Louisiana iris in places that are wet in the spring, old roses, thirty different kinds of citrus, a collection of rainlilies and crinums, and over forty ginger plants. I am a frequent visitor to a factory that fabricates concrete columns and other architectural pieces; they have a boneyard of leftovers and I pick up pieces to create different kinds of raised beds for this area. There's also a picnic table, and my neighbors are free to enjoy this part of my garden any time they wish."

BELOW Brick and flagstone paths invite exploration; Japanese stone lanterns light the way at night. **RIGHT, ABOVE** The aviary is home to exotic birds and plants. **RIGHT, BELOW** A bench overlooks a pond, one of Lee's favorite features—he has named every koi.

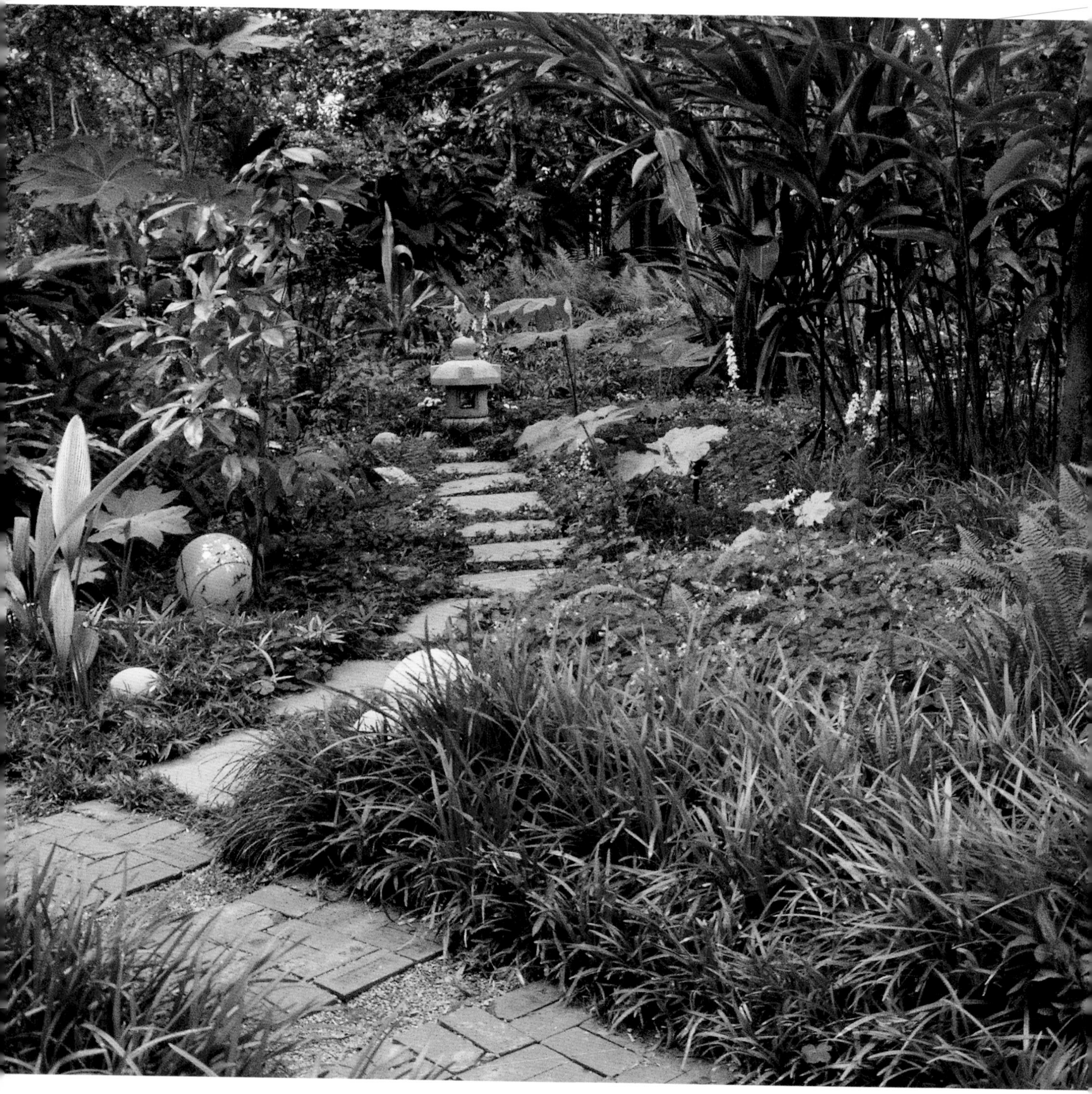

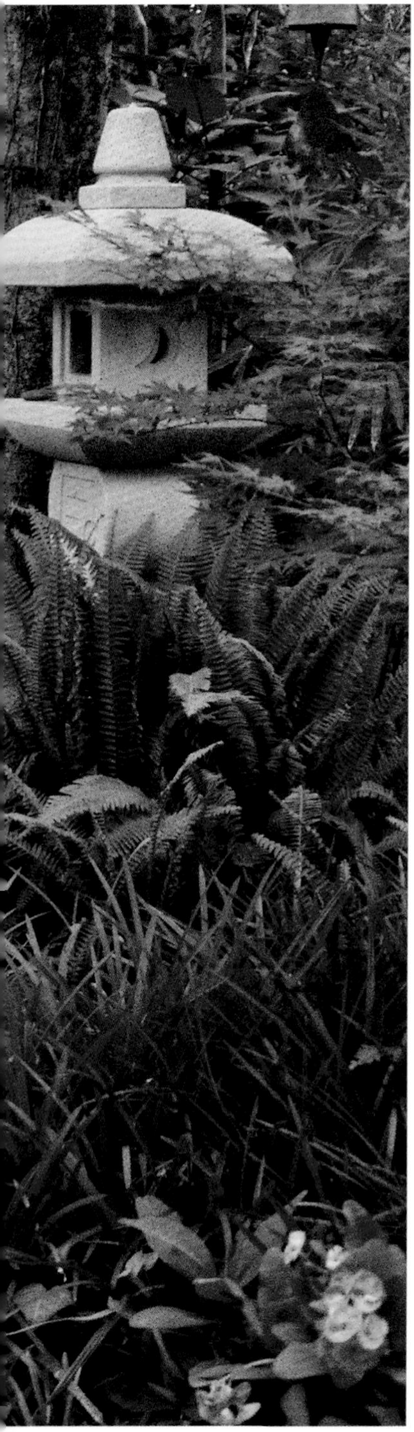

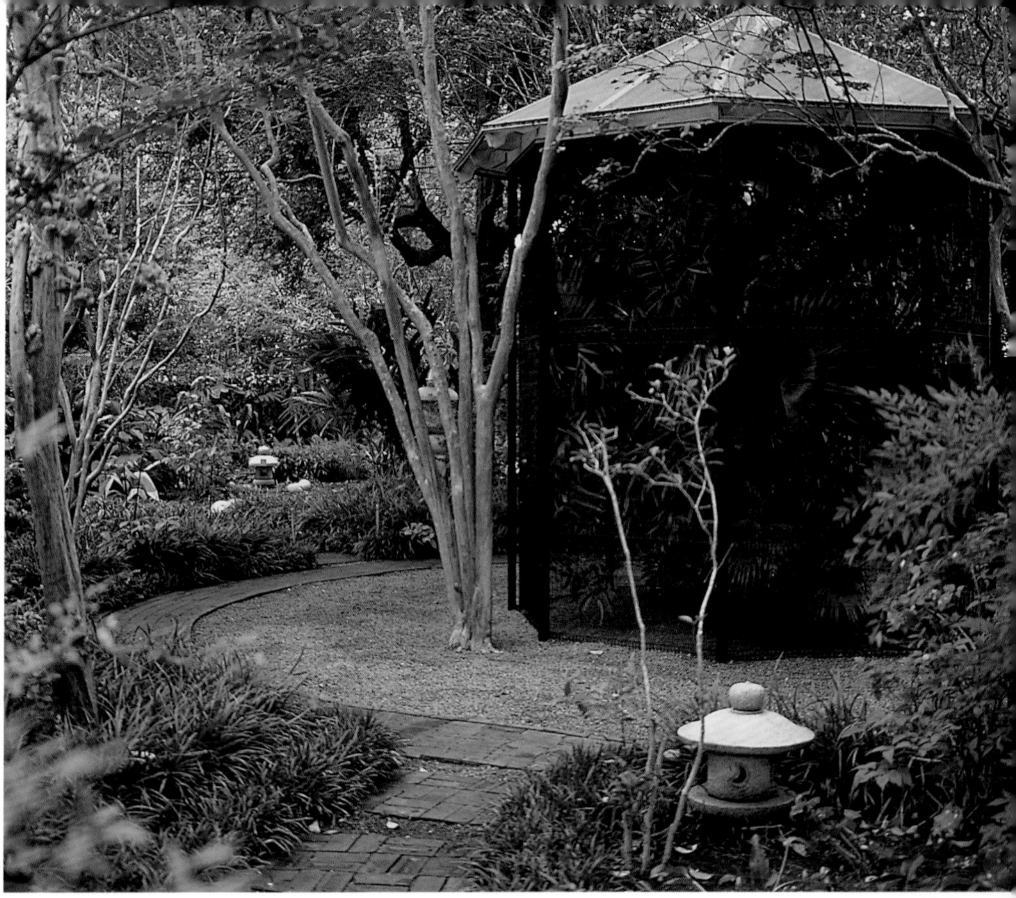

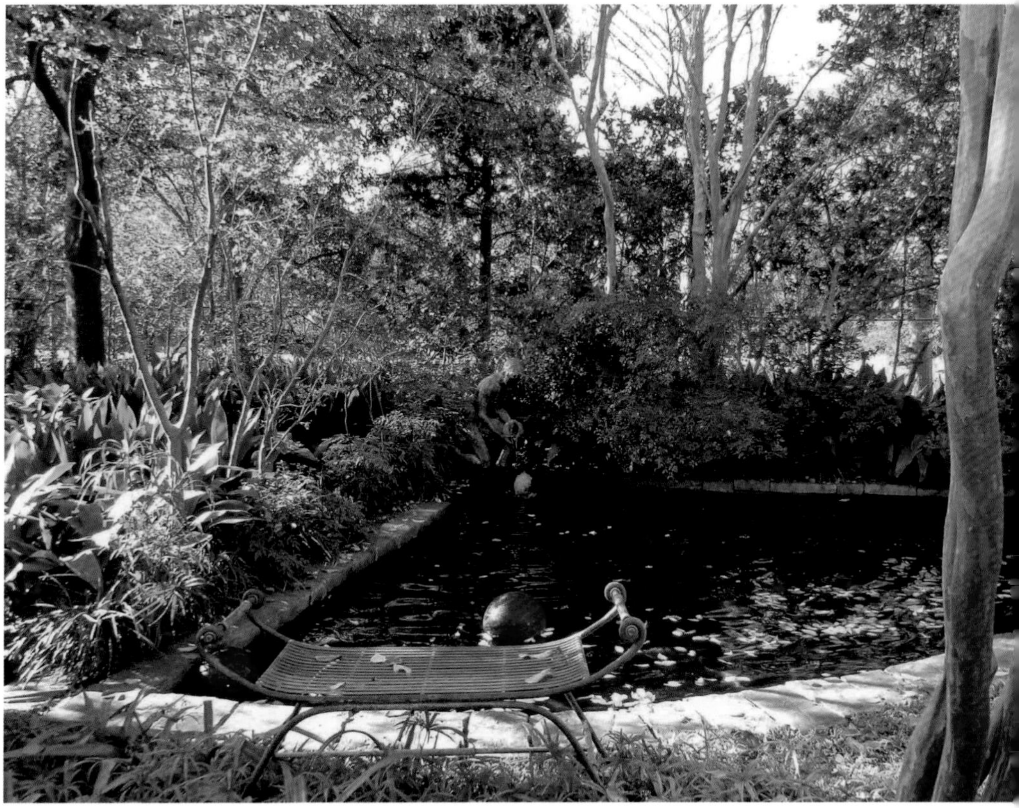

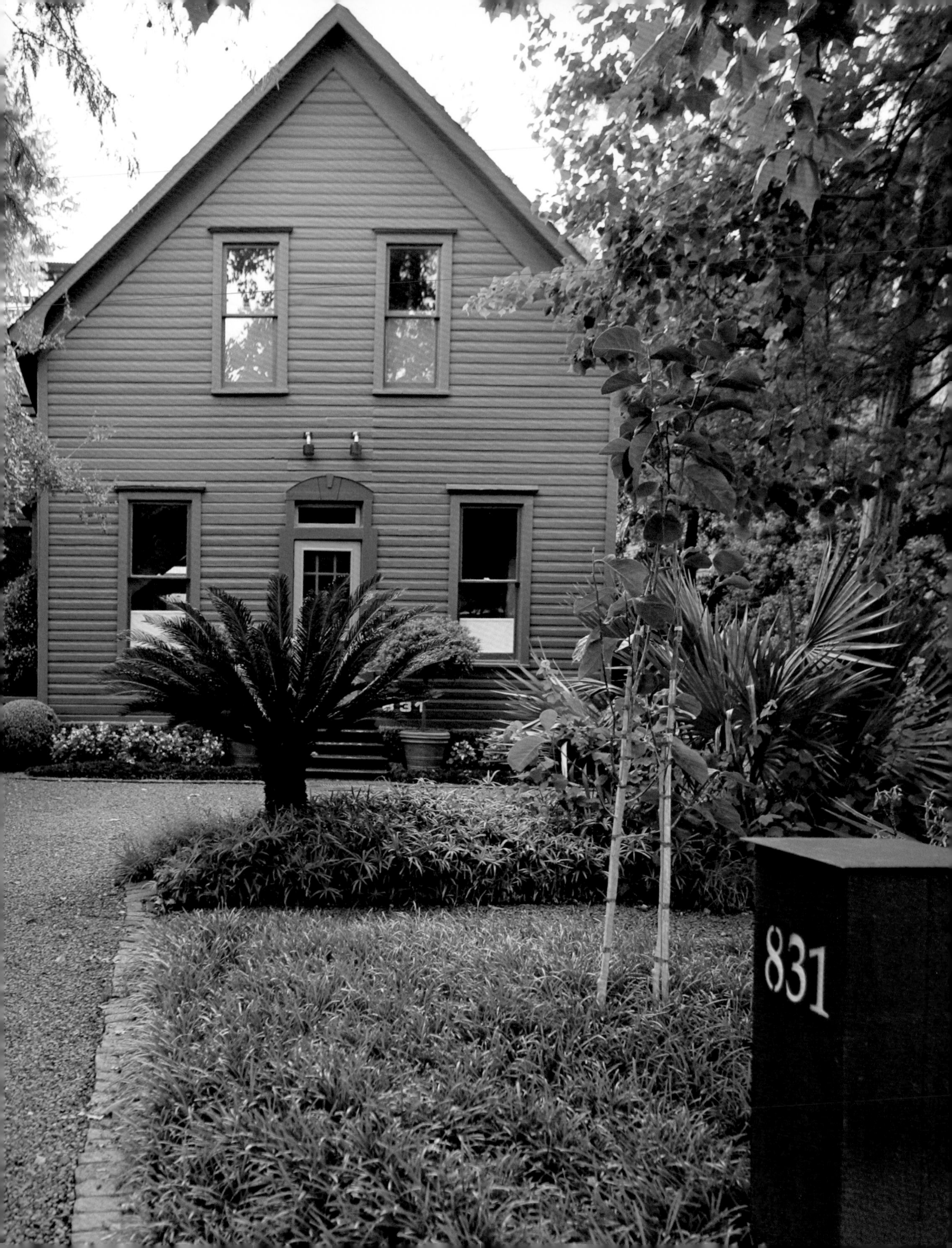
831
831

Houston landscape architect Mark McKinnon went looking for a contemporary house in 1988, but wound up purchasing a 1907 house instead. He admits, "This home is the one that was meant to be—the lot was the most heavily wooded on the block, so I built on what was there."

A gate made from bronzed plowshares opens onto a walk along the south side of the house, the birch alley. It adds to the sense of arrival, though its real gift is to the interiors. "In all seasons the light and shadow play is exceptional," McKinnon notes. "Sunlight piercing delicate green shades dances on the interior surfaces of a morning reading room, stairwell, and dining room. In the fall, the yellow foliage intensifies the mango walls of the dining room. Midwinter, the walls of the morning room match the Gulf Coast winter blue sky visible through the peeling birch branches."

A covered porch on the west side of the main house, overlooking the lawn and water garden, serves as an all-weather entertaining area. An 8-foot-high breezeway connects the main structure to a garden house, completed in 2004, for his mother. "From the beginning I knew a breezeway would be key to the project for permit purposes," he says. "The project became an 'addition' to the original home." Each dwelling is 1,400 square feet, yet they both feel larger, thanks to carefully planned views into the yard. Thick vegetation around the property's perimeter maintains privacy on the urban lot, however.

The yard's other most prominent features include a sunken water garden and lawn. The self-contained sunken water garden does more than please the eyes and ears. Storm water is directed to its main basin, filtered first by the gravel paths around the structures that serve as French drains. Heavy storm runoff overflows this basin into a second storm basin, allowing it to slowly percolate into the ground. The water in the main basin is filtered as it is recirculated through a fountain and a raised container planted with potted red-stemmed thalia, black *Alocasia,* and maidenhair ferns. As these plants fade in the fall, white calla lilies emerge and bloom from late winter to May. There is also a 35-foot-high lookout tower with a translucent roof to allow light in. McKinnon considers the tower the main organizing feature of the garden. "I like to get up high and experience the long vista," he says.

"The gardens are important to me for hearing and olfactory engagement," McKinnon says. "As I age, I find I become more sensitive to noise and its stresses. Sound from the flora and the fauna the garden attracts is fascinating—it offers a connection with nature unusual for a city setting. Day and night, sitting on any of the terraces, or inside with the doors and windows open, the sounds soothe. Bamboo rustles. Birds, crickets, owls, toads—it is a symphony. And then there's fragrance—sweet olive in cool weather, the smell of wet sycamore leaves, of healthy soil—I swoon with pleasure."

McKinnon says the greatest compliment he's ever received on his garden, however, came by way of his regular pizza delivery person, who suffers ADHD and once told him, "I feel a calming force just walking to your front door."

RIGHT AND BELOW Both houses on the site are connected by a breezeway that encloses a central court with a prominent water garden, accented by raised containers planted with red-stemmed thalia, black *Alocasia*, and maidenhair ferns; it also mediates sudden storm runoff created by Houston's frequent heavy rainstorms.

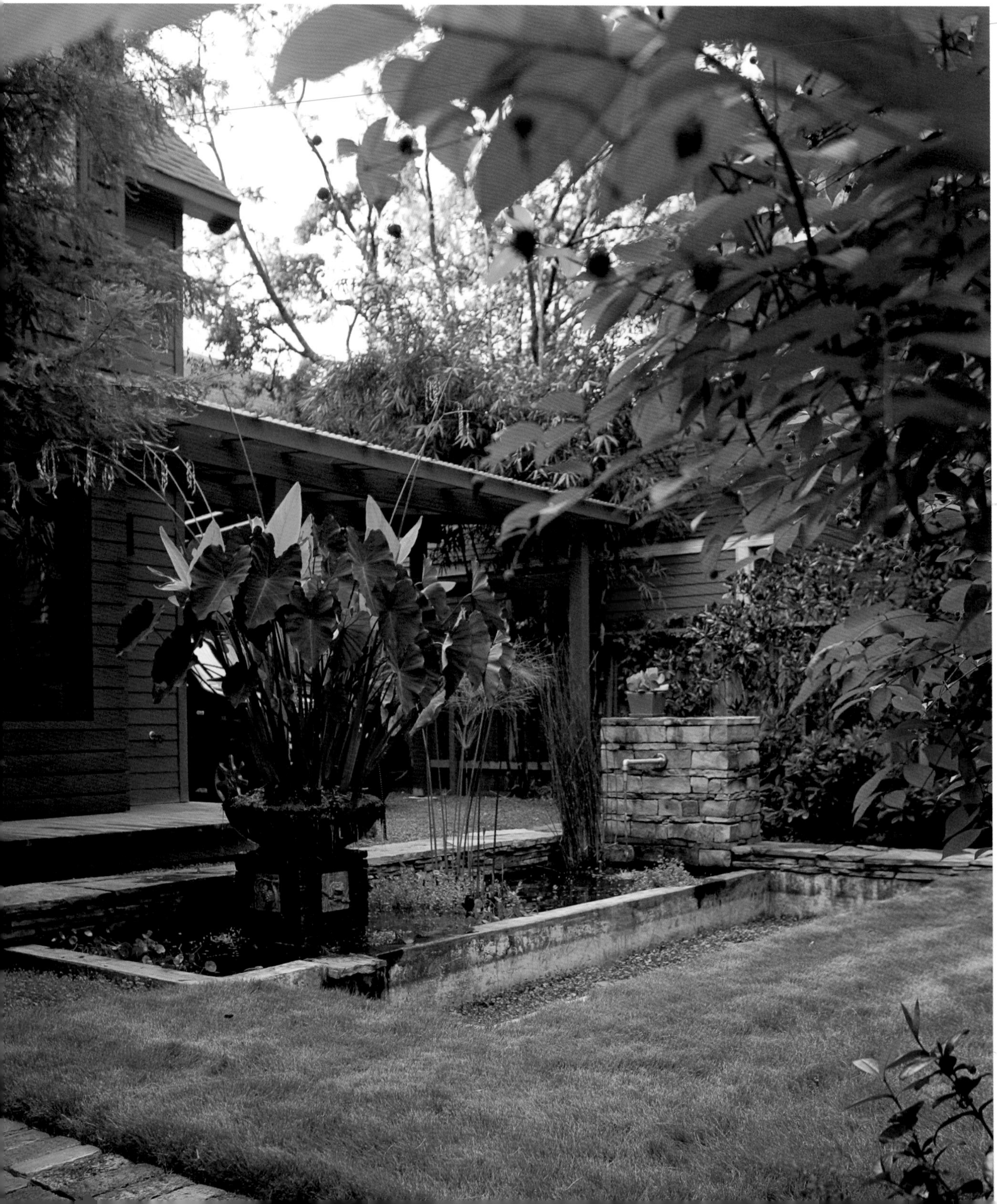

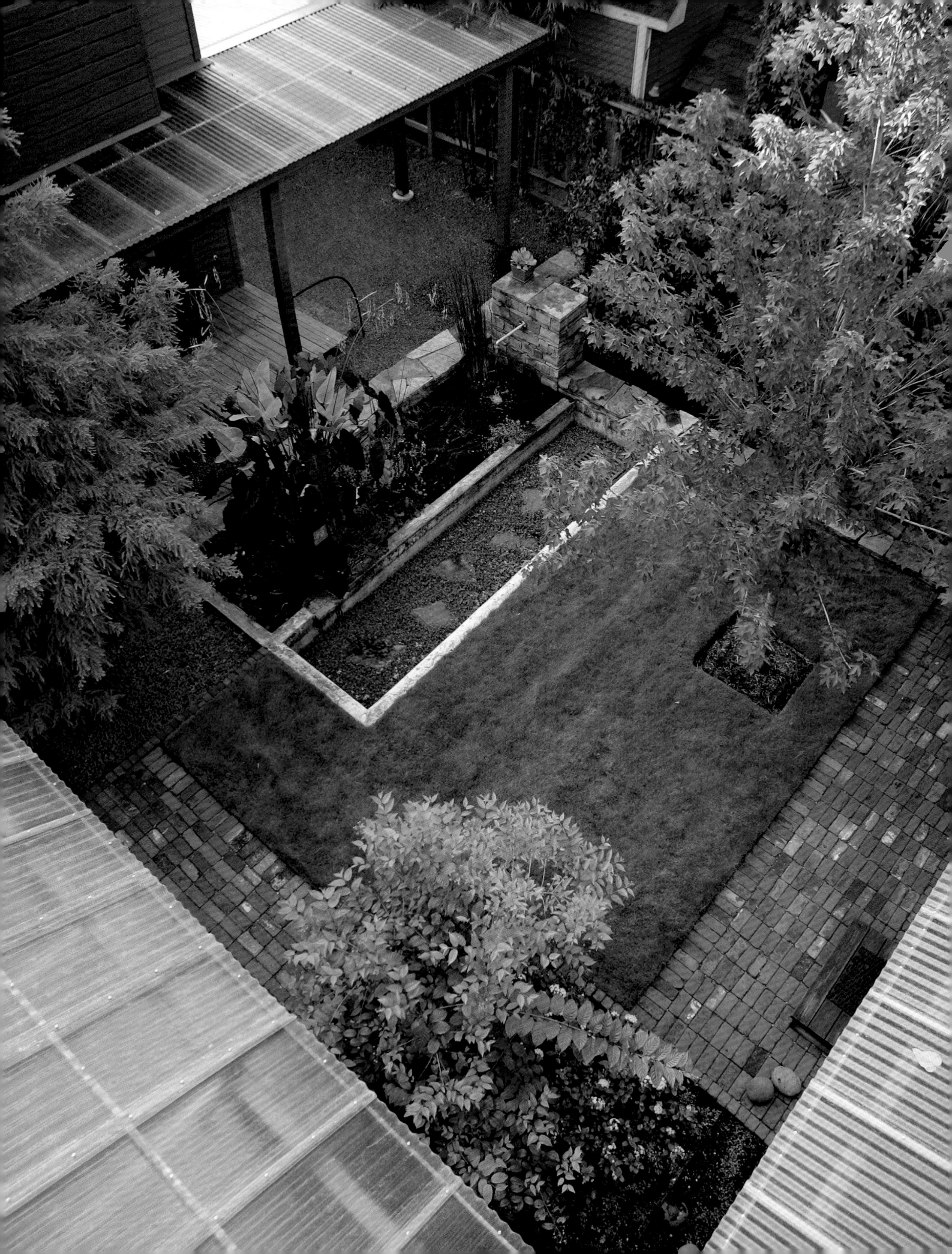

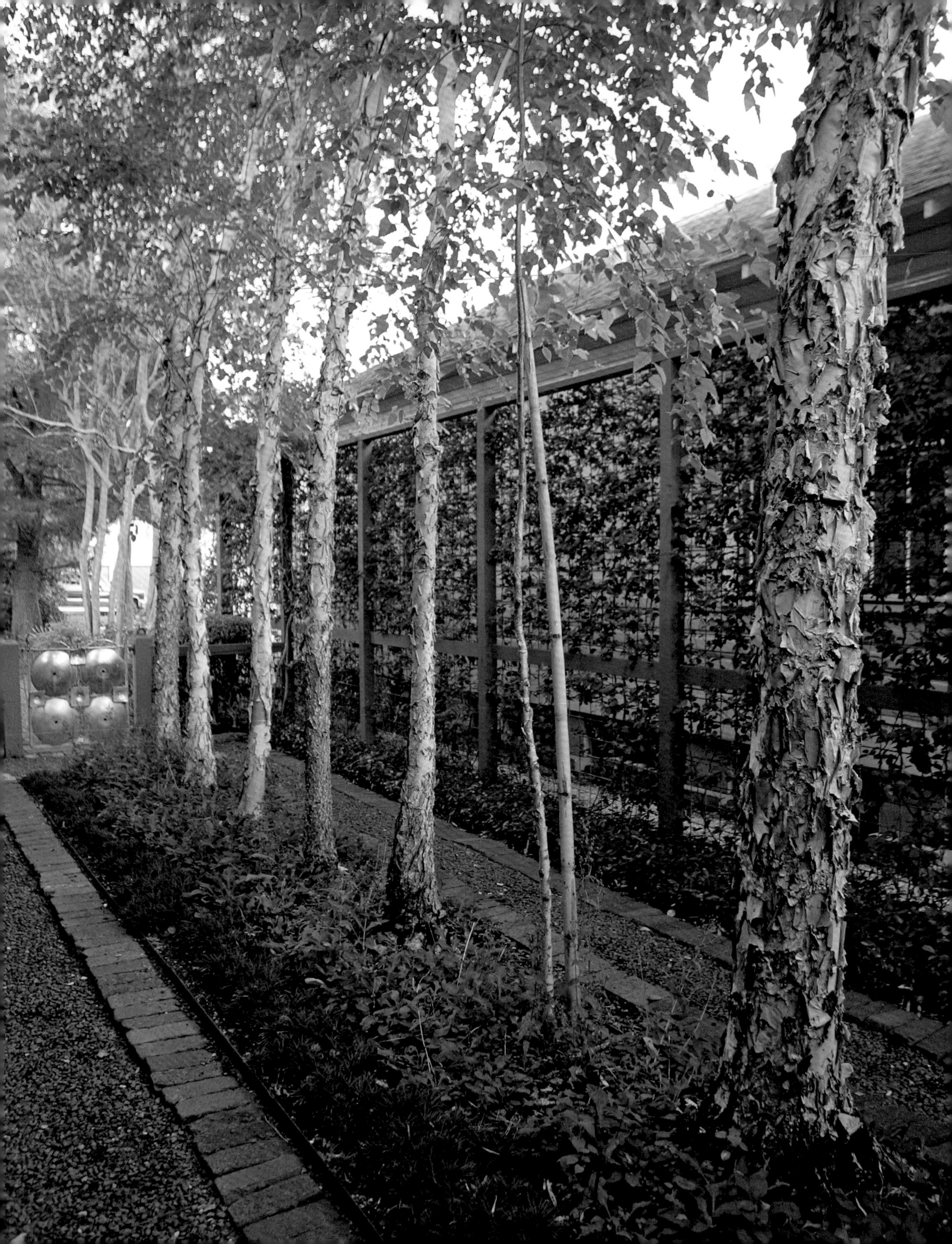

LEFT AND BELOW A gate made from bronzed plowshares by metalsmith Lars Stanley opens onto an allée of river birches that leads to the inner courtyard; the trees also create an interplay of shadow and light for rooms on the house's interior.

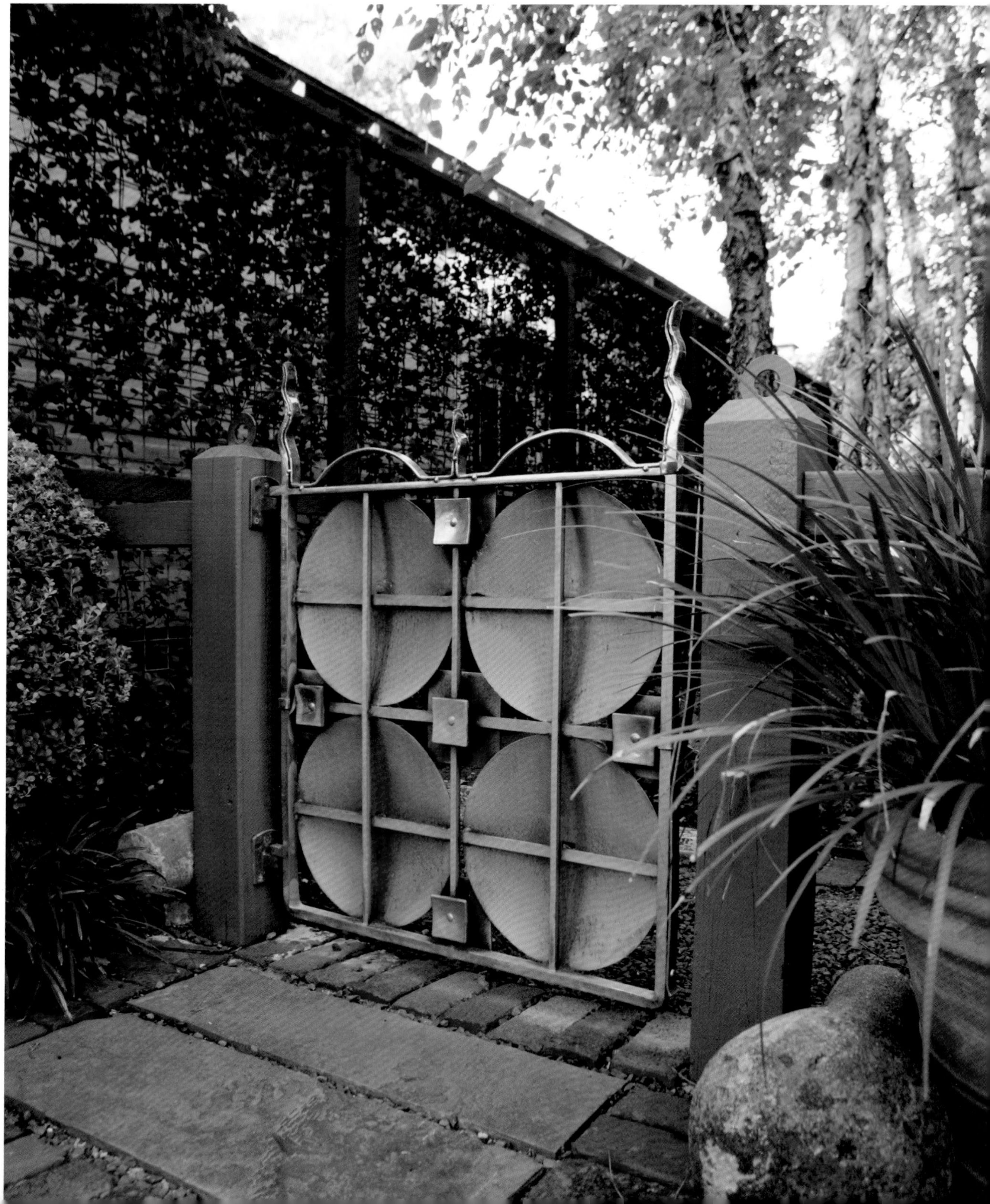

BELOW Bold leaf textures on palms, sycamores, and agaves add to the small courtyard's drama. **RIGHT** A 35-foot-high lookout tower is the garden's major feature. **OVERLEAF** The breezeway McKinnon built to connect his house to his mother's doubles as a space for all-weather entertaining, and looks out onto the central courtyard and water garden.

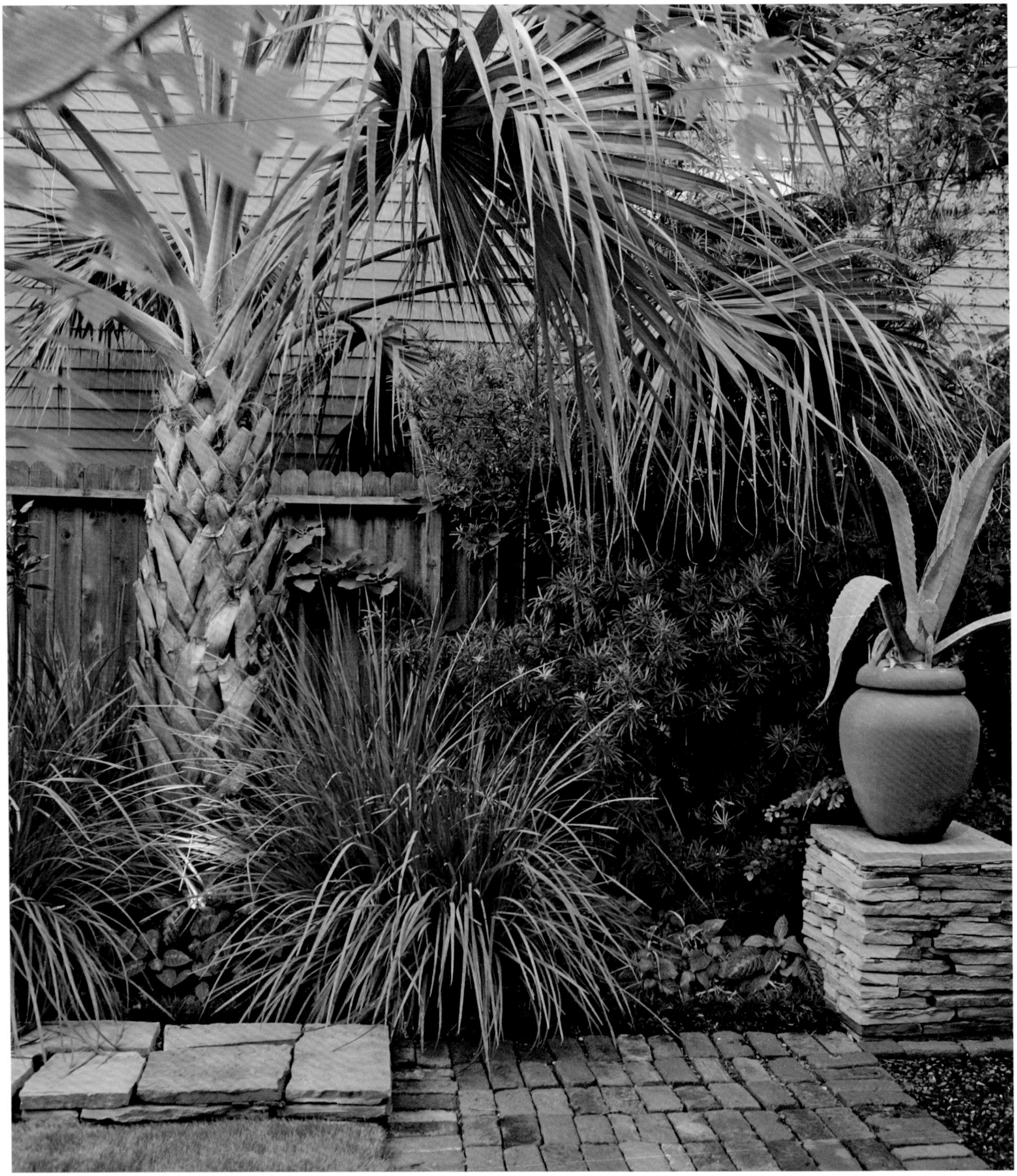

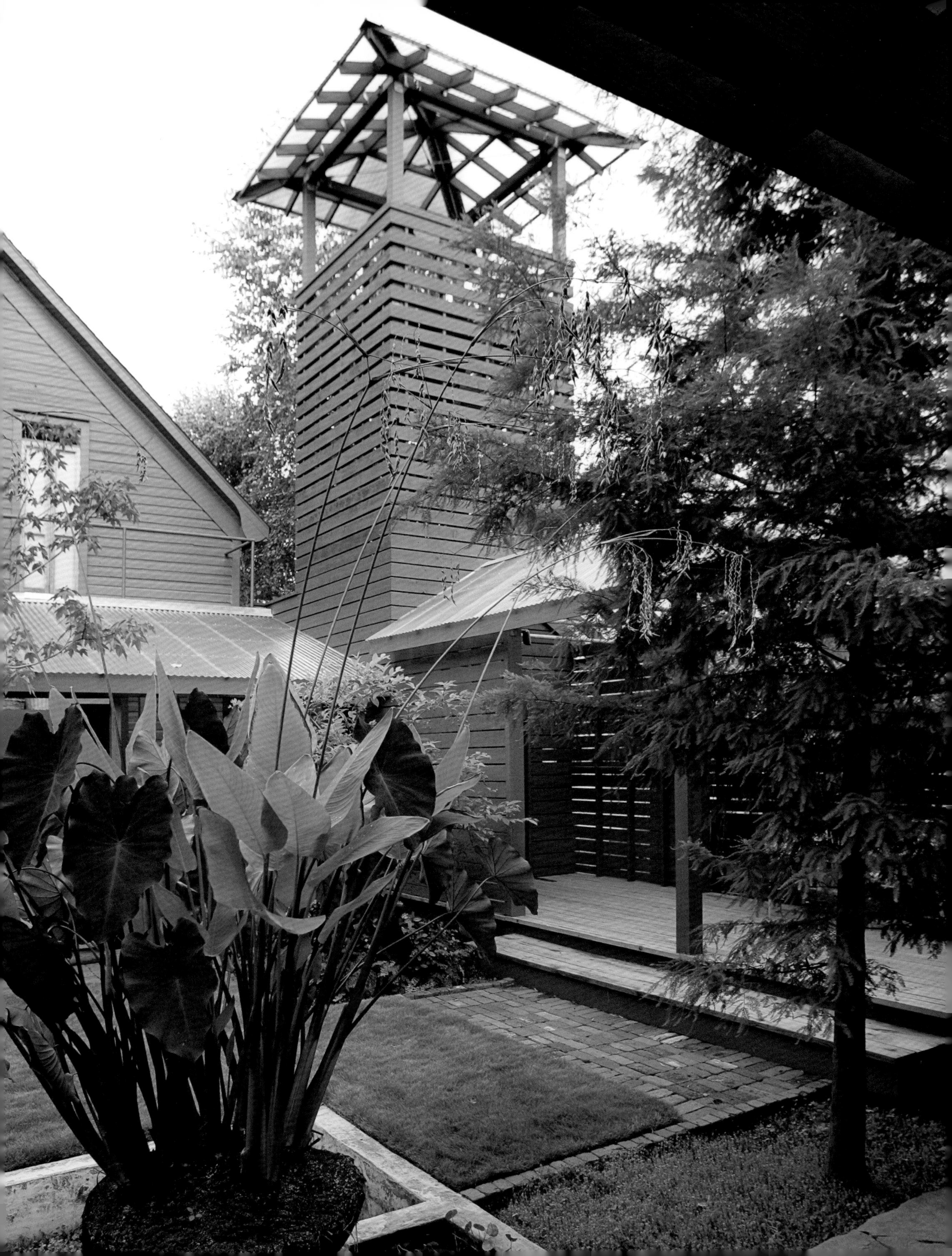

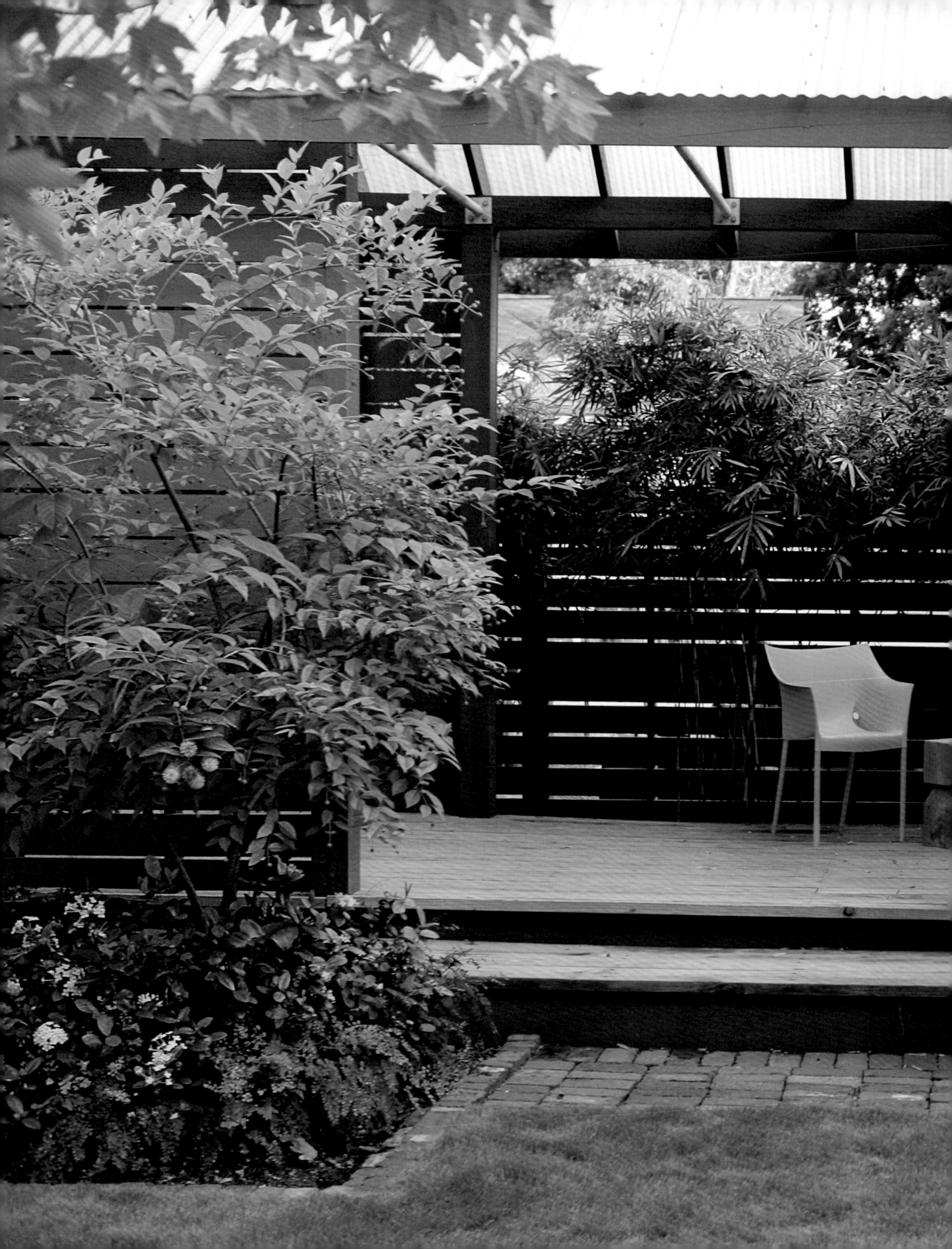

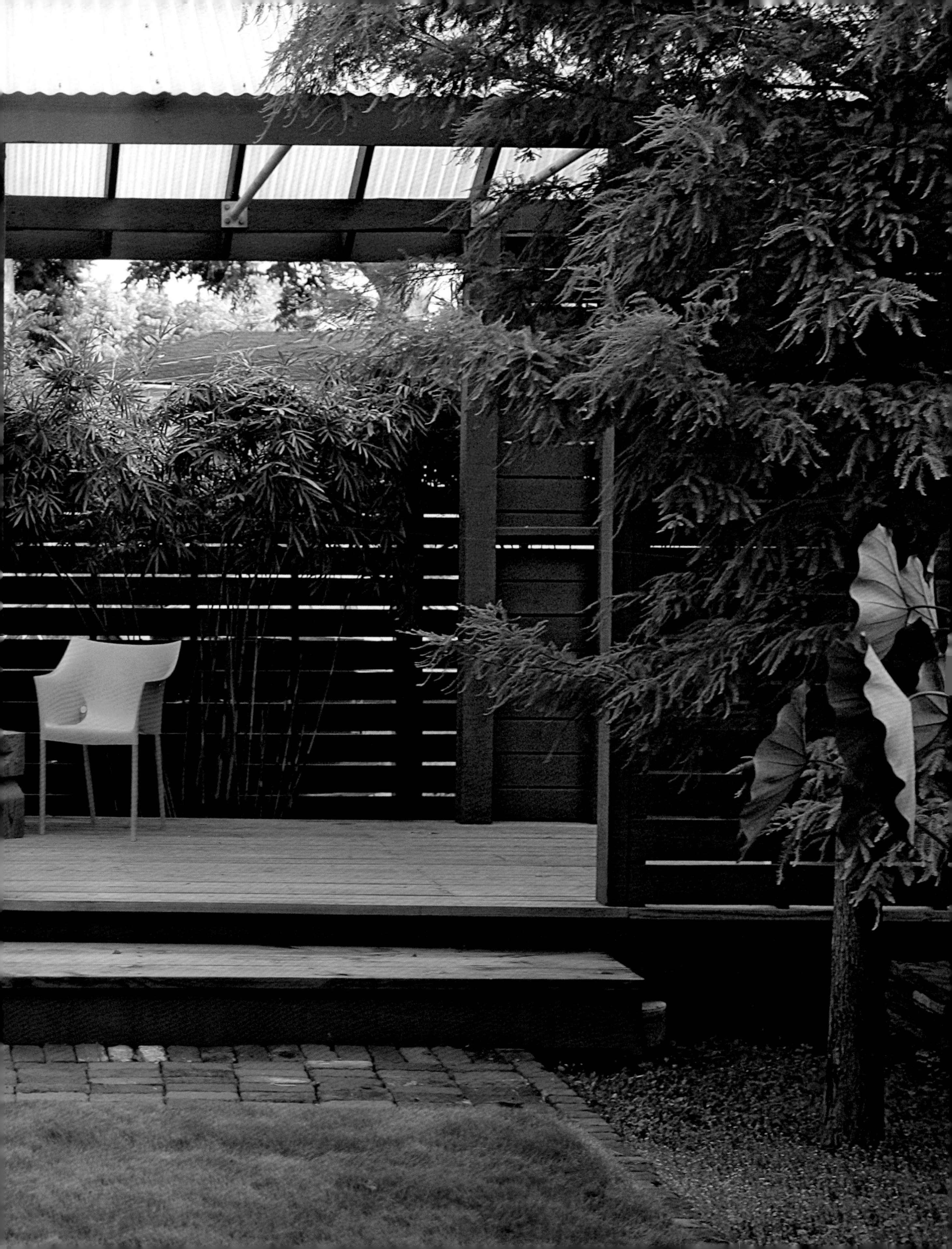

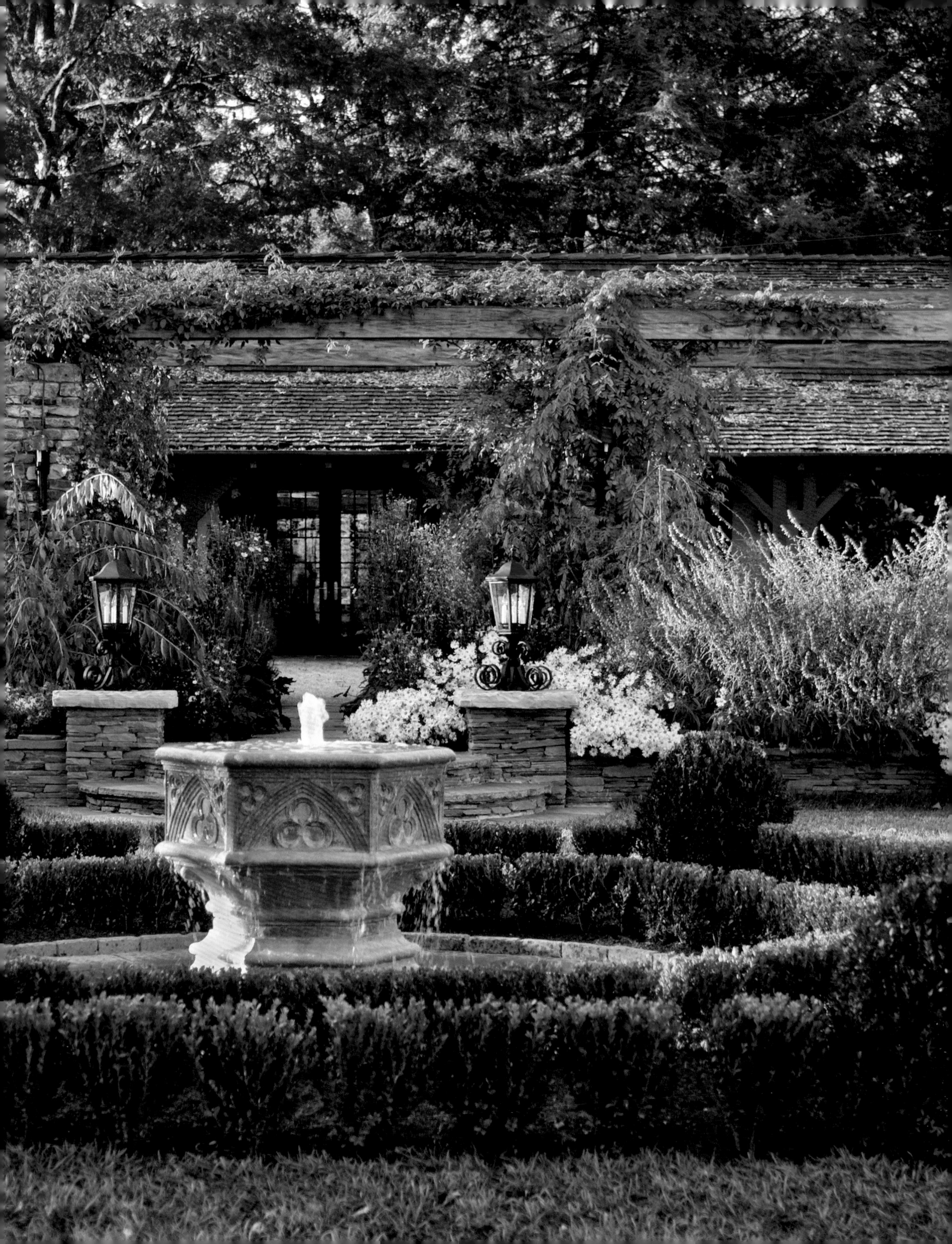

HILL TOP FARM

Knoxville, Tennessee • *Ryan Gainey with Dorothy and Caesar Stair*

A chance meeting of Georgia-based plantsman Ryan Gainey with Dorothy and Caesar Stair at their property in Knoxville, Tennessee, in 2001 led to the creation of a garden full of intimate "rooms" opening onto sweeping vistas. Gainey engaged Atlanta architect Marc B. Mosley to collaborate on the design. The 7-acre site, known as Hill Top Farm, has been in the Stair family since 1956, and its Prairie-style house, dating to 1916, is where Caesar grew up. Today, a practicing lawyer, he says the gardens are where his cares dissipate.

Rather than create a master plan at the outset, Gainey says the modus operandi was to develop one garden room at a time. Early in the planning process, the Stairs toured English gardens, and Caesar came home enthusing over the pergola at Hestercombe, in Somerset. Gainey's response was to suggest re-creating it on a smaller scale here. Designed by Mosley, the Stair pergola is a masterful blending of the rustic and the sophisticated. It features stacked stone columns topped with rough-hewn cypress beams and serves as the centerpiece for a bounteous garden of vines and herbaceous plants in the presence of a formal lawn. One of the featured plants, *Aster oblongifolius* 'Rachel Jackson,' is of historical significance. Gainey rediscovered it in the gardens at The Hermitage in Nashville, the former home of President Andrew Jackson. It is named for his wife.

The addition of a pool house led, in turn, to a pavilion, a fireplace that serves as a focal point for the formal garden, and a demilune aerial hedge that Gainey calls "a hedge on sticks," inspired by a similar structure at Dumbarton Oaks, in Washington, D.C., which was designed by Beatrix Farrand. "The hedge serves as a colonnade," Gainey says, "and is underplanted with white hydrangeas, one of Caesar's favorite plants. At times there are as many as ten thousand hydrangea blooms. Looking out over them to the distant view, you have the illusion of walking on clouds."

Another project was to develop a garden in front of the pergola, in an area that overlooks the Tennessee River and the foothills of the Great Smoky Mountains. Here Gainey chose plants that would bloom from late summer into late fall, in colors that would echo autumn colors seen in the distance. All display hues of purples and yellows. Gainey emphasizes that because purple and gold are naturally harmonious, plants in these colors make a garden intuitively satisfying.

Recently an outdoor sitting room was added off the kitchen, featuring a hexagonal, carved-limestone font framed by a boxwood hedge that mirrors its shape. A second hedge just inside the hexagonal one also repeats a circular, triform motif expressed on its sides.

While the Stairs take immense personal pleasure in their gardens, sharing them with friends and family is of primary importance. Two sons have been married in the gardens, and they are also the site for fundraising events to benefit the local opera and other cultural institutions. "The gardens at Hill Top Farm constitute a complete aesthetic experience," Gainey says. "They embody arts and crafts, the theater, and creative gardens—all in a natural surround."

RIGHT The wisteria-draped pergola is the garden's defining element and frames many views both to the house and out into the landscape beyond. **BELOW** Stone from the house's original 1916 chimney served as the inspiration for the stone chosen for the pergola.

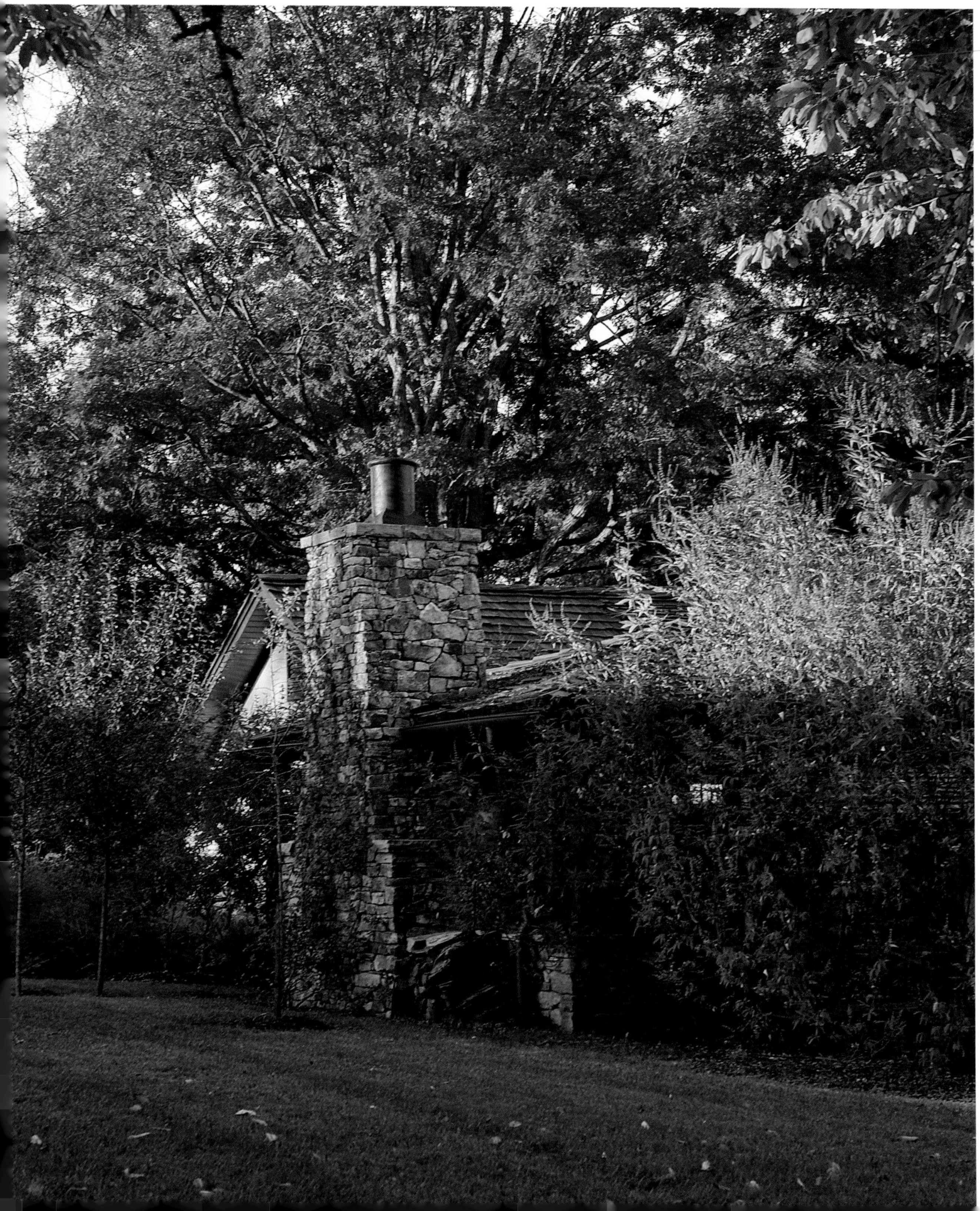

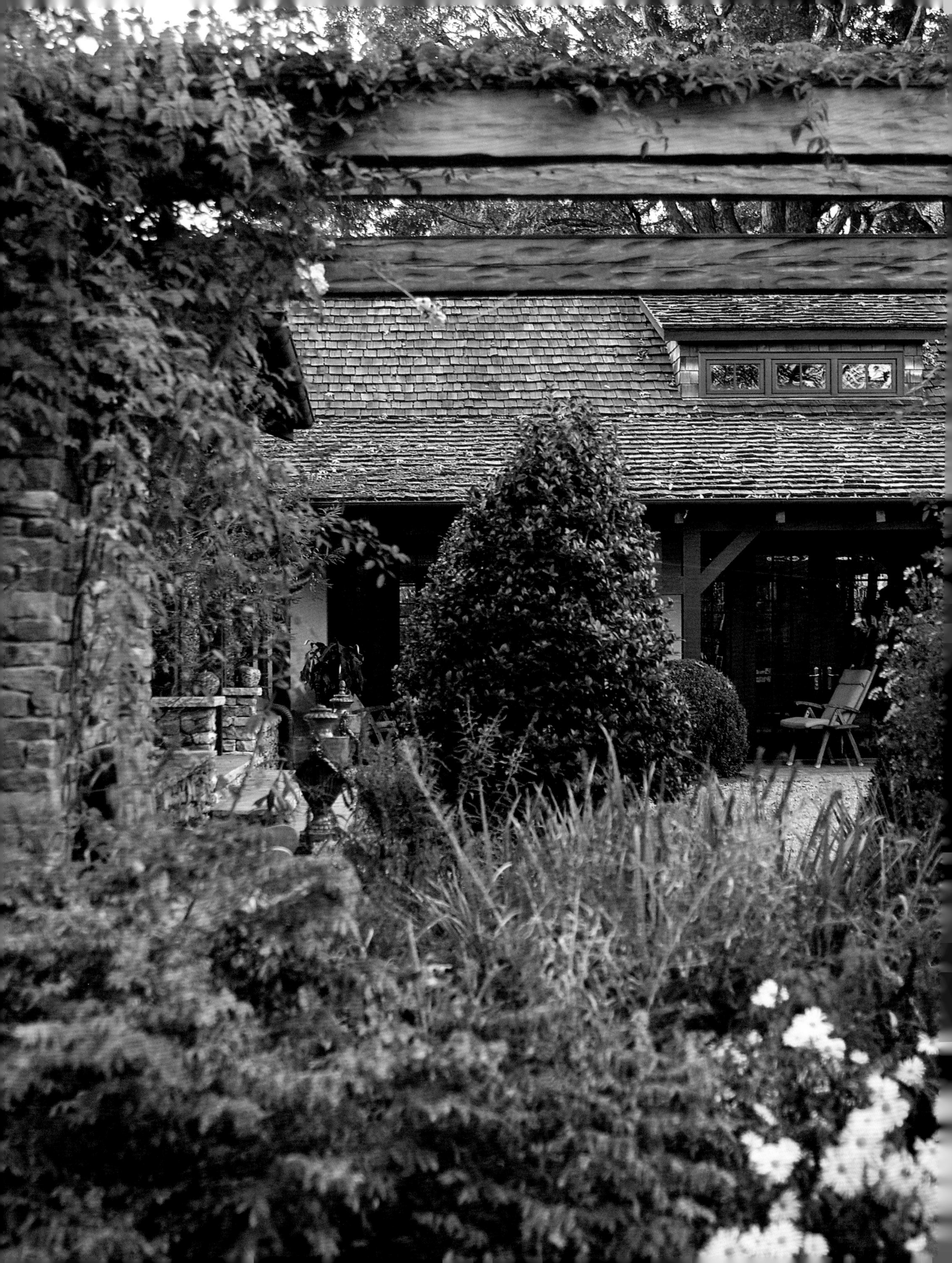

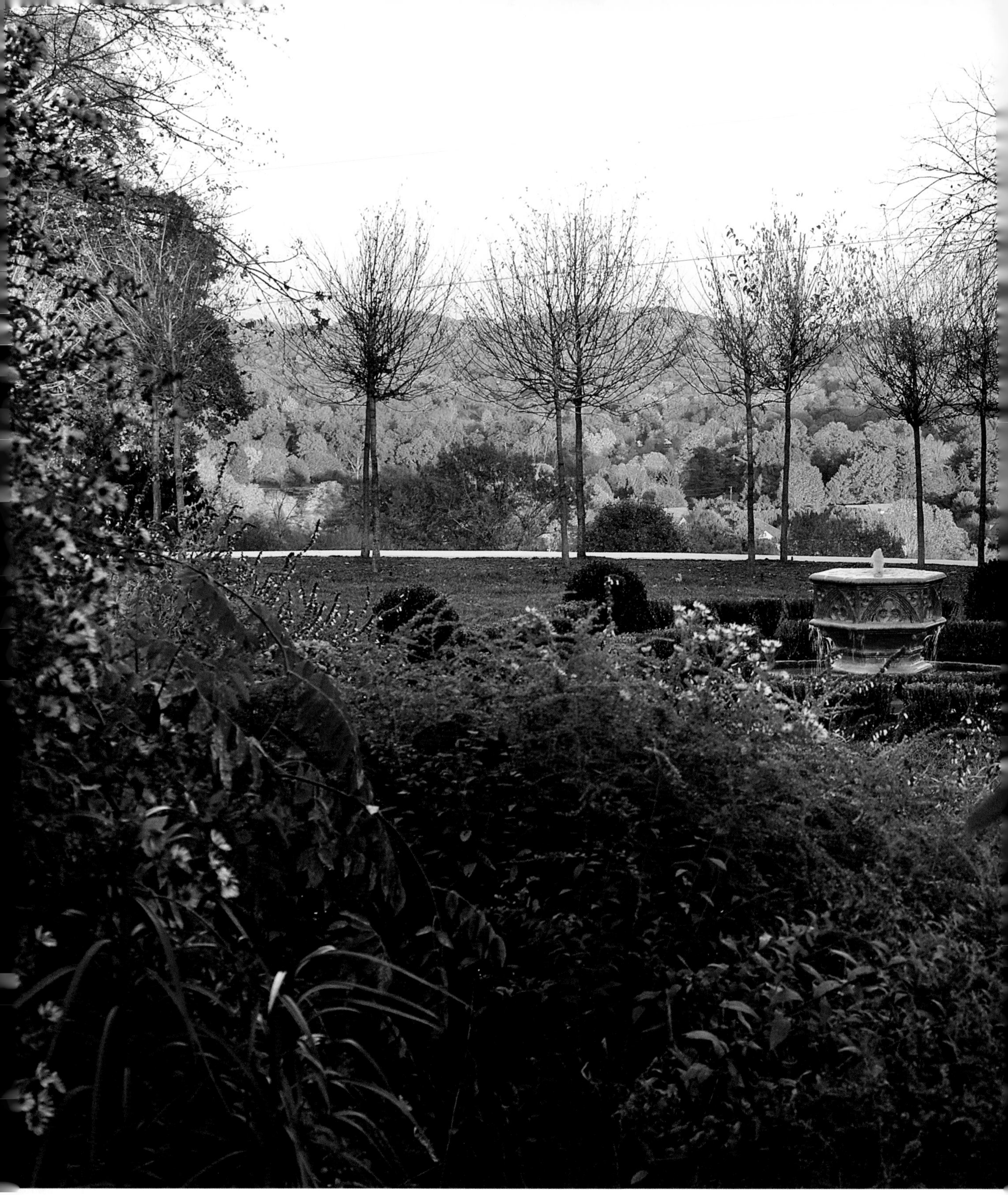

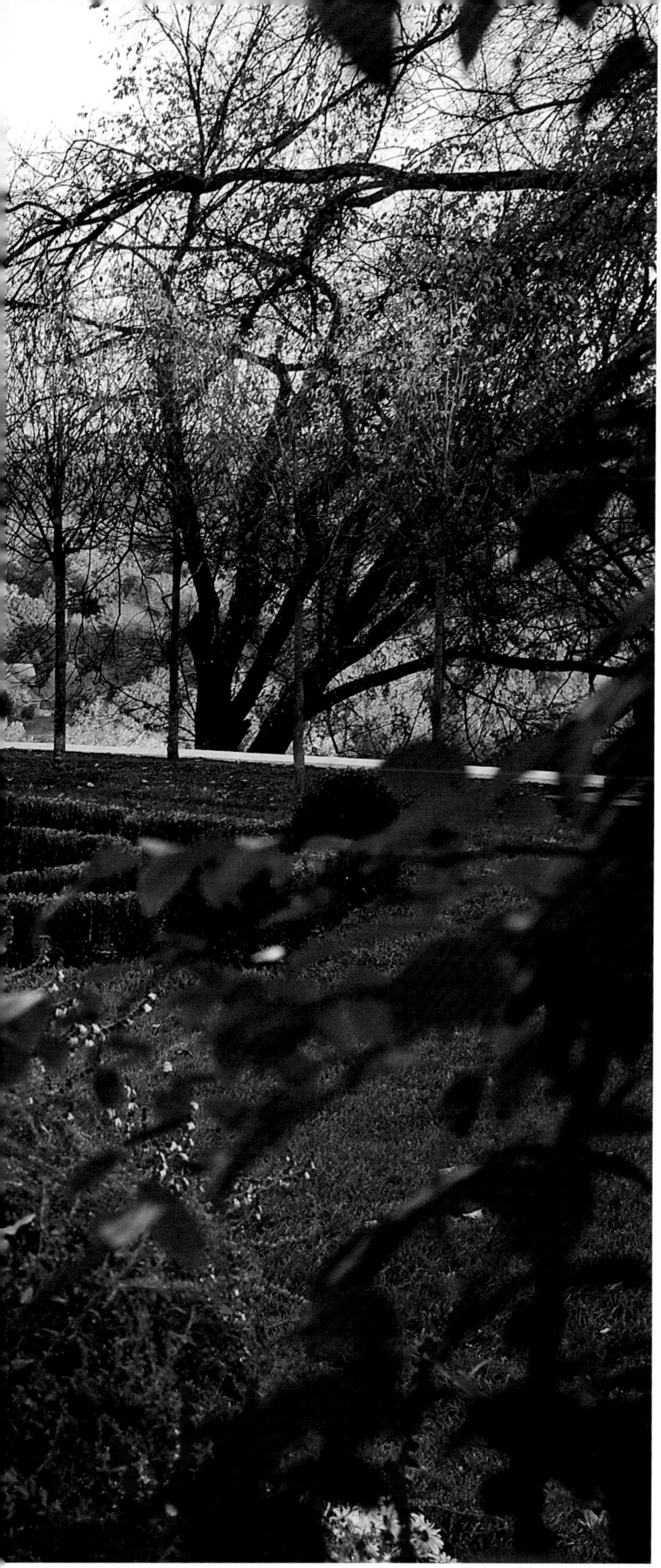

LEFT High-limbed elms were chosen to create the colonnade Gainey refers to as a "hedge on sticks" to allow views out to the landscape beyond. **BELOW** Sweet bay trees in terra-cotta pots echo the structure of the columns of a walkway outside the kitchen.

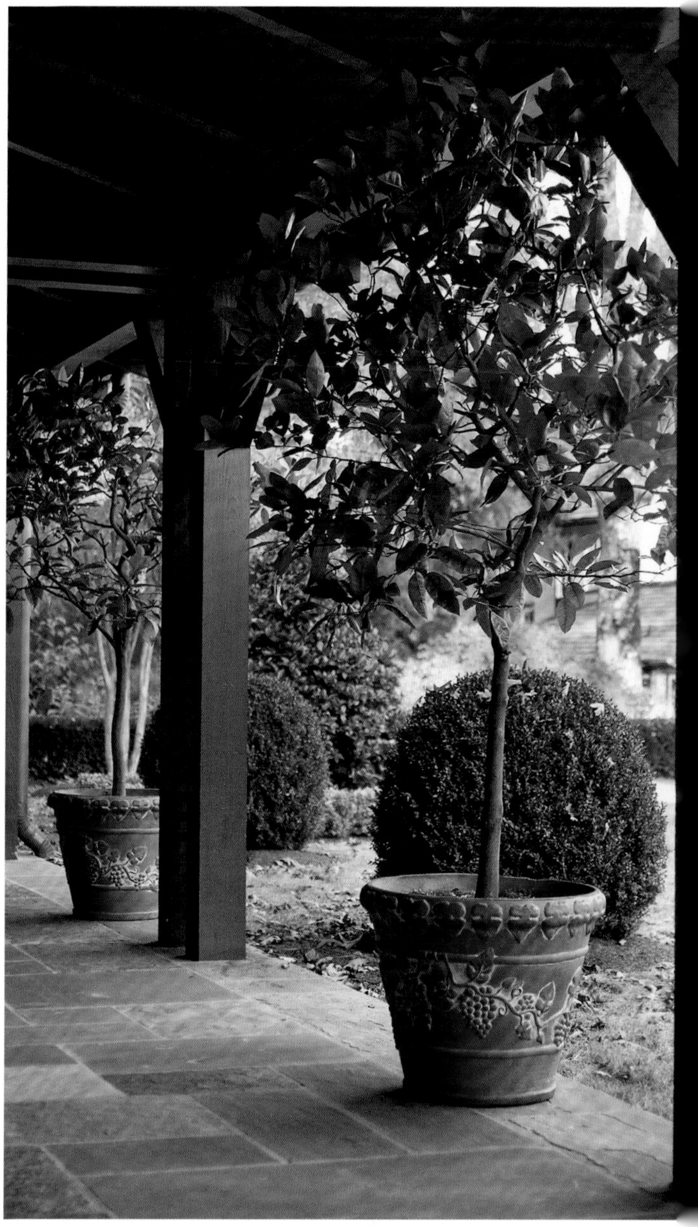

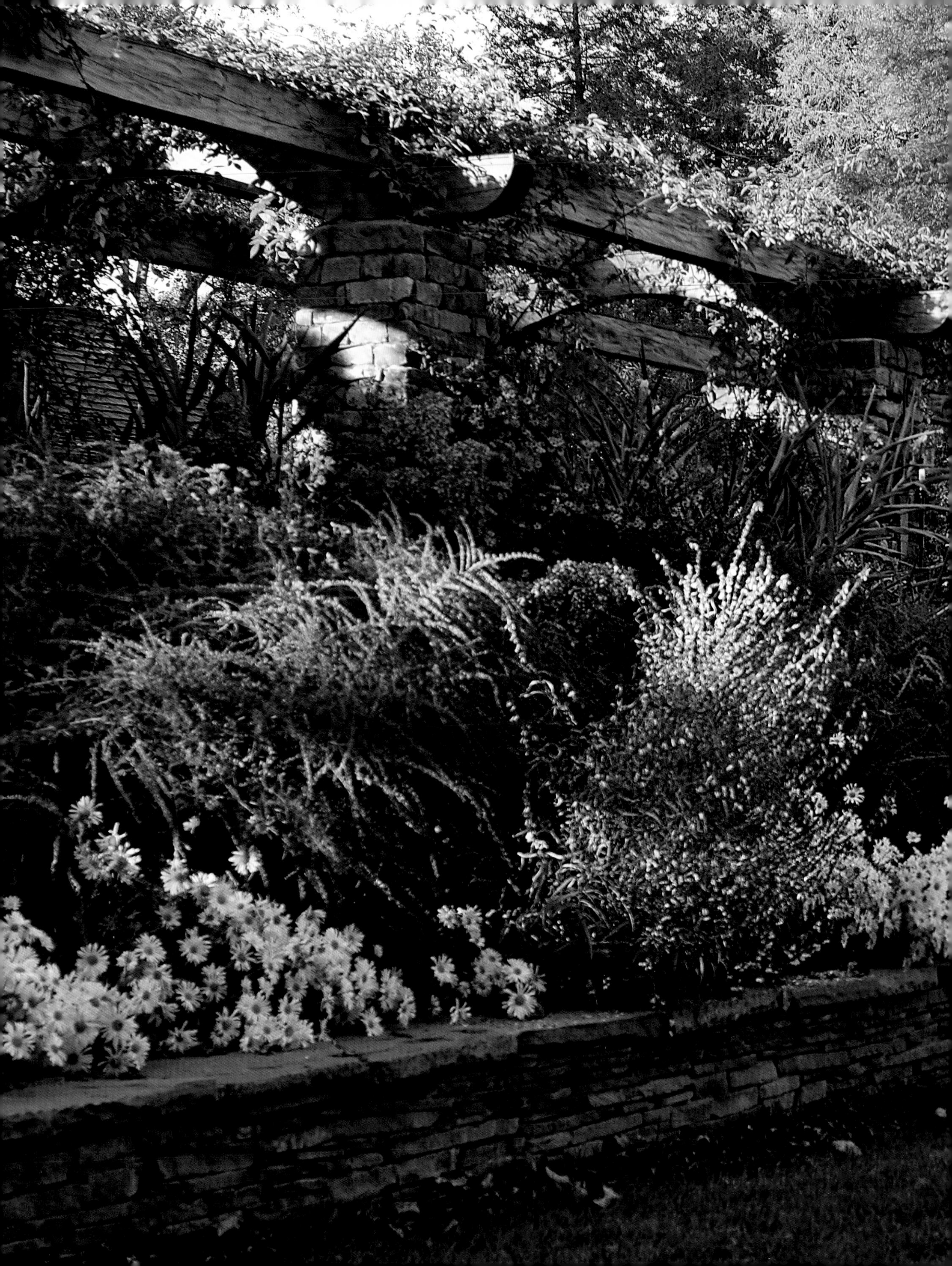

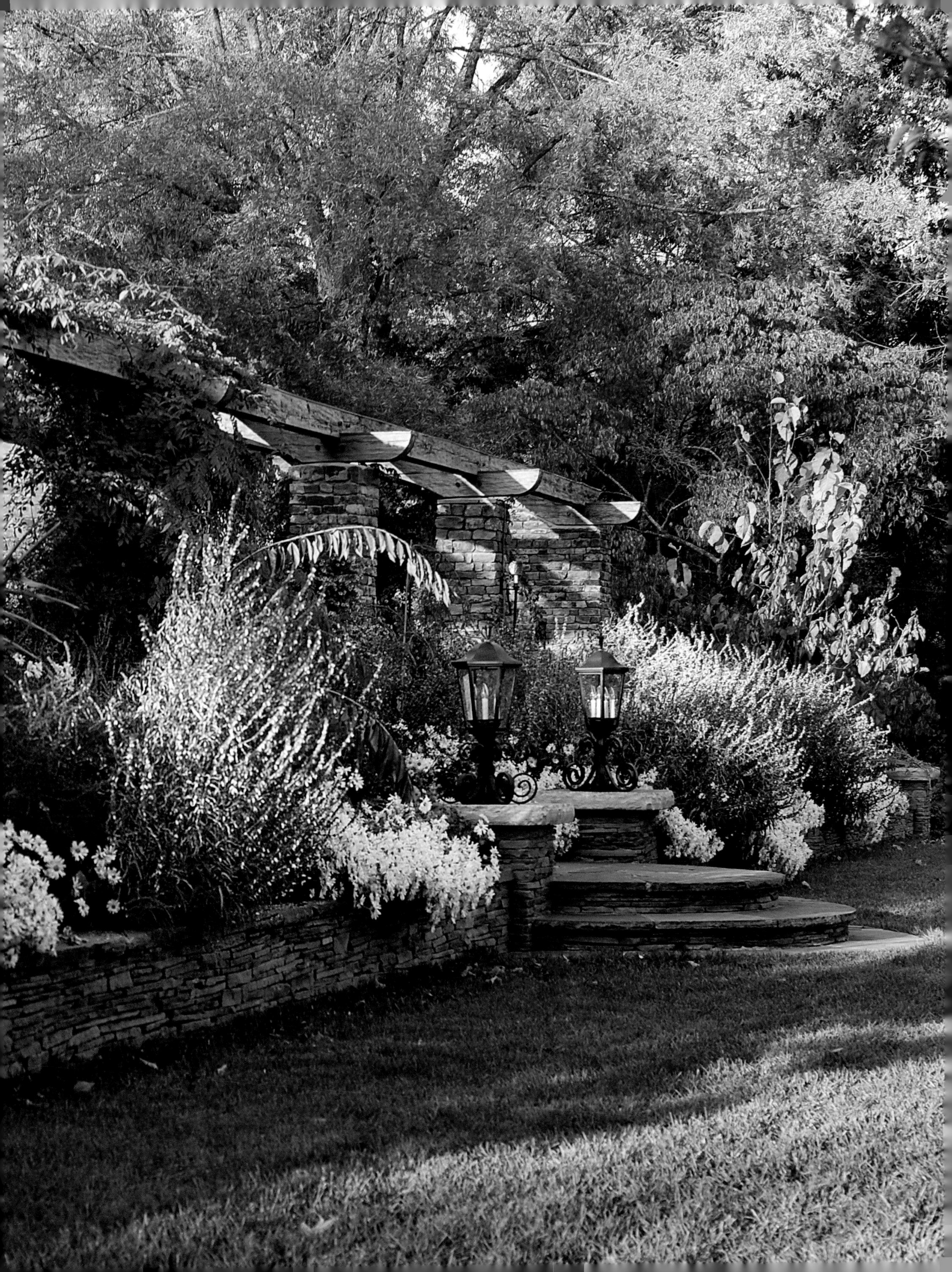

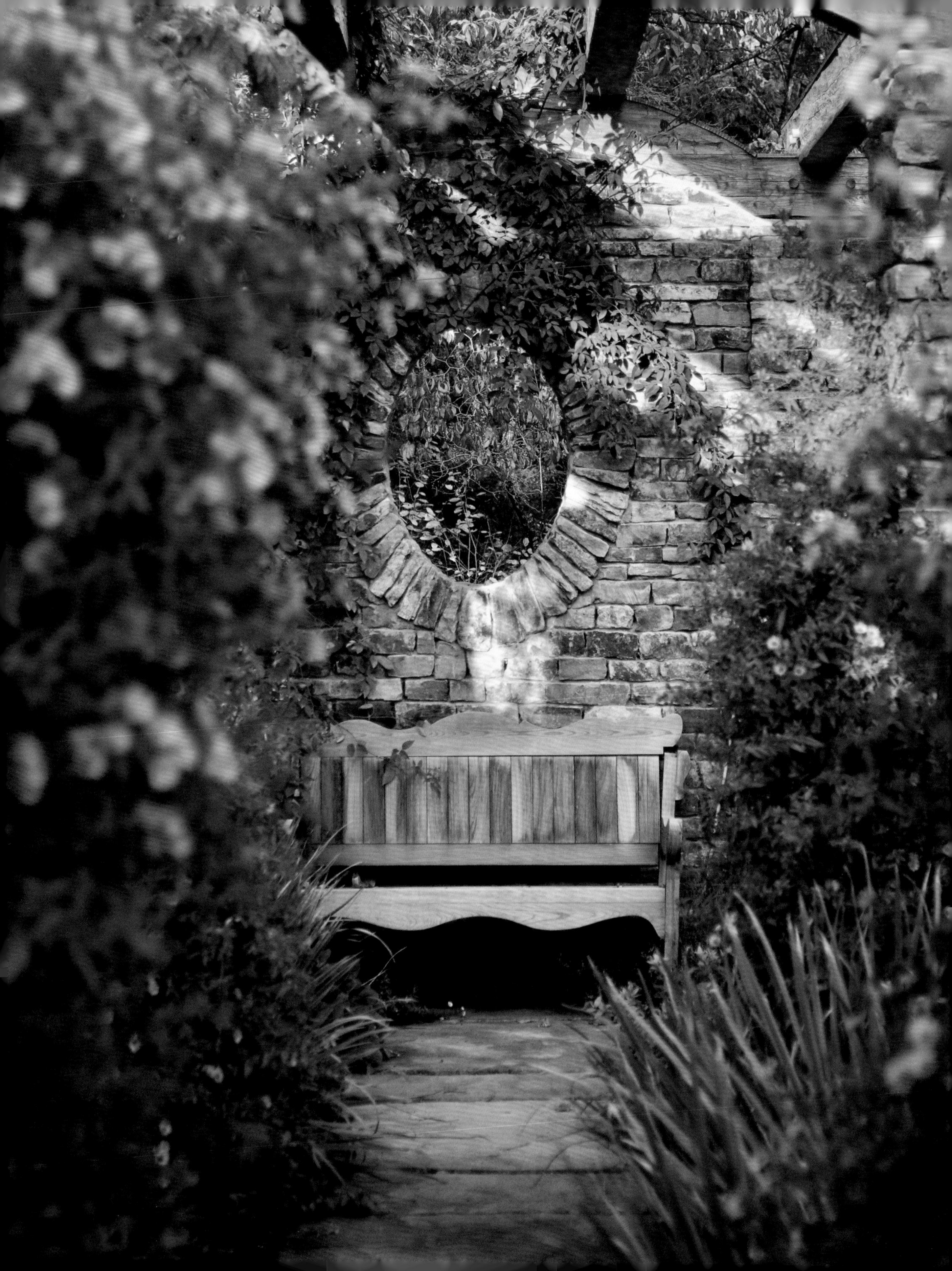

LEFT AND BELOW A rare vining aster, *Ampelaster carolinianus*, climbs the pergola's stone columns, framing brilliant fall foliage beyond through an oculus at one end. **PREVIOUS PAGES** Late-summer hues of pale yellow and purple created by *Chrysanthemum* x *morifolium* 'Ryan's Yellow' and Russian sage cascade out from the front of the long pergola inspired by Hestercombe in Somerset, England.

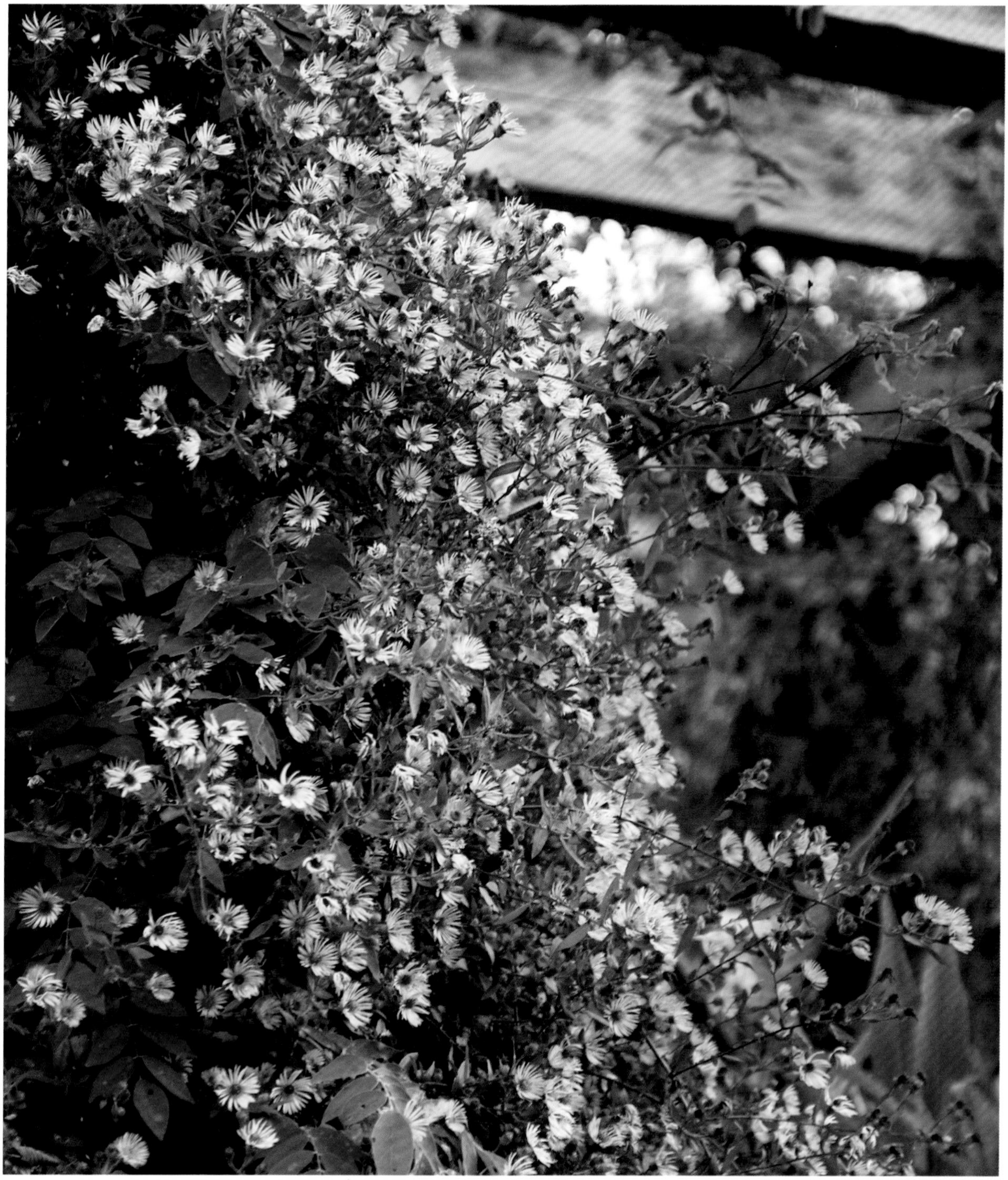

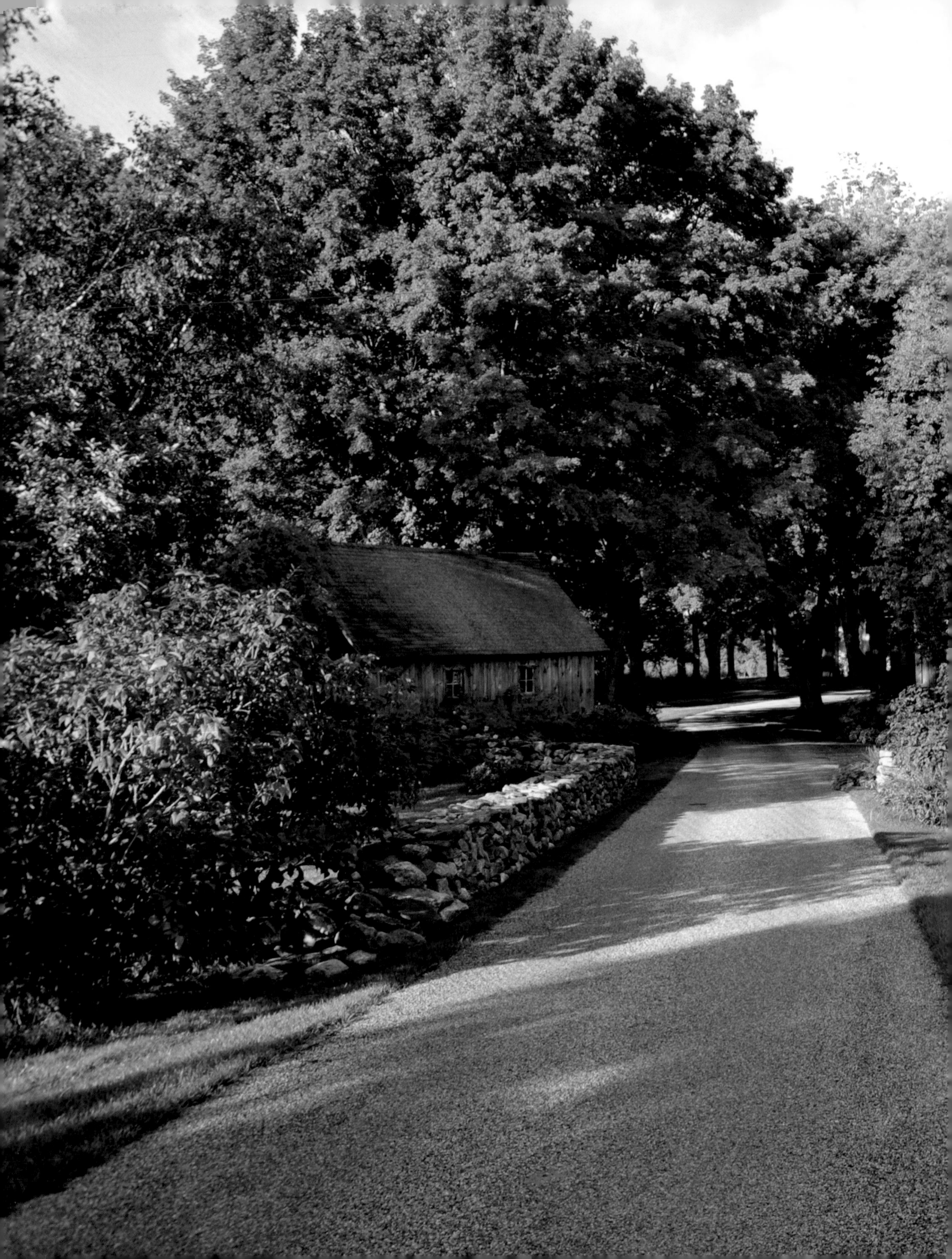

midwest

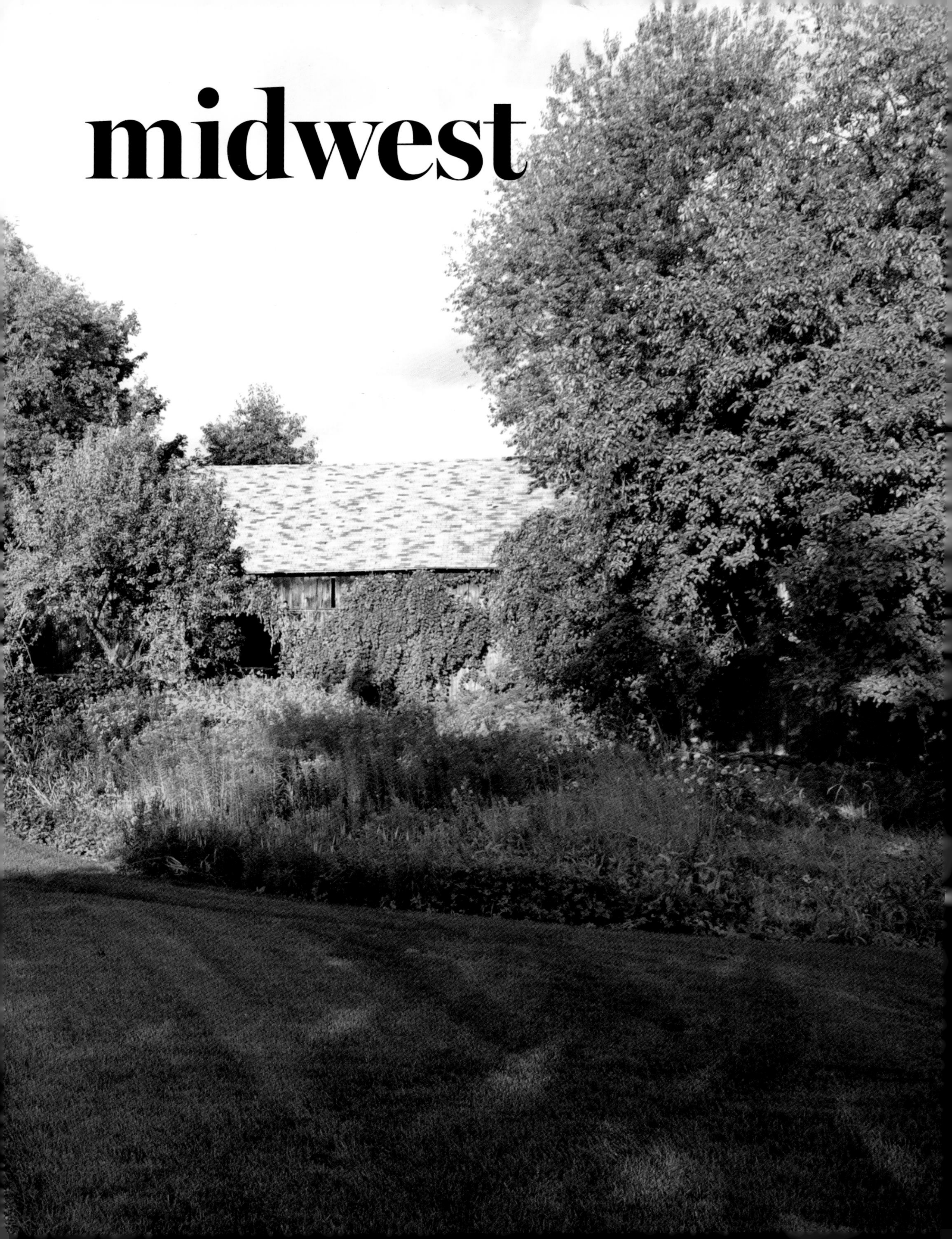

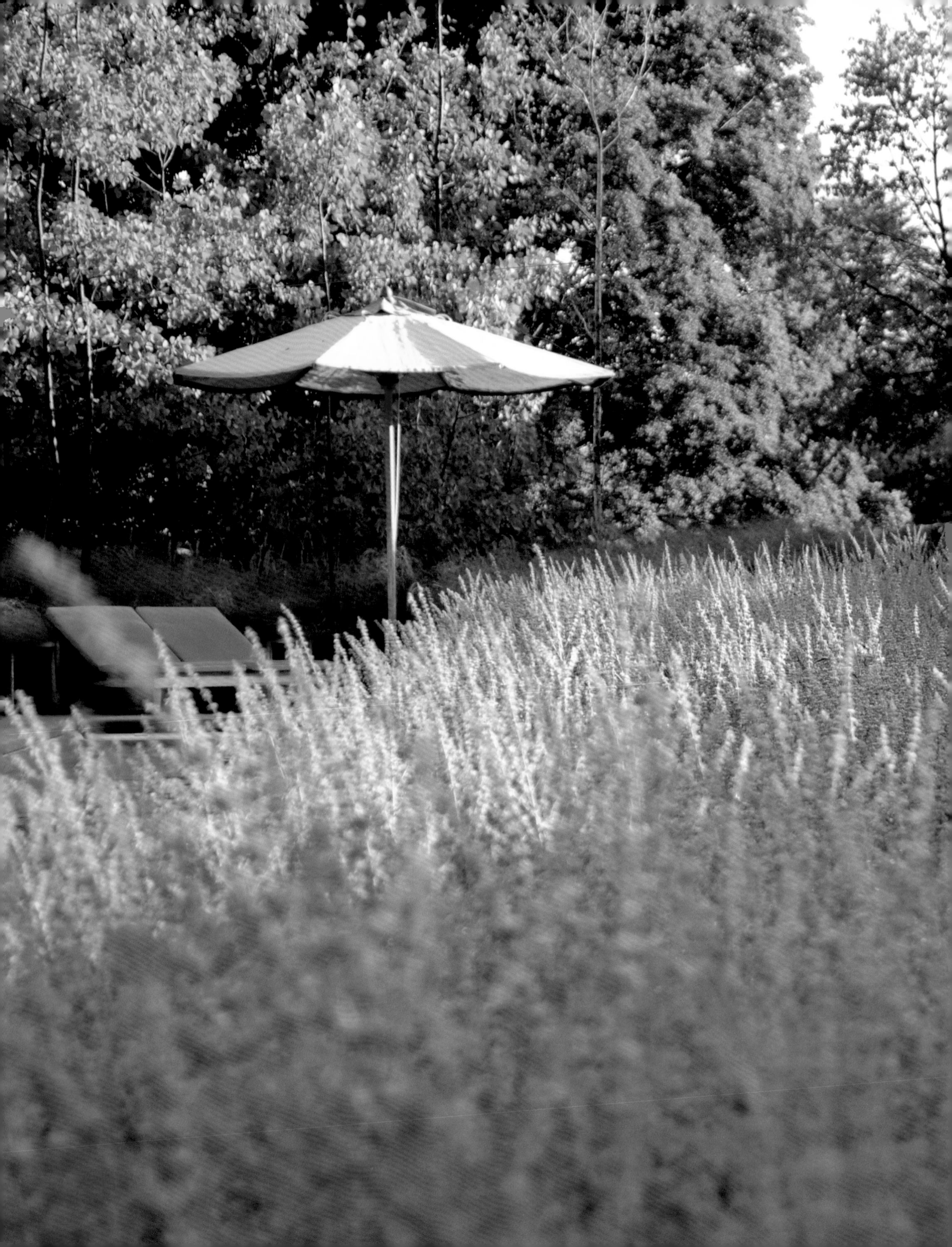

BOLD MEADOWSIDE GEOMETRY

Harbor Springs, Michigan

Hoerr Schaudt Landscape Architecture

Two avid travelers worked with Chicago landscape architect Douglas Hoerr to design this 18-acre garden in Harbor Springs, Michigan. "The landscape celebrates a sense of calm, quiet order introduced by the contemporary architecture," Hoerr says, "but it is simultaneously responsive to its native northern Michigan context—farms, woods, horizon and sky, native plants, and wild overgrowth that pushes at any boundary."

The entry drive passes remnants of the site's history—a barn and outbuildings. To enhance the feeling of history, along a portion of the drive, Hoerr added a wall that appears to be crumbling with age and subtle plantings around the buildings.

The house's central court is serene and peaceful, the most structured, or as Hoerr says, "designed," of the landscape spaces on the site. It draws on the architectural features of the house surrounding it for its scale and shapes. The original layout gave those looking down the U-shaped courtyard a view only of parked cars, whereas the new design incorporates a water feature reminiscent of an artesian well as a focal point. At the opposite end of the courtyard, visitors cross an angular, bridged pool to the glass entrance of the home, which seems to float above it. Water from this pool also gives the impression that it flows under and out of the back of the house.

Plantings in the courtyard were selected for form and texture over color. They feature Amur and Japanese maples, evergreen ground cover, boxwood in bold geometric forms, rhododendron, cotoneaster, and dwarf conifers. A bluestone walkway patterned into an abstracted grid and large native-stone boulders reference the material used in the drive's stone walls.

The sunken east terrace, off the master bedroom, functions as a private outdoor space designed for yoga, meditation, and swimming. A meadow of native plantings—panicum grasses, sumac, and quaking aspen—is held in check by a stone retaining wall and the strong, simple forms of a lawn and elongated lap pool that run parallel to the house. At the north end of the pool, natural drifts of plantings spill over into the remainder of the landscape.

By contrast, the west terrace is raised and offers views of the native landscape in the distance through a carefully ordered bosque of maples. The choice of gravel for the terrace, a material often used on Midwestern farms, changes the perception that it can't be elegant. It's tactile in a sophisticated way, yet not polished or urban. "At least two walls of every room feature large windows that face the landscape," Hoerr says. "In many ways the integration of landscape and architecture makes you feel you are in the garden even when you are in the house."

Instead of lawn, native meadow plantings create a natural Michigan landscape of an envelope around the house. Every plant was chosen to look like it's always been there. Hoerr also used mature specimens in the garden from the outset. "The naturalized meadows and native areas took a couple of years to mature," he says, "but the bones of the garden were fully expressed from the first day."

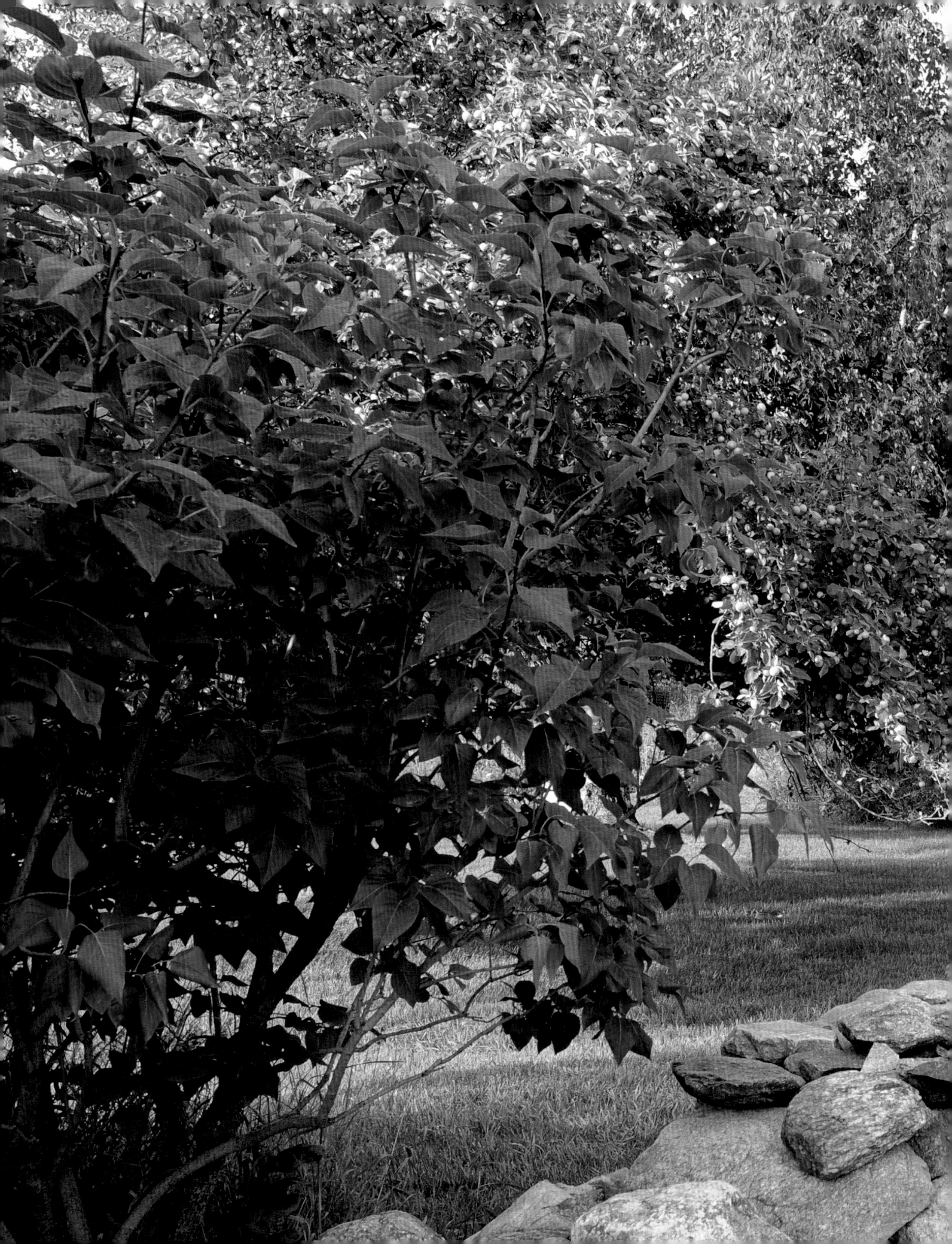

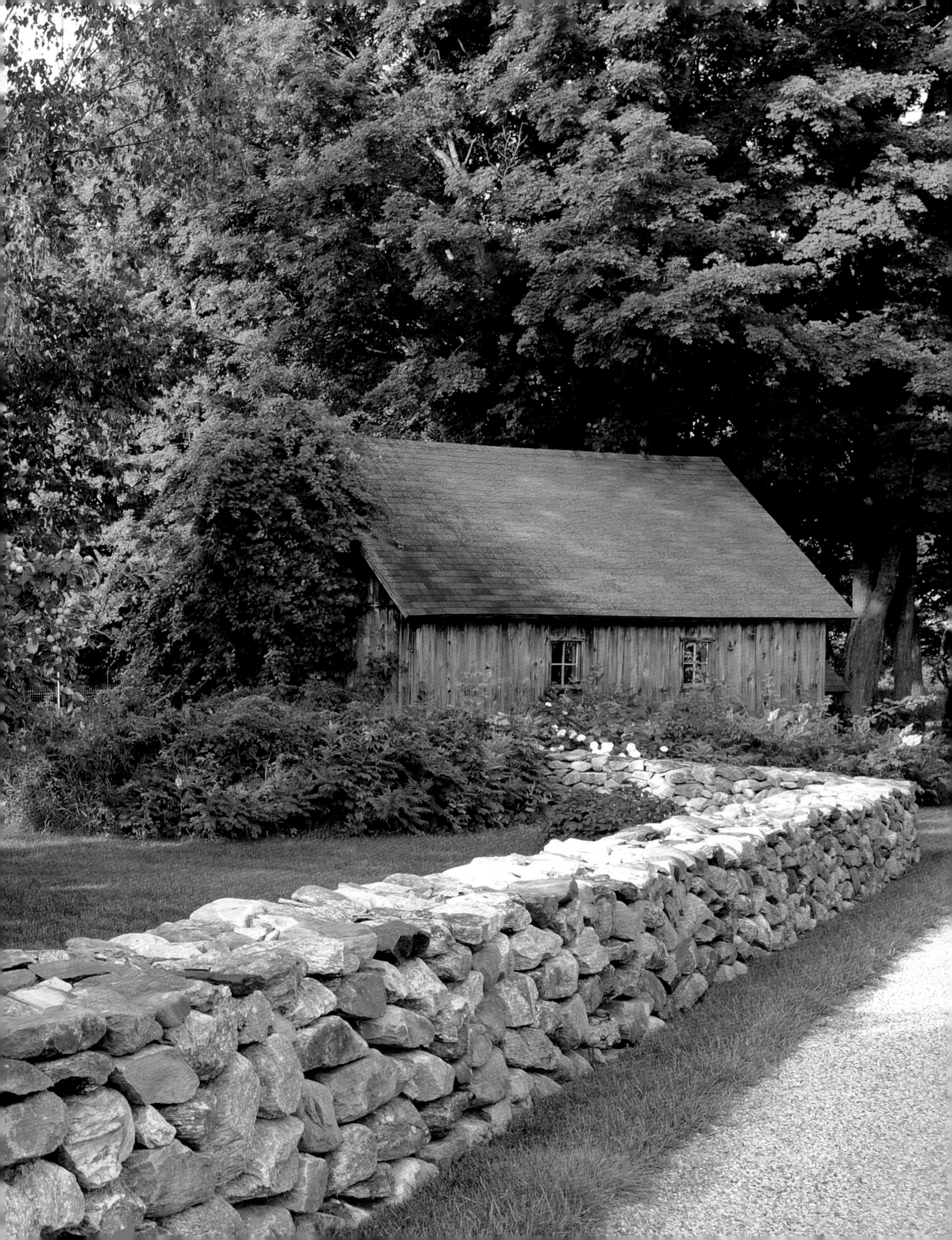

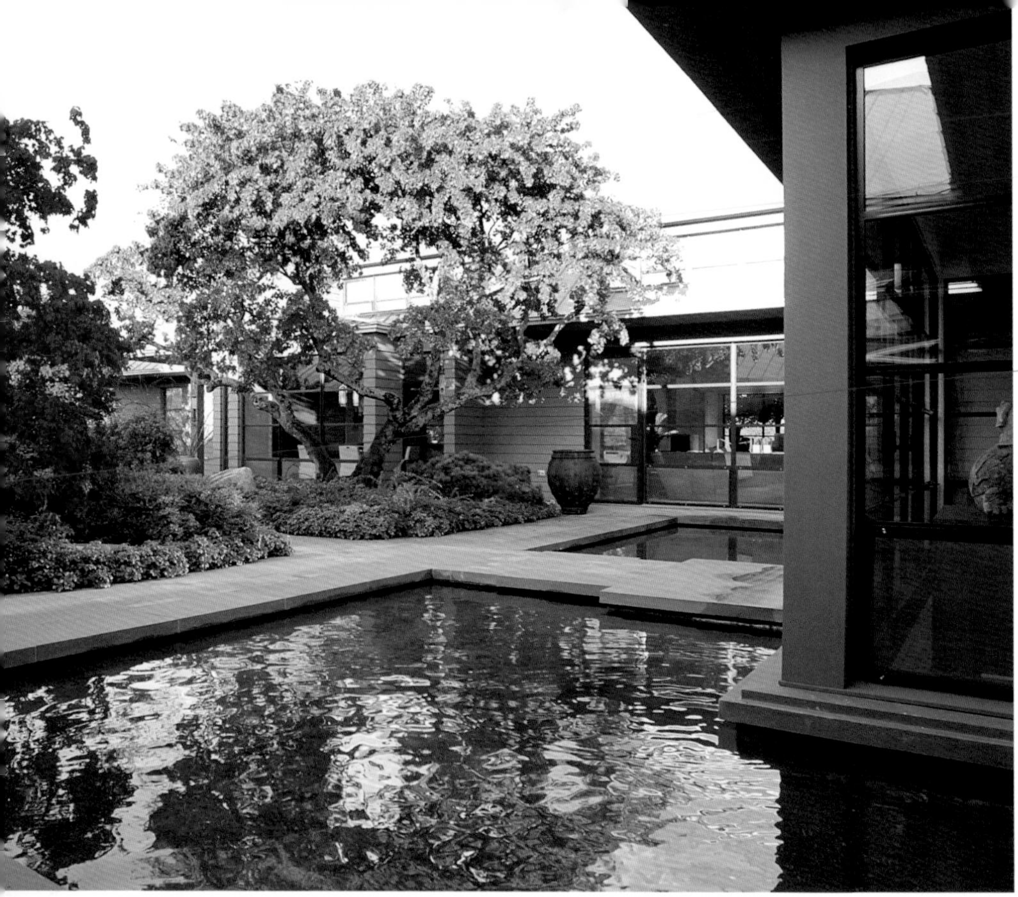

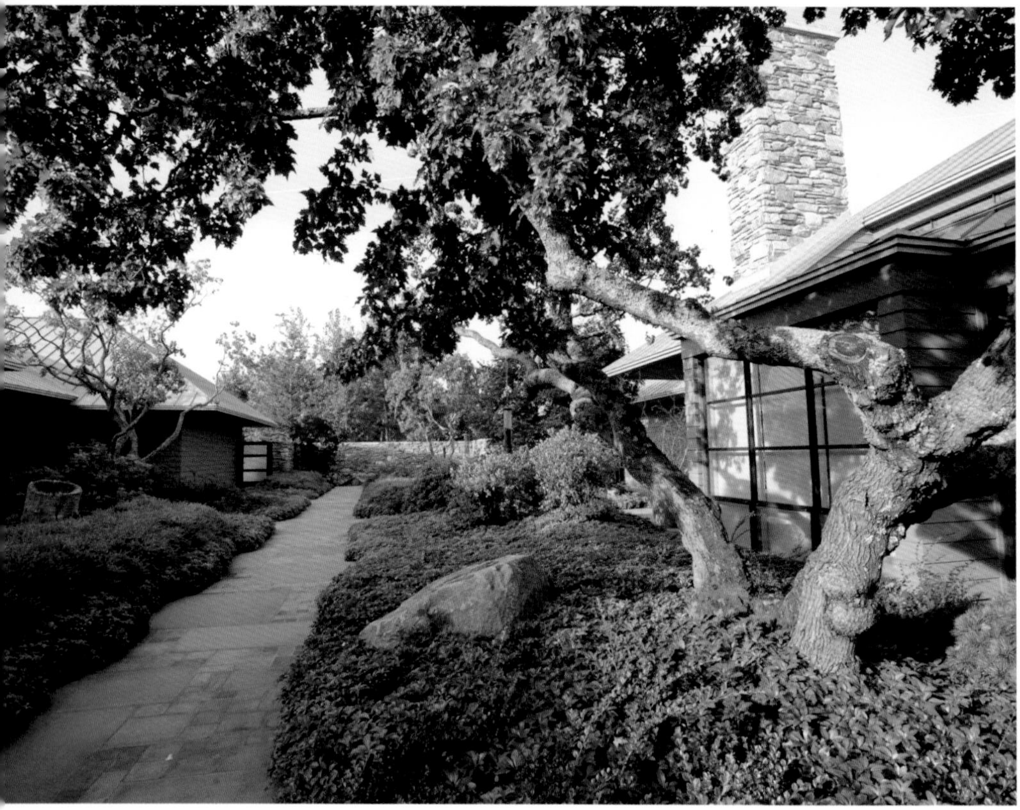

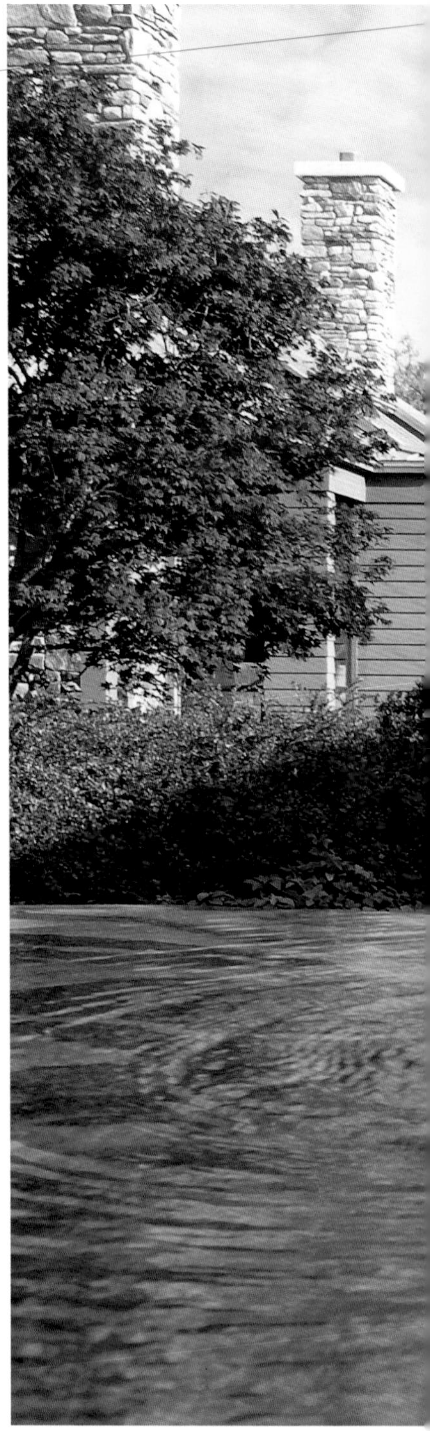

BELOW Bubbling water rising from a large, circular pool reminiscent of an artesian well greets visitors in the house's entry court. **OPPOSITE, ABOVE** An angular entry path bridges over calm pools of water that appear to flow out from beneath the house. **OPPOSITE, BELOW** Loose, natural edges along the entry walk contrast pleasantly with the architecture.

PREVIOUS PAGES The site's original outbuildings add a sense of history to the landscape, as do rambling masses of geraniums and ranunculuses—flowers landscape architect Douglas Hoerr associates sentimentally with old barns—planted at their bases; a new stone wall likewise crumbles intentionally at its terminus to evoke age.

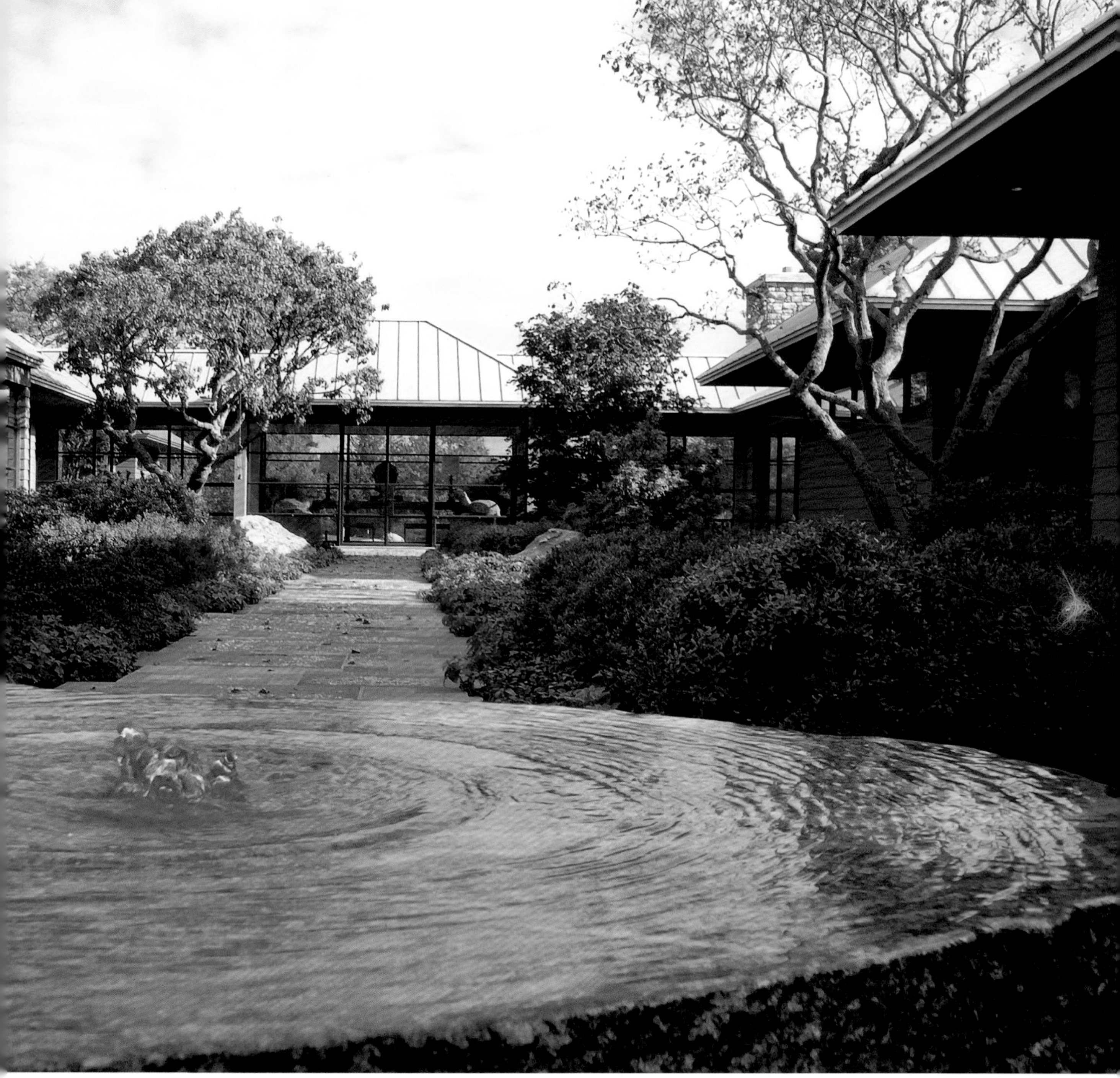

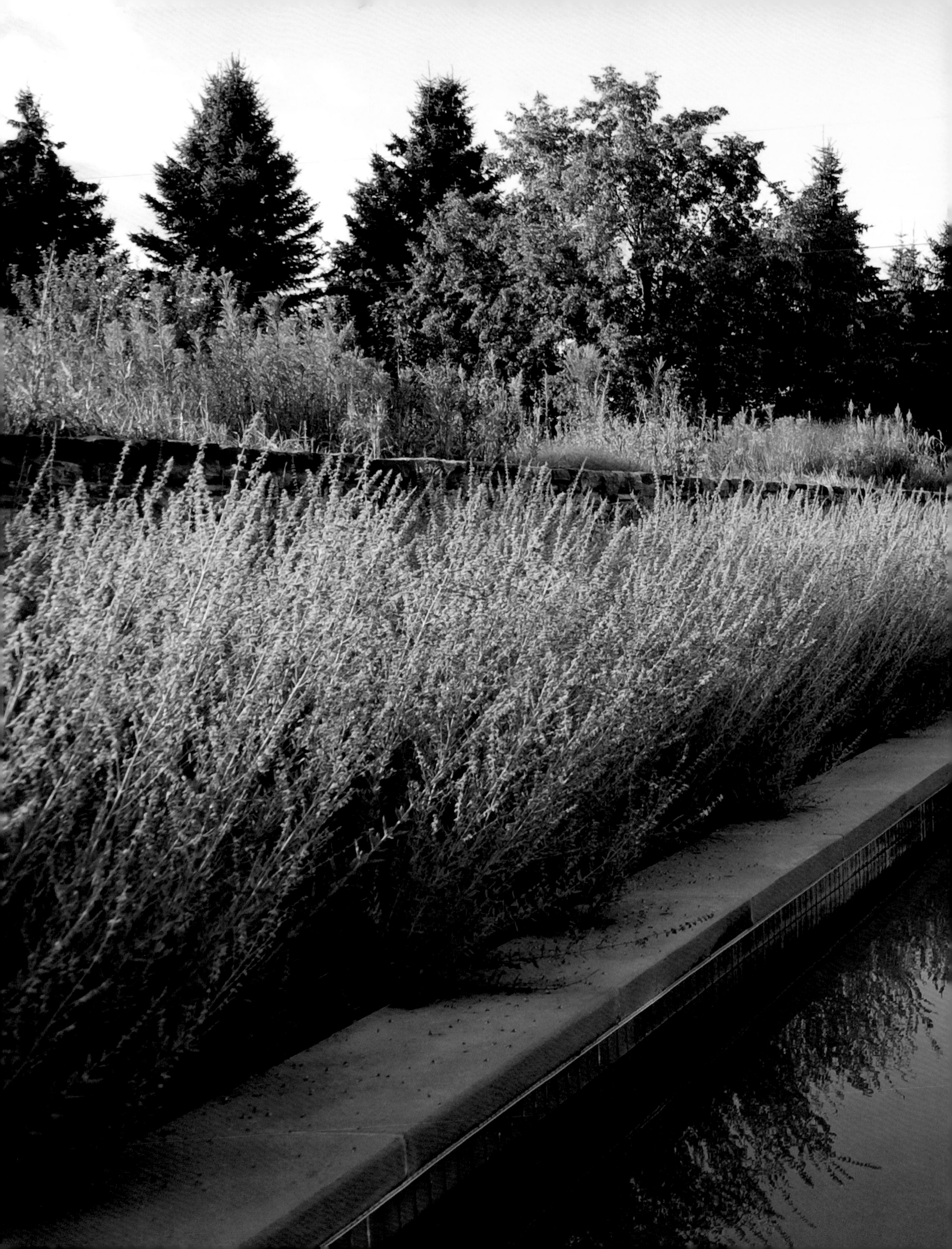

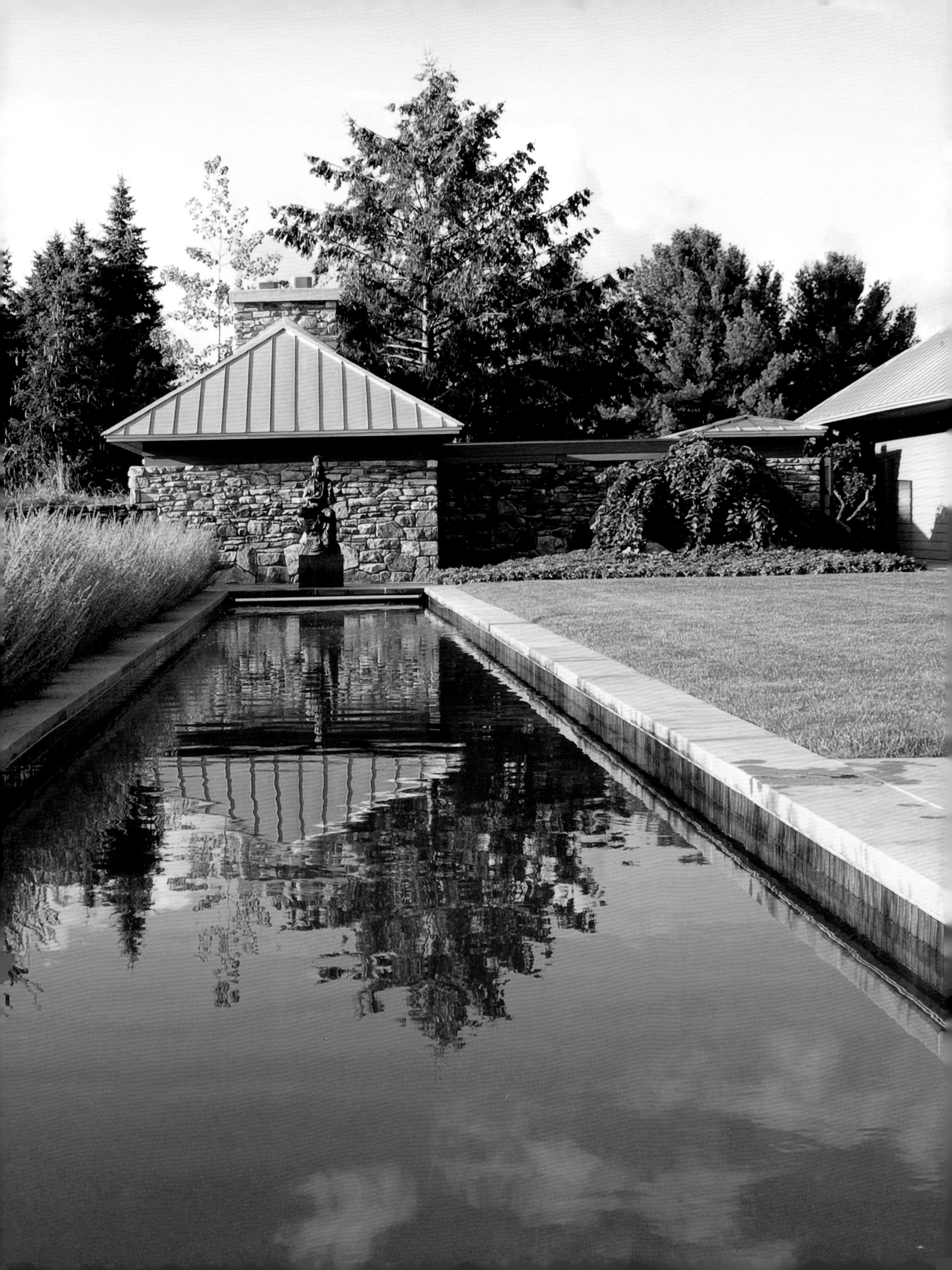

OPPOSITE Precise geometry in the form of cut-slate paving, trim stone walls, and a carefully ordered maple bosque makes an effective counterpoint to the pastoral woodland surroundings. **BELOW** The west terrace is raised to offer views of the native landscape in the distance. **PREVIOUS PAGES** Expanses of turf, water, and meadow flowers define the sunken east terrace. Russian sage blooms along the lap pool from summer into fall; a similar effect is created in spring by hundreds of *Allium giganteum* bulbs planted directly below. **OVERLEAF** Herbs and vegetables grow in contemporary containers of varied heights.

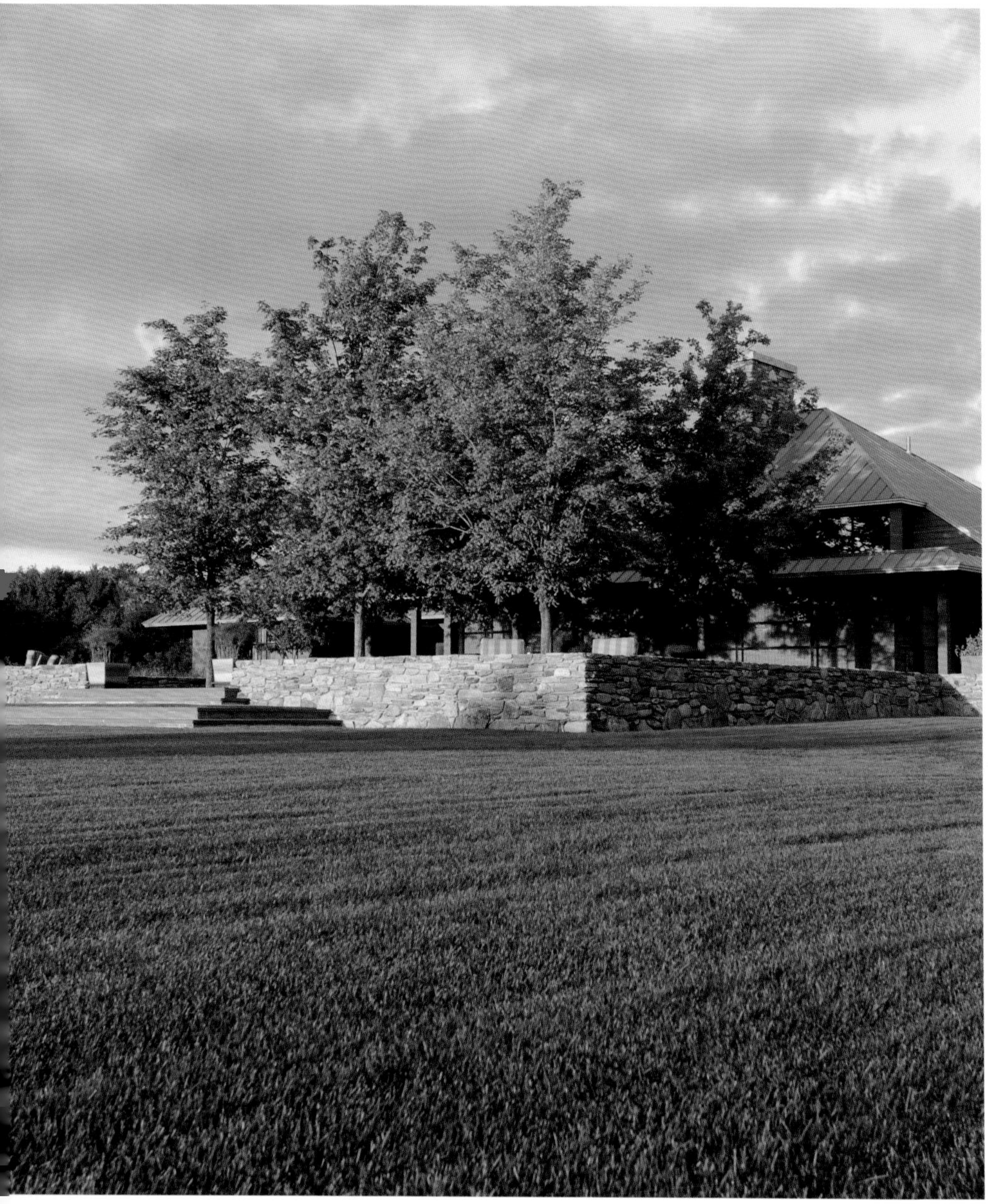

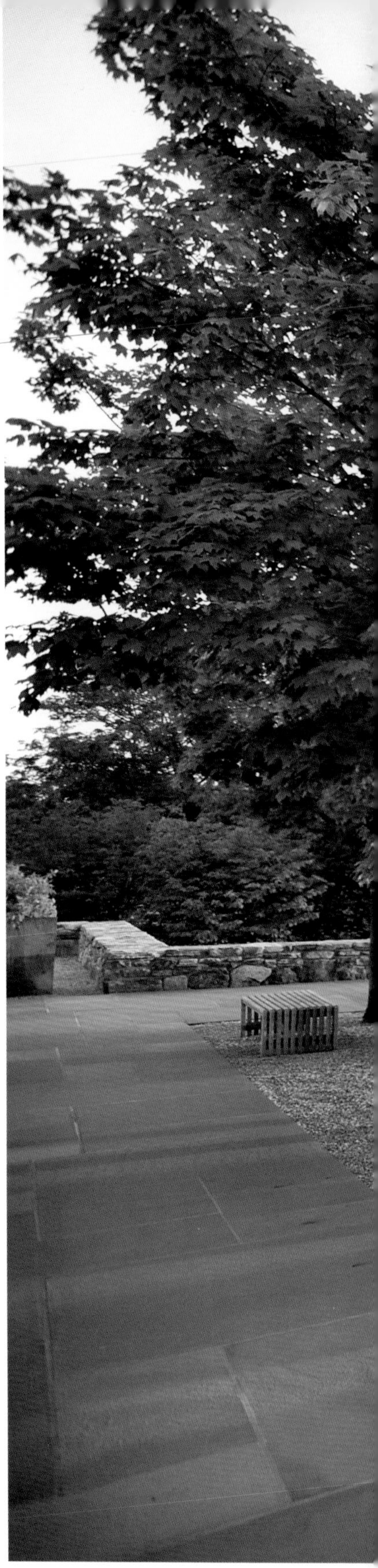

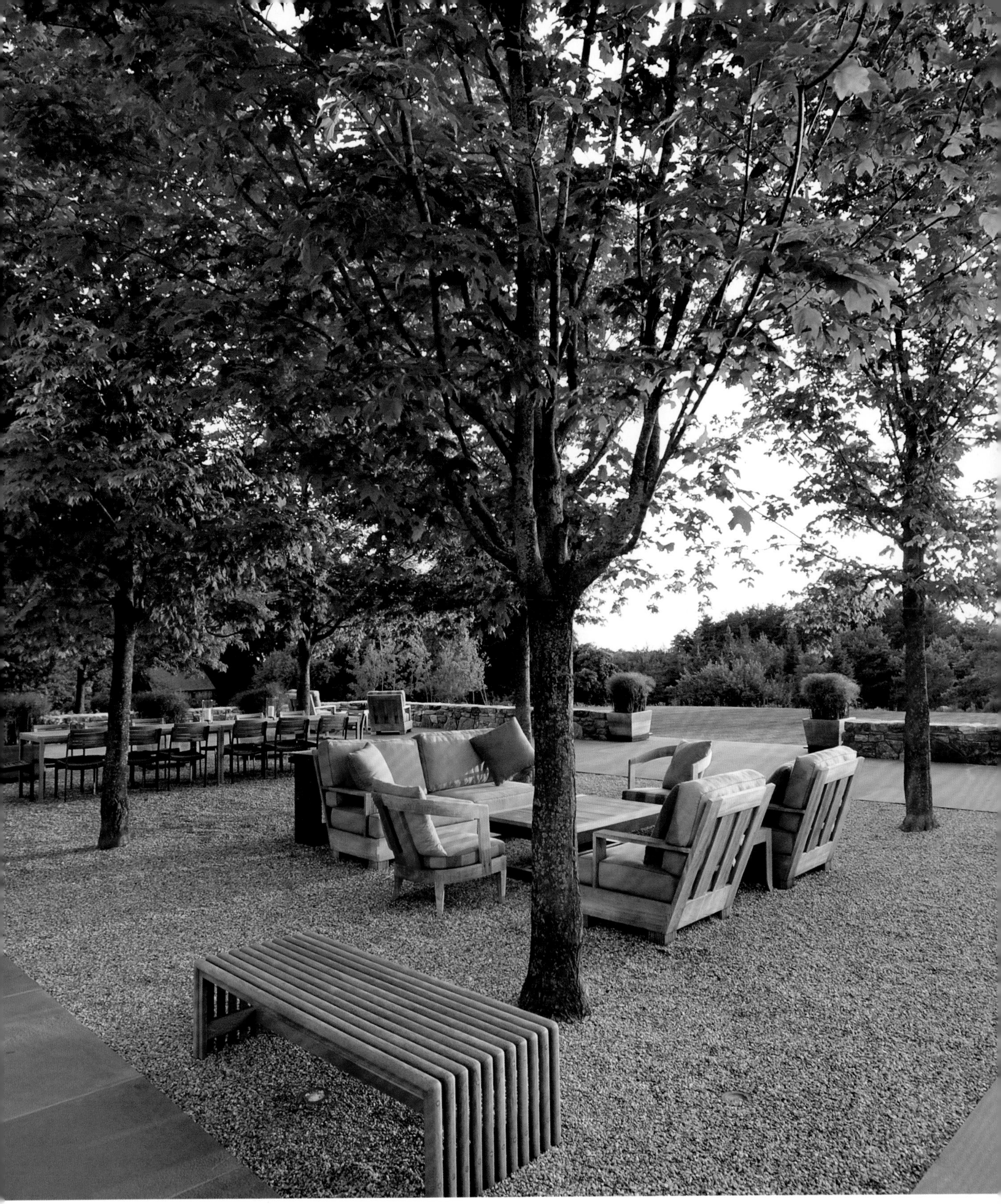

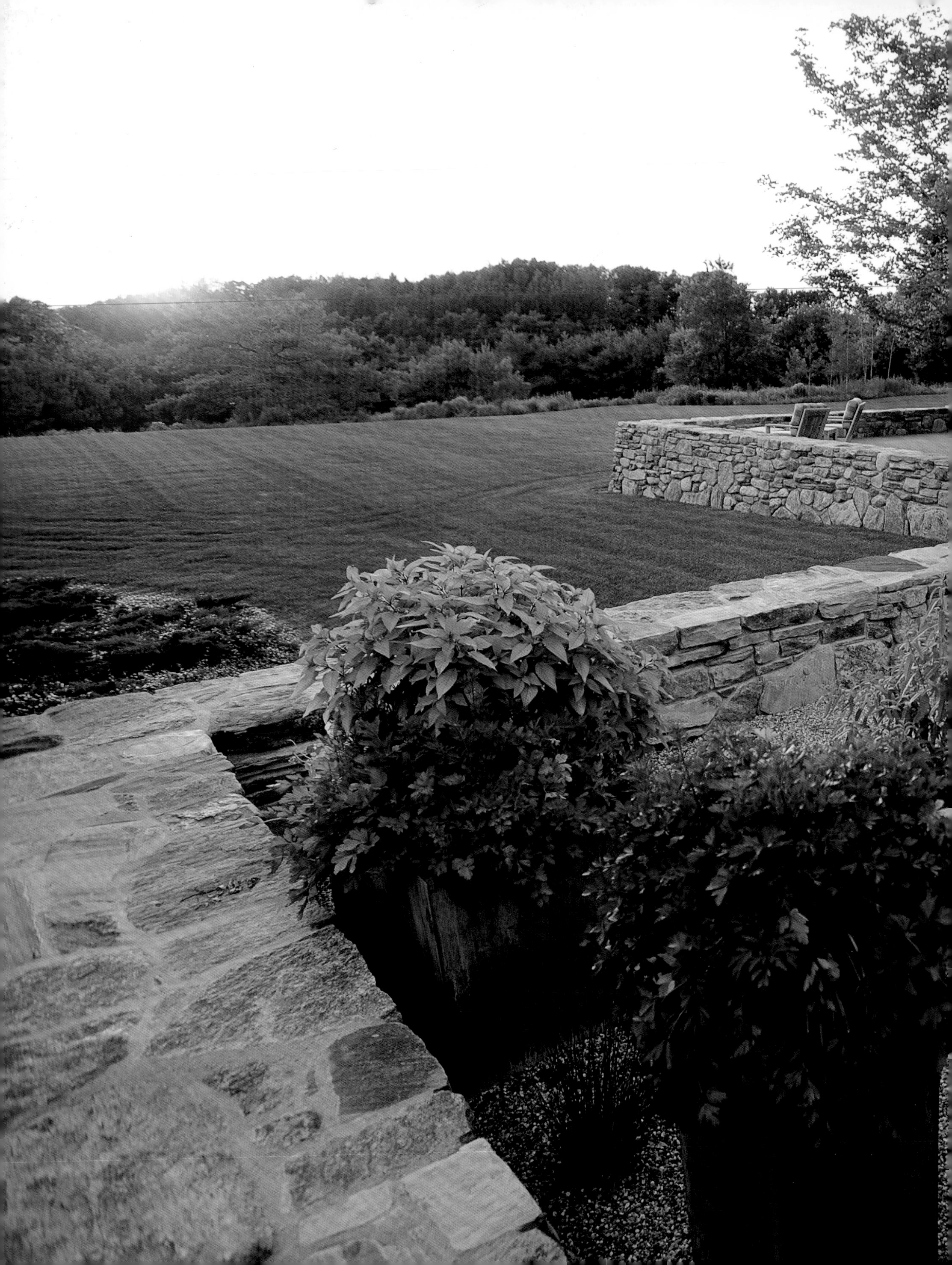

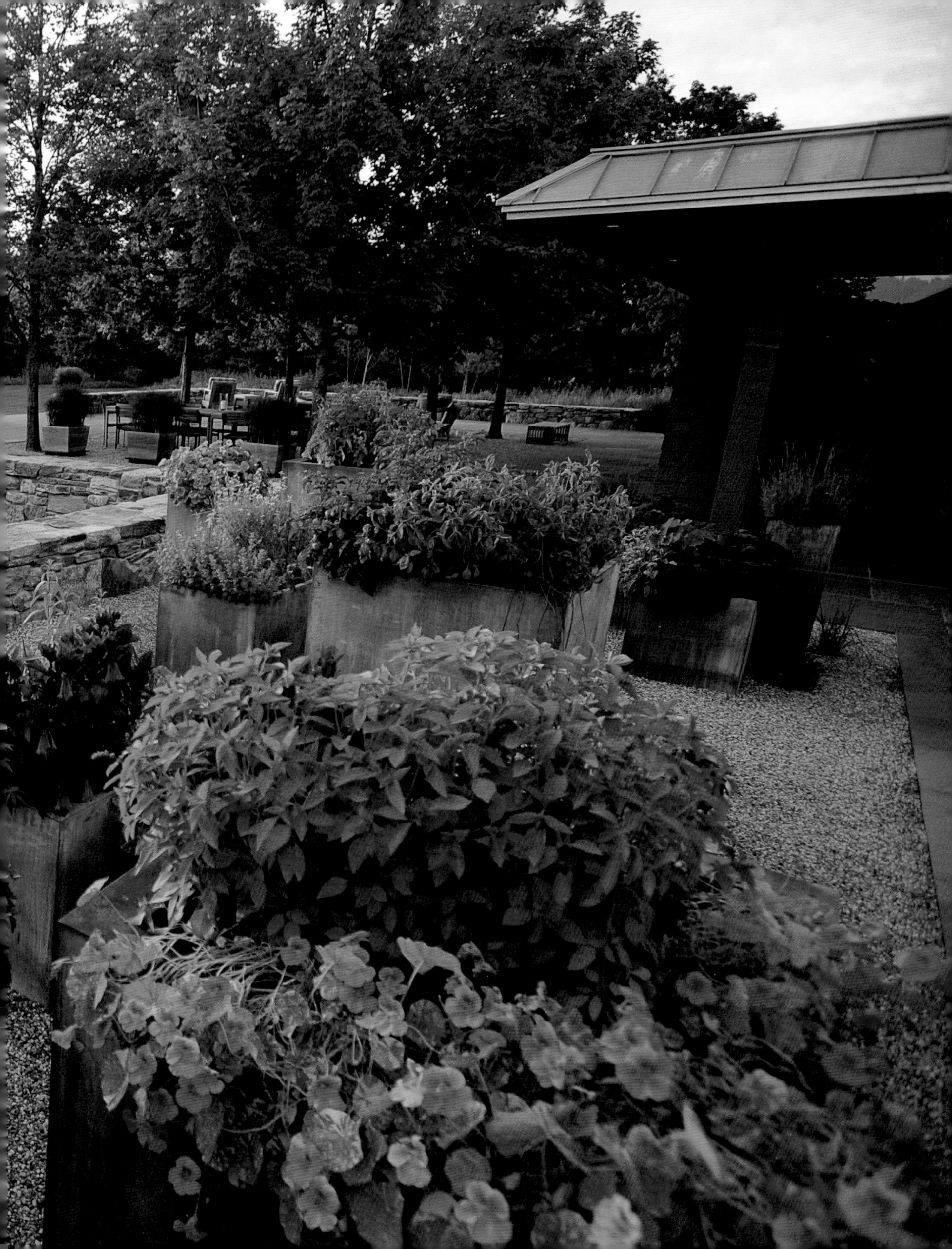

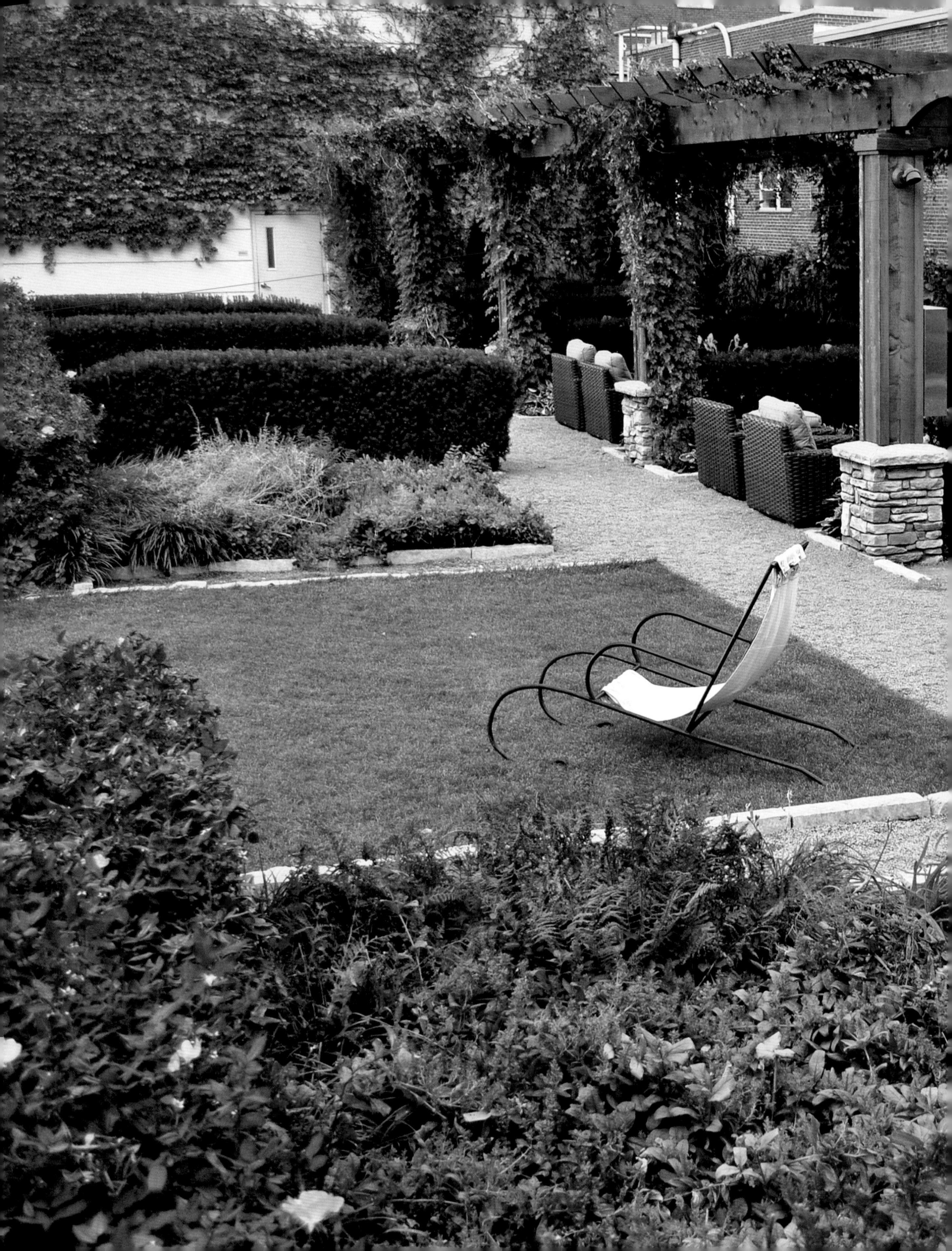

The tallest apartment building in Missouri, 909 Walnut in Kansas City, is a landmark thirty-four-story property built in 1930–31, recently renovated to create mixed-use space. When the developers decided to carve 161 condos from the interior, they also constructed a new eight-story parking garage to accommodate residents' vehicles. To their credit, they made a decision to include an amenity most apartment dwellers only dream of: a green roof on top of it, masquerading as a lush garden.

Jeffrey Bruce, designer of the 16,000-square-foot rooftop garden, says his plant selection was driven by two goals: providing bird nesting opportunities and creating food sources for them. "We can proudly say that we've spotted the endangered and rare peregrine falcon on the shade structure," Bruce says.

The developer recognized the value of providing a recreational space in the densely populated downtown neighborhood, and was a staunch supporter of the concept, funding the green roof without even tapping into public funds available for sustainable projects.

The garden consists of four distinct spaces: the open lawn, the focus of active recreation and sunbathing; a row of gazebo cabanas, seven small, enclosed garden spaces beneath a flowering trellis, designed to evoke a private resort setting; an elevated plaza on the south end, which serves as an outdoor gathering space for meetings, performances, and program events for the commercial tenants; and the north plaza, another hardscape surface available for program use primarily by residential tenants.

Special soil depth profiles, 6 inches for the lawn area and 6 inches for landscape beds, were designed to meet the site's diverse needs. All soil mixes and construction materials also had to be placed on the roof deck using cranes and buggies, which added to the complexity of the installation.

Plant choice was driven by a focus on a burst of color in the summer—when the garden is most used—and also minimal maintenance and water conservation. Native plants were favored for their ability to adapt to the harsh environment; unique wind vortexes and the height of surrounding structures, as well as elevated temperatures create an urban "heat island" effect.

The green roof is often the setting for intimate dinners, large parties, and fundraisers. Films are projected on the surrounding walls on summer Fridays. Once a week, a professional chef also sets up an outdoor kitchen in the garden and cooks anything the residents bring down from their apartments, creating a neighborly social event.

One of the primary challenges in designing any green roof garden is to create a vegetative canopy. Neither limited soil depths nor weight restrictions encourage trees. "We did not want only a carpet of green on the ground," Bruce says. "Since we believe a garden should envelop the visitor in green, we decided to incorporate green vertical surfaces and elevated growing planes to provide a sense of three-dimensional space and foliage. We encouraged vines to cover most vertical surfaces, and the trellis structure also gets green into the air."

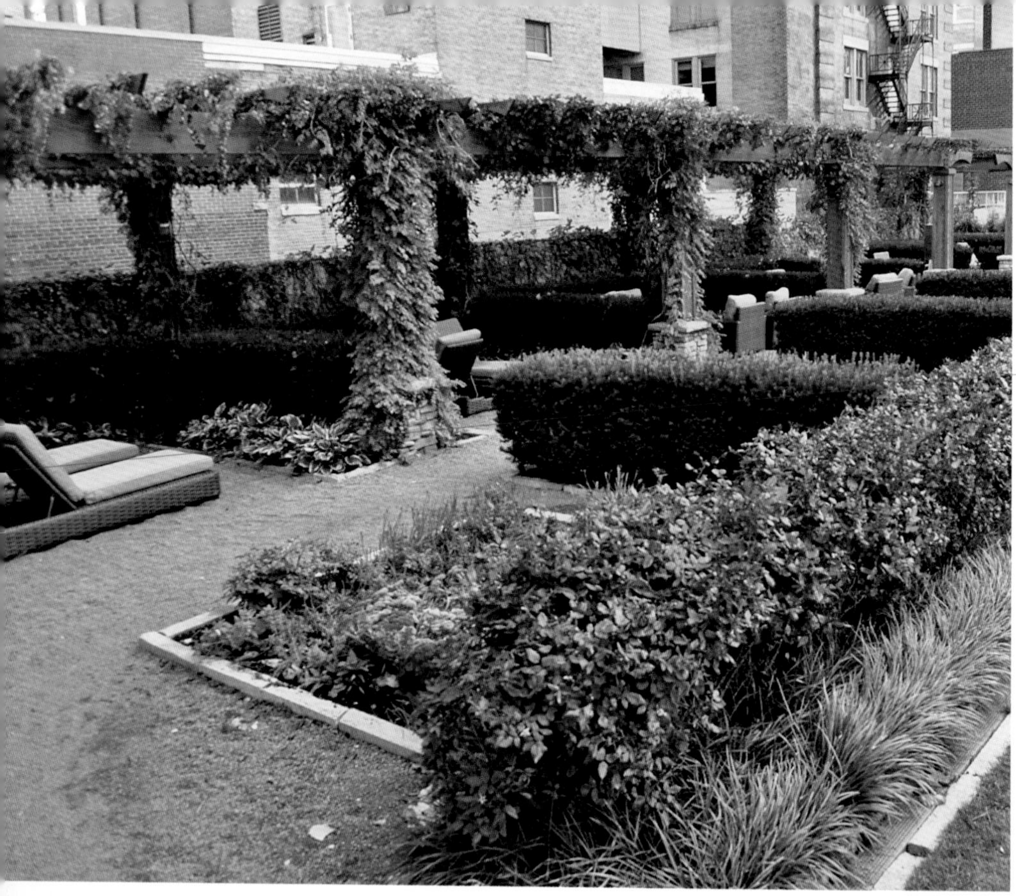

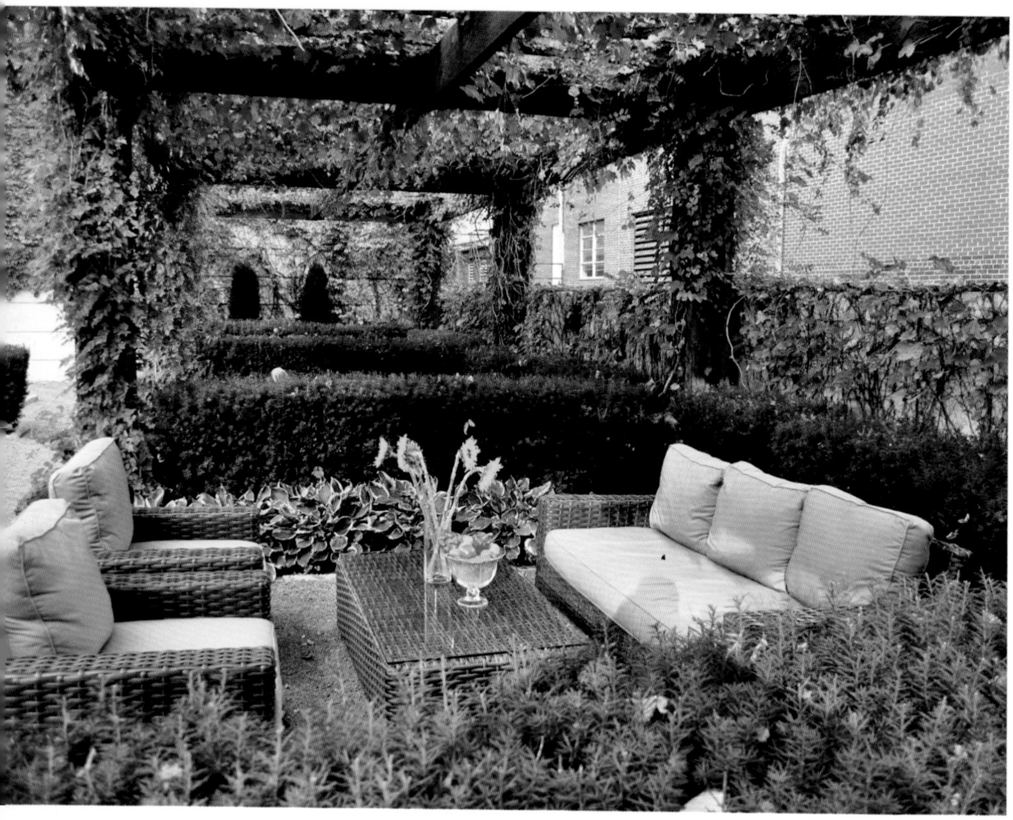

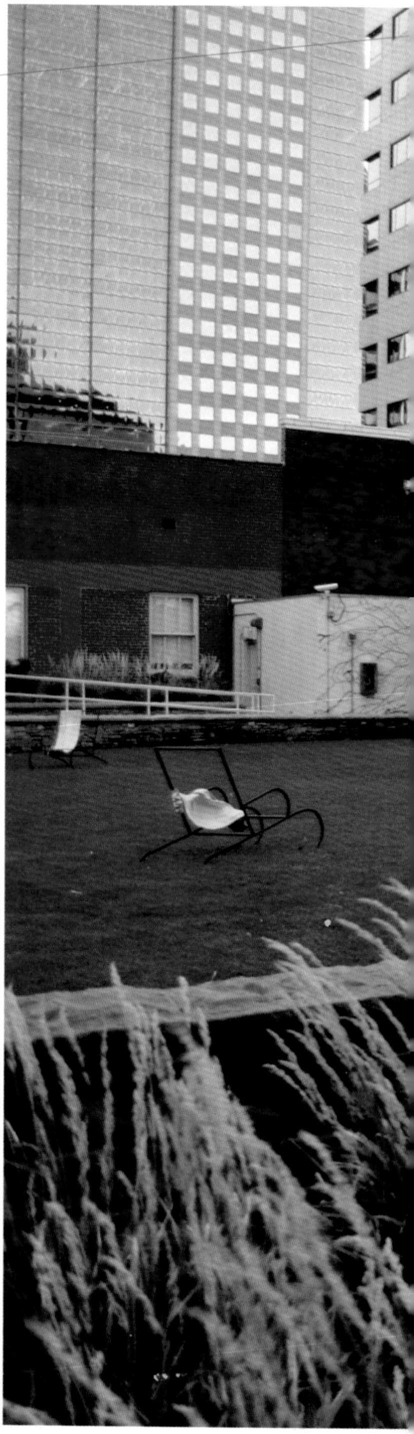

BELOW The roof garden's four distinct spaces—open lawn, gazebo cabanas, trellis area, and elevated plaza—connect via a decomposed granite walkway. **OPPOSITE, ABOVE AND BELOW** A luxurious canopy of vines wraps a shade structure, creating lush, intimate spaces and thriving even in the roof's thin soil profile and elevated temperatures. **OVERLEAF** Seven small, enclosed garden spaces under a flowering trellis are designed to evoke a luxury resort setting.

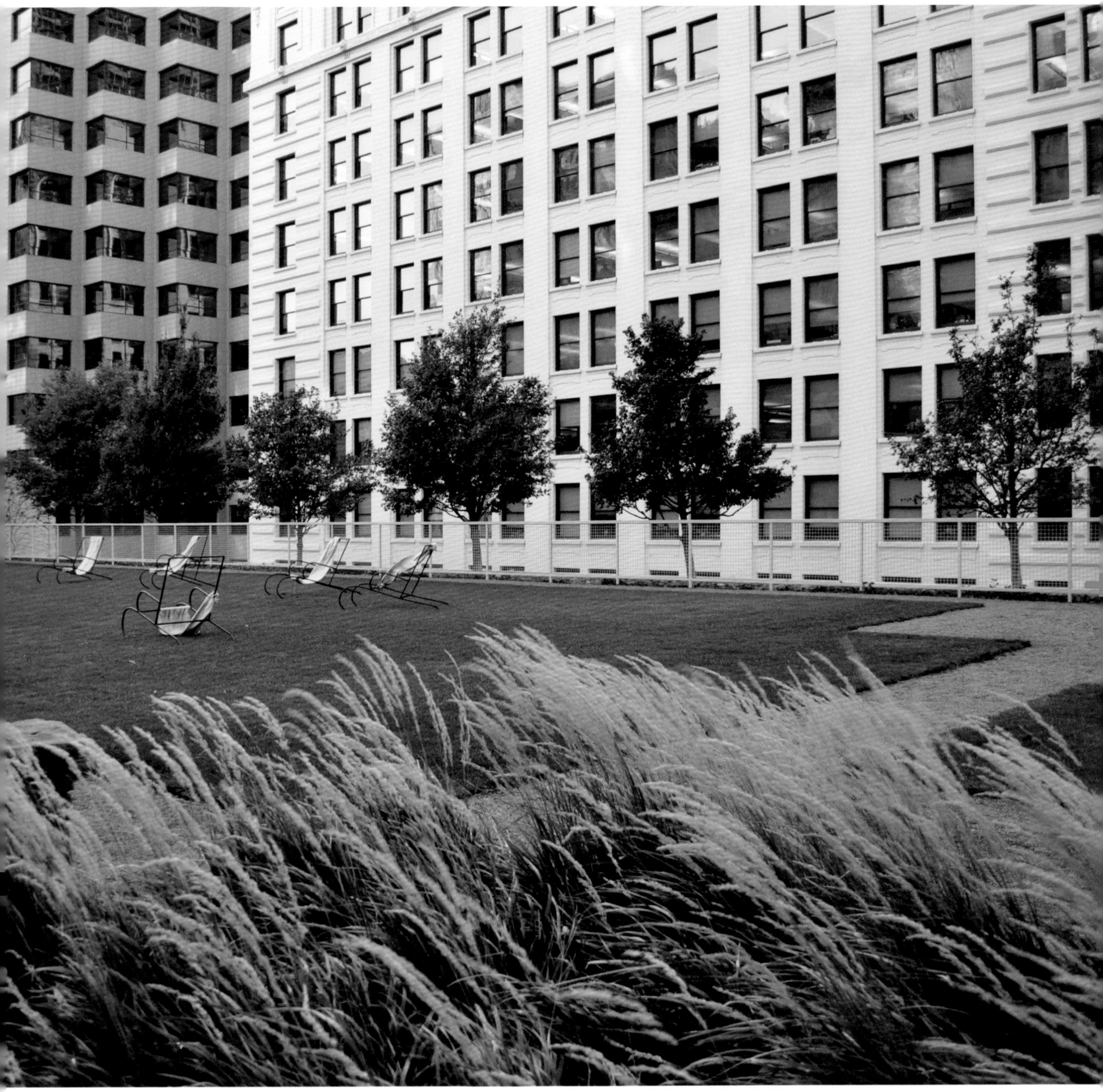

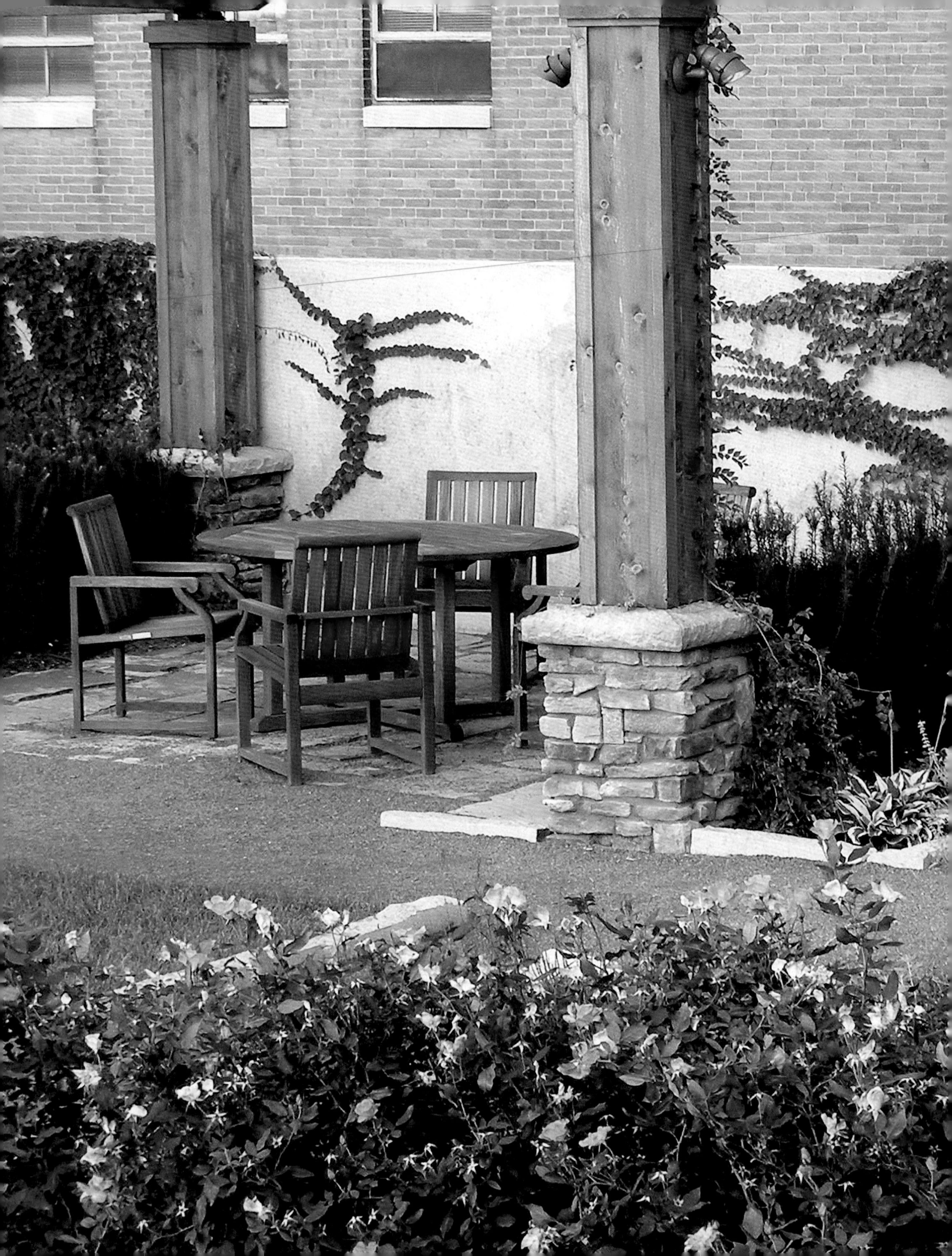

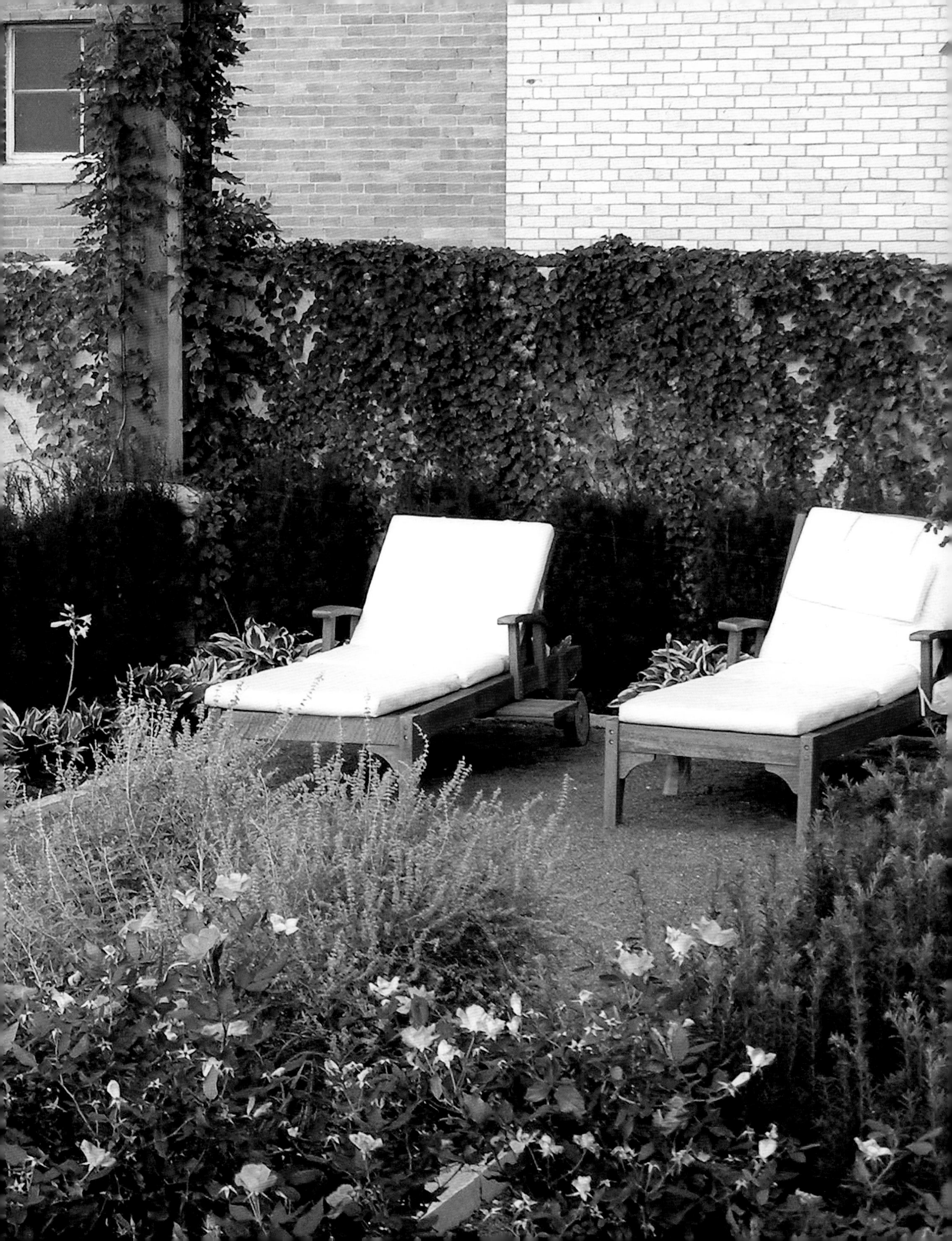

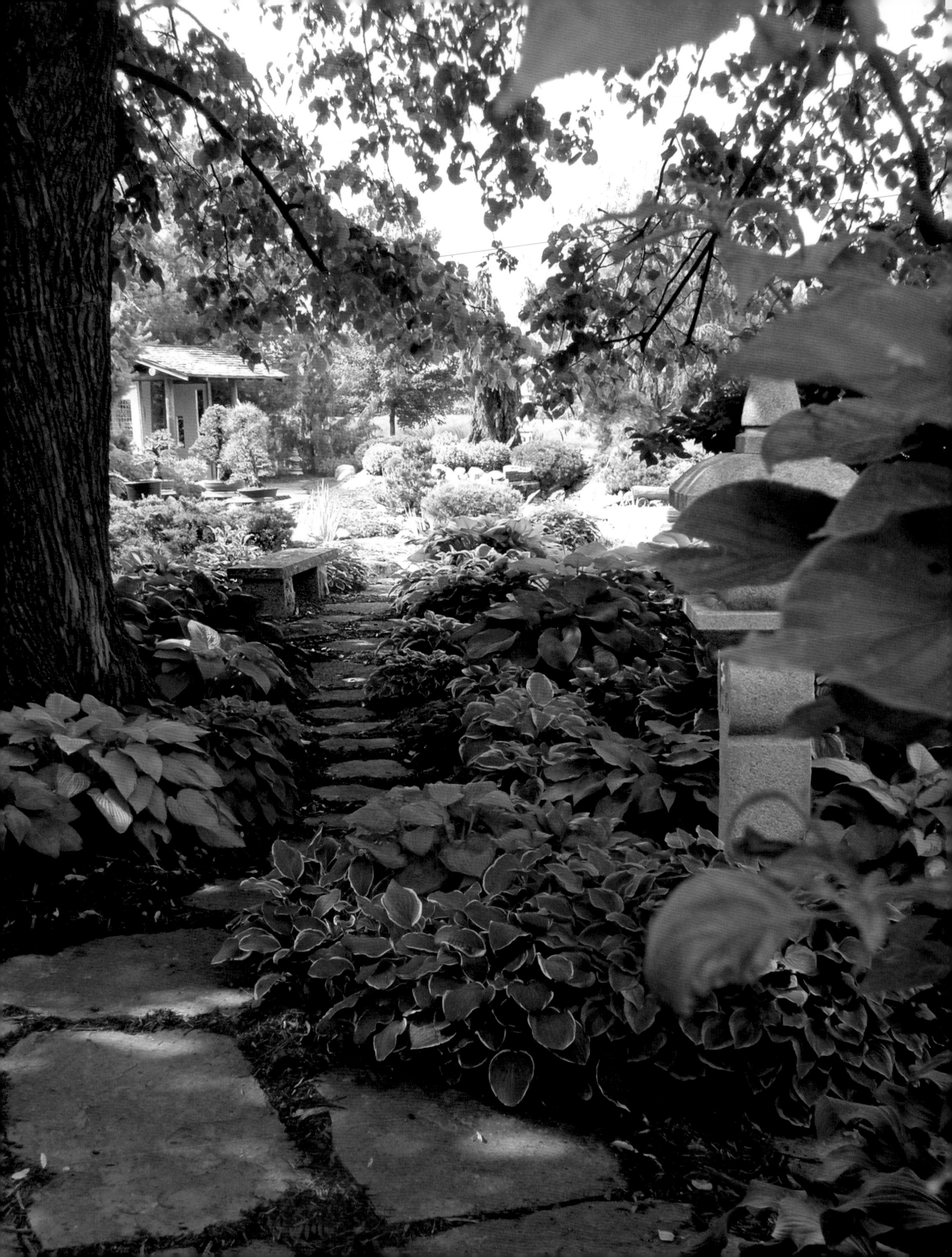

Alan Magruder, a retired college professor, and his wife, Helene, live on a farm near Indianola, Iowa, surrounded by fields of corn and soybeans. On their world travels visiting gardens, the couple fell in love with the Japanese landscape style and saw that it could be expressed on their property, especially because Helene developed a passion for training bonsai trees. "There was originally a riding area east of the house and north of the barn," Alan says. "It was no longer being used, so we decided to turn it into a more pleasant view and to build a place where we could display Helene's bonsai. We incorporated the three basic elements of a Japanese garden—stones, water, and plants—arranged to invite strolling."

A flagstone path set between two small, dry gardens leads the way into the main space. The gate at the entry contains a diamond-shaped cutout to provide a sneak preview of what lies ahead. The motif is also repeated along the top of the fence that surrounds the entire garden. Just past the gate is an area with several bonsai trees on stands to the left and a pond to the right. At the far end of the pond, past three stepping stones, a waterfall cascades beneath three large weeping evergreen trees that the owners refer to as "the three dragons." A stone pagoda peeks out from behind them.

The pond is edged with stones and a blanket of Blue Rug juniper groundcover. Continuing around the pond to the left, more bonsai trees sit on stands in a gravel bed next to a large Japanese water jar. This is followed by a berm containing several varieties of conifers including threadleaf cypress, prostrate junipers, a large weeping hemlock, and Mugo pines shaped like stones. This swath of greenery leads to a small building shaded by a large white pine and a Chinese pine. This structure, nicknamed the "Meditation House," which Alan built, catches cool breezes and is positioned to overlook a bamboo dripper trickling water tranquilly into a stone basin.

The path continues, lined with tall grasses on one side and a dry waterfall on the berm. It eventually leads to a weeping willow and a small secret garden with a bench surrounded by tall grasses, a large pine, and Amur maples. Still farther on, around the pond and up a short flight of steps, a hosta garden is shaded from the strong Midwest sun by an ancient linden tree. A large stone pagoda-shaped lantern is nestled among the hostas. Although hostas flourish in many garden settings, they are native to eastern Asia, making them look most at home in this Japanese-style landscape.

Enclosed by a cedar wall, the farthest dry garden contains more specimen bonsai trees on stands. A pergola shades the most tender bonsai, and a nearby deck incorporates another bonsai growing bench. A stone patio anchors the garden and is sited to provide an overall view.

The Magruders added a large windowed room to their home to serve as Helene's bonsai studio, so she could care for the little trees year-round. In the world of bonsai, she is a rarity—a female accorded the honor of the title Bonsai Master.

RIGHT Three weeping conifers, which the Magruders call "the three dragons," surround masses of variegated iris planted in a sunny pool. **BELOW** Bonsai trees on platforms dot the garden.

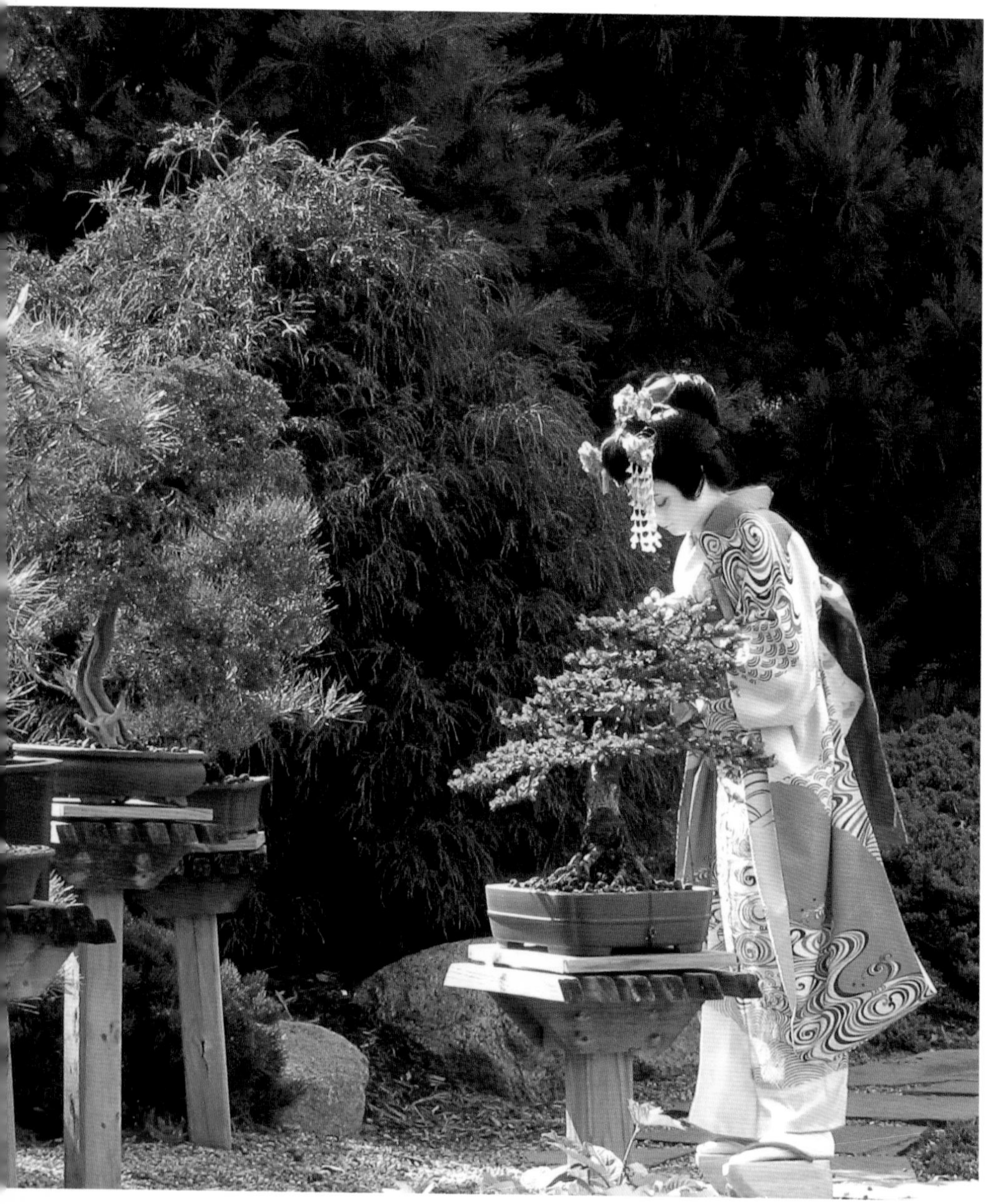

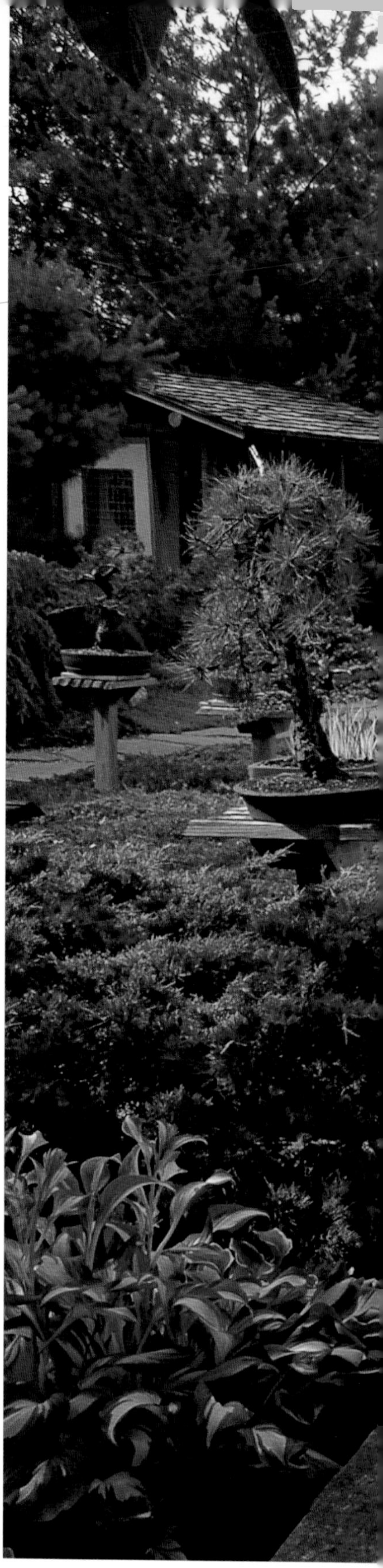

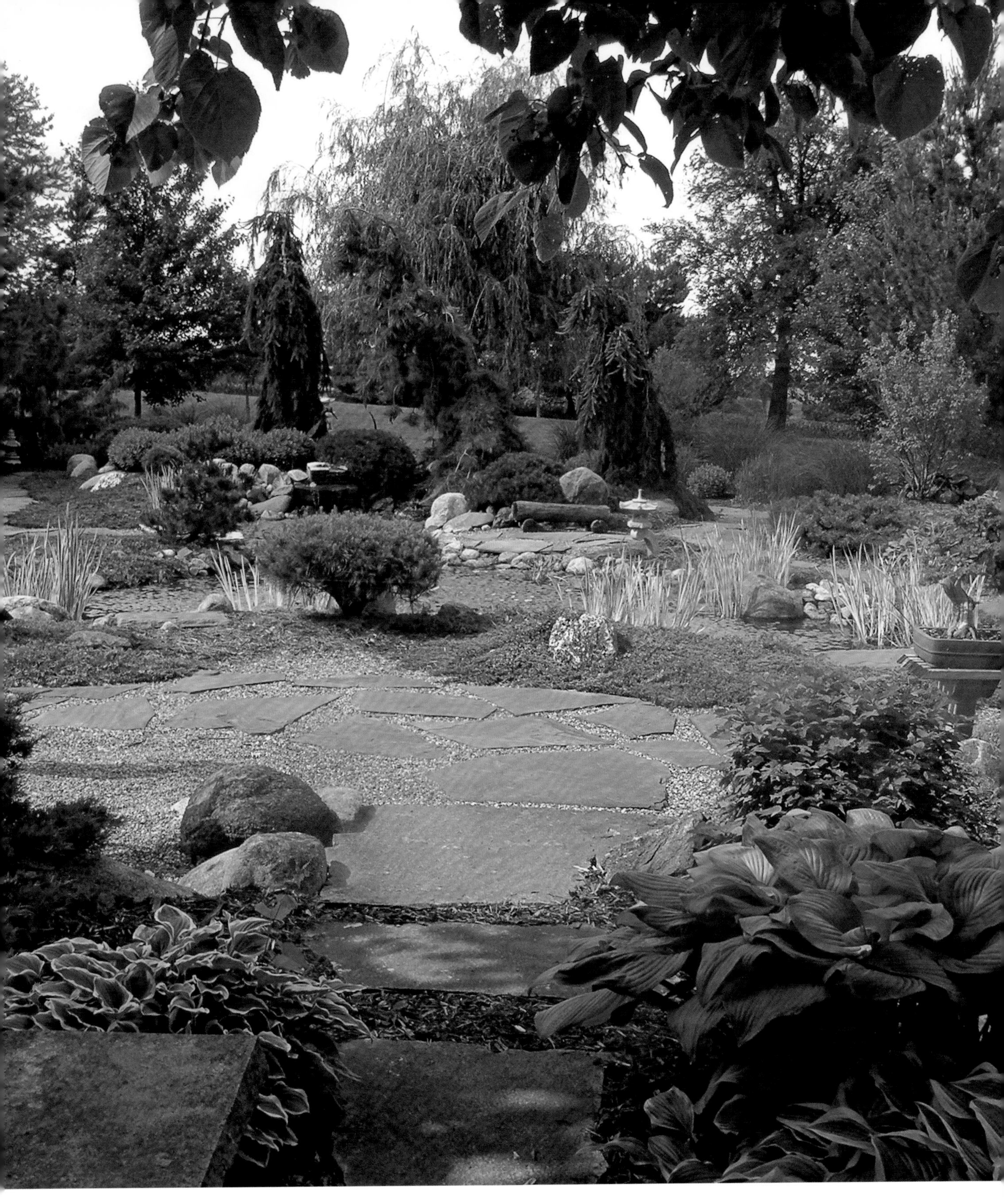

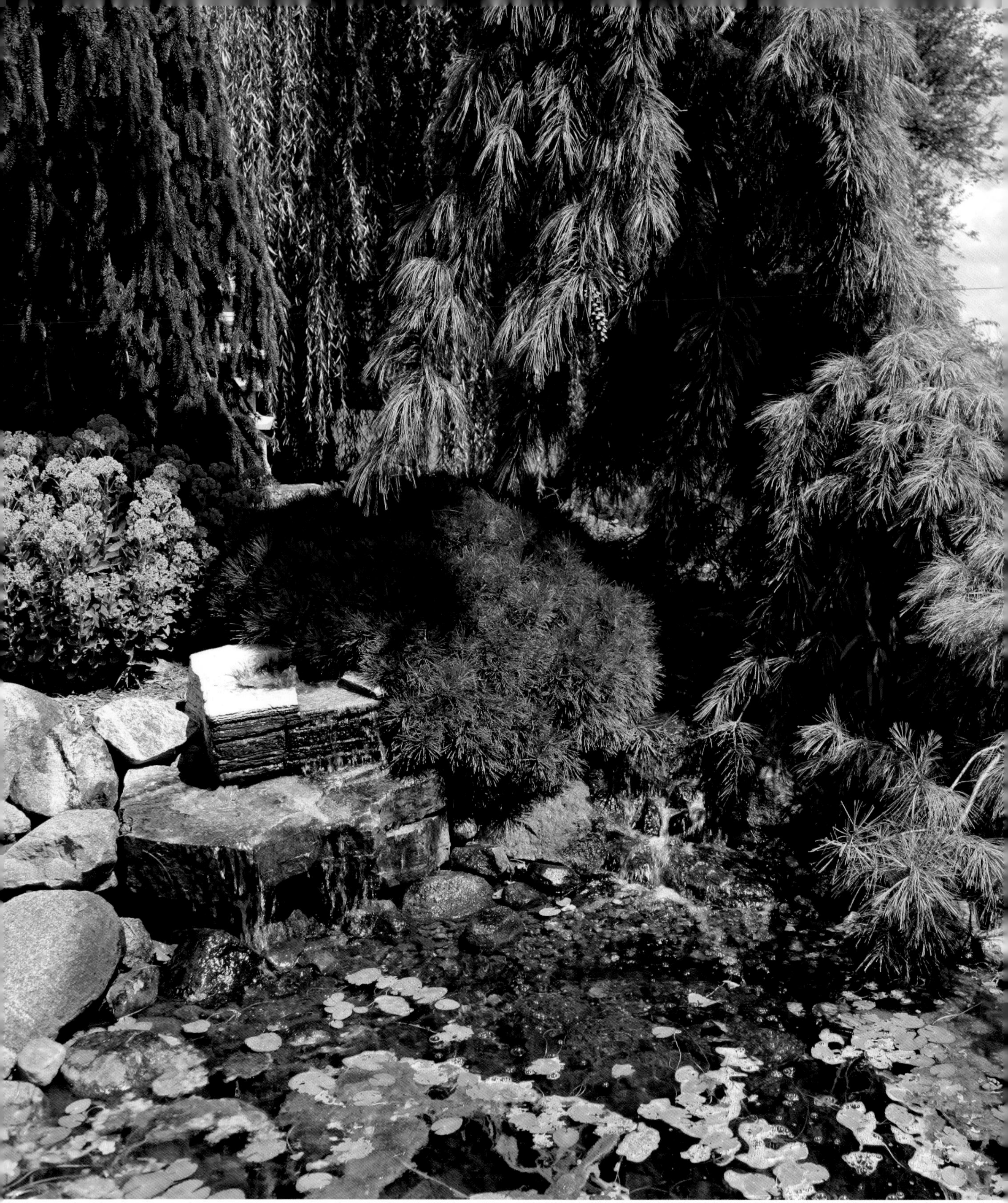

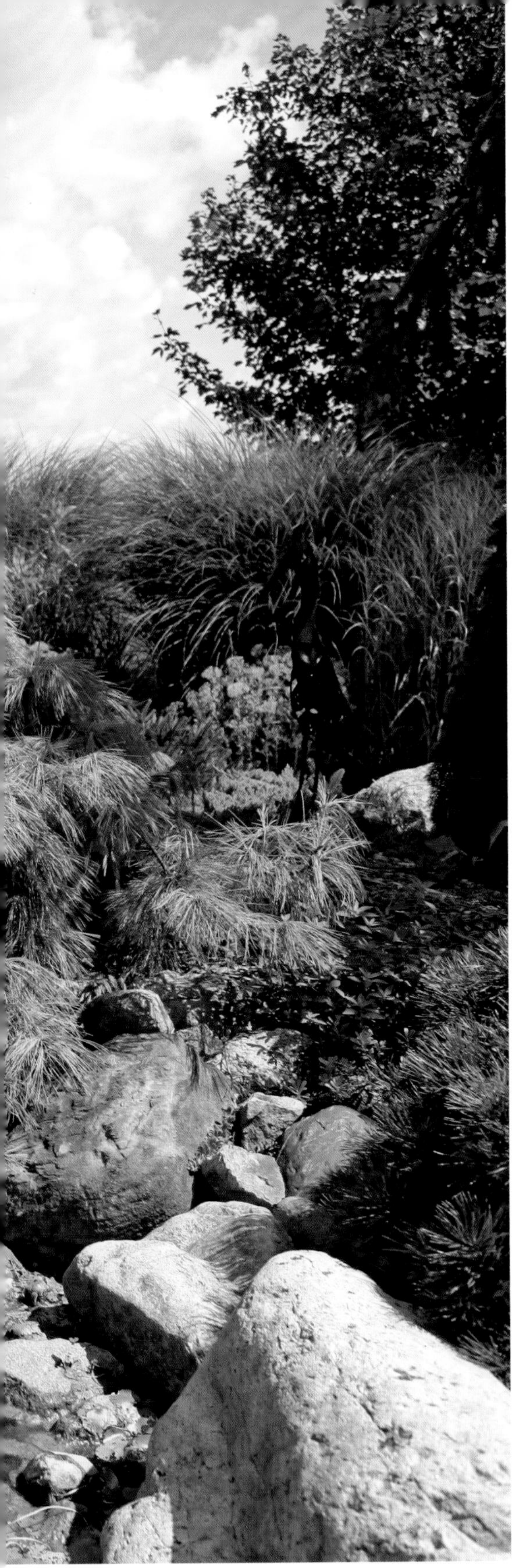

OPPOSITE Branches of a weeping white pine echo the movement of a waterfall as it cascades over stones. Mounds of dwarf Mugo pine and sedum 'Autumn Joy' similarly mimic rounded boulders nearby. **BELOW** Hostas, native to East Asia, play a significant role in this themed garden. Cultivars with yellow- and white-variegated leaves add a hit of light to shady areas. **OVERLEAF** A meditation house, inspired by the form of traditional Japanese tea houses, is positioned to catch breezes and offer a view of the pond. A nearby bamboo fountain, or *shishi odoshi,* adds to the garden's serene feeling by creating a soothing trickling-water sound.

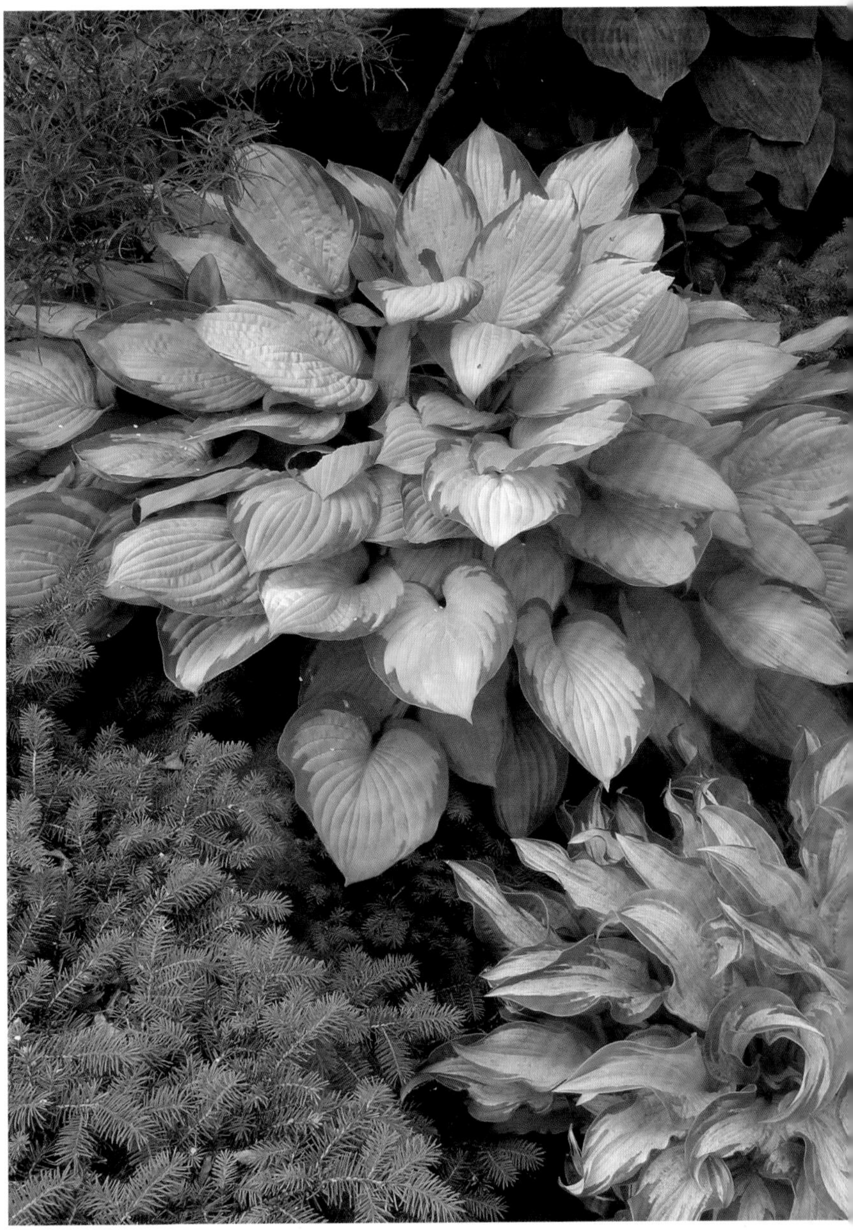

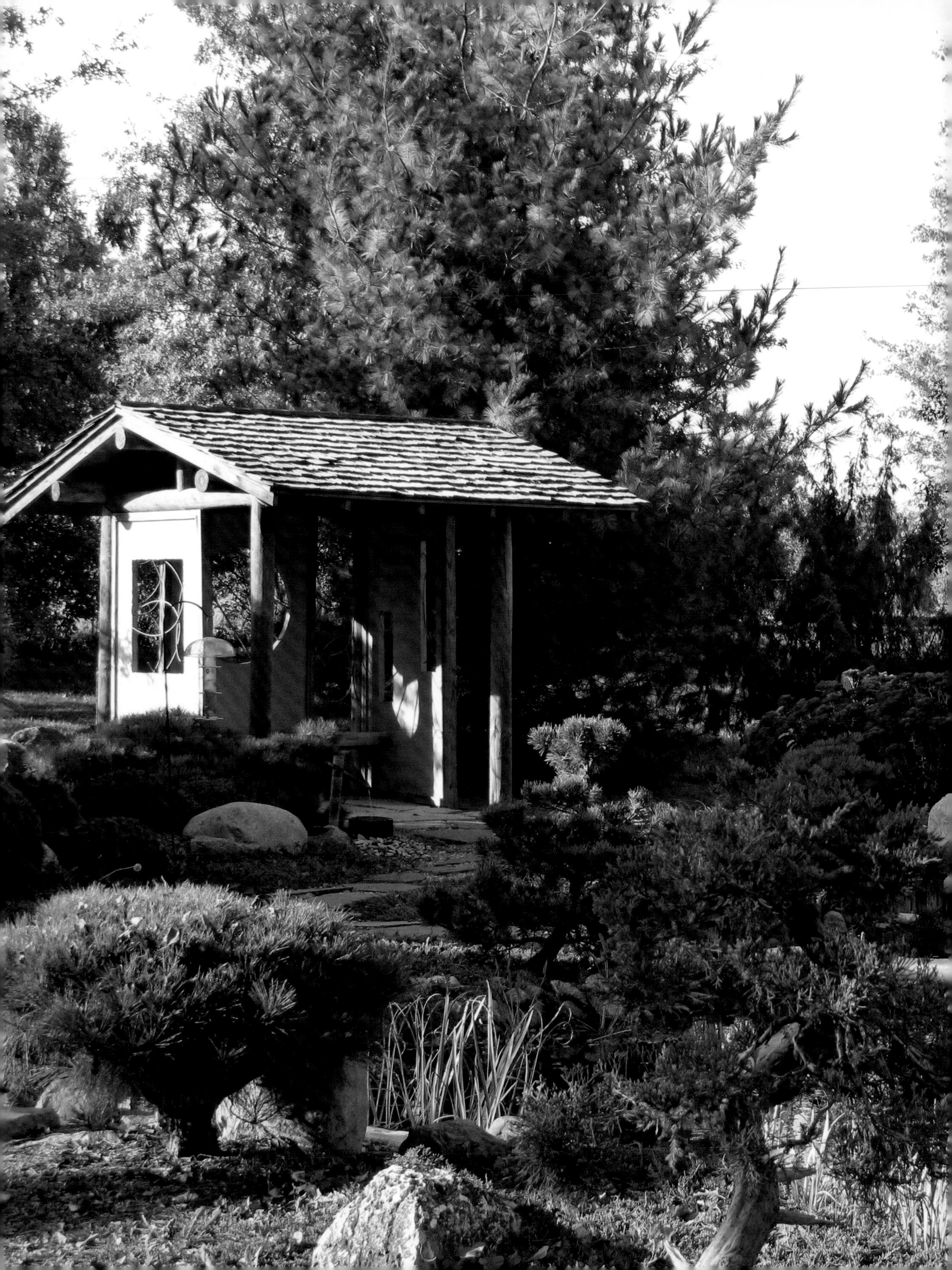

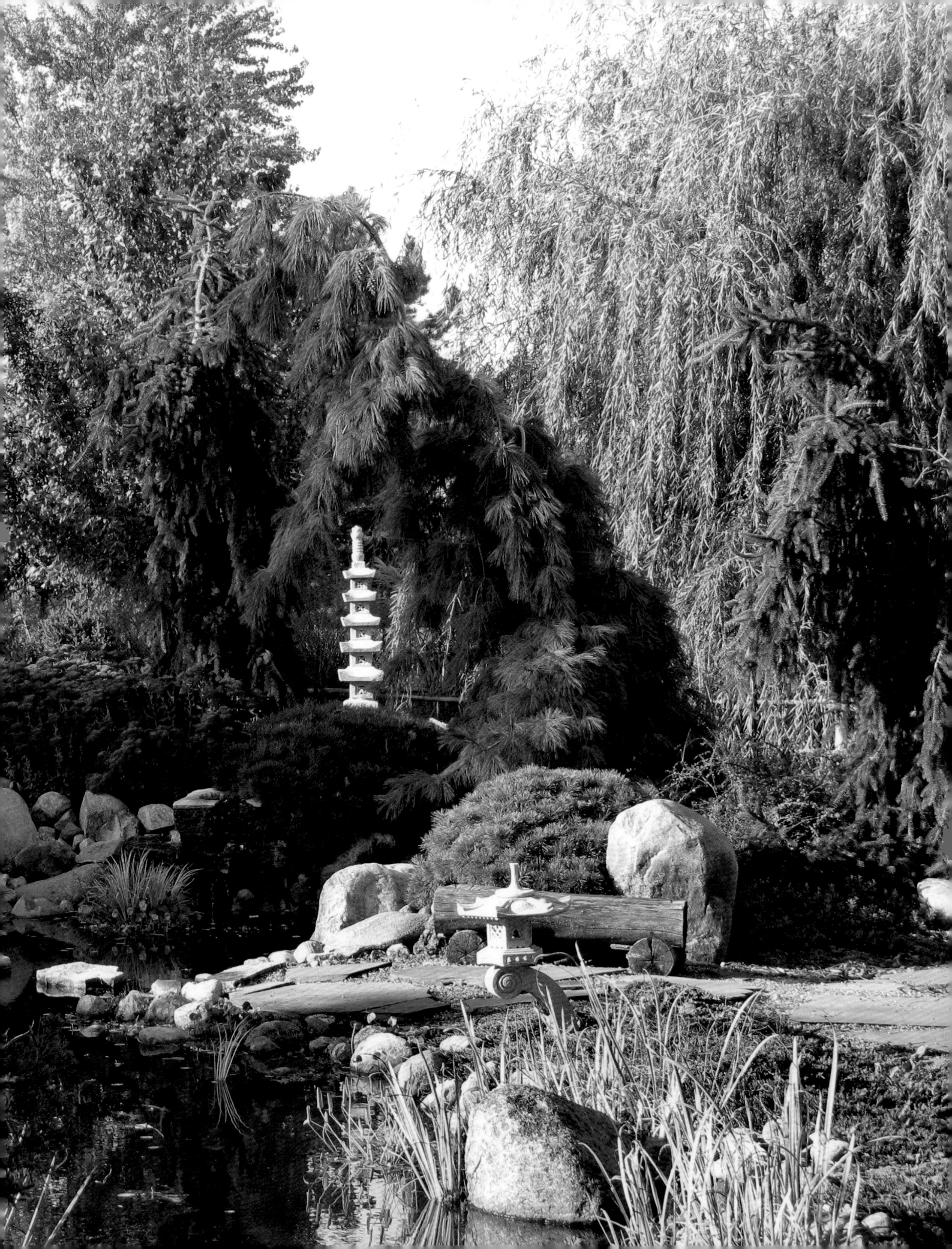

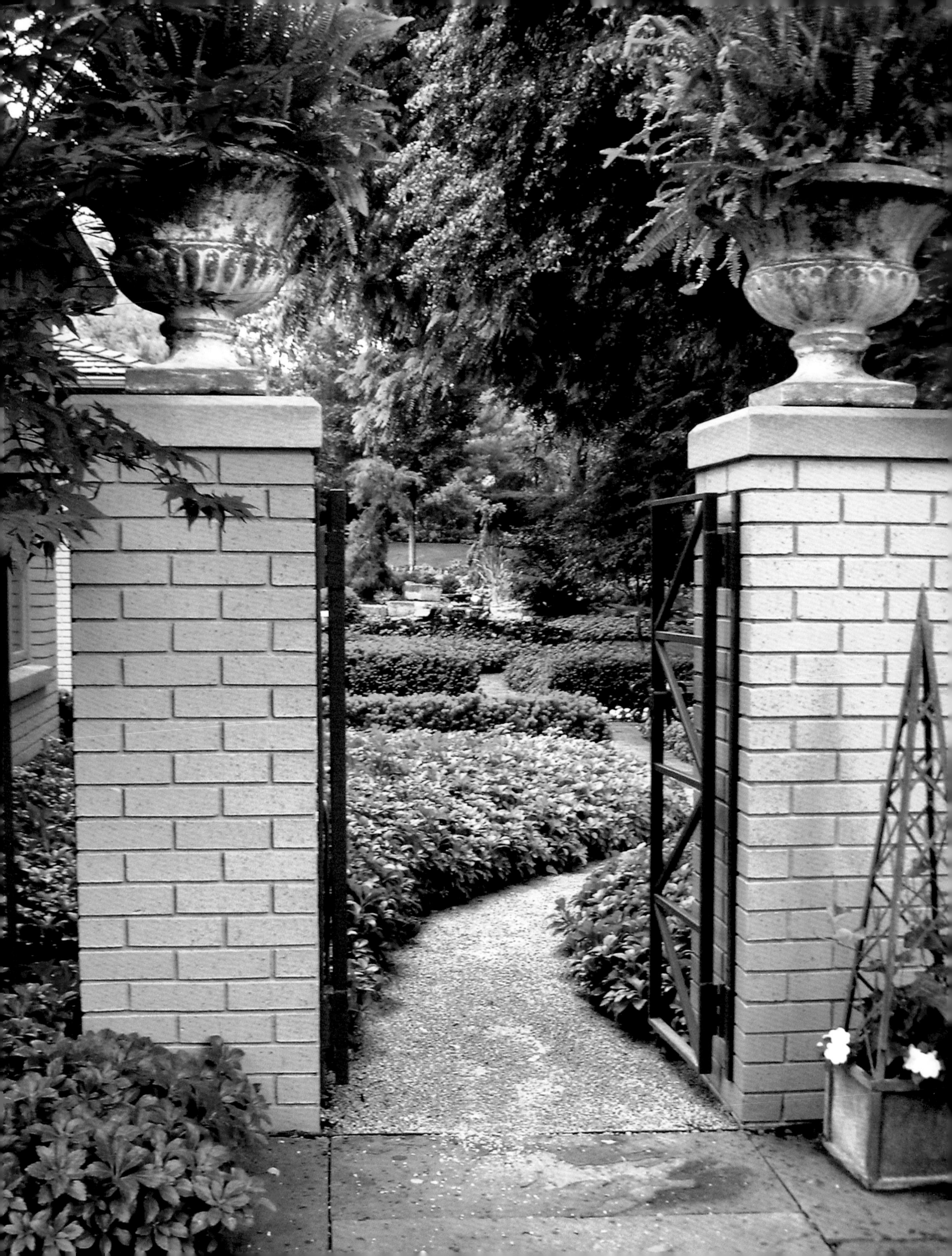

Landscape architect Richard Nielsen began this garden for an Omaha surgeon in the spring of 2005. "The property consisted of grass, grass, and more grass," he says. "It was completely devoid of any structure that might indicate a garden—unless you count a row of misshapen yews as a foundation planting." To add interest, Nielsen leveled part of the sloping lawn and added a wall and stairs. "Using centuries-old European techniques, I tucked away the ramped maintenance routes to the upper spaces to invisibly facilitate the movement of the lawn mower and wheelbarrow."

The house's architecture lent itself to the creation of two complementary courtyards that bring the landscape design deep into the main living space. Crushed stone paths radiate in either direction from the back courtyard. One meanders past a centuries-old French well head, turned vertically, that now floats sculpturally over low ground cover. A gate opens onto an informal, private stone-paved court featuring a raised, screened pavilion, water feature, grill, and informal seating areas. "This is the heart of the garden where friends gather for intimate dinners," Nielsen says. "It overlooks the deep wooded ravine and natural creek bed."

A stone path leads out from this dining area to a natural pond and waterfall. From this level, a wall and steps made of broad stones lead up to a sweeping lawn surrounded by perennial borders. Numerous seating areas and paths traverse this area; the most notable path ends at a winding stone stairway leading 12 feet down to a natural creek bed.

Coinciding with Nielsen's work, the owner spent nearly a year working closely with an architect to remodel the midcentury dwelling. New windows were added or replaced to maximize views to the garden. A new floor plan makes the most lived-in rooms flow into one another, then into the outdoor spaces.

"My client wanted the house to have an indoor/outdoor feel," Nielsen says, "a serene environment, an escape from a busy work schedule. He loves working in the yard and walking the grounds with morning coffee. Most entertaining is on a small scale, although on occasion he hosts a crowd to raise funds for the local opera company and has even had opera singers perform in the gardens."

Most areas contain massings of plants to create a clean, manicured appearance. A screened pavilion was added to the top edge of a steep slope to allow for outdoor living when the insect population escalates in the spring. "It is a grand place to sit and enjoy the rains," Nielsen says.

The bones of the garden were essentially completed in a year, but Nielsen notes, "Things are constantly evolving: growing, not growing, a new piece of sculpture here and there. My goal was for it to be timeless. Other than for the lawn maintenance, the owner himself cares for the gardens, finding the work satisfying and relaxing."

There has been one surprise: the owner is unable to realize his hope of keeping fish stocked in the pond because of the hungry mink population that lives in the nearby creek.

RIGHT Groups of gold-leaved spiraea contrast with the dark greens of the balsam firs and create a manicured border along the lawn. **BELOW** Sweeping lawns bordered with masses of perennials act as turf-covered paths for exploring the garden.

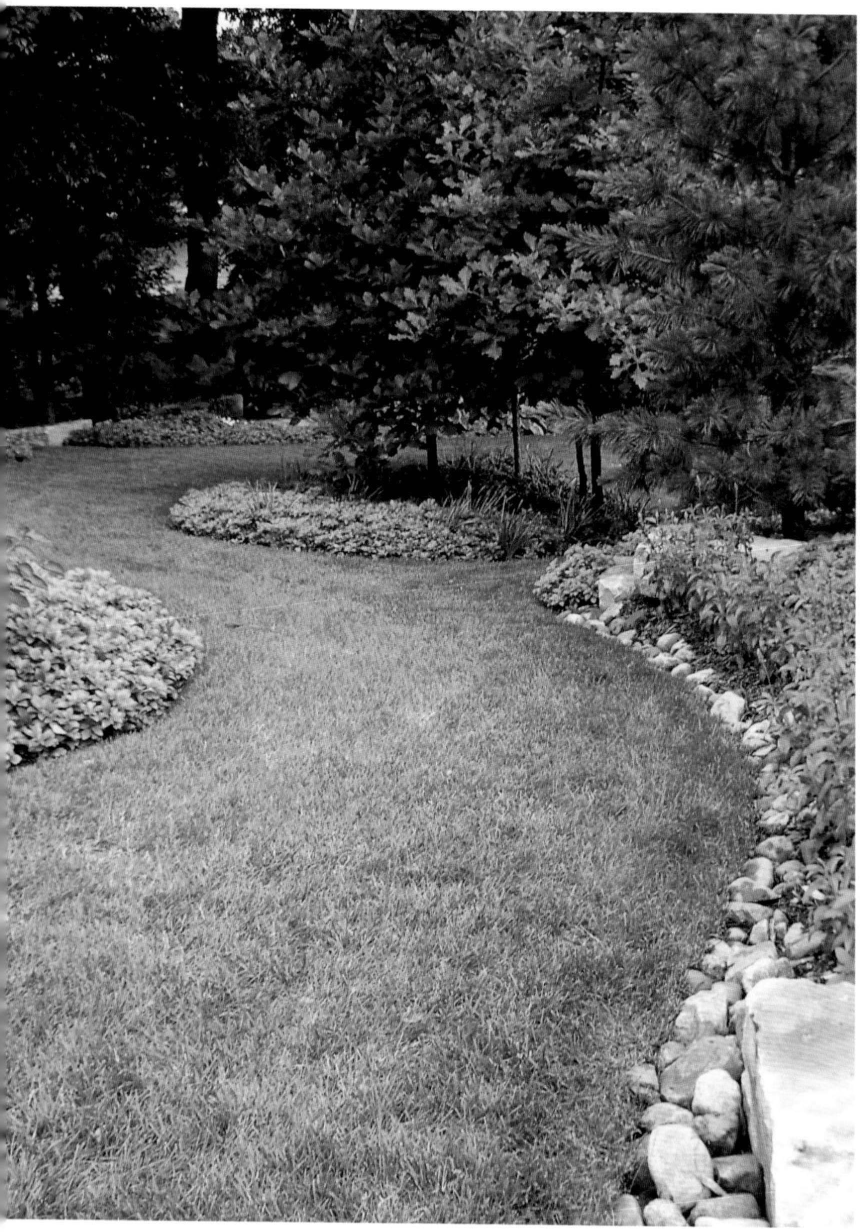

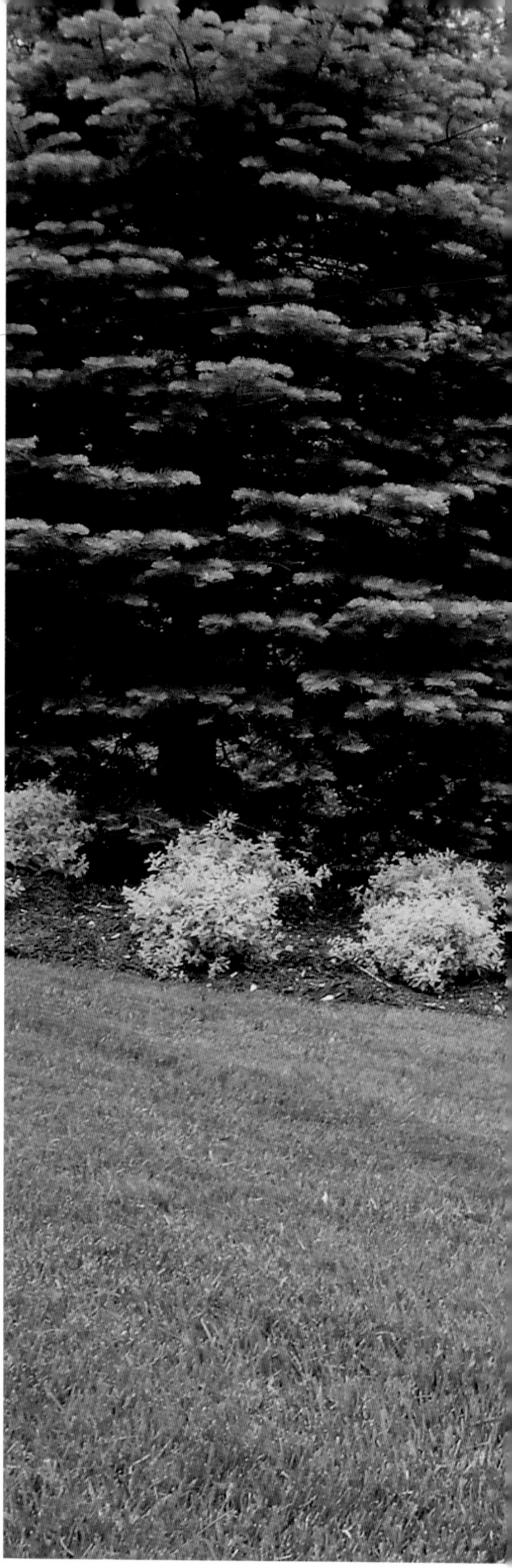

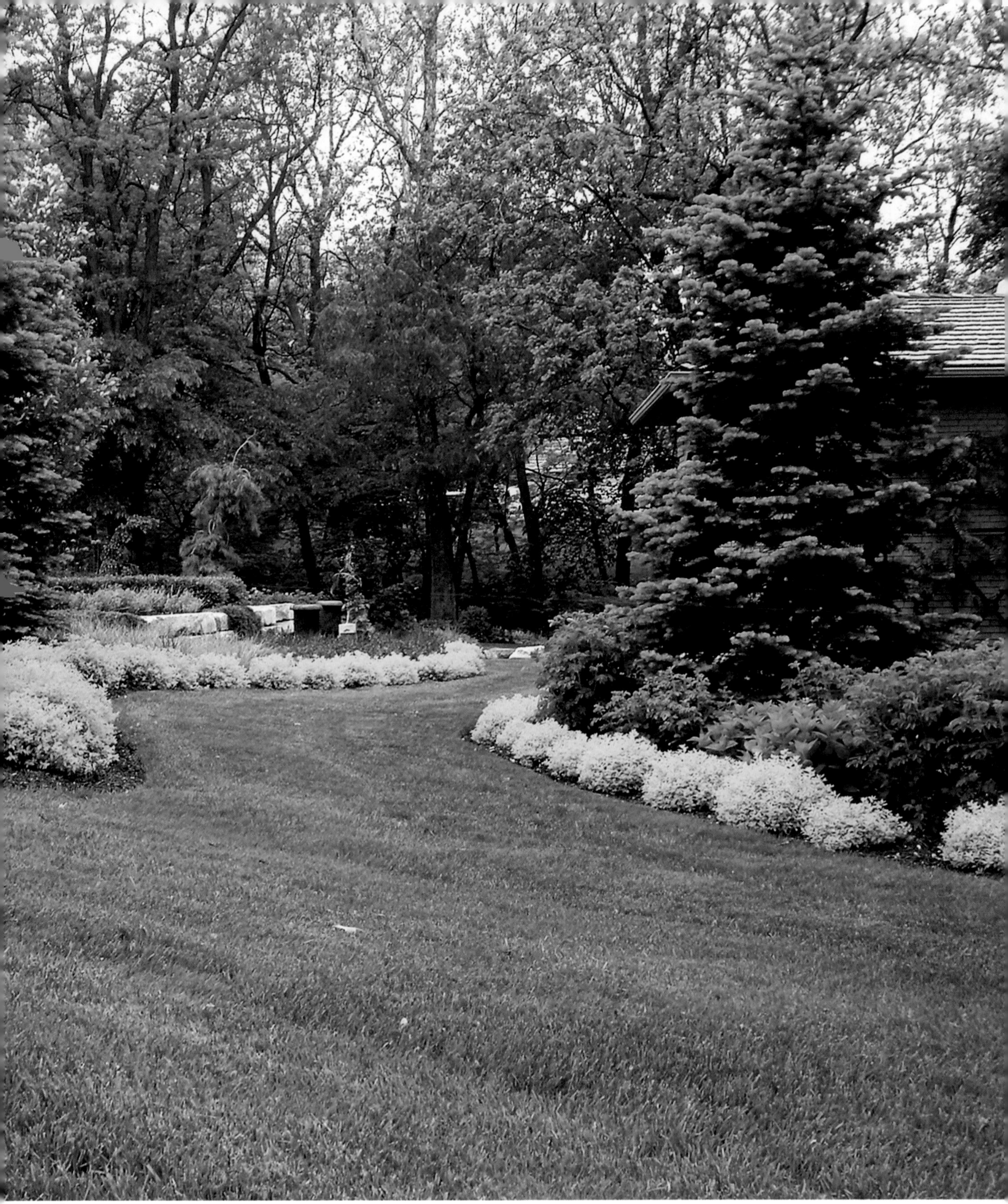

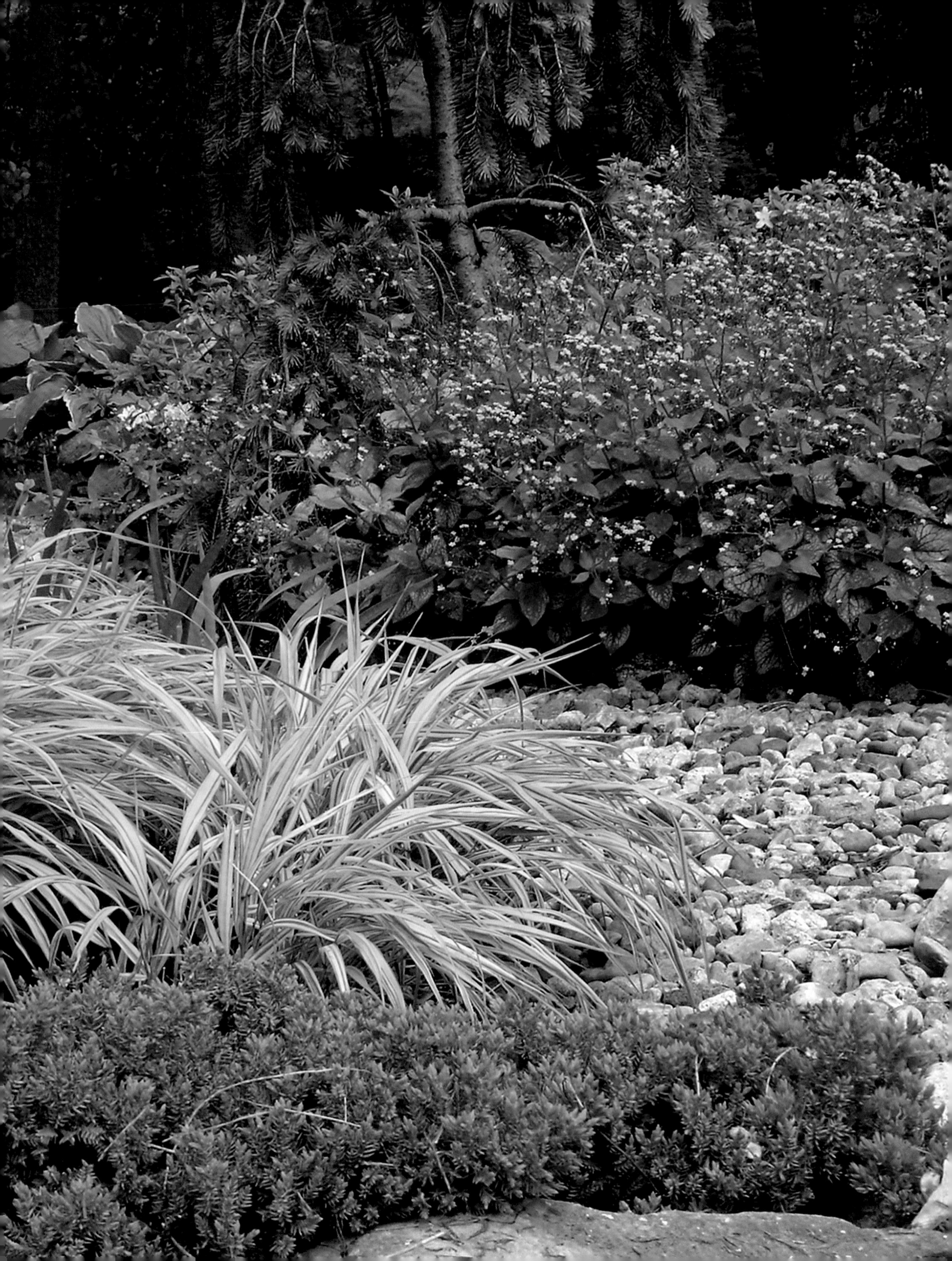

BELOW The bright-green leaves of hosta and pachysandra contrast with the dark tones of heuchera 'Palace Purple' and the red tones of a garden sculpture by Tom Sitzman. **LEFT** Masses of foamflower and hosta thrive in the shade beneath trees, while variegated Hakone grass and creeping phlox emerge in sunnier areas.

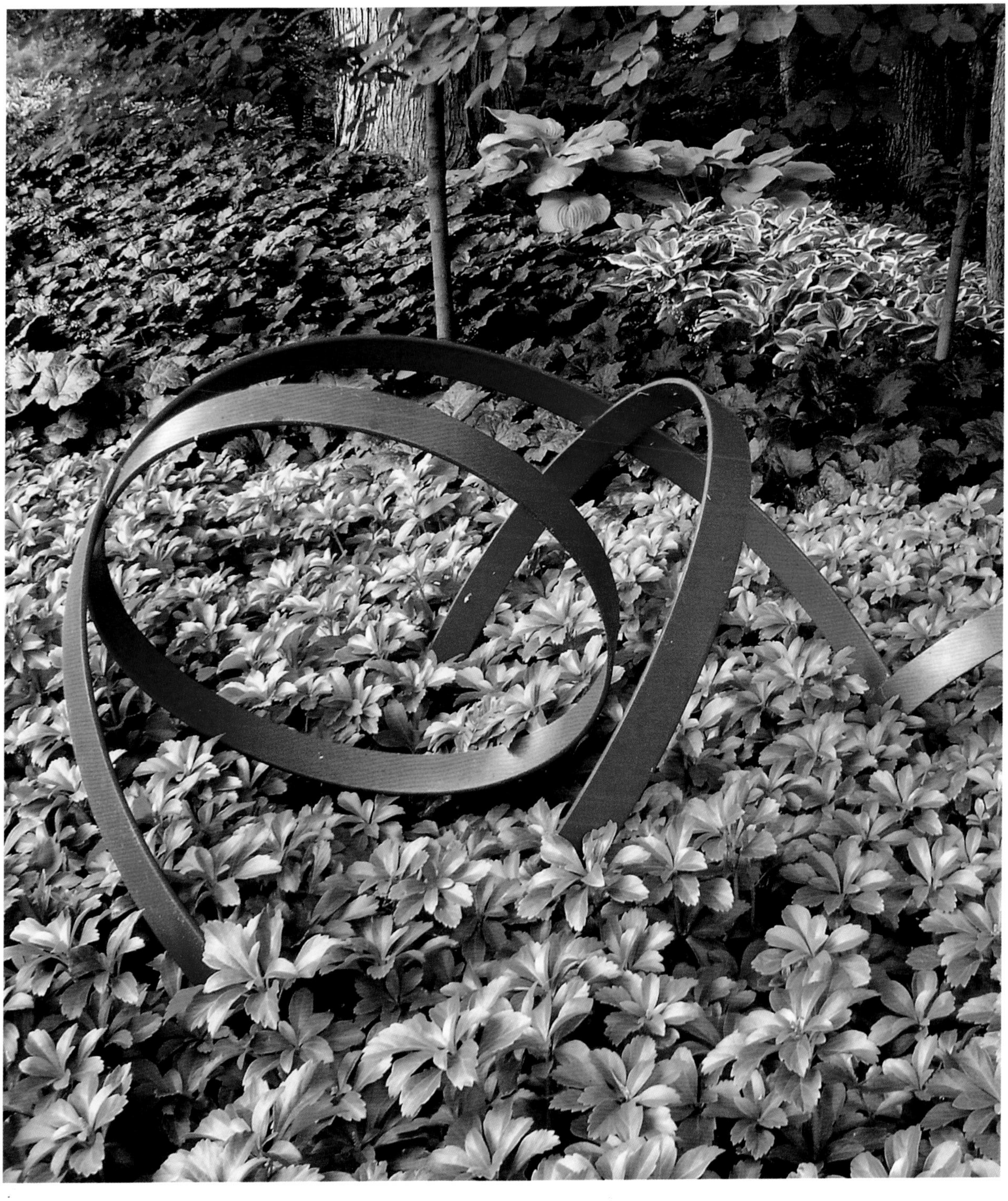

OPPOSITE Pockets of perennials give seasonal color to a landscape otherwise devoted to extended season effects. *Allium giganteum* and salvia 'May Night' add splashes of early-summer purples. **BELOW** A screened pavilion overlooking a fern-laden ravine and creek is a favorite place for the owners to sit during rainstorms.

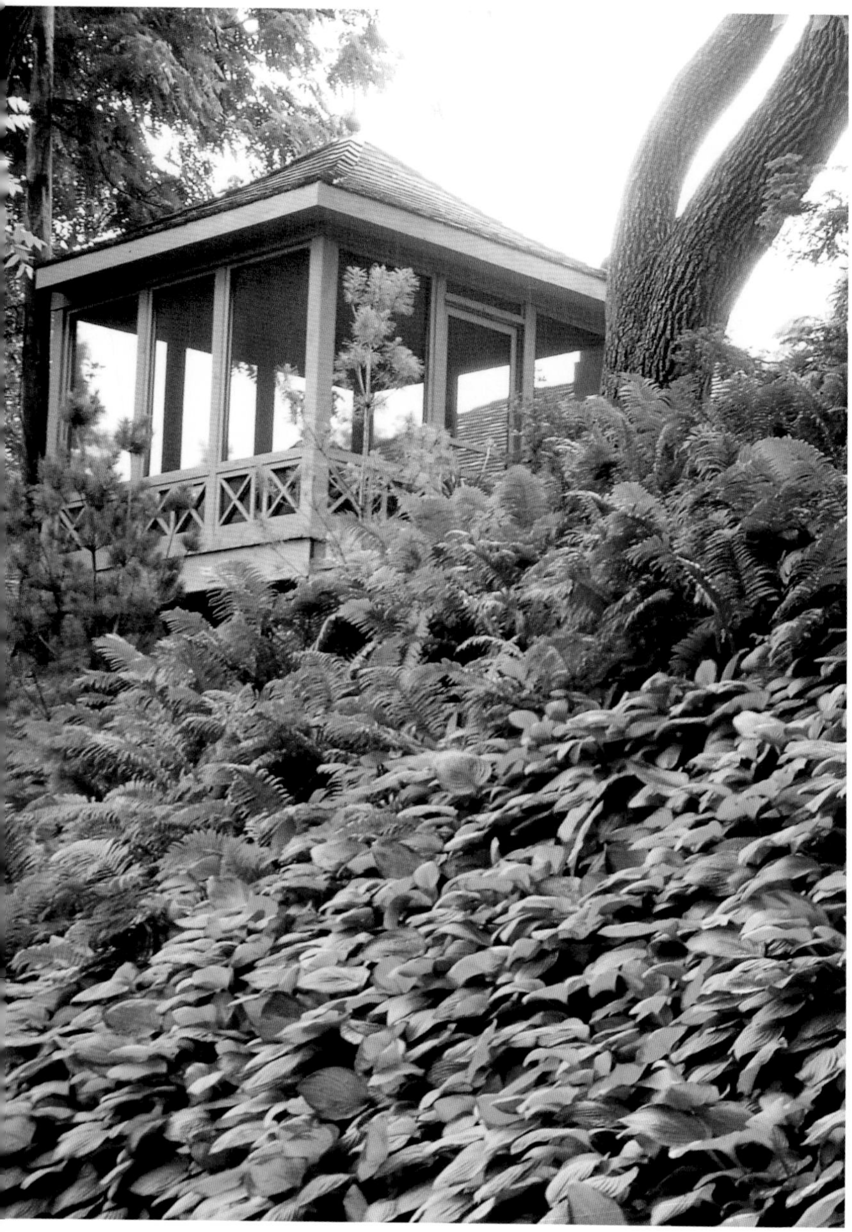

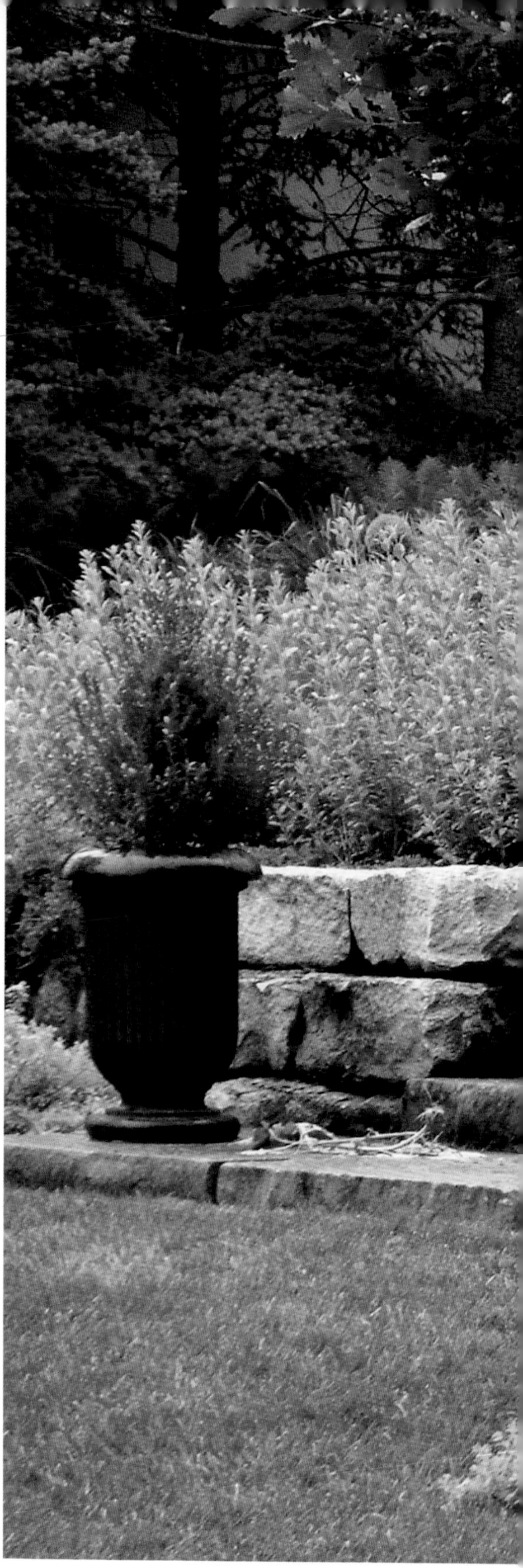

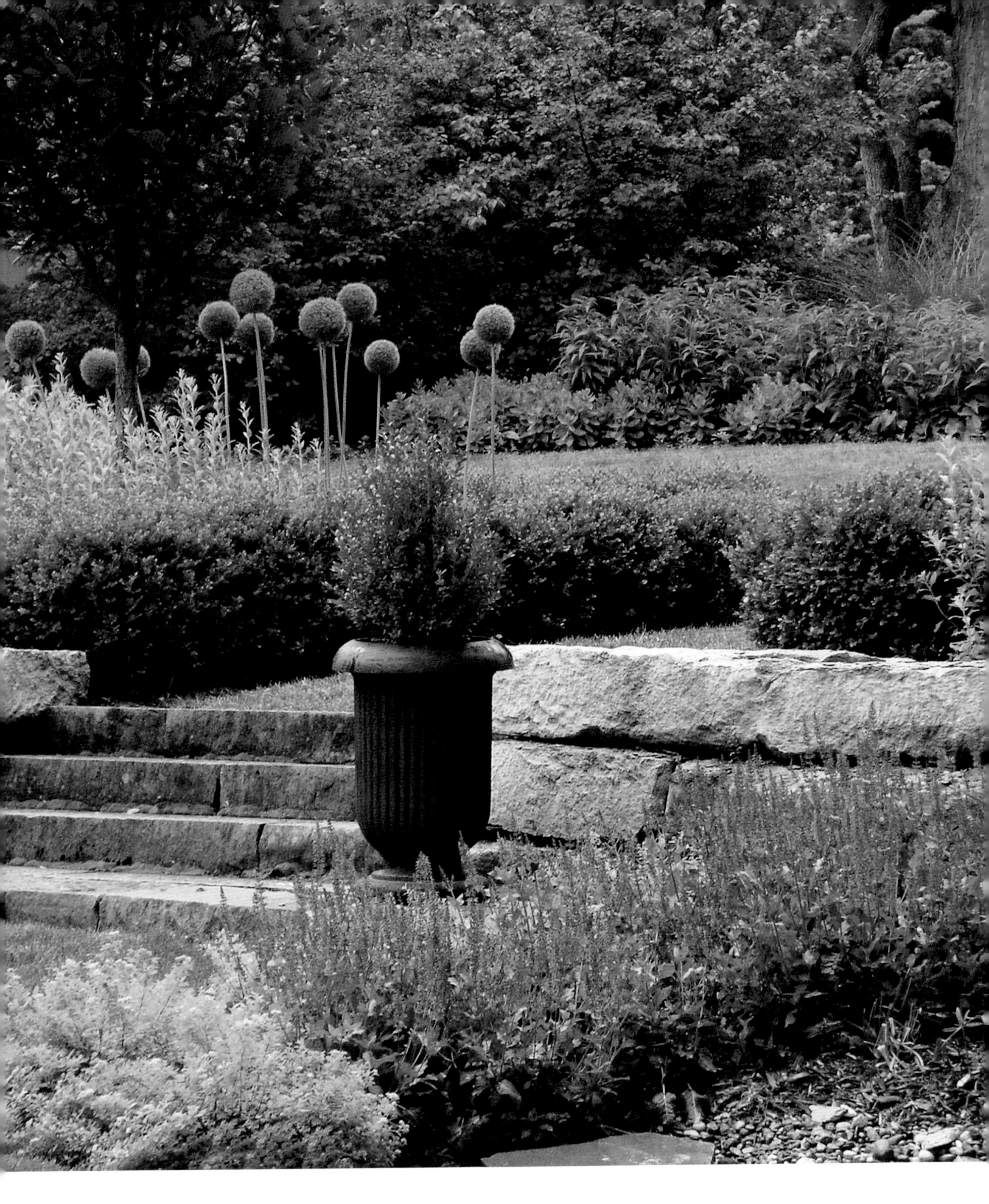

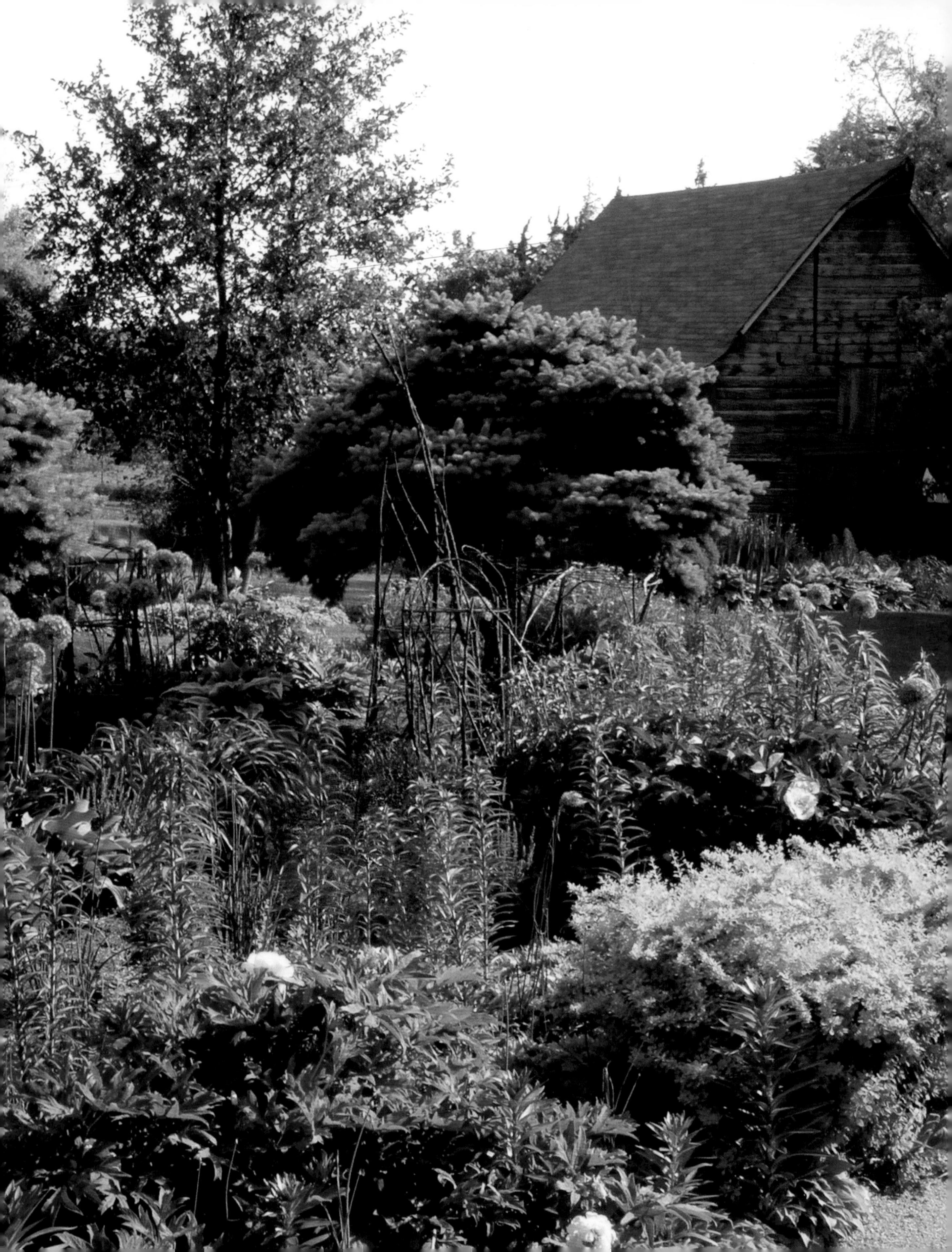

K aren Strohbeen and Bill Luchsinger are internationally known artists who happen to make their home in the Iowa countryside about an hour's drive southwest of Des Moines. They purchased their 80 acres in 1981 from a woman devoted to English-style gardening, then set about reorganizing her plantings into a modernist grid.

Strohbeen knew she wanted to take an approach Russell Page set out in his book *The Education of a Gardener.* Page said that if he ever had a garden of his own, there would be lots of square beds in which he could experiment with plant combinations without concern for a larger context. Luchsinger constructed fifty-four 4-foot-square raised planting beds with 2-foot walkways separating them on a hillside. At this point Strohbeen departed from Page's concept, coding each bed by color and bloom time, aiming for seasonal harmonies and repetitions. "We've always enjoyed caring for these beds," she says, "because you can plant or weed one in a few spare minutes and have a sense of accomplishment."

Under the influence of Adrian Bloom, the artist-gardeners next set out a series of island beds featuring ornamental grasses, peonies, lilies, hydrangeas, alliums, and conifers—which the deer promptly "pruned" into fantastical shapes. Wide swaths of lawn set off the islands and invite strolling.

While creating *The Perennial Gardener* for PBS in the late 1990s, the artists added a kitchen garden with fences, to keep the deer out, and raised planting beds. This proved so successful that they continued to fence all the acreage immediately surrounding the house and gardens. Their latest innovation was to add a series of raised planting beds, pavilion structures for verticality, and boardwalks that connect with a series of decks to the house. The underlying agenda is to make the garden more readily accessible as its keepers age.

In the same vein of thought, the island beds have also been changed to lower necessary maintenance. While ornamental grasses are generally touted as care-free, the pair found that, over time, the required annual pruning was more arduous than pleasurable. "Their last spring we chainsawed them to the ground," Luchsinger says, "and then we smothered the roots with layers of plastic. It wasn't a pretty sight for that season, but for relatively little effort we gained room for experimenting with more perennials and bulbs."

Despite gardening on a property that hovers between USDA Hardiness Zones 4 and 5, the couple says they are able to enjoy dining outdoors from as early as late March until Halloween. It is their style to set out a variety of just-picked vegetables, olives, nuts, and condiments to complement something grilled—asparagus spears on toast points, for example. And there is always at least one breathtakingly beautiful flower on the table.

BELOW Peonies and *Salvia x superba* provide late spring color. **OPPOSITE** A few of the fifty-four raised planting beds Strohbeen and Luchsinger use for experimenting with plant combinations.

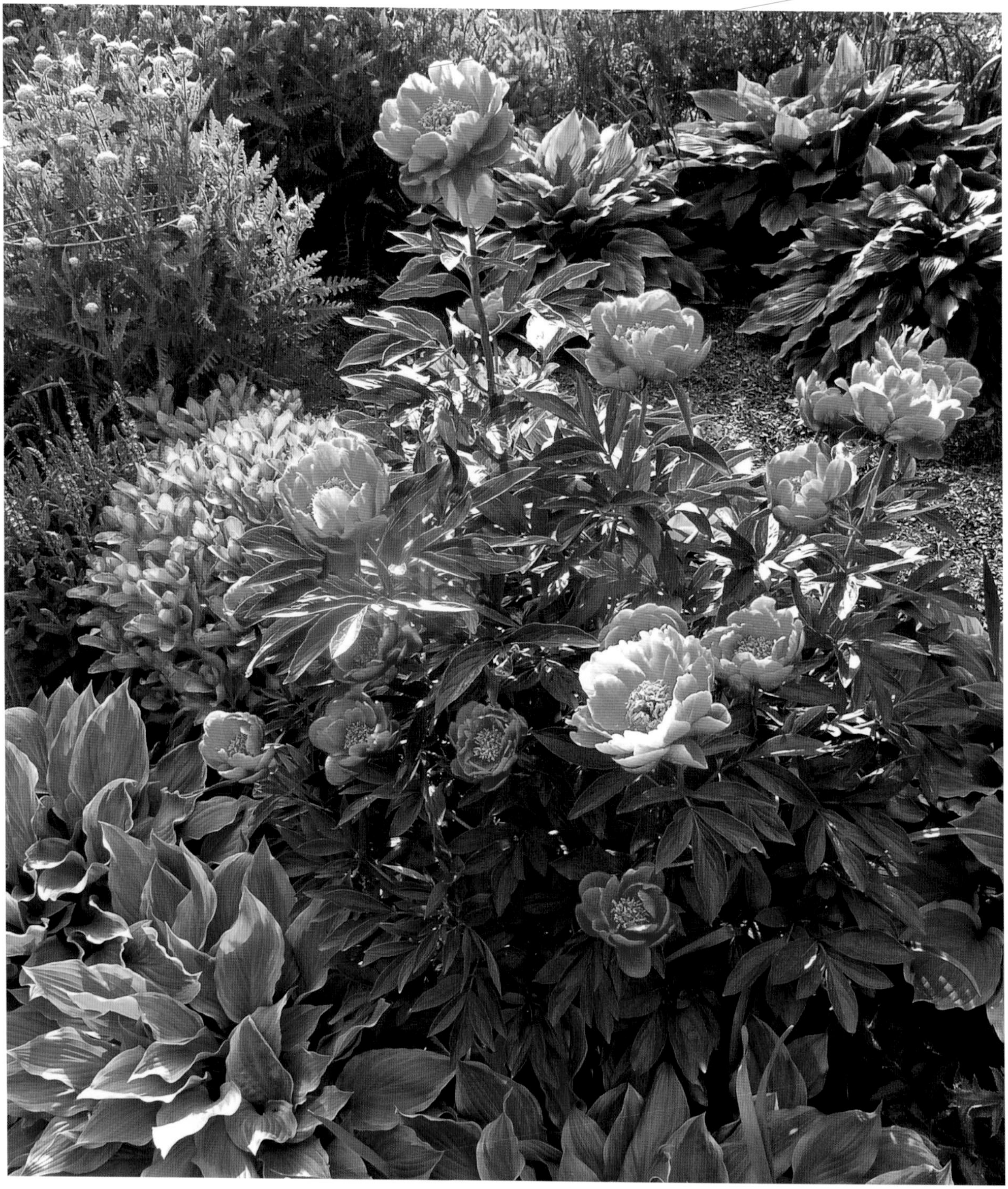

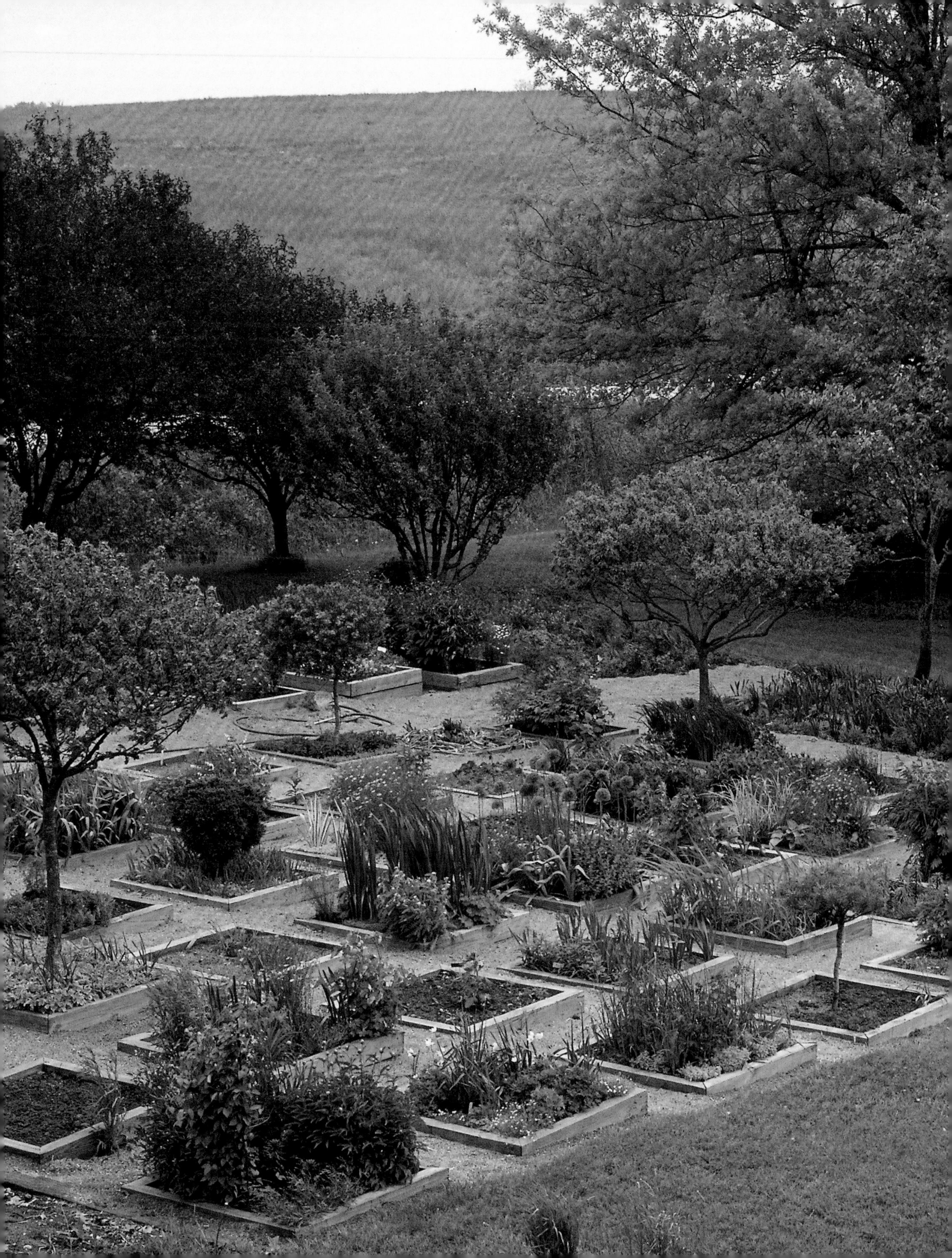

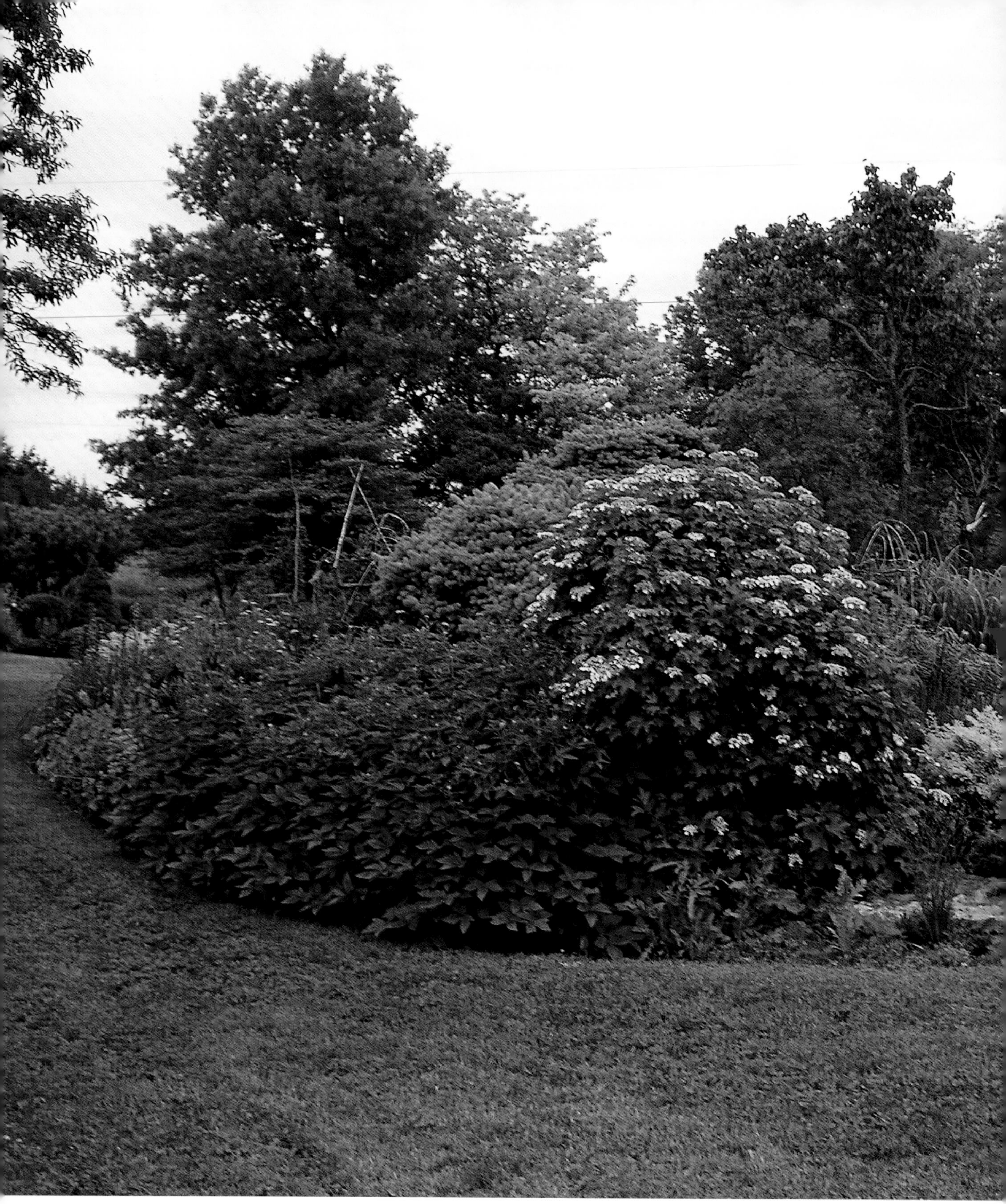

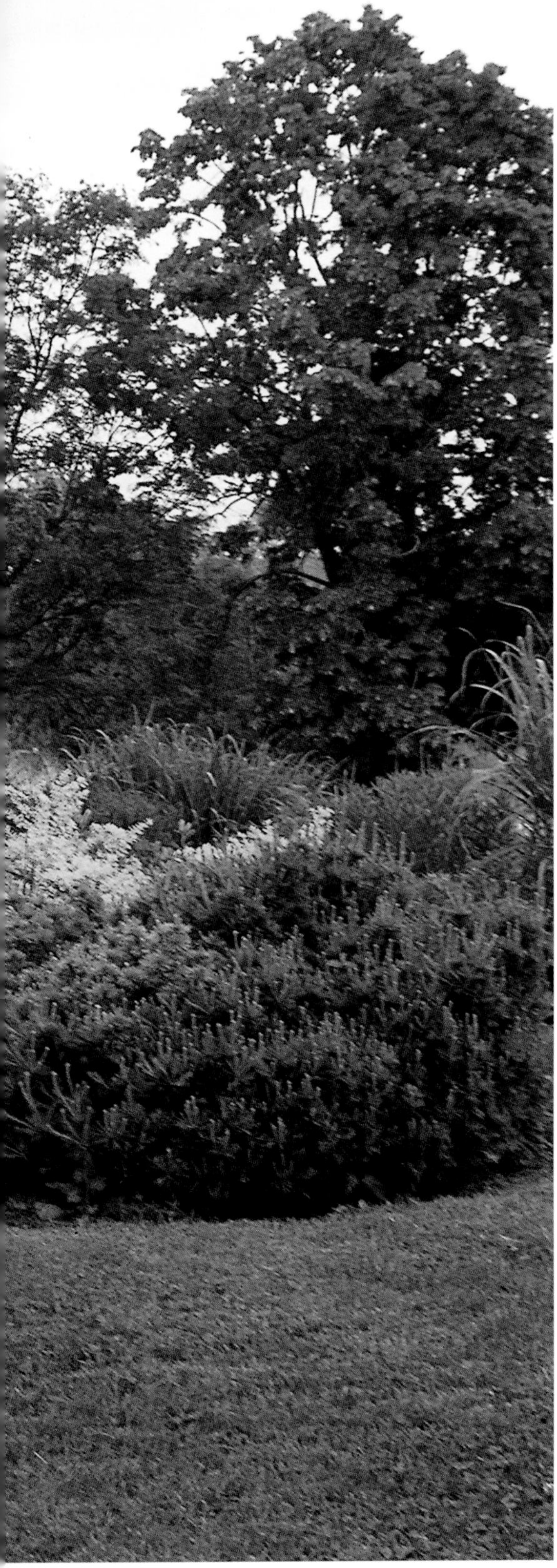

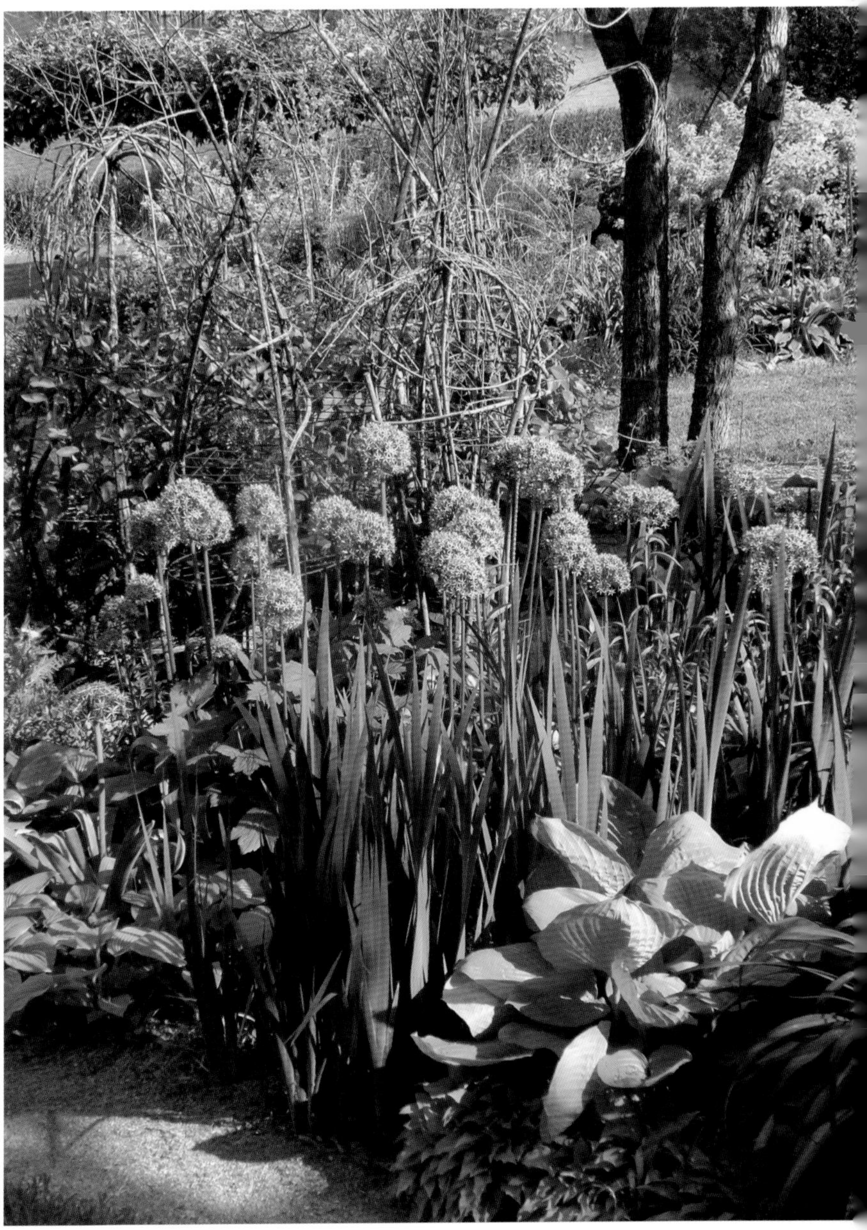

LEFT Island beds feature a sophisticated interplay of form, texture, and seasonal color that reflect their creators' artistic talents. Wide sweeps of lawn invite strolling. **BELOW** Allium and natural-looking training cages created by Strohbeen and Luchsinger from branches found on the property.

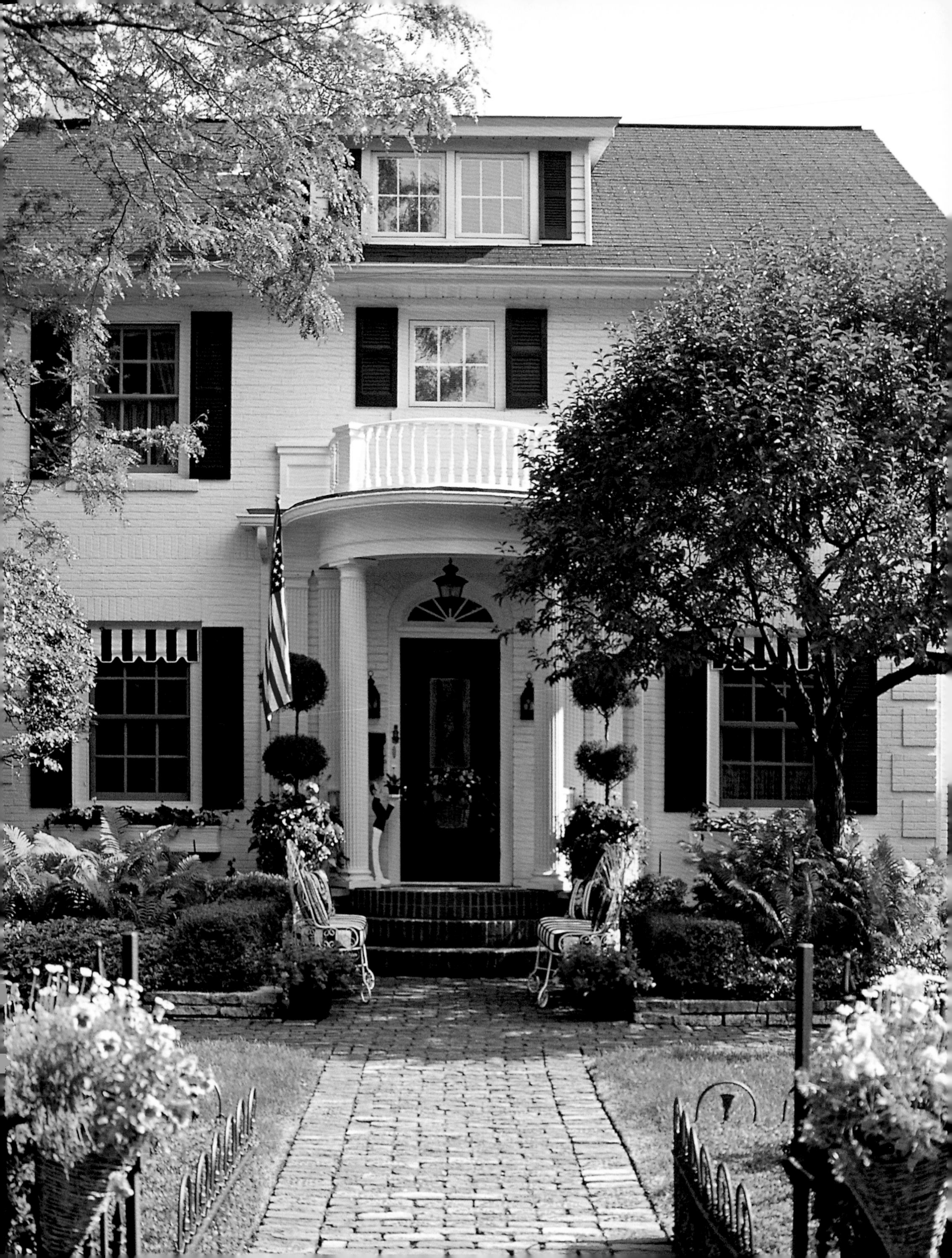

D iamonds are a girl's best friend," says Marie Trader, and then smiles as she adds, "but in my case, not the kind you might think. I love pattern, and when I find one I like, I repeat it. Blue diamonds are painted on the wood floor of my breakfast room, and there are black-and-white diamonds in the back entry."

Trader decided to extend the motif out into the garden, where she selected aggregate stepping stones separated by narrow grass strips to create sure footing for garden furniture. "I wanted a big surface that didn't say 'hardscape' and that let you see enough green to look like softscape. I keep it trimmed with a small push-powered reel mower."

When the Traders first moved here, nearly thirty years ago, the house was all red brick in a sea of overgrown shrubs and trees, which they removed along with a front porch. Then they painted the house white and added black shutters and black-and-white awnings. Next came the front garden, where Marie envisioned "the graciousness of Charleston." To accomplish that feeling, they added a broad, straight walk from the sidewalk to the front door composed of repurposed bricks. They also installed new wrought-iron fencing and a custom gate, designed from snapshots they had taken of other gates they admired.

Sixteen years later, she received a birthday surprise from her husband—a card that said, "This entitles you to a garden design by Craig Bergmann." The timing was perfect, as it allowed them slightly more than a year to prepare the yard as the location for their daughter's wedding. Bergmann recalls their first meeting: "Marie was prepared. She told me that her favorite gardens were English and Southern, with lots of boxwood and roses, and that she loved a 'country' or 'grandmother's garden' look."

The result of their collaboration utilized the diamond pattern as its dominant theme, and carved several distinct areas out of what was one undefined space. "The lattice fencing around the perimeter frames the largest space," Bergmann says, "and then each area flows into the other."

An espalier of the purple-leaved flowering crab apple 'Royalty' along the fence between the garage and the house takes the diamond pattern in an unexpected direction. To establish it, cabling had to be attached to grommets installed in the wall. "We planted a one-year whip at the base of each diamond," Trader explains, "then tied in place any growth that fit the design and pruned off any that didn't."

One of her favorite features of the garden, however, is one most visitors never get to see: a secret cutting garden behind the garage. It measures 24 by 24 feet and is accessed through an arch, one of three in the yard covered with 'New Dawn' roses that create a living screen. The walkways are pea graveled, and its four square beds for annual cut flowers are edged with antique fencing.

Trader confesses to preferring perennials, but she still uses unexpected empty spaces as places to try out different annuals. "I never tire of updating the interior of my home, and I find the same is true of my garden," she says.

BELOW A bench with a cushion covered in stripes—the garden's second graphic motif—near a pond filled with lily pads. **RIGHT** Espaliered dwarf purple-leaf plums and concrete pavers set into the lawn reinforce the garden's prominent diamond theme.

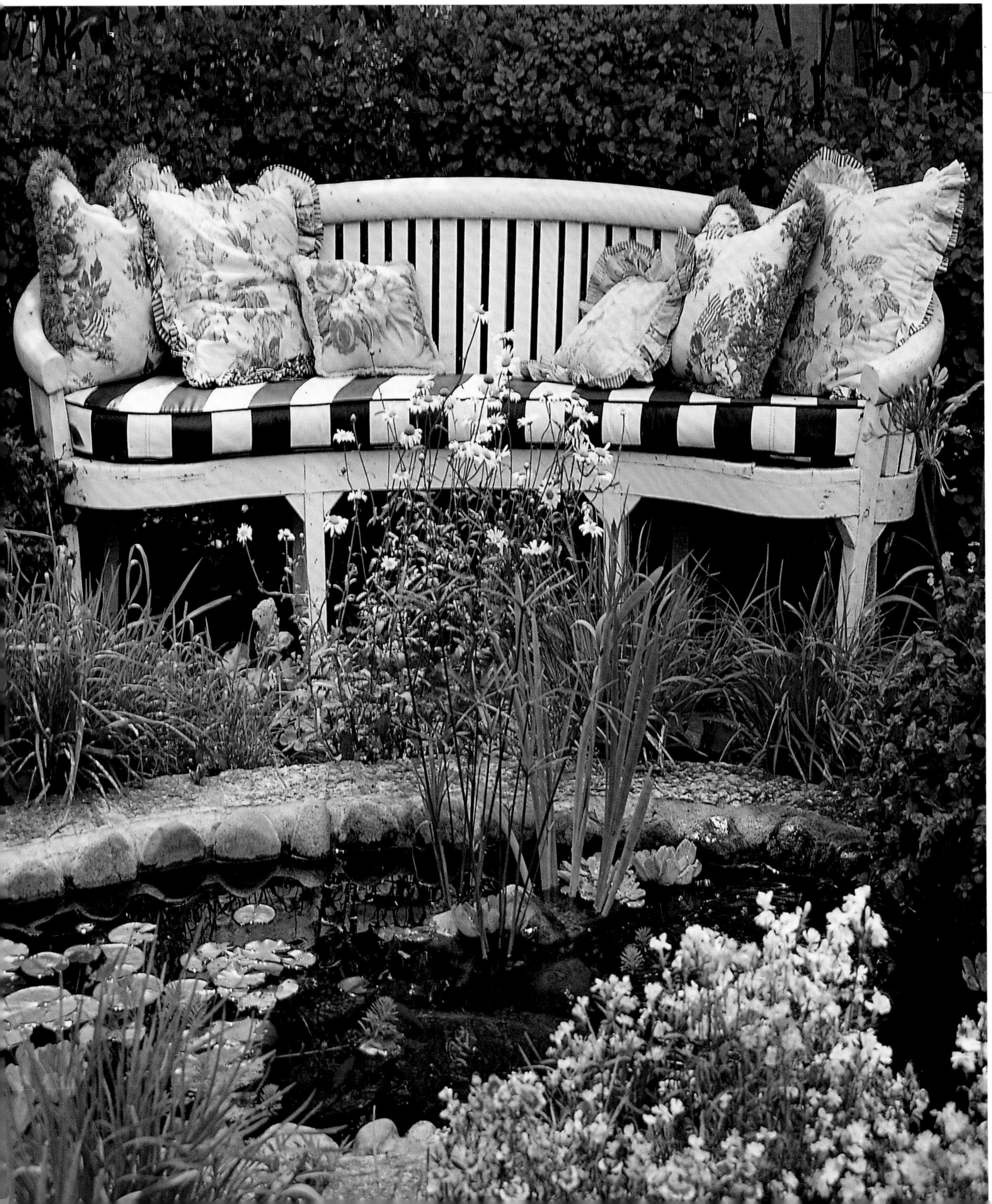

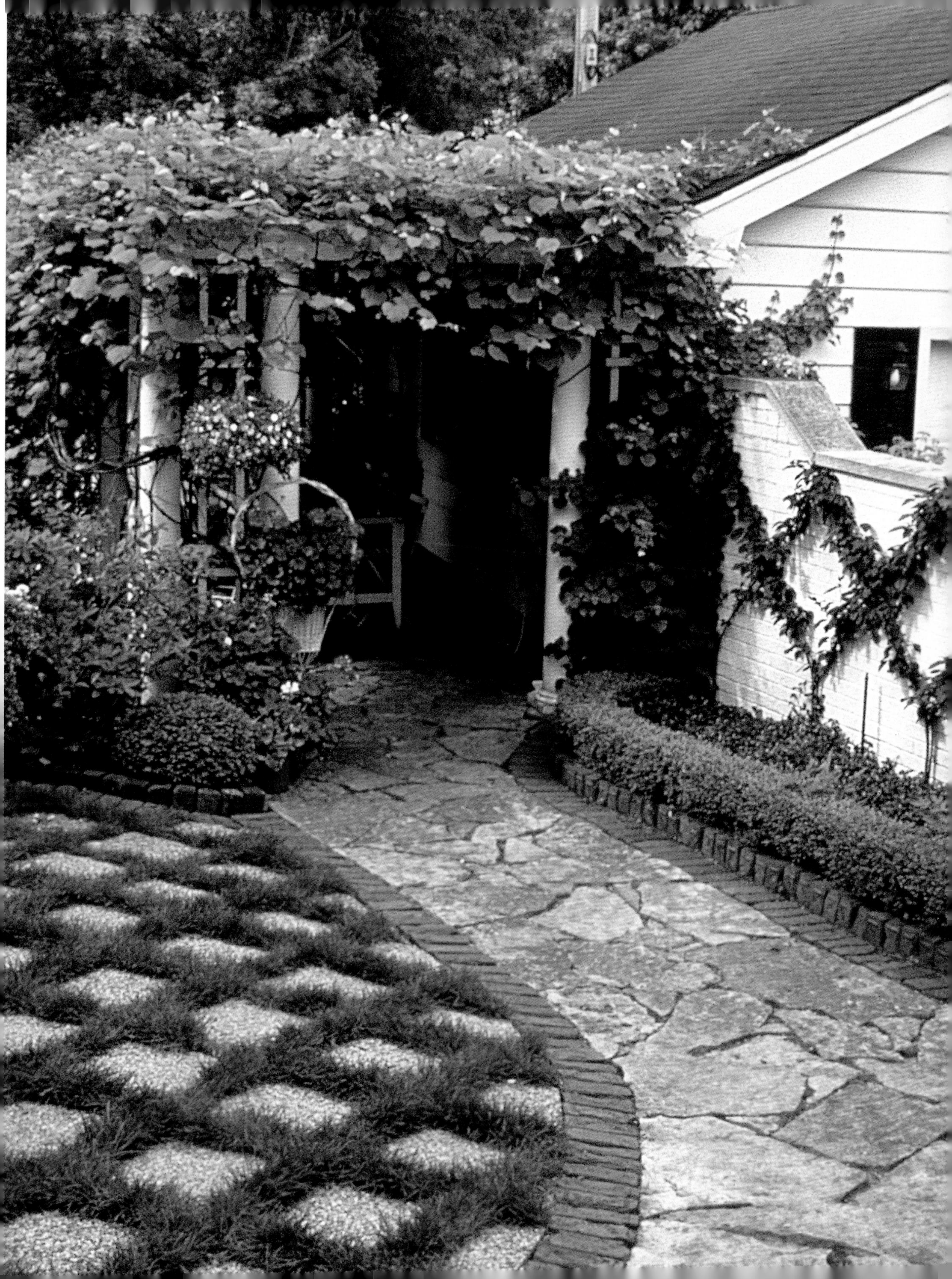

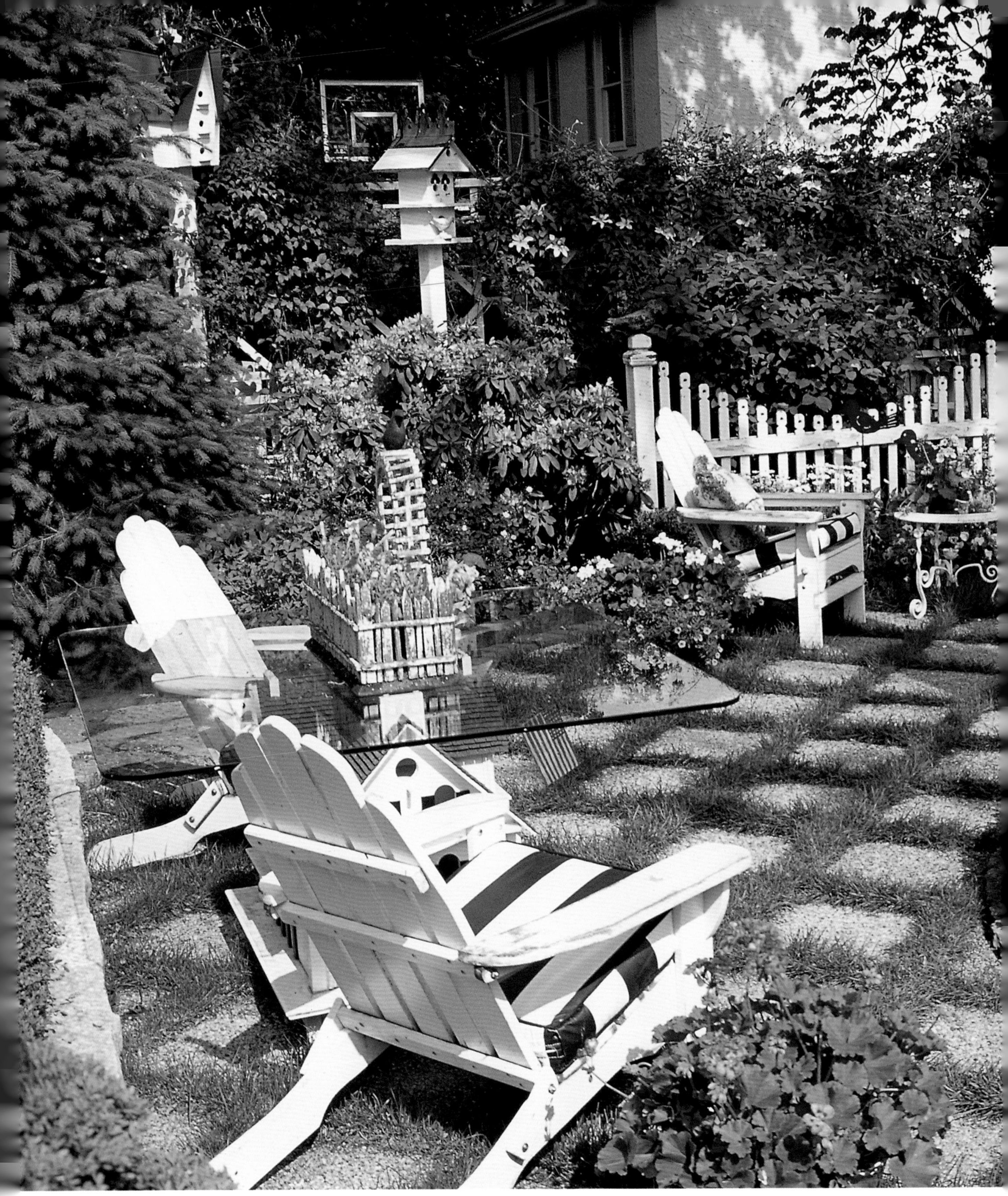

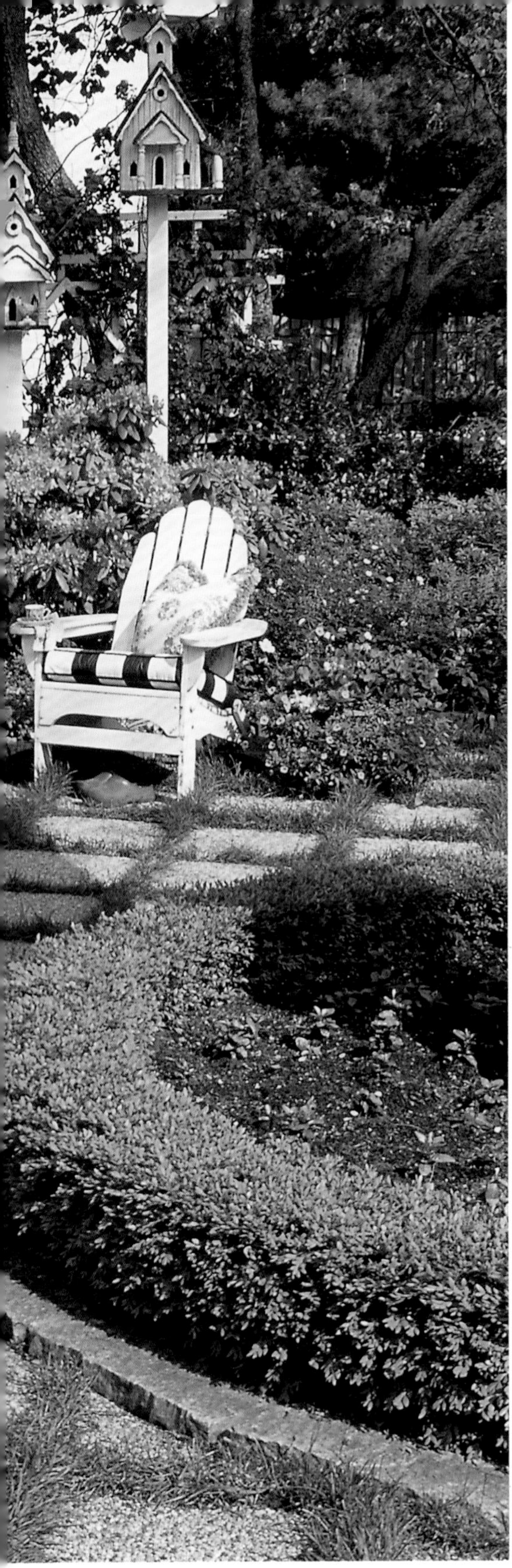

LEFT Visitors to this welcoming outdoor parlor are often greeted by the chatter of birds, which live in dozens of birdhouses dotted throughout the garden. **BELOW** Soldier-course brick mowing strips outline the planting beds.

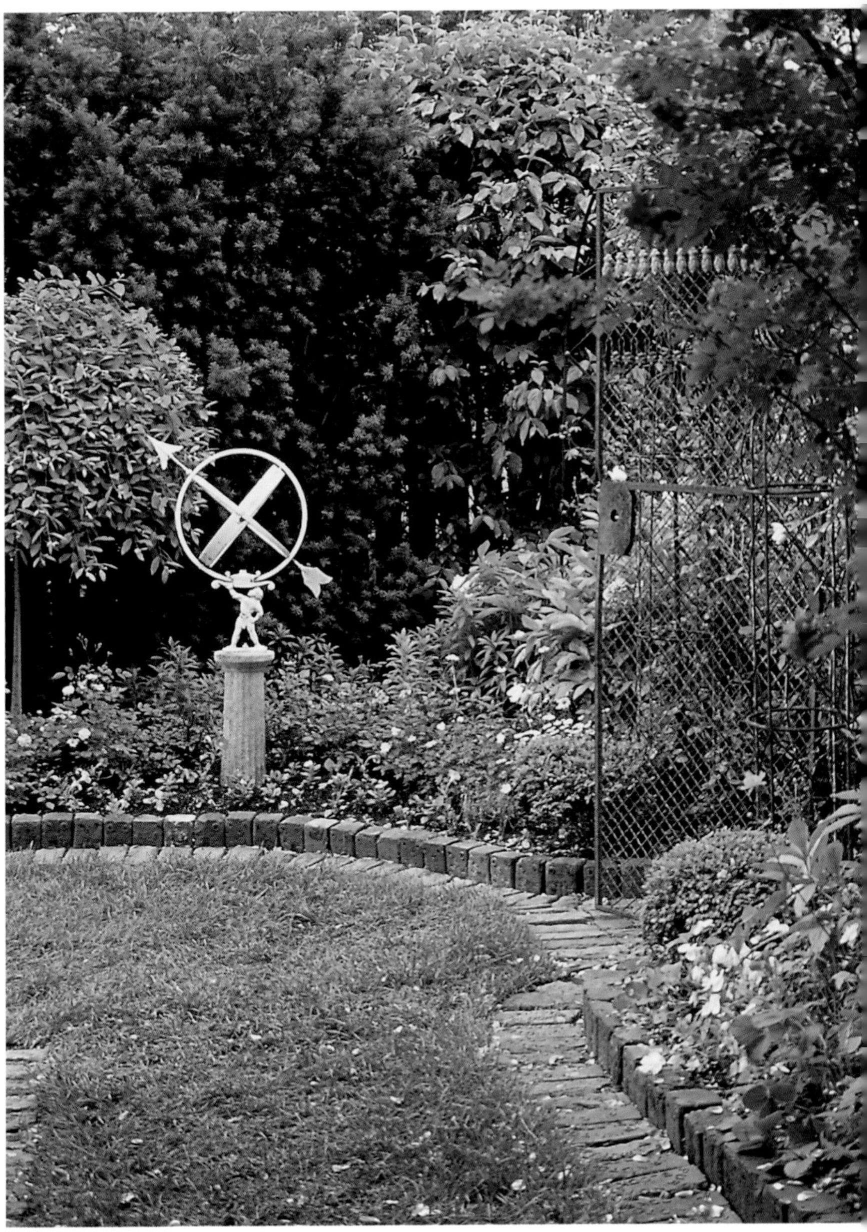

RIGHT 'William Baffin' roses climb over a romantic arbor fitted with a black-and-white striped cushion—another of the owner's favorite design motifs. **BELOW** Delicate pastel-pink roses are set off by the soft silver of woolly lamb's ears and a vintage English terra-cotta rhubarb forcer.

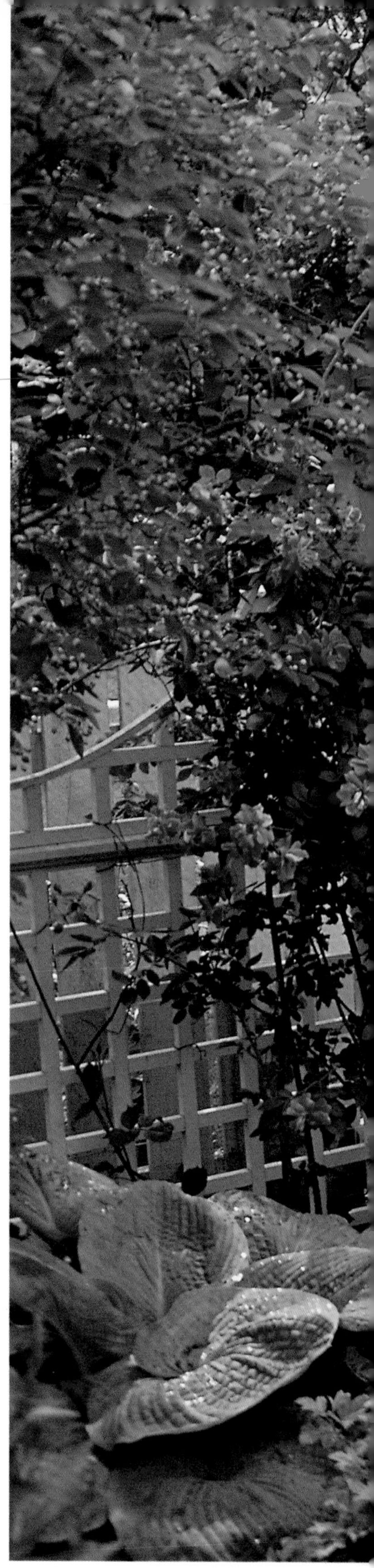

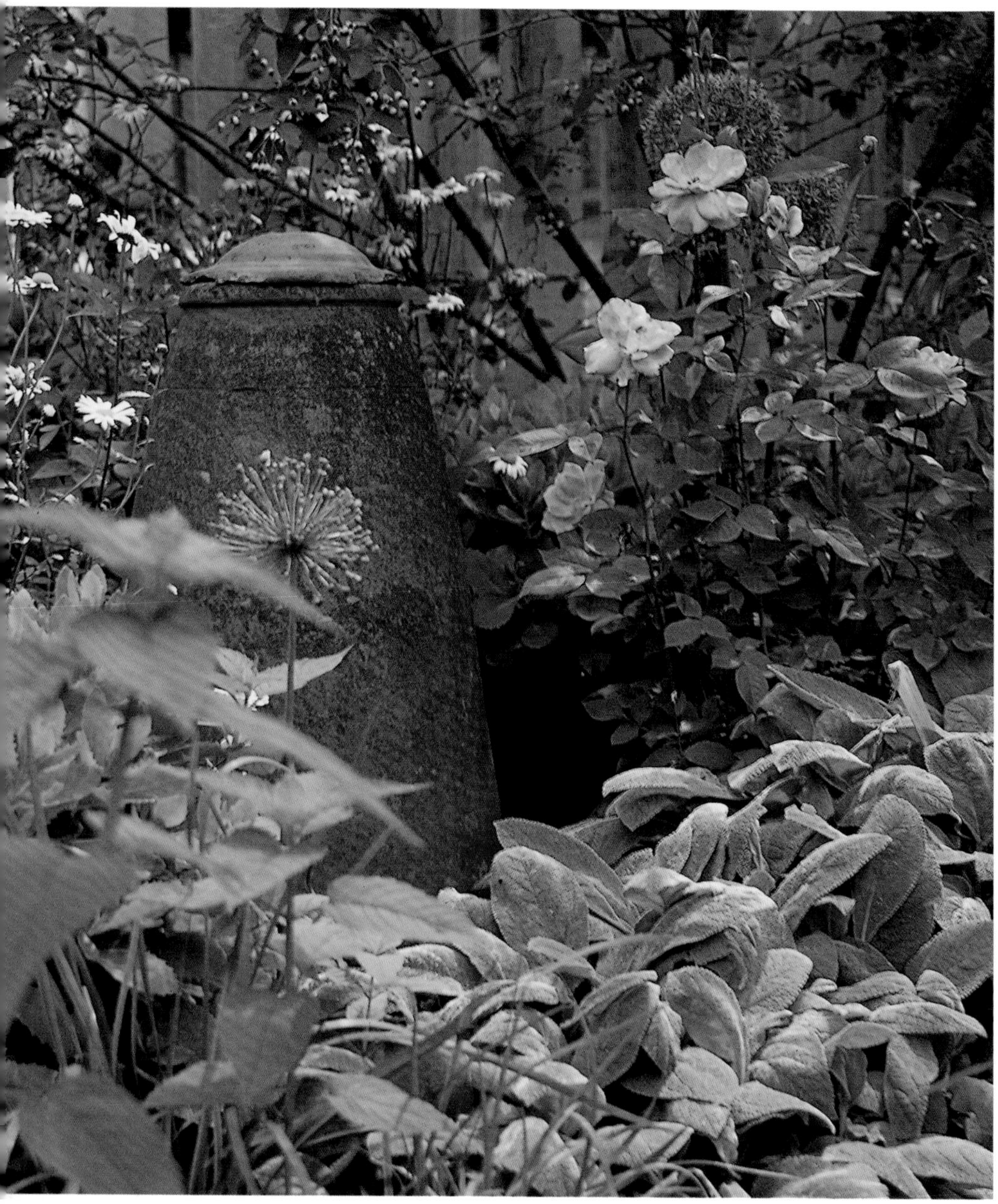

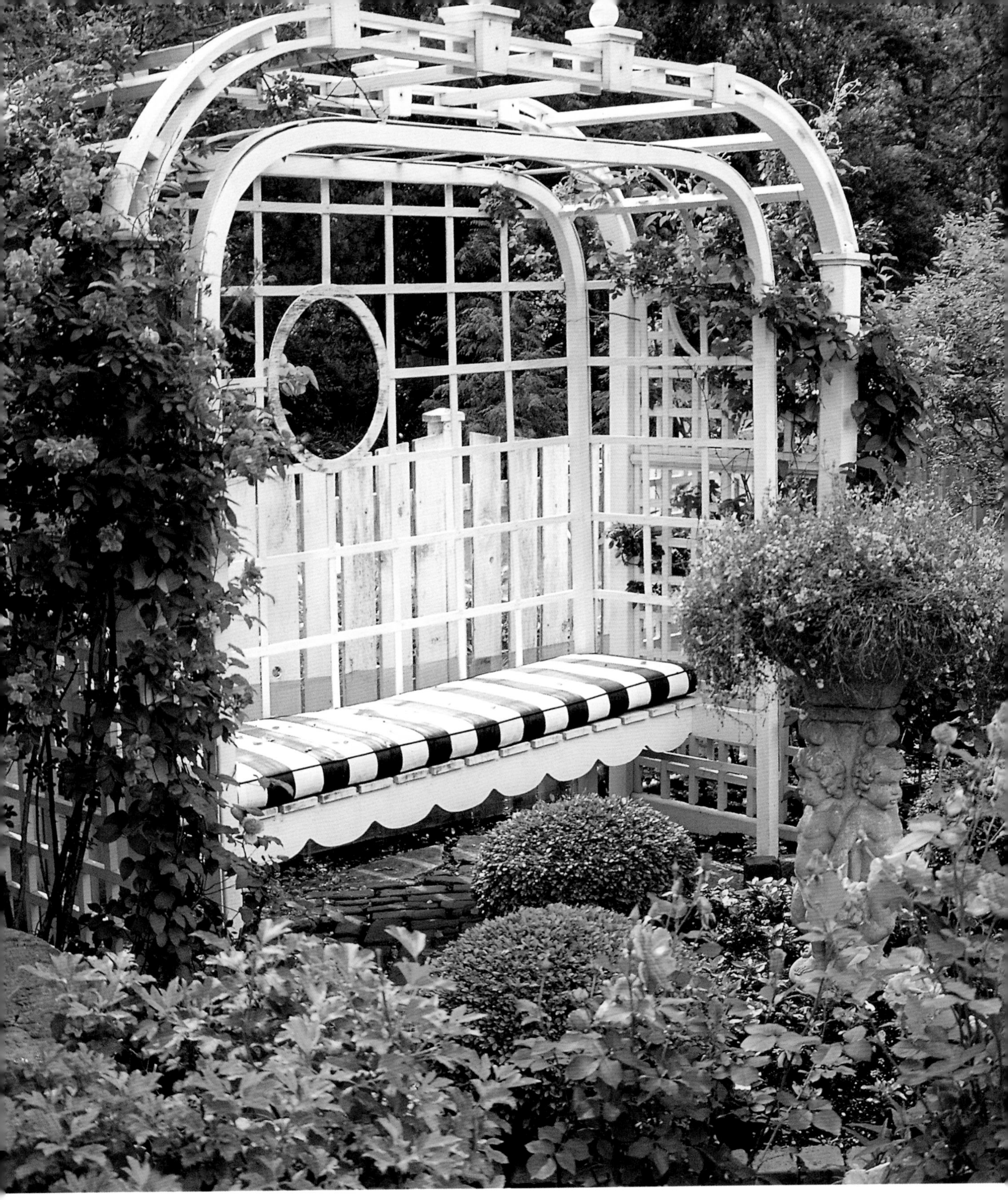

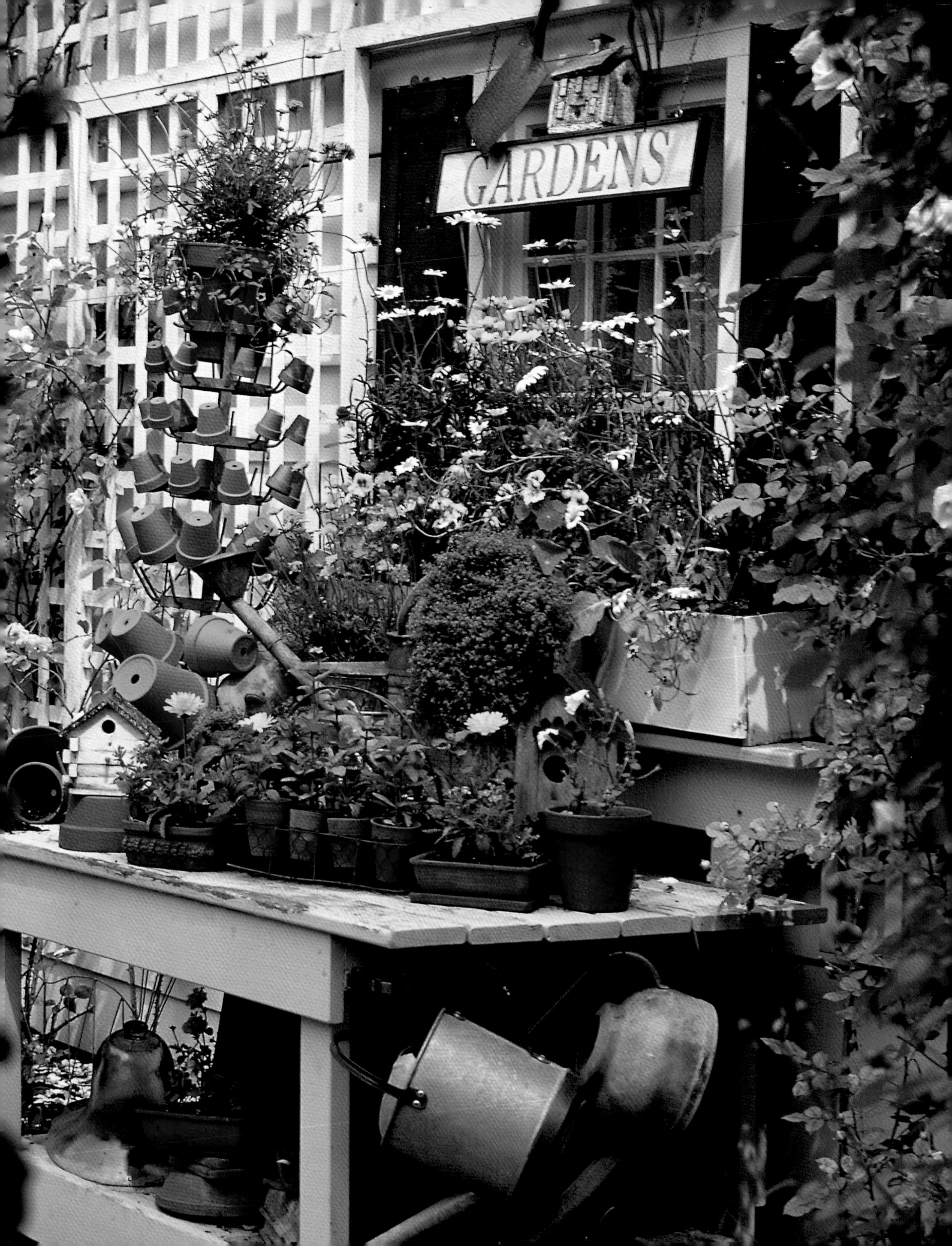
GARDENS

BELOW Small details await at every turn in this garden; a table nestled among pink and white roses and Shasta daisies holds an antique beehive. **OPPOSITE** Even utilitarian areas in this garden reflect a sensibility for design; a vintage bottle drier is repurposed for pot storage on a well-appointed potting bench.

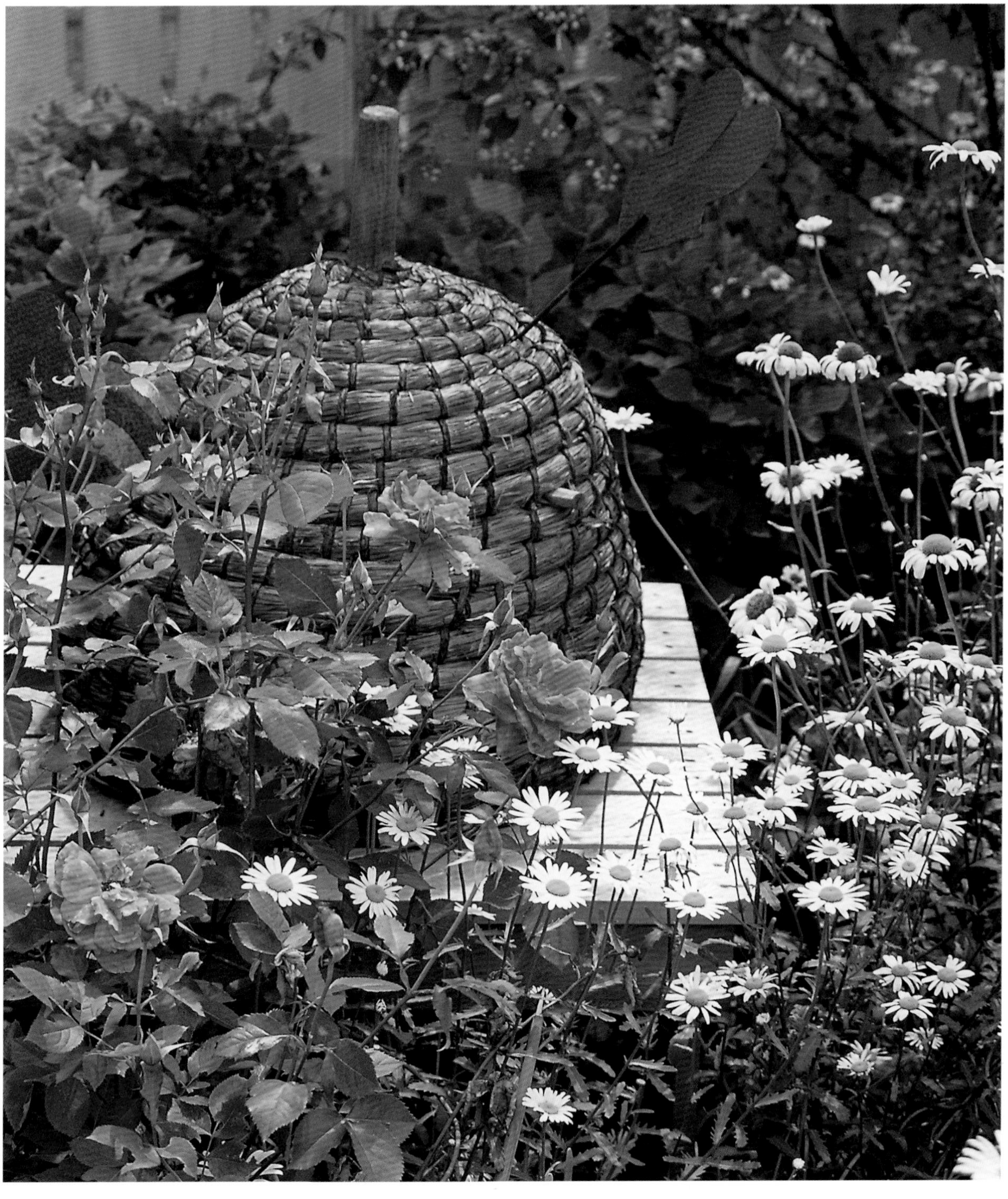

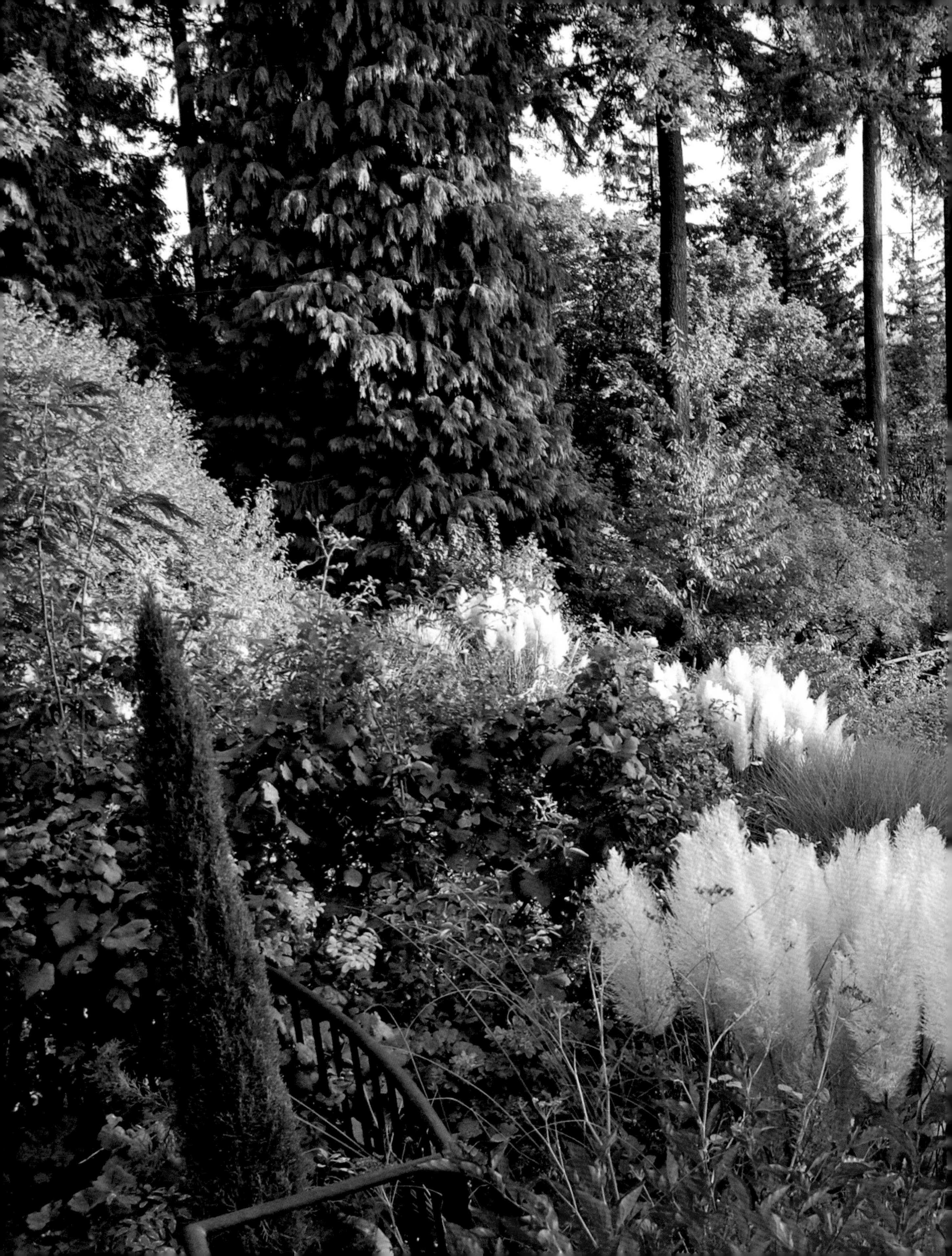

northwest

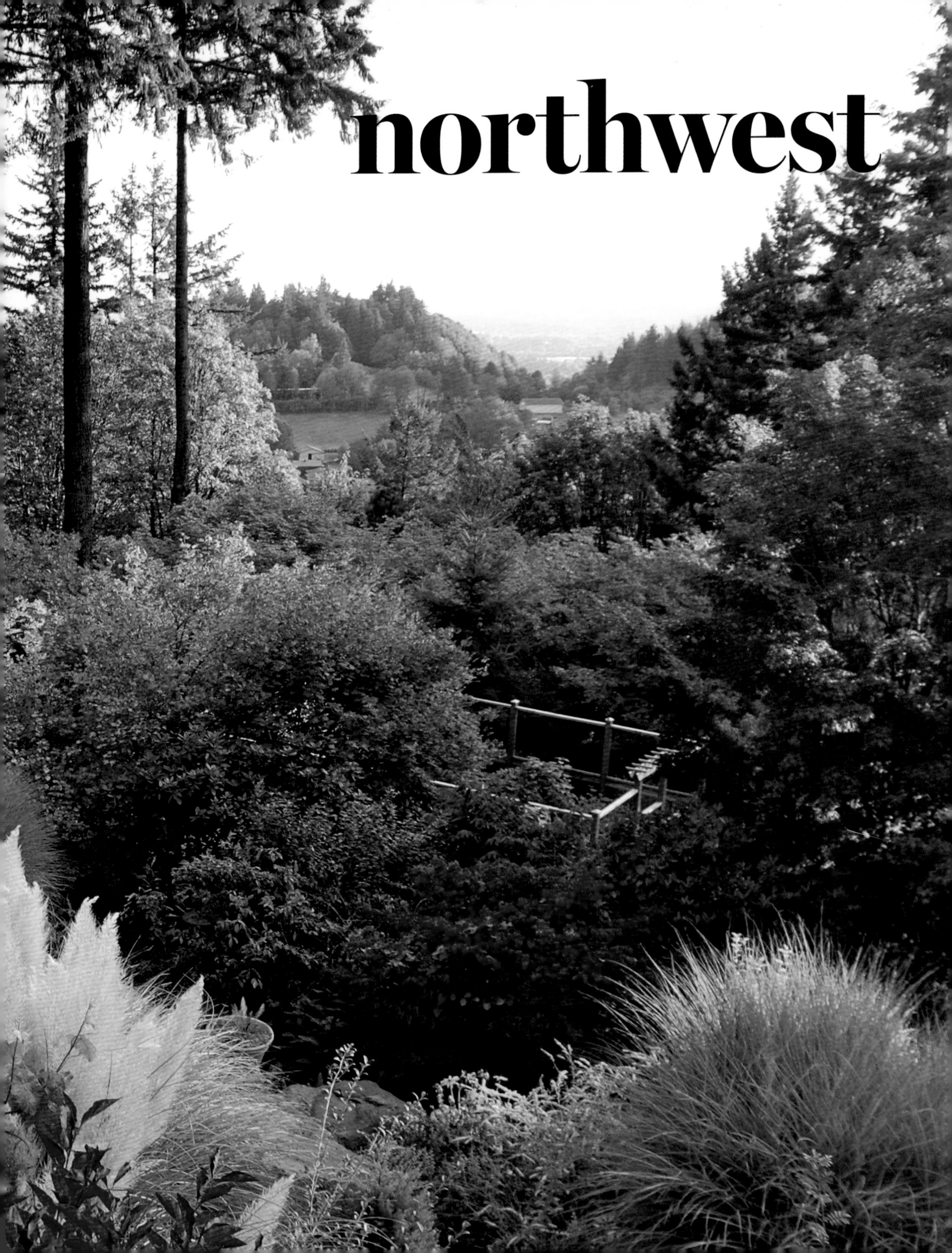

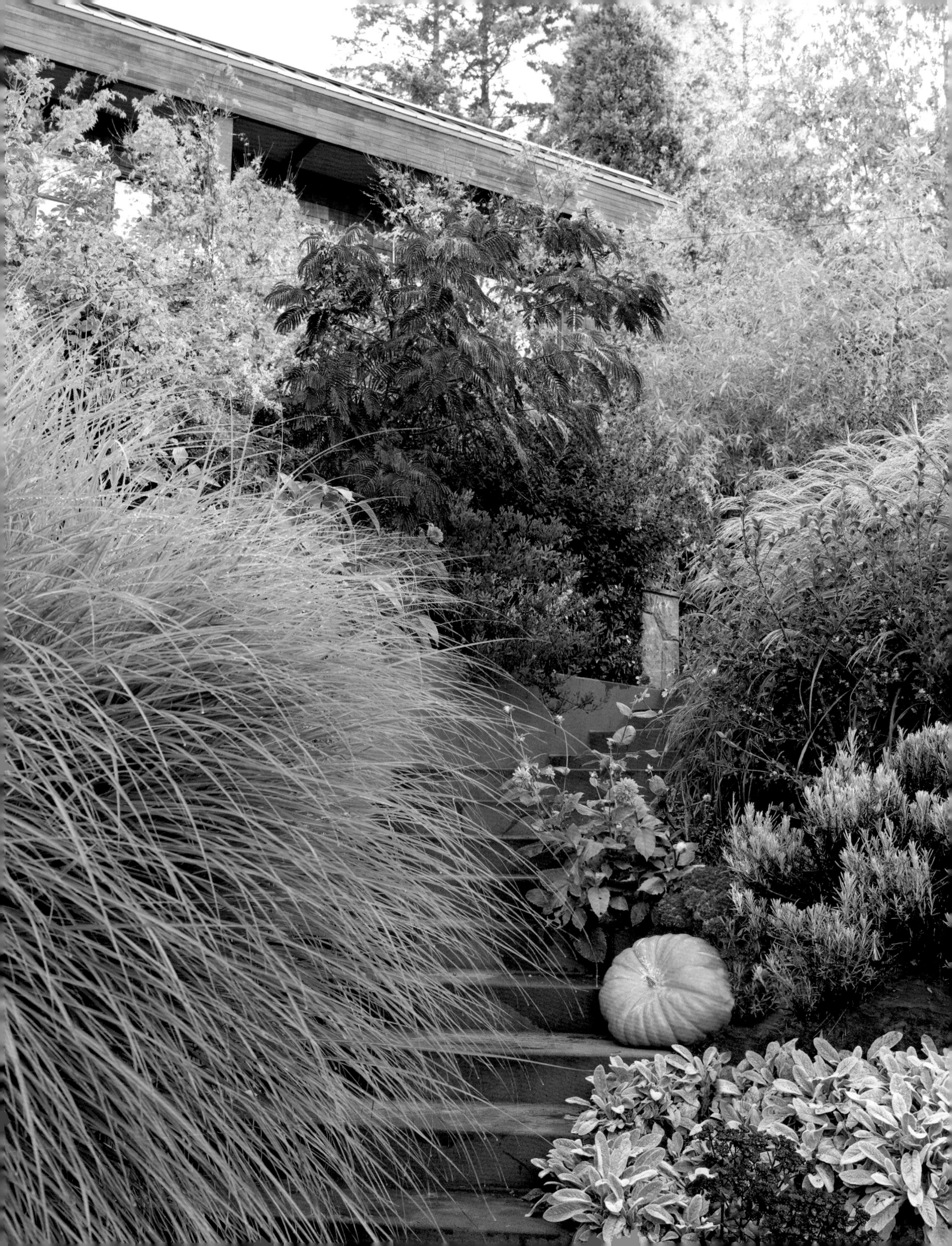

P artners Tom Barreto and Brian Sinclair live on 2 dramatically sloped acres ten minutes from downtown Portland, Oregon. "We purchased the property in 2000 for the south-facing view, proximity to the city, and the privacy afforded by the wooded location," Barreto says. "The cedar-shake-clad dwelling nestles into the hillside and its boomerang shape offers views of the Tualatin Valley from every room." Their 1950s modernist house was designed by John Storrs, an early pioneer of Northwest Style.

The house stands on the property approximately 50 feet below the road. Just after Barreto and Sinclair moved in, the neighbor above them cut down twenty-two Port Orford cedars lining a protective berm at the top of the property to improve his valley view, leaving the new owners with a line of ugly stumps along their driveway. Between that and a rickety stairway that brought visitors precariously down the berm from the street, they determined that the initial view of their property was not terribly welcoming.

At this point landscape architect Michael Schultz was hired to help them redesign the property. Their main goals were to create a better flow among the back-yard pathways, to provide a sound barrier from the busy street above, and to develop an extended outdoor living space in the backyard that integrated the house more smoothly with the land.

The owners, who had just returned from a trip to the hill towns of Tuscany, had become enamored by its country homes' walled terraces that framed views and added recreational space. Schultz proposed a three-tiered design based on that vision. A primary terrace with a flagstone-and-Camas-basalt half wall arcs around the house, providing plenty of seating for large gatherings. This steps down to a second terrace, composed of a dark aggregate stone surface, which in turn leads to a third patio of flagstone. Other parts of the patio and its retaining walls are made of a textured, tinted sand/concrete mixture that ties together the flagstone, aggregate, and basalt.

This design also serves a practical purpose: helping people get down to the lower part of the property quickly. Prior to landscaping, the pathways were simply wide switchbacks that zigged and zagged broadly from one side of the property to the other. Today the garden has eight defined levels filled with unique shrubs that satisfy Barreto's interests as a plant collector. There are also large swaths of *Miscanthus sinensis* 'Adagio' and *Phygelius* x *rectus* 'Winchester Fanfare,' and the garden is dotted with dwarf pampas grass to give the eye an occasional focal point or resting place.

A 25-by-50-foot fenced area for vegetables, herbs, and bush fruits, namely blueberries and raspberries, is close to the bottom of the property. "The only problem with the vegetable garden is that it's located so far from the house," Barreto says. "To go grab some greens for a quick salad is quite a trek, especially back uphill to the house! There are always challenges, whether it's slugs, deer, the steep slope, or the heavy rains during the winter—but it's all worth the rewards in the other three seasons."

RIGHT AND BELOW Grasses and meadow flowers appear as though naturalized, in a celebration of color. **OVERLEAF** Fall color cascades down the slope; Japanese maples and yellow *Amsonia tabernae-montana,* along with ornamental grasses, play a dominant role in the meadow-themed garden.

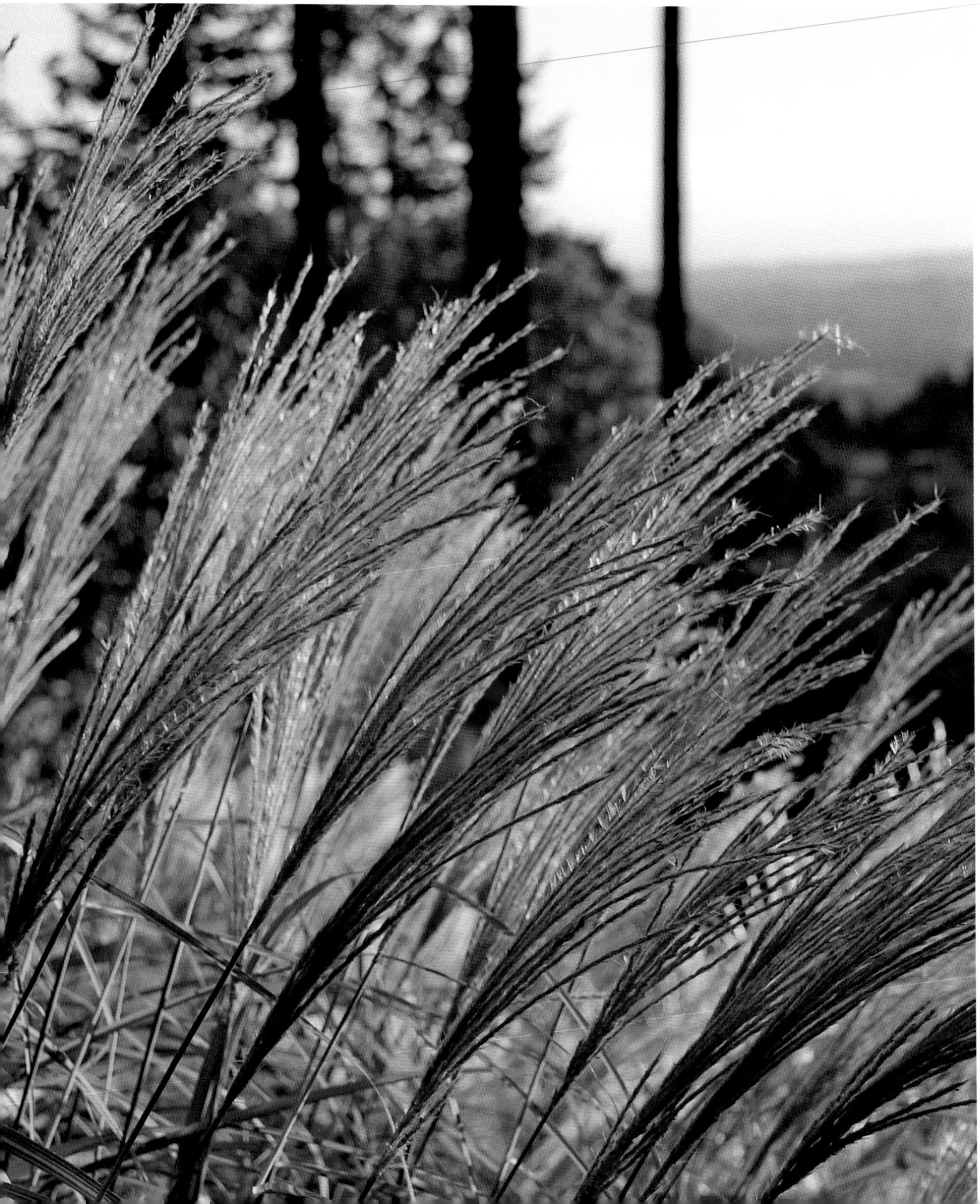

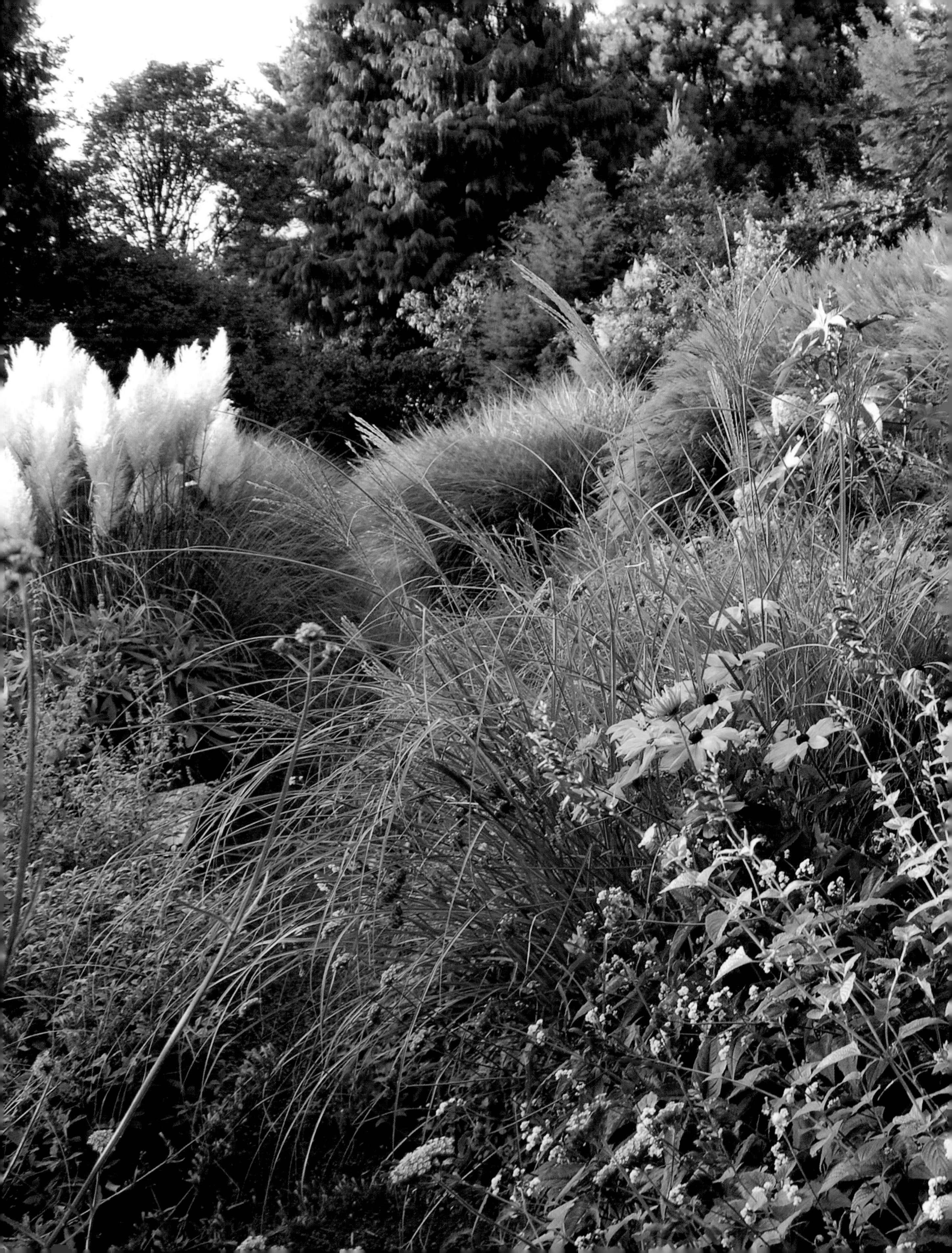

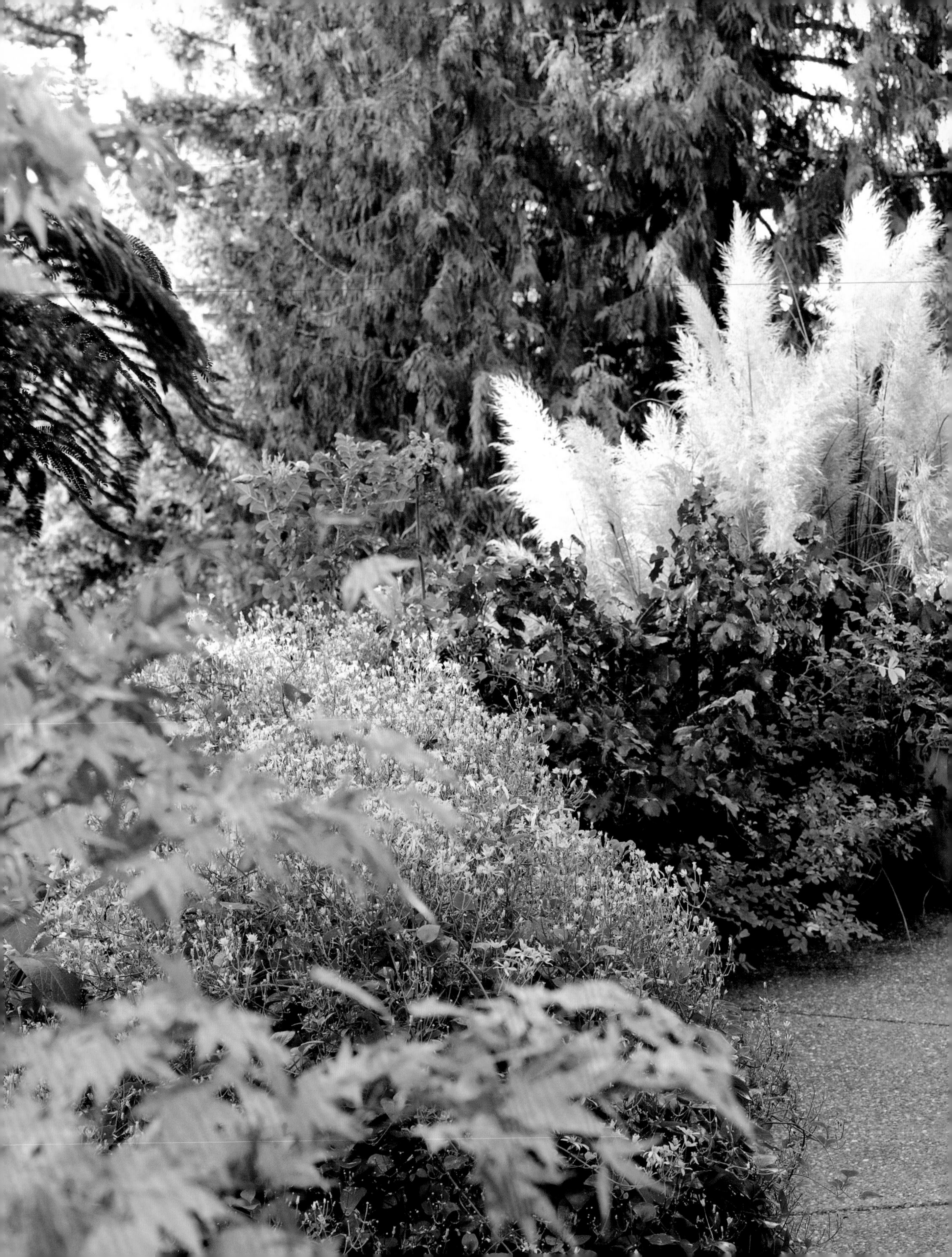

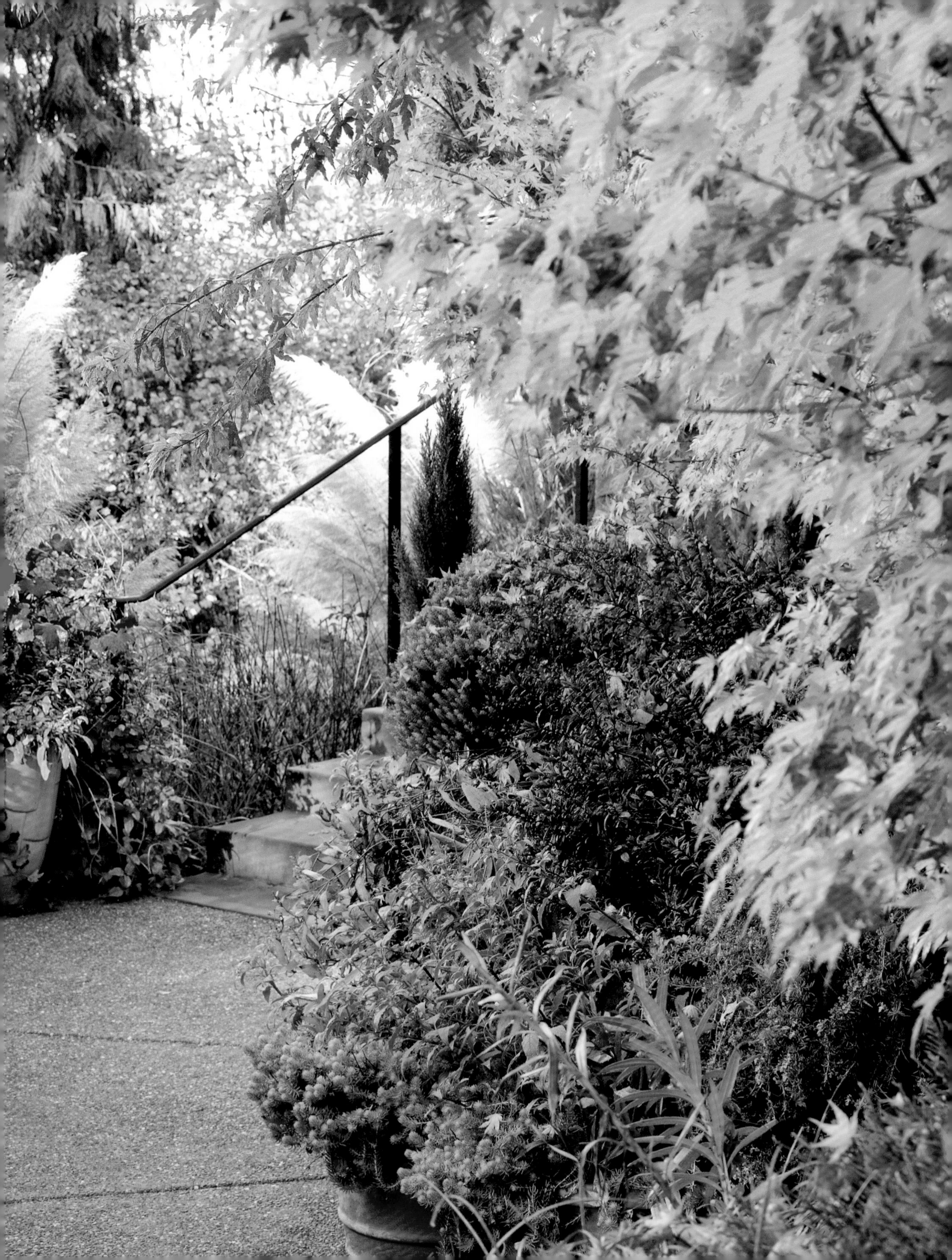

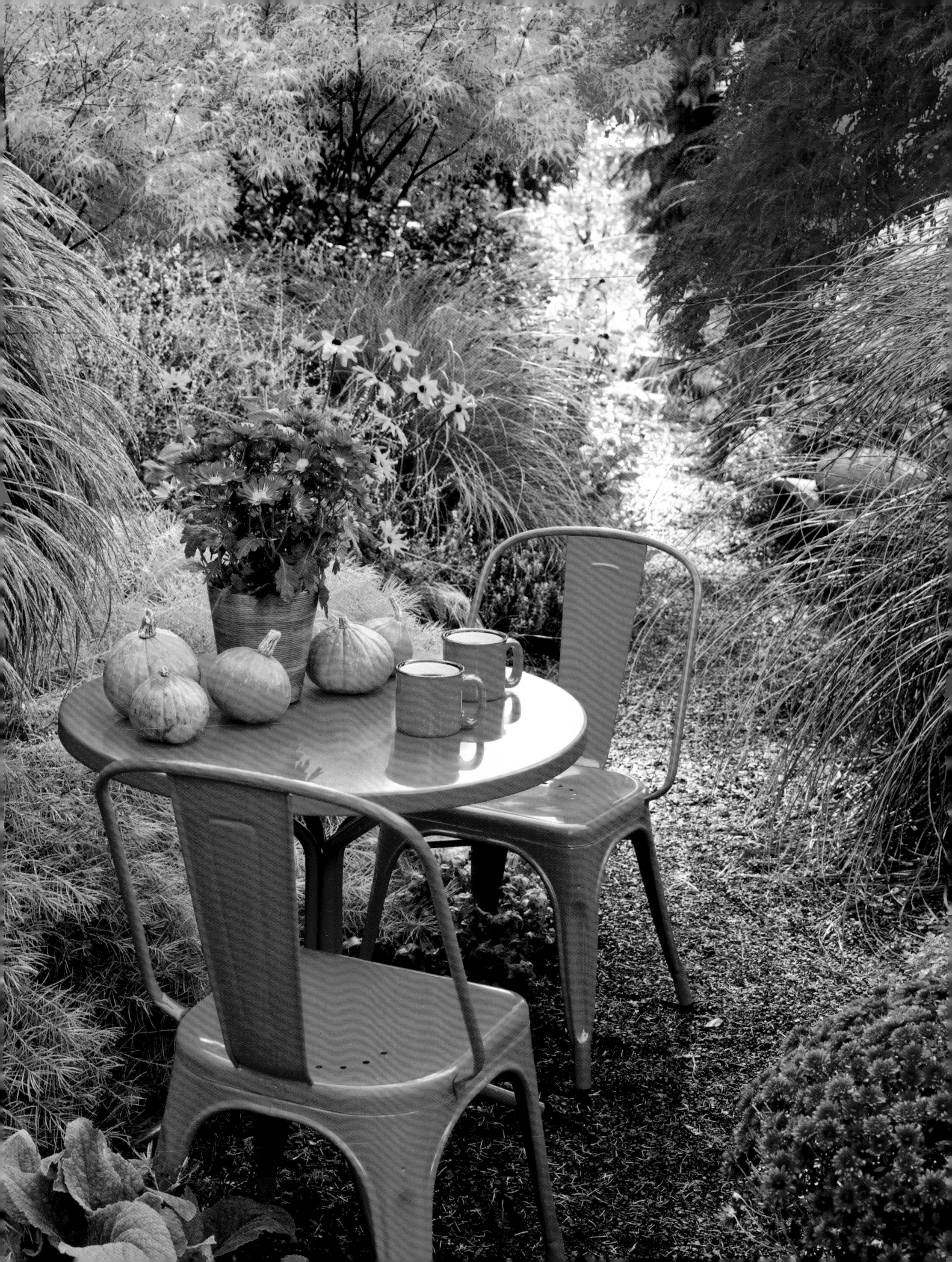

LEFT An intimate dining area situated amid a brilliant nest of Japanese maples. **BELOW** A flagstone-and-Camas-basalt half wall arcs around the house on the uppermost terrace.

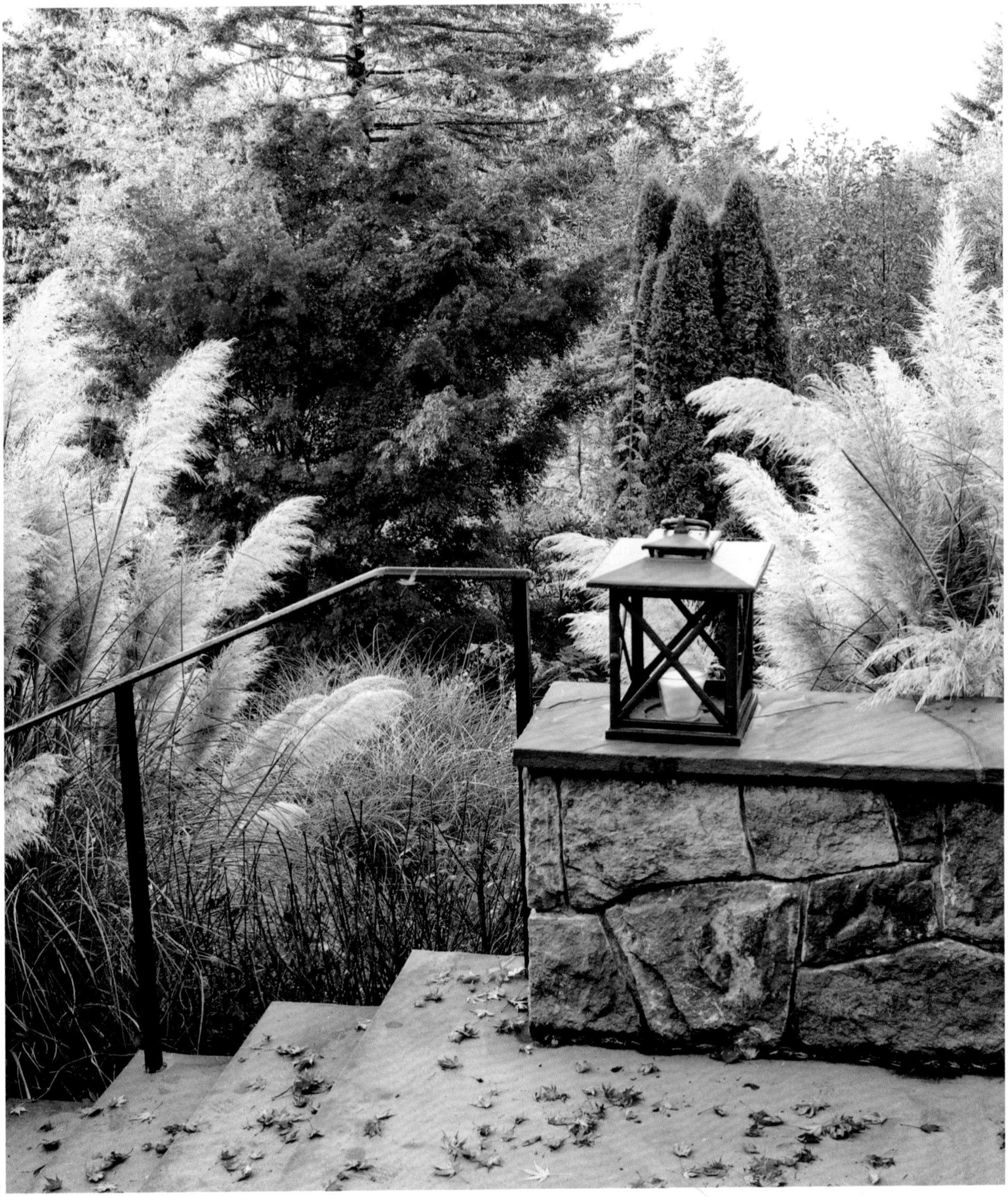

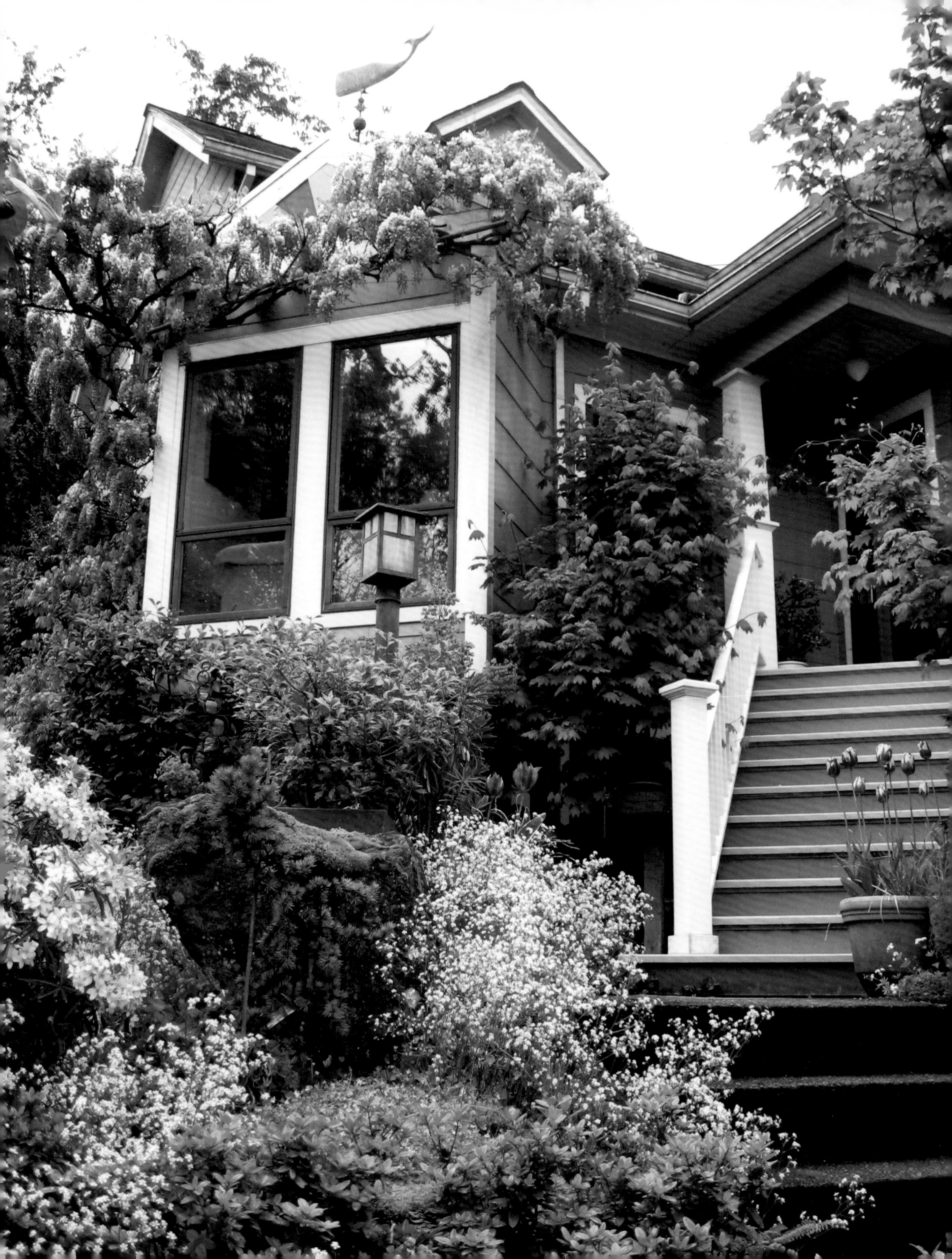

When Anne Marsh started gardening on two city lots in the historic John's Landing neighborhood of Portland, Oregon, over thirty years ago, she was a health researcher. When she met Gary Fear, an engineering draftsman, they began to realize that their native talents were complementary: Gary was drawn to structure, Anne to content. Today they are in business as Marsh & Fear Garden Solutions.

Her 1895 house originally stood high on a grassy slope that contained only a few poorly placed trees and shrubs that provided little privacy; the banks have been replaced by large boulders, to create a north-facing rock garden. The 100-foot-long street frontage today contains mixed plantings of evergreen and deciduous trees, ornamental shrubs, and perennials. "I designed the plantings to have variations in height," Anne says. "Some of my favorites in this long border include magnolias 'Betty' and 'Susan,' *Choisya ternata* 'Aztec Pearl,' *Cotinus coggygria* 'Royal Purple,' *Enkianthus campanulatus, Hamamelis* x *intermedia* 'Diane,' *Camellia sasanqua* 'Jean May,' *Viburnum* x *bodnantense* 'Pink Dawn,' and *Itea virginica* 'Henry's Garnet.'"

The house sits on a corner lot, leaving the second 50-by-100-foot property to the east of the dwelling open for gardening. "We treat it as our own private park," Anne says, "and at one corner of this lot on the street side, Gary designed and built a screening gate that encloses a storage space for all things gardening that won't fit in the basement. Owing to the age of the house, there is no garage, so compost and other necessities needed a place to be stashed."

Many bulbs reside in the border, and she planted them with sequence in mind so that some of the earliest, such as *Galanthus,* or snowdrop, often begin pushing through the soil by early January. The garden is also punctuated with plants that sprout or grow quickly, and therefore invite frequent, rewarding visits in the early season, when gardeners are eager to see progress. Some of Anne's choices include *Corydalis,* crocuses, daffodils, epimediums, euphorbias, hardy geraniums, hellebores, trilliums, and tulips.

The current design evolved in two stages, beginning in 1993, when the boulders were placed over the front bank and a bluestone meandering path was constructed on the east side of the house. "These new hardscape elements made it much easier to plan plantings—they established a structure to work within," Anne says. The second stage began in 2000, when Gary designed and built the back garden stream and pond, arbors, screening fences, gates, and rock walls to surround planting beds. "By 2002 all the new areas were planted, and our renovated garden spaces began to welcome us with the kind of natural environment we formerly had to drive far outside the city to truly experience."

Anne and Gary improved these formerly nondescript lots in three main ways: by using hardscape to define a slope and various rooms or types of gardening areas within the overall garden; adding water flow to override the sounds of city life; and adding arbors and fences to encourage plants to grow vertically while screening out the neighbors.

RIGHT An outdoor dining area provides the owners with the kind of natural environment they formerly had to drive outside the city to experience. **BELOW** A burbling stream meanders through the side garden, masking city noises, as it makes its way down a slope.

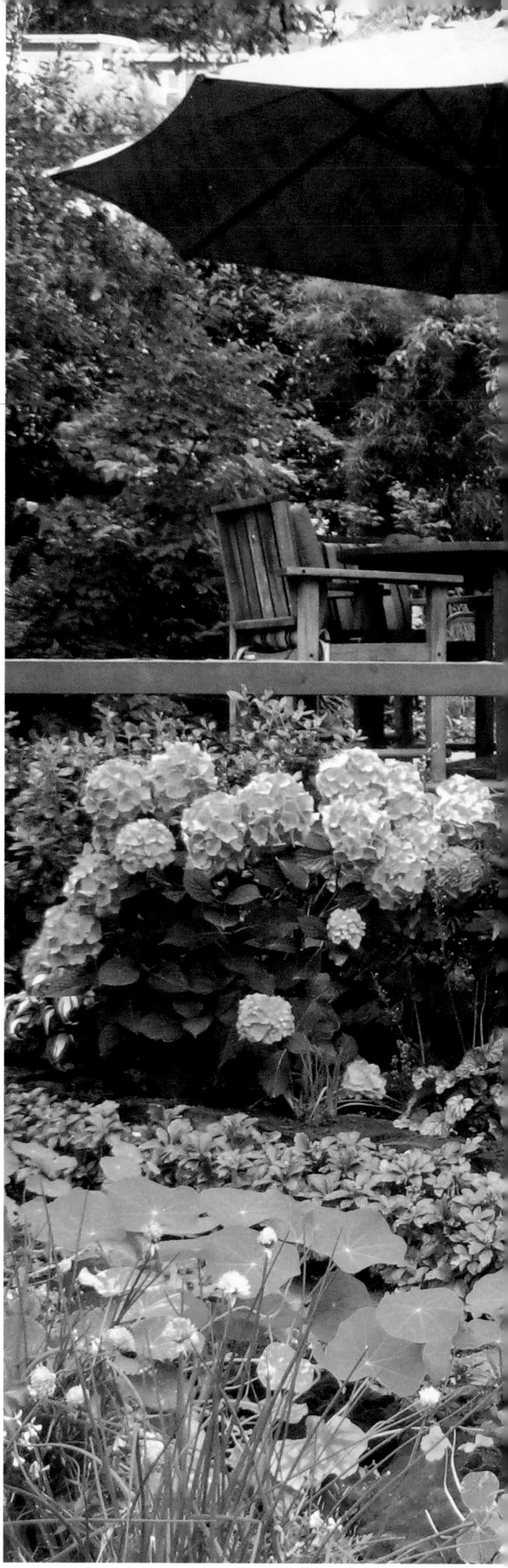

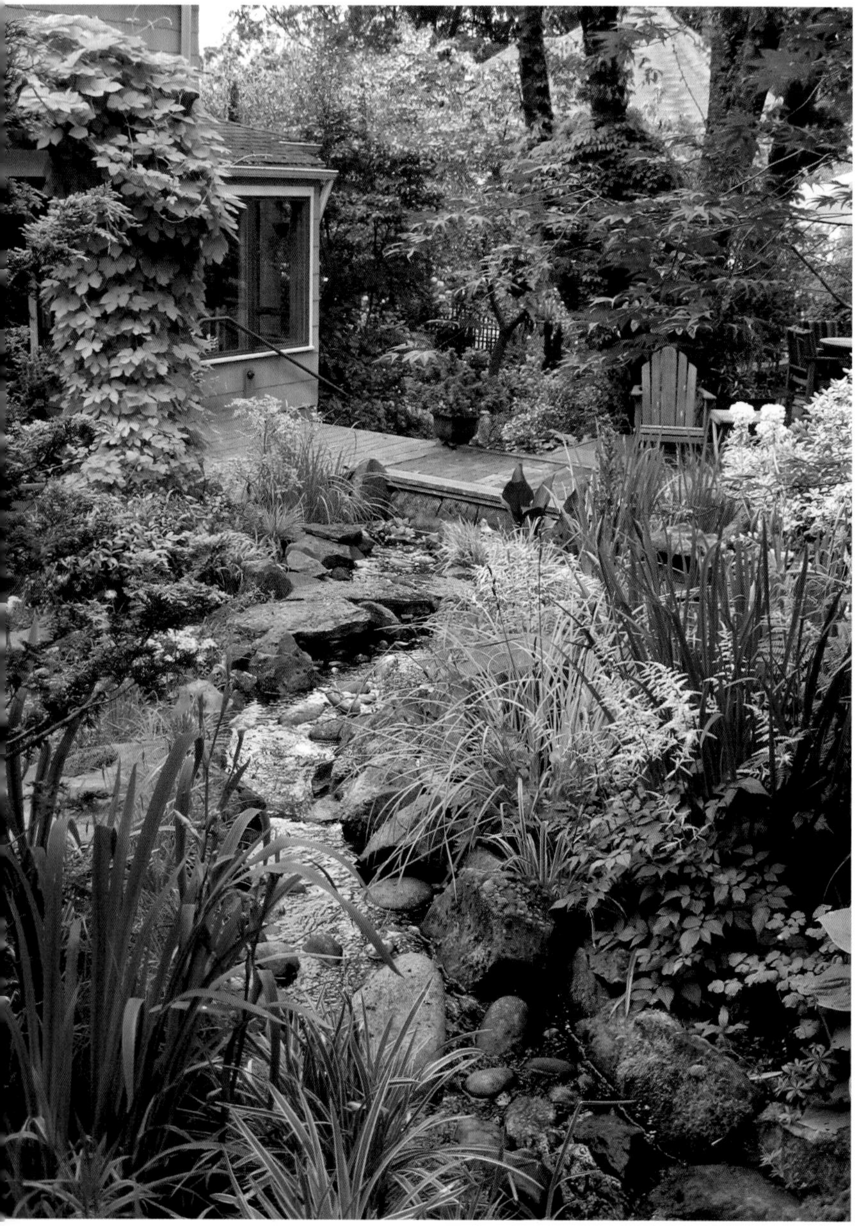

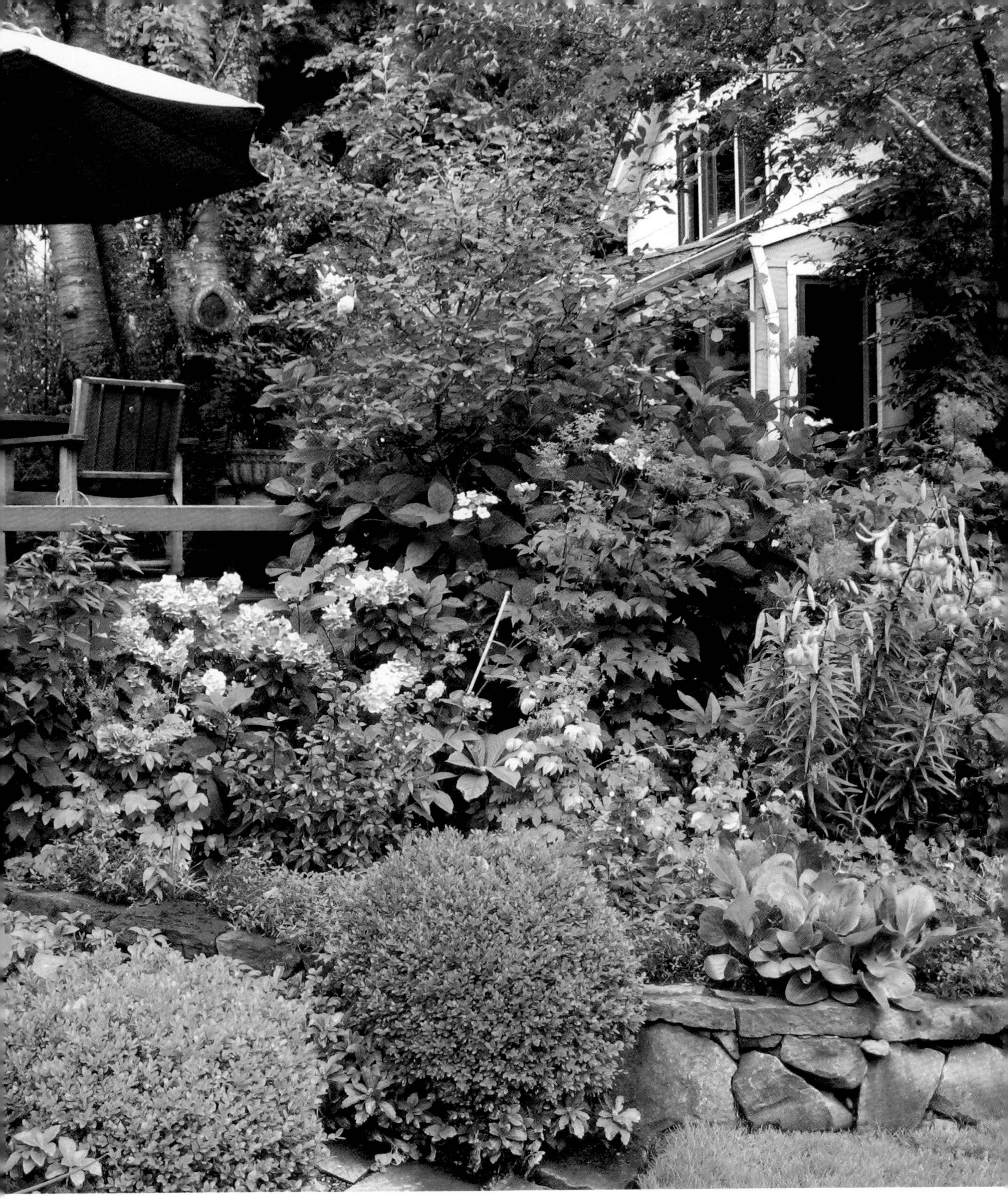

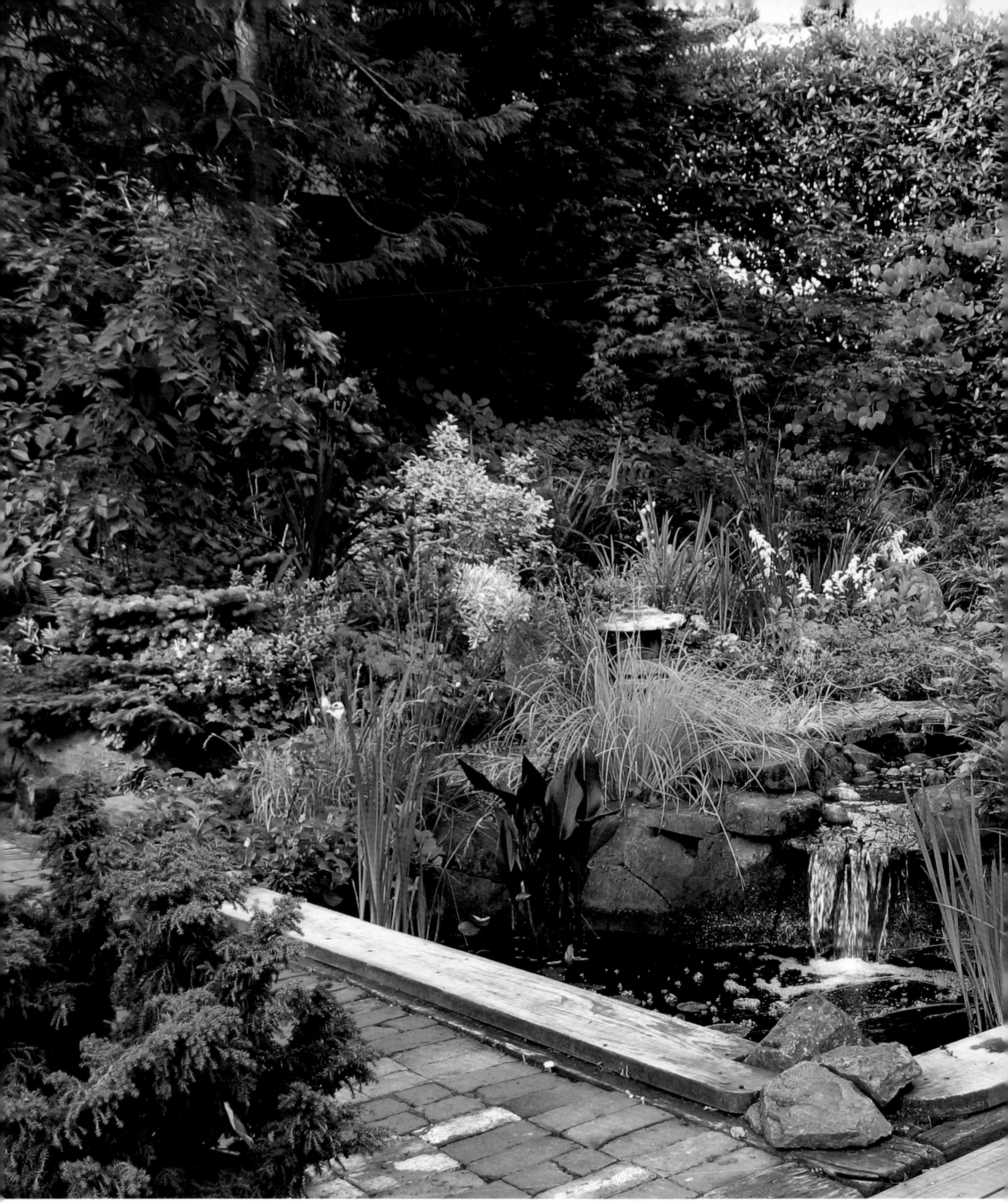

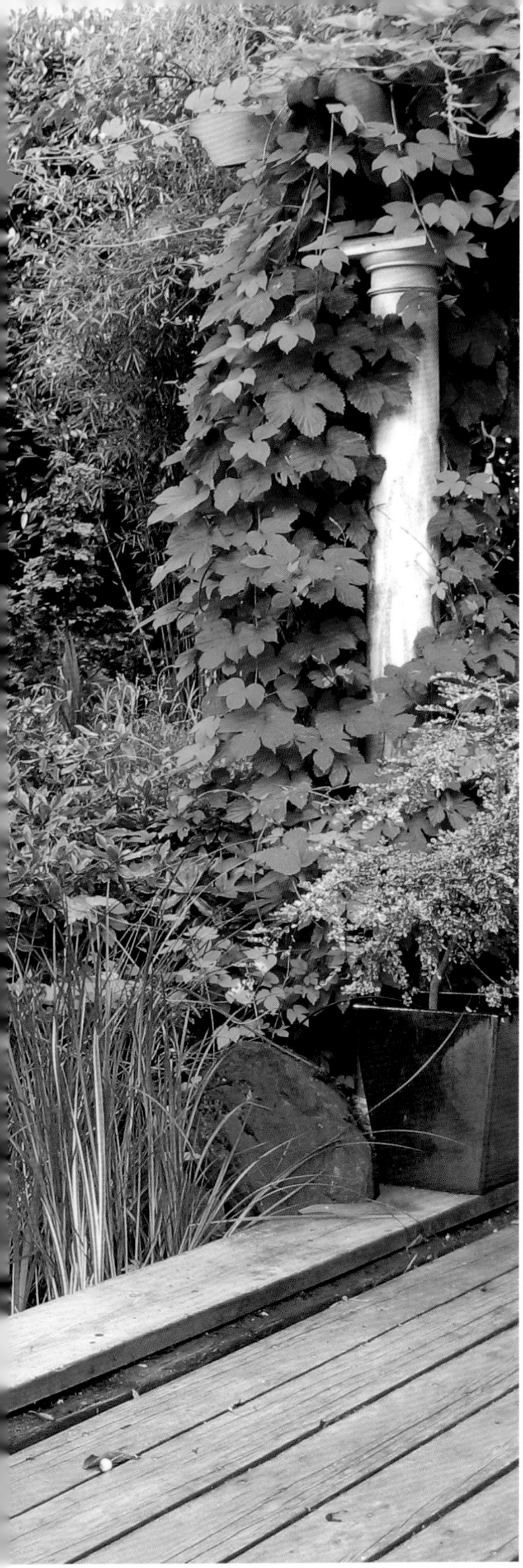

LEFT Vertical screening from hedges, the music of a small waterfall, and pergolas that support dense vines combine to make the backyard a quiet, private oasis in the middle of town. **BELOW** White astilbe and Japanese iris sparkle alongside a small stream.

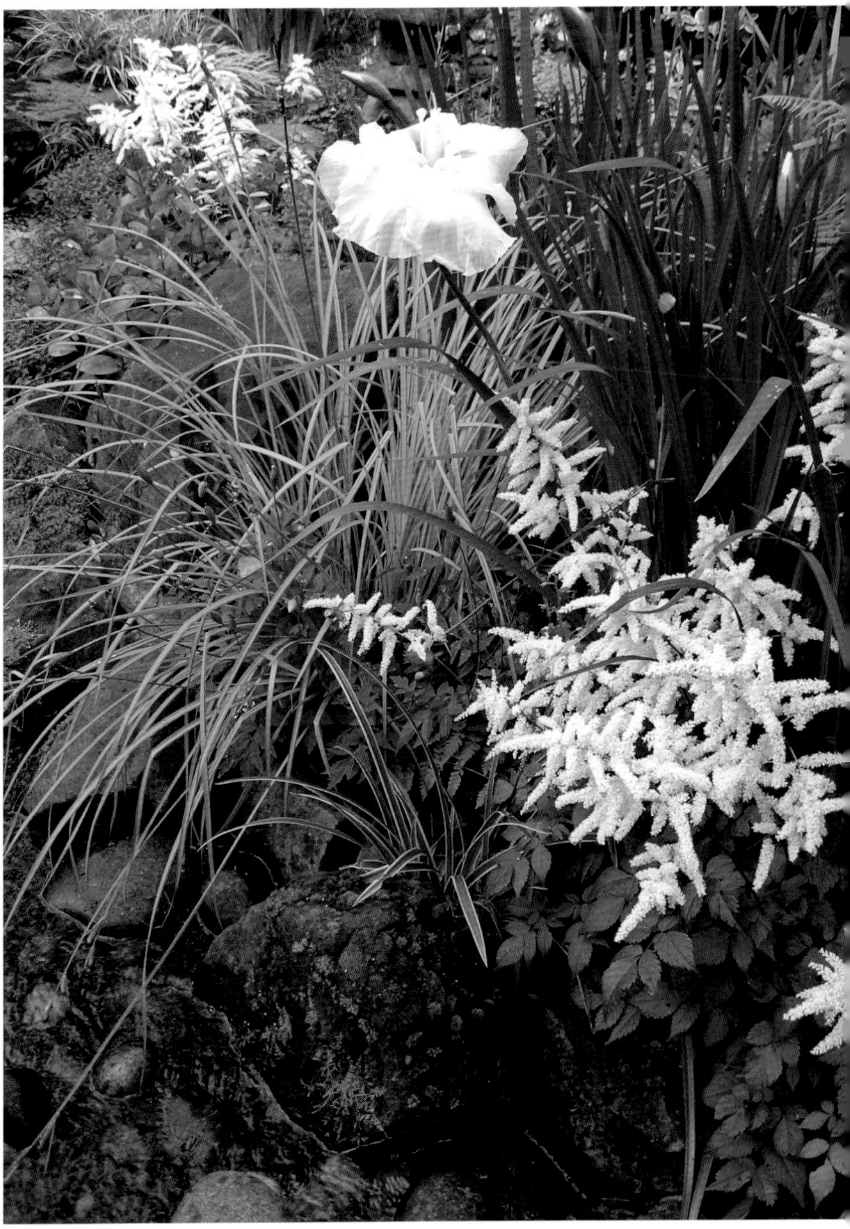

BELOW A screening fence encloses a storage space for garden equipment, which is reached via a small path through a colorful border. **RIGHT** Meandering flagstone pavers lead from the garden's main entrance to the cottage-style side garden, featuring roses mixed into a perennial border.

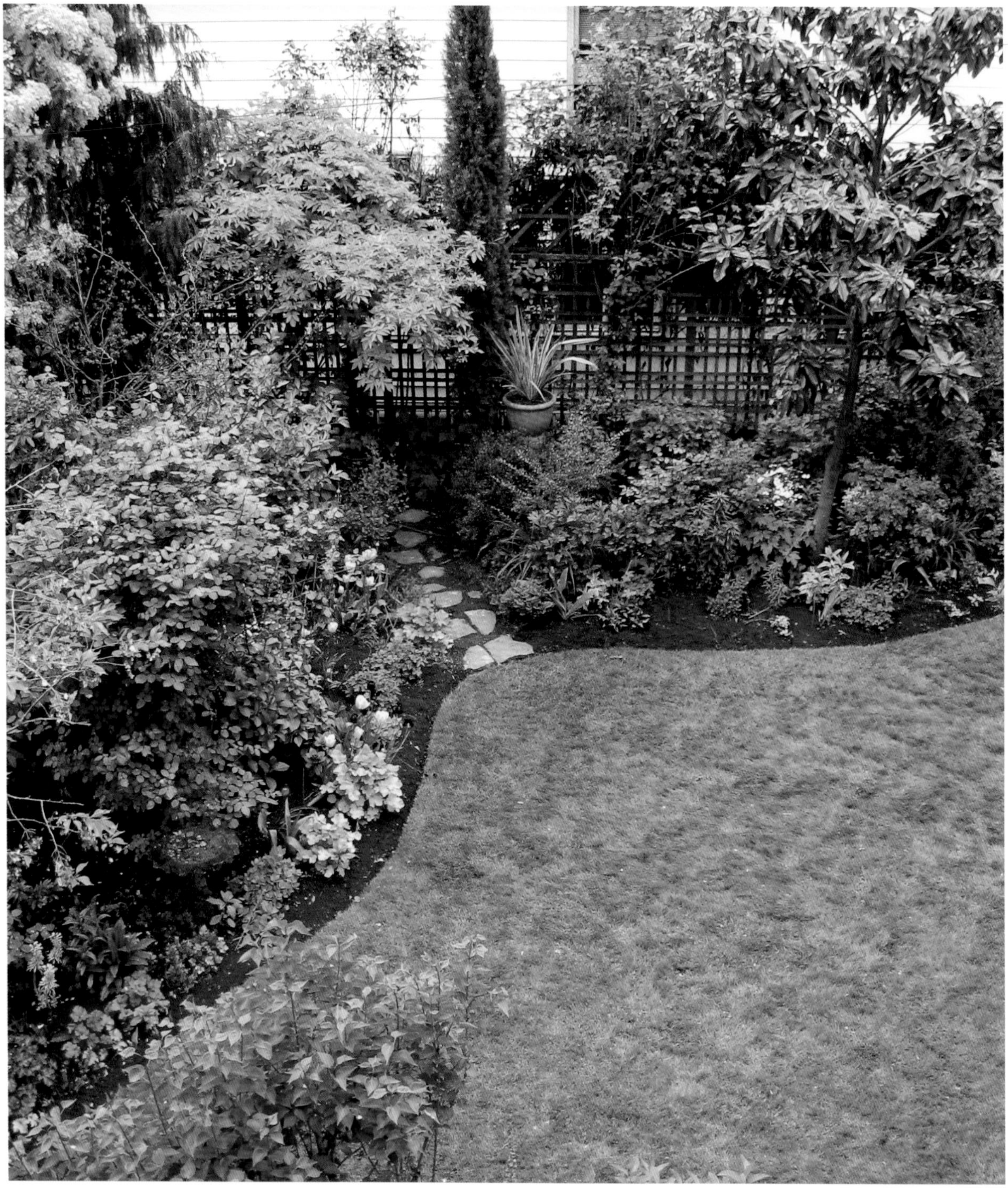

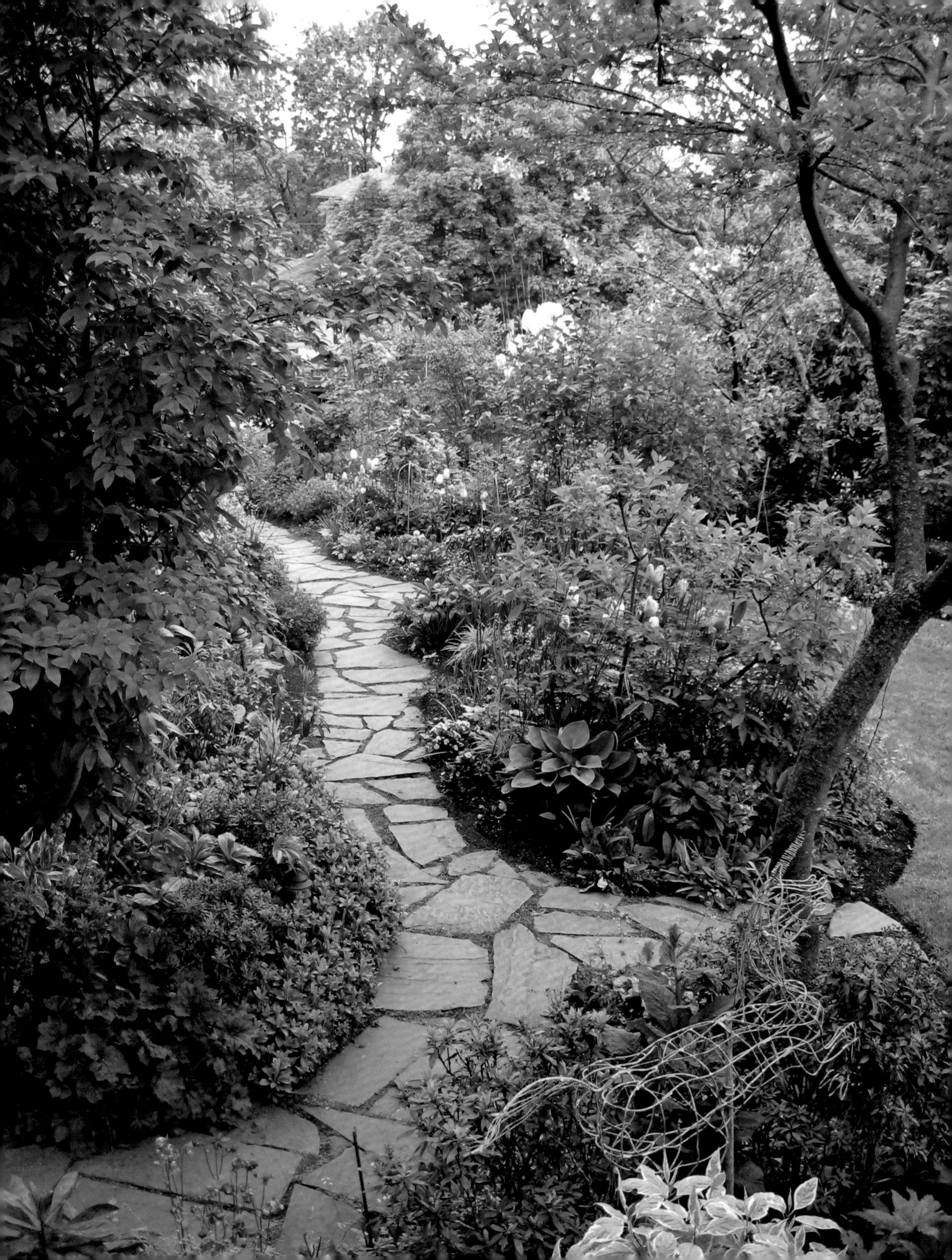

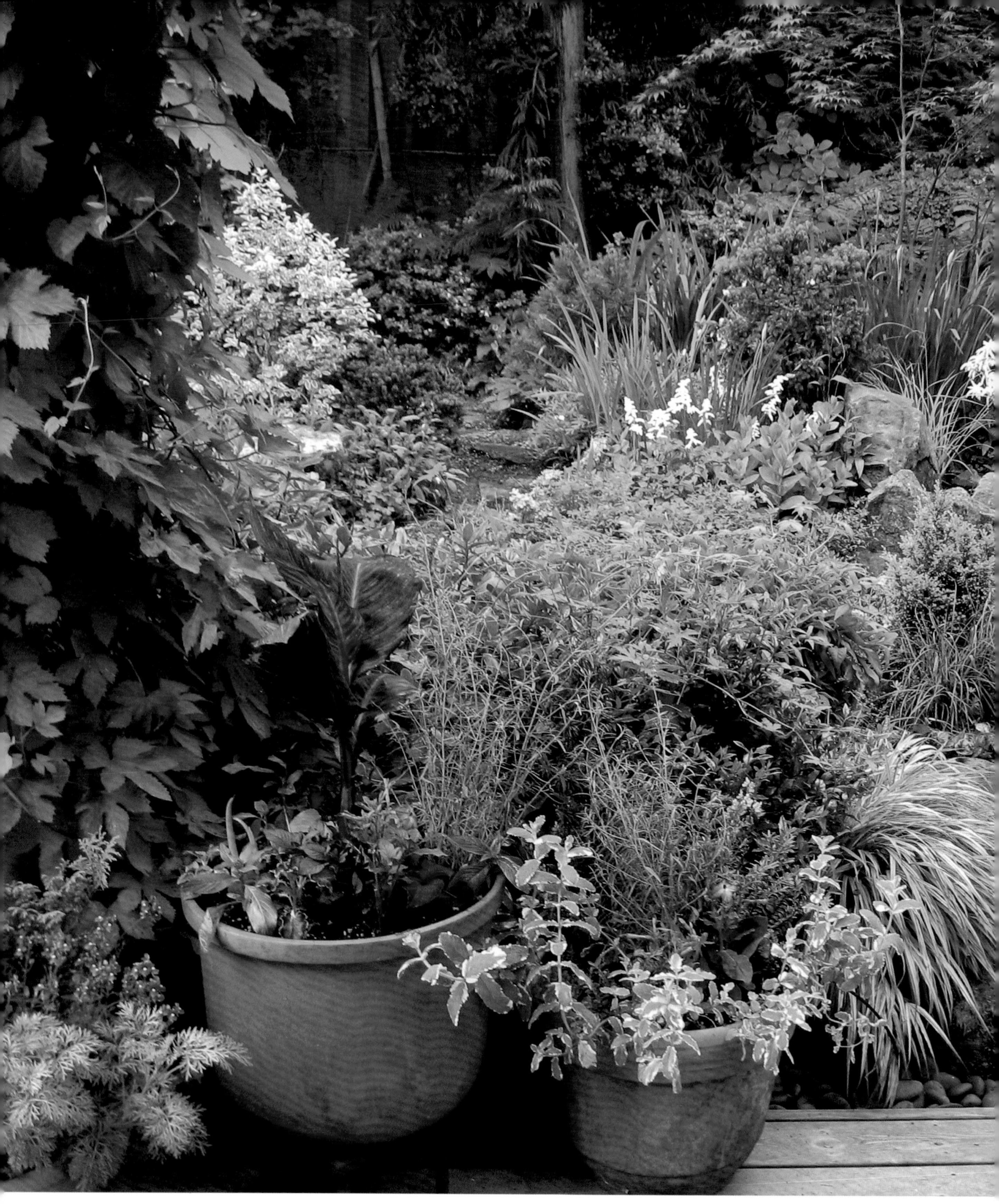

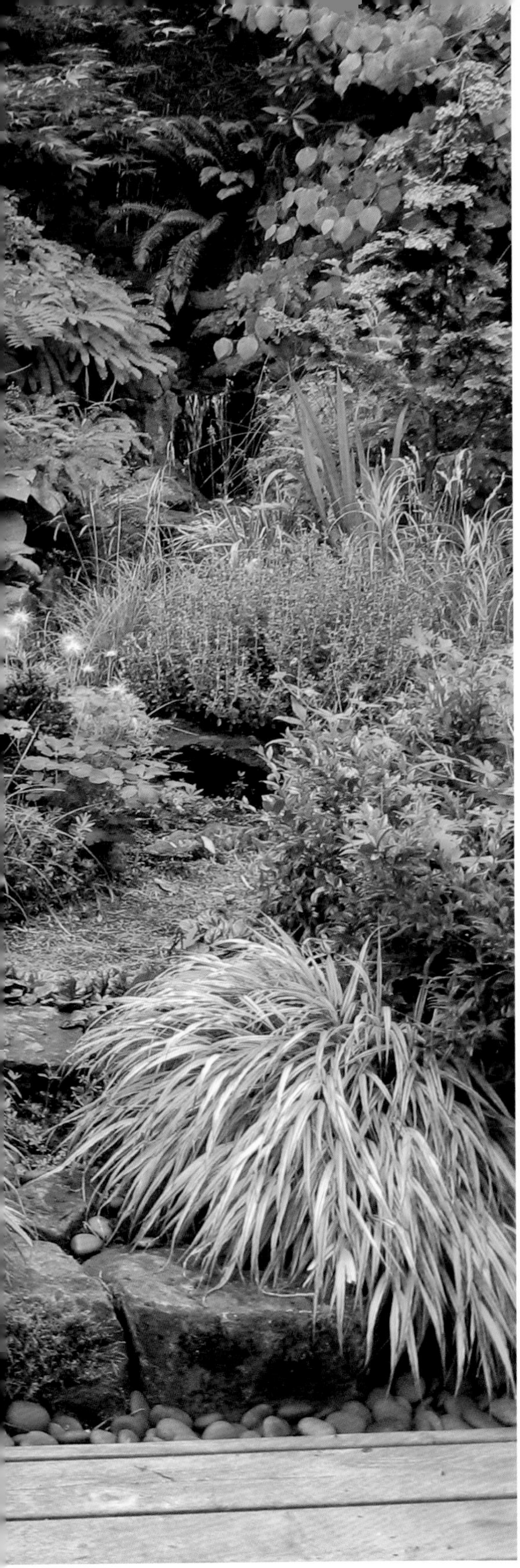

LEFT Masses of golden Japanese forest grass *Hakonechloa macra* 'Aureola' serve as beacons that entice visitors into the woodland garden area. **BELOW** A border that receives full sun features tall shrubs and perennials—including meadowsweet, lilies, and oakleaf hydrangea—that screen out neighbors' houses.

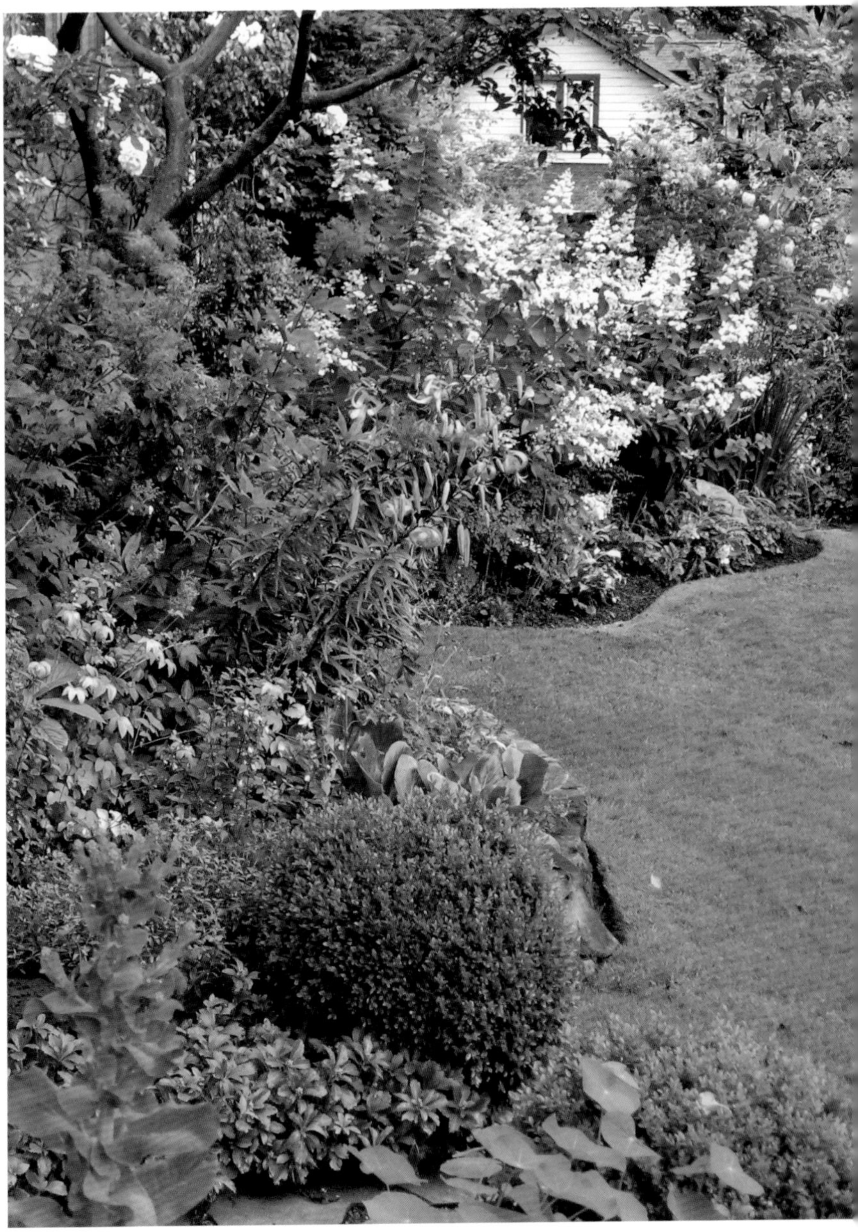

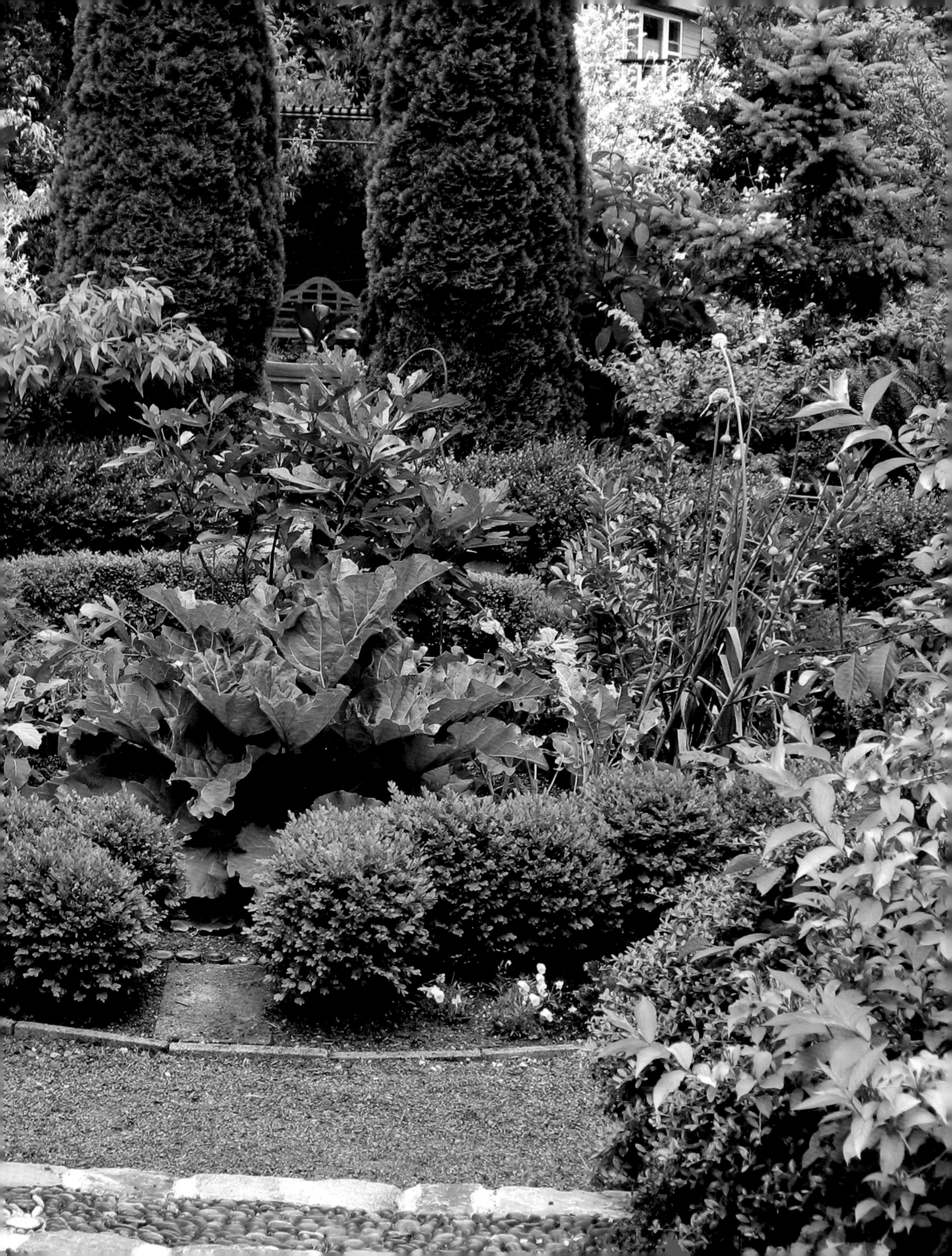

Portland, Oregon, landscape designer Vanessa Gardner Nagel and her husband, Michael, began focusing on their own garden twenty years ago, when their children moved out. "Roughly a third of our acre is wild ravine," Vanessa says. "We keep it that way for the birds and other wildlife." The house and the garden occupy the remaining two-thirds of the property.

Calming vistas and the sense of tranquility the garden exudes today belie the daunting problems the Nagels encountered while they improved the land. As soon as they began truly inspecting the plants, they discovered half of their Douglas fir and big-leaf maple trees had to be removed, owing to a root disease. Then a leaky heating oil tank had to be dug out and replaced; the 13-acre forest next door was cleared and replaced with a housing development; and a neighbor removed a forty-year-old hedge and installed a fence instead of more greenery. Vanessa says, "These are a few of the factors that make me think our garden design was almost completely reactive."

A gravel drive along the north side of the property comes up from the street, crosses a creek, and proceeds through the ravine to a parking area east of the house. They refer to this sunny upper driveway border as the "orange grove," because as spring begins, a welcoming show of mainly orange flowers emerges: crocosmia, daylilies, echinacea, *Epilobium, Geum, Helianthemum, Kniphofia, Phygelius,* and poppies bloom into November among grasses and shrubs. In the winter the red-orange twigs of *Cornus sanguinea* 'Midwinter Fire' are exposed for seasonal interest.

"Our uncomplicated architecture allows us to follow a contemporary and Asian-influenced design," Vanessa says, "although our travels have led us to infuse small tucked-away areas with Mediterranean touches." Vanessa found a bronze Chinese bell during a work trip, when she visited the Dirt Market in Beijing. The central feature of the garden, a circular dragon pebble mosaic, is a few steps away to the right.

Three other areas, formerly devoted to lawn, continue the circle motif, which is based on the ancient ouroboros symbol of a serpent devouring its own tail. Near the first, a Thai spirit house welcomes each visitor and is surrounded by grasses, Russian sage, and boxwood spheres. "Its pattern is based on a flattened crop pattern we found online," Vanessa says, reinterpreted with upturned wine bottles and dwarf boxwood arranged to form a pattern. The second circle is planted with herbaceous, variegated *Carex.* The third is referred to as the "blue meadow" and is filled with blue-tinged *Carex flacca* and the blue flowers of *Allium caeruleum* and *Camassia leichtlinii.*

"Our garden is a feast for all seasons," Vanessa says. "It has good winter bones, but its spring blooms and fall color are my favorites. Gravel is the primary paving material, because it allows water to absorb slowly back into the ground. This is a fully organic garden, and we have woven exceptional exotic plants in with natives. We take our responsibility as stewards of the environment seriously, because we observe many types of birds and animals in our garden every day that call the ravine and creek home."

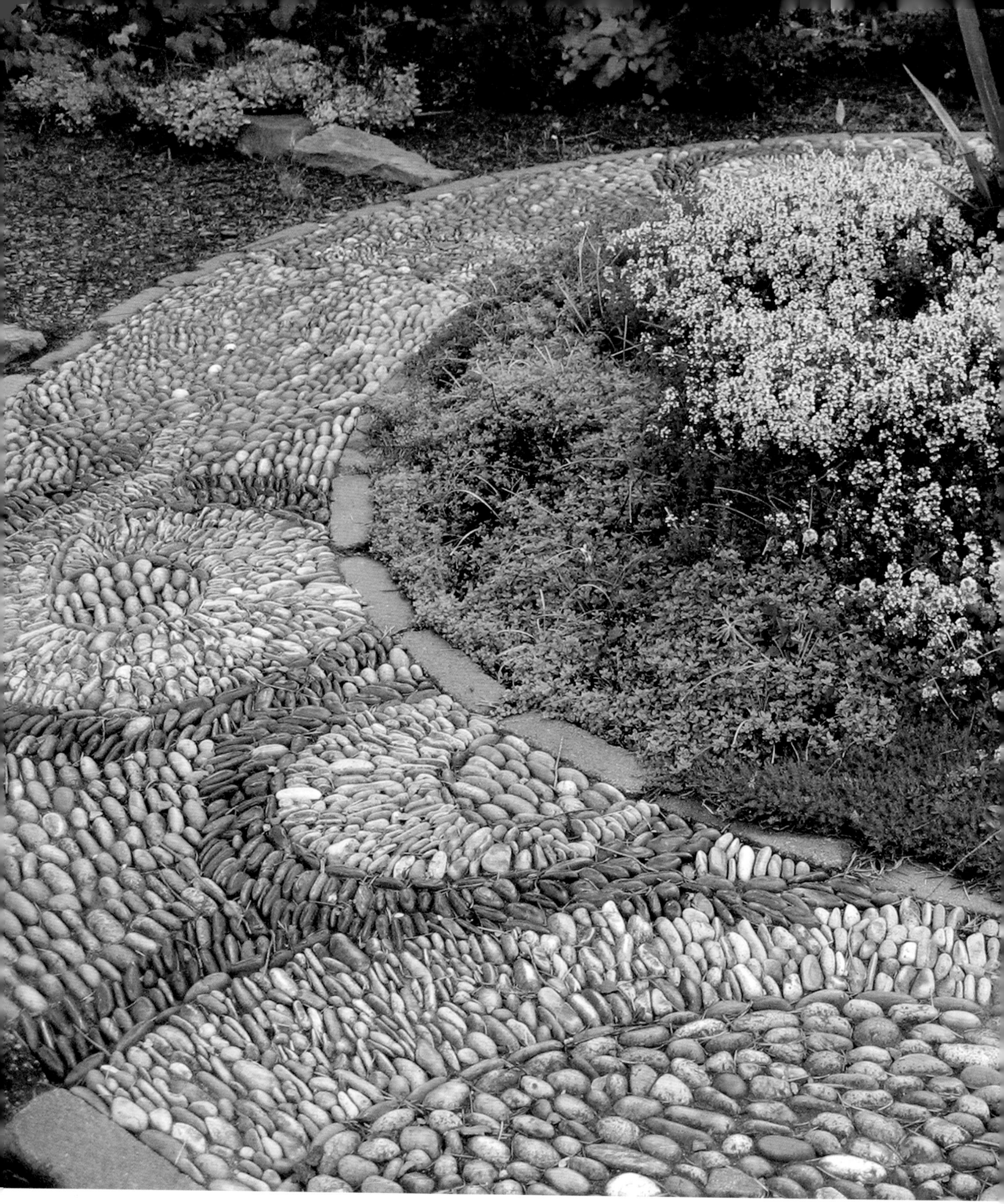

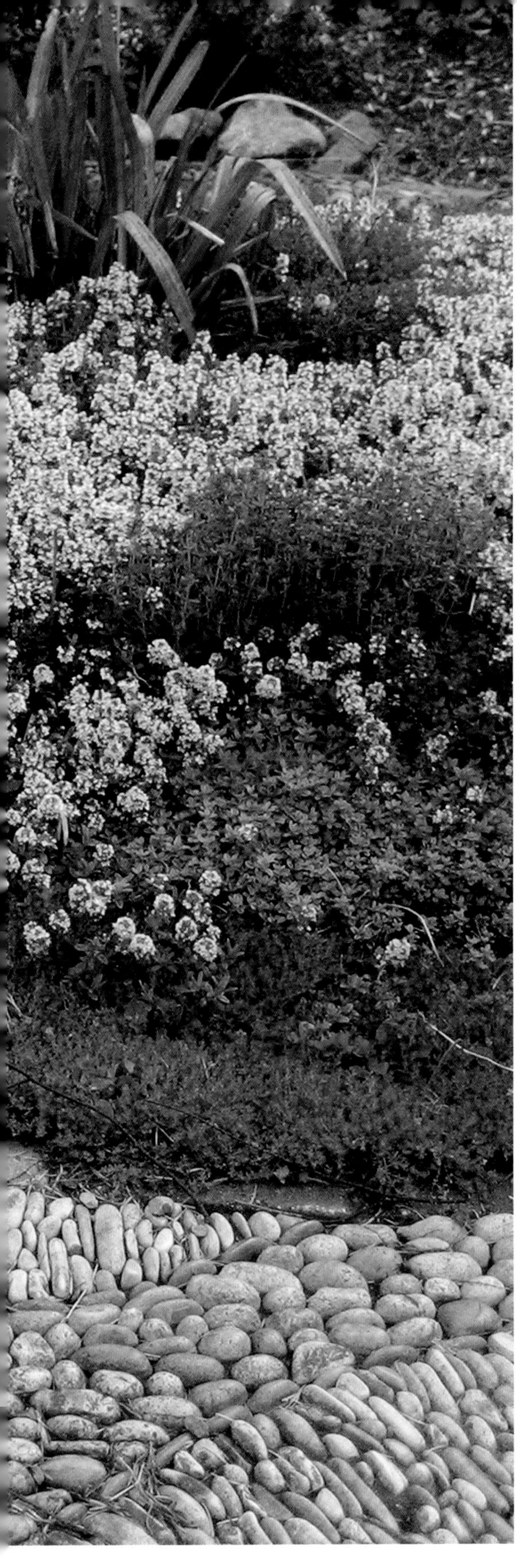

LEFT The central feature of the garden is a circular, pebbled dragon mosaic, a representation of the cyclical renewal of life and infinity; creeping thyme blooms in the center. **BELOW** Agapanthus, bell-flowers, and hostas provide a blue theme for a shady spot in the garden with both their blooms and foliage.

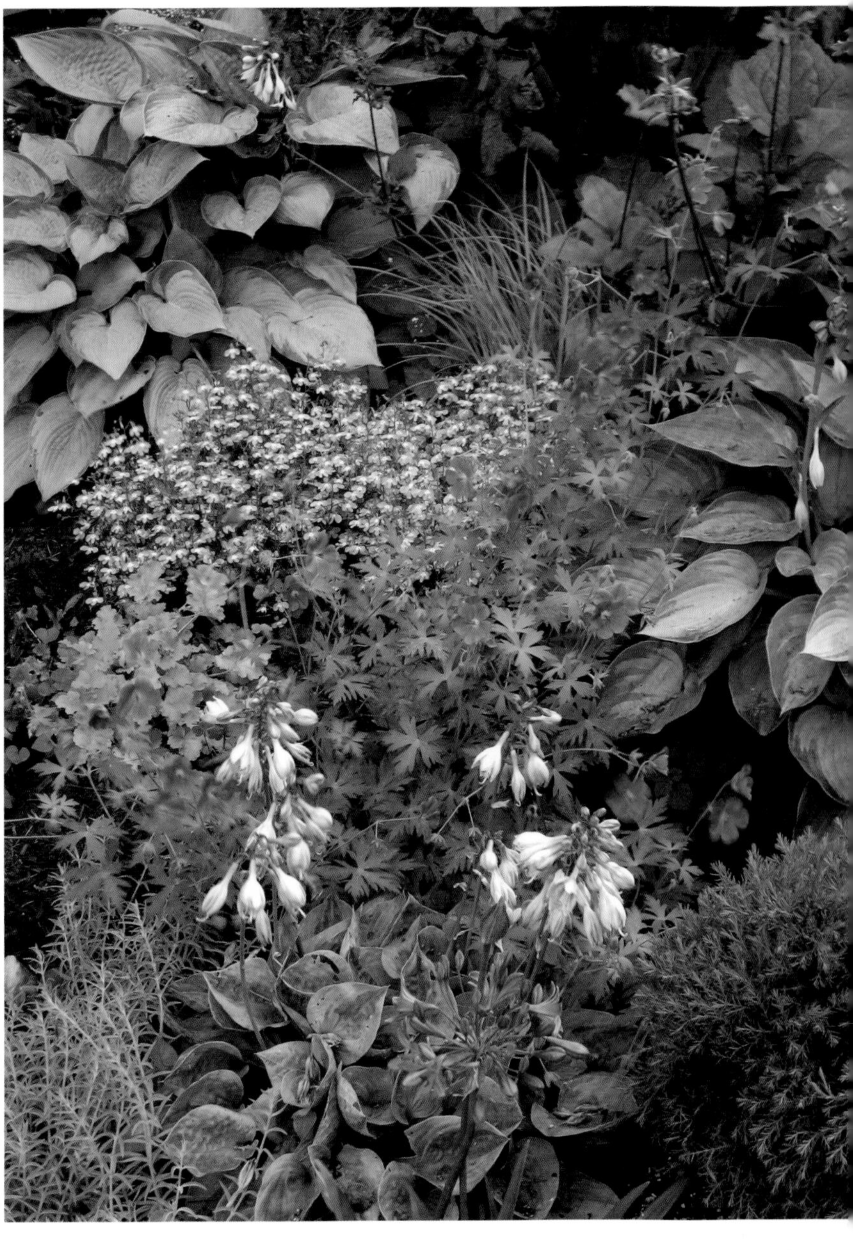

BELOW The cut-leaf textures of fernleaf peony, parrot tulips, and sword fern complement each other. **RIGHT, ABOVE** *Kniphofia* and oatgrass seeds form part of the "orange grove" border that lines the upper driveway.

RIGHT, BELOW English lavender and a bicolored German iris extend the blue garden's theme to the purple end of the spectrum.

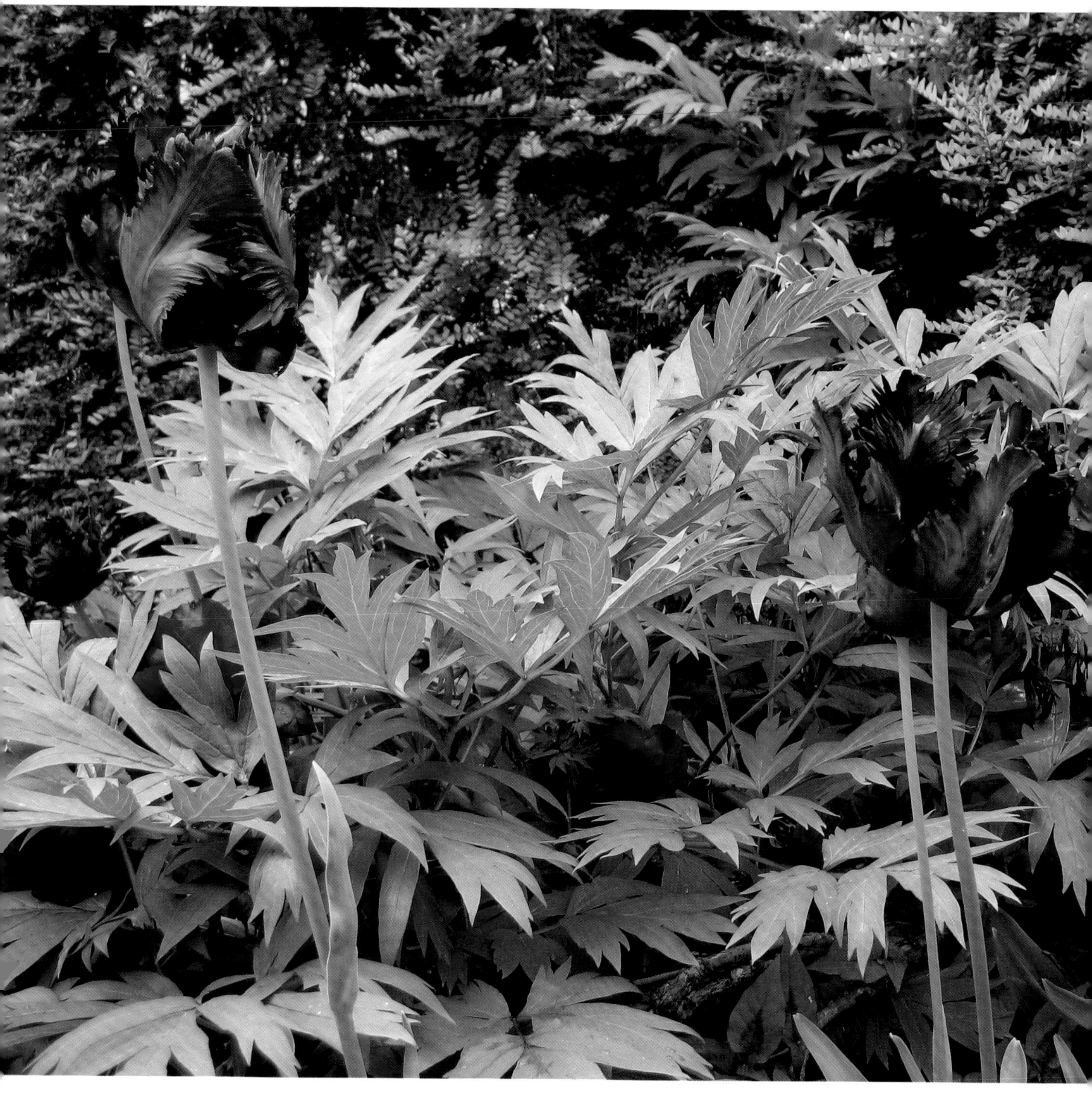

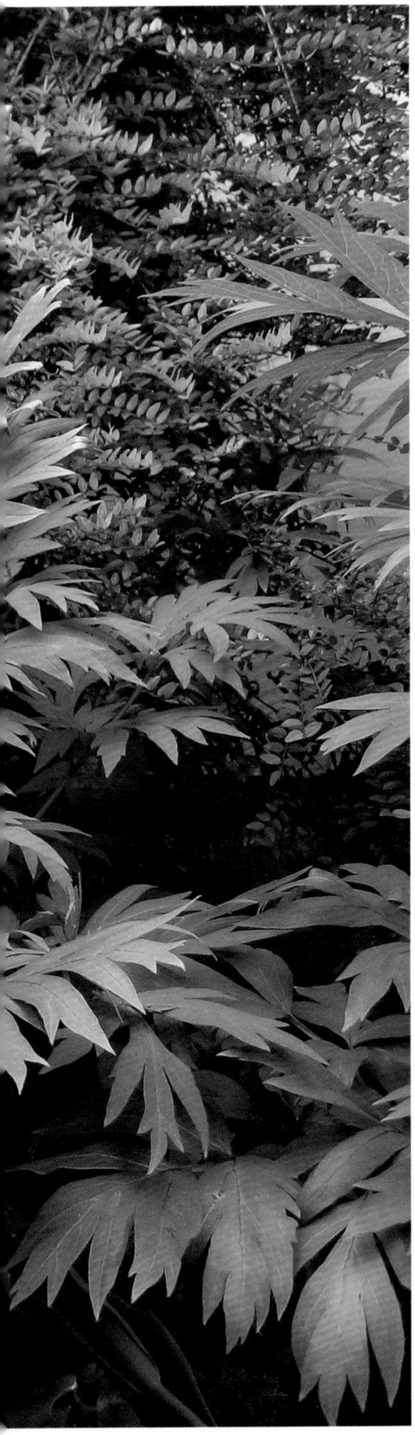

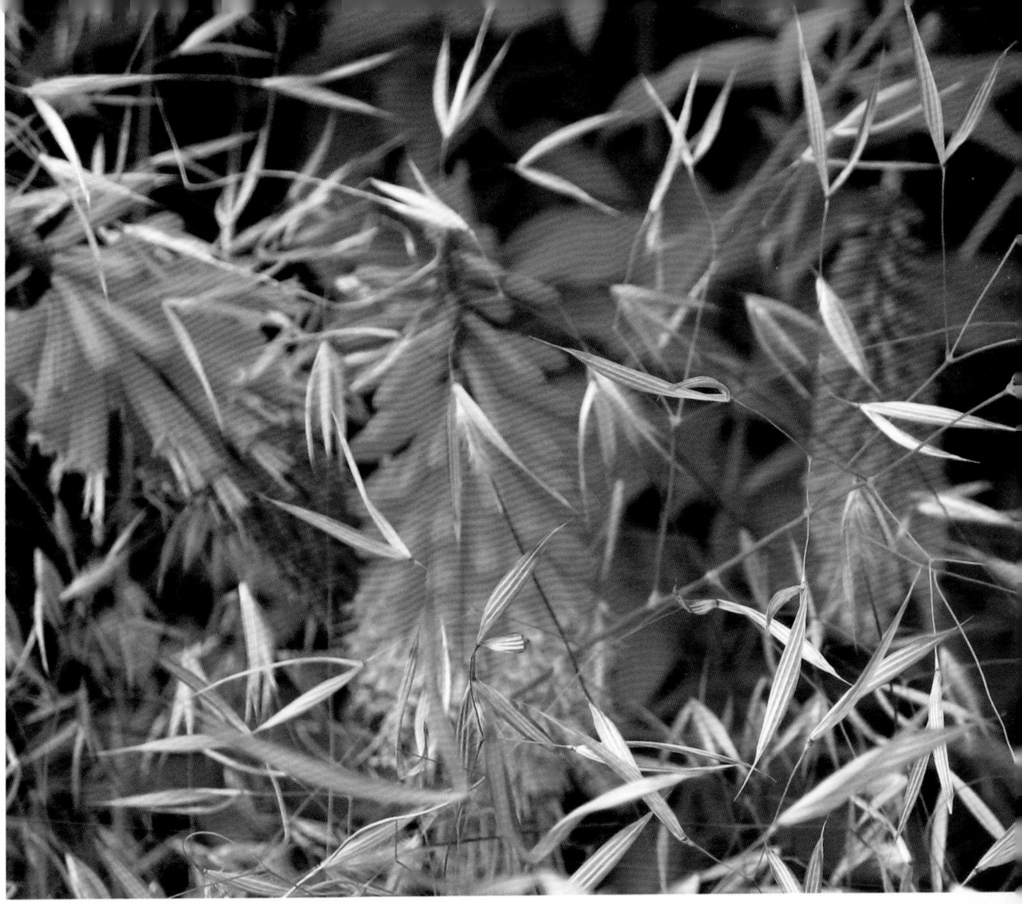

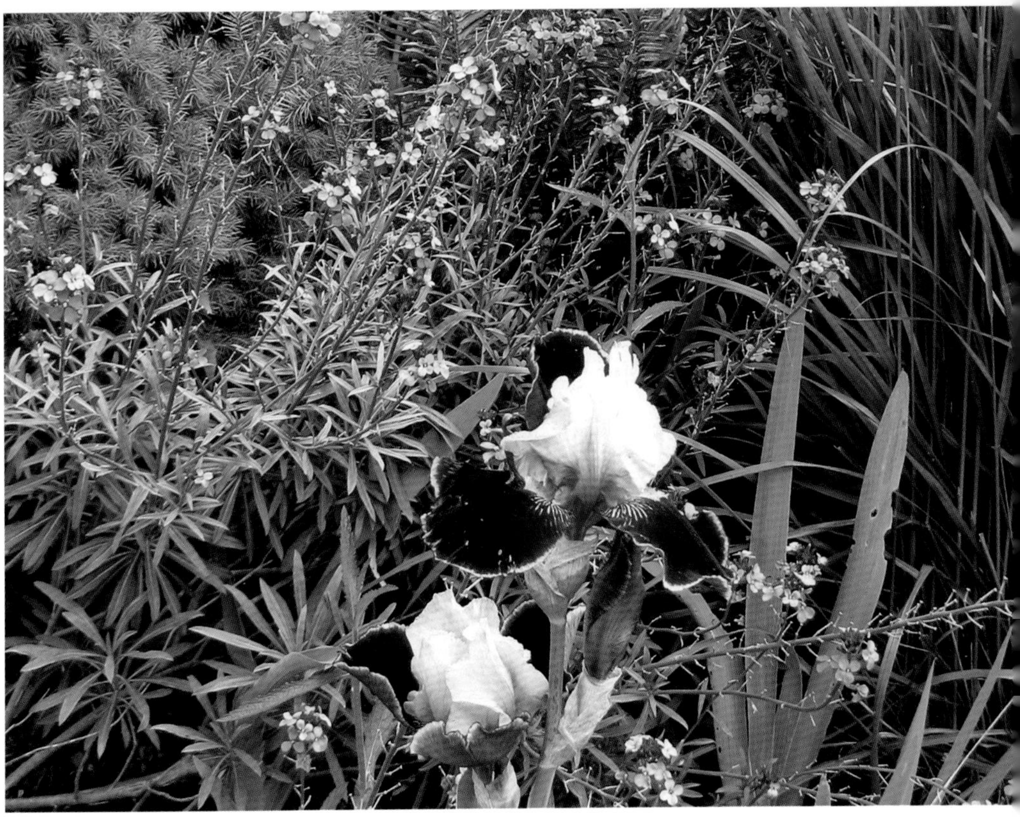

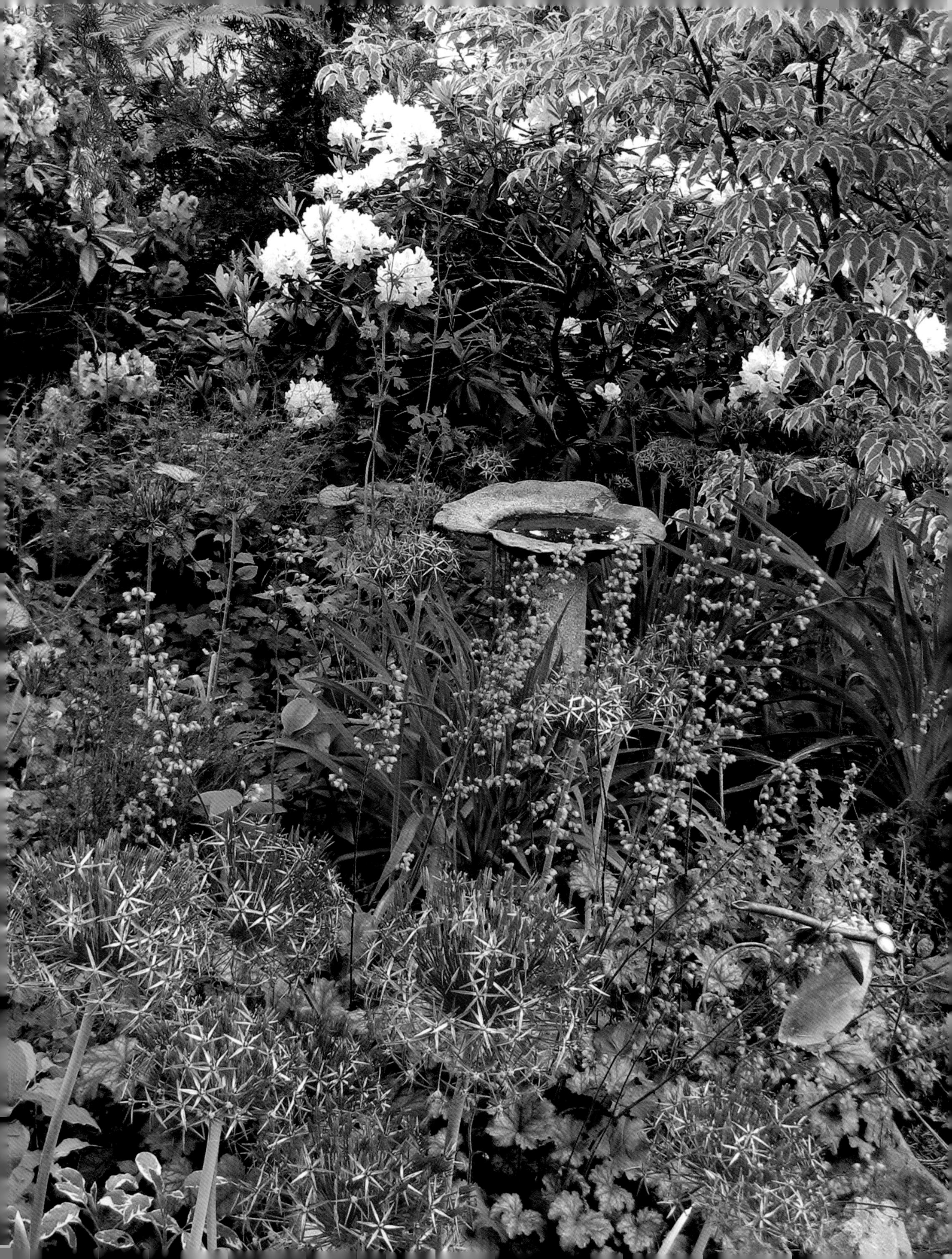

BELOW A bird nesting box sits surrounded by late-summer seed heads of stipa and miscanthus grasses, and the vibrant orange blooms of crocosmia.
LEFT This birdbath, nestled in a bower of *Allium caeruleum,* coralbells, and rhododendrons, attracts many song-birds, to the delight of the owners.

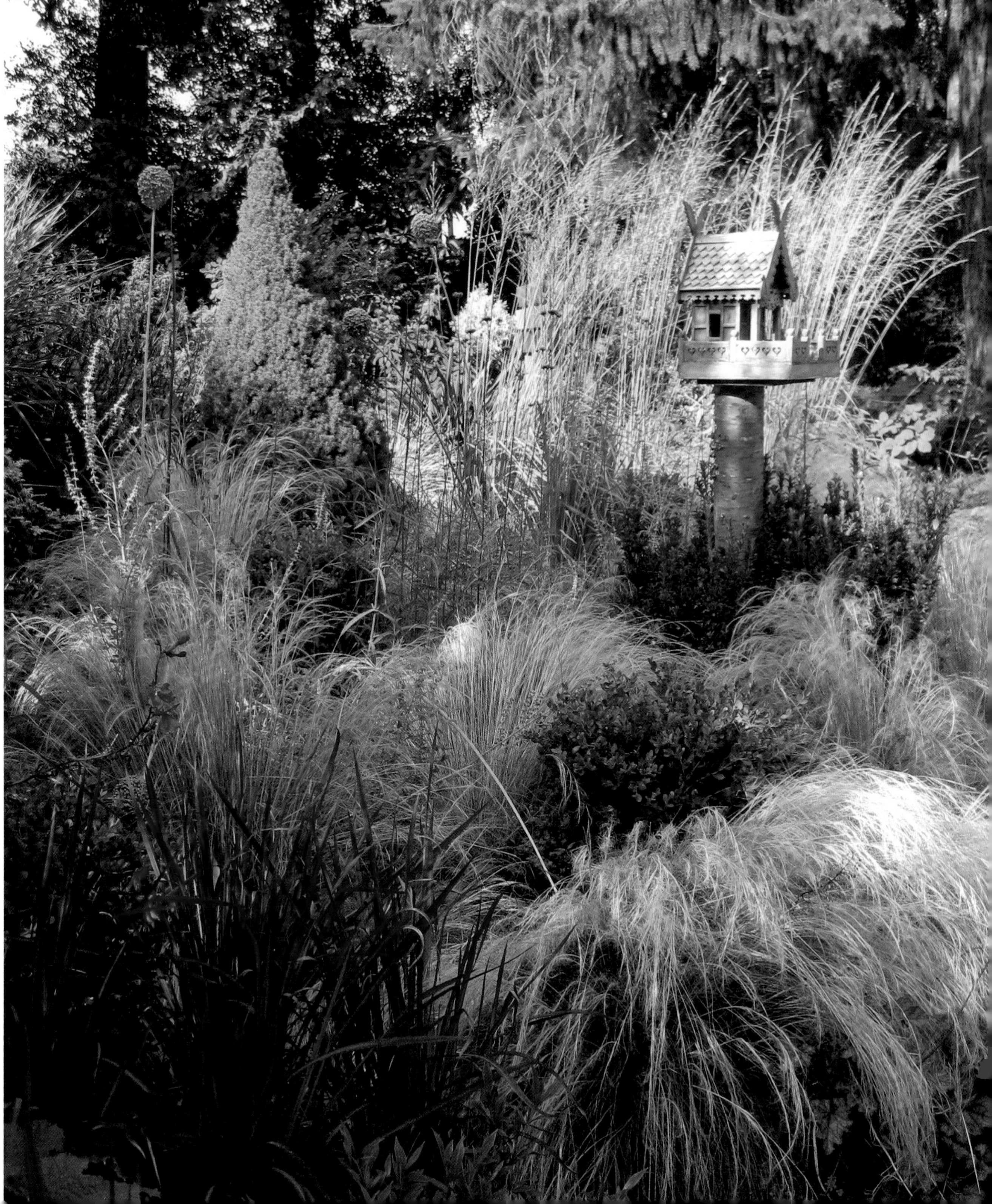

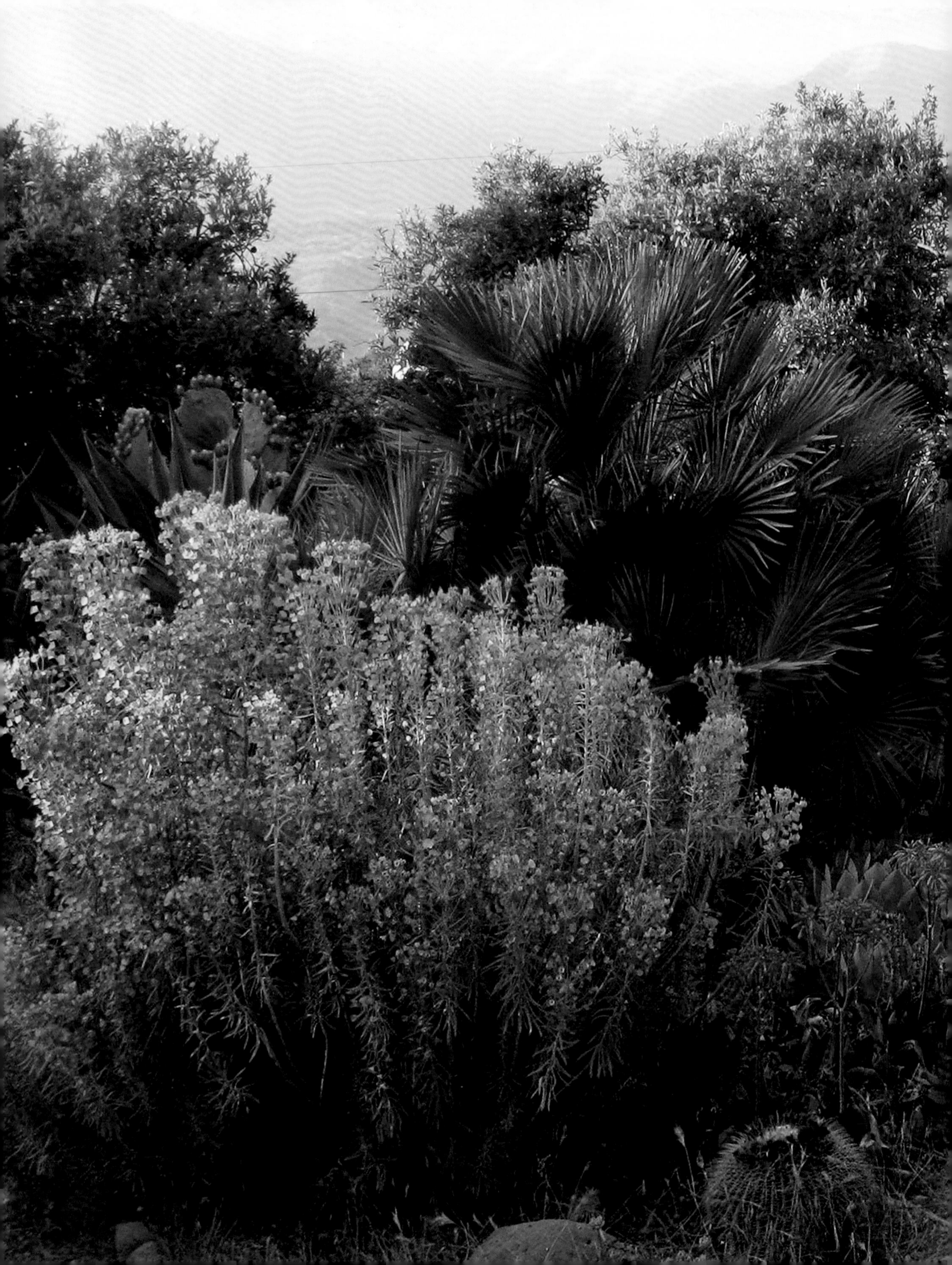

west

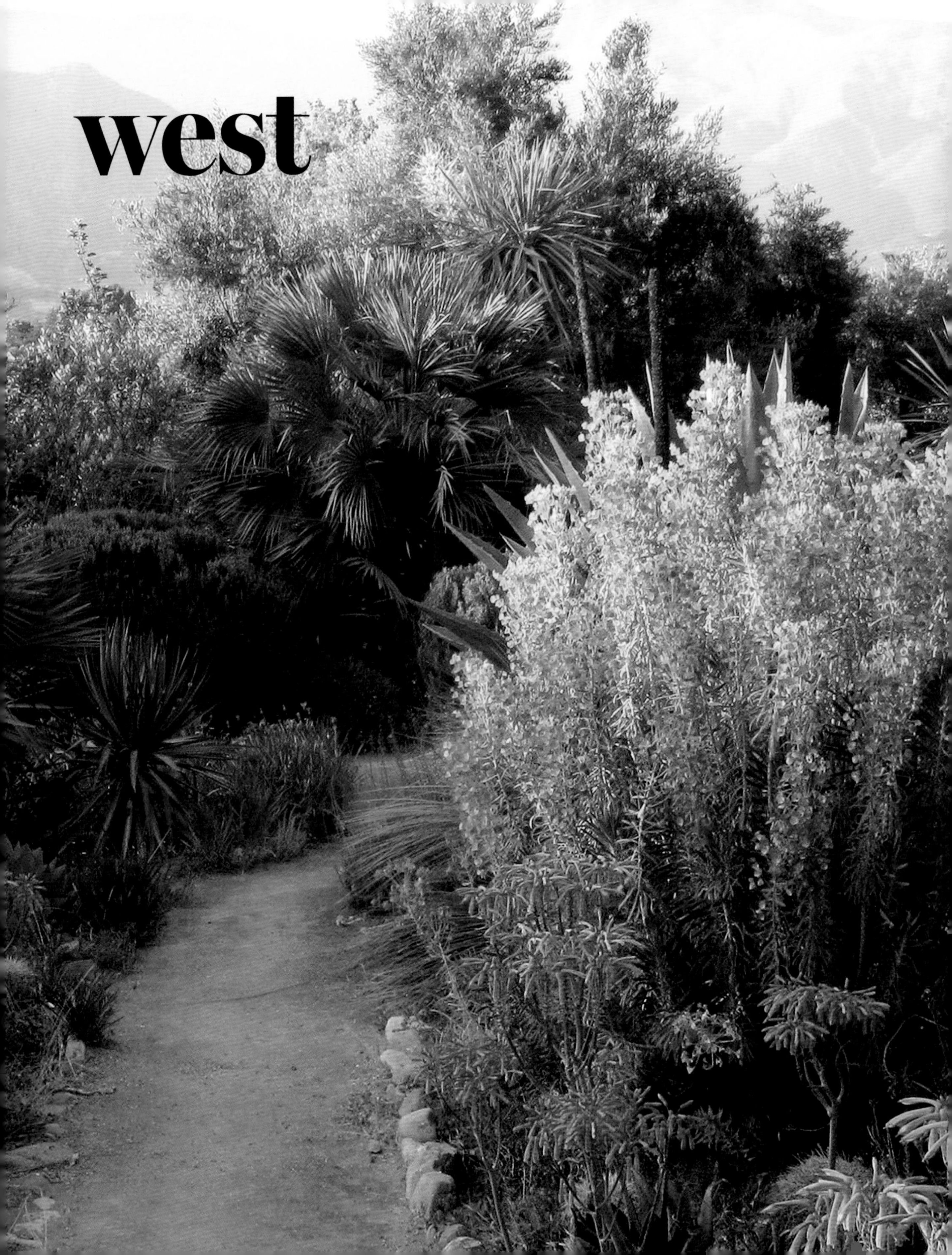

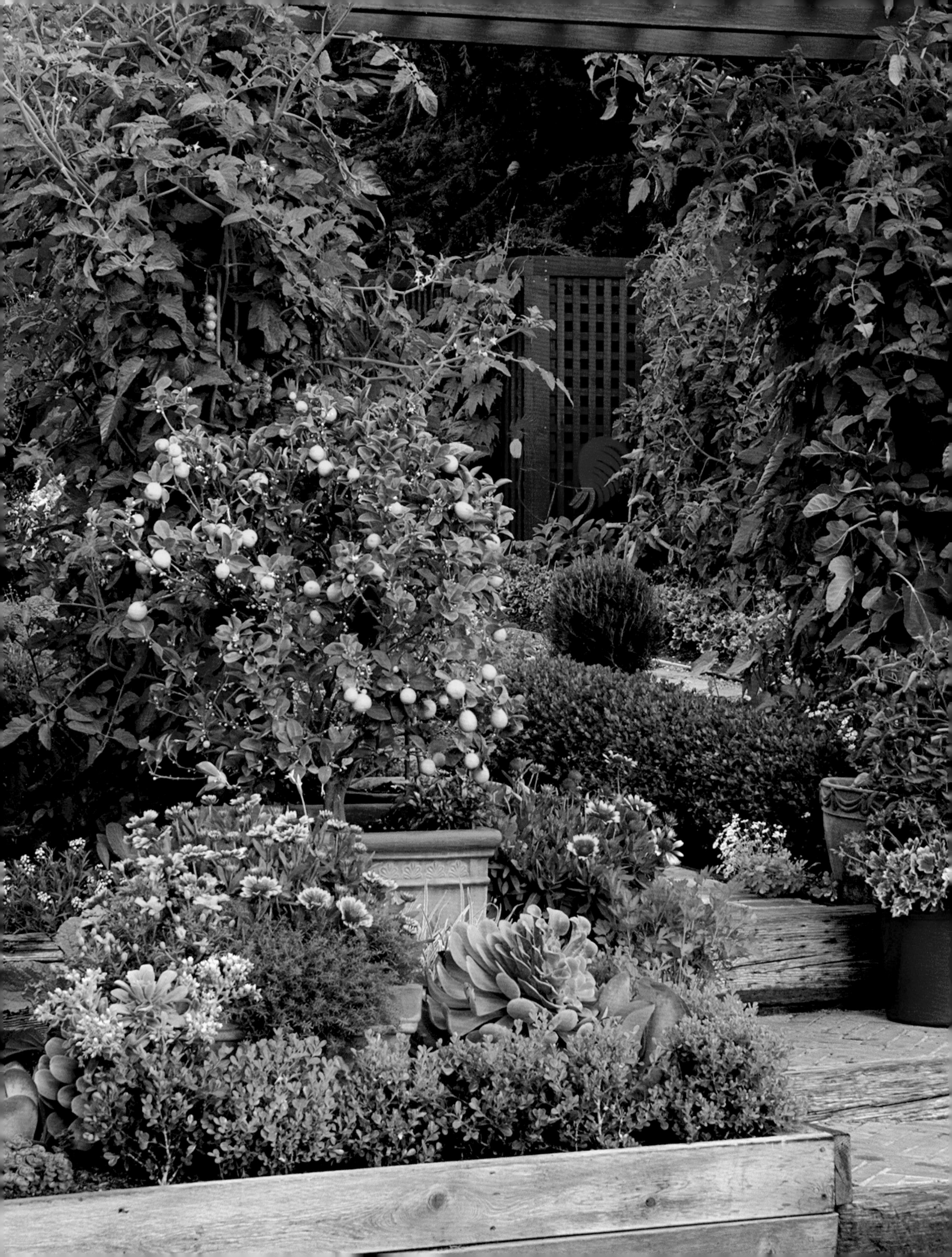

A pioneer in edible landscaping, Rosalind Creasy practices what she preaches on a quarter-acre lot in Los Altos, California. The front yard, where most of the gardening happens, is a mere 1,200 square feet—a yard size typical of the Bay Area, even in affluent communities. "Views of the neighbors are unavoidable," she says. "I have learned to accept them as part of the scene."

The success of the front landscape is dependent on three components: strong bones provided by wood walls, arbors, and fencing that can be repainted often; structure provided by defined or raised beds, fruit trees, and shrubs; and a backyard holding and storage area. An organic approach is a given.

Creasy's garden is unique in that it is at once a personal garden, a photo studio, a design laboratory, and a demonstration garden—functions that support her own roles of cook, professional garden designer, educator, and activist. "Edible plants in a decorative setting never cease to amaze people," she says. "I thrive on changing things around at least twice a year, trying new combinations of vegetables, herbs, and flowers— all edible. Roses, calendulas, and violets picked from organically grown plants are as tasty as they are beautiful. And I do like to repaint the woodwork in new, surprising colors."

Much to Creasy's consternation, she finds that local or community bylaws favoring activism for responsible environmental stewardship are often later overturned to serve other interests. "That's what led me to make my front garden a living example of what I believe in," she says. "If I can grow organic food in my small space, anyone can."

Involvement with the neighborhood's children gives Creasy immense psychic and spiritual contentment, and she welcomes them into her garden at any time, to pick and eat things. It's no wonder they love her. "My garden is where the kids hang out," she says proudly. Over the years, they've inspired her to do whole theme gardens for them: an *Alice in Wonderland*, a *Wizard of Oz* fantasy, and a rainbow vegetable patch. "If it weren't for the kids, I would never have done all this." She's had many children return to visit as grown-ups over the years as well.

"I live in an unusual neighborhood for modern suburbia," Creasy says. "We call it the 'Assisted Living Street,' because everyone helps everyone else. At least once a week the whole street gets together for a party with margaritas, usually here in my garden. I like to think of it as the soul of the street. The neighbors are my big family, always welcome to come pick whatever is in season."

Organic and sustainable are Creasy's bywords. There is no chemically dependent lawn, no gratuitous foundation planting. She says, "I thrive on change and always look forward to trying something different— a spring salad garden expressing a new design or a summer theme of Italian specialties. And who can resist heirloom varietals—beets the size of volleyballs and huge, meaty tomatoes?"

BELOW Sweet strawberries growing in the pockets of a vertical planter contrast in taste with the peppery leaves and flowers of edible yellow nasturtiums. **RIGHT** The grid of a purple raised bed holds both neat rows of edible lettuces and less-structured plantings of hens and chicks.

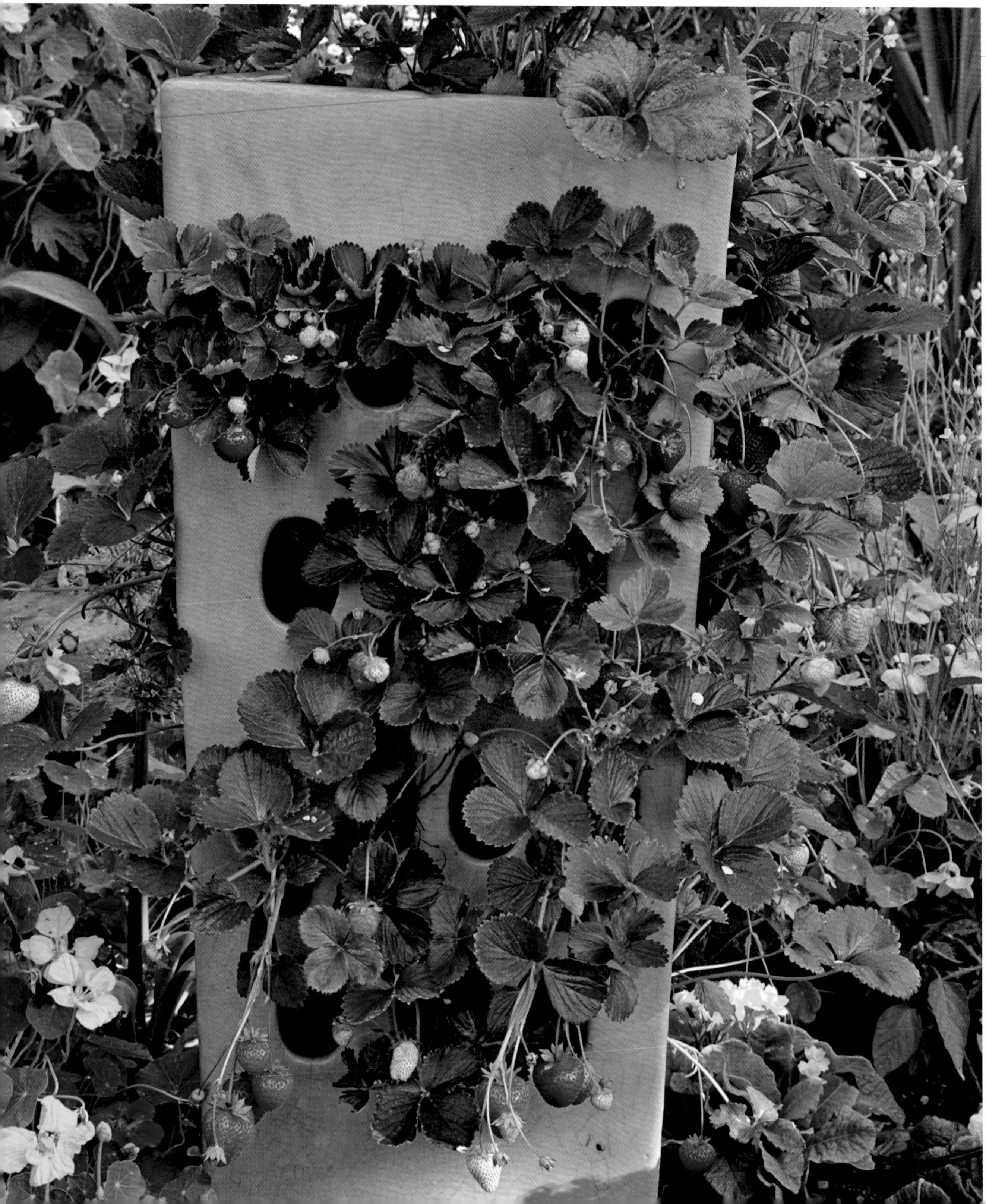

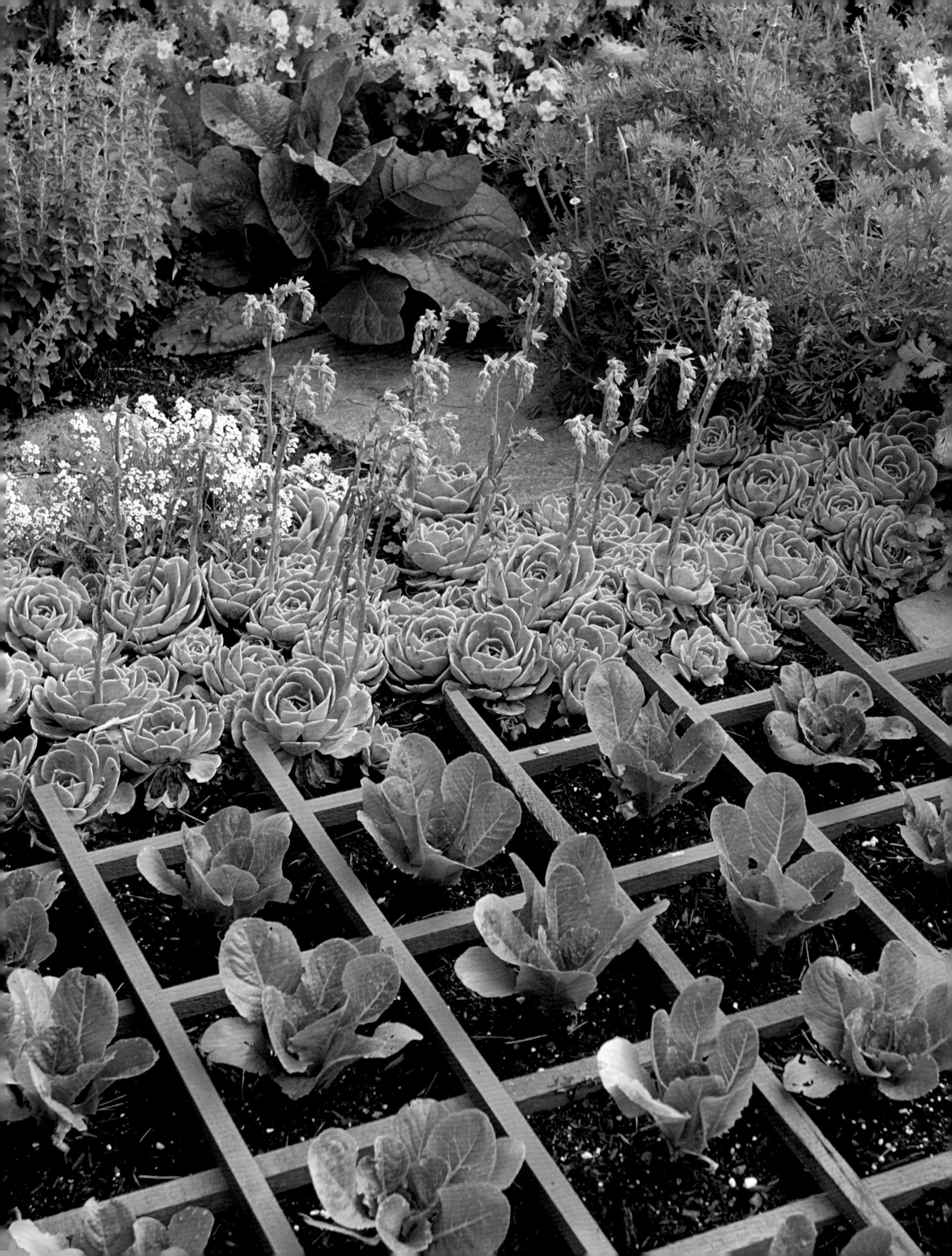

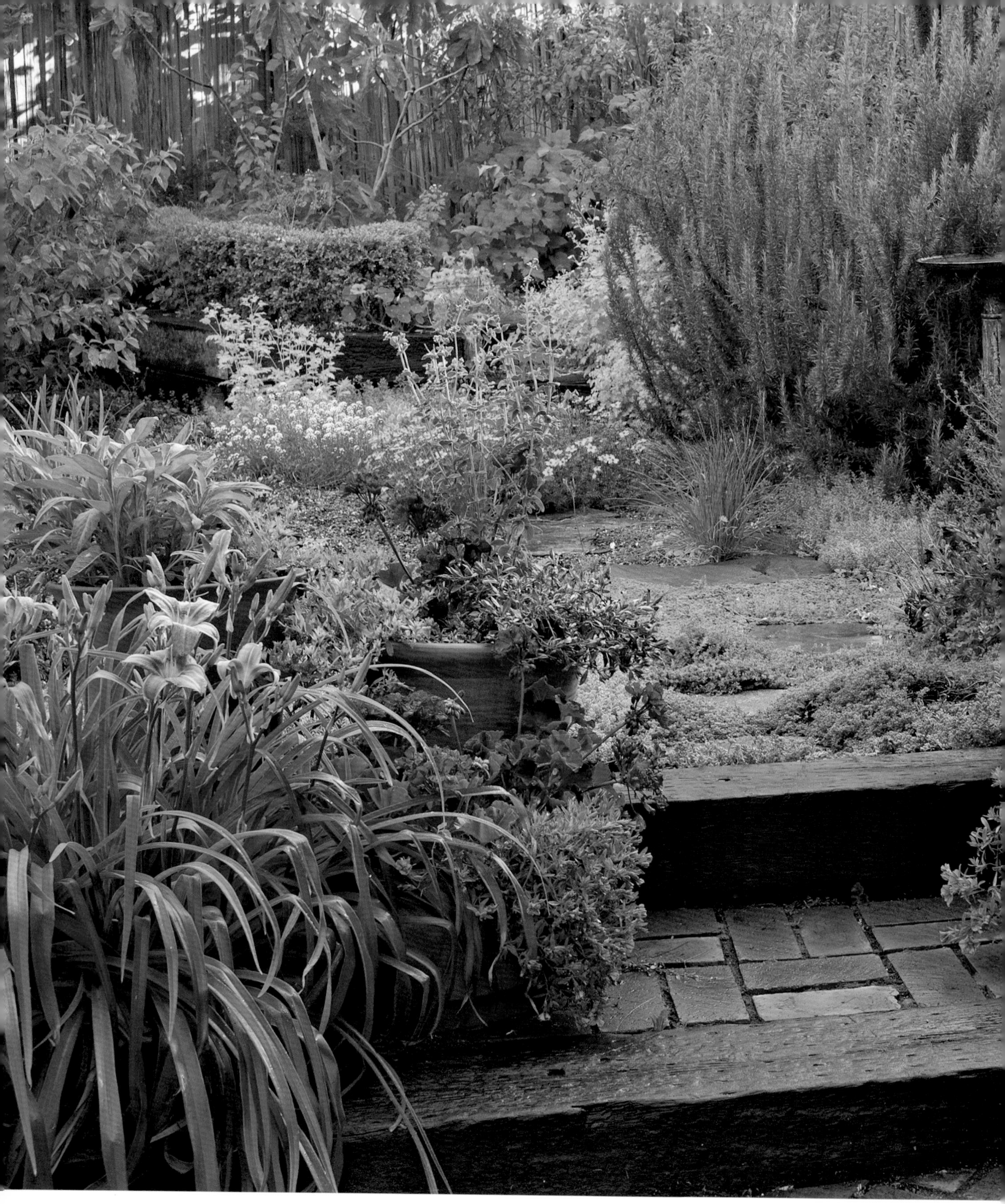

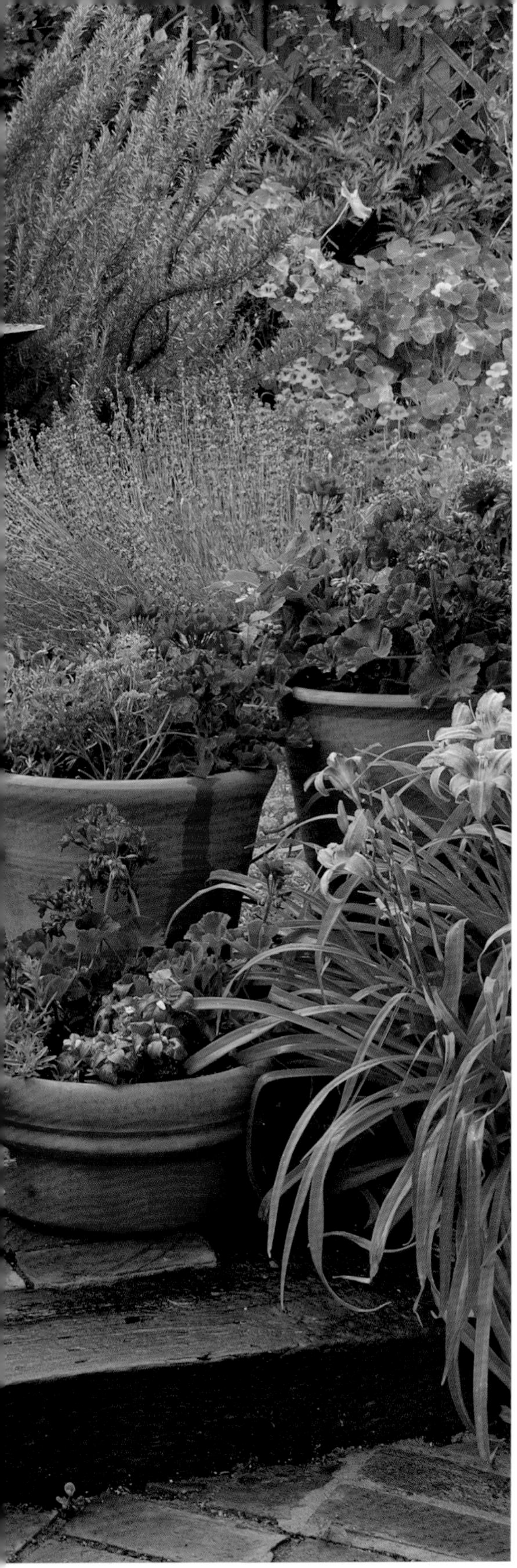

LEFT Nearly every plant in the herb garden is edible—even daylily buds can be put in salads or stir-fried. **BELOW** A mirror placed against a wall bordering a neighbor's yard creates the illusion of greater space in this small city lot. **OVERLEAF** In a garden that appeals to all the senses, a patchwork of creeping thyme, Corsican mint, and chamomile planted around flagstone pavers provides scent even underfoot.

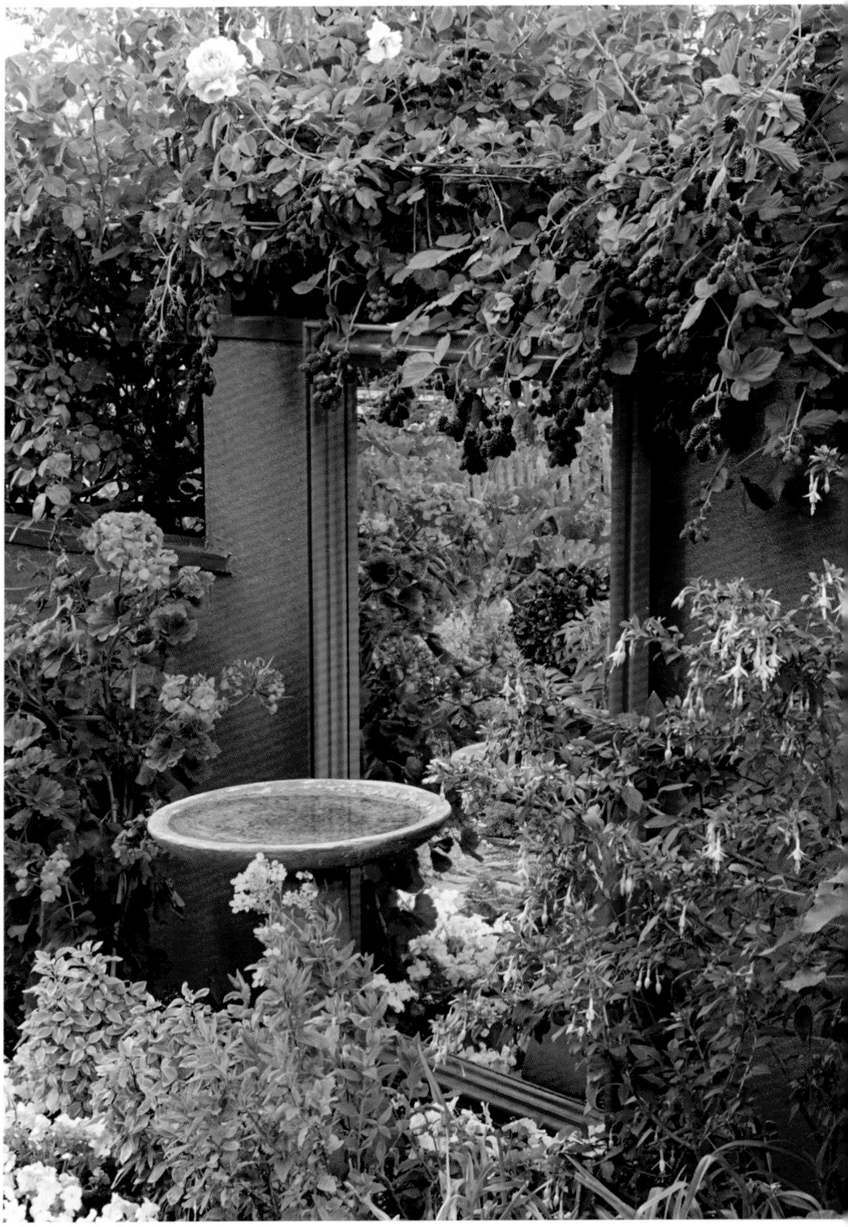

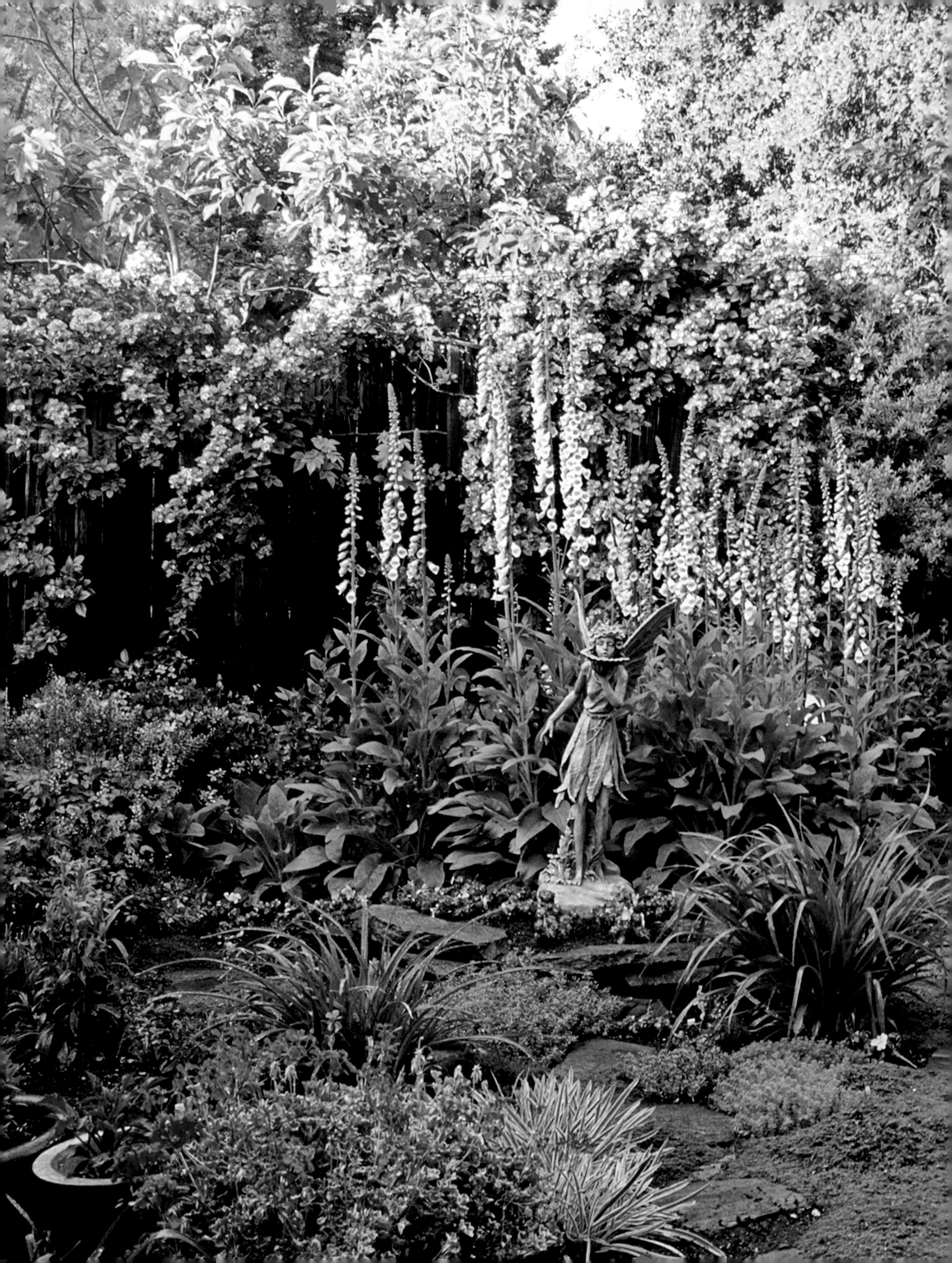

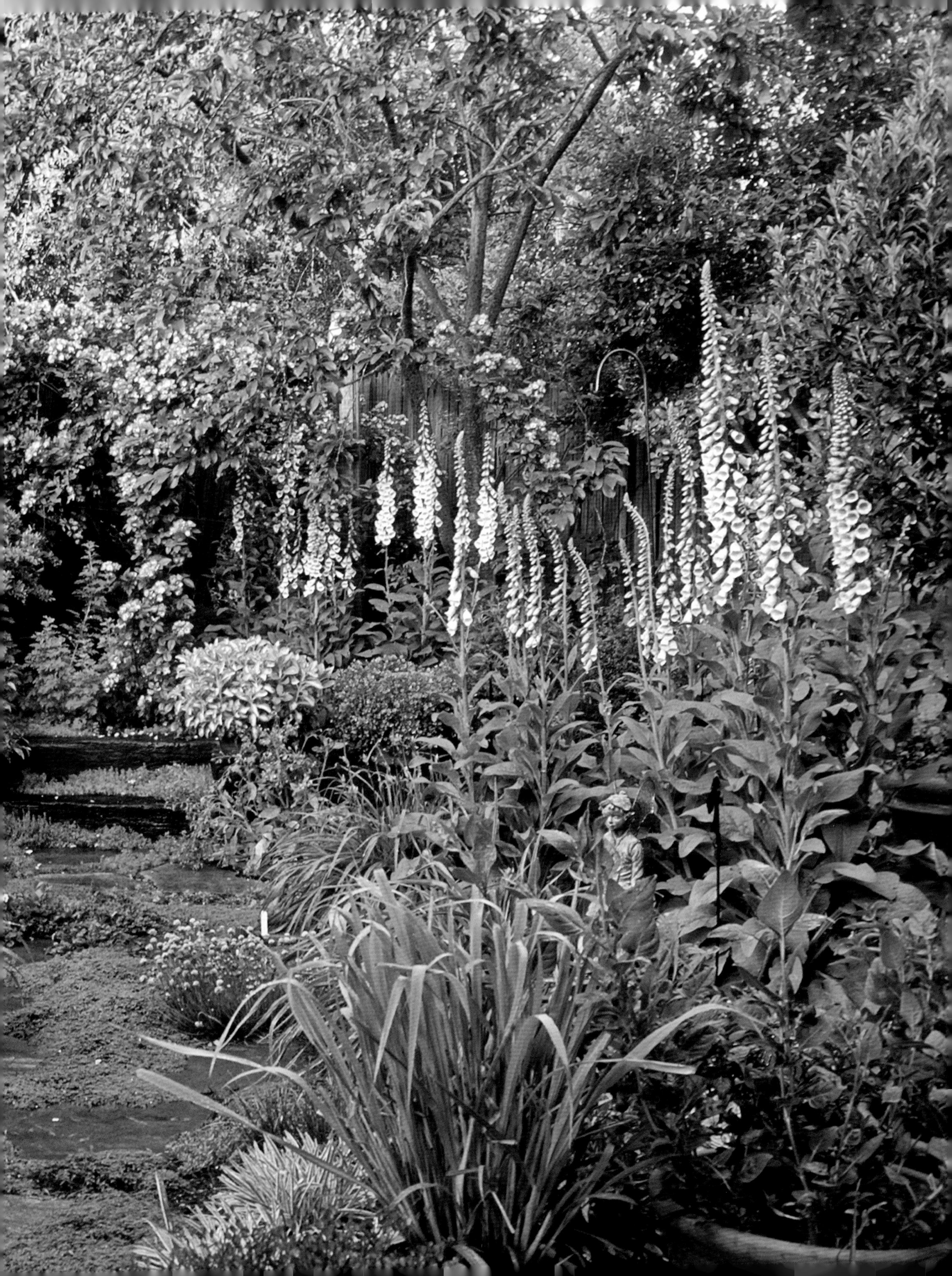

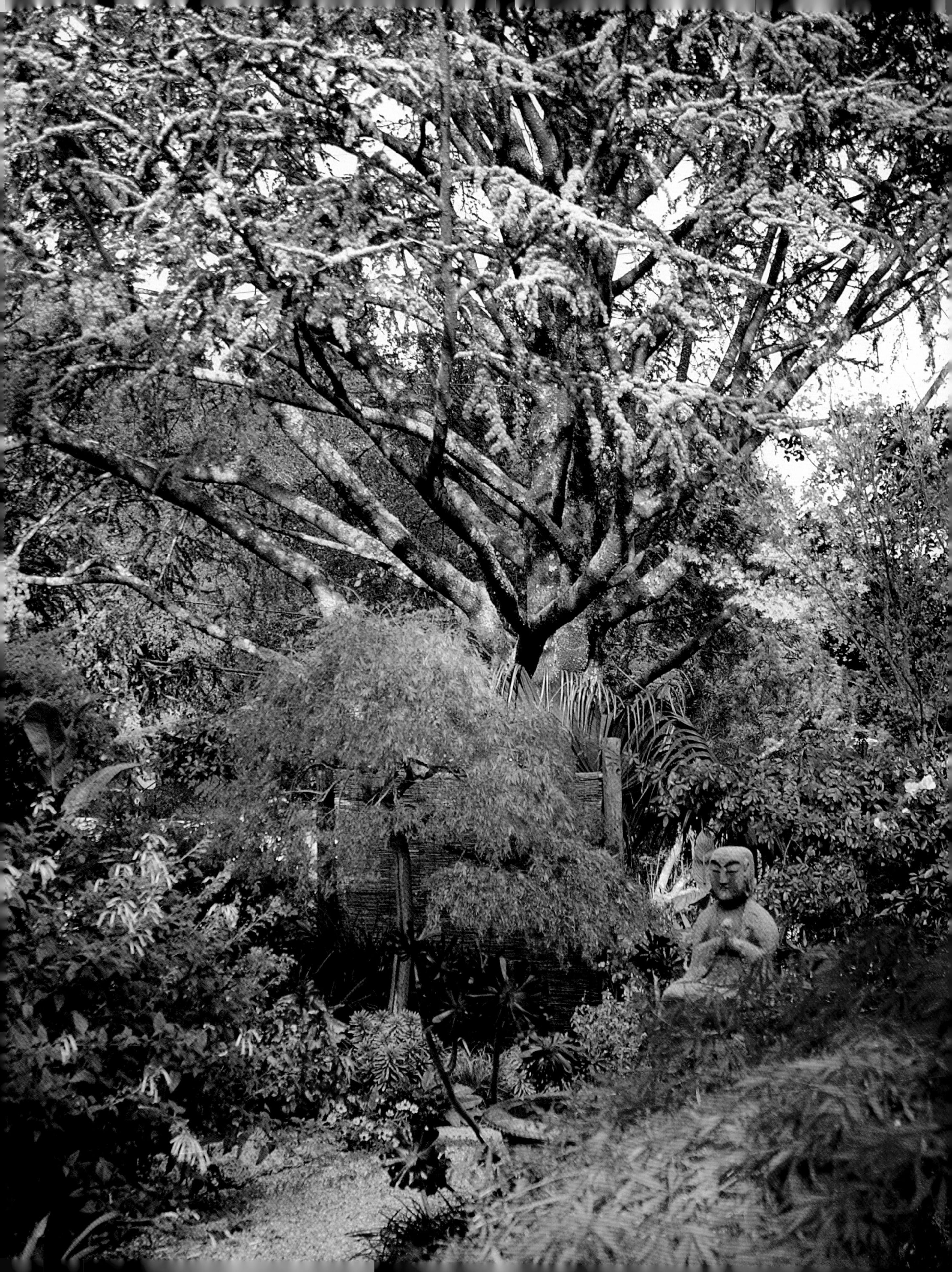

H

igh in the Cascades near Fairfax, California, rests garden designer Davis Dalbok's half-acre property. It is set in a hilly, temperate oak forest, but, once inside, visitors are transported to a much more tropical locale. "The garden is definitely a world apart from the surrounding properties," he says. "I regularly get handwritten notes in my mailbox from the many hikers and bicyclists who pass by, asking if I would share a viewing—especially in late summer when the 60-foot-long hedge of yellow kahili ginger blooms along the fence that borders the road. I'm all for 'borrowed scenery' and have opened up and created vistas that capture the peak of Mt. Tamalpais and a grove of Deodar cedars two properties over." The garden is sited on a southwest-facing plateau that slopes away on three sides.

Dalbok says when he first began to plan the garden, fourteen years ago, his goal was to create a true retreat for himself, family, and friends. "I commute Monday through Friday, and when I get home, I need to be worlds apart—in sanctuary. I love to collect plants, sculpture, and artifacts, and this garden is the venue where I can play with all of those elements. I believe a garden should be a massage for all the senses and that it should be restorative for the soul. The sound of water moving in a garden is essential."

Entry to the property is through reed-thatched gates, but the driveway is rarely used for autos. "It's been commandeered as a staged nursery, both for my garden and for holding plants destined for client projects." A specimen Atlantic blue cedar overhangs the drive and provides light shade for tree ferns, rhododendrons, sobralia orchids, and a collection of Japanese maples below.

Another focal point is the lotus pond, which is constantly replenished with water rushing down from a large, naturally created feature rock. The pond is also visible from the entry hall's glass front door. Dalbok says, "This direct visual relationship brings the garden into the home both night and day. I always replace solid doors with glass in situations that could potentially link the garden to the interior."

An avid swimmer, Dalbok completely renovated the house's original 1950s swimming pool and tiled the water line in "hot aqua" Italian tile. "I wanted the visual quality of the water to emulate my memories of swimming in the warm, aquamarine ocean waters of Southern Thailand," he says. He chose pinkish Arizona sandstone for the coping, which conjoins Chinese slate on the terrace.

"A garden is a laboratory," Dalbok says, "where the flux and change of season, time itself, and plant temperaments are always at play. My job when designing for a client is to incorporate their essence and desires into the design, coupled with the sensibility of my honed aesthetic. When I play in my garden, it's for me. I am always happiest in the warm tropics, so this garden pushes the envelope of zonal challenge. I collect cycads, palms, vireyas, and cold-hardy orchids including species cymbidiums, sobralias, masdevallias, oncidiums, and laelias. They cling to tree fern trunks and I move the potted ones all over the garden when in bloom."

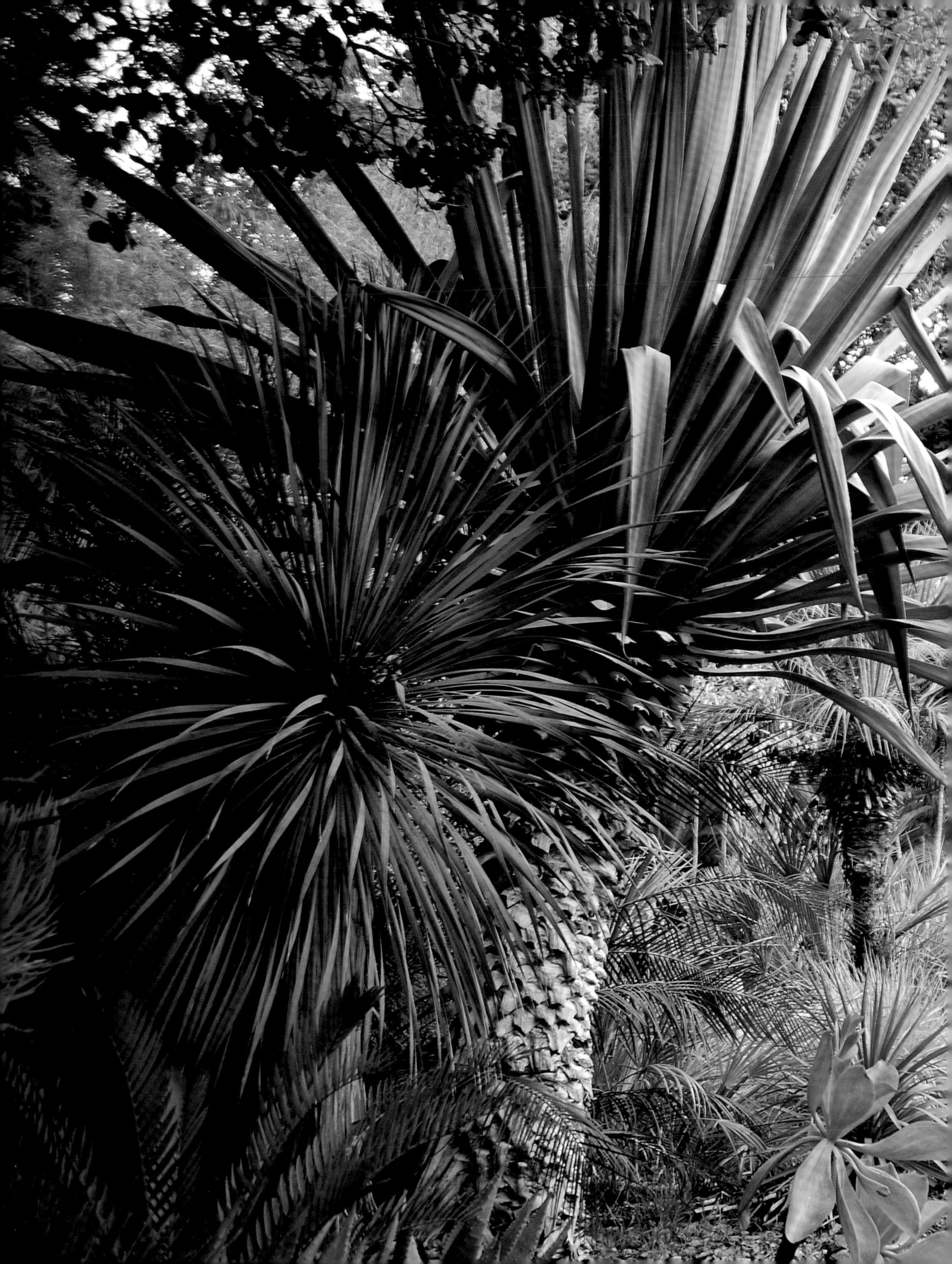

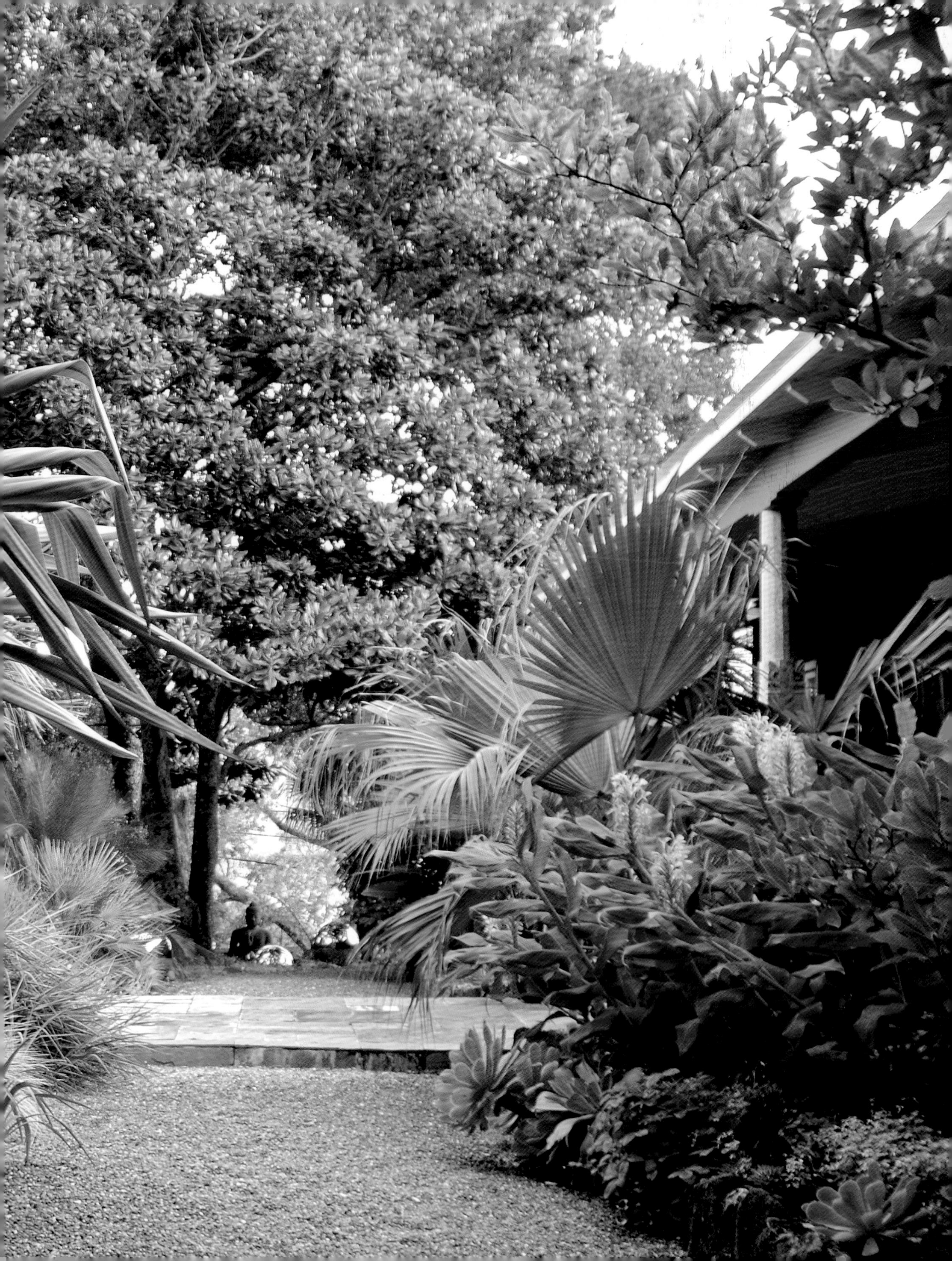

BELOW The boldness of a yellow Kahili ginger is juxtaposed with a cabbagelike aeonium succulent. **RIGHT** A thatched-roof entry gate fitted with antique Chinese gates sets the tone for the Asian-themed garden beyond. **PREVIOUS PAGES** Tree yuccas, gingers, palms, aeonium, and cycads—a host of tropical plants with bold leaves and forms—populate the exotic garden.

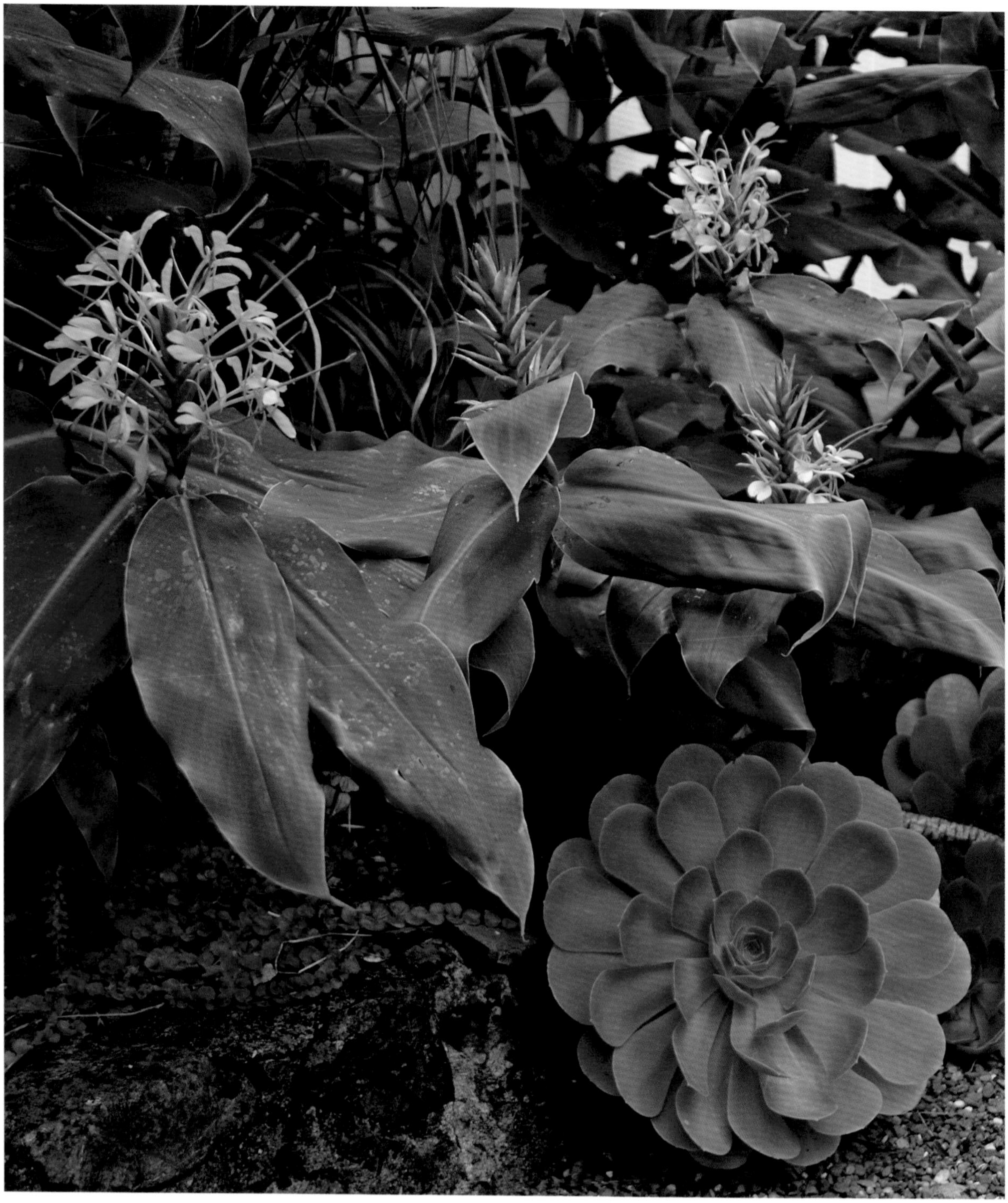

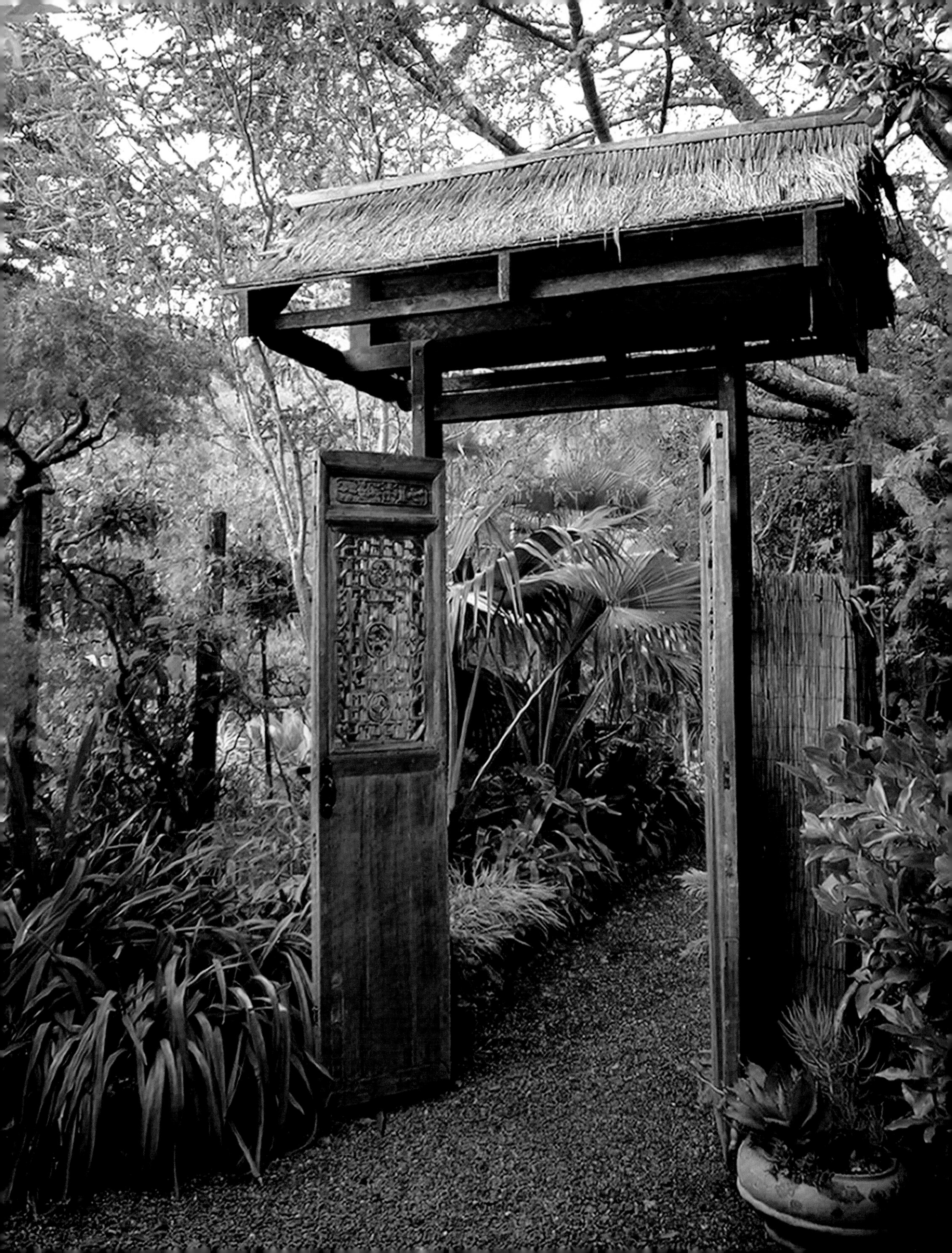

BELOW Low-growing, evergreen echeveria 'Duchess of Nuremberg' blooms in spring and summer. **RIGHT** Tree yuccas, a ponytail palm, agave, bamboo, and lotuses reflect Dalbok's Thai inspiration, while the nearly black rosettes of aeonium 'Schwarzkopf' lend mystery to the grouping.

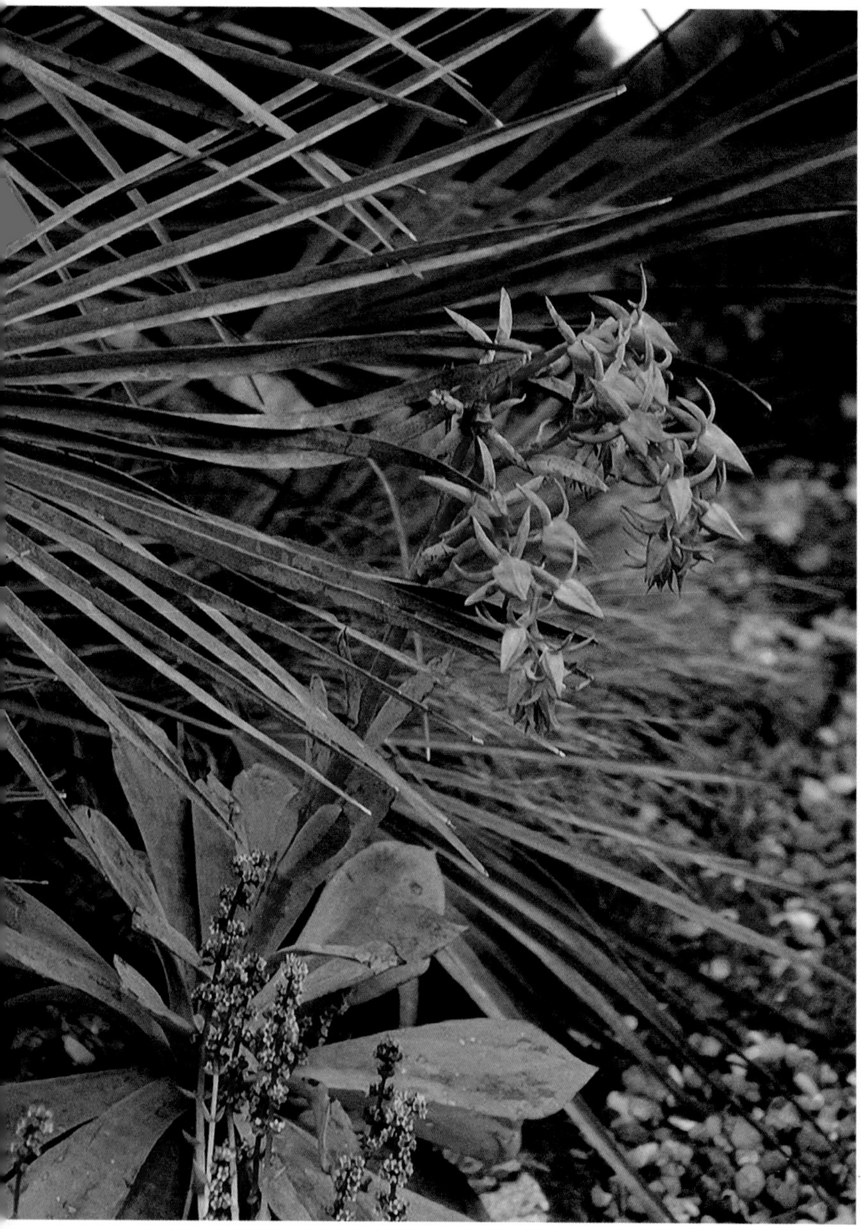

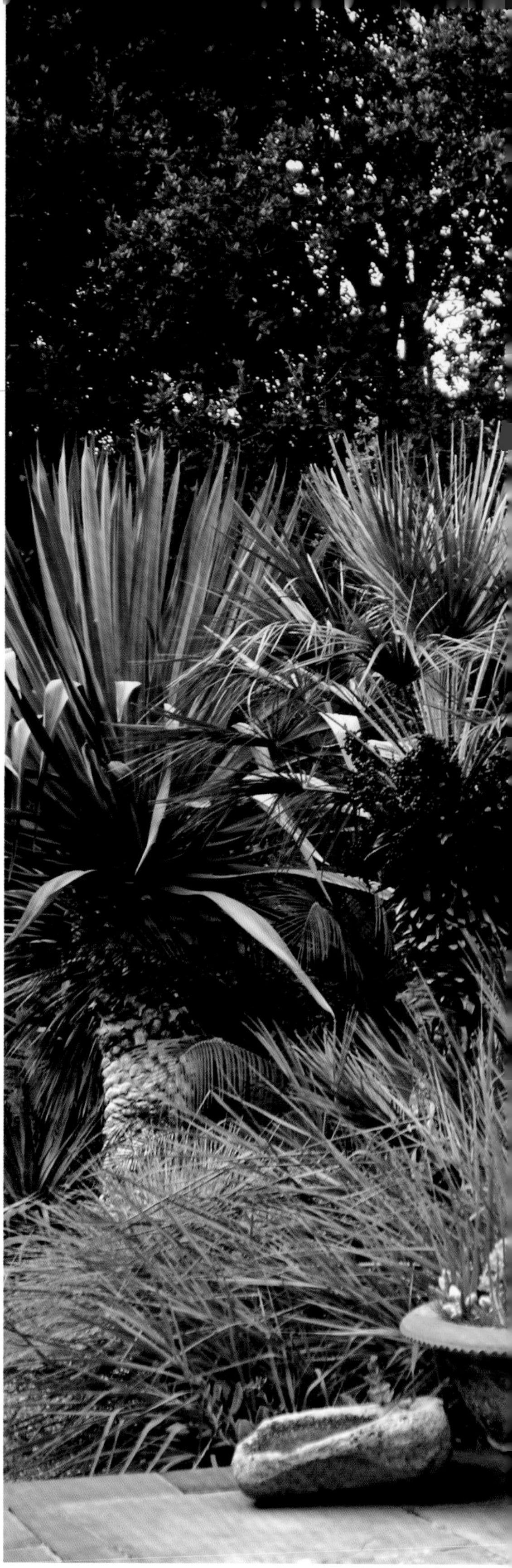

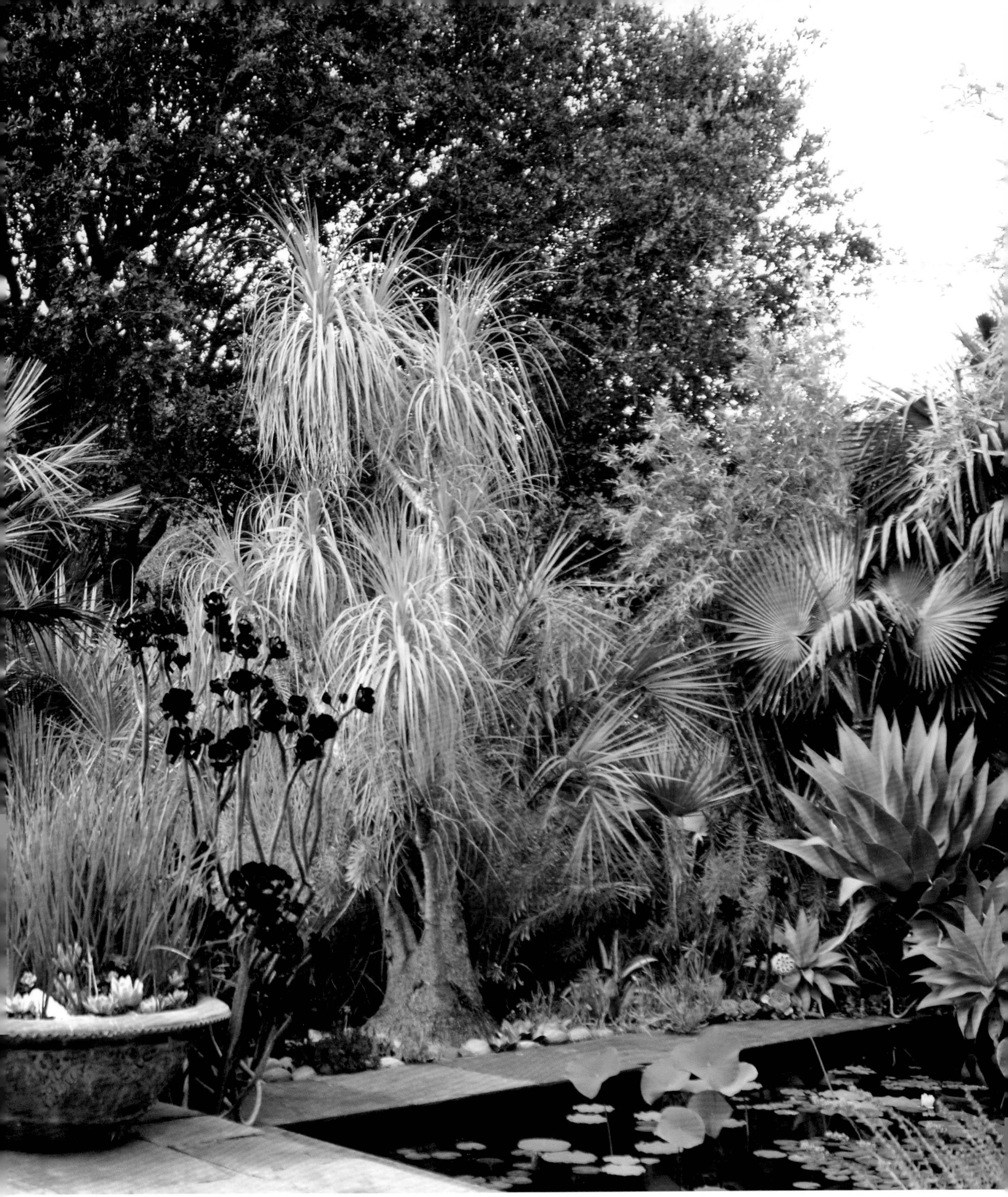

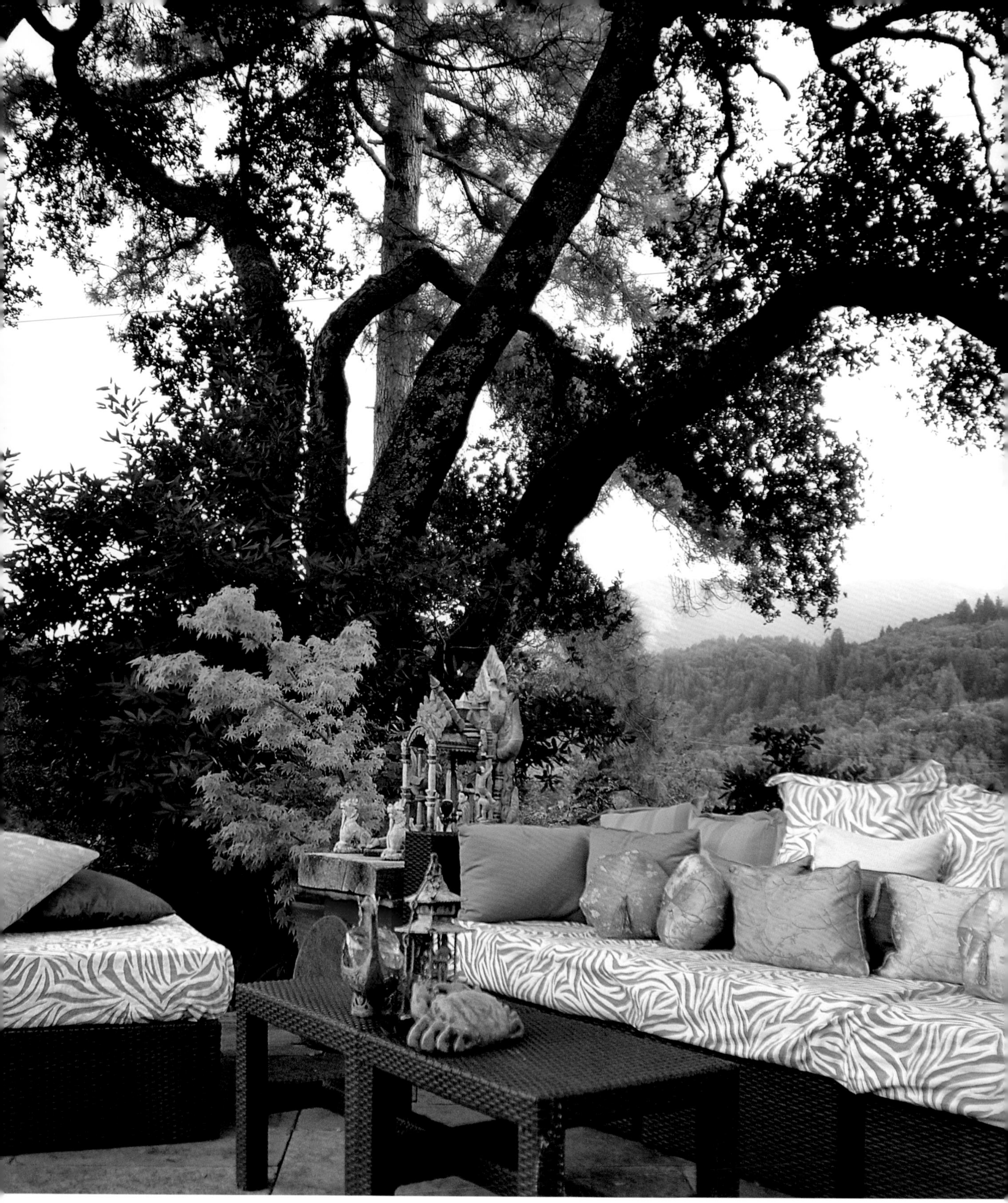

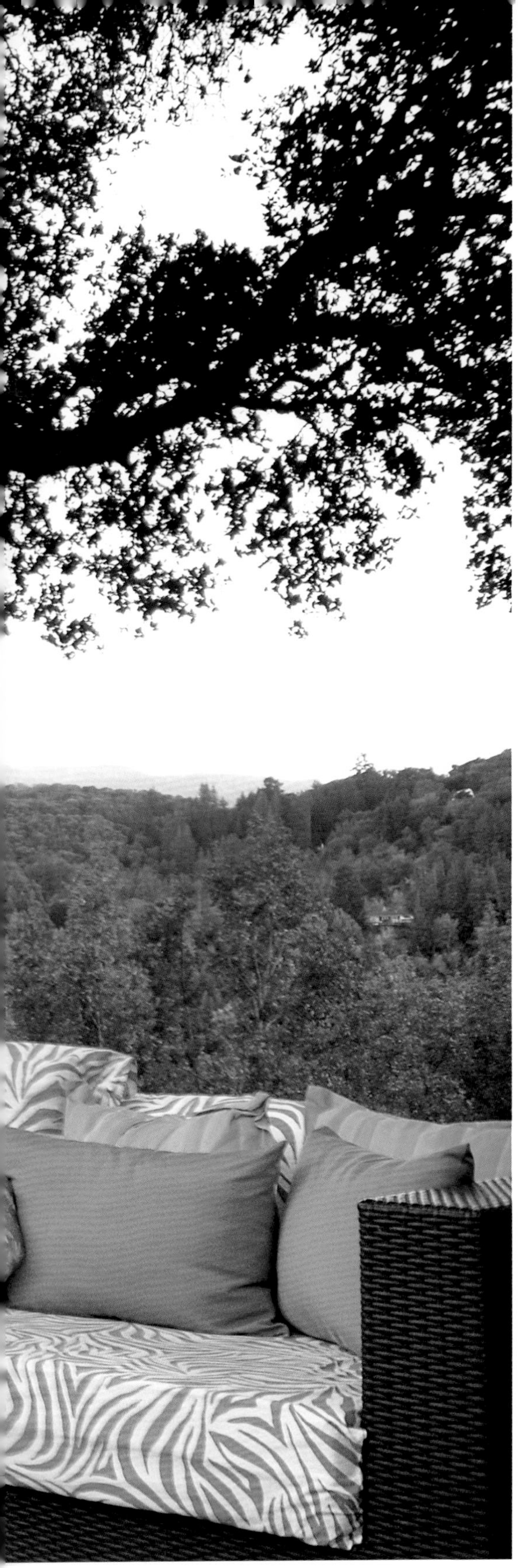

LEFT AND BELOW Comfortable seating for gatherings large and small and vivid green columns announce entry to the pool area.

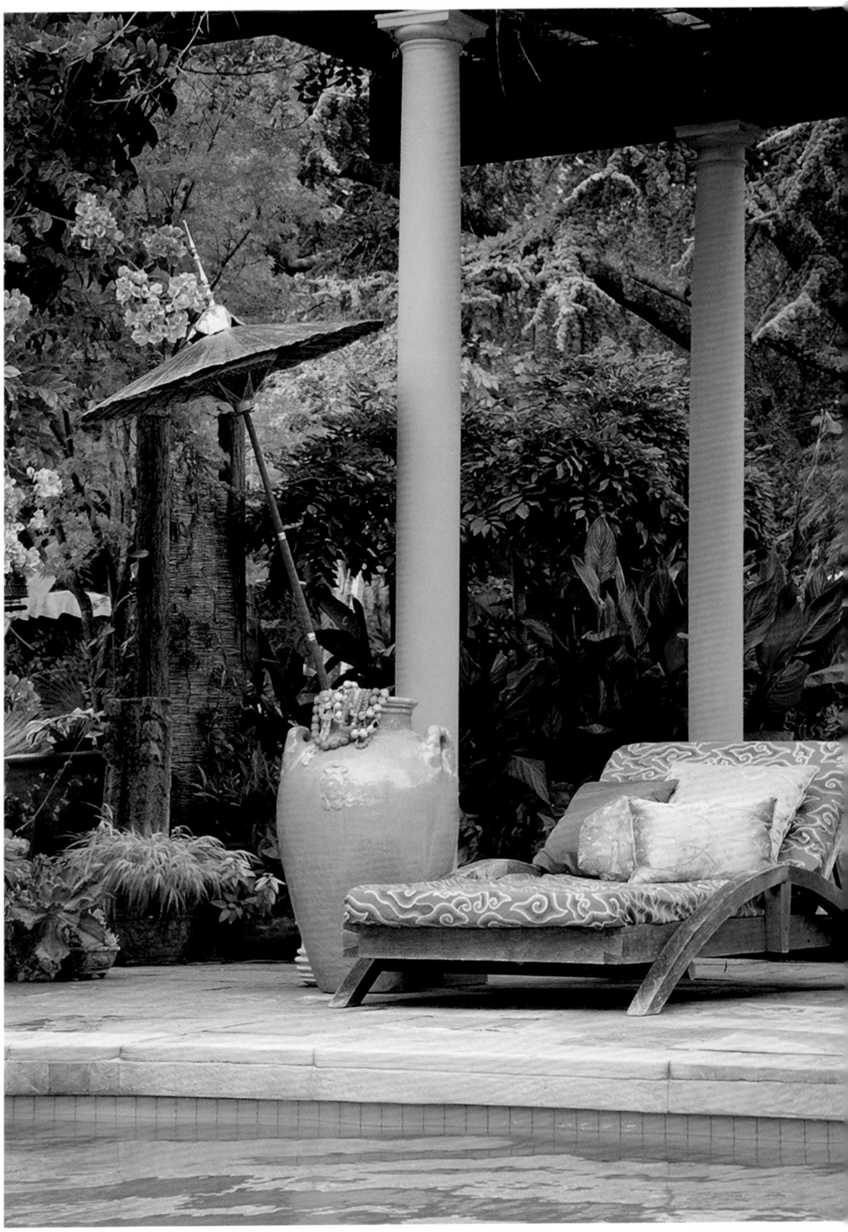

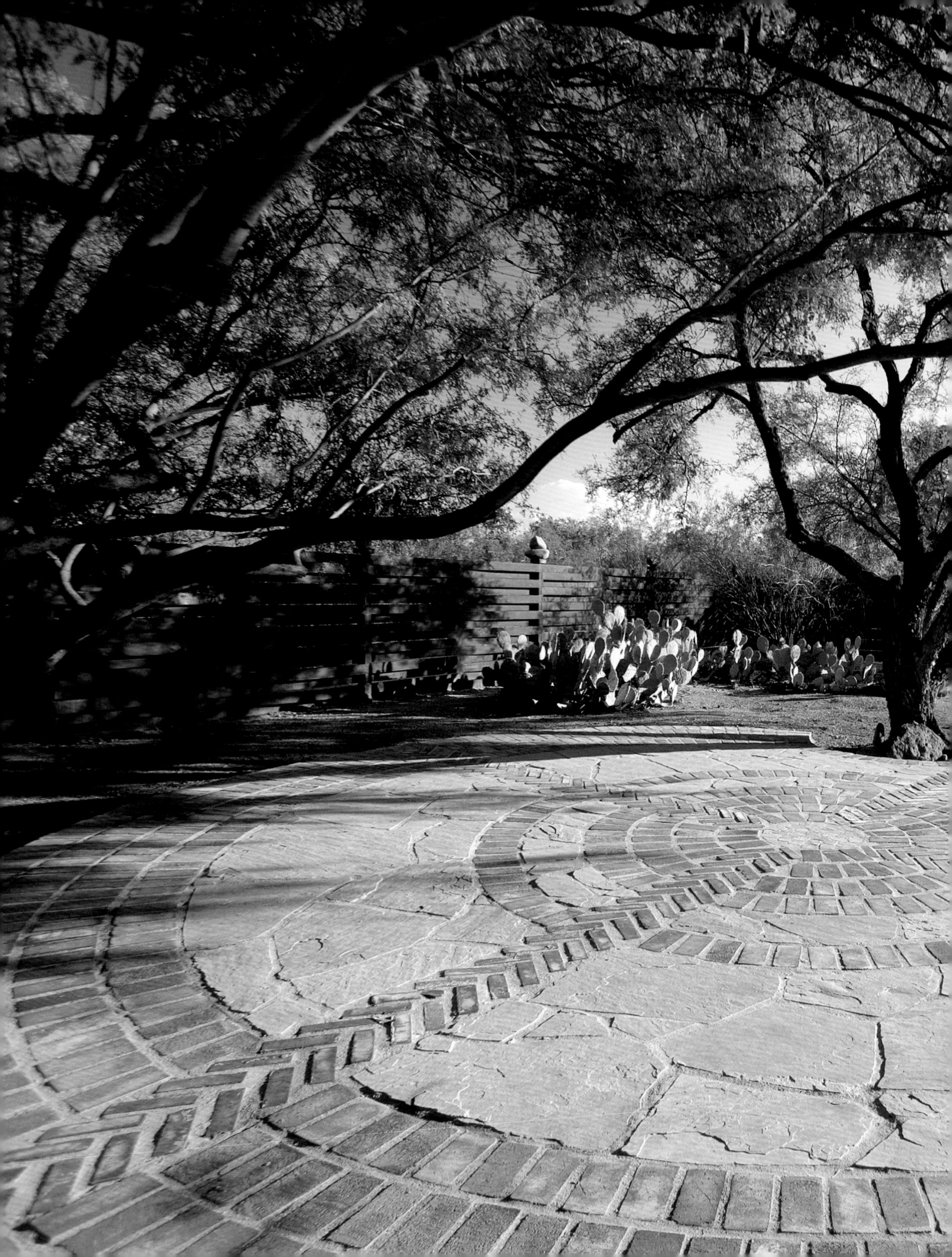

Landscape architect Margaret Joplin's 1-acre garden is in the center of the city of Tucson, and, as she says, "You definitely know you are in the middle of the desert. I focused on creating shade, harvesting water, and plants that can withstand the harsh environment. Our soil is rocky and filled with caliche, which makes digging a challenge. Understanding the unique conditions is essential—and also how they change drastically over just a small distance."

A circular driveway of stabilized ¼-inch minus decomposed granite provides the first impression of Joplin's property. "The Soil-Shield product on the driveway combines the look of hard-packed dirt with the stability of asphalt," she says. "This provides a natural-looking alternative to concrete or asphalt and is fitting to this desert setting."

The planting in the driveway island is a mix of a large native mesquite; golden barrel, prickly pear, and trichocereus cacti; yuccas; and aloes. In addition, a large date palm dating to the 1950s, when the house was first built, anchors the design. Colored concrete pots filled with ocotillo and more cacti grace a planting shelf above the front windows. "The front yard is designed to be low maintenance," Joplin says. "Owing to the large animal population of peccary, coyotes, and rabbits, only the strong survive!"

Entering the backyard from the house, visitors pass through a typical Arizona room, with windows made of louvered glass, then a covered patio with a round dining table to one side and a set of lounge chairs to the other. Potted plants are placed throughout this area. The paving throughout the backyard is an acid-washed, colored concrete called Flagstone Brown. Semicircular, poured-in-place benches of the same material, 12 inches wide by 18 inches high, provide secondary seating for entertaining and separate the patio from planting areas. The paving layout allows for versatility—dancing or dining. A group of three feels as comfortable here as one of seventy or one hundred.

A rectangular grass area from the original landscape design remains but has been reduced. "This area is great for lawn sports, bocce ball, badminton, croquet," Joplin says. "Large trees edge the lawn area to the south and create definition and screening from an area I call 'the outback.' I designed the woven steel fence to create some privacy and a usable space. A 24-foot-round patio of salvaged brick and flagstone between the mesquite trees' canopy was designed as a tranquil space and includes a small fire pit."

Steel sheets, 5-by-10-foot pieces of Cor-Ten purchased as scrap after mailbox flags were laser-cut from them, adorn the garden wall and act as a sculptural element. "The garden has enriched my family's life more than I expected," Joplin says. "It gave my daughter a setting to collect cactus spines instead of the usual bugs. It demonstrated the importance of night lighting. It has given me ways to use my repurposed steel. It has connected me with the people who helped me to develop it. It has given me a testing ground for new ideas. Most of all, it gives me joy!"

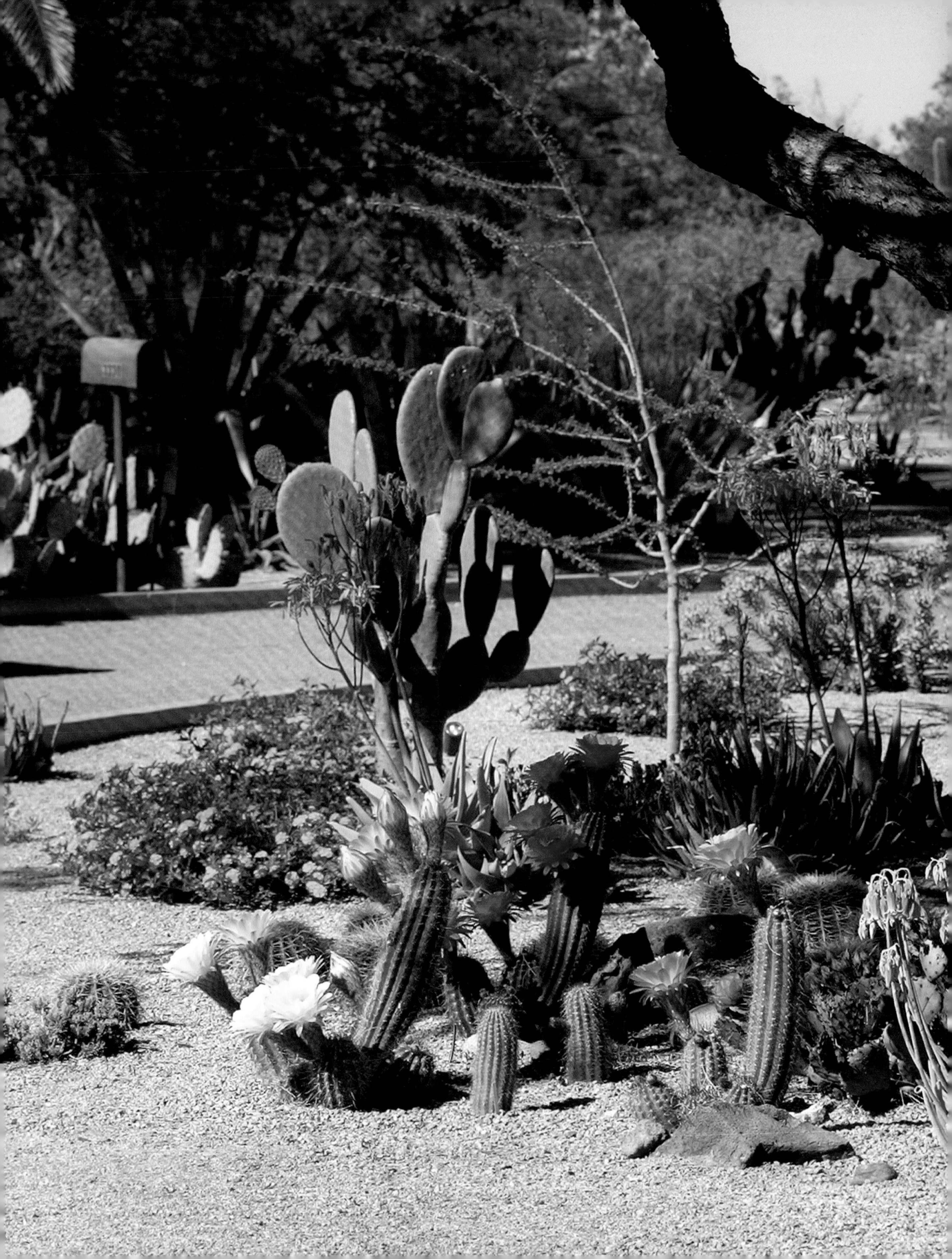

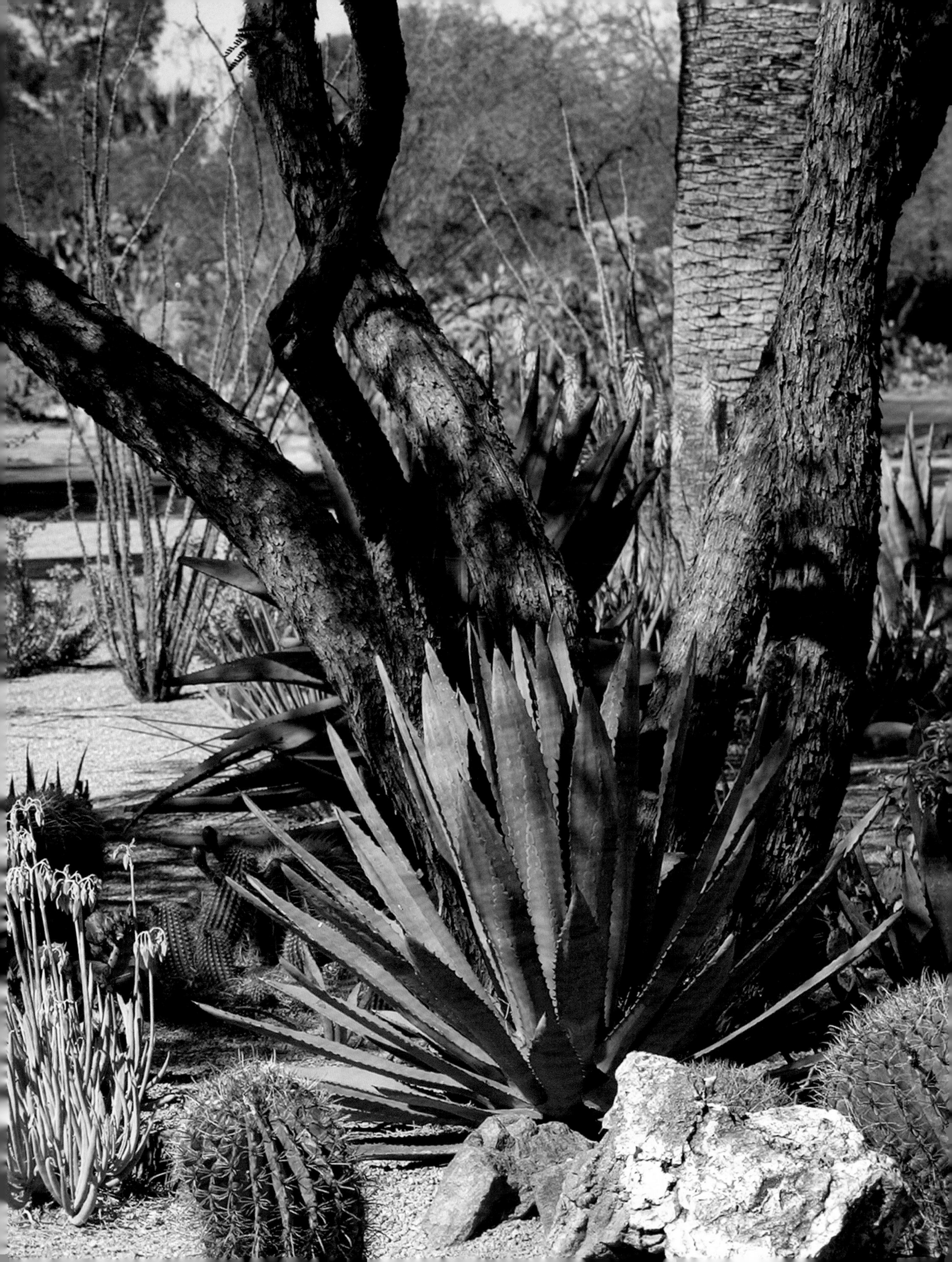

BELOW Container plants, found throughout the garden, also appear on shelves fit into a metal trellis. **OPPOSITE** A low colored-concrete wall was designed to serve as an impromptu seating option during Joplin's many spontaneous parties. **PREVIOUS PAGES** Aloes, desert marigolds, golden barrel, prickly pear, trichocereus cacti, and yuccas create a proud grouping of drought-tolerant plants along the driveway.

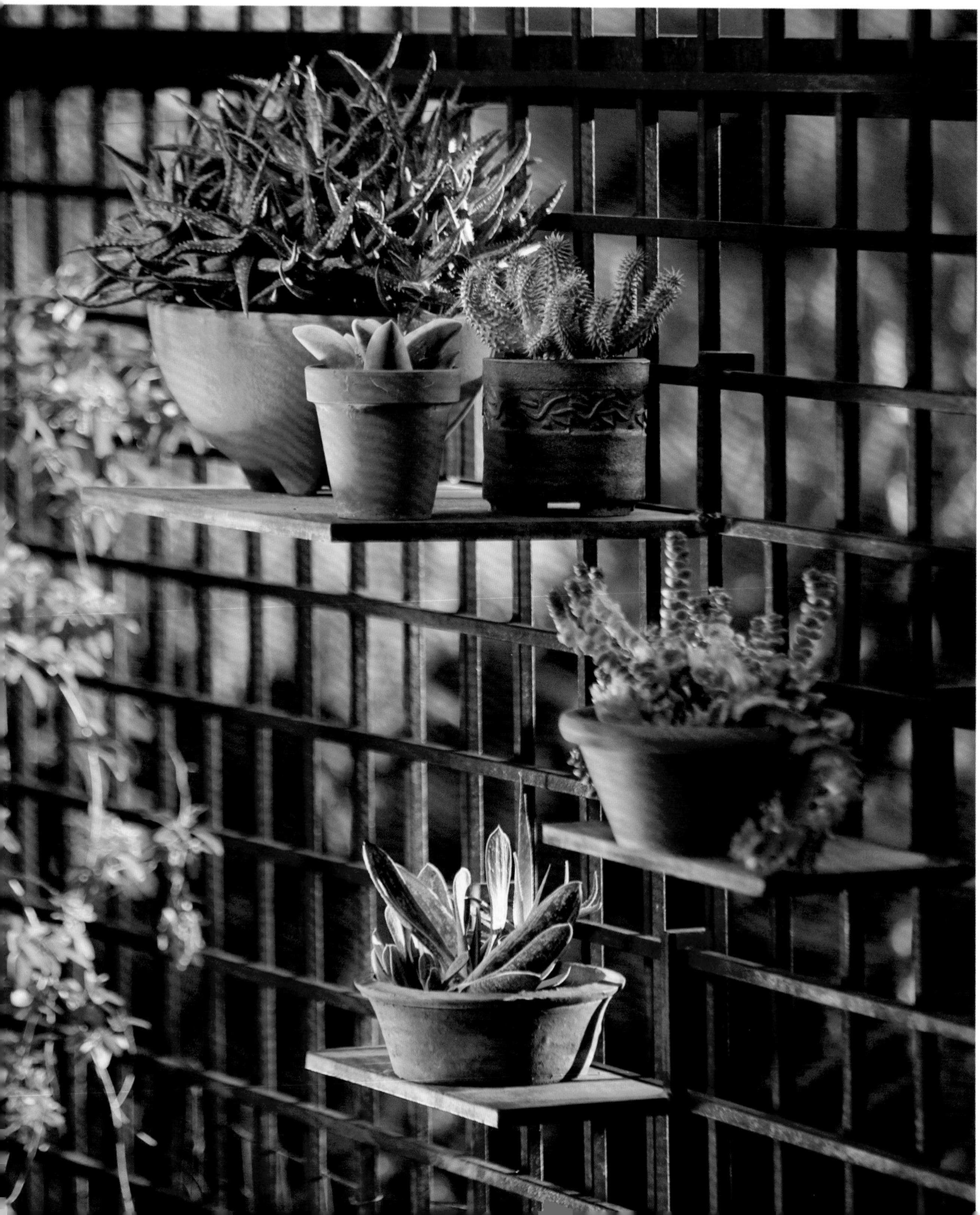

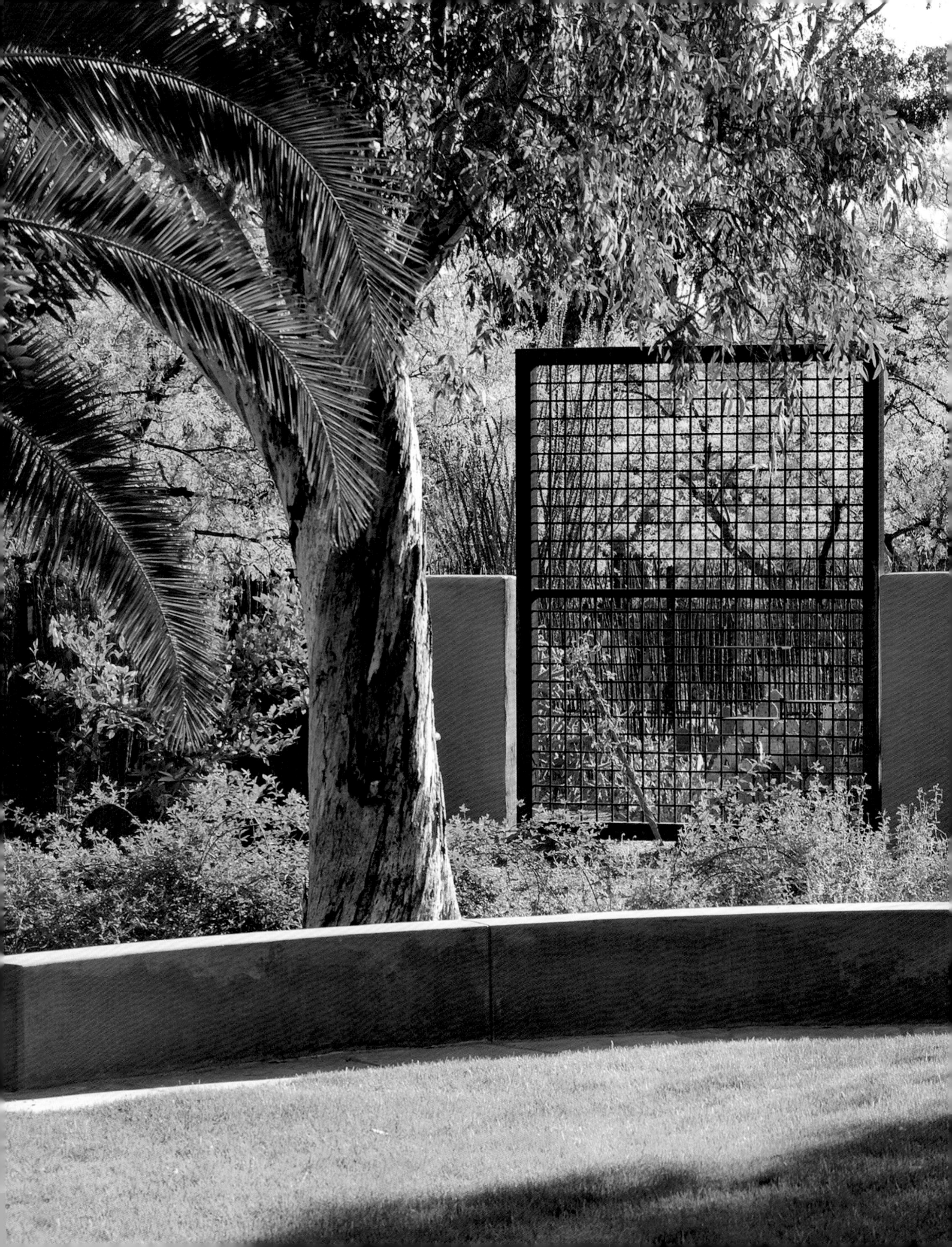

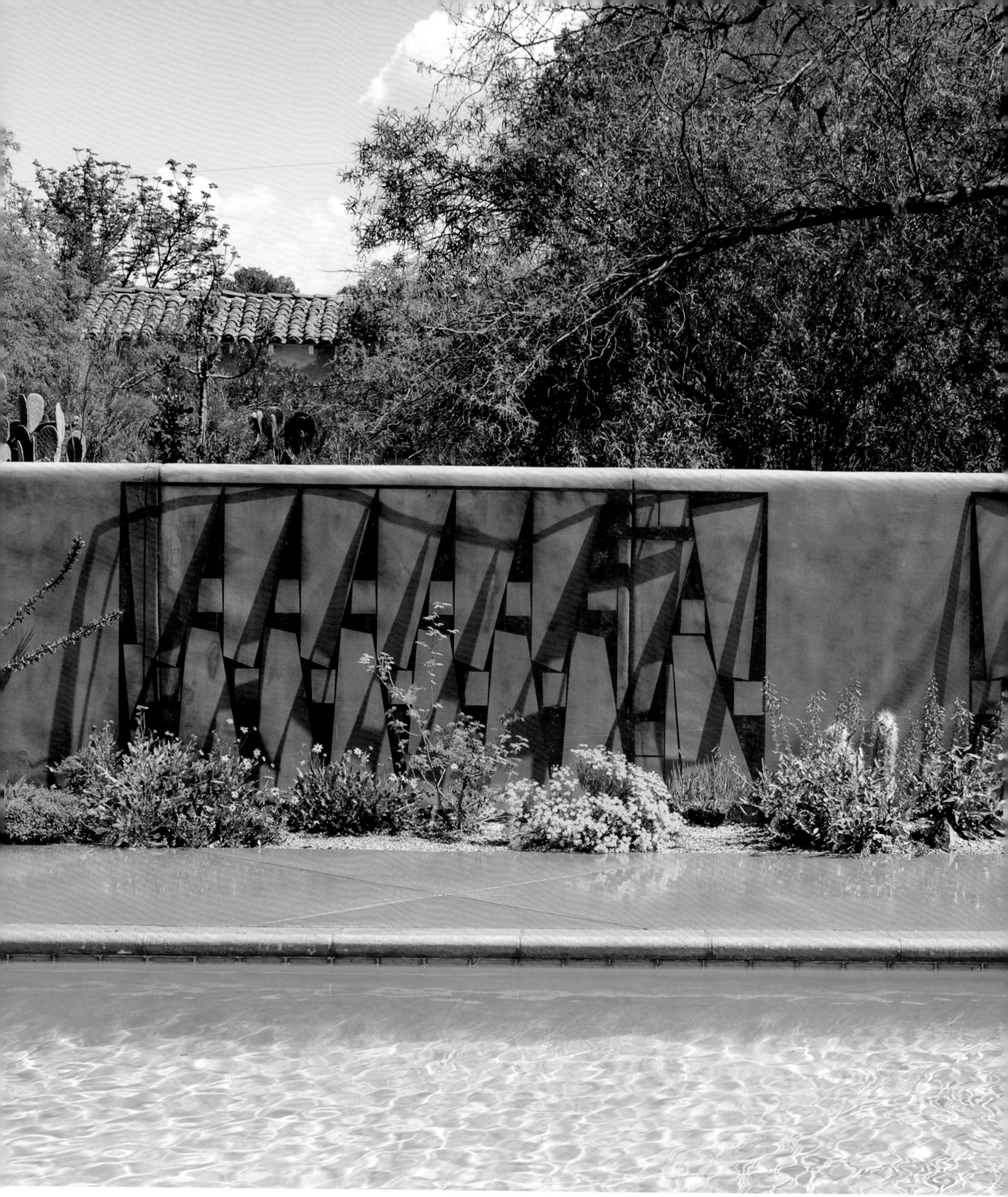

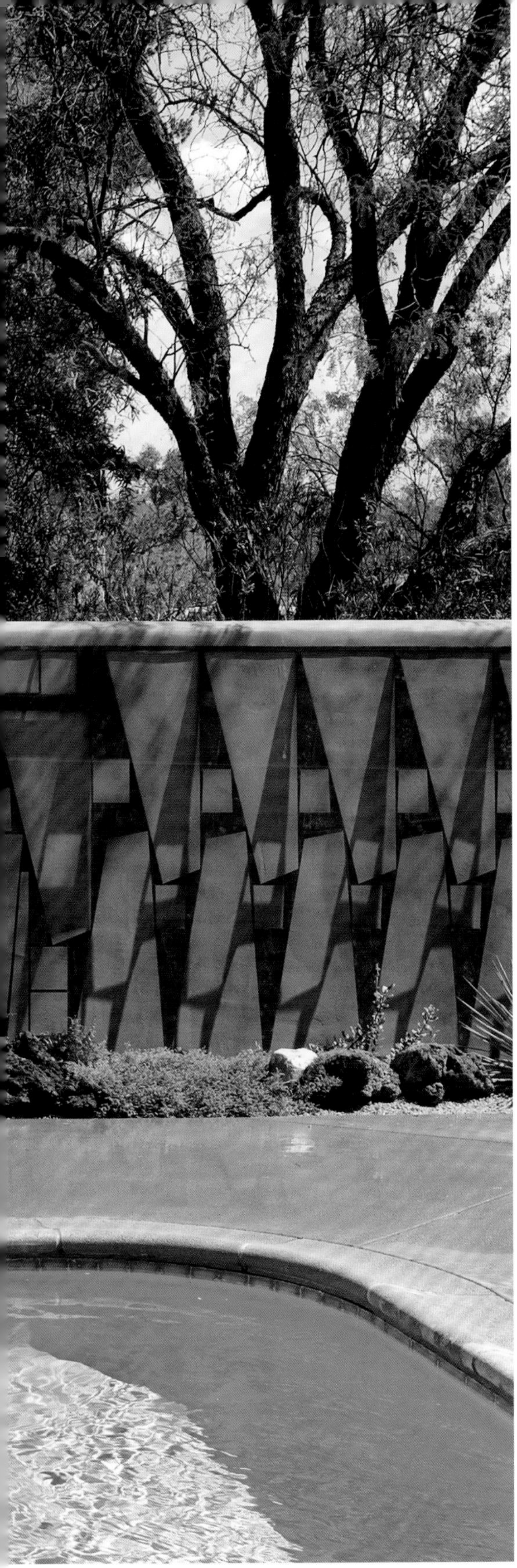

LEFT A sculptural wall made of Cor-Ten steel plate remnants from a mailbox factory lends a dramatic decorative touch to the pool area. **BELOW** Pot marigolds provide a vibrant foil to the purple leaves of a Moses-in-the-Cradle plant.

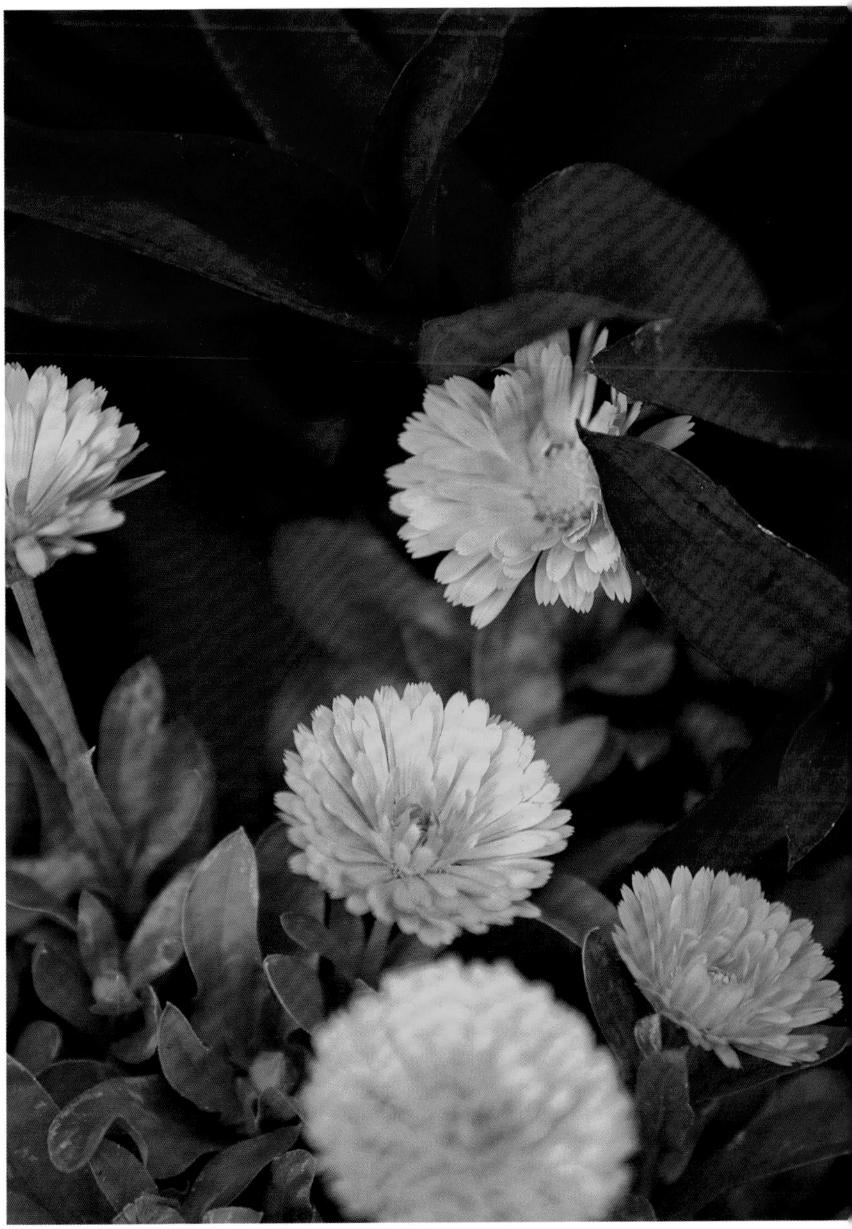

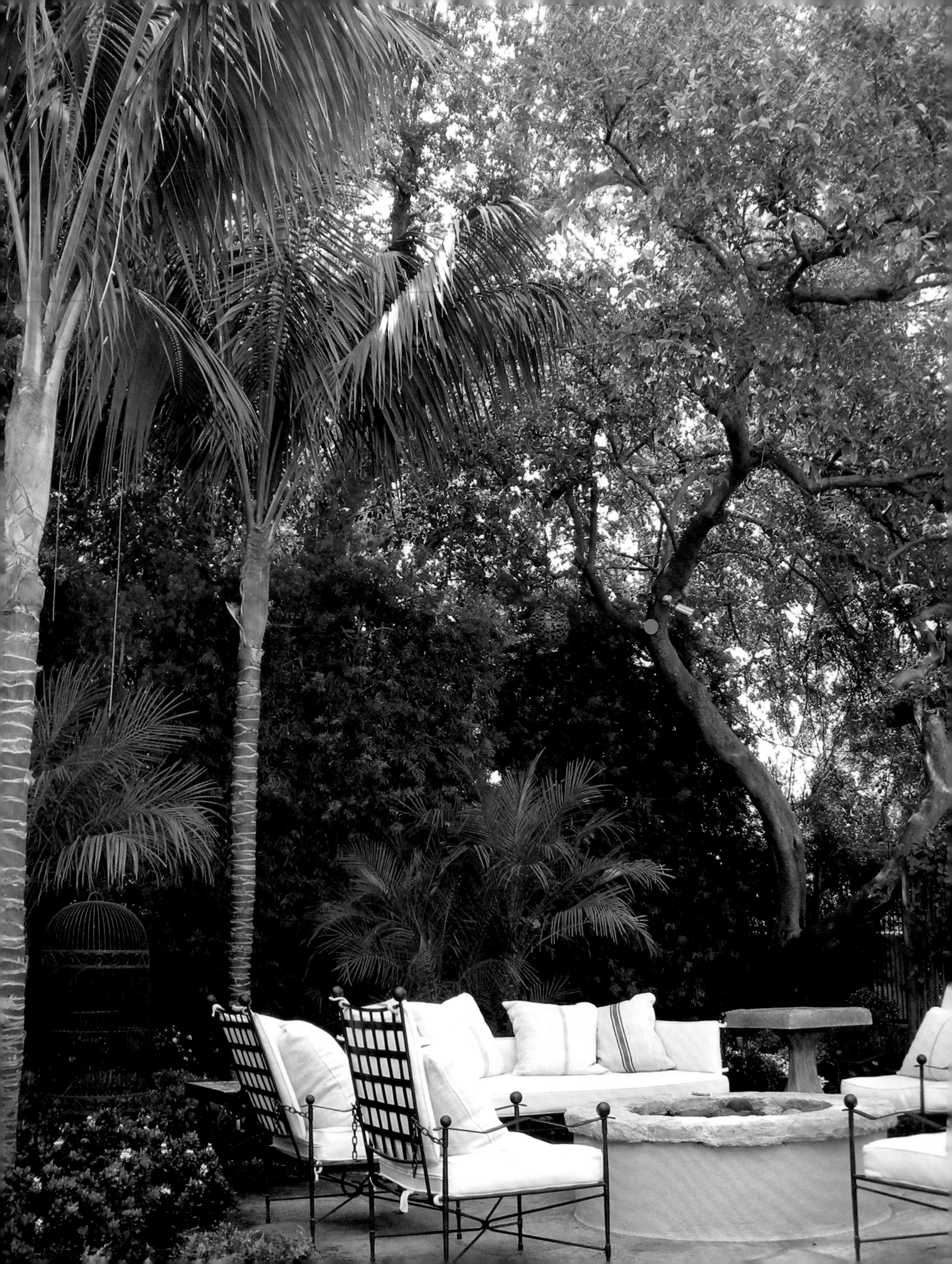

F ormally trained in England, Los Angeles–based garden designer Paul Robbins brings much of that country's style, where floral bounty overflows structure, to his work, and continues to be amazed at how fast things grow in a ten-month season. His clients for this property in Hancock Park, one of the oldest neighborhoods in the city, are a young couple with three daughters.

"The original house was built in 1923 in the Mediterranean style," Robbins says. "Rolling front yards are a characteristic feature of the area. The garden reflects the architecture and, in fact, frames it. There are mature elm trees on the street, and other streets nearby feature mature camphor, cedar, and magnolia trees."

The generous entry walk is paved with antique Spanish tile flanked by agapanthus and pittosporum. The style of landscaping in the neighborhood reflects large lawns adjacent to the sidewalk, so those are also retained here. The oldest tree on the property, the *Arbutus* 'Marina,' or strawberry tree, is the front yard's main focal point. Other plants are grouped in large swaths for maximum impact and consist largely of evergreen shrubs and perennials suited to year-round viewing. The Spanish tile changes from a rectangular running pattern after the inner courtyard to a hexagonal shape as a subtle marker of transition.

The main gardens are seen and approached from numerous French doors in the house's living room, sun room, and kitchen. Terrace materials continue the theme of earth tones but are more rustic in form than the entry tile—randomly shaped sandstone pavers and gravel pathways in a complementary color. Plantings range from subtropical specimens to citrus and olive trees, cycads, and palms. Like the front, the unifying element is the use of massed plants: a single variety of cistus under the olives, myrtus beneath the citrus trees, and unusual ferns beneath the angel trumpets.

Robbins's design approach was to create a subtle and harmonious link between the indoor and outdoor worlds while suiting the character of the house. "My clients have restored and decorated their house to its original glory," he says. "They use it as a home office, enjoy it with family and friends, and sometimes host large parties that spill into the garden spaces. I was hired to unify some existing spaces, create new entertaining areas, and replant the whole garden, which included moving existing palm trees. I also redesigned hardscape areas. The clients wanted seasonal interest with plantings, but within an evergreen frame. For edible produce, they asked for lots of lettuce and herbs—especially an abundance of mint, the wife's favorite."

The main purpose of the garden is to serve as a true extension to the house. The family cooks and entertains in real outdoor rooms, each of which has a distinct personality. There are places to view fountains, focal points such as vintage pots, and shaded areas at every time of day. Garden lighting is also important. Scents from the trees, shrubs, and flowers provide a sense of calm to a couple always on the move. Most important, however, are the mature trees that give privacy on the city lot.

BELOW Angel trumpets add an exotic flair and an intoxicating fragrance near a Moroccan-themed fountain. **OPPOSITE** Containers brimming with succulents help create a sense of cozy intimacy in a small seating area.

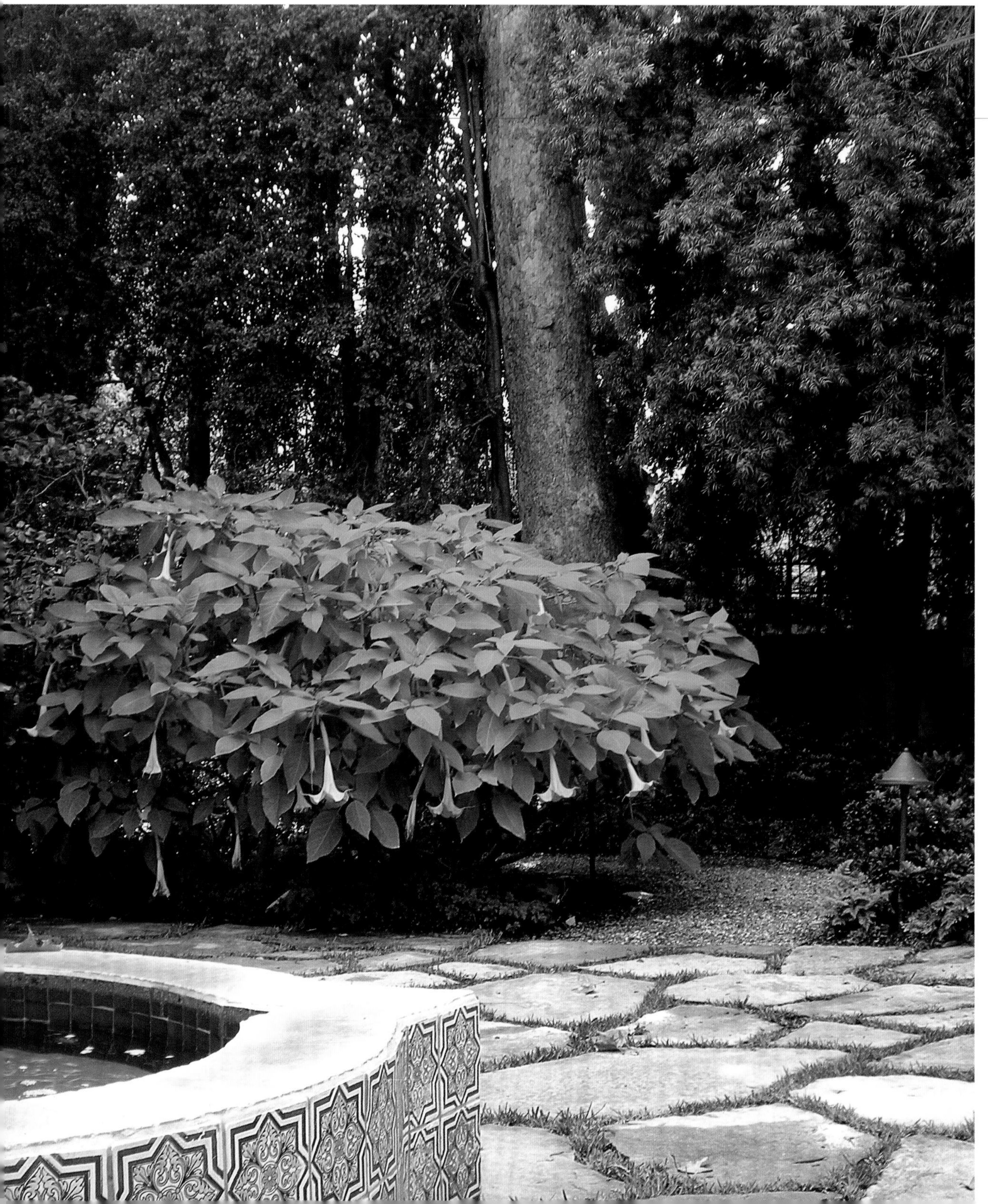

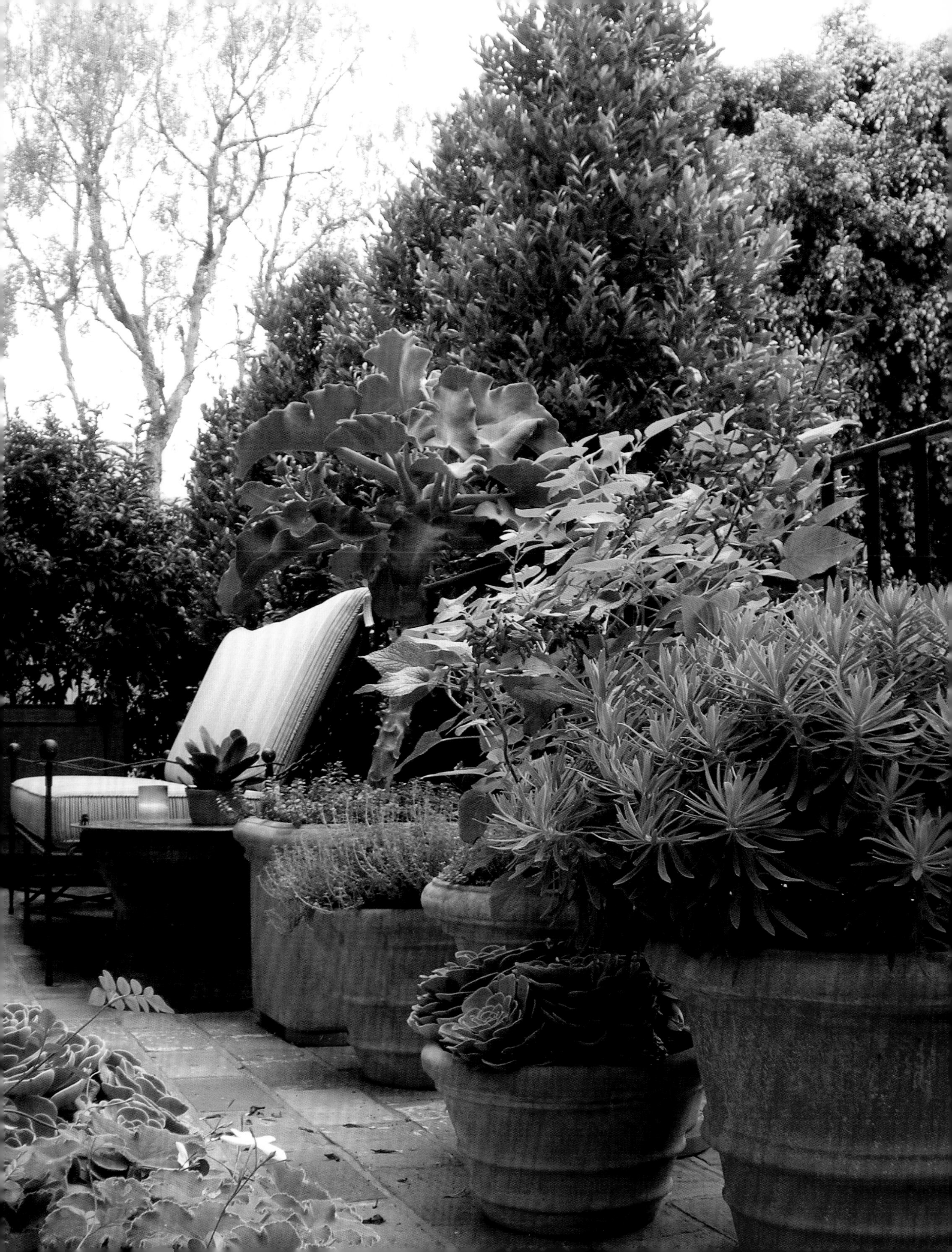

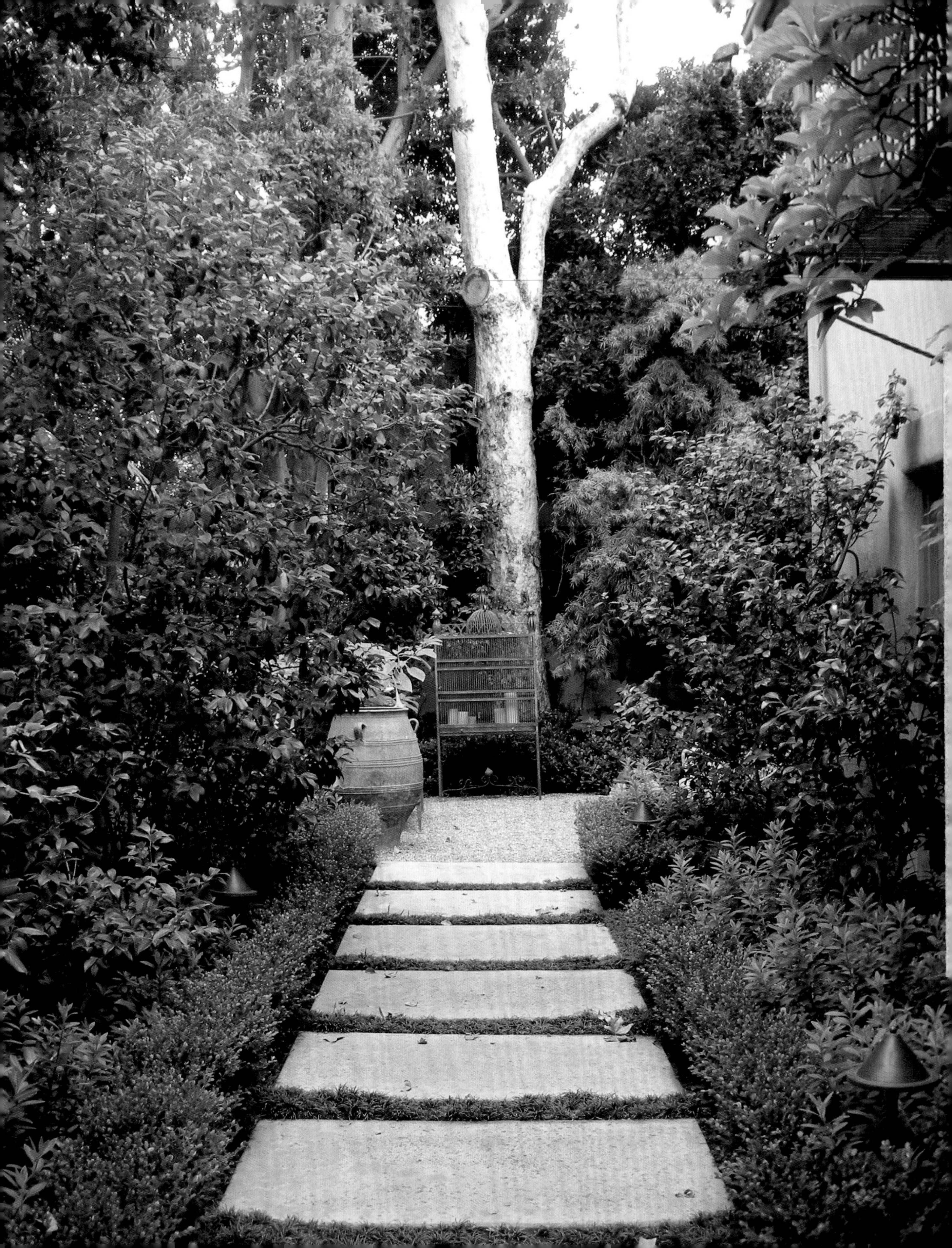

BELOW Connected courtyards and dining and entertaining terraces embrace the Southern California outdoor lifestyle. **LEFT** A courtyard edged in boxwood and framed by camellias and azaleas showcases a mature sycamore tree, the area's focal point.

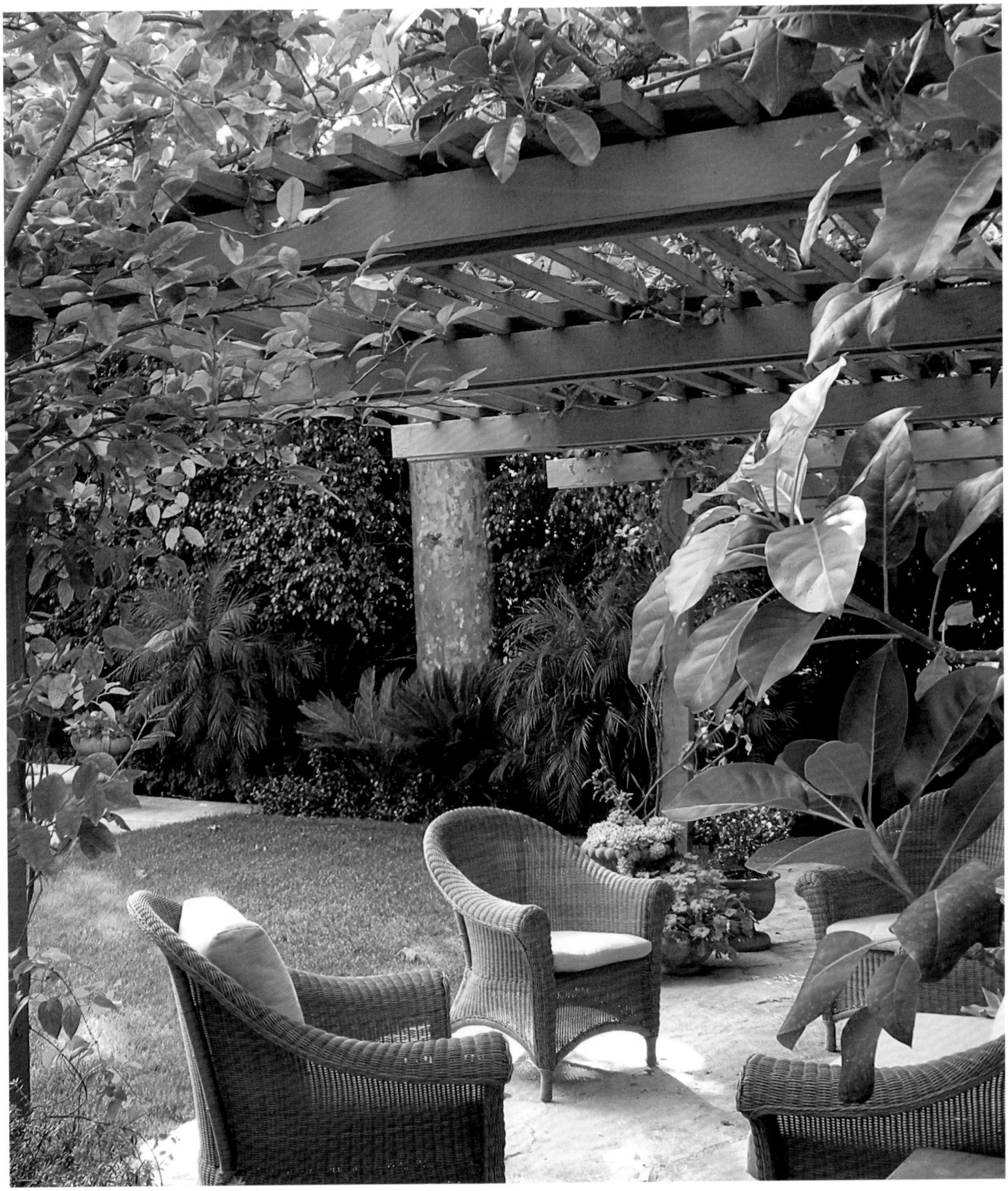

RIGHT Borders of agapanthus flank the house's curvilinear entry path to create a gracious welcome.
BELOW The silvery leaves of lavender, Jerusalem sage, and aloe resonate with the residence's Mediterranean architecture.

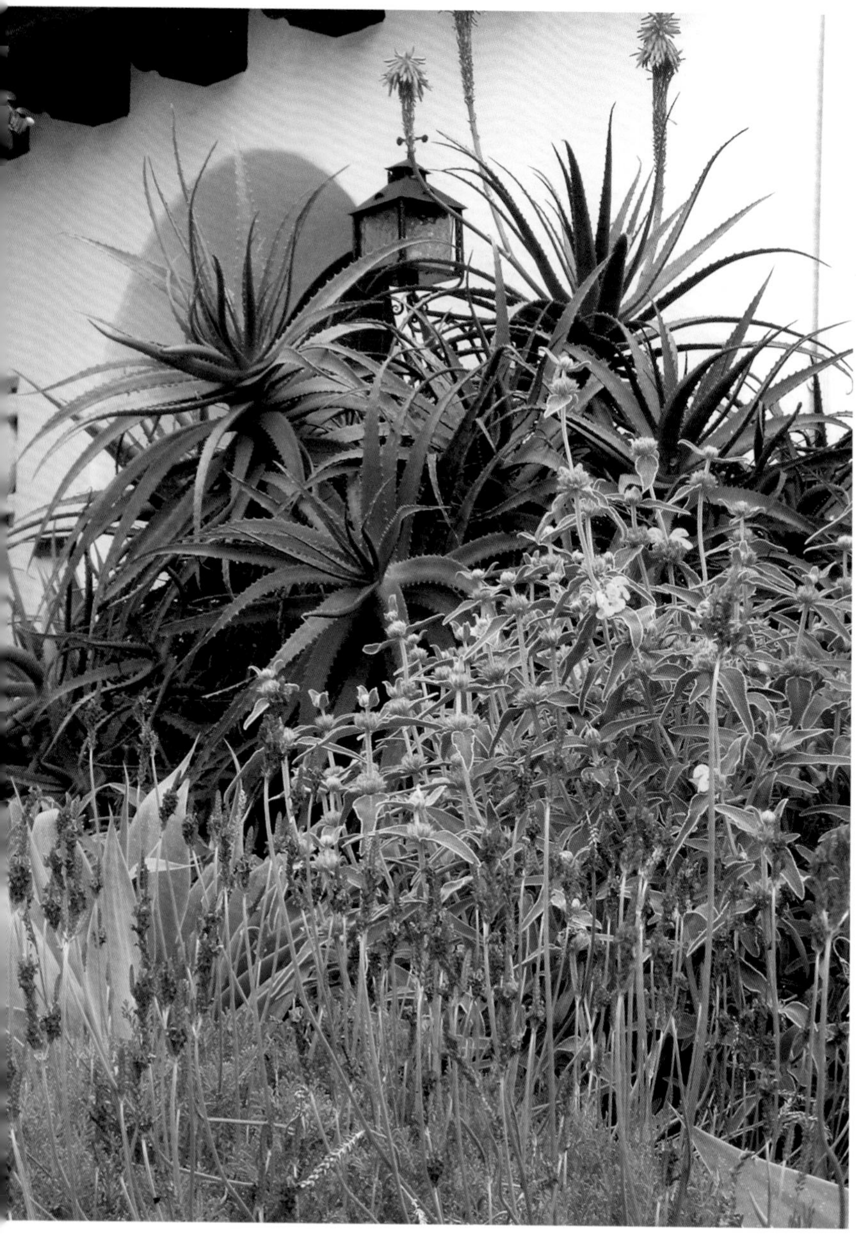

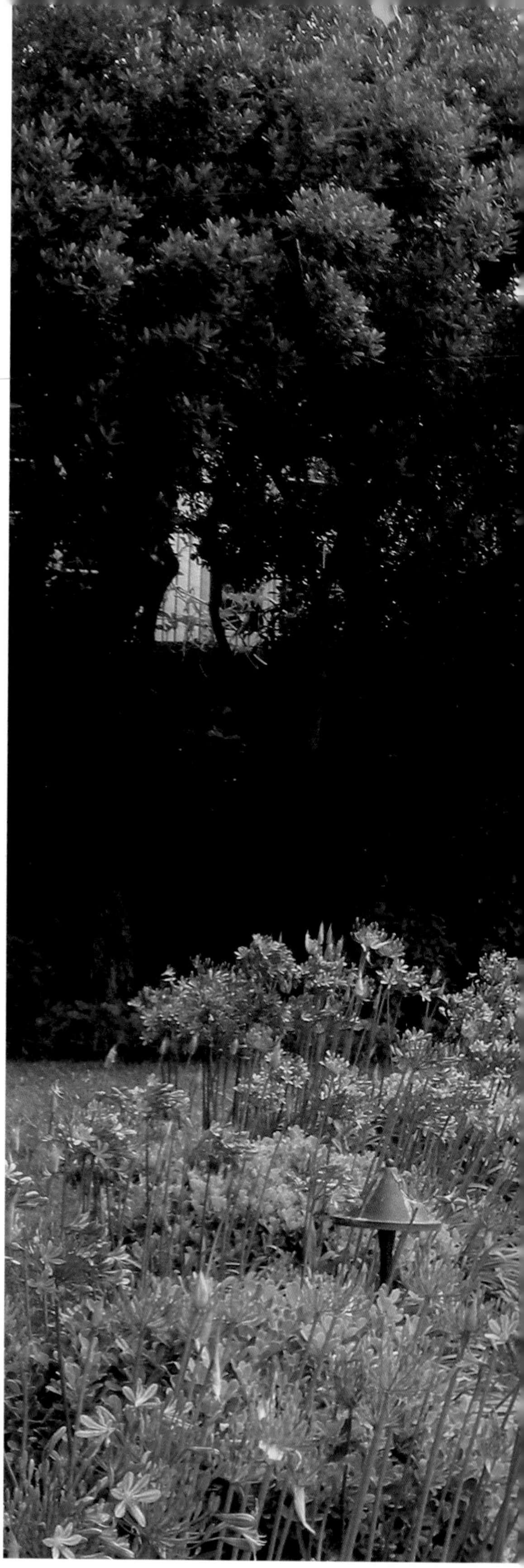

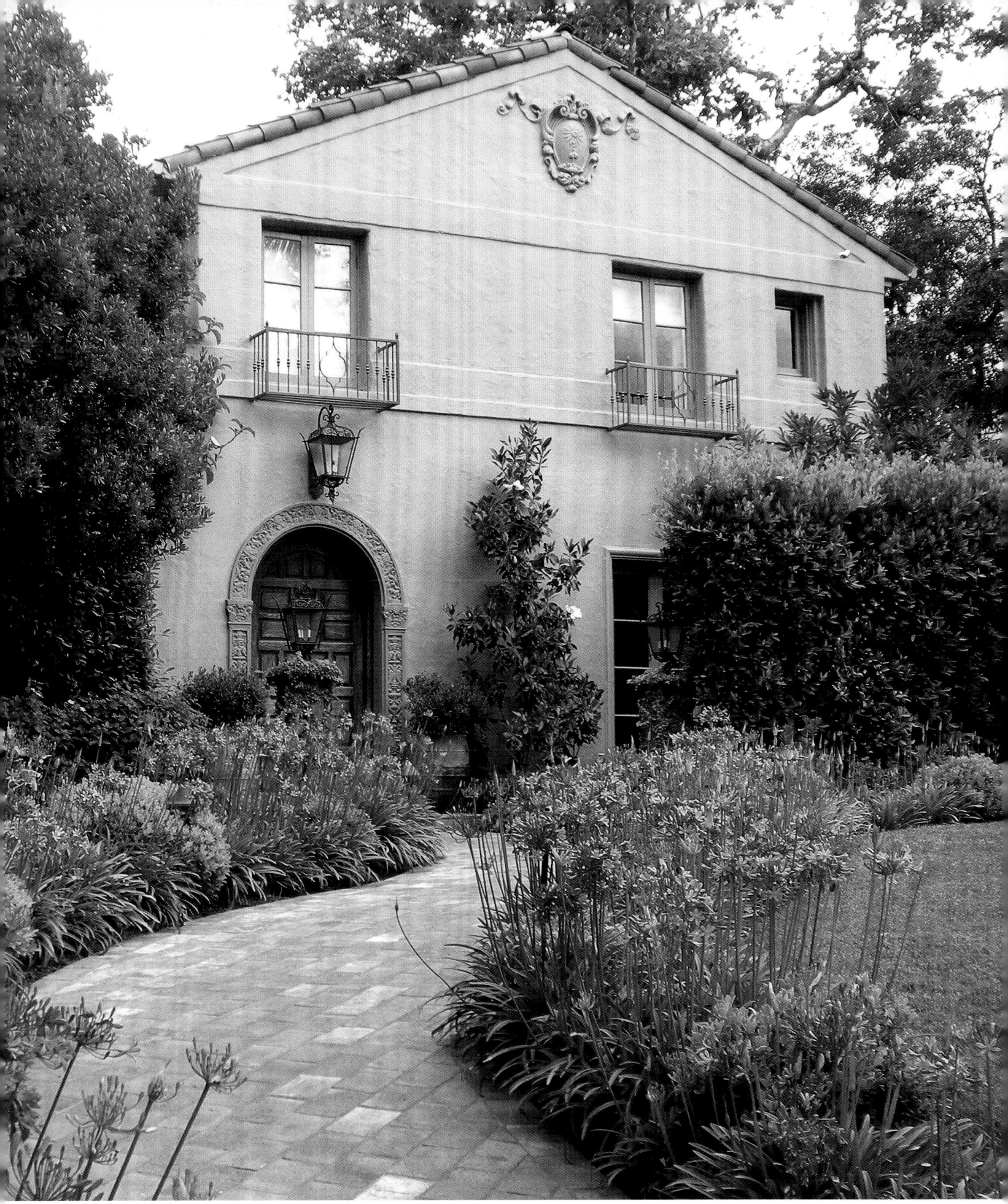

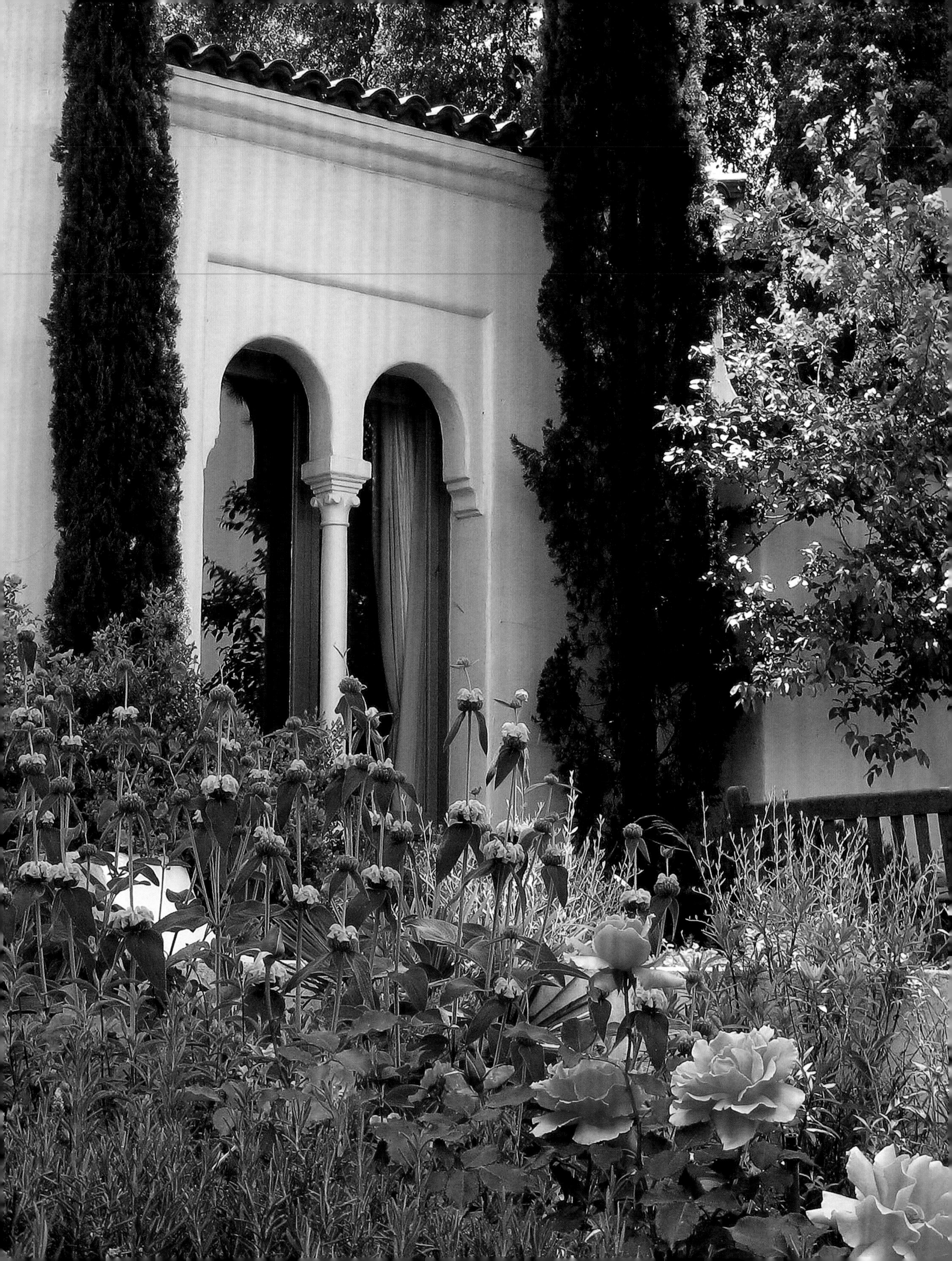

P eter Strauss graduated from Northwestern University in 1969 and immediately headed for Hollywood to pursue an acting career. When he got there, he found that despite all of the city's other glamour, it was the "white stucco walls covered with purple bougainvillea" that impressed him the most. "I was hooked," he says. "I started visiting arboretums and botanic gardens. *Sunset* magazine's *Western Garden Book* became my bible and still is. My wife thinks it's weird bedside reading."

Strauss now has his own garden in Ojai, California, about ninety minutes northwest of Los Angeles and twenty minutes inland from the coast. The house sits on 4 acres above a 30-acre citrus orchard, a legitimate farming enterprise. "I've hypothetically divided the garden into sections," he explains. "There's a formal entry, river garden, rose garden, native garden, Mediterranean garden, perennial border, and cactus garden. That sounds very structured, but actually there's no telling where I may decide to plant something simply because of color or architecture."

The soil is fast-draining—essential for citrus and Mediterranean plants—sandy loam with a relatively neutral pH. Strauss counts this a blessing, along with "lots of sunshine, water even if it's costly, and the availability of a gardener. That's me."

He says that as the different gardens have evolved, he has been guided by simply considering which plants he likes and wants to grow, then finding a place for them. "Once those defined areas were realized, I did try to be loyal to what belonged in each garden, i.e., native plants were kept native, and anything in the Mediterranean garden had to be from that region. Then I began to contrast and complement color and form. As with most gardeners, reality takes over. Mistakes can be glaring or turn into happy accidents. I suppose if I had a large staff, things might be more disciplined. I'd love to do a white garden or a water garden, but nature has her own plans. You don't know the effect the right rose can have against an agave until you try it."

Strauss is an extremely hands-on gardener. "The garden is a daily effort," he says. "I have actually sorted its monthly care charts into computerized folders. This gives me a record so I can track when any particular plant needs pruning back, or what fertilizer it may need when. I know I can cover the whole garden's maintenance in a week's time. This is sometimes tedious and exhausting—but I love it!"

The most thrilling time in the garden is from April through May, when everything blooms. And fall brings a respite from intense summer heat and the potential for rain. "Winter in Ojai can mean a freeze, which is always worrisome," Strauss says. "I have lost the citrus crop twice, literally losing 440 tons of fruit— and trust me, the bougainvillea was not happy!"

Strauss likes to quote Russell Page, his favorite garden writer and landscaper, who said, "Gardening is the humanization of Nature." What attracts Strauss to gardening is its unique demand on plain old work ethics, its artistry, its science, its spirituality, and the way it teaches him patience and tolerance.

RIGHT The entry court is anchored by a Spanish Colonial fountain adorned with container plants; Jerusalem sage and white centranthus flank the path. **BELOW** Thirty acres of the property are devoted to a working citrus orchard that produces 440 tons of Valencia oranges each season. **OVERLEAF** Arching branches on a massive native oak and a long view across the valley beckon visitors to explore the Mediterranean-themed garden.

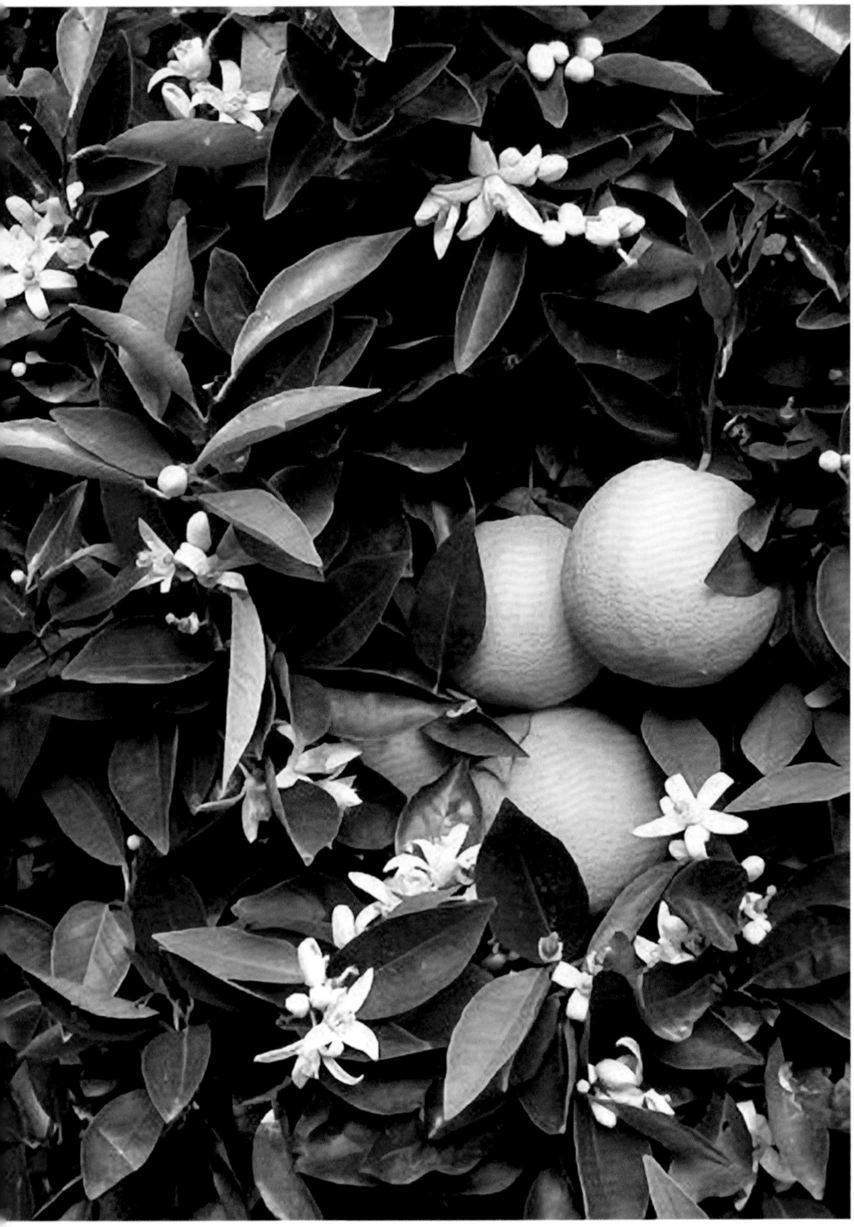

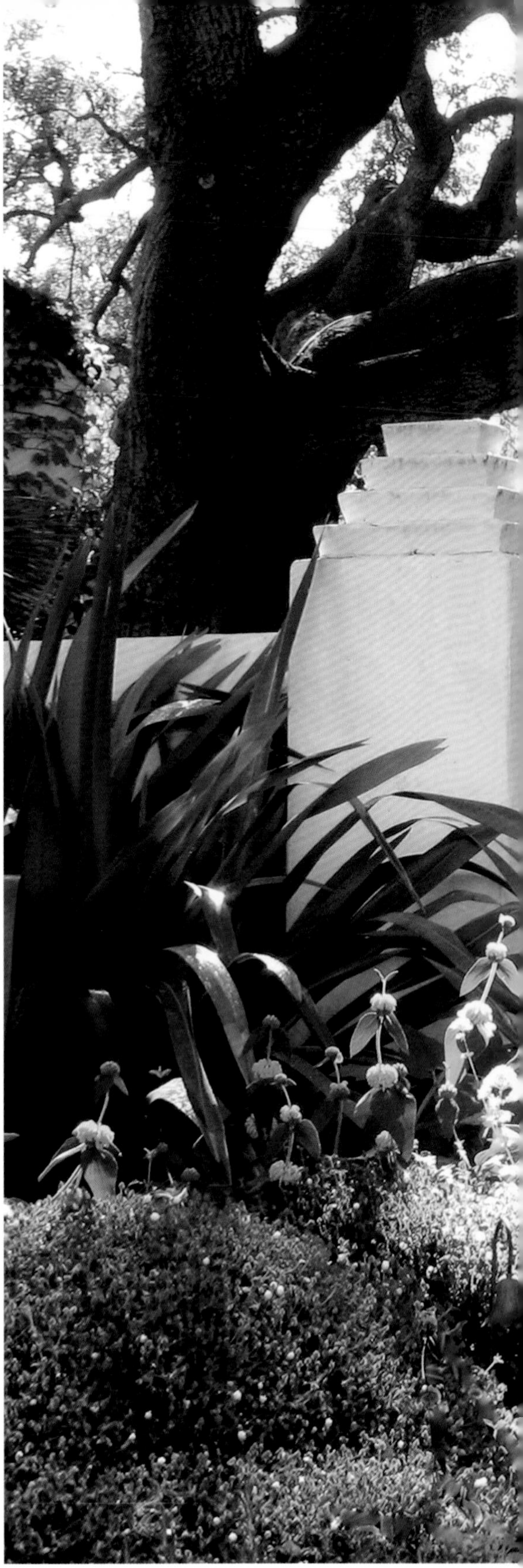

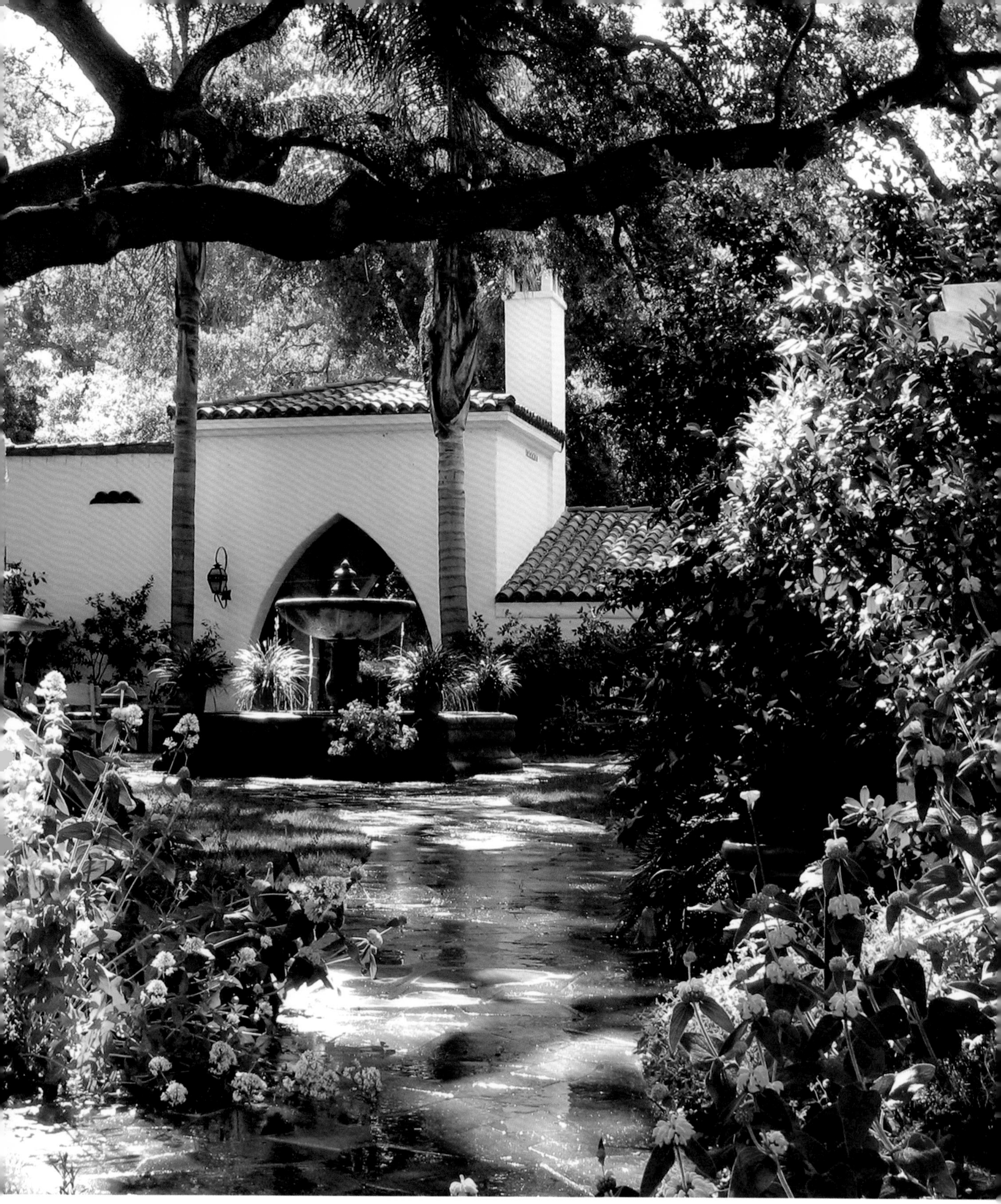

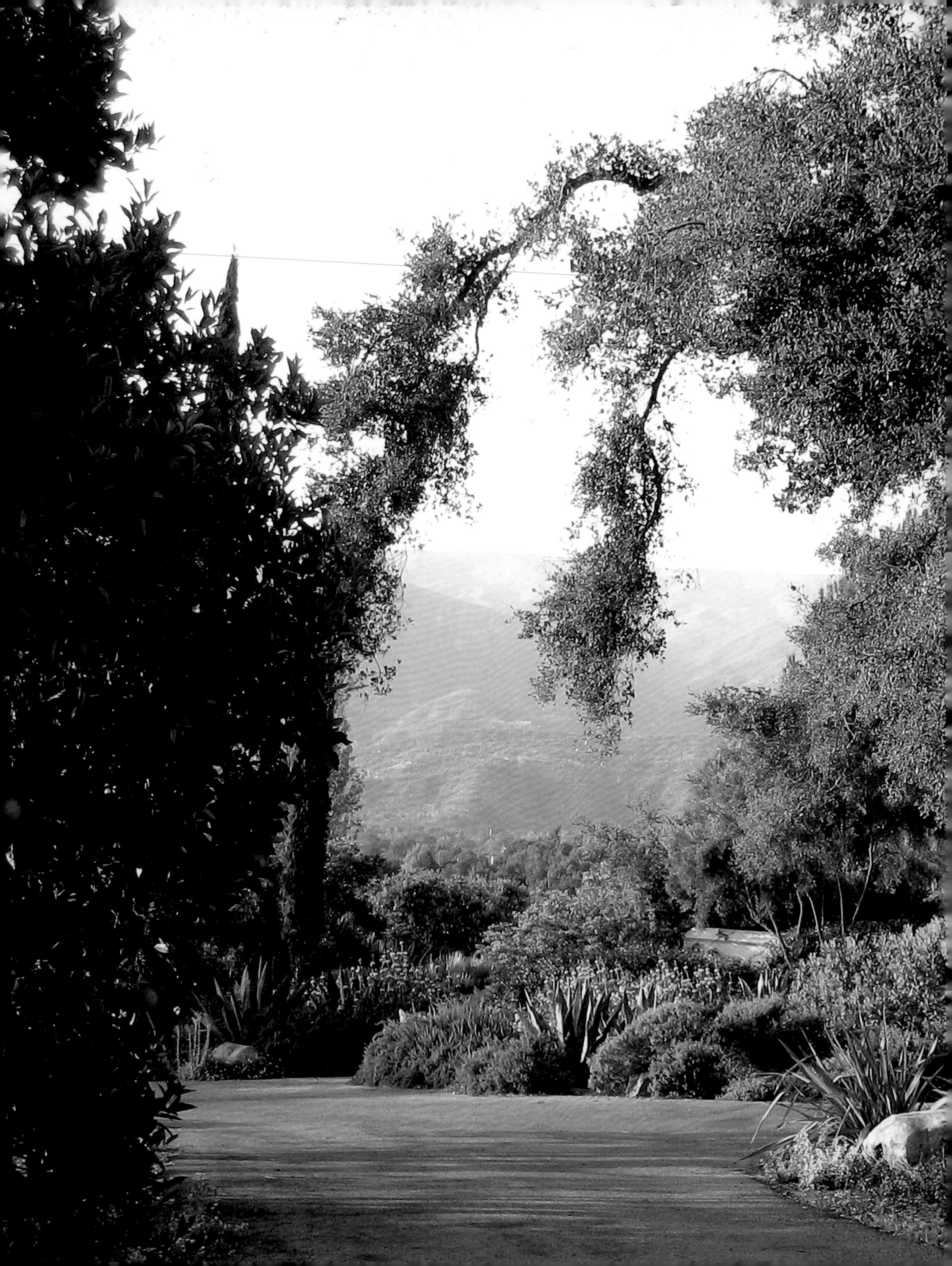

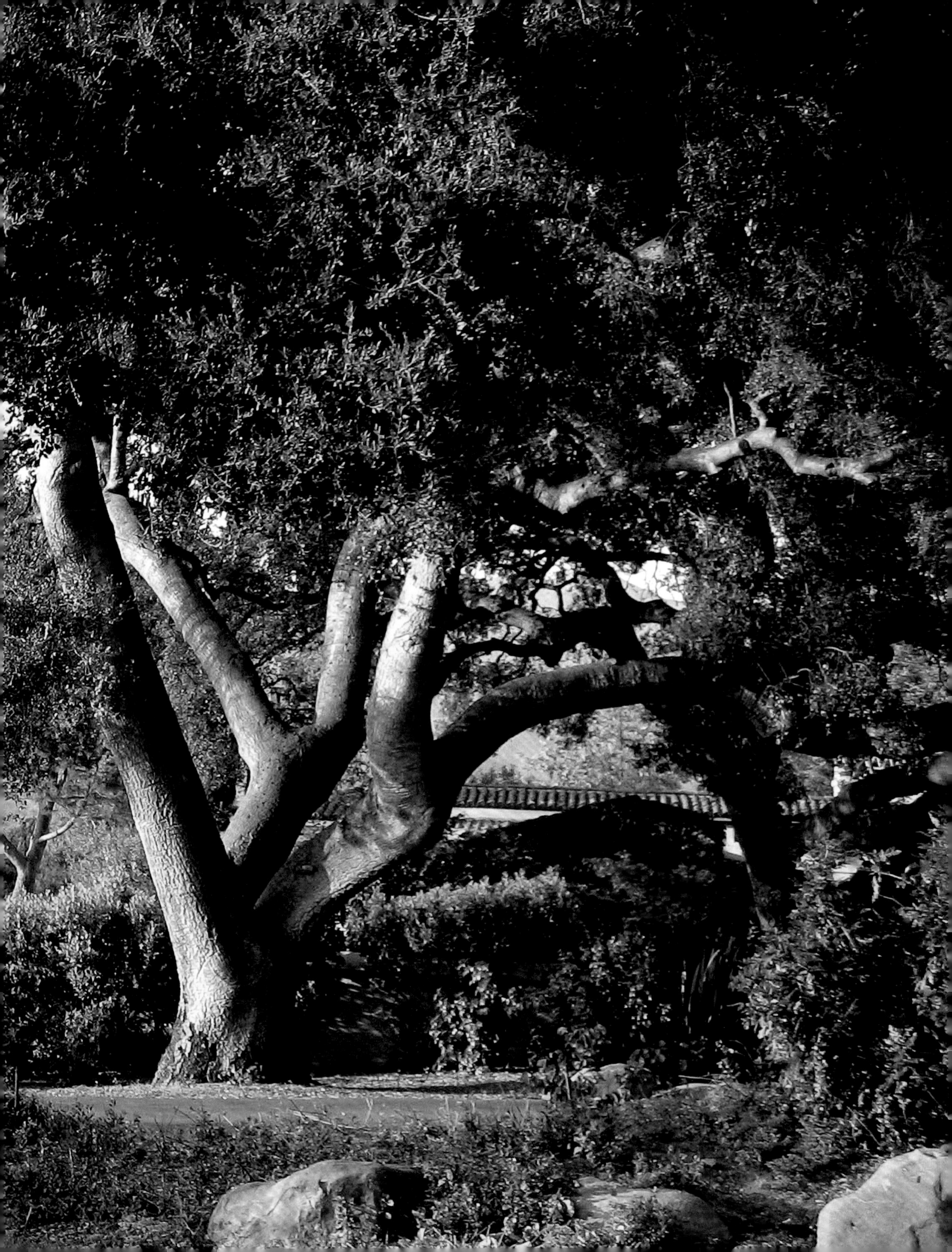

BELOW In the "desert garden," agaves, dwarf blue fescue grass, old man cactus, and sedums create a compelling vignette. **OPPOSITE** Agaves, aloes, euphorbias, palms, and tree yuccas make the arid setting surprisingly lush.

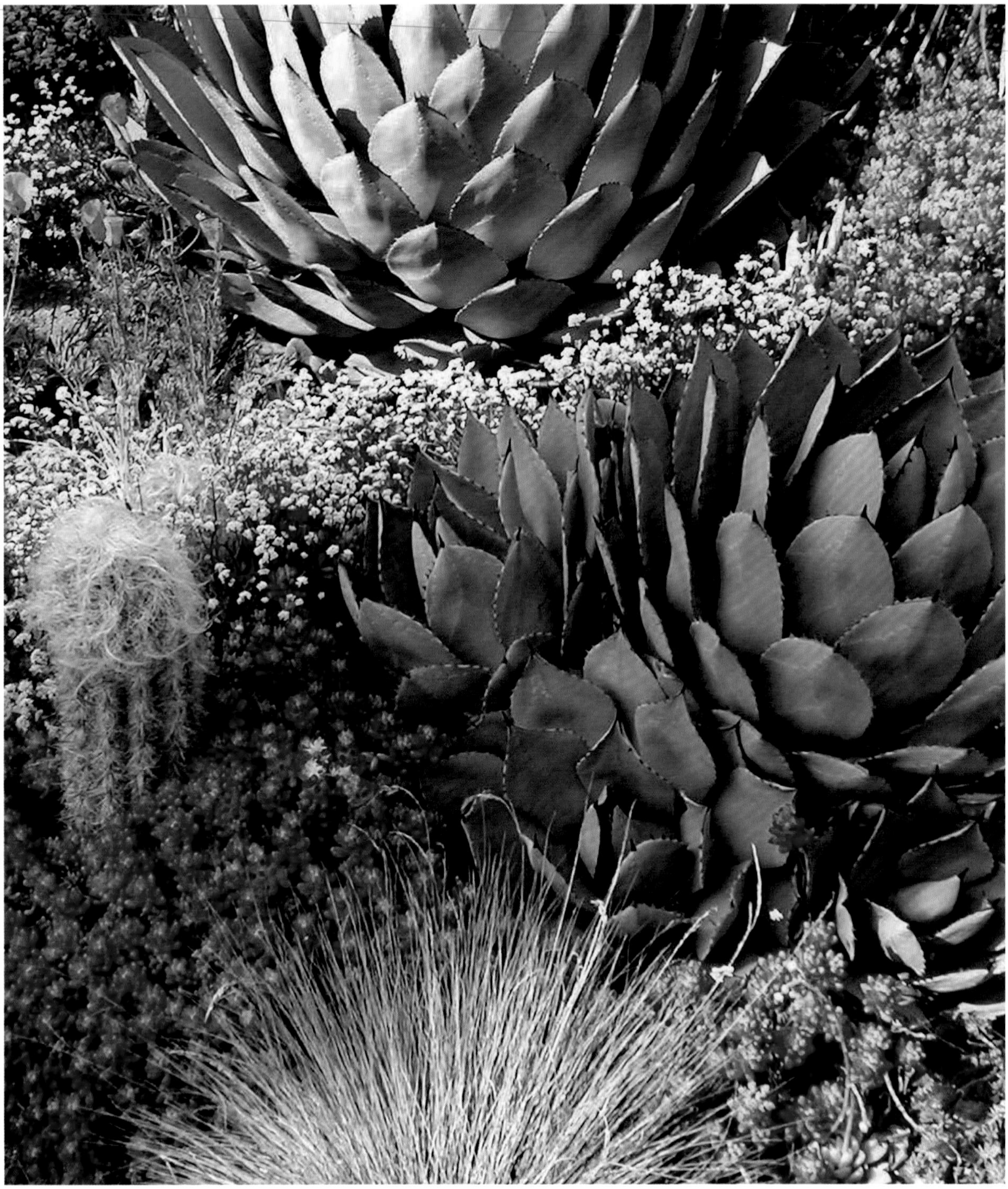

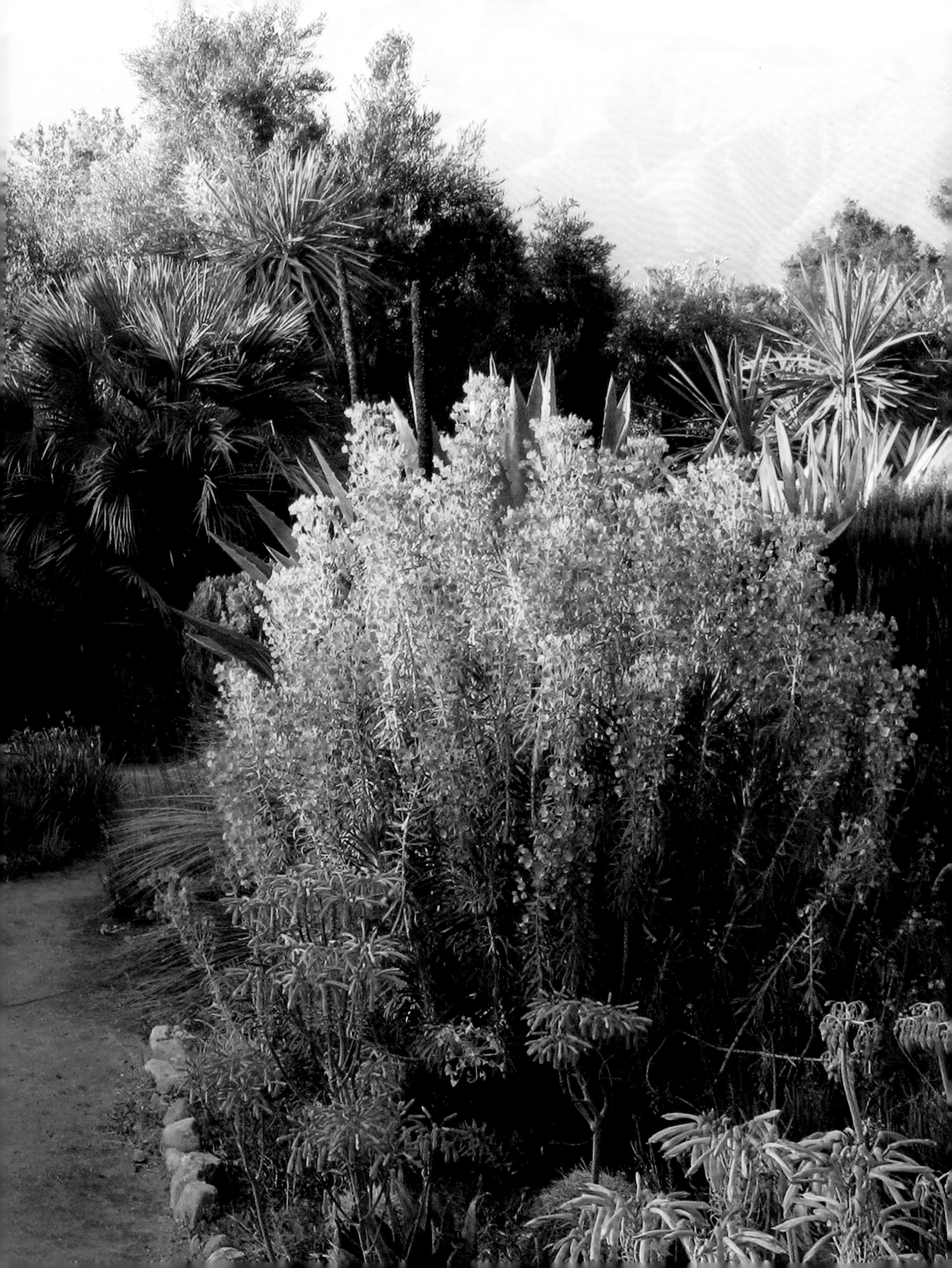

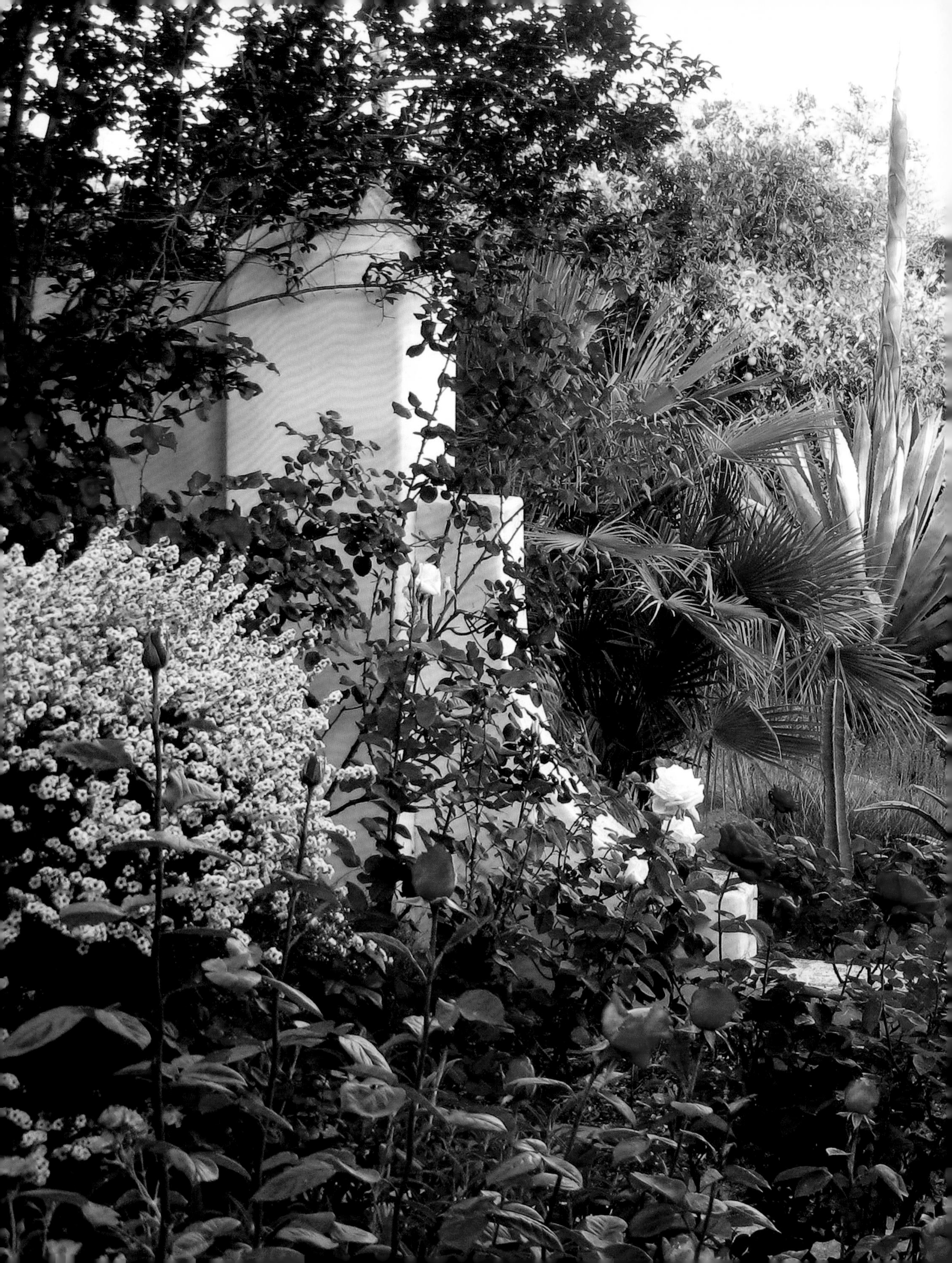

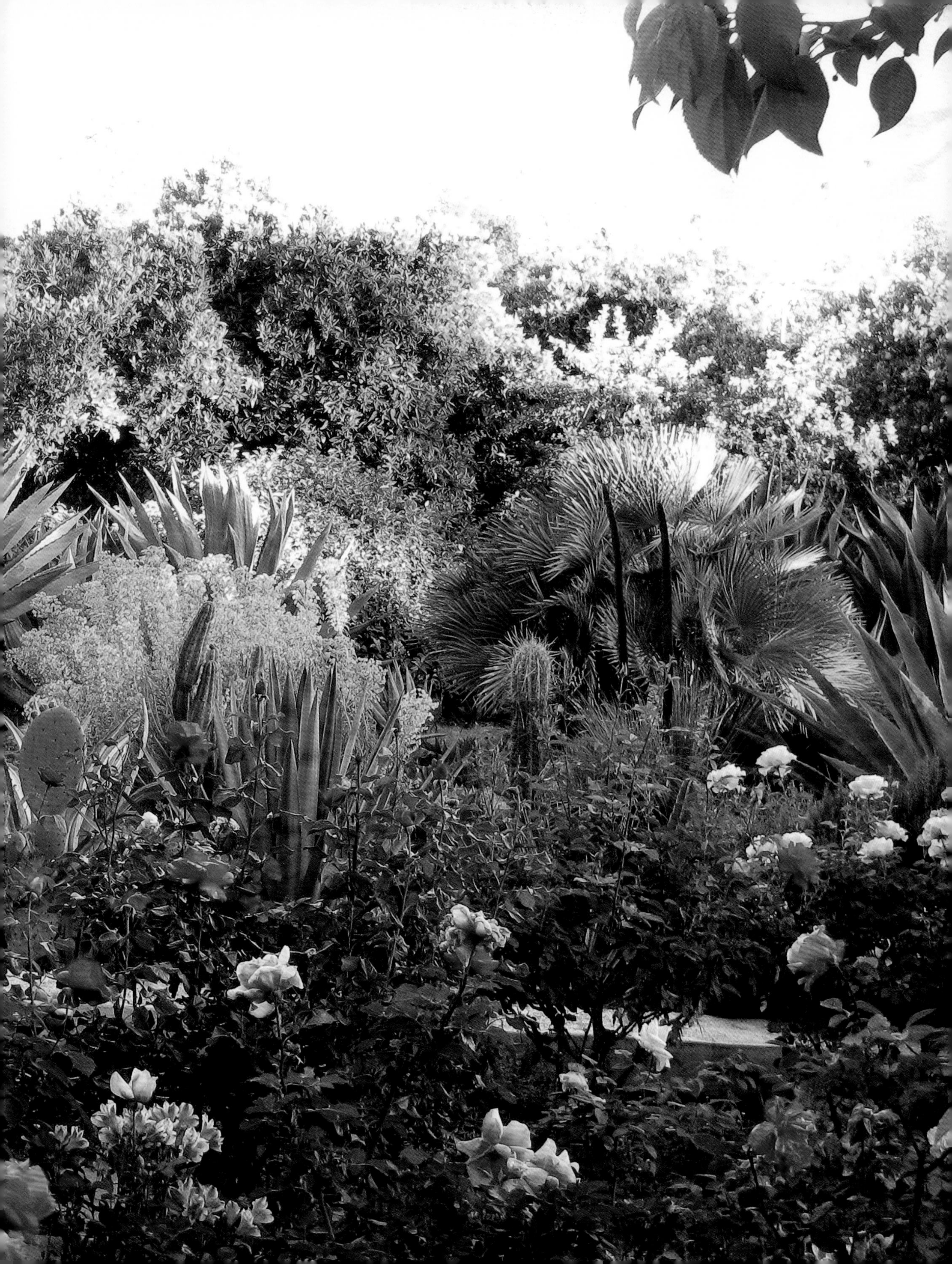

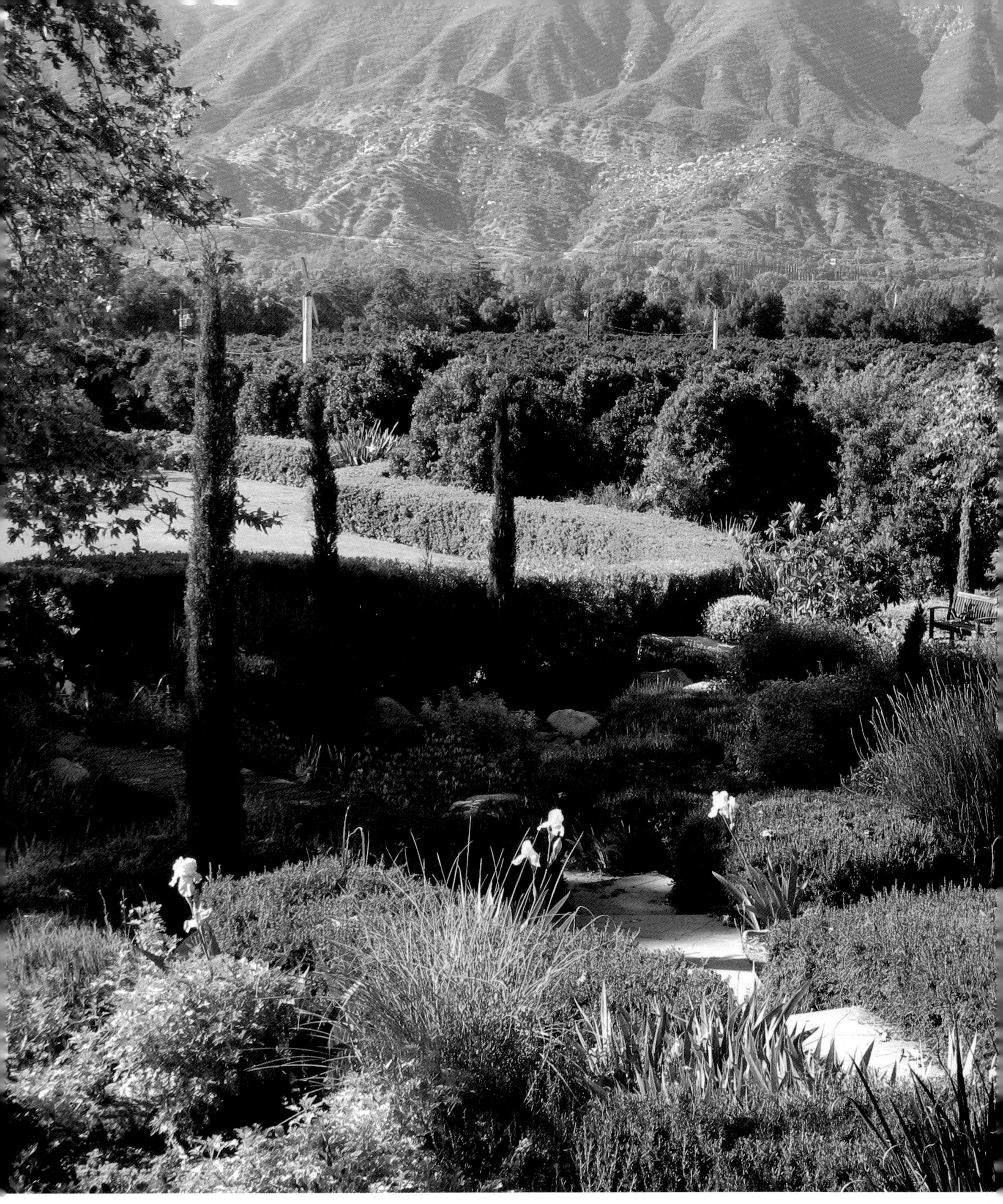

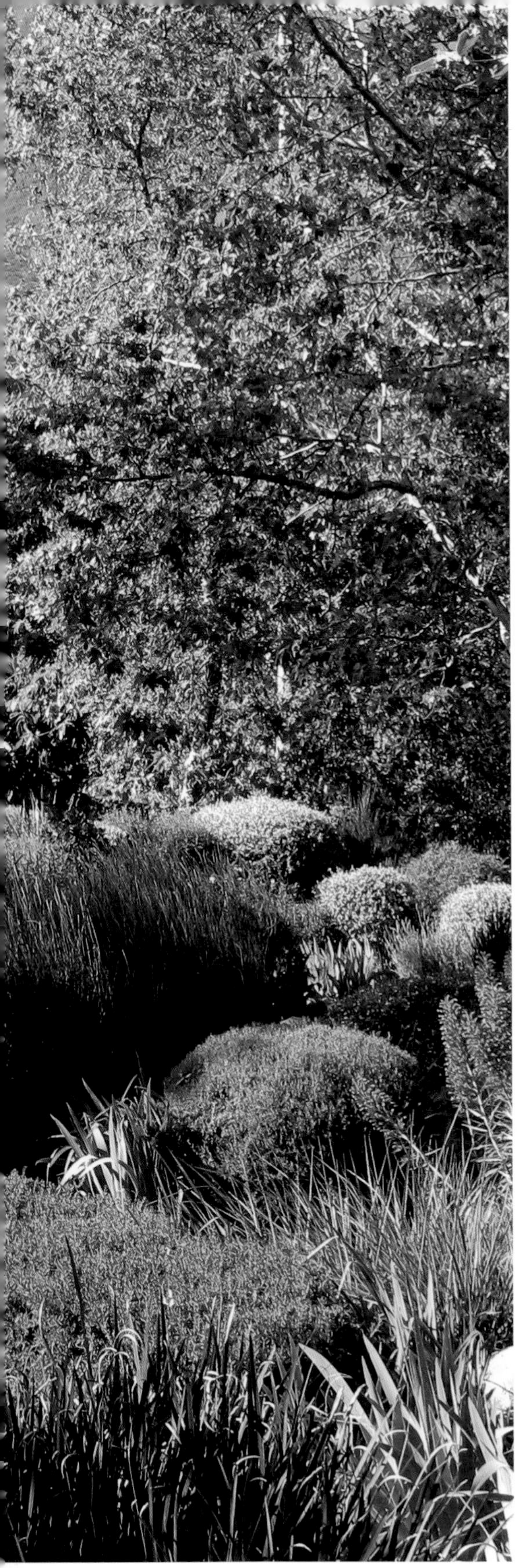

LEFT Framed by boxwood hedges and Italian cypress trees, the "Mediterranean garden" path leads the eye to the cultivated citrus grove beyond. **BELOW** A gate at one end of the pool leads to the untamed wildness of the California hills. **PREVIOUS PAGES** The "rose garden" outside the bedroom frames the "cactus garden" beyond; a century plant is beginning to throw what will become a 30-foot-high bloom stalk.

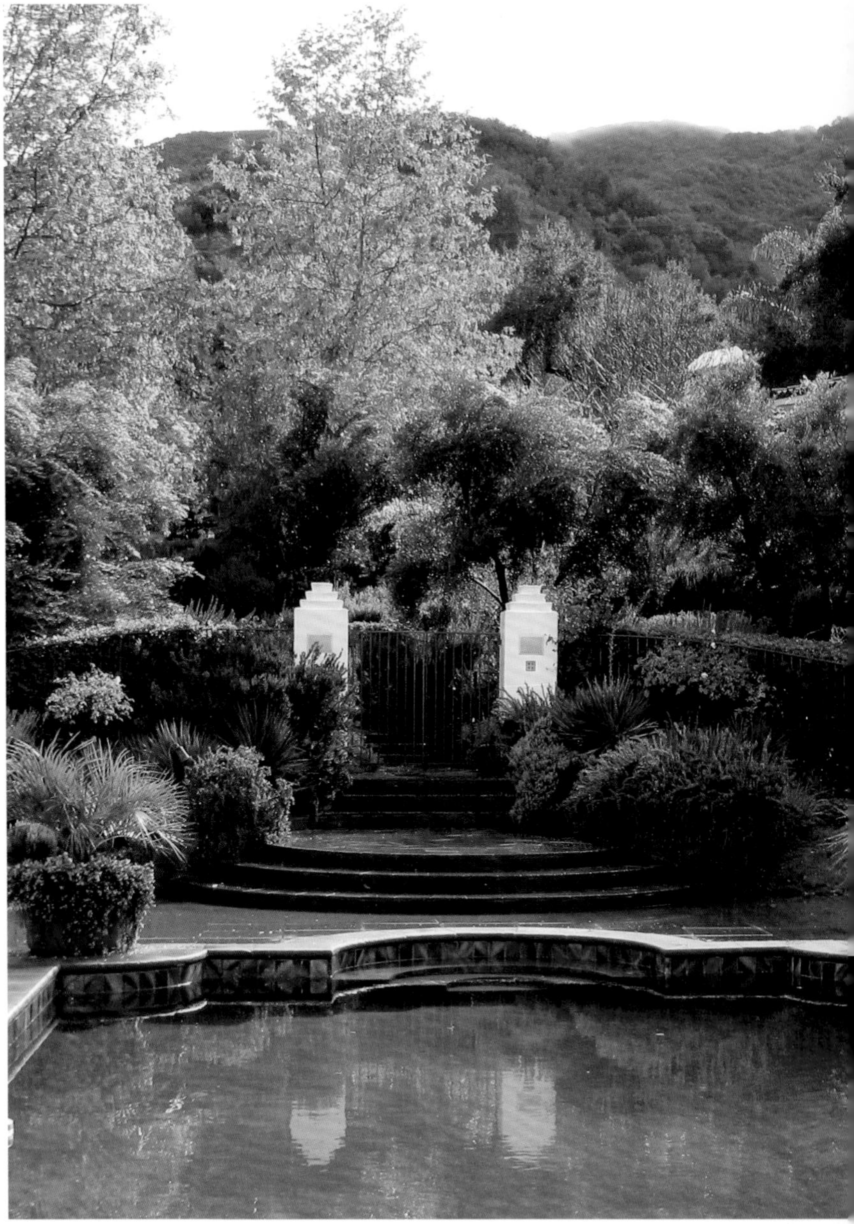

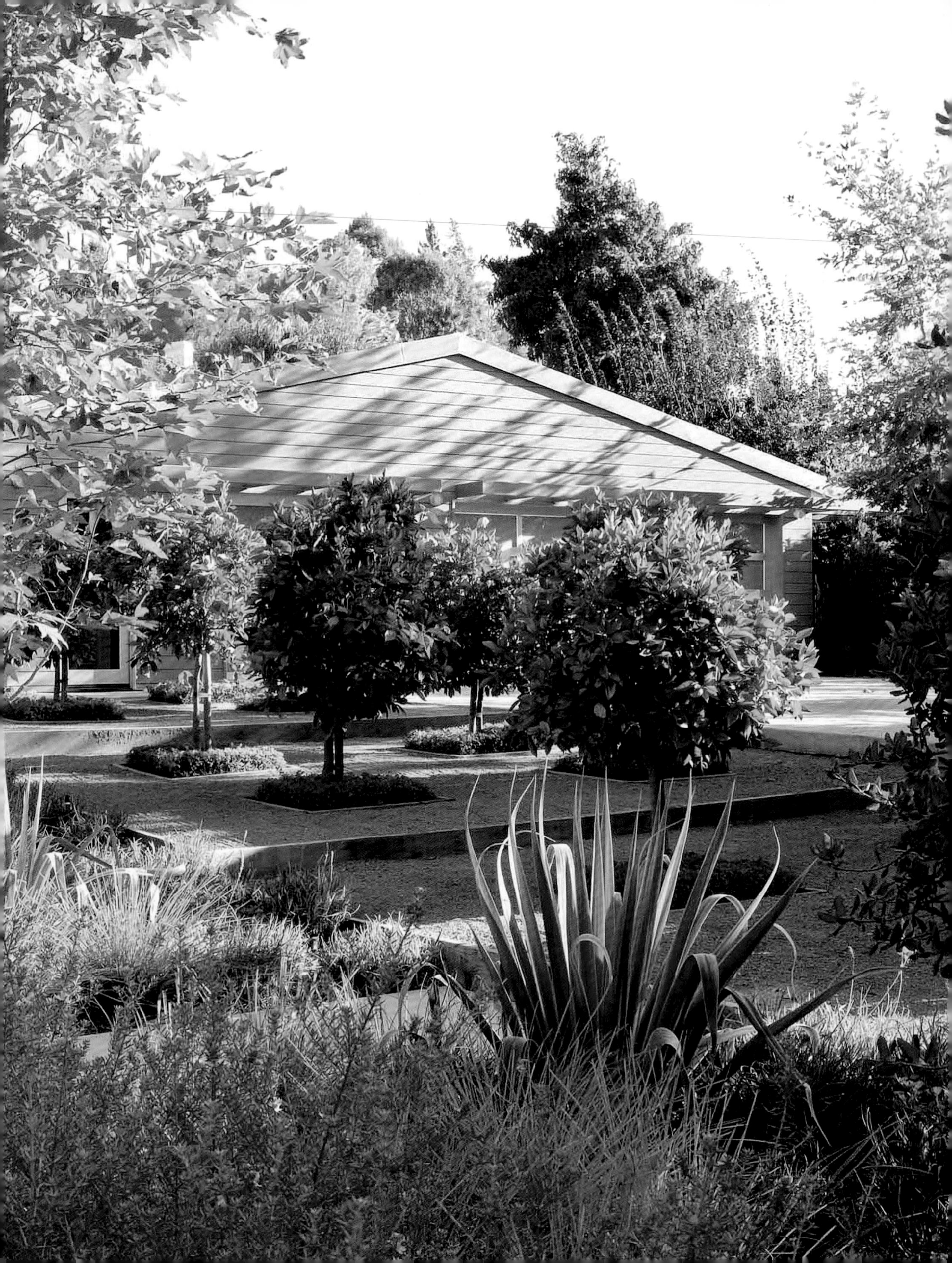

Landscape architect Mark Tessier's design of this garden in California's San Fernando Valley takes its cue from the architecture of the house, designed by Scrafano Architects. They turned a 1953 house into a sleek, modern version of ranch house vernacular. They opened up the house by installing large windows to allow more light in and also to take full advantage of the views. The interior of the 5,000-square-foot structure was completely updated, and a new two-story, 1,000-square-foot studio and guesthouse was added.

Tessier envisioned the landscape as a series of distinct garden spaces, each with its own identity. "I saw them as reflections of adjacent interior spaces," he says. "The client desired a garden strongly rooted in environmentally responsible and sustainable design principles, which could still address the needs of a growing family's lifestyle."

A new entry for the property was created at the street edge by taking the front door of the house and moving it close to the street. Zig-zag bridges from traditional Chinese gardens based on the principles of feng shui provided inspiration for the staggered, floating wood bridge and sunken succulent garden that now defines the entry experience. A modern cast-in-place concrete water basin, drawing inspiration from a *tsukubai*, a Japanese purification fountain, provides a soothing and peaceful sound.

Referencing the valley's agrarian past, a grove of Valencia orange trees introduces an organized geometry to the landscape that continues, later, into the rear yard. "The orange grove makes a strong connection between the main house, guesthouse, the multipurpose parking court, and sport court," Tessier explains.

The back of the house received new outdoor terrace spaces. "The hardscape and planting of the rear garden plays off the architect's rectilinear forms with long axes and crisp geometry," Tessier says. "It was envisioned as an open lawn for children's play and entertaining. I saw the lawn panel as a special element or rectilinear 'rug' of grass rather than a design more like wall-to-wall carpeting."

The forms of the main outdoor space are dominated by a breathtaking view of the San Fernando Valley and the borrowed landscape beyond, with its hues of gray, sage green, and the dusty greens of the native California sycamore. Many native species are also planted extensively on the property in small groups, as they would exist naturally in the surrounding foothills and canyons.

A secret garden for adults wraps around the opposite side of the house, providing the connection between the backyard lawn and the playroom. A complex series of angular paths, trails, and vegetative mounds creates a shaded respite from the Southern California sun and a framework for informal play. A permeable, decomposed granite surface contrasts purposefully with the more refined concrete finishes found in other areas of the garden. Tessier says, "The use of local materials helps pull in and connect the environment and landscape to the renovation, which has been awarded high honors."

BELOW A secret garden connects the lawn and pool to the children's outdoor playroom; playful angles, landscaped mounds, and shade create a setting for informal play. **OPPOSITE** Landscape architect Mark Tessier designed the rear garden to play off the house's rectilinear forms by using long axes and crisp geometry.

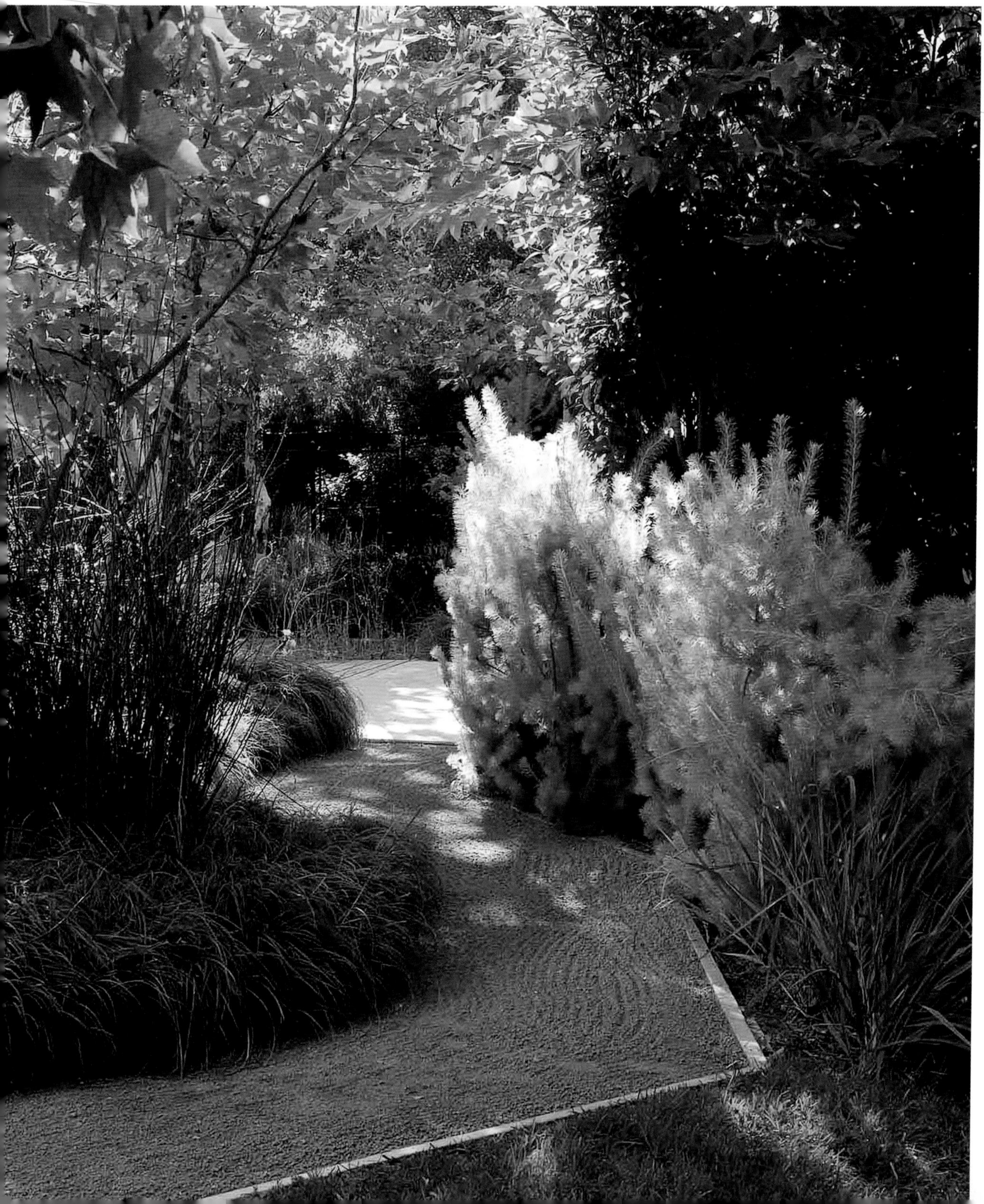

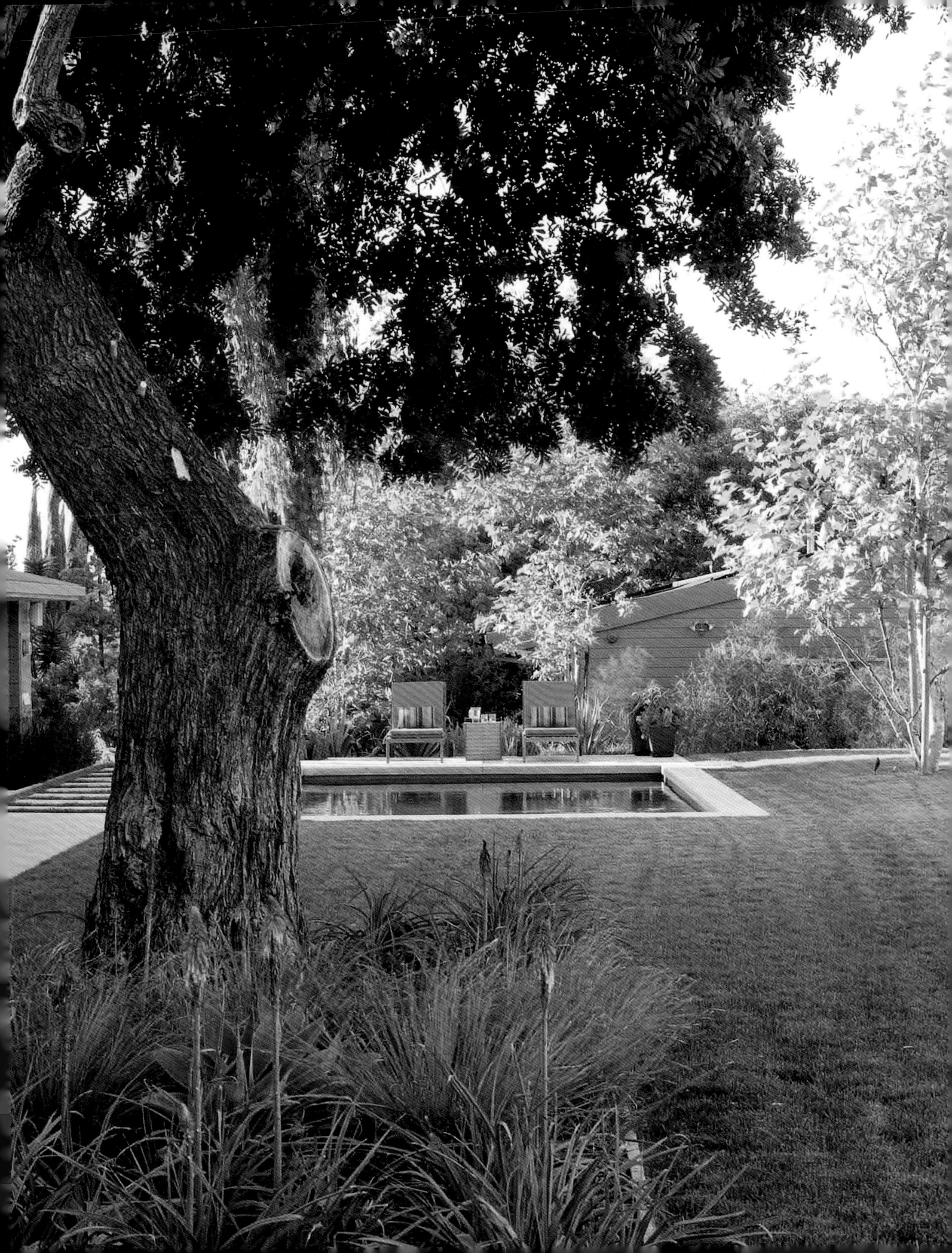

RIGHT The new outdoor living space at the back of the house looks out over the open lawn designed for play and entertaining. **BELOW** The rectilinear pool and panels of grass carry the eye out to the scenery of the San Fernando Valley.

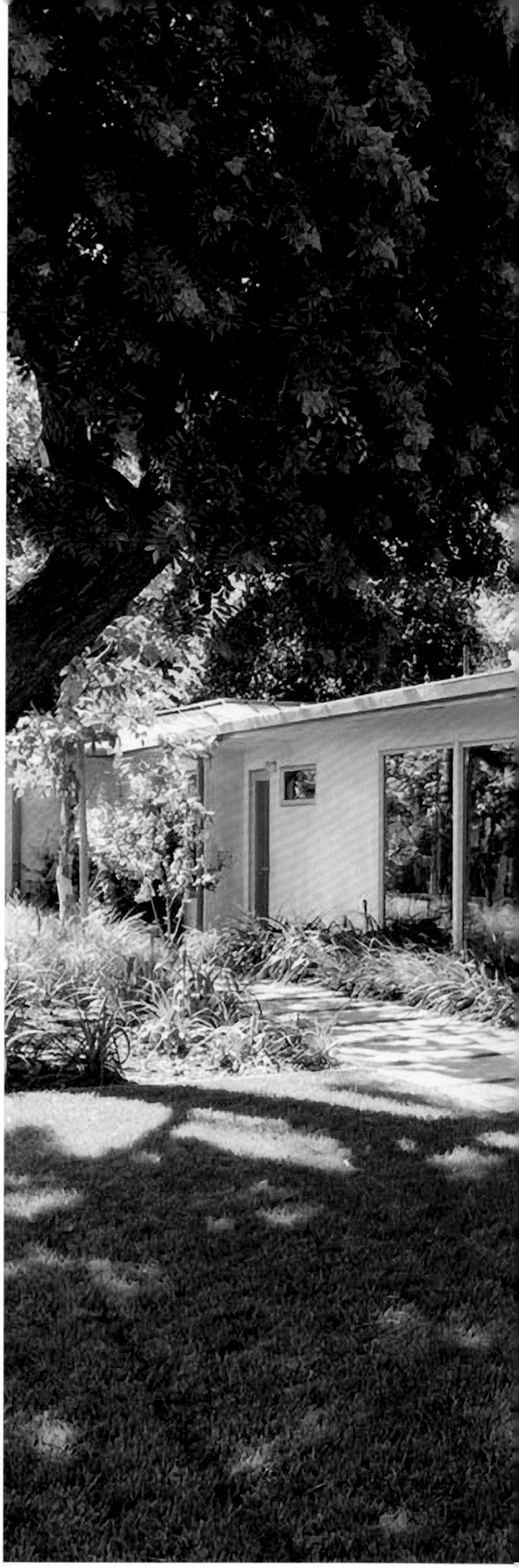

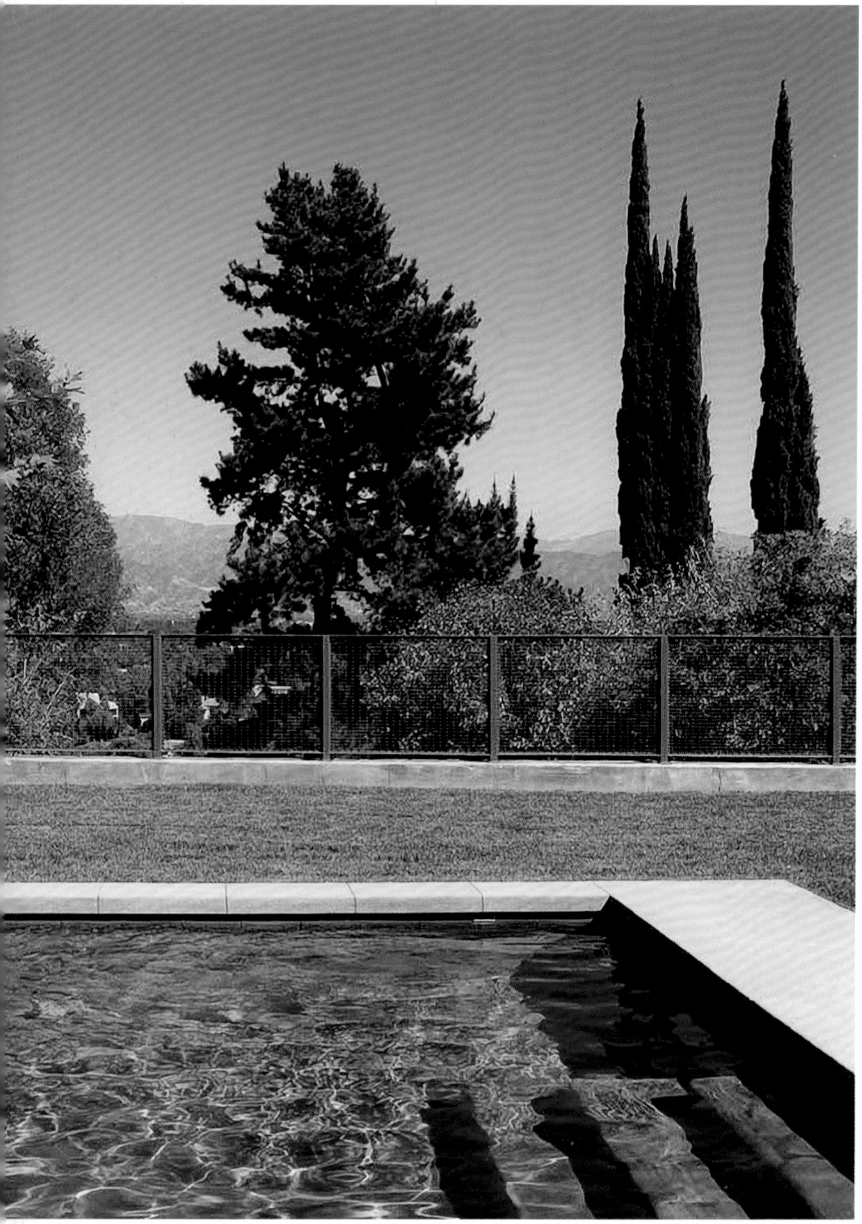